American Higher Education
in the Twenty-First Century

# American Higher Education in the Twenty-First Century

**Social, Political, and Economic Challenges**

FOURTH EDITION

*Edited by*

Michael N. Bastedo, Philip G. Altbach, and Patricia J. Gumport

Johns Hopkins University Press
*Baltimore*

© 1998, 2005, 2011, 2016 Johns Hopkins University Press
All rights reserved. Published 2016  •
Printed in the United States of America on acid-free paper
9  8  7  6  5  4  3  2  1

Johns Hopkins University Press
2715 North Charles Street
Baltimore, Maryland 21218-4363
www.press.jhu.edu

Library of Congress Cataloging-in-Publication Data

Names: Bastedo, Michael N. editor. | Altbach, Philip G. editor. | Gumport,
    Patricia J. editor.
Title: American higher education in the twenty-first century : social,
    political, and economic challenges / edited by Michael N. Bastedo,
    Philip G. Altbach, and Patricia J. Gumport.
Description: Fourth Edition. | Baltimore : Johns Hopkins University Press,
    2016. | Third edition lists Philip G. Altbach as the first editor. | Includes
    bibliographical references and index.
Identifiers: LCCN 2015031662| ISBN 9781421419893 (hardcover :
    acid-free paper) | ISBN 9781421419909 (pbk. : acid-free paper) |
    ISBN 9781421419916 (electronic) | ISBN 1421419890 (hardcover :
    acid-free paper) | ISBN 1421419904 (pbk. : acid-free paper) |
    ISBN 1421419912 (electronic)
Subjects: LCSH: Education, Higher—Aims and objectives—United States. |
    Education, Higher—Social aspects—United States. | Education, Higher—
    Political aspects—United States.
Classification: LCC LA227.4 .A45 2016 | DDC 378.00973—dc23 LC record
available at http://lccn.loc.gov/2015031662

A catalog record for this book is available from the British Library.

*Special discounts are available for bulk purchases of this book. For more
information, please contact Special Sales at 410-516-6936 or specialsales@press
.jhu.edu.*

Johns Hopkins University Press uses environmentally friendly book
materials, including recycled text paper that is composed of at least
30 percent post-consumer waste, whenever possible.

*To*
*Robert O. Berdahl*
*Scholar, Teacher, and Friend*

# Contents

# Preface

Whether we look at advances in information technology, organized social movements, or income inequality and stratification, higher education serves as a lens for broader issues in American society. We kept this in mind as we prepared this fourth edition during a period when higher education is the focus of intense interest and considerable scrutiny by the public, the media, and government.

This volume seeks to capture several crucial dynamics in the nexus of higher education and society. We analyze the relationship between colleges and universities and their external environments as higher education becomes increasingly salient to the nation's future. In a system of higher education as large and decentralized as the one in the United States, it is difficult to assess the cumulative record of strains and transitions comprehensively, much less reassess the priorities needed for higher education to survive and prosper. But it is worth the attempt, for there is analytical utility in examining the affairs of colleges and universities within their changing social, political, and economic contexts.

Accordingly, the editors of this volume and its contributors share a view of colleges and universities as social institutions embedded in the wider society and subject to society's constraining forces. We stress that in view of the obviously changing agenda of issues, the importance of the policy process becomes magnified. In trying to assess the validity of criticisms of American higher education, it is helpful to bring a broader perspective to the process.

For the new edition, existing chapters have been revised extensively to reflect these new realities. One of our goals has been for the chapters to represent a broader spectrum of higher education institutions and students than has been represented previously. Chapters have been revised to focus on more types of institutions—such as for-profit colleges and online education—and to reflect more deeply the racial, ethnic, and socioeconomic diversity within higher education. New chapters were added with these themes in mind.

Another goal has been to answer questions of intense public interest in higher education. What are the drivers of cost escalation in higher education? What do we know about the effectiveness of MOOCs (massive open online courses) and other technologies? What is the impact of student diversity on college student learning and campus climates? All of these questions and more are answered in the chapters that follow.

We hope these changes make the text more engaging and useful for our audience of newcomers to higher education scholarship, practitioners in higher education institutions, and members of the public interested in learning more about a social sector of increasing national and international importance.

We should note changes in our editorial team for this edition. Philip G. Altbach, the founder and lead for this series through many successful editions, has decided to step back from this position. New to this edition is Michael N. Bastedo, a professor of education at the University of Michigan, who is now the lead editor of the volume. Patricia J. Gumport completes our editorial team, as she has through all of the editions with Johns Hopkins University Press.

This edition is dedicated to Robert O. Berdahl, an editor of this volume for many years, who passed away on December 10, 2014. Professor Berdahl leaves a significant legacy of work, particularly on issues of accountability, autonomy, and state coordination in higher education. He was also a wonderful person and an advocate for social justice, having marched with the Congress of Racial Equality in the 1960s. Bob was a supportive colleague and mentor, a welcoming and vigorous presence in higher education research. He will be missed.

PART I / Core Enduring Missions

# Chapter One

# The Ten Generations of American Higher Education

Roger L. Geiger

We study the history of higher education because things change and because some things do not change. Continuity is evident in individual institutions in which circumstances or self-images of origin and development continue to influence current activities. Basic forms persist as well, perhaps most notably in the centrality of the American college. Issues also recur, particularly those concerned with curriculum, institutional mission, and student development. But change is an irreducible reality and must, by its nature, be analyzed in a temporal dimension. The key elements here are understanding the processes of change and aggregating such changes to discern fundamental transformations in the entire system of higher education. This last element forms the premise of the analysis that follows: that the character of American higher education has perceptibly shifted in each generation, or approximately every thirty years. The exploration of the successive generations is intended to illuminate these historical dynamics as well as the underlying processes that shape them.

The ten generations of American higher education, from the founding of Harvard to the current era, are characterized here in terms of what was taught, the experience of students, and the array of institutions. Existing knowledge was and is screened by institutions and their faculty for certified acceptance into the curriculum. That curriculum, in turn, has an implied relationship with subsequent uses. Next, the place of higher education in the lives of students can be captured in the phrase "origins and destinations." The expansive nature of American higher education has meant that student origins have tended to be broad and diverse. Yet expectations about culture and career destinations have largely motivated college attendance, and these same expectations have inspired crucial interventions by third parties—whether governments, churches, foundations, or individuals. Between origins and destinations lies the college experience itself, certainly one of the most critical variables. Finally, there is institutional order—all the institutions offering higher education and their internal makeup. This chapter's organizational scheme is intended to be heuristic, highlighting central features for monitoring change over time without necessarily excluding any factors impinging on higher education.

## Generation 1: Reformation Beginnings, 1636–1740s

Each of the first three colleges in the British colonies of America was unique, but all may be described as "schools of the Reformation."[1] Harvard College, the College of William and Mary, and Yale College were established as adjuncts of their respective churches, which in turn were integrally related to the colonies' civil governments. The long head start enjoyed by Harvard gave it a special, settled character. A true product of the Wars of Religion when it was chartered in 1636 by Puritans fleeing religious persecution, it evolved in the eighteenth century into a more cosmopolitan and tolerant institution. This evolution away from strict Calvinism reflected the spreading heterodoxy of Puritan society and the support of the more secular and mercantile elements in that community. The College of William and Mary was formally linked with the Church of England. Its founder, James Blair, and his successors were titular heads of the church in Virginia. Originally operated as a grammar school, William and Mary did not offer collegiate instruction until the 1730s. It then embodied the relative tolerance of official Anglicanism, a stance congenial to the planter families who dominated the colony.[2] Only Yale attempted to preserve and cultivate the sectarian zeal of the Reformation era into the middle of the eighteenth century.

Some original features persisted long after the Reformation era. External governance was a natural outgrowth of viewing the colleges as an emanation of the polity. Both Harvard and William and Mary had dual structures, consisting of an immediate governing body and boards of overseers or visitors. Yale was guided by a single board, originally consisting of ten Congregational ministers, but it looked to the General Assembly of Connecticut for financial support and legal backing.[3] This combination of provincial authority external to the college and the clerical authority lodged within it generated recurring conflicts. Control of Harvard was contested among old-line Puritans and more liberal Congregationalists. Yale's minister-trustees, left to themselves, disagreed over where to locate the college. And at William and Mary, the inability of the board of visitors to control the faculty was a perpetual problem. All three colleges nevertheless received financial support from their respective colonies.

A relatively powerful college president eventually emerged as the natural complement to lay authority. A circumscribed role remained to be played by the faculty of tutors, who were usually recent graduates preparing for the ministry. The curriculum of the colleges in this era was adapted from the Arts course of medieval universities. Its aim was to provide students with a liberal education, which meant facility with classical languages, grounding in the three basic philosophies of Aristotle—ethics, metaphysics, and natural philosophy or science—and a grounding in logic. In order to be admitted, students had to show knowledge of Latin, the language of instruction, and a bit of Greek. The first two years were devoted for the most part to polishing linguistic skills and then learning logic in order to engage in disputations. Philosophy and general subjects were taught in the final two years. The education offered was a practical one for the seventeenth and early eighteenth centuries, when most learned texts were in Latin. The process of education was undoubtedly as valuable as the content. The collegiate way of living and the constant presence of tutors gave students complete immersion in both religion and learning. Delivering declamations and engaging in disputations inculcated a facility with language that was indispensable to the oral public culture they would enter.

The founding documents of all three schools speak to the aim of educating ministers. Indeed, except at William and Mary, this was the chief expectation associated with college matriculation. Actual ministerial training, nevertheless, followed upon a liberal education. Nearly two-thirds of the graduates of seventeenth-century Harvard entered the ministry, but nonministerial students were both welcomed and expected. William and Mary sought to make youths "piously educated in good Letters and Manners"; the founders of Yale intended to provide education "for Publick employment both in Church & Civil State."[4]

The nexus between college and the ministry would erode slowly during the eighteenth century. Under president John Leverett (1708–24), Harvard already possessed a clientele of young gentlemen who took scant interest in studies or piety. At William and Mary, where a ministerial career required a journey to England for ordination, most sons of the Virginia gentry sought only a patina of liberal education, and almost none graduated.

By the third decade of the eighteenth century, Harvard surmounted the narrow role of a Reformation college in another way. Gifts from Thomas Hollis created two professorships, in divinity (1721) and in mathematics and natural philosophy (1727). The hiring of individuals who could specialize over the years in a single field of knowledge overcame an inherent curricular limitation. By the next generation, learned professors, in addition to young tutors, would be sought by the colonial colleges.[5]

## Generation 2: Colonial Colleges, 1745–1775

The mold of Reformation colleges was broken with the founding of the College of New Jersey (Princeton University) in 1746. A compromise between Presbyterians and the colony of New Jersey produced a board of trustees having twelve ministers, ten laymen, and the governor of the colony as ex officio presiding officer. The college was rooted in the colony yet served a far wider constituency of Presbyterians; it was denominational in nature yet tolerant of other Protestant sects. The next four colleges to be founded followed this same pattern of "toleration with preferment," although for somewhat different reasons. King's College (Columbia University, 1754), as an Anglican founding, had to assuage fears of institutionalizing a state religion. The College of Philadelphia (University of Pennsylvania, 1755), successor to the academy that Benjamin Franklin had helped to found, practiced toleration in the spirit of the Enlightenment amid a context of considerable religious diversity, but was led by a prominent Anglican. Baptists, too, believed in toleration, even while insisting on control over the College of Rhode Island (Brown University, 1765). New Hampshire's eagerness to launch a provincial college prompted it to entice Eleazar Wheelock to found Dartmouth College (1769). Only the creation of Queen's College (Rutgers University, 1771), by and for the New Jersey Dutch Reformed community, introduced an exclusive (and unsuccessful) model at the end of this period.[6]

Harvard and William and Mary also conformed to the new model of provincial colleges. Yale under Thomas Clap (1740–66), however, resisted this form in the name of doctrinal purity but, in doing so, demonstrated that the theocratic ideal of the Reformation was no longer tenable. Clap's rearguard action to defend Yale against the doctrines of the Great Awakening, against an Anglican presence in Connecticut, and, finally, against the Connecticut General Assembly ironically ended when he lost control of the college to rebellious students.

On the eve of the Revolution, the colonial colleges enrolled nearly 750 students, but 450 of them attended Harvard, Yale, and Princeton.[7] These schools—

and Philadelphia—exemplified instruction that had become more secular in its curriculum and purpose. Fewer than half of the graduates of Princeton pursued careers in the ministry. In the small but vital urban centers of the colonies, a sizable class of gentlemen now existed, consisting of professional men and successful merchants. At King's College perhaps 40 percent of the students originated from that milieu, and the proportion at Harvard may well have been higher. Still, many students clearly came from more humble circumstances, chiefly the sons of farmers. They were more likely to be destined for the ministry, while gentlemen's sons more typically followed the path that led to law and public life.[8] Students at the three largest colleges formed literary societies to cultivate debate, belles lettres, and good company.

At the outset of this period, the curriculum was an incoherent amalgam of works predicated on both the old, theocentric universe and the new, enlightened views reflecting the writings of John Locke and Sir Isaac Newton. The doctrines of the "Moderate Enlightenment" gradually prevailed.[9] The enlightened spirit also included a more thorough teaching and appreciation of classical authors. Latin and Greek thus remained at the heart of the curriculum, but Latin ceased to be a language of instruction. Classical authors introduced the generation of the Founding Fathers to the political forms and lessons of the ancient world. Scottish "common-sense philosophy," as taught by John Witherspoon (1768–95) at Princeton, reconciled Christian doctrines and the new knowledge. Students also received more competent instruction in these decades, as college teaching became a settled occupation, attracting a few men of genuine learning.[10]

In sum, during the colonial generation the colleges balanced duties to both church and province, offered a richer and more secular intellectual fare, and served, among others, a constituency of aspiring gentlemen. The new nation soon called upon them to make a still larger contribution.

### Generation 3: Republican Education, 1776–1800

The revolt against England ignited political sentiments in the colleges. However, college life was disrupted for much of the War for Independence and then developed slowly before the nation was united under the Constitution in 1788. Despite this triumph of federalism, political passions rose to a crescendo at the end of the century.

The ideal for collegiate education in this period sought a harmonious joining of disparate elements. First was the notion of republican education—instilling selflessness, patriotism, and virtue in the citizens and leaders of the new republic.

Such an outlook was conveyed through the choice of texts, topics for student oratory, and the widely touted (though unsuccessful) introduction of the study of law. Second, Enlightenment learning was welcomed as never before, although the fiscal limitations of colleges made realization fall far short of aspirations. Indeed, these years mark the zenith of Enlightenment influence in American colleges, a time in which theology sought to accommodate the truths of science and reason. Samuel Stanhope Smith (1795–1812), who succeeded Witherspoon at Princeton, epitomized both the ascendancy and the fragility of this "republican Christian Enlightenment": learning was valued in the colleges, and higher education was valued in the polity.[11]

After independence, the newly sovereign states made provision for collegiate education for their citizens. States that had no colleges chartered new institutions—Maryland (1782 and 1784), Georgia (1785), South Carolina (1785), North Carolina (1789), and Vermont (1791)—although some years passed before most of these institutions were able to open. Elsewhere, this same impulse sometimes became entwined with controversial changes in existing colleges. The board of visitors of William and Mary imposed a reorganization of the faculty in 1779, dispensing with classical languages. That same year, Pennsylvania supplanted the College of Philadelphia with a "public" institution (the two were merged in 1791 to form the University of Pennsylvania). The superstructure of the University of the State of New York was erected in the 1780s, in theory to oversee Columbia and future colleges. Where continuity was the rule, state officials were made ex officio trustees of colleges (Massachusetts, Connecticut, New Hampshire, and New Jersey), and financial support was sporadically provided. Denominationally sponsored colleges found few students and little influence in these years. The new colleges founded near the frontier often reflected close-knit denominational communities, but they, too, assumed a public outlook.

The vision of republican higher education was undermined considerably by the material weakness of the colleges. The nation's most solid institution, Harvard, had just three professors at the turn of the century. Collegiate enrollments for the last quarter of the century did not keep pace with population growth, despite the proliferation of new institutions. Where roughly 1 percent of a four-year male cohort attended college in 1775, the corresponding figure for 1800 was 0.75 percent. In some new colleges, like North Carolina, the absence of experienced teachers for a time fomented chaotic conditions. Student unruliness was a particular blight at institutions associated with Jeffersonian republicanism, such as William and Mary and Dickinson College. Public subsidies for state-sponsored colleges were soon terminated, leaving these institutions in an exceedingly weak state. At the end of the eighteenth century, there was no functioning model of a state college.[12]

Ironically, popular sentiment now began to turn decisively in support of religion, but the religion of the heart, not the head. In this respect, as in others, the consequences of the dissolution of republican education were realized after 1800.

## Generation 4: The Passing of Republican Education, 1800–1820s

The first generation of the nineteenth century is perhaps the least understood in American history. It has largely been associated with negative developments. Indeed, the most widely known historiographical treatment interprets it as the beginning of a "great retrogression."[13] Signs of trouble are not hard to find. The underpinnings of republican education were dislodged by popular egalitarianism, to the horror of the Federalists who dominated most colleges, and by the upsurge of religious spirit known as the Second Great Awakening. The most popular churches—Methodists and Baptists—opposed colleges and college-trained ministers before 1830. In addition, most institutions were in a parlous state. In a plea some other colleges might have echoed, Columbia trustees described the college's sorry state as "mortifying to its friends, [and] humiliating to the city."[14] The universities of Maryland and of North Carolina lost their state support; and such major institutions as Princeton and William and Mary entered prolonged declines.

Such a picture, however, portrays only misfortune. Harvard, Yale, Brown, and Union College all strengthened notably, and even Columbia was much improved by the 1820s. Moreover, an important group of institutions opened their doors shortly after 1800—Transylvania University, Bowdoin College, and the state colleges of Georgia and South Carolina. College enrollments slowly recovered, except during the depression caused by the War of 1812, bringing male participation back to 1 percent by the end of the 1820s. Underlying the fortunes of individual institutions, nevertheless, lay fundamental questions stemming in large measure from the obsolescence of the putative republican model: Who owned the colleges? What was their mission? What should students be taught? And how could they be controlled?

In the first three decades of the century, colleges experienced the worst student violence of their histories. Unruliness had long been endemic in all-male residential colleges, but these years were distinguished by episodes of collective resistance to college authority.[15] They invariably began with some relatively minor transgression of college rules, but what followed was the key. In certain cases, students deemed disciplinary action, based on measured degrees of public disgrace, to be unjustly severe. Believing their rights and dignity to have been violated, they would either remonstrate or commit further acts of insubordination. The colleges invariably won these contests of will, but at considerable cost. Numerous unrepentant students were expelled, and the college's reputation was besmirched. Such riots at Princeton and William and Mary were factors in precipitating their decline; Harvard endured its periodic riots more stoically; North Carolina forfeited public support.

Steven Novak interpreted student riots as the stimulus for college leaders to shift the emphasis of the curriculum back toward ancient languages. Latin and Greek were considered safe, and their difficult study promoted behavioral as well as mental discipline. However, "having embraced [this] curriculum for the wrong reasons—as a bulwark against dangerous ideas—academics were never able to bring it to life."[16] Other factors played a role here as well. Most conspicuous was the collapse of efforts to construct a republican curriculum of scientific and professional subjects, due to the lack of suitable teachers or interested students. Moreover, attempts to deemphasize classical languages threatened to undermine the entire enterprise. At Transylvania, the college course without Latin and Greek lasted just two years; and Dickinson students in 1800 demanded and were granted a reduction of the course to a single year. Socially, some knowledge of the classical languages was a badge of cultural distinction appropriate to gentlemen. As a practical matter, lax entrance requirements brought immature and poorly prepared students to campus. Most established colleges thus made concerted efforts to raise their entrance requirements, impose a minimum age, and strengthen instruction in Latin and Greek.

This restandardization of the classical curriculum corresponded to a refocusing of institutions on their collegiate missions. In a reciprocal development, the links between professional education and the colleges were dissolving. This trend has seldom been noted. Yale and other colleges sprouted professional schools during these years and appeared to become fledgling universities. Yet, few institutions followed this path, and professional schools in those that did were largely proprietary undertakings with little organic connection to the parent college. They resembled, in fact, the independent professional schools that began to flourish in this era.

The most vigorous law school after 1800 operated independently—in Litchfield, Connecticut. Unlike earlier attempts to teach law in the colleges, which were intended for civic education, Litchfield Law School prepared students for professional practice. In medicine, the dominant institution was the University of Pennsylvania. With enrollments exceeding four hundred, this medical school was the largest higher education unit in the country. But its students paid the professors directly for lectures, making the school virtually autonomous and quite overshadowing the college. Other medical schools either sought similar proprietary status or else they collapsed. The Columbia medical school faltered and was absorbed by another school; Harvard's medical school achieved greater autonomy by moving to Boston; and Brown's medical school folded when the college sought to control its faculty.[17] The most consequential change for the colleges, nevertheless, concerned the training of ministers.

The preparation of ministers was an implicit mission of the colleges, even though ministerial training had always followed the undergraduate course. When New England Congregationalists reacted to the Unitarian capture of Harvard by establishing Andover Theological Seminary (1808), a new alternative became available. During the next two decades, more schools for ministerial training were opened than new colleges. These institutions were, in a sense, alternatives to collegiate education and, as in the case of the Princeton Theological Seminary (1812), were votes of no confidence in the colleges. The leading seminaries became the locus for serious scholars of language and philology (and, hence, German academic scholarship), and they attracted gifts that might have gone to colleges.[18] Most consequential, they distanced colleges from the function of ministerial training, thus abetting a secular curriculum.

The final issue hanging over the colleges was the ambiguous mix of public function and private control. Controversies arising from this situation had plagued the colleges since the Revolution. What proved to be a definitive resolution had to await the justly celebrated Dartmouth College case (*Dartmouth College v. Woodward*, 1819). When the US Supreme Court ruled that New Hampshire could not without cause alter the charter of an "eleemosynary corporation" like Dartmouth College, it effectively provided colleges with a shield against unwanted intrusions of democratic legislatures. More significantly, it resolved an implicit question of ownership that had plagued virtually every college. In Massachusetts, for example, the composition of the board of overseers had been altered by the legislature three times in the 1810s. Justice Joseph Story, a member of that board, was undoubtedly as concerned with the autonomy of Harvard as with that of Dartmouth when he supported the trustees. Years passed before the import of the Dartmouth College case became fully apparent; the colleges continued to present both public and private personae, but an agenda of privatization clearly triumphed. Not only did the eastern provincial colleges become fully private institutions, but the way was also cleared for the establishment of a new type of unambiguously private denominational college.[19]

## Generation 5: The Classical Denominational Colleges, 1820s–1850s

Generation 5 began in the 1820s, with widespread challenges to the classical college, and was superseded in the 1850s by new waves of reform. The first efforts largely failed, but the second produced permanent change. In between, the private denominational college emerged as the characteristic institution of American higher education. Its success drove a rapid expansion in both the number of colleges and total enrollments. At the same time, sectional differences created distinctive patterns for higher education in the Northeast, the South, and the trans-Appalachian West.[20]

Criticism of the classical college in the 1820s in part reflected the success of efforts to bolster the curriculum. Now colleges were attacked for their obsession with dead languages, for neglecting practical subjects and science, and for the continued unruliness of apparently disgruntled students. A flurry of specific reforms occurred in the middle of the decade.[21] George Ticknor, after a student insurrection at Harvard, managed to reform his own modern languages department, offering advanced courses outside the rigid boundaries of the separate classes. Thomas Jefferson's University of Virginia (1824) provided an entirely new departure, aimed at achieving the nation's first true university. And Eliphalet Nott created a parallel scientific course at Union College (1827). Little lasting change resulted from this ferment of reform. The efforts of Ticknor and Nott remained isolated achievements, and the University of Virginia proved an incongruous (if congenial) setting for the sons of southern planters. Instead, the reforms provoked a magisterial defense of the classical college—the Yale *Reports* of 1828.

In defending the classical curriculum, the *Reports* defined the purpose of college as "to lay the foundation of a superior education."[22] The object, above all, was to discipline the mind and only secondarily to provide content, or "furniture." The classical languages were championed as the ideal vehicle for instilling mental discipline as well as culture and "balance." From these premises, the report could argue that all other forms of education—for practical training or advanced learning—should be relegated to other kinds of institutions. This position rationalized the de facto undergraduate focus of the colleges. The cogency of the Yale *Reports*, moreover, seemed to grow over time and became the principal defense of the classical course for the next fifty years.

The classical college drew on deeper strengths than the arguments of the Yale *Reports*. Furthermore, it had rather different histories on the eastern and western sides of the Appalachians. In the Northeast, generally, the colleges preserved their narrow focus on preprofessional liberal education and were content to serve the relatively limited clientele who valued such an expensive badge of cultural distinction. Student life in these institutions changed profoundly during this era and served to fortify this sense of distinction. As the colleges relaxed their oppressive discipline, the students themselves developed a rich extracurriculum of their own, including the rapid rise of fraternities. Student life was transformed into a self-contained world of activities and social ceremony that engendered deep loyalties instead of intense hostility.[23] In the West, the most salient development of this era was the proliferation of denominational colleges in territories that had, only short years before, been considered the frontier.

The prototypical denominational college nevertheless emerged in the East in the 1820s. The definition given by the Lutherans of Pennsylvania College (Gettysburg College, 1832) cut to the heart of the matter: noting that its students, teachers, trustees, and benefactors all were church members, they concluded that the college "may then with truth be said to belong to that Church." These colleges were established by religious minorities (some of whom had previously disdained advanced education for their ministers) primarily to educate and retain the loyalties of their members. The education of ministers was left to theological seminaries. Regional church organizations generally played an important role in founding denominational colleges as well as in their governance. Thus, Baptists established Waterville College (Colby College, 1820) and Columbian College (George Washington University, 1821). Episcopalians broke the Yale monopoly in Connecticut in 1826 (Trinity College). And Methodists joined the collegiate movement by opening Wesleyan University (1831) and Randolph-Macon College (1832). State legislatures required that the charters of these colleges impose no religious tests, nor had they any desire to since they served all local students. Like the Gettysburg Lutherans, the churches wanted their own colleges to educate their own communicants.

On the western side of the Appalachians, where colleges were virtually non-existent in 1820, denominational colleges soon proliferated. The earliest exemplars were founded by Congregational or Presbyterian missionaries almost as soon as the frontiers were settled. Later foundings tended to be sponsored by regional church organizations. In both cases, a crucial role was played by local boosters, who believed that a college would enhance the cultural and economic standing of their towns.[24] The western colleges were capable of notable experiments, especially where student access was concerned. Manual labor schemes were tried repeatedly—and unsuccessfully—in the 1830s and 1840s, and Oberlin College became the first college to admit women and African Americans. Pedagogically, though, they initially replicated the classical curriculum. Given denominational sponsorship and clerical leadership (often from graduates of Yale or Princeton), this path was a natural course to follow. Colin Burke argues that these institutions need to be viewed in a different framework from the established colleges of the East: they served the basic need for educational upgrading for their localities by becoming multipurpose colleges. Nearly all found it necessary to establish preparatory departments, for example. Over time, they tended to add diverse educational programs to the classical core in spite of limited means. The average size of western colleges in 1860 was about fifty-six collegiate students (compared with 174 in New England), and costs were kept low for their far-from-wealthy students. By 1860 the Southwest and Midwest contained 59 percent of colleges and 43 percent of students.[25]

A somewhat different institutional pattern, characterized by dominant state universities, emerged in the South during this era. The College of South Carolina (1803) and the University of Virginia (1824) were the region's strongest institutions and the only universities in the country to receive regular state appropriations before the Civil War. Both institutions catered to sons of the planter aristocracy, who dominated their states politically and socially. Such students, with exaggerated notions of personal honor, made student unrest endemic in southern universities. Denominational colleges in such milieus developed later and attracted a more humble clientele. The pattern of strong state universities spread throughout the Cotton Belt but conspicuously failed in states like Kentucky and Tennessee, where social and religious fragmentation favored denominational colleges.

The 1820s and 1830s were two of the most expansive decades for higher education. Enrollments jumped by roughly 80 percent in each decade, fueled by the establishment of denominational colleges. The 1840s, however, were years of comparative stagnation: they were no doubt hampered by the severe economic downturn that followed the crash of 1837 and by the limited appeal of the classical course in the East. Exasperation with these conditions prompted another spasm of reform. Brown president Francis Wayland (1827–56) diagnosed the weakness of the eastern colleges: they catered solely to the professional class and furnished students with only a preprofessional education—precisely the narrow focus advocated in the Yale *Reports*. Entirely neglected were practitioners of industry and commerce, who were responsible for the transformation taking place in the American economy.[26] However, these were the polemics of the 1820s in a more sophisticated guise. Wayland's attempt to restructure Brown in order to appeal to this new class proved disastrous. Ironically, his failure occurred at the opening of one of the most dynamic eras of American higher education. The ensuing generation, rather than displacing the classical college, created new institutions and studies to complement it.

### Generation 6: New Departures, 1850s–1890

The Civil War has long been the conventional dividing line for the history of American higher education. However, most of the new departures associated with the postbellum years emerged in preliminary form in the 1850s, if not earlier. German-style universities, offering graduate education, are associated with the opening of Johns Hopkins University in 1876, but Henry Tappan (1853–63) transformed the University of Michigan in these same directions. The Morrill Land Grant Act of 1862 can lay exclusive claim to neither "schools of science" nor agricultural colleges. Daniel Coit Gilman estimated that twenty such institutions existed before 1860, including Yale's Sheffield Scientific School, which had evolved from a few extracurricular courses into a department in which both practical and advanced subjects could be studied.[27] In addition, at least four agricultural colleges were chartered in the 1850s, in Pennsylvania, Michigan, Maryland, and Ohio.

In the same decade, collegiate education was broadened to include other than white males. More than forty women's institutions were chartered to offer collegiate degrees before Matthew Vassar presumed to give women "a college in the proper sense of the word."[28] Ashmun Institute (Lincoln University, 1854) in Pennsylvania and Wilberforce University (1856) in Ohio provided college education for free African Americans.

Perhaps the greatest continuity from antebellum to postbellum years existed for denominational colleges. They began a second period of proliferation in the

1850s, which carried through to the early 1870s. The dynamics of this expansion derived from a dual process of extension and elaboration. Through extension, colleges followed close behind the ever-moving frontier into the trans-Mississippi West. Once again, the agents of these initial foundings were largely missionaries from the principal denominations. In the wake of this movement, and indeed throughout the Midwest, a second process of elaboration occurred as denominations without colleges made provision for the education of their church members. These colleges were inherently multipurpose. They still preserved the classical core, but added degree courses in English and science or practical courses in business and teaching. In keeping with this impulse to serve their denominations broadly, these multipurpose colleges were often coeducational, except for denominations opposed to this in principle (Roman Catholics, Presbyterians, German Lutherans). This great expansion of denominational colleges proceeded unfazed by the dawning age of the university, until conditions changed radically after 1890.[29]

The Morrill Land Grant Act still largely determined the character of the new utilitarian education. Enthusiasm among the industrial classes for education in agriculture or the mechanical arts turned out to be sparse. True, well-publicized Cornell University attracted the nation's largest entering class in 1868, but these initial students were mixed in their aspirations and qualifications. Only 10 percent eventually graduated. Outside of New England, preparatory departments overshadowed collegiate ones in the new land-grant colleges. After a slow start, enrolments in engineering grew in the 1880s and then accelerated after 1890. Matriculants in agriculture, however, remained few and far between. Reformers simply failed to find ways to connect farming with advanced education.

Contrary to the conventional view, land-grant colleges did not meet an exigent popular demand, nor did they appreciably democratize higher education. Had they been dependent on enrollment, many undoubtedly would have failed. However, the circumstances of their beginnings gave them an assured, if meager, income as well as an implicit relationship with their respective states. They were thus sustained long enough through their sickly infancy for social and economic conditions to catch up to the expectations that had prompted their somewhat premature founding. In 1890, after intensive lobbying by land-grant presidents, the Second Morrill Act gave these institutions direct annual infusions of federal funds, a crucial advantage at a time when universities were entering their most dynamic era of growth.[30]

The first Morrill Act nevertheless set the most important precondition for utilitarian education when it stipulated the establishment of "at least one *college*" in which these subjects would be taught "without excluding other scientific and classical studies."[31] Unlike continental Europe, where modern languages and useful subjects were taught in less-prestigious institutions than those offering classical and theoretical studies, in the United States the progeny of the industrial classes would eventually study in the same institutions as those from the professional classes.

Despite the salience of the Morrill Act, these years were characterized far more by private initiatives and, particularly, single acts of philanthropy. Gifts of hitherto unprecedented size sought to fill lacunae in American higher education. Matthew Vassar, Henry Wells, Sophia Smith, and Henry Durant (Wellesley College) founded colleges for women between 1865 and 1875 that were intended to equal the best men's colleges.[32] Ezra Cornell and John Purdue enhanced the effectiveness of land-grant colleges. Trustees of estates were responsible for establishing the Stevens Institute of Technology and the Johns Hopkins University. This era culminated with the most spectacular new institutions (after Hopkins)—Clark and Stanford universities and the University of Chicago.

The American university is the most enduring legacy of these developments, even though its ascendancy over American higher education would have to await the next generation. Charles Eliot said in 1869 that no university yet existed in the United States, and prior to 1890 it was uncertain what form an American university would assume. Indeed, Daniel Coit Gilman, G. Stanley Hall, David Starr Jordan, and William Rainey Harper each independently attempted to invent such an institution (at Johns Hopkins, Clark, Stanford, and Chicago, respectively). The chief conundrum was the relationship between advanced learning, or graduate education, and the American college.

The true paradigm of the American university evolved instead at the country's paramount institution. Charles W. Eliot assumed the presidency of Harvard in 1869 with a clear sense of the changes that were needed in both college and professional schools. For the college, he sought to replace recitations and the classical curriculum with an elective system of taught courses that could accommodate true learning. This reform took a decade and a half, but by then the old regime was vanquished at Harvard and in retreat elsewhere. Eliot also attacked the decadence of the professional schools at the outset of his presidency. A learned, full-time faculty replaced proprietary-teachers; a mandatory curriculum was put in place; and professional education was eventually defined as requiring a bachelor's degree. Eliot's instincts were by no means as sure when it came to graduate education. But as the elective system allowed him to appoint many more learned professors, a distinguished faculty emerged, capable of scholarship, research, and advanced instruction. In 1890 the scientific school and the college faculty were merged into the Faculty of Arts and Sciences. The Graduate School of Arts and Sciences was its other face. Finally, Eliot felt that Harvard was "now well on the way to the complete organization of a university in a true sense." The American university would be an institution in which the instruction of large numbers of undergraduates would support a numerous, specialized faculty who would also teach graduate students. Not even the ingenious William Rainey Harper could devise anything better. Moreover, this model was a natural one for the more vigorous state universities, whose growth was about to explode. The next generation of American higher education would see the efflorescence of this powerful combination of mixed purposes.[33]

## Generation 7: Growth and Standardization, 1890 to World War I

The character of growth in American higher education changed profoundly around 1890. During the previous generation, enrollment growth had been absorbed into an increasing number of institutions, but during generation 7 the net number of institutions remained fairly stable, while enrollments swelled. The average institution in 1870 had 10 faculty and 98 students; in 1890, these figures had grown to just 16 faculty and 157 students; but in 1910, they were up to 38 faculty and 374 students. Moreover, the largest institutions led this growth: in 1895 the ten largest universities averaged nearly 2,000 students; in 1910 they approximated 4,000; and in 1915, 5,000.[34]

At the other end of the spectrum, colleges that failed to grow were threatened with extinction. The institutional order was anything but stable; the founding of new colleges continued unabated into the 1890s, but many institutions expired during these years.

One important source of growth was the assimilation of women into higher education. In 1890 the majority of female students were found in single-sex colleges, most of which were regarded by contemporaries as inferior. This situation changed abruptly with the opening of the elective curriculum and the expansion of universities. The proportion of women students grew slowly, from 32 to 37 percent (1890–1913), but the proportion of women in coeducational institutions nearly doubled, to 68 percent. The gulf between the educational experiences of women and men narrowed even further in the next generation.[35]

The standardization of the universities after 1890 is the central theme of Laurence Veysey's classic study. His deliberate emphasis on the intellectual history of this subject, however, may slight some of the more mundane features, largely caused by similar adaptations to a common environment. The rapid growth of universities resulted from the growth of their several parts. Most added units in engineering, business, and education, plus different combinations of other smaller specialties (e.g., mining, forestry, dentistry, pharmacy, veterinary medicine, art, architecture, and music), in addition to schools for graduate study, medicine, and law. Universities became compartmentalized institutions, whose parts shared little common subject matter. Administrative structures were necessary to serve these intellectually autonomous compartments and especially to secure ever more resources to fulfill their needs.[36]

By 1908 it was possible to define the standard American university. It admitted only bona fide high school graduates. It provided them with two years of general education followed by two years of advanced or specialized courses. It offered doctoral training in at least five departments, appropriately led by PhDs, and had at least one professional school. A sizable list of possible options might be added: summer sessions, extension work, correspondence courses, a university press, and the publication of learned journals. Idiosyncrasies faded away in this environment, such as Eliot's free elective system and proposed three-year bachelor's degree. Outliers moved closer to the norm: Johns Hopkins enrolled more undergraduates and lengthened the bachelor of arts course to four years; the Massachusetts Institute of Technology established units for research and graduate education.

The universities, in turn, were the most powerful force in generating standards for the rest of higher education, chiefly by defining academic knowledge and the academic profession. From about 1890 to 1905, all of the major disciplinary associations assumed their modern form. In a parallel development, the departmental structure of colleges and universities replicated these contours. Academic disciplines henceforth possessed a dual structure, whereby scientific recognition was embodied in disciplinary organizations while the most consequential positions, those commanding the means to advance these fields, were in university departments. As teaching positions were increasingly reserved for faculty who contributed to the knowledge base of disciplines, the universities imposed a definition on the academic profession. University faculty then took this definition a step further by organizing the American Association of University Professors (1915) to champion their professional rights, particularly academic freedom.[37]

Probably much more apparent to contemporaries was the "Collegiate Revolution"—the explosion of student-run organizations and activities on campus, with the rise of football being the most prominent. Younger alumni with business careers in urban centers, in particular, appreciated the social qualities that were instilled by extracurricular activities. Their ability to contribute badly needed funds gave their wishes weight among college trustees and eventually influenced the selection of modernizing presidents. Denominational doctrines were soon deemphasized in favor of broad, middle-of-the-road Protestantism, epitomized in the soaring popularity of the campus YMCA. New kinds of students began to matriculate, eager to throw themselves into campus activities and consciously destined for careers in the business world. Intercollegiate athletics tended to be the catalyst in this process, galvanizing the enthusiasm of students and the loyalties of alumni.[38]

The collegiate ideal developed first out of the unique traditions of the Ivy League schools, especially Harvard and Yale. It quickly captured imaginations among the principal eastern colleges and spread to include state universities. The older generation of university leaders, such as Charles Eliot, had scant regard for such activities, but the next generation—Eliot's successor, Abbott Lawrence Lowell (1909–33), and above all Woodrow Wilson (1902–10) at Princeton—sought to amalgamate the collegiate ideal with their own concern for enhancing undergraduate learning. The collegiate ideal projected clear normative standards emphasizing the college experience outside the classroom, while another form of standardization found champions after 1900.

In 1905 the Carnegie Foundation for the Advancement of Teaching was chartered to provide pensions for college teachers. That same year, the General Education Board reoriented its activities toward promoting "a comprehensive system of higher education in the United States." Both foundations sought to alleviate the "chaos" and "confusion" they perceived in American higher education. The former promulgated stringent criteria of eligibility for its pensions, and institutions scrambled to conform. The latter worked more subtly by providing matching endowment grants that forced colleges to appeal to their alumni.[39] Neither required an institution to have a football team, but they validated the types of schools that did: residential colleges with strong alumni support.

Following the model of the Land-Grant College Association (1887), successive associations were formed in this era, and their efforts also furthered standardization. The National Association of State Universities formulated the definition of the "standard American university." The Association of American Universities

(AAU), formed to set standards for graduate education, soon became, in effect, an accrediting agency for colleges.[40]

A generation of standardizing activities gave much greater definition to the American system of higher education, even if it left the system still highly diverse and decentralized. By World War I, American colleges and universities by and large conformed to a single pattern in terms of admissions, credit hours, offerings, majors, and so on. The large divergence among institutions pertained chiefly to the level of resources each commanded for the fulfillment of this pattern. Differences in resources would henceforth produce a steep and increasingly apparent hierarchy among American institutions of higher education.

## Generation 8: Mass Higher Education and Differentiation between the Wars

Enrollments in higher education approximately doubled during the 1920s, and this expansion triggered qualitative changes analogous to what Martin Trow would later identify as the transition from elite to mass higher education.[41] Elite patterns are characterized by full-time residential students, by cultural ideals of liberal learning and character formation, and by destinations in high-status professions. In contrast, mass forms of higher education cater to part-time or commuting students, convey applicable knowledge, and prepare students for employment in technical or semiprofessional positions. American higher education had always been somewhat hierarchical in terms of resource levels and admissions requirements. Between the two world wars, however, it became much more explicit. Emerging forms of higher education fulfilled "mass" roles, and educational leaders deliberately sought to offer qualitatively different kinds of instruction for different levels of students.

The growth of a mass sector in American higher education was apparent in the burgeoning junior colleges, teachers colleges, and service-oriented, urban universities.[42] Teachers colleges resulted from the process of continuously upgrading normal schools. This process began in the 1900s, although the majority of normal schools were converted in the 1920s. During this period most teachers colleges were confined to education degrees for mostly primary school teachers. In addition, education departments of traditional universities offered superior credentials for higher positions. But as heirs to the normal schools, they provided access to higher education for a broad segment of the population, especially women.

The expansion of higher education to serve city dwellers included both new and existing institutions. The free municipal university established in Akron

(1913) exemplified the former. It aimed to produce employable graduates for the region, typically with programs in engineering, home economics, commerce, and teaching. The College of the City of New York was perhaps the most spectacular exemplar of this phenomenon, growing to more than 24,000 students during the 1920s. Private municipal universities shared in this growth, especially New York University. Both types combined a variety of professional schools and programs with special courses for part-time students. In 1930, for example, part-time and summer students exceeded full-time students at New York, Northwestern, Southern California, Boston, and Western Reserve universities. By that date, the biggest American institutions were no longer research universities, but municipal universities with large, irregular enrollments.

True junior colleges first appeared in the decade of the 1900s but multiplied in the 1920s. They provided local access to higher education for both sparsely populated areas of the West and cities. By 1940, 11 percent of college students were enrolled in junior colleges, many of which were still attached to local high schools. The emergence of junior colleges nevertheless profoundly affected thinking about the structure and purpose of American higher education.

The waves of mass higher education lapping the shores of traditional institutions produced largely defensive reactions. President Ernest Hopkins of Dartmouth caused a stir by declaring that "too many young men are going to college." Perhaps the most vehement critic was Abraham Flexner, who charged that universities had become "'service' stations for the general public."[43] A number of educators took inspiration from the apparent success of junior colleges and concluded that democratic access should extend through the sophomore year of college. The University of Minnesota created a two-year, terminal General College for students deemed unfit for its regular programs. Another clear rationalization of hierarchical differentiation was the Carnegie Foundation's 1932 report, *State Higher Education in California*, which defined separate roles for the university in Berkeley, regional state colleges, and largely vocational junior colleges. This document was resisted in California, but represented widespread opinion that sought to define the junior colleges as terminal programs.

Determined efforts by the leaders of higher education had the effect of hardening the outlines of the mass sector of higher education, which had emerged almost spontaneously. Similarly, purposeful actions were required to define the upper reaches of American higher education. As with the mass sector, this was a matter combining, all at the same time, social origins and destinations, manner or style of attendance, and links with higher learning.

Three general criteria could be used to claim elite status. The *collegiate ideal*, especially popular in the 1920s, was determined by the peer society of students, by extracurricular activities, and by expectations of subsequent careers in the business world. *Quality of undergraduate learning* was a persistent concern; not only did colleges attempt to raise their standards, but many educators also sought to re-create the elusive ideal of liberal education. In universities, the imperative of *advancing knowledge* was an end in itself, the touchstone of research and graduate education, but also a distinguishing feature of only a handful of institutions.

At the leading private institutions, financial constraints and rising applications prompted limits on the number of students after World War I. At the same time, these institutions became more sensitive to the social composition of their students and the implications it had for their collegiate image. Columbia pioneered a form of selective admissions in which social criteria were used to limit the proportion of Jewish students, and the same discriminatory procedures were soon copied by Princeton, Yale, and Harvard.[44] Selective admissions were part of a larger pattern of fashioning elite status. These institutions shaped the peer society and collegiate environment not only by excluding supposedly nonconforming social types, but also by widening their recruitment pool to encompass the entire country. They simultaneously became national rather than regional institutions, culling the weakest academic performers from among their traditional clientele and raising the level of study, at least slightly. As these institutions prospered in the 1920s, they vastly increased educational spending on each student. When Yale launched higher education's largest endowment drive in 1927, it promised "to make a finer, not a bigger Yale."[45]

For elite universities, additional wealth was invested in more and better faculty—in scientists and scholars actively engaged in the advancement of knowledge. This phase of development was strongly assisted by philanthropic foundations, particularly the Rockefeller trusts. Participation in research also conferred prestige and elite status. Recognition in this dimension lay outside of universities, in international communities of scholars. It thus created an altogether different set of imperatives, which universities could scarcely ignore. It was no paradox, then, that a Jew could be a physics professor at Princeton but not an undergraduate: universalism prevailed in the former sphere but not in the latter.

Probably the most difficult course for sculpting an elite status was to excel in only undergraduate education. However, Swarthmore, under president Frank Aydelotte (1921–39), was a notable success in this regard. Inspired by his Oxford experience as a Rhodes Scholar, Aydelotte established an honors program to provide a rigorous course of study for able and motivated students. At the same time, he progressively deemphasized the underpinnings of the collegiate ideal—sororities, fraternities, and big-time football. The honors program was used to attract academically ambitious students and soon made Swarthmore one of the most academically selective colleges in the country. The high cost of this education was met with help from Abraham Flexner and the General Education Board, who supported high academic standards.[46]

The hierarchical differentiation of the institutional order between the wars simultaneously moved American higher education in several different directions with respect to elite and mass sectors, access, and the curriculum. American higher education became open to virtually all high school graduates, a category that grew from 9 to 51 percent of age cohorts between 1910 and 1940. Yet social exclusiveness among many elite institutions increased, too, as nativist prejudice strengthened. The system was only weakly meritocratic and largely mirrored the social biases prevailing in the workplace. In curricular matters, the expanding mass sector was dominated by vocationally oriented programs, including attempts to define terminal tracks. A preoccupation of the era was nevertheless the persistent desire to fashion a true liberal education. At the same time, the implacable advancement of the academic disciplines weighed ever more heavily on the structure of college courses. Which trends predominated? The answer would become apparent during the next generation of American higher education: democratic access triumphed over social exclusiveness; academic development raised the stature of mass institutions, even as elite ones became more meritocratic; and an academic revolution confirmed the ascendancy of the academic curriculum.

### Generation 9: The Academic Revolution, 1945–1975

The thirty years following the end of World War II were possibly the most tumultuous in the history of American higher education. Two fundamental movements nevertheless underlie these myriad developments: expansion and academic standardization. Beginning with the flood of returning soldiers, supported by the Servicemen's Readjustment Act of 1944 (the GI Bill), and concluding with the tidal wave of community college students in the early 1970s, this period was the most expansive in the American experience. The proportion of young people attending college tripled, from 15 to 45 percent; from 1940 to 1970, undergraduates grew almost fivefold, and graduate students almost ninefold; and the 1960s alone registered the largest percentage growth of any decade.[47]

While previous growth spurts, like the 1920s, were associated with new types of institutions reaching new clienteles, the postwar period was characterized by an implacable movement toward common academic standards. Not only did institutions become more alike in terms of curricular offerings, faculty training, and administrative practices, but students migrated toward studies in the arts and sciences. The principal dynamics of this era fortified these developments.

Excess demand for college places existed through most of the era, allowing institutions to supply education largely on their terms. This phenomenon arose when returning veterans took advantage of the GI Bill in unprecedented and unanticipated numbers. In 1947, 1.1 million ex-GIs were enrolled, compared with 1.5 million total students before the war. This surge did little to raise standards, though, as overcrowded institutions were forced to run year round, shorten courses, and curtail requirements. This interlude nevertheless rebuilt depleted institutional treasuries and boosted morale as well. In the wake of this experience, most institutions sought to consolidate and bolster their programs.

Enrollment backtracked only slightly in the early 1950s, before larger cohorts began coming of age and seeking college places. Student numbers grew by approximately 50 percent in the 1950s. By the end of the decade, however, the baby-boom generation had already filled the high schools. The 1960s experienced a double effect: participation rates increased by half (from 30% to 45%), and the eighteen- to twenty-one-year-old age cohort grew even more (from 9 million to 15 million). This flood of students flowed into flagship state universities, which expanded to their limits and then became increasingly selective. Private institutions, which had more difficulty funding expansion, tended to optimize their efforts by building stronger academic programs for a more select student body. A large portion of the new students found places at burgeoning regional state institutions. Formerly teachers colleges, these institutions eagerly expanded academic programs, ventured into graduate education, and became regional universities. The final component of this growth came from new public community colleges which, from 1965 to 1972, were opened at a rate exceeding one per week.

Higher education expanded in another way by opening to previously excluded minorities, most dramatically African Americans. The 1954 *Brown v. Board of Education* decision outlawing segregation had little immediate impact on southern colleges and universities. Instead, often violent confrontations achieved no more than token integration. Only the 1964 Civil Rights Act overcame the obstruction of southern politicians and allowed a genuine process of desegregation to begin. At the same time, northern colleges and universities began to undertake proactive efforts to reverse the grievous underrepresentation of African American students.

The idealism suffusing higher education after the war lent support for the basic arts and sciences. Institutions emphasizing these subjects had assumed preponderant prestige in the interwar years. Now, a consensus formed endorsing the Harvard report *General Education in a Free Society* (1945), which pronounced that a judicious sampling of the basic disciplines would comprise the foundation for a liberal education.[48] The pattern of institutional expansion also supported this trend toward arts and sciences. Service institutions that had embraced vocational-professional programs (or were confined to teacher education) in the interwar years gradually fortified disciplinary departments. A shift in student majors ensued in the 1960s, when bachelor's degrees awarded in the arts and sciences rose to a peak of 47 percent.[49]

These trends were powerfully fortified by a prodigious expansion of research and graduate education, largely due to federal support.[50] Federal sponsorship of research initially took place within the channels established for the wartime emergency. For more than a decade after World War II, the bulk of the increased funding for academic research came from the defense establishment and was skewed toward the physical sciences. However, a new federal relationship with higher education emerged after the Sputnik crisis of 1957 sparked national resolve. For about a decade after Sputnik, huge increases in funding for academic science came from the civilian side of the federal government: the National Science Foundation, the National Aeronautical and Space Administration, and, most prolifically, the National Institutes of Health. Moreover, this bounteous support was accompanied by assistance for universities to support graduate students, build laboratories, and develop new science programs. Sputnik also provoked Washington to support higher education directly, first through the National Defense Education Act and later through direct aid for buildings and students. Federal largess, superimposed on mushrooming enrollments and state support, produced an ephemeral golden age in American higher education.

Christopher Jencks and David Riesman characterized the transformation that occurred during this era as "the academic revolution."[51] They meant the process by which the theoretical and specialized academic outlook of graduate schools was conveyed throughout the institutional order. It was a process that transcended the sciences, ultimately affecting virtually every school and department. The agents were the new PhDs, trained in burgeoning graduate programs, who staffed the expanding universities. Their teaching and their writings brought the most current and specialized academic knowledge into the classrooms of all types of institutions. Ultimately, however, the expectations and idealism of the academic revolution set the stage for a backlash that arose in the late 1960s. Its chief manifestation was the great student rebellion.

The student movement crystallized from the Free Speech Movement at the University of California at Berkeley and Students for a Democratic Society. The national issues of the war in Vietnam and racial injustice largely propelled its evolution toward increasing radicalism and militancy. Although the major campuses suffered their greatest disruption from the fall of 1967 to the spring of 1970, the enduring impact altered the prevailing atmosphere of higher education. The momentum of the academic revolution was checked. The university's relation to students was profoundly altered, from paternalism to exaggerated permissiveness. And universities retreated for a time to an ivory-tower aloofness. The student rebellion was the crescendo to the tumultuous postwar generation, but it only partially foreshadowed the dawning new era.

## Generation 10: Privatization and the Current Era, 1975–2010

To extend historical analysis beyond the point at which documentation is available and ensuing consequences can be known is perilous. Nonetheless, it is now apparent that the 1970s represented a transitional decade for higher education, and that since 1980 significant developments have altered the demographics, politics, and social relations of American higher education.

In 1975, enrollments in higher education topped 11 million, but then an unprecedented change occurred: student numbers for the first time ceased to grow. In the ensuing years there was an upward creep, but twenty years later the number of full-time students had grown by just 20 percent. Never before had enrollments been so stagnant for so long. One important dynamic was nevertheless at work: whereas 55 percent of students were male in 1975, 55 percent were female in 1995.

Higher education's relationship with the federal government changed in these years. Federal investment in higher education increased significantly in the 1970s, with the new funds being used to support access through student financial aid. The 1972 amendments to the Higher Education Act were a watershed in two respects. First, they formalized a major commitment to provide aid to students on the basis of financial need. Second, the 1972 amendments extended the government's regulatory control over higher education. The student rebellion of the 1960s had, in effect, staked the claim for a greater presence in higher education for minorities and women. Title IX now provided the means for legal enforcement. It was perhaps the most significant of a number of measures by which federal regulation became an inescapable presence in higher education.

One clarion call of the student rebellion was for greater relevance in university studies. Relevance indeed became a hallmark of the new era, but in ways not anticipated by student activists. They had advocated a tendentious relevance predicated on the university's role as an aloof critic of society. Thus they urged universities to study and seek to ameliorate problems stemming from the Vietnam War, racial inequality, poverty, and the environment. These topics long remained preoccupations on campuses, but 1970s students sought a more tangible form of relevance by turning away from the arts and sciences toward more vocational or professional majors. Bachelor's degrees in arts and sciences plummeted to just over one-quarter of the total, barely more than the number awarded in business alone.

Beginning around 1980, American higher education entered a new era of privatization. Whereas the previous generation had been characterized by increasing government investments, higher education now began to extract a growing proportion of revenues from the private sources. Most prominent was rising absolute and relative levels of tuition. From the 1950s to 1980, average tuition in both the public and private sectors had been stable, as a percentage of median family income. These figures doubled in both sectors by the late 1990s and then rose steeply again after 2001.[52] These increases made possible higher levels of spending especially in private colleges and universities. In public institutions the burden for these expenditures was shifted from states to students and parents. Several conditions made this possible.

Private colleges and universities adopted a strategy of "high tuition–high aid," whereby large tuition increases were accompanied by financial aid for students with financial need. The increasing availability of federal student loans after the Middle Income Student Assistance Act (1978) touched off the development of a loan culture that has grown ever since. However, private schools amplified the impact of federal student aid by offering additional institutional aid—tuition discounts—to allow students to meet escalating prices. Differential pricing and loans thus prevented demand from falling due to lack of affordability. Private schools also benefited from a soaring demand for high-priced, high-quality education at selective colleges and universities. Rising monetary returns to a college education and media publicity for college rankings encouraged this "selectivity sweepstakes." Some of these same factors affected the public sector, although not tuition discounting. However, public institutions had to adapt to the stagnation of state appropriations. Real spending per student peaked in the late 1970s and fluctuated at somewhat lower levels since then. Rising tuition thus compensated for the relative shrinkage of public support.[53]

The consequences of this financial aid revolution have been mixed. Private colleges and universities have enjoyed unparalleled prosperity, with the wealthiest institutions receiving the greatest bounty from burgeoning student demand, rising tuition revenue, large donations, and outsized investment returns. At the same time, despite programs to recruit diverse students and provide greater student aid, the wealthiest institutions predominantly enroll wealthy students, and in fact depend on them to pay the high tuition that is necessary for high financial aid. For American higher education as a whole, rising prices have been accompanied by increasing social stratification. In the public sector, regional campuses and community colleges have, on the whole, been weakened by declining appropriations. Public research universities have adapted by raising tuition and performing an ever-increasing volume of research.

Privatization in university research began decisively in 1980, with a succession of federal actions designed to encourage the transfer of university technology to private industry and the commercialization of university inventions. During the current era, the expectation that university research can or should contribute to economic development has become an article of faith in many circles. This rationale, in turn, has justified a healthy growth of private, state, but mostly federal investments in academic research. On campuses, research has grown far more rapidly than instruction or faculty, thus increasing its relative weight in the balance of university activities. Controversy over university involvement in commercial pursuits has accompanied these developments. But, undeniably, the current era has seen an enormous expansion of university research, a corresponding strengthening of most research universities, and greater contributions to society.[54]

The economic turmoil of 2008–10 almost certainly signaled the passing of generation 10 and the probable inception of new trends as yet too inchoate to identify. Nonetheless, the experience of generation 10 will no doubt shape the nature of future developments. The achievements of American research universities first excited the envy of the world and now have stimulated growing competition. The United States has long been the most educated society in the world, but due to enrollment stagnation, our college graduation rates now trail more than a dozen countries. National commitments to rectify this situation will need to overcome the high price of tuition and an excessive reliance on student loans. Yet the demand for places in public four-year and community colleges is growing, even while public investment is declining. The next generation will be challenged to sustain the immeasurable contributions that colleges and universities make to American society, let alone to improve on them.

## NOTES

*References have been limited to principal secondary works and quotation sources. The first eight generations are examined more thoroughly in Roger L. Geiger,* The History of American Higher Education: Learning and Culture from the Founding to World War II *(Princeton: Princeton University Press, 2015). For additional bibliography, see Christine A. Ogren, "Sites, Students, Scholarship, and Structure: The Historiography of American Higher Education in the Post-Revisionist Era," in* Rethinking the History of American Education, *ed. William J. Reese and John L. Rury (New York: Palgrave Macmillan, 2008).*

1. Jurgen Herbst, *From Crisis to Crisis: American College Government, 1636–1819* (Cambridge, MA: Harvard University Press, 1982), 1–61.

2. Samuel Eliot Morison, *Three Centuries of Harvard, 1636–1936* (Cambridge, MA: Harvard University Press, 1936), 53–82; Richard Hofstadter, *Academic Freedom in the Age of the College* (New Brunswick, NJ: Transaction, 1996 [1955]), 98–113; Susan H. Godson, Ludwell H. Johnson, Richard B. Sherman, Thad W. Tate, and Helen C. Walker, *The College of William and Mary: A History*, 2 vols. (Williamsburg, VA: King and Queen Press, 1993), vol. 1, 3–80; J. David Hoeveler, *Creating the American Mind: Intellect and Politics in the Colonial Colleges* (Lanham, MD: Rowman and Littlefield, 2002).

3. Herbst, *From Crisis to Crisis*, 38–47; Richard Warch, *School of the Prophets: Yale College, 1701–1740* (New Haven, CT: Yale University Press, 1973).

4. Bruce A. Kimball, *The "True Professional Ideal" in America: A History* (Cambridge, MA: Blackwell, 1992), 75–84; Herbst, *From Crisis to Crisis*, 1.

5. William D. Carrell, "American College Professors: 1750–1800," *History of Education Quarterly* 8 (1968): 289–305.

6. Herbst, *From Crisis to Crisis*, 82–137; Howard Miller, *The Revolutionary College: American Presbyterian Higher Education, 1707–1837* (New York: New York University Press, 1976), 65–75; Hoeveler, *Creating the American Mind*; Roger L. Geiger and Nathan M. Sorber, "Tarnished Icon: William Smith and the College of Philadelphia," *Perspectives on the History of Higher Education* 28 (2011): 1–32.

7. Beverly McAnear, "College Founding in the American Colonies: 1745–1775," *Mississippi Valley Historical Review* 42 (1952): 24–44.

8. David C. Humphrey, *From King's College to Columbia, 1746–1800* (New York: Columbia University Press, 1976), 199; Robert McCaughey, *Stand Columbia: A History of Columbia University* (New York: Columbia University Press, 2003); Morison, *Three Centuries*, 102–3; James McLachlan, introduction to *The Princetonians, 1748–1768: A Biographical Dictionary* (Princeton, NJ: Princeton University Press, 1977).

9. Edmund S. Morgan, *The Gentle Puritan: A Life of Ezra Stiles, 1727–1795* (Chapel Hill: University of North Carolina Press, 1962), 47–57; Henry F. May, *The Enlightenment in America* (New York: Oxford University Press, 1976); Hoeveler, *Creating the American Mind.*

10. Mark A. Noll, *Princeton and the Republic, 1768–1822: The Search for a Christian Enlightenment in the Era of Samuel Stanhope Smith* (Princeton, NJ: Princeton University Press, 1989), 16–98; Miller, *Revolutionary College,* 82–94.

11. Noll, *Princeton and the Republic,* 185–213, 297–99; David W. Robson, *Educating Republicans: The Colleges in the Era of the American Revolution, 1750–1800* (Westport, CT: Greenwood, 1985), 143–77.

12. Robson, *Educating Republicans,* 247.

13. Hofstadter, *Academic Freedom,* 209–53. However, see Roger L. Geiger, "The Reformation of the Colleges in the Early Republic," *History of Universities* 16, no. 2 (2000): 129–81.

14. *A History of Columbia University, 1754–1904* (New York: Columbia University Press, 1904), 100. See also McCaughey, *Stand Columbia.*

15. Geiger, "Reformation of the Colleges," 133–39; Steven J. Novak, *The Rights of Youth: American Colleges and Student Revolt, 1798–1815* (Cambridge, MA: Harvard University Press, 1977); Leon Jackson, "The Rights of Man and the Rites of Youth: Fraternity and Riot at Eighteenth-Century Harvard," in *The American College in the Nineteenth Century,* ed. Roger L. Geiger (Nashville, TN: Vanderbilt University Press, 2000), 46–79.

16. Novak, *Rights of Youth,* 166. However, see also Caroline Winterer, *The Culture of Classicism: Ancient Greece and Rome in American Intellectual Life, 1780–1910* (Baltimore: Johns Hopkins University Press, 2002).

17. Alfred Z. Reed, *Training for the Public Profession of the Law* (New York: Scribner, 1921), 116–60; William F. Norwood, *Medical Education in the United States before the Civil War* (Philadelphia: University of Pennsylvania Press, 1944).

18. Natalie A. Naylor, "The Theological Seminary in the Configuration of American Higher Education: The Ante-Bellum Years," *History of Education Quarterly* 17 (1977): 17–30; Glenn T. Miller, *Piety and Intellect: The Aims and Purposes of Ante-Bellum Theological Education* (Atlanta: Scholar's Press, 1990).

19. Herbst, *From Crisis to Crisis,* 232–43; Leon Burr Richardson, *History of Dartmouth College* (Hanover, NH: Dartmouth College Publications, 1932), 287–346; John S. Whitehead and Jurgen Herbst, "How to Think about the Dartmouth College Case," *History of Education Quarterly* 26 (1986): 333–50; Geiger, *History,* 160–70.

20. Geiger, *History,* chap. 6.

21. Stanley M. Guralnik, *Science and the Ante-Bellum American College* (Philadelphia: American Philosophical Society, 1975), 18–46.

22. David B. Potts, *Liberal Learning for a Land of Colleges* (New York: Palgrave Macmillan, 2010); *Reports on the Course of Instruction in Yale College; By a Committee of the Corporation and the Academical Faculty* (New Haven, CT: H. Howe, 1828).

23. Frederick Rudolph, *Mark Hopkins and the Log: Williams College, 1836–1872* (New Haven, CT: Yale University Press, 1956); Roger L. Geiger, with Julie Ann Bubolz, "College as It Was in the Mid-Nineteenth Century," in *American College,* ed. Geiger, 80–90.

24. Charles H. Glatfelter, *A Salutary Influence: Gettysburg College, 1832–1985*, 2 vols. (Gettysburg, PA: Gettysburg College, 1987), vol. 1, 175; David B. Potts, "'College Enthusiasm' as Public Response: 1800–1860," *Harvard Education Review* 47 (1977): 28–42.

25. Colin Burke, *American Collegiate Populations: A Test of the Traditional View* (New York: New York University Press, 1982); Roger L. Geiger, "The Era of Multipurpose Colleges in American Higher Education, 1850–1890" in *American College*, ed. Geiger, 127–52.

26. Francis Wayland, *Report to the Corporation of Brown University on Changes in the System of Collegiate Education* (Providence, RI: G. H. Whitney, 1850).

27. Daniel Coit Gilman, "Our National Schools of Science," *North American Review* (Oct. 1867): 495–520; Richard J. Storr, *The Beginnings of Graduate Education in America* (Chicago: University of Chicago Press, 1953), 60–65, 112–17.

28. Thomas Woody, *A History of Women's Education in the United States*, 2 vols. (New York: Science Press, 1929), vol. 1, 145–47; Christie Anne Farnham, *The Education of the Southern Belle: Higher Education and Student Socialization in the Antebellum South* (New York: New York University Press, 1994); Sidney Sherwood, *The University of the State of New York* (Washington, DC: U.S. Government Printing Office, 1900), quotation on 447.

29. Roger L. Geiger, "The Era of Multipurpose Colleges in American Higher Education, 1850–1890" in *American College*, ed. Geiger, 127–52; Doris Malkmus, "Small Towns, Small Sects, and Coeducation in Midwestern Colleges," *History of Higher Education Annual* 22 (2002): 33–66.

30. Roger L. Geiger, "The Rise and Fall of Useful Knowledge," in *American College*, ed. Geiger, 153–68; Roger L. Williams, *The Origins of Federal Support for Higher Education: George W. Atherton and the Land-Grant College Movement* (University Park: Pennsylvania State University Press, 1991).

31. "The Morrill Act, 1862," in *Higher Education: A Documentary History*, 2 vols., ed. Richard Hofstadter and Wilson Smith (Chicago: University of Chicago Press, 1961), vol. 2, 568–69 [emphasis added].

32. Helen Lefkowitz Horowitz, *Alma Mater: Design and Experience in the Women's Colleges from Their Nineteenth Century Origins to the 1930s* (Boston: Beacon, 1984).

33. Hugh Hawkins, *Between Harvard and America: The Educational Leadership of Charles W. Eliot* (New York: Oxford University Press, 1972); Morison, *Three Centuries*, 323–99, quotation on 361; Laurence Veysey, *The Emergence of the American University* (Chicago: University of Chicago Press, 1965).

34. Roger L. Geiger, *To Advance Knowledge: The Growth of American Research Universities, 1900–1940* (New York: Oxford University Press, 1986), 270–71.

35. Roger L. Geiger, "The 'Superior Instruction of Women,' 1836–1890," in *American College*, ed. Geiger, 183–95; Barbara Miller Solomon, *In the Company of Educated Women: A History of Women and Higher Education in America* (New Haven, CT: Yale University Press, 1985); Lynn D. Gordon, *Gender and Higher Education in the Progressive Era* (New Haven, CT: Yale University Press, 1990).

36. Veysey, *Emergence*; Geiger, *To Advance Knowledge*, 14–19; enrollments by professional school or department are given in Edwin E. Slosson, *Great American Universities* (New York: Macmillan, 1910).

37. Geiger, *To Advance Knowledge*, 30–39; Walter P. Metzger, "Origins of the Association," *AAUP Bulletin* 51 (1965): 229–37; Roger L. Geiger, "Professionalization of the American Faculty in the Twentieth Century" in *Shaping the American Faculty*, ed. Roger L. Geiger, Perspectives on the History of Higher Education 31 (New Brunswick, NJ: Transaction, 2015).

38. Geiger, *History*, chap. 9; W. Bruce Leslie, *Gentlemen and Scholars: College and Community in the "Age of the University,"* 1865–1917 (University Park: Pennsylvania State University Press, 1992); Ronald A. Smith, *Sports and Freedom: The Rise of Big-Time College Athletics* (New York: Oxford University Press, 1988); David P. Setran, *The College "Y": Student Religion in an Age of Secularization* (New York: Palgrave Macmillan, 2007).

39. Geiger, *To Advance Knowledge*, 45–47; Ellen Condliffe Lagemann, *Private Power for the Public Good: A History of the Carnegie Foundation for the Advancement of Teaching* (Middletown, CT: Wesleyan University Press, 1983), 3–53.

40. The AAU established an "approved list" of colleges whose graduates were presumed to be prepared for graduate study: Hugh Hawkins, *Banding Together: The Rise of the National Associations in American Higher Education, 1887–1950* (Baltimore: Johns Hopkins University Press, 1992), 107–10.

41. Martin Trow, *The Transition from Elite to Mass Higher Education* (Paris: Organisation for Economic Co-operation and Development, 1974).

42. David O. Levine, *The American College and the Culture of Aspiration, 1915–1940* (Ithaca, NY: Cornell University Press, 1986).

43. Geiger, *To Advance Knowledge*; Abraham Flexner, *Universities: American, English, German* (New Brunswick, NJ: Transaction, 1994 [1930]).

44. Jerome Karabel, *The Chosen: The Hidden History of Admission and Exclusion at Harvard, Yale, and Princeton* (Boston: Houghton Mifflin, 2005); Harold Wechsler, *The Qualified Student: A History of Selective Admissions in America* (New York: Wiley, 1977); Marcia G. Synnott, *The Half-Opened Door: Discrimination in Admissions to Harvard, Yale, and Princeton, 1900–1970* (Westport, CT: Greenwood, 1977); Geiger, *To Advance Knowledge*, 129–39.

45. Geiger, *To Advance Knowledge*, 206 and appendices for institutional finances.

46. Burton R. Clark, *The Distinctive College* (New Brunswick, NJ: Transaction, 1992 [1970]), 184–232.

47. Enrollment data are from the National Center for Education Statistics, *Digest of Education Statistics*, http://nces.ed.gov/programs/digest/. For postwar academic development, see Richard M. Freeland, *Academia's Golden Age: Universities in Massachusetts, 1945–1970* (New York: Oxford University Press, 1992); Roger L. Geiger, *Research and Relevant Knowledge: American Research Universities since World War II* (New York: Oxford University Press, 1993).

48. Harvard University, *General Education in a Free Society* (Cambridge, MA: Harvard University Press, 1945).

49. Roger L. Geiger, "Demography and Curriculum: The Humanities in American Higher Education, 1945–1985," in *The Humanities and the Dynamics of Inclusion since World War II*, ed. David A. Hollinger (Baltimore: Johns Hopkins University Press, 2006), 50–72.

50.  The following draws on Geiger, *Research and Relevant Knowledge*.

51.  Christopher Jencks and David Riesman, *The Academic Revolution* (Chicago: University of Chicago Press, 1968); Geiger, *Research and Relevant Knowledge*, 198–203.

52.  Claudia Goldin and Lawrence F. Katz, *The Race between Education and Technology* (Cambridge, MA: Harvard University Press, 2008), 276.

53.  Roger L. Geiger, *Knowledge and Money: Research Universities and the Paradox of the Marketplace* (Stanford, CA: Stanford University Press, 2004).

54.  Geiger. *Knowledge and Money*, 132–231; Roger L. Geiger and Creso M. Sá, *Tapping the Riches of Science: Universities and the Promise of Economic Growth* (Cambridge, MA: Harvard University Press, 2009).

# Chapter Two

# Academic Freedom

*Past, Present, and Future*

## Robert M. O'Neil

The subject of academic freedom has been a central theme throughout much of the history of American higher education. Within the collegiate community, there have been widely differing perspectives on certain key issues—for example, whether academic freedom applies as fully to students as to professors, how far beyond the classroom and laboratory such protection extends, and what circumstances might warrant the curtailment of academic freedom to serve broader societal interests. This chapter explores the meaning and scope of academic freedom in four phases: its origins and early historical development, its current status in the courts and in institutional policy, challenges that are certain to arise as teaching and learning occur increasingly in an electronic environment, and the fate of academic freedom in the years since the terrorist attacks of September 11, 2001.

### Academic Freedom's Roots and Legacy

The origins of the concept of academic freedom lie deep in the history of teaching and scholarly inquiry.[1] German universities long recognized the concept of *Lehrfreiheit*, or freedom of professors to teach, with a corollary *Lernfreiheit*, or freedom of students to learn. Other countries recognized the distinctive status of university teachers and students in different ways and in widely varying degrees. What is most striking about the importation of these concepts to the United States is the recency of any systematic protection for academic freedom in a currently recognizable form. As late as the second decade of the twentieth century, some of our most eminent universities could discharge—or refuse even to hire—professors solely because their views on economic or social issues were deemed radical or subversive. While many within the academic community found such actions abhorrent, and many governing boards took a more tolerant view of outspoken scholars, the establishment of clear principles protecting the expression of unpopular views within or outside the classroom occurred surprisingly late in our history.

The formal origins of academic freedom in this country almost certainly lie in the issuance in 1915 of a "declaration of principles" by a committee of senior scholars who had been convened by the fledgling American Association of University Professors (AAUP). That declaration, some twenty pages in length, canvassed a wide range of issues. Walter Metzger, the preeminent historian of academic freedom, describes the declaration in this way: "Utilitarian in temper and conviction, the theorists of 1915 did not view the expressional freedoms of academics as a bundle of abstract rights. They regarded them as corollaries of the contemporary public need for universities that would increase the sum of human knowledge and furnish experts for public service—new functions that had been added to the time-honored one of qualifying students for degrees."[2] The drafters of the declaration thus characterized the emerging university of their time as an "intellectual experiment station, where new ideas may germinate and where the fruit, though still distasteful to the community as a whole, may be allowed to ripen until finally, perchance, it may become part of the accepted intellectual food of the nation and the world."[3]

Such an institution must, the declaration went on to insist, be prepared to tolerate a range of views on controversial issues. It must also tolerate those members of its faculty who expressed such aberrant views. Academic institutions that sought to repress or silence such views simply did not deserve the respect of the higher education community. Thus, concluded the declaration, any university that placed restrictions on the intellectual and expressive freedom of its professors effectively proclaimed itself a proprietary institution and should be so described in making any appeal for funds, and the general public should be advised that the institution has no claim to general support or esteem.

The reception of these views was not entirely harmonious, even in intellectual circles. The *New York Times*, in an editorial fairly representative of the more conservative media of the time, scoffed at the newly declared principles: "'Academic freedom,' that is, the inalienable right of every college instructor to make a fool of himself and his college by . . . intemperate, sensational prattle about every subject under heaven . . . and still keep on the payroll or be reft therefrom only by an elaborate process, is cried to the winds by the organized dons."[4] The reference to "an elaborate process" was not entirely unfair, since a major element of the declaration was a cornerstone of what would become the concept of academic tenure—the precept that academic freedom entailed procedural due process for the dismissal of faculty as much as a limitation on the reasons for which such dismissal might occur.[5]

Thus by the time the United States entered World War I (an event that would create new tensions between professors and society), three vital elements were already in place. There was a rather elaborate and forceful declaration of the basic principles of academic freedom. There was the nucleus of a guarantee of tenure, in the form of procedures that should be followed in the event an institution wished to remove or terminate a professor. And there was an organization, created by and for the benefit of university faculty, committed not only to promulgating and publicizing the new principles, but also to enforcing those principles by investigating egregious departures from them and disseminating the results of such inquiries in a form that would eventually become known as "censure."

The next major milestone along the route to broader recognition of academic freedom was a statement adopted in 1940 as a joint effort between the AAUP and the Association of American Colleges (now the Association of American Colleges and Universities), a longtime partner in this enterprise. The 1940 "Statement of Principles of Academic Freedom and Tenure" soon drew the support and adherence of many learned societies and academic organizations. By the time of its sixtieth anniversary at the turn of a new century, the Statement had the formal endorsement of more than 150 such groups, representing virtually every facet of academic life and every scholarly discipline, as well as the endorsement of the great majority of research universities and liberal arts colleges.[6]

The 1940 Statement remains nearly as inviolate as the US Constitution. There have been a few "interpretive comments" added over the years (and codified in 1970), and the gender-based language of the original document was modified to achieve neutrality in 1990. The core of the Statement is a declaration, remarkably brief, that university professors are entitled to academic freedom in three vital dimensions—freedom in research and in the publication of the results of research, freedom in the classroom in discussing the subject matter of the course and when speaking or writing as citizens, and freedom from institutional censorship or unwarranted sanction. Each of these freedoms entails corollary responsibilities and limitations. With regard to research, for example, the Statement cautions that "research for pecuniary return should be based upon an understanding with the authorities of the institution." In the classroom, college professors "should be careful not to introduce . . . controversial matter which has no relation to their subject." Teachers, when speaking or writing as citizens, "should at all times be accurate, should exercise appropriate restraint, should show respect for the opinions of others, and should make every effort to indicate that they are not speaking for the institution."

The balance of the 1940 Statement defines the basic elements of faculty tenure, including the need for every institution to adopt a clear statement of the terms and conditions of appointment; a finite probationary period (recommended, but not mandated, to last for seven years), during which a nontenured teacher on the tenure track fully enjoys academic freedom; and rigorous procedures for the handling of charges that might lead to dismissal for cause. The Statement also envisions that tenured and continuing appointments might be terminated for demonstrated "financial exigency," or when a program or department is eliminated for sound academic reasons, or when the subject has a proven medical disability.

Over the years since 1940, the AAUP has adopted many statements and policies, most of which appear today both in the Redbook (most recently revised in 2000) and on the association's website, www.aaup.org. Especially cogent to the evolution of professorial interests is the 1994 "Statement on the Relationship of Faculty Governance to Academic Freedom." This statement notes the crucial link between meaningful faculty participation in the governance of a university and the probable condition of academic freedom on that campus. Central to such freedom is the right of a faculty member, without fear of reprisal or loss of influence, to criticize the administration and the governing board on matters of faculty concern. Thus the nexus between governance and academic freedom is vital, as this statement serves to remind those on both sides of this relationship.

It is not only the endorsement of virtually all learned societies and very many universities that has given the 1940 Statement such stature as a source of academic common law. The US Supreme Court in one major case, and the lower federal and state courts on numerous occasions, have cited the Statement as an exemplar, guide, and template of the principles of academic freedom.[7] "Probably because it was formulated by both administrators and professors," observed a federal appeals court in a 1978 case, "all of the secondary authorities seem to agree [that the 1940 Statement] is the 'most widely accepted academic definition of tenure.'" Another federal court of appeals approvingly cited the AAUP policy on nonrenewal of continuing appointments, noting that its language "strikes an appropriate balance between academic freedom and educational excellence on the one hand and individual rights to fair consideration on the other."[8] Judges have also recurrently invoked AAUP standards for determining financial exigency as a prelude to the dismissal of tenured faculty. On most issues of that sort, there simply are few, if any, other credible and widely accepted sources to guide lawyers and judges. Moreover, AAUP standards tend to emerge from practical experience at the campus level and have often been revised in light of further and constantly changing experience in the field. Thus it is not surprising to discover the degree of judicial reliance and respect they have received.

The actions and practices to which these standards are addressed have changed substantially over time as well. In the early years, those faculty members at greatest risk were economists and others in the social sciences who had spoken and written unpopular views about the nation's foreign policy or its domestic economic system, making the business and government leaders who comprised typical boards of trustees and alumni officers acutely uncomfortable. The pressures that such leaders brought to bear on the administration led even so illustrious an institution as the University of Pennsylvania to discharge the nonrevolutionary Marxist Scott Nearing from the faculty of its Wharton School; for the next several years, Nearing was an unemployable pariah in higher education, until finally the University of Toledo offered him a teaching position.[9] There were other egregious cases of outspoken critics of capitalism who were either not hired at all or, if their controversial views became known after they began teaching, were summarily dismissed, even by the most prestigious universities.

Of course there were also striking cases to the contrary. Some universities fought to keep, and to protect, "radical" or "subversive" professors, even without the application of the full force of academic freedom and tenure—much less, at this early stage, without contemplating the prospect of an AAUP investigation that might result in censure. Harvard's example was notable in this regard. President A. Lawrence Lowell refused in 1916 to discipline a prominent professor for his avowedly pro-German statements and outspoken opposition to US entry into World War I. Lowell wisely observed that a university that officially condemns faculty views it dislikes would quickly find attributed to it—simply by the absence of such condemnation—a host of professorial utterances from which it had not formally distanced itself.

Though there were a few serious breaches during the 1920s and 1930s, the gravest challenges to academic freedom and tenure occurred during the Mc-Carthy era of the late 1940s and early 1950s. Many professors (as well as screenwriters, actors, and others) were summoned before federal and state antisubversive legislative hearings. Often there was no evidence that the target of such inquiry had personally done anything remotely "subversive" or "anti-American," much less actually joined the Communist Party. Rather, the witness had often befriended, collaborated, or simply casually met one or more suspected Communists or front-group members. Many professors summoned under such conditions either declined to appear at all, fearing that their mere presence would place them at risk, or appeared and (while sometimes candidly describing their own activities and associations) refused to identify suspected colleagues, describe political gatherings they had attended, or in other ways jeopardize long-standing relationships of trust within the academic community.

In many such cases recalcitrance led to demands for reprisal. Few administrations and governing boards, especially at public institutions, were able to resist such pressures completely. The stakes were too high, the publicity too intense, and the forces too powerful to avoid taking some action against faculty members who invoked constitutional claims to avoid compelled testimony, even when many had nothing of their own to hide. Ellen Schrecker, the preeminent chronicler of faculty fates in those unhappy times, has reported that nearly 170 tenured or tenure-track professors were dismissed during the McCarthy era, mostly for suspected disloyalty that was never convincingly documented.[10] The most reputable (and normally most protective) institutions were among the most culpable—Harvard, Michigan, Rutgers, the University of Washington, and other top research institutions.

Much of the damage to faculty freedoms came not through outright dismissals, but in subtler (if no less insidious) forms, such as the exaction of disclaimer-type loyalty oaths. When all University of California professors were required to sign such oaths in the early 1950s, some principled nonsigners simply left the faculty as a matter of conscience, though they had nothing to hide or conceal. Others brought a lawsuit in state court, which yielded a classically Pyrrhic victory. The California Supreme Court agreed with the professors that, given the constitutional autonomy of the university and its regents, they could not be made to take an oath prescribed by the legislature for all state employees. Instead, in a bitter irony, they were left subject to the even more intrusive and distrustful loyalty oath devised by the regents exclusively for University of California faculty and staff. It was not until 1967, long after the political climate had changed, that the California courts finally invalidated all loyalty oaths, following the lead the US Supreme Court had set several years earlier.

Since the McCarthy era happened just a decade after the issuance of the AAUP's 1940 Statement, and after most of the academic community had signed on, it is fair to ask whether academic freedom and tenure failed their first critical test. This is a difficult and complex question, to which at least two contrasting views are responsive. One view is that the academic community, which is especially vulnerable at all times and was unusually suspect during this perilous time, would have fared even worse had not such safeguards existed—that many careers were in fact saved because protective administrators and trustees could tell livid legislators and angry alumni that "our hands are tied since he/she has tenure." Some evidence supports that hypothesis; for example, the fact that no faculty were fired at institutions like Indiana University (despite pressure from an extremely conservative congressional delegation) because the insiders gave the outsiders an unwelcome but irrefutable account of the legal protections that professors enjoyed. The contrary view takes to task not only those eminent universities that caved in under anti-Communist pressure, but also notes that the AAUP, as well as organizations such as the American Civil Liberties Union (ACLU), were slow to respond. During the later stages of the McCarthy period, these groups did become active both on campus and in court in ways that undoubtedly afforded some protection, even if, arguably, it was too little and too late. Thus the jury remains out on the question of whether the 1940 Statement failed its inaugural test; surely a less auspicious time for a debut could hardly be imagined.

The end of the McCarthy era brought a period of relative calm to the academic world. The 1960s launched a massive expansion of higher education, during which the demand for young scholars grew geometrically and strongly diminished the likelihood of reprisals against those with unconventional views. Besides, this was a time when young people were expected to have and express unconventional views, with college professors likely to be leading the pack. The later years of the Vietnam War did bring some institutional pressures to bear on outspoken faculty, both for publicly expressed attacks on US policy in Southeast Asia, and for such collateral actions as "reconstituting" courses to focus on the rising disenchantment with Vietnam policy, as well as on poverty, racism, and the environment. But the sanctions were few and relatively mild and dismissals (at least by major institutions) almost unknown. The AAUP's investigative caseload, which certainly did not diminish during these years, consisted disproportionately of mishandled personnel actions at smaller and less-sophisticated institutions, relating more to strained finances or lack of experience than to aberrant faculty voices.

The more recent history of academic freedom contains one other promising feature. While those who teach in private colleges and universities cannot claim the protection of the First Amendment against their institutions—it applies only to government action—state university professors enjoy not only the speech rights of citizens, but also a special sensitivity that courts have shown for the academic setting. Starting with a 1950s case that barred a governmental demand for a teacher's lecture notes, through several key rulings in the next decade that struck down loyalty oaths, to later judgments invalidating laws of other sorts that repressed campus speech, the courts consistently recognized a special role for academic freedom. Perhaps the clearest statement is that of Supreme Court Justice William J. Brennan, Jr., in sounding the death knell for New York State's loyalty oath in 1967:

> Academic freedom . . . is of transcendent value to all of us and not merely to the teachers concerned. That freedom is therefore a special concern of the First Amendment, which does not tolerate laws that cast a pall of orthodoxy over the classroom . . . The classroom is peculiarly a marketplace of ideas. The Nation's future depends upon leaders trained through wide exposure to its robust exchange of ideas which discovers truth out of a multitude of tongues, [rather] than through any kind of authoritative selection.[11]

Although the Supreme Court has never retreated from that view of academic freedom—indeed, the court has amplified it in such varied contexts as race-sensitive admission policies of state universities—there has been some erosion in lower federal courts. In cases during the late 1990s and the first years of the twenty-first century, several appeals courts effectively created a new tension between individual and institutional academic freedom. When a faculty member challenges on First Amendment grounds a government policy by which the institution is bound, several cases seem to favor the institutional interest, to the detriment of the individual professor's interest. Most dramatically, when the Fourth Circuit Court of Appeals sustained a 1996 Virginia law that bars the use of state-owned or state-leased computers by state employees to access sexually explicit material, save with official approval for "bona fide research projects," the majority expressly rejected a professorial academic freedom claim, recognizing only an institutional interest.[12] Scholars and chroniclers of academic freedom have written critically of that and several other rulings that similarly disparage individual academic freedom claims.

Despite occasional setbacks, and despite important differences between court-declared and institutionally shaped academic freedom precepts, these two sources interacted and blended throughout the twentieth century in ways that, as William Van Alstyne notes, constantly reinforce one another. Although the First Amendment does not bind them, most major private universities pride themselves on voluntary adherence to standards (typically those crafted by the AAUP) that are at least as rigorous as the standards legally imposed on their state-supported counterparts. The historic development of academic freedom, covering as it does most of the twentieth century, reflects gradual and, at times, checkered progress toward enhanced security for professorial speech and political activity. During the Cold War era, a number of professors were targeted and a few were even dismissed. Yet that history suggests, in the main, how much less well the American professoriate would have fared had there not emerged, early in the last century, a set of widely accepted principles and a nearly universal commitment to fair procedures for the termination of faculty appointments.

### Academic Freedom and Academic Tenure

Despite wholly understandable confusion, academic freedom and faculty tenure remain quite distinct concepts, and for several vital reasons. For one, given its constitutional grounding in the First Amendment, academic freedom fully protects only those who teach and pursue research in publicly supported institutions. With the sole exception of courts in New York State, the First Amendment and state constitutional guarantees of free expression simply do not apply to nonpublic colleges and universities; only those institutions that are governmentally supported and regulated are compelled to observe and apply the safeguards of free speech and press. Faculty colleagues in the independent sector, although typically enjoying comparable safeguards by reason of benign governing board policies (usually embedded in faculty handbooks and websites), and cannot insist upon legal protection for free expression and inquiry. Another distinction is easily overlooked. While organizations like the AAUP almost universally embrace the concept of tenure, they do not categorically require a tenure system. Indeed, Hampshire College in western Massachusetts has from its inception in the 1960s adopted a different form of protection. This eminent liberal arts college offers its full-time faculty renewable five-year contracts, which are usually extended after the initial term, although they may occasionally be terminated beyond the normal seven-year probationary period for tenure-track appointments. Hampshire's commitment, in contrast, is to insist on rigorous procedural standards for later nonrenewal and—even more crucial—to provide assurance that termination or nonextension did not abridge basic principles of free speech and inquiry. Several other institutions have experimented with Hampshire-like term appointments but eventually embraced more traditional personnel policies.

The century-old AAUP premise is that a formal and consistent tenure system best serves the interests of both individuals and institutions. It is not only the likeliest guarantor of academic freedom but offers other benefits as well. Tenure provides continuity and stability of employment in a profession whose members often engage in long-term research and where institutions need to be able to project their curriculum and staffing needs well into the future. Finally, a traditional tenure system also compels—typically within a year of the close of the probationary period—a critical review and assessment of the potential of every junior faculty member. In short, such review demands a rigorous up-or-out judgment at the critical moment. The scholarly quality of an academic community invariably reflects the impact of such a process.

Despite these virtues, even the strongest champion of tenure would admit having some reservations. First, to be sure, the current system is far from perfect. More rigorous review of the performance of those seeking tenure would undoubtedly benefit them and their careers, as well as their students and the entire institution. Moreover, those who have already achieved tenure are not—and should not be—immune from continuing scrutiny despite the greater security they enjoy; while this is clearly not the occasion for analyzing controversial post-tenure review policies that some universities have recently adopted, the prospect of complete disregard for faculty accountability is troubling. Finally, tenure invites the risk of an exaggerated hierarchy within the academic profession. There have surely been abuses by senior scholars of junior colleagues who should be seen as their protégés. It is hardly surprising that some younger teachers, even without tenure, view the current system with ambivalence or resentment. The tradeoff between enhanced protection for those who survive the system and hardship for those who fall along the wayside may seem to create an excessive cost or burden. The quest for better alternatives should therefore continue, while even the most securely tenured professors should incur some responsibility to improve the current and admittedly imperfect faculty personnel system.

A closely related aspect of free expression in the college community, with special value to faculty organizations like AAUP, is the matter of sanctions for violations of academic freedom. Free speech and political activity have been notably less protected in certain types of institutions, mainly those with weak or nonexistent traditions of shared governance. For example, in some religiously affiliated institutions curbs on faculty speech not only serve special theological needs but go well beyond theology in ways that have no secular counterpart. Indeed, AAUP policy since 1940 has declared that "limitations of academic freedom because of religious or other aims of the institution should be clearly stated in writing at the time of the appointment"[13]—an implicit indication that AAUP declines to compel adherence to (or avoidance of) matters of faith or doctrine even if such precepts are distasteful to the vast majority of the academic community.

Meanwhile, there is no monopoly on academic freedom violations at small and campuses; in recent years the AAUP's list of censured administrations has included such eminent institutions as New York University and Southern California (both having eventually taken appropriate steps to remove such a sanction). The censure list increasingly involves procedural violations in the handling of sensitive personnel matters rather than direct reprisals for outspoken statements of unorthodox views or faculty activities. (One small but important technical comment is in order: AAUP censure, when warranted, is imposed not on the governing board but rather on the administration; with one single exception—the Angela Davis case in California—such a sanction cites the campus administration rather than the trustees or regents.)

Meanwhile, terminating academic appointments for reasons of financial exigency continues to invite AAUP scrutiny and, on occasion, litigation. Association policies and court decisions define a clear and legally acceptable path to declaring perilous financial conditions, and if necessary to reducing faculty in a way that will pass strict inspection. Comparable to the procedure for terminating an academic appointment on the basis of "cause" (a deliberately and inevitably enigmatic if portentous term) or the parallel process for "bona fide elimination of an [academic] program or department,"[14] the manner in which such an action is taken may generate far greater concern and scrutiny—including the potential for censure—than the substance of that action itself.

It may be useful to elaborate briefly the vital distinction between public and independent or private academic institutions. Several universities that are usually characterized as "public" share certain qualities that might be termed "private." Brown, Yale, and Tulane, all private institutions, have from their inception included public officials as ex officio board members. MIT and Cornell, although also private, are land-grant institutions. Cornell is a curious hybrid: Four of its professional schools or colleges are also units of the State University of New York, which provides most of the financial support for students there. Alfred University in Western New York and Syracuse University are for most purposes independent or private, but are also hosts to SUNY so-called contract colleges (the New York State College of Ceramics at Alfred University and the College of Environmental Science and Forestry at Syracuse). Other curious anomalies also merit attention: The universities of Vermont and Delaware, both land-grant campuses, are hybrids; Delaware describes itself as "a state-assisted, privately governed institution," while Vermont "blends the traditions of both a private and public university."

Laws in two states also confuse the distinction between public and independent institutions. In New York State, students and faculty of otherwise private campuses are enabled by a section of the Civil Practice Act (Article 78) to seek relief against their governing boards to ensure compliance with their internal rules and legal duties. Thus in a host of cases state courts have intervened where it was alleged that the institution had failed to follow its own hearing or review procedures in the discipline of a student or the dismissal of a faculty member. Such judicial intervention occurs only in New York State, where the impact of Article 78 has been substantial. Finally, there is the special case of the so-called Leonard Law in California uniquely imposes on private secular (though not religiously affiliated) campuses the same First Amendment obligations as apply to the Golden State's abundant public colleges and universities. That statute creates a private cause of action for students alleging a violation of such a rule or regulation. Ironically, Stanford University witnessed the legal demise of its speech code, while nearby University of California and Cal State campuses escaped such intrusion both because the Leonard Law applies only to independent or private campuses and simply because no aggrieved student ever sought relief from a court. More could be said about the anomalous distinction between the public and independent sectors, though this brief summary may well suffice.

### Academic Freedom in the Digital Age

As new technologies convey an ever-growing share of academia's intellectual exchanges, challenges to academic freedom will invariably arise in new and sometimes profoundly different ways. There are, of course, some obvious differences between print and electronic messages. A digital message may reach thousands (if not millions) of recipients within a fraction of a second, while the source of that message may be far harder to trace than the same message on paper. The absence on the Internet or within digital or electronic messages of comparable and more familiar print media may curiously evoke anxiety or even fear at the other end of the process to a far greater degree than likely occurs imprint. Yet academic freedom must perforce adapt to cyberspace, however uncomfortably.

When it comes to the potential scope of academic freedom in digital media versus traditional means, striking differences emerge. For example, the sanctity of the university classroom and of communication taking place within that physical space have always been at the core of academic freedom. Yet when an instructor creates a course home page, or when a growing portion of verbal exchanges between teacher and student occur through e-mail or social media, we need to ask whether such media are merely an extension of the brick-and-mortar classroom or whether they should invite a wholly different analysis. Clearly the distinction between the expressions "on campus" and "off campus" needs to be redefined when applied to an electronic environment.

We should also ask whether expressive freedoms even apply to digital or electronic communications. When it comes to basic constitutional safeguards, the Framers clearly never anticipated digital or electronic material as "speech" or "press," and while early courts eventually recognized nonverbal messages as presumptively protected (invoking, for example, the precedent of the Boston Tea Party), they could hardly have envisioned the current cyber world. Yet there seems no logical reason why a message entitled to protection in print form should not be comparably protected when it travels by electronic means. A brief historical retrospective may be helpful in framing an answer to this central question.

Until the late 1990s the scope of constitutional speech and press remained limited under applicable US Supreme Court rulings. Basically, only traditional media were fully protected. Such formats as motion pictures, licensed broadcasting, and cable television were not entitled to unfettered protection under the First Amendment until 1997, when the court fully embraced the Internet as the only fully protected medium other than books, newspapers, and oral declarations. The court stressed in this seminal judgment (*Reno v. ACLU*, 521 US 844[1997]) the emergence of "a unique and wholly new medium of worldwide communication." Noting that "anyone with access to the Internet may take advantage of a wide variety of communication and information retrieval methods," the court was keenly aware of vital differences. Contrary to the assumptions of critics who might simply have viewed the Justices as naïve or inattentive, the

Court's members had been in fact amply prepared for the emerging digital era; they had been fully exposed in the process of preparing for oral argument to a broad range of challenging sexually explicit visual material.

Providentially, the AAUP has long conveyed a keen interest in precisely these issues. In a 2004 subcommittee report, the association's Committee on Academic Freedom and Tenure declared "academic freedom, free inquiry, and freedom of expression within the academic community may be limited to no greater degree in electronic format than they are in print, save for the most unusual situation where the very nature of the medium itself might warrant unusual restrictions—and even then only to the extent that such differences demand exceptions or variations."[15] (The need for passwords to gain access would, for example, illustrate and limit the scope of this proviso.)

Over a decade later, in early 2014, a successor AAUP group substantially updated the initial report. This time, while retaining the earlier commitment to the principles of academic freedom, the association shifted its focus to the burgeoning status of social media. In its new report, AAUP noted that a survey showed 70 percent of all faculty responding reported having visited a social media site for personal use during the prior month. Of even greater import is that 55 percent of faculty respondents noted having made professional use of social media outside the classes they taught on at least a monthly basis, while 41 percent reported having used social media in their classroom teaching.

While such data illustrate the rapid rise in the use of social media, two vital cautions emerge. On the one hand, the AAUP report highlighted an alarming deficiency in the shaping of applicable policies. Specifically, most institutions of higher learning "have yet to formulate policies regarding social media usage by faculty members."[16] Moreover, in the strikingly few instances where such rules have been crafted, the results have been disappointing.

In April, 2015, the Kansas State board of regents adopted new regulations under which faculty members might be suspended or dismissed for "improper use of social media," although "improper"[17] was defined only in the broadest and vaguest sense, specifically, communication that is "contrary to the best interest of the university" or which "impairs discipline by superiors or harmony among co-workers [or] . . . interferes with the regular operation of the university or otherwise adversely affects the university's ability to efficiently provide services."[18] The event that triggered the Kansas policy was a tweet by David Guth, a journalism professor at the University of Kansas, following the September 2013 Washington Naval Yard shooting. Guth's online comment was highly critical of the

National Rifle Association; although Guth retracted the tweet and apologized, he was placed on administrative leave. The national AAUP conveyed its concern following the incident: "[I]f faculty members seek to communicate opposition to this policy . . . via electronic media they risk being suspended or terminated for 'acting contrary to the best interests of the University for impairing discipline or . . . harmony among co-workers.' "[19]

The reaction of the Kansas State Board of Regents was hardly unusual; what evoked so much attention was the contrast between the policies governing faculty outrage and indignation conveyed orally and in traditional print media, and digital declarations. Had the board of regents sought to punish or discipline Guth for airing his anti-NRA views in a more conventional medium, the recently issued policy would clearly have been declared in violation of the First Amendment. Yet there has been remarkably little discussion or analysis of the import of this contrast between print and digital media even with regard to closely analogous content.

Even more notable was the summary withdrawal by the University of Illinois of the imminent promotion of a long-tenured—and quite outspoken—professor of American Indian Studies, Steven Salaita, triggered by angry and volatile tweets he unleashed about tensions in the Middle East. While hardly models of civil discourse, and containing vulgar and taboo epithets reflecting anti-Semitic rage, his tweets were no more opprobrious than language Salaita had used on other occasions during his years as a Virginia Tech professor. Perhaps most striking about the withdrawal of Salaita's promotion was the barely noted distinction between digital and print media. Had he uttered such volatile and offensive epithets from a podium or plaza, or included them in a letter to the campus newspaper or a local underground weekly, outrage and offense would undoubtedly have followed, along with administrative and alumni pressure to demand his dismissal. The University of Illinois' board of trustees in early 2015 finally foreclosed any further relief for Salaita—leaving open the intriguing question of whether, had he used comparably offensive language in a flier, editorial, or any other print medium, free speech and print precepts would have ensured a different level of protection.[20]

Obviously many critical legal issues await clarification. The Supreme Court and lower federal courts have, meanwhile, steadily refined the applicable standard of "intent" with regard to regulation of verbal attacks and hateful speech. Meanwhile, remarkably few colleges and universities have made even modest adaptations to their policies to reflect the dramatic change in digital and electronic messages as we have moved from simple e-mail communications to Facebook, Twitter, and other formats. Perhaps the best advice in this respect (as with others where rapid change seems inevitable) is "stay tuned." In a decade or less, most of us will probably not even recognize the landscape of cyberspace.

## Virginia's Singular Ban on Digital Indecency

Among several anomalies in the recent evolution of digital and electronic communication, none more clearly merits scholarly attention than Virginia's ban on digital indecency. Perhaps in the expectation that other states would soon follow the lead of Old Dominion, Virginia lawmakers in 2000 enacted a law that specifically barred state employees (including but not limited to state college and university professors) from using state-owned or state-leased computing equipment to access digital material that was not legally obscene nor involved child pornography. A group of Virginia college professors, led by Melvin Urofsky, a professor at Virginia Commonwealth, immediately filed suit, challenging the statute's constitutionality on free speech and free press grounds including its potential intrusive impact upon faculty-initiated research projects.

The case came in scheduled rotation before federal judge Leonie Brinkema of the Eastern District of Virginia. She had the singular distinction among the judiciary of having served for over a decade as a professional librarian before earning a law degree and eventually attaining the federal bench. Given her background, it was hardly surprising that Judge Brinkema ruled the challenged law abridged free speech, due process, and academic freedom in several respects. The statute did contain two possibly mitigating exceptions, including an invitation to Virginia public campuses to exempt certain designated personnel for the pursuit of "bona fide research projects"—a term never adequately defined.[21] The law also clearly implied that Virginia public employees might avoid the ban by accessing such material from personally owned computers.

The commonwealth promptly appealed Judge Brinkema's ruling. A sharply divided three-judge panel of the Fourth Circuit Court of Appeals soon reversed the district court in a cursory opinion. The full (active or not yet retired) Federal Court of Appeals for the Fourth Circuit (based in Richmond) agreed to review US District Judge Brinkema's decision in the Federal Eastern District of Virginia and eventually reversed, with three separate opinions. The majority of the judges in turn deferred to the Virginia General Assembly, ruling that a restriction on accessing sexually explicit digital material constituted a valid condition on use of publicly owned or leased computing equipment. The majority accepted in passing both the exceptions that Judge Brinkema had essentially disregarded—the invitation to exempt staff members engaged in pursuit of "bona fide research projects" and the gratuitous opportunity to access such suspect material on personally owned computers.

Four more liberally inclined Fourth Circuit judges dissented at length on traditional free speech and academic freedom grounds, essentially following Judge Brinkema's lead. That left one judge—J. Harvie Wilkinson (a former clerk to Justice Lewis Powell and a University of Virginia law professor). Though Wilkinson ultimately joined the majority in reversing Brinkema's ruling, his opinion said much more about academic freedom than about state regulation of salacious images in digital form. In his long and thoughtful opinion, Wilkinson wrote more as a reluctant dissenter, noting that "by embracing the Commonwealth's view that all work-related speech by public employees is beyond public concern, the majority sanctions state legislative interference in public universities without limit."[22] Late in his opinion, Judge Wilkinson observed with similar unease that "Internet research with all its potential falls outside the majority's conception of public concern."[23]

Given the tenor of Judge Brinkema's comprehensive ruling against the Virginia statute, there was limited opportunity for amicus briefs for such faculty voices as those of the AAUP or the Thomas Jefferson Center for the Protection of Free Expression. In their joint filing, which preceded the Fourth Circuit's full-court press, the two organizations added several salient arguments in support of the case for free expression and academic freedom. First, the amici noted the anomaly that a ban on accessing material that was sexually explicit but not otherwise unlawful directly abridged precedents like *Sweezy v. New Hampshire* (1957) and *Keyishian v. Board of Regents* (1967). Second, this joint brief highlighted the sharp contrast between the Fourth Circuit's views in *Urofsky v. Gilmore* and divergent rulings in the Sixth, Second, and Ninth circuit courts, which had struck down similar laws in other states on free speech and academic freedom grounds. Finally, the AAUP/TJC brief stressed the dissonance between *Urofsky v. Gilmore* and the broader constitutional context of public employee speech. Under such conditions, the US Supreme Court's predictable refusal to review *Urofsky v. Gilmore* simply left an anomalous division among circuits on this important issue. And had the justices taken up the case, the best possible outcome would likely have been an extension of Judge Wilkinson's ambivalent embrace of academic freedom. Given that prospect, the high court's action in leaving the *Urofsky v. Gilmore* saga intact seems merciful if not providential.

## Academic Freedom and Free Expression Reunited: 2015 and Beyond

Until the late 1960s, few government workers could insist on broader or deeper safeguards than their neighbors or colleagues who held comparable jobs in the private sector. Save for quite limited protection for California workers employed by private companies, corporate managers retained virtually unlimited discretion to hire—and fire—outspoken staff members. When junior employees openly criticized their bosses, they quickly found themselves seeking new jobs. But all that changed when an outspoken Illinois public school teacher was dismissed on the basis of a contentious letter he sent to a local newspaper, in which he addressed the school system's fiscal priorities. While the state courts refused any relief to the aggrieved teacher, the Supreme Court dramatically altered the legal landscape, establishing dramatically more protective principles of free speech and press.[24] At least when speaking on a "matter of public concern" rather than airing personal gripes or grievances, government workers for the first time enjoyed significantly greater safeguards.

Despite this dramatic improvement, however, the scope of such protection remains to this day surprisingly incomplete. When, for example, such expression disrupts the efficiency of the public workplace or endangers or impairs employee morale, unduly preempts assigned duties, undermines client confidence, or simply demonstrates a serious lack of competence, sanctions may follow even in the public sector. Yet for the first time outspoken government workers at least enjoyed partial First Amendment protection unless they displayed "reckless disregard" of the truth or deliberately falsified their statements, limitations that reflect the Supreme Court's catalytic shift in the *New York Times v. Sullivan* libel case of 1964.[25]

During the years that followed, courts assumed that when a government worker spoke "pursuant to official duties," a public employee's expression deserved constitutional protection under the First Amendment. Indeed, every federal appeals court that had ruled on that question simply assumed that such speech merited at least substantial constitutional protection despite the potentially confusing link between the speaker or writer and his "official duties." Such accord among the circuits persisted until a California federal judge ventured a dissenting view in the case of a junior district attorney who had openly criticized the agency for which he worked.[26] The Supreme Court seemed eager to grant review of that case, and soon signaled its readiness to adopt a strikingly less congenial view of a public worker's "official duties." At this point a heretofore complacent academic community feared an imminent reversal of the principles that governed speech on "official duties." Nomenclature added to the confusion. While the outspoken California assistant DA was named Ceballos, the case quickly became known by the agency head's name as *Garcetti.*

By a narrow majority, the US Supreme Court reversed the presumption of protection for the outspoken prosecutor and redefined the status of "official duties"and thus seemed seriously to undermine Pickering's established First Amendment protection for outspoken government workers, at least when the speaker or writer was engaged in "official duties." But the Court was sharply split in so ruling. Justice Anthony Kennedy, while joining his more conservative colleagues, added a cautious corollary: "[T]here is some argument that expression related to academic scholarship or classroom instruction implicates additional constitutional interests that are not fully accounted for by this Court's customary employee-speech jurisprudence."[27] Justice David Souter, speaking for the four liberal justices, went substantially further and conveyed his concern that the majority's sharp reversal of the "official duties" doctrine could "imperil academic freedom in public colleges and universities."[28] The import of this potential shift for university faculties remained uncertain; AAUP and other organizations immediately shared Justice Souter's misgivings, while embracing Justice Kennedy's reservation on the link to "academic scholarship."

A bit more might be said about the perverse nature of this case. As the dissenters and Justice Kennedy noted, there is an ironic reverse correlation between a professor's assigned subject matter and the proximity of a possibly contentious statement by such a scholar. A professor who discourses on issues quite remote from his or her assigned specialty seems to be fully protected. But the genuine expert who publicly conveys views much closer to the subject matter is likely to incur correspondingly greater risk, when in fact the reverse ought logically to be the case.

There is a second and related risk: The line that separates speech within one's official duties and speech as a citizen—often unclear even for a custodian or food service worker—seems hopelessly vague when it comes to the genuine academic expert. Hence the special irony of this perverse correlation: While the scope of First Amendment protection for professorial speech—which should logically have been far more extensive than comparable safeguards for a custodian or other junior staffer—turned out in the majority's view to be precisely the reverse or opposite. Thus a professor who speaks out on issues remote from his or her academic expertise is essentially offering little more than a layperson's insight, while the genuine expert seems perversely (at least initially) to incur greater risk when basic First Amendment values should operate in precisely the reverse fashion.

Meanwhile, the official duties issue had already become the focus of at least three federal cases—one in southern California,[29] a second in Milwaukee,[30] and the third in Delaware[31] (thus encompassing three separate circuits). Two of these courts inexplicably disregarded Justice Kennedy's reservation on "academic scholarship" and Justice Souter's dissenting caution. The third court was at least willing to recognize the existence of the problem, though eventually it ruled against the outspoken academic's free speech claims. It was at this point that the AAUP and the Thomas Jefferson Center for the Protection of Free Expression entered the fray, filing *amicus curiae* briefs in several additional cases.

The first post-*Garcetti* case to break new ground involved Michael Adams, a tenured sociology professor at the University of North Carolina at Wilmington. When Adams' department colleagues and dean denied him a promotion, to which he felt entitled on the basis of his demonstrated scholarship and teaching, he filed suit against the university, alleging First Amendment retaliation and viewpoint discrimination, denial of equal protection under the Fourteenth Amendment, and religious discrimination under Title VII of the 1964 Civil Rights Act. Adams, who described himself as the department's only true conservative, made an adequate if not overwhelming case for promotion. The department chair and senior faculty reviewed Adams' scholarship and deemed it insufficient to warrant his advancement to full professor. The district court granted summary judgment for the university on all counts. Adams appealed, with active support from the conservatively inclined Alliance Defense Fund, reflecting Adams' publicly expressed views on religious and campus issues. The Fourth Circuit Court of Appeals reversed the district court with regard to Adams' free speech and retaliation claims, while affirming it on the equal protection claim and remanding on other constitutional matters.

In the spring of 2011, the Fourth Circuit was ready for the first time to embrace Justice Kennedy's *Garcetti* reservation and Justice Souter's plea for recognition of academic freedom. Without resolving the internal dispute over the adequacy of Adams' scholarship, the three-judge panel avoided that complex issue by means of a dispositive end run. The appellate court declared unequivocally that "*Garcetti* would not apply in the academic context of a public university as represented by the facts of this case. Our conclusion is based on the clear reservation of the issue in *Garcetti*, Fourth Circuit precedent, and the aspect of scholarship and teaching reflected by Adams' speech."[32] Despite the Fourth Circuit's mixed record on free speech and academic freedom issues (including the sharp division over Virginia's statutory ban on sexually explicit digital material in *Urofsky*) its readiness to embrace Justice Kennedy's reservation in *Garcetti* seemed appropriate and welcome. Moreover, invoking as it did the *Garcetti* exception for "academic scholarship" allowed the court to neatly sidestep other questions, such as the quality and quantity of Adams' publications. Meanwhile, the coincidental docketing of an appeal from "the department's only true conservative" may have proved providential—though of course nothing need be said to embrace Justice Kennedy's reservation beyond the statement of a congenial set of facts in the first post-*Garcetti* case.

Academic freedom champions now eagerly anticipated a more congenial environment in which to press faculty interests. That opportunity providentially emerged in the case of Washington University State journalism professor David Demers, who had consistently advocated the reorganization or realignment of his own professional school (appropriately named for Edward R. Murrow, its most illustrious graduate). Inclined to vigorous rhetoric, Demers wrote forcefully in support of his plan to split the Murrow School into two tracks or divisions—a plan which senior administrators (and for the most part his colleagues as well) did not welcome. Demers eventually filed suit in federal district court in Spokane, arguing that he had been a victim of retaliation on the basis of his wide distribution of a brief pamphlet setting forth his case for reorganization. The district judge ruled that Demers' advocacy failed to address a matter of public concern as defined in *Garcetti* and beyond, and was thus not protected speech.

The Ninth Circuit panel, however, profoundly disagreed early in 2014, and reversed the lower court. This court noted that Demers' advocacy clearly reflected his views on matters of public concern; moreover, the panel ruled that his First Amendment protection was not diluted or impaired by a claimed nexus between his public statements and his official duties. He had served, for example, on a Murrow School committee on "structure" but was not deemed for that or other reasons to have acted simply within his official duties. Along the way, the Ninth Circuit panel perceptively noted an inescapable ambiguity regarding the crucial term "public concern." Accordingly, this court declared that some statements made by public employees may not properly be protected by the First Amendment, such as those made during a "classic personnel struggle" or purely personal gripes or grievances.[33] But in the *Demers* case, there could be no serious question about the applicability of the "public concern" concept, given Professor Demers' clearly demonstrated and widely circulated advocacy of a major change in the structure of the academic school of which he was a senior faculty member. Leaving no doubt, the Ninth Circuit panel ruled that "there is an exception to *Garcetti* for teaching and academic writing" which clearly embraced Demers' statements.[34] The *Demers* case happily reflects the sensitive First Amendment views of two congenial appeal court judges—William Fletcher and Raymond Fisher—whose commitment to and understanding of academic freedom and scholarship were shaped by their mutual mentor, Supreme Court Justice William J. Brennan, Jr.

The post-*Garcetti* landscape was thus extended beyond tenured and tenure-track college teachers to the growing constituency of those who are described as contingent faculty. A late 2014 case served to advance dramatically the scope of protection for the speech and advocacy of part-time and adjunct teachers. A downstate Illinois community college, Moraine Valley, had summarily dismissed Robin Meade, an adjunct faculty member who headed the local teacher's union, on the basis of her consistent criticism of and disagreements with the college administration over myriad issues. Meade had, for example, detailed her concerns about inadequate salaries and lack of benefits, which "created a chilling effect which affects adjunct performance."[35] The district court dismissed the case out of hand. But the Chicago-based appeals court for the Seventh Circuit took a markedly different view, declaring that Meade was protected by the First Amendment in publicly expressing her views, at least as long as the issues she addressed were matters of public concern. This court also declared that even a contingent or part-time college teacher had a reasonable expectation of continued employment at that institution. The Seventh Circuit further ruled, in a sensitive opinion, that Meade was "not alone in expressing concern about the treatment of adjuncts."[36] This court broke important new ground by observing that "colleges and universities across the country are targets of increasing coverage and criticism regarding their use of adjunct faculty."[37] Such a realistic appraisal of the often-overlooked and under-appreciated contingent faculty—most especially in the community college world—also served to enhance academic freedom for full-time tenured and tenure-track teachers.

Finally, in 2014, Philip Lee of the University of the District of Columbia Law School published *Academic Freedom at American Universities: Constitutional Rights, Professional Norms, and Contractual Duties*. In it, Lee argues that the time has come for careful analysis of contract law as a medium of legal protection, in addition to the more traditional guarantees of academic freedom and due process. Specifically, he suggests that such a focus might erase the difference between the public and independent sectors with regard to academic freedom and free speech, because the pervasive application of contract law would treat both sectors comparably.

Lee also argues that "collective bargaining agreements can provide express terms that merge professional norms with contractual duties" as a growing number of such relationships already offer protection.[38] In addition, even absent explicit contract protection, courts occasionally recognize the legal force of implicit or implied-in-fact contracts. Moreover, as Lee observes, the state courts of New York have applied quasi constitutional precepts to private colleges and universities under Article 78 of the Code of Civil Practice.

In the fascinating case of Ward Churchill, a University of Colorado professor whose 2001 essay on the 9/11 attacks described some of the victims as "little Eichmanns," Lee finds an instructive analogy to contract law. After outrage from public officials over his essay caused Churchill to relinquish his administrative role at the Boulder campus, the university ruled that such statements were First Amendment protected despite their deeply offensive character. However, a prestigious faculty panel then claimed that Churchill had engaged in inexcusable "research misconduct"—a judgment which the board of regents unanimously affirmed and that Churchill decried as retaliation. That action of course eventually rendered moot Churchill's academic freedom and free expression claims.

Invoking the Churchill case, Lee argues that—even in the absence of explicit academic freedom safeguards—"Churchill could turn to implicit terms that were not written in the contract, but established by the conduct of the parties." This is indeed a novel and engaging approach. It not only serves to reinforce more traditional guarantees of academic freedom, but does so at the very time when state lawmakers have launched heightened attacks on due process and intellectual liberty.

This timely and welcome insight on Lee's part serves to bring the analysis full circle. Of course common law contract principles do reflect ancient roots, as well as familiar parallels to private campuses in New York's state courts under Article 78. Most important, such recognition of the utility of contractual safeguards should remind scholars, trustees, and litigants that an aggrieved or beleaguered professor seeking legal recourse now has two strings to his or her bow.

NOTES

1. See Walter Metzger, "The 1940 Statement of Principles on Academic Freedom and Tenure," in *Freedom and Tenure in the Academy*, ed. William W. Van Alstyne (Durham, NC: Duke University Press, 1993).

2. Ibid., 13.

3. "General Report of the Committee on Academic Freedom and Academic Tenure," *AAUP Bulletin* 17 (1915): 1.

4. Quoted in "The Professors Union," *School and Society* 175 (1916): 3.

5. See Metzger, "1940 Statement," 9.

6. See American Association of University Professors, *Policy Documents and Reports* (Washington, DC: American Association of University Professors, 2000), 3–10.

7. See *Tilton v. Richardson*, 403 U.S. 672, 681–2 (1971); *Jiminez v. Almodovar*, 650 F.2d 363, 369 (1st Cir. 1981); *Krotkoff v. Goucher College*, 585 F.2d 675, 679 (4th Cir. 1978); *Gray v. Board of Higher Education*, 692 F.2d 901, 907 (2d Cir. 1982); *Levitt v. Board of Trustees*, 376 F. Supp. 945, 950 (D. Neb. 1974). See also Matthew W. Finkin, ed., *The Case for Tenure* (Ithaca, NY: Cornell University Press, 1966); Ralph S. Brown, Jr., and Matthew W. Finkin, "The Usefulness of AAUP Statements," *Educational Record* 59 (1978): 30–44.

8. See *Krotkoff v. Goucher College*, 588 F. 2d 675 (4th Cir. 1978); *Kunda v. Muhlenberg College*, 621 F.2d 532 (3d Cir 1980).

9. See "Report of the Committee of Inquiry on the Case of Professor Scott Nearing of the University of Pennsylvania," *AAUP Bulletin* 127 (1916): 2.

10. Ellen Schrecker, *No Ivory Tower: McCarthyism and the Universities* (New York: Oxford University Press, 1986).

11. *Keyishian v. Board of Regents*, 385 U.S. 589, 603 (1967).

12. *Urofsky v. Gilmore*, 216 F.3d 401 (4th Cir. 2001).

13. AAUP, "1940 Statement of Principles on Academic Freedom and Tenure," 1970 Interpretive Comment #3.

14. Ibid.

15. See American Association of University Professors, "Academic Freedom and Electronic Communications," April 2014, at www.aaup.org/report/academic-freedom -and-electronic-communications-2014.

16. See www.insidehighered.com.news/2013/12/19.

17. Ibid.

18. Ibid.

19. Ibid.

20. See www.aaup/report/UIUC.

21. Va. Code Ann.S.1-805 (as amended Michie Supp. 1998).

22. *Urofsky v. Gilmore*, 216 F.3d 401 (4th Cir 2000).

23. Ibid.

24. *Pickering v. Board of Education*, 391 U.S. 563 (1968).

25. In the seminal case of *New York Times v. Sullivan* (376 US 254 [1964]), the Supreme Court established a dramatically more protective standard governing cases brought by a public official (or later a public figure) seeking damages for defamation against critics of his or her official conduct.

26. *Garcetti v. Ceballos*, 547 US 410 (2006).

27. Ibid.

28. Ibid.

29. *Hong v. Grant*, 516 F. Supp. 516 F. Supp. 1158 (C.D. Cal. 2007).

30. *Renken v. Gregory*, 541 F.3d 769 (7th Cir. 2008).

31. *Gorum v. Sessons*, 564 F.3d 179 (3d Cir. 2009).

32. *Adams v. Trustees of University of North Carolina-Wilmington*, 640 F.3d 550 (4th Cir. 2011).

33. *Demers v. Austin*, 2014 US App. LEXIS 1811 (9th Cir. 2014).

34. Ibid.

35. *Meade v. Moraine Valley Community College*, No. 13 C 7950, ____F.3d ____ (7th Cir. 2014).

36. Ibid.

37. Ibid.

38. Phillip Lee, *Academic Freedom at American Universities: Constitutional Rights, Professional Norms, and Contractual Duties* (Lanham, MD: Lexington Books, 2015), 103–11.

# Chapter Three

# Curriculum in Higher Education

*The Organizational Dynamics of Academic Reform*

Michael N. Bastedo

The curriculum in American higher education is often characterized as a pendulum swinging from one extreme to another: from religion to secular science, from prescribed study of the classics to curricular pluralism, and from tradition and conservatism to experimentation and growth. Indeed, these have been some of the major tensions in the American higher education curriculum over the past three centuries, and conflict over these issues has often been intense within academic communities. The need for curriculum reform can be understood as emanating from changes in the broader society, such as scientific advancement, evolving conceptions of knowledge, changing student demographics, and, more recently, labor market demands. These have often provided compelling rationales for some forms of curricular change.

We must also recognize, however, that these explanations have often been egregiously simplified. Over thirty years ago, Douglas Sloan accused historians of treating the higher education curriculum as a "morality play," where the forces of science, growth, and *Lernfreiheit* (student freedom to learn) fought the good battle against the forces of religion, stagnation, and prescription.[1] In reality, those who fought for a prescribed curriculum often struggled with how to provide some form of academic freedom to students; those who were fervent and pious followers of the Christian faith were often equal believers in the need for education in the basic sciences; and those who believed that knowledge must be conserved were also committed to change and innovation. There are identifiable tensions in the curriculum, but they are not simplistic dichotomies.

In short, we must come to a more nuanced understanding of the reciprocal relationship between the curriculum and society. While the curriculum can be seen as a lens for social change, it can also serve society by defining the boundaries of knowledge and thus serve as a force for social change itself, as we will see in the development of technology and the study of women and racial minorities. And while social forces undoubtedly influence the curriculum, a full understanding is only possible when we understand how those changes have unfolded over time. Toward that end, we must identify the agents of change, the ways in which they organized for social action, and the dynamic relationship between actors in the university and organizations and leaders in society at large.

With these aims in mind, this chapter provides a broad overview of the organizational dynamics of curriculum reform since the early days of the American college. Using three major tensions in curriculum reform—prescription and election, stability and growth, and conservation and innovation—historical developments are considered analytically to understand how early reforms have influenced contemporary debates. In the final section, I briefly consider some conceptual frameworks for understanding the dynamics of curriculum reform, as well as some emerging policy issues for the coming decade.

## Prescription and Election

The curriculum of the early American college was strongly influenced by the medieval English university, which trained the Calvinist ministers who founded early American colleges in the seventeenth century. There was one curriculum for all students, designed to prepare them for a career in law or the clergy. Incoming classes were quite small; until the 1760s, all of the colonial colleges combined did not yield more than one hundred graduates per year.[2] Students themselves were generally only fourteen to eighteen years old and were often taught by the college president himself. In later years, recent graduates, themselves only eighteen or nineteen years old, assisted him as tutors.[3]

Training for the Protestant ministry required learning the major languages of biblical texts—Latin, Greek, and Hebrew—so that students could understand them in the original. Study of the classical languages was also highly valued for its perceived ability to shape the human mind; the complexity of the grammatical structures of ancient languages was believed to train students to think at a more advanced level than was possible in the vernacular or other modern languages. Although a basic knowledge of Latin and Greek was often required for admission, teaching in these languages comprised much of the first two years of study, with the addition of logic, grammar, and some rhetoric. Logic was highly valued for its usefulness in teaching students to think rationally and critically, as it had been in the English university. In the final two years, a greater portion of the curriculum consisted of rhetoric, poetry, literature, ethics, arithmetic, and philosophy. Teaching itself consisted of lectures, verbatim recitations, and public disputations.

Emerging topics that did not fit into the ordinary curriculum were covered in weekly "extracurricular" lectures to the student body. Extracurricular topics were also occasionally taught in courses that were stated to be Latin or logic. Student literary societies served an important curricular role, promoting the reading of poetry, literature, science, and other topics that were not a priority in the standard curriculum.[4] Beyond simply reading the works, debates on these subjects were often organized by competing societies for the benefit of the campus. As is often true today, a great deal of learning in the early American college took place outside of the classroom.

As students and faculty became excited by new knowledge, they made extensive efforts to incorporate new materials into the curriculum, both formally and informally. After Yale hired Timothy Dwight as president in 1795, the senior class successfully petitioned the trustees to allow students to take lectures from him in rhetoric, history, poetry, and literature.[5] The evolution of the Scientific Revolution in European universities also could not be ignored; American faculty returned from Europe fired up to teach these new and daring subjects to eager students. Gradually, courses in physics, anatomy, chemistry, and more advanced mathematics were added to the final two years of the college curriculum.

With new topics emerging at a rapid pace, many openly considered allowing students to select their courses. At the turn of the nineteenth century, the American college curriculum was in a state of conflict over the knowledge and skills necessary for a liberal education in contemporary society. As the interests and career goals of incoming students became more catholic, as society expected higher education to cover an increasing number of subjects, and as faculty grew restive, the curriculum came under attack from progressives for its intensive focus on ancient languages and theology. The result was an unplanned growth of subjects in the curriculum without an overarching philosophy, which to some meant chaos and confusion. According to historian Frederick Rudolph, "higher education behaved in harmony with a culture that built canals and railroads in seemingly endless number and for reasons that were often more consistent with the national psychology than with sound economic and engineering practice."[6] Students were also getting older; the age of the average college student rose throughout the nineteenth century, making the idea of an elective curriculum increasingly acceptable as students grew from boys to men.

Yet there were many who were opposed to such changes, for reasons both traditional and contemporary. The defense of the classical curriculum by the president and faculty of Yale College in 1828 was often seen as the last bulwark against the radical changes being proposed by students and society. The Yale Report famously defined the purpose of liberal education as providing "the *discipline* and *furniture* of the mind."[7] Intensive study of Latin and Greek, they argued, was necessary for students to expand their memory; logic and scientific experiments were required to teach students to think through complex problems. Ordinary Americans could be trained on the job for careers in "subordinate" positions. Yale's purpose, they argued, was to train young men from the upper classes who would serve as society's enlightened leaders and decision makers.[8]

Despite widespread acceptance of the report, Yale and the other elite colleges could not single-handedly resist the demands of a changing society and the propulsion of increasingly rapid knowledge change. As state, community, and denominational competition drove the creation of hundreds of colleges throughout the nineteenth century, those states, communities, and denominations expected college curricula consonant with their needs and interests. Advanced education was increasingly necessary for professions outside of the law and the clergy, and students expected a more rational connection between their course work and future career opportunities. Faculty and students, seeing emerging knowledge being created in new academic fields such as science, economics, and sociology, expected to find that knowledge reflected in the curriculum. The complexity of these demands by college constituents made reform virtually irresistible.

Once the classical curriculum was dismantled, it happened with remarkable speed. Although Frances Wayland had instituted an elective curriculum at Brown University by 1850—and, as a result, increased enrollment by 40 percent—Harvard president Charles Eliot, in embracing reform, popularized the new curriculum throughout higher education, despite being appointed nearly twenty years after Wayland inaugurated changes at Brown.[9] By 1879, only the freshman year was prescribed for Harvard undergraduates, but there was still intense conflict over the elective reforms. Numerous public debates among high-ranking college presidents were conducted throughout the late nineteenth century. Indeed, presidents and faculty were often conflicted within themselves about the choice between prescription and election.

The changes at Brown and Harvard led to similar moves throughout higher education, part of what David Riesman has described as a "meandering snakelike procession" of ideas through colleges and universities.[10] Nevertheless, there was widespread unhappiness with the rapid decline in standards that accompanied the adoption of the elective system; students increasingly enrolled in entry-level courses and abandoned logic and languages in droves, leading to charges that universities were educating a generation of sophists and dilettantes. The appointment of A. Lawrence Lowell to the Harvard presidency in 1909 was, in large degree, a response to Eliot's radical overhaul of undergraduate education. Lowell's mandate was to institute a set of distribution requirements to ensure that all students received a liberal education, a plan he outlined at his inauguration, with Eliot sitting next to him on the dais.

An idea that worked in theory never seemed to work well in practice. Distribution requirements forced students to select courses from particular categories, but there was still no common curriculum for all undergraduates. Proponents of a rigorous liberal education were still around to make plenty of trouble for the new system. Dissent crystallized around Robert M. Hutchins, who took over the University of Chicago in 1919, at the age of twenty-nine. Hutchins was driven by a desire to elevate the common man through standards of culture, thought, and morality, and thus to elevate society as well. The only way to accomplish these goals, Hutchins believed, was a prescribed program of general education.

The development of general education programs would be facilitated by institutional changes in the disciplines. Historians, who needed to introduce students to their rapidly developing field, shaped broad courses that covered Western history from Greece to the present.[11] These courses were the basis for War Issues courses developed during World War I, whose purpose was to create solidarity between future American soldiers and their European counterparts by educating them on their common heritage.[12] These courses, in turn, led to the "Great Books" movement launched in the 1940s and 1950s and discussed later in this chapter.

The response to the concerns of Hutchins and his sympathizers within higher education was exemplified by Harvard's famous Red Book.[13] The Red Book was a report written by a committee of Harvard faculty charged with evaluating the state of general education for undergraduates. The committee for the 1945 Red Book did not go as far as Hutchins or Mortimer J. Adler might have hoped, but they did acknowledge that distribution requirements were inadequate and recommended that all students be exposed to the major areas of knowledge. Tension between prescription and election is evident throughout the monograph, an artifact not only of the prevailing views of the country, but also of the conflicting views of the faculty on the committee.[14] Once again, the Harvard plan proved to be popular, and it became a model for general education programs throughout the country.

Twenty years later, Columbia University faced concerns about its general education program, but from the opposite direction. Columbia's Contemporary Civilization program required a single course sequence in the classics for the entire first-year class, leading to attacks claiming that it restricted the academic freedom of students and consisted of works largely irrelevant to contemporary social concerns. Daniel Bell, a prominent sociologist at the university, was asked to write a report on the subject for the consideration of the faculty. His 1966 book, *The Reforming of General Education*, was a thoughtful, pragmatic approach to the problem of general education. Bell argued that since college takes its place between secondary school, which emphasizes facts, and graduate school, which emphasizes specialization, "the distinctive function of the college must be to teach modes of conceptualization, explanation, and verification of knowledge."[15] The selection of canonical texts included in Columbia's program broadened the mind, he said, because the works were presented as contingent, allowing the reader to draw conclusions that differed from those of the professor. Material presented merely as fact or dogma, Bell argued, would lead only to specialization and vocationalism, thereby undermining the goals of general education.

Despite his defense of Columbia's core curriculum, Bell's pragmatic argument provoked those who believed that the classics were worthwhile in and of themselves. This view was most clearly expressed by Leo Strauss, a political philosopher at the University of Chicago. "Liberal education is education in culture or toward culture . . . The finished product of a liberal education is a cultured human being," Strauss wrote. "We are compelled to live with books. But life is too short to live with any but the greatest books."[16] Robert Belknap and Richard Kuhns later took an even more reactionary stance, arguing that contemporary students were ignorant, and that universities had failed to integrate the disciplines by instead placing a premium on specialization. "Universities and schools," they said, "have lost their common sense of what kind of ignorance is unacceptable."[17]

Allan Bloom extended this argument in 1987 in *The Closing of the American Mind*. Bloom derided the culture of American college students and the curriculum of American colleges, both of which, he believed, encouraged an unhealthy cultural pluralism. Teaching students merely to be open to new cultures was wrongheaded, he said, because it is natural to prefer your own culture, just as it is natural to prefer your own child over another's. Without this proprietorship of culture, students were left in a "no man's land between the goodness of knowing and the goodness of culture, where they have been placed by their teachers who no longer have the resources to guide them."[18] Students, Bloom argued, no longer had a cultural orientation with which to organize the world around them, leaving them unable to construct meaning from a stream of facts and opinions. In a society characterized by torrents of information, Bloom said, colleges have abandoned students by their ideology of openness.

Bloom's tract led to a flood of books on the state of the American college generally and liberal education specifically. In 1991, Dinesh D'Souza, in *Illiberal Education*, argued that the problem was not that colleges taught non-Western culture, but that it was taught ignorantly. Instead of teaching classic non-Western texts such as the *Analects* of Confucius or the *Ramayana*, he said, faculty taught explicitly political works like *I, Rigoberta Menchu* and *The Wretched of the Earth*, books that were written by Westerners and served merely to reflect liberal Western conceptions of non-Western peoples.[19] Thus D'Souza advocated a prescriptive but not ethnocentric curriculum that identified essential texts from multiple traditions. D'Souza strongly supported *50 Hours*, a similar curriculum published in 1989 during the Reagan administration, under the auspices of the National Endowment for the Humanities.[20]

In the 1990s, a few scholars emerged to defend the university against these often vituperative critiques.[21] They were united in their opinion that most discussion of liberal education was oblivious to its history, and they emphasized how the curriculum has always been a contested area full of controversy and disagreement. The curriculum, even in its classical period, was never entirely static—new books gained entrance (for example, Austen, Twain, James, Freud) and old books were discarded. In this way, the curriculum has always responded to changing fashions in scholarship, taste, and the demands of an evolving society.

They said further that the new demographics of higher education mandated the inclusion of new authors in general education programs that reflected an increasingly multicultural society. University of Chicago philosopher Martha Nussbaum, for example, has argued that shaping citizens remains a vital function of higher education. Students must be prepared for a culturally diverse and international world, she said, and doing so requires understanding the perspectives of a wide variety of cultures. Nevertheless, she saw the Western tradition as remarkably consonant with emerging demands for pluralism. Books in the Western tradition can help students with the critical examination of people and cultures, including one's own, and develop the ability to think about the emotions and values of people in other cultures. This ability "to step out of your own shoes," she concluded, was key to living in a world marked by people's diversity in race, class, gender, and sexual orientation.[22]

Debate over the nature and necessity of the prescribed college curriculum continues to this day, although it has abated substantially in the wake of concerns about access, funding, and accountability. Most recently, the burden of defending the case for a prescribed curriculum has fallen to the American Council of Trustees and Alumni (ACTA), a conservative advocacy group that has issued a series of reports alleging the failures of American higher education to hold students to rigorous academic standards. By their criteria, in 2014 only 18.3 percent of undergraduate programs require an acceptable course in US government, just 37.5 percent require a course in literature, and only 13.1 percent require the study of a foreign language.[23] They note courses that meet history requirements around the country include "Horror Films and American Culture," "Leisure and Marketing in America," and "Vampires: History of the Undead."

There are remarkable parallels between debates over the elective system in the 1880s and 1890s and more recent debates over general education since the 1980s. In both cases, the degree to which knowledge evolution and changing student demographics demand curricular reform is a key point of contention. Both sides have engaged in significant debates on the utility of more traditional curricula compared with emerging subjects. The primary question is always, what do college students need to learn to be educated members of society? Ultimately, general education does not exist in a vacuum, and it must be as dynamic as the rest of the curriculum.

## Stability and Growth

Persistent debates on the state of general education have occurred amid the massive expansion of knowledge and the development of organizational structures to support them. During the 1880s and 1890s, as the implementation of the elective system was negotiated in colleges across the country, the modern disciplines were also beginning to emerge. In a process that Walter Metzger has called *subject parturition*, the disciplines that we have come to understand as the foundation of the modern university were organized into distinctive and recognizable units.[24] As knowledge created in the university became increasingly complex and differentiated, new subjects emerged to help define the boundaries of that knowledge. In their early days, professors in these fields often struggled for legitimacy with professors in more established areas of knowledge. Over the years, through a process Metzger termed *subject dignification*, these fields gradually gained legitimacy through the creation of scholarly societies, academic journals, and distinctive and rigorous methodologies.

Subject parturition was led in the nineteenth century by the sciences, which began to break out from the more general and humanistic approach taught in the colonial and antebellum colleges under the rubric "natural philosophy." As scientific modes of investigation were incorporated and PhDs returned from advanced study in Germany, the study of science seemed increasingly differentiated from other subjects. Before the widespread adoption of the elective system, chemistry, geology, astronomy, physics, and biology were already recognized as distinct subjects at most colleges.[25] The social sciences quickly followed, with economics emerging from political economy, and sociology emerging from economics. These new fields were supported by scholarly societies like the American Anthropological Association, founded in 1802, and journals such as the *American Journal of Sociology*, founded in 1895.[26]

New forms of knowledge and methodologies for their investigation led to new forms of classroom pedagogy. The lectures and recitations of the early American colleges were simply ineffective methods for science education or for advanced students at the graduate level. Laboratory sections were added to courses to facilitate the empirical investigation of scientific phenomena. While the lecture would remain the primary mode of instruction for most of the twentieth century, the seminar was implemented for graduate students and then gradually diffused to advanced undergraduates.[27] Having learned the basic foundations of their field, graduate students and advanced undergraduates were deemed capable of engaging in direct dialogue with professors and colleagues.

The disciplines became increasingly specialized over the course of the twentieth century. Universities helped to define what forms of knowledge were worth knowing by the disciplines' placement in the curriculum, and researchers themselves established new modes of inquiry. These changes were then diffused throughout the academic community through scholarly societies and journals, and transmitted to society by graduating students and faculty who interacted with people outside the university. The curriculum was transformed further as faculty sought to teach more specialized courses, resulting in a greater differentiation of courses and degrees. The professional self-identification of faculty changed concurrently. Whereas once faculty members might call themselves psychologists or biologists, later they would declare themselves to be Jungians or neuroendocrinologists.[28]

Subjects outside of the traditional disciplines have also been accommodated, particularly in fields that are closer to the economy. Schools in medicine, law, education, social work, and public health emerged to meet the needs of an increasingly professionalized society, and to certify and elaborate professional knowledge.[29] Academic work in these schools was often a laboratory for increasing specialization and the interdisciplinarity of knowledge. Technical and vocational subjects have become a core mission for the community colleges, ranging from automobile repair to medical technology and radiation therapy. This is not to say that vocational subjects were solely the realm of community colleges; on the contrary, students across the spectrum of both public and private colleges became increasingly vocational in their orientation and demanded curricula relevant to their needs.[30]

In recent years, the humanities have been an increasingly fertile field for the development of new programs and departments within the university. Unlike those founded in earlier periods, these programs were often explicitly connected to organized social movements led by students.[31] The civil rights movement of the 1950s and 1960s inspired student groups to demand black studies programs at more than eight hundred colleges and universities. Black faculty worked in concert with the students, making strenuous efforts to increase scholarship in the emerging field. Funding was often provided by the Ford Foundation, whose grants helped to establish many black studies programs across the country.[32]

Over the course of the 1960s, however, black students increasingly associated themselves with the Black Power movement, a more militant attempt to force society to recognize the rights of black Americans. Students inspired by the Black Power movement often thought black faculty, tainted by their socialization in the academy, were "too white" to reflect an authentic black culture, and they demanded programs that explicitly rejected the involvement of the traditional disciplines and incorporated community members into the curriculum.[33] Their goal was not simply to establish a separate curriculum, but to transform the curriculum of the university as a whole and to address racism in society more broadly.

Women's studies programs followed a similar path in the early 1970s.[34] Feminism was a powerful influence on young women entering the university, who demanded that the study of women and women's issues be incorporated into the curriculum. Female faculty who pursued graduate work during the 1960s often risked their careers by writing dissertations in women's studies and, once they were hired, faced sharp critiques from their disciplinary colleagues that their work was methodologically weak or "too political." Women's studies faculty and students, like those in black studies, explicitly sought to change the curriculum of the university and to rectify institutionalized sexism and misogyny in society. Similar identity-based movements can be seen today in efforts to promote Chicano studies, Asian American studies, and Queer studies in the curriculum.[35]

Further growth in the higher education curriculum has resulted from interdisciplinarity, the integration of two or more disciplines to form a new content area or mode of inquiry.[36] Interdisciplinarity creates fundamental tensions as new organizational spaces are created in the university. Many will advocate for an entirely new interdisciplinary program to establish a foothold in the curriculum and, not incidentally, to make a permanent claim in the university budget. Inevitably, another faction will argue that interdisciplinary programs should exist only across the existing departments, so as to wait until the field matures, retain disciplinary legitimacy for scholars, and maintain faculty hires in the departments.

Interdisciplinary inquiry has occurred almost since the foundation of the disciplines; recently, however, there have been movements to organize new subjects in separate departments and programs. Interdisciplinary programs are in evidence across the fields of knowledge, from biostatistics and biopsychology to area studies of Latin America, Eastern Europe, and Africa. The disciplines themselves have also become increasingly interdisciplinary, as subfields of the disciplines have grown ever closer to their neighbors. Thus we see areas of study such as economic sociology, where sociologists have directed their energies into areas previously claimed by economists, and behavioral economics, where economists have taken on insights from psychology to paint a more realistic picture of economic behavior. Growth in the disciplines is therefore increasingly fractal, as each discipline differentiates within itself into smaller and smaller parts, but in ways that are highly and predictably patterned through social, philosophical, and methodological lenses.[37]

Finally, growth in the curriculum can be seen in areas that serve to segregate students and academic programs within colleges and universities.[38] In the past, the differentiation of students generally occurred among colleges; increasingly, this separation also occurs *within* individual colleges, particularly at public universities.[39] Separate admissions standards are often established for popular academic programs, especially at community colleges, forcing some students into less-lucrative or less-popular fields. Honors colleges, which provide special sections and other benefits to enrolled students, are a rapid growth industry in higher education; fully one-quarter of all honors programs were established at public colleges in the decade from 1989 to 1999.[40] Underprepared students are often shunted into remedial education courses with low pass rates, preventing students from accumulating credits toward a college degree. Each of these trends has significant implications for equitable access to higher education, particularly within the public sector.

Amid all the talk of growth, there are fields in sharp decline. Those associated with agriculture—botany, horticulture, veterinary medicine, and animal science—have declined sharply since 1975. Home economics programs have fallen nearly 40 percent, and most of those programs were eliminated before 1975. Programs such as journalism, library science, and speech have been systematically eliminated across the country, and European languages like French and German have been hard hit. These trends have been summarized by sociologist Steven Brint and his colleagues as "Old Economy," "Old Media," and "Old Culture/Identity."[41]

Despite all of these pressures toward change and differentiation, impressive stability has accompanied this tremendous growth. Disciplines established over a century ago—and some older than that—remain at the core of the academic enterprise today. If anything, there is greater consensus within the disciplines on appropriate modes of inquiry and the established domains of content. Societal demands on the university and on knowledge construction have certainly become more complex over time, but the university has often adapted by accommodating those changes within its existing organizational structures. Despite seemingly unending specialization, conflict, and change, the university curriculum is a recognizably stable entity that has adapted remarkably to social, economic, and political demands.

## Conservation and Innovation

One of the main forces for stability in the curriculum has been academic culture. Scholars have been trained to believe that one of the core missions of the university is to preserve the knowledge of past generations. The classical curriculum, while dynamic in some ways—through extracurricular lectures, literary societies, and the gradual adoption of new subjects—remained remarkably consistent for most of the colonial period and well into the nineteenth century. In an era when it was plausible to believe that Latin and Greek were essential for any man who considered himself liberally educated, the forces of stability were a powerful influence in the American college.

The effect of Christianity on the college curriculum cannot be underestimated. Although the central role of colleges in the preparation of ministers gradually declined, Christianity nevertheless remained infused throughout student life and the curriculum. Protestant revivalism, as expressed through the Great Awakenings of the 1740s and the early 1800s, found fertile ground in the American college. Indeed, one of the major sources of the Second Great Awakening was Yale University, and one historian has described colleges during this period as "revival camps."[42] The curriculum and Christianity were thus mutually reinforcing; faculty concern for the salvation of their students was paramount, and it was transmitted to students in courses such as ethics, literature, and theology.

Although science was certainly on the rise throughout the nineteenth century, there was not as sharp a divide between science and religion as is often perceived today. After the *Summa Theologica* of Thomas Aquinas, the major intellectual project of the Middle Ages was the resolution of biblical revelation with classical science and philosophy. Thus the people who were founding new colleges as an expression of religious faith were also the same people establishing science departments in these colleges, and they saw no contradiction in those two actions. The scientific method, far from undermining religion, was, rather, an instrument for the revelation of sacred truth.

Nonetheless, a gradual secularization of the Protestant university took hold over the course of the nineteenth and twentieth centuries. As new subjects were added to the curriculum at a rapid pace, their connection to the religious mission of the college was often increasingly tenuous. Protestant leaders, for their part, valued religious tolerance and a unified American culture, making it difficult to retain denominational separatism and distinctive religious missions.[43] As the nature of the multiversity became the secular pursuit of knowledge, religion grew increasingly unimportant to the college mission, and leaders of the academy themselves were drawn from prominent academics rather than ministers. The declining influence of Christianity was quite gradual; Wellesley College, for example, did not eliminate required chapel until 1968.[44]

The secularization of the university was not entirely welcomed, and neither was the liberalization of academic requirements. Robert M. Hutchins, the University of Chicago president who led the attack on distribution requirements during the 1930s and 1940s, began to think about resurrecting more traditional curricula that would meet the standards of an earlier era. He was encouraged by John Erskine's General Honors course at Columbia University, which was an extension of the War Issues course developed by Erskine for outgoing American soldiers during World War I. Erskine designed the course in response to what he saw as the increasing specialization and vocationalism in college education, and his students read fifty-two classics—from Homer to William James—in a single year.[45] Hutchins soon taught a course of his own, first to high school students, and then as a Great Books course at the University of Chicago, limited to twenty students by invitation.

The Great Books idea was highly influential both inside and outside of the university, leading to a small industry of book publishing and discussion groups during the 1940s and 1950s. This was initiated by the publication of Hutchins's caustic *The Higher Learning in America* in 1936, which derided the vocationalism and intellectual content of higher education and prescribed a new course centered on the classics.[46] His book was an instant bestseller despite—or perhaps because of—its rather elitist attitude toward college education. Ten years later, Hutchins left the Chicago presidency to assist the Great Books movement, which had inspired a charitable foundation, discussion groups throughout the country, and a rather lucrative company that published approved selections as *The Great Books of the Western World*.[47]

Adherents of the Great Books method were so pleased with the results of the courses at Columbia, Chicago, and elsewhere that they were eager to revamp an entire college based on the premise. The opportunity presented itself when two-hundred-year-old St. John's College announced that it would close, due to budget problems.[48] Stringfellow Barr and Scott Buchanan, Great Books adherents at the University of Virginia, decided to try and save the college by instituting a four-year prescribed course in the classics. The "New Program" curriculum that they developed, based on the Chicago and Columbia models but with the addition of a substantial amount of science and mathematics, has remained largely as it was since its creation in 1939.[49]

St. John's College as it exists today was only one of many experimental colleges founded during the postwar period, with the 1950s and 1960s being a particularly fertile time. In its willingness to upend the foundations of the college curriculum, this period is virtually unmatched in American history. Prominent examples include the University of California at Santa Cruz (UCSC), whose cluster colleges tried to break down the multiversity into manageable organizational units, each with its own distinctive character. As one example, UCSC's Kresge College experimented with using T-groups in courses inspired by the 1960s encounter movement, founded by Carl Rogers, which allowed students to interact through problem solving and role playing exercises.[50] Another example is Black Mountain College, which attracted famous writers and artists from across the country to its utopian community in North Carolina until its collapse in 1956.[51]

The 1960s served as a period of experimentation even within traditional colleges. The emergence of national student movements and the breakdown of social conformity that characterized the post–World War II era pressured colleges to alter traditional curricular and pedagogical practices. For student activists, the curriculum had become far too abstracted from relevant political and social concerns. The best-known group was Students for a Democratic Society (SDS), which formed in 1960 to organize students around the social concerns of the period, primarily social justice issues and the Vietnam War.[52] Because the university graduated the future leaders of the country, the SDS viewed reforming the university as essential to promoting social change.

Resistance to the idea of "politicizing" the university curriculum was strong, so SDS members moved to create "free universities" where any student could study or teach, and where individuals in the university community, regardless of academic qualifications, were welcome to participate. In free universities, the political neutrality of courses and instructors was explicitly rejected, because the mission was to encourage political activism to improve society. Any form of grading was often eliminated as irrelevant to the learning process. Over time, free universities were widely accepted at colleges across the country. Indeed, they were so successful that militant students, seeing that free universities were peacefully coexisting with the traditional curriculum, became disenchanted with their ability to transform the university and eventually abandoned them.[53]

As the 1960s came to a close, many students and faculty became cynical about the ability of universities to inspire social change. The persistence of the Vietnam War and the student killings at Kent State and Jackson State universities in 1970 coincided with an overall contraction in university growth. Student activism declined dramatically, reaching record lows in the 1980s and 1990s. The major curricular experiments in higher education had, one by one, failed to achieve their goals, leading to further cynicism and apathy. In future decades, curricular reforms would be significantly less ambitious, but would nevertheless influence the core of the educational enterprise. In an incremental manner, these changes would ultimately have more impact on the curriculum than the most ambitious experimental colleges.

The influence of technology on the modern curriculum is undeniable.[54] The information technology revolution of the 1970s and 1980s has transformed how students conduct their work and how they expect to obtain and transmit information. Improving a student's ability to use technology is often explicitly stated as part of the core educational mission of undergraduate education, and the "digital divide" is a key issue among those concerned with equity and access. The widespread adoption of the Internet by colleges and universities during the 1980s and 1990s has revolutionized our ability to obtain vast quantities of information and synthesize it in a short time. Classroom teaching itself has been changed through the use of computer laboratories, "clickers," flipped classrooms, and massive open online courses (MOOCs).

New forms of learning have emerged to take advantage of new technologies. Online education, which allows instructors and students to connect visually across multiple classroom locations, has expanded access to higher education for those who live far from a university or who are determined to seek out programs that are outside their local communities. The Internet has created innumerable opportunities for online education, where students communicate solely by discussion groups, e-mail, video chat rooms, podcasts, and instant messaging. More recently, even mainstream programs have begun to experiment with combining both traditional and virtual modes of instruction as the needs of students, faculty, and the subject dictate. Although proclamations of the death of the traditional university have proved to be premature, there has been an undeniable change in the nature of academic work for many students and faculty.

Other forms of curricular experimentation are making their claims on the university as well, often with remarkable success. One prominent example is the development of experiential education and service-learning programs. Service learning emerged in the experimental fervor of the 1960s from the same social movements that led to the creation of the SDS and the free universities.[55] Consonant with the ideals of the time, service learning was a means for students to engage and transform society through efforts that were rewarded with academic credit by the university. At first, service learning was simply a loosely defined group of internships and volunteer activities, many with a political or nonprofit bent. As notions of community service expanded into society throughout the 1980s and 1990s, service-learning programs grew in importance and were co-opted, becoming increasingly apolitical. Over time, service learning has emerged as an identifiable and legitimate mode of inquiry, with applications across the fields of study, and it serves as a demonstration of the university's commitment to public service.

Curriculum reform has also been aimed at improving student persistence and graduation rates, particularly at community colleges and public comprehensive universities. In "learning communities," groups of students enroll simultaneously in a sequence of courses, or even an entire academic program, instead of choosing those courses separately. These courses often have a unifying theme that draws students and faculty together to study one topic intensively. Although research in this area remains embryonic, learning communities seem to promote student persistence by providing classroom experiences that are more meaningful for students, and by building support structures among the students themselves.[56] Another effort to address dropout rates has been to use "supplemental instruction" in the classroom, which provides coursework in basic skills for underprepared students enrolled in traditional credit-bearing courses, rather than segregating them into separate remedial courses. Data on these programs suggest that students in supplemental instruction earn higher grades and are more likely to persist than their peers.[57]

There may well be a strong relationship between curriculum structures and student success, particularly at institutions with lower graduation rates. Using a wealth of data from community colleges around the country, scholars recently argued that two-year colleges can substantially increase their persistence and graduation rates by providing "guided pathways" in the curriculum rather than a cafeteria-style menu of options.[58] In future years, research on the "choice architecture" of colleges and universities should expand, leading to new insights about how to promote student success.

## Organizing Curricular Change

For many observers, the curriculum is an "academic graveyard" where ideas for educational reform go to die. It is widely believed that the curriculum simply does not change, and that reforms never move forward, but merely swing from one extreme to the other over the course of time. On the contrary, significant changes in the curriculum have occurred in American higher education throughout its history. Although revolutionary change in the curriculum has been rare, incremental changes have often accumulated over time to create significant and lasting impacts.[59] By using the curriculum as a lens for social change, we can see the effect of society's demands on higher education, and how universities have sought to define the boundaries of knowledge and thereby influence how the public views social issues.

Knowledge differentiation is certainly a key factor in curricular change. For some, knowledge is the prime unit of analysis, putting constant pressure on the university organization to adapt to its increasing complexity.[60] To cope with these unrelenting pressures, the curriculum must accommodate them by altering the content and form of courses, as well as the requirements and organization of programs and departments. Unending differentiation thus yields an organization that is remarkably adaptable to the range of demands placed upon it, but it faces increasing problems of integration, since students and faculty have less in common when they move further and further apart. In this perspective, general education for all students can never be resurrected, because it is impossible to build a consensus across the university on which types of knowledge are most valuable to undergraduates.[61]

Curricular change can also be understood as an inhabitant of the organizational culture that supports it.[62] In this view, the curriculum is socially constructed among the constituents of the university, who interact with one another to create meaning. The curriculum itself signifies changes in the faculty's underlying assumptions about what counts as knowledge, what knowledge is most worthy of transmission, and what organizational forms are most appropriate. The curriculum also serves as a form of organizational culture for students, socializing them into the content and skills needed to navigate the world of the university. From this perspective, in order to understand curricular change, we must first understand the organizational culture of the university, and then identify the mechanisms by which faculty and students interact within the curriculum to construct the meaning of knowledge.

Social movements can also be a key motivator for curricular change.[63] Traditional accounts of curricular change have often cited changing student demographics—increasing numbers of racial and ethnic minorities, women, and sexual minorities in the university—as the main causal factor behind change in the curriculum. With this explanation, there has been little understanding of how these demographics have led to actual change in the curriculum. One answer is social movements, which have organized students and faculty around political and identity-based causes so as to make demands for new programs and departments in the curriculum. Earlier, we saw how the Black Power movement, leftist movements, and feminists have marshaled themselves to create new content and produce new organizational structures in the curriculum.

The construction of the curriculum can also be connected to powerful political and economic actors in society.[64] As both the government and profit-seeking corporations have become increasingly involved in the funding of university research activities, their influence on the curriculum in departments and programs closely connected to those agencies has become apparent. For-profit corporations make grants to science departments and business schools; the government pours substantial funds into medical schools, science departments, and schools of education. In addition, nonprofit foundations are often significant providers of funds in the humanities and the social sciences. Although it is not yet clear how these connections yield specific changes in coursework or organizational structures, these actors are undoubtedly powerful resource providers exerting a marked influence on research-oriented faculty.

Finally, we must consider efforts to influence undergraduate education through state policy. Nonpartisan organizations, including the Education Commission of the States and the National Center for Public Policy and Higher Education, have been sharply critical of the inability of states and colleges to improve teaching or monitor progress on student learning.[65] State policymakers in Ohio and Massachusetts have been equally disparaging about faculty productivity and about more time being spent on research and service than on teaching.[66]

These opinions have been reinforced by research showing the weak impact of college on critical thinking skills, in books such as *Academically Adrift*.[67] Increasingly, states are considering the use of measures such as Graduate Record Exam scores, critical-thinking inventories, and even high-stakes graduation exams to improve and assess undergraduate instruction. Regional accreditation agencies now routinely require institutions to use assessment instruments that evaluate student learning outcomes. Although many of these ideas are still in their early stages, they may well be a major policy issue in the next decade.

NOTES

1. Douglas Sloan, "Harmony, Chaos, and Consensus: The American College Curriculum," *Teachers College Record* 73 (1971): 221–51.

2. Frederick Rudolph, *Curriculum: A History of the Undergraduate Course of Study since 1636* (San Francisco: Jossey-Bass, 1977). Rudolph's work is still the standard for historical examination of the college curriculum, and his influence can be seen throughout this chapter.

3. John D. Burton, "The Harvard Tutors: The Beginning of the Academic Profession, 1690–1825," *History of Higher Education Annual* 16 (1996): 1–17.

4. James McLachlan, "The 'Choice of Hercules': American Student Societies in the Early 19th Century," in *The University in Society*, ed. Lawrence Stone (Princeton, NJ: Princeton University Press, 1974), vol. 2, 449–94; Rudolph, *Curriculum*, 95–98.

5. Although this effort was successful, the lectures were not incorporated into the standard curriculum, and attending students were required to get permission from their parents. See Rudolph, *Curriculum*, 39.

6. Ibid., 55.

7. "The Yale Report of 1828," in *American Higher Education: A Documentary History*, ed. Richard Hofstadter and Wilson Smith (Chicago: University of Chicago Press, 1961), vol. 1, 275–91 (emphasis in the original).

8. For an extensive discussion of the Yale Report, see Jack C. Lane, "The Yale Report of 1828 and Liberal Education: A Neorepublican Manifesto," *History of Education Quarterly* 27 (1987): 325–38; Melvin I. Usofsky, "Reforms and Response: The Yale Report of 1828," *History of Education Quarterly* 5 (1965): 53–67; Rudolph, *Curriculum*. Rudolph has been strongly criticized for overestimating the effect of the Yale Report. See David B. Potts, "Curriculum and Enrollments: Some Thoughts on Assessing the Popularity of Antebellum Colleges," in *The American College in the Nineteenth Century*, ed. Roger Geiger (Nashville, TN: Vanderbilt University Press, 2000).

9. Hugh Hawkins, *Between Harvard and America: The Educational Leadership of Charles W. Eliot* (New York: Oxford University Press, 1972); Phyllis Keller, *Getting at the Core: Curricular Reform at Harvard* (Cambridge, MA: Harvard University Press, 1982).

10. David Riesman, *Constraint and Variety in American Education* (Garden City, NY: Doubleday, 1958).

11. Gilbert Allardyce, "The Rise and Fall of the Western Civilization Course," *American Historical Review* 87 (1982): 695–725.

12. Carol S. Gruber, *Mars and Minerva: World War I and the Uses of the Higher Learning in America* (Baton Rouge: Louisiana State University Press, 1975).

13. Paul H. Buck et al., *General Education in a Free Society: A Report of the Harvard Committee* (Cambridge, MA: Harvard University Press, 1945).

14. Ironically, the Harvard faculty never formally adopted the report, and it had far more influence outside of Harvard than within it. See Bruce A. Kimball, *Orators and Philosophers: A History of the Idea of Liberal Education* (New York: College Entrance Examination Board, 1995).

15. Daniel Bell, *The Reforming of General Education: The Columbia College Experience in Its National Setting* (New York: Columbia University Press, 1966), 8.

16. Leo Strauss, *Liberalism Ancient and Modern* (New York: Basic Books, 1968), 3, 7.

17. Robert L. Belknap and Richard Kuhns, *Tradition and Innovation* (New York: Columbia University Press, 1977), 23.

18. Allan Bloom, *The Closing of the American Mind* (New York: Simon and Schuster, 1987), 37.

19. Dinesh D'Souza, *Illiberal Education* (New York: Free Press, 1991).

20. Lynne V. Cheney, *50 Hours: A Core Curriculum for College Students* (Washington, DC: National Endowment for the Humanities, 1989).

21. W. B. Carnochan, *The Battleground of the Curriculum: Liberal Education and the American Experience* (Stanford, CA: Stanford University Press, 1993); Lawrence W. Levine, *The Opening of the American Mind* (Boston: Beacon Press, 1996); John K. Wilson, *The Myth of Political Correctness: The Conservative Attack on Higher Education* (Durham, NC: Duke University Press, 1995).

22. Martha Nussbaum, *Cultivating Humanity: A Classical Defense of Reform in Liberal Education* (Cambridge, MA: Harvard University Press, 1997). See also Fareed Zakaria, *In Defense of a Liberal Education* (New York: W. W. Norton, 2015).

23. American Council of Trustees and Alumni, *What Will They Learn? A Survey of Core Requirements at Our Nation's Colleges and Universities* (Washington, DC: American Council of Trustees and Alumni, 2014).

24. Walter P. Metzger, "The Academic Profession in the United States," in *The Academic Profession*, ed. Burton R. Clark (Berkeley: University of California Press, 1987), 123–208. See also Laurence R. Veysey, *The Emergence of the American University* (Chicago: University of Chicago Press, 1965), 121–70.

25. Metzger, "Academic Profession," 128.

26. On the beginnings of the social sciences, see Dorothy Ross, *The Origins of American Social Science* (Cambridge: Cambridge University Press, 1991); Thomas Haskell, *The Emergence of Professional Social Science* (Urbana: University of Illinois Press, 1977).

27. For a brilliant discussion of the origins of the research seminar and the fall of the disputation, see William Clark, *Academic Charisma and the Origins of the Research University* (Chicago: University of Chicago Press, 2006).

28. For more on the differentiation of knowledge, see Burton R. Clark, *The Higher Education System* (Berkeley: University of California Press, 1983); Patricia J. Gumport and Stuart K. Snydman, "The Formal Organization of Knowledge: An Analysis of Academic Structure," *Journal of Higher Education* 73 (2002): 375–408.

29. The definitive statement on professions is by Andrew Abbott, *The System of Professions: An Essay on the Expert Division of Labor* (Chicago: University of Chicago Press, 1988).

30. Steven Brint, "The Rise of the Practical Arts," in *The Future of the City of Intellect: The Changing American University*, ed. Steven Brint (Stanford, CA: Stanford University

Press, 2002), 231–59. For an empirical analysis, see Steven Brint, Mark Riddle, Lori Turk-Bicakci, and Charles S. Levy, "From the Liberal to the Practical Arts in American Colleges and Universities: Organizational Analysis and Curricular Change," *Journal of Higher Education* 76 (2005): 151–80. On the increasing vocational orientation of traditional liberal arts colleges, see Matthew S. Kraatz and Edward J. Zajac, "Exploring the Limits of the New Institutionalism: The Causes and Consequences of Illegitimate Organizational Change," *American Sociological Review* 61 (1996): 812–36.

31. Philip G. Altbach, *Student Politics in America: A Historical Analysis* (New York: McGraw-Hill, 1974); Sheila A. Slaughter, "Class, Race, and Gender and the Construction of Post-Secondary Curricula in the United States," *Journal of Curriculum Studies* 29 (1997): 1–30; Julie A. Reuben, "Reforming the University: Student Protests and the Demand for a Relevant Curriculum," in *Student Protest: The Sixties and After*, ed. Gerard DeGroot (New York: Longman, 1998), 153–68.

32. Fabio Rojas, *From Black Power to Black Studies: How a Radical Social Movement Became an Academic Discipline* (Baltimore: Johns Hopkins University Press, 2007).

33. Joy Ann Williamson, *Black Power on Campus: The University of Illinois, 1965–1975* (Urbana: University of Illinois Press, 2003).

34. Marilyn J. Boxer, *When Women Ask the Questions: Creating Women's Studies in America* (Baltimore: Johns Hopkins University Press, 1998); Patricia J. Gumport, *Academic Pathfinders: Knowledge Creation and Feminist Scholarship* (Westport, CT: Greenwood Press, 2002).

35. Thomas J. La Belle and Christopher R. Ward, *Ethnic Studies and Multiculturalism* (Albany: State University of New York Press, 1996); Janice L. Ristock and Catherine G. Taylor, *Inside the Academy and Out: Queer Studies and Social Action* (Toronto: University of Toronto Press, 1998). Growth in these fields is demonstrated in Steven Brint, Kristopher Proctor, Scott Patrick Murphy, and Robert A. Hanneman, "The Market Model and the Growth and Decline of Academic Fields in U.S. Colleges and Universities, 1980–2000," *Sociological Forum* 27 (2012): 275–299.

36. Lisa R. Lattuca, *Creating Interdisciplinarity* (Nashville, TN: Vanderbilt University Press, 2001). For a longitudinal examination of the growth of interdisciplinary programs and fields, see Steven Brint, Lori Turk-Bicakci, Kristopher Proctor, and Scott Patrick Murphy, "Expanding the Social Frame of Knowledge: Interdisciplinary, Degree-Granting Fields in American Colleges and Universities, 1975–2000," *Review of Higher Education* 32 (2009): 155–83.

37. Andrew Abbott, *Chaos of Disciplines* (Chicago: University of Chicago Press, 2001). For a compressed version of the argument, see Andrew Abbott, "The Disciplines and the Future," in Brint, *Future of the City of Intellect*, 205–30.

38. Michael N. Bastedo and Patricia J. Gumport, "Access to What? Mission Differentiation and Academic Stratification in U.S. Public Higher Education," *Higher Education* 46 (2003): 341–59; Patricia J. Gumport and Michael N. Bastedo, "Academic Stratification and Endemic Conflict: Remedial Education Policy at the City University of New York," *Review of Higher Education* 24 (2001): 333–49.

39. See Michael N. Bastedo, "Convergent Institutional Logics in Public Higher Education: State Policymaking and Governing Board Activism," *Review of Higher Education* 32 (2009): 209–34.

40. At private colleges, the figure is 39 percent. See Bridget Terry Long, "Attracting the Best: The Use of Honors Programs and Colleges to Compete for Students," working paper, Harvard University.

41. Brint et al., "Market Model," 282.

42. Sloan, "Harmony, Chaos, and Consensus," 227–32.

43. George M. Marsden, "The Soul of the American University: A Historical Overview," in *The Secularization of the Academy*, ed. George M. Marsden and Bradley J. Longfield (New York: Oxford University Press, 1992).

44. Ibid.

45. James Sloan Allen, *The Romance of Commerce and Culture* (Chicago: University of Chicago Press, 1983); Joan Shelley Rubin, *The Making of Middlebrow Culture* (Chapel Hill: University of North Carolina Press, 1992).

46. Robert M. Hutchins, *The Higher Learning in America* (New Haven, CT: Yale University Press, 1936).

47. Allen, *The Romance of Commerce and Culture*; Robert M. Hutchins, ed., *The Great Books of the Western World* (Chicago: Encyclopedia Britannica, 1952). See also Alex Beam, *A Great Idea at the Time: The Rise, Fall, and Curious Afterlife of the Great Books* (New York: PublicAffairs, 2008).

48. Gerald Grant and David Riesman, *The Perpetual Dream: Reform and Experiment in the American College* (Chicago: University of Chicago Press, 1978).

49. Ibid., 40–76. Outside of St. John's, very few Great Books programs exist today. Prominent holdouts are the general education programs at Columbia University and the University of Chicago, and Stanford's Structured Liberal Education option.

50. Grant and Riesman, *Perpetual Dream*, 77–134.

51. Martin Duberman, *Black Mountain: An Exploration in Community* (New York: E. P. Dutton, 1972).

52. Altbach, *Student Politics in America*, 221–26; Reuben, "Reforming the University."

53. Reuben, "Reforming the University," 156. Few of the free universities exist today. At Oberlin, the Experimental College (ExCo) sponsors dozens of student-taught courses every year, and students may earn up to five ExCo credits toward graduation either by teaching or by enrolling in these courses.

54. Robert C. Heterick, Jr., *Reengineering Teaching and Learning in Higher Education: Sheltered Groves, Camelot, Windmills, and Malls* (Boulder: CAUSE, 1993); Martin J. Finkelstein, *Dollars, Distance, and Online Education: The New Economics of College Teaching and Learning* (Phoenix: Oryx Press, 2000). For a more critical perspective, see David F. Noble, *Digital Diploma Mills: The Automation of Higher Education* (New York: Monthly Review Press, 2001).

55. Timothy K. Stanton, Dwight E. Giles, Jr., and Nadine I. Cruz, *Service-Learning: A Movement's Pioneers Reflect on Its Origins, Practice, and Future* (San Francisco: Jossey-Bass, 1999); Janet Eyler and Dwight E. Giles, Jr., *Where's the Learning in Service Learning?* (San Francisco: Jossey-Bass, 1999).

56. Vincent Tinto, "Classrooms as Communities: Exploring the Educational Character of Student Persistence," *Journal of Higher Education* 68 (1997): 599–623; Faith Gabelnick, Jean MacGregor, Roberta S. Matthews, and Barbara Leigh Smith, *Learning*

*Communities: Creating Connections among Students, Faculty, and Disciplines* (San Francisco: Jossey-Bass, 1990).

57. Deanna C. Martin and David R. Arendale, *Supplemental Instruction: Increasing Achievement and Retention* (San Francisco: Jossey-Bass, 1994).

58. Thomas R. Bailey, Shanna Smith Jaggers, and Davis Jenkins, *Redesigning America's Community Colleges: A Clearer Path to Student Success* (Cambridge, MA: Harvard University Press, 2015).

59. For a framework for understanding incremental change in the curriculum, see Larry Cuban, *How Scholars Trumped Teachers: Change Without Reform in University Curriculum, Teaching, and Research, 1890–1990* (New York: Teachers College Press, 1999); see also David Tyack and Larry Cuban, *Tinkering Toward Utopia: A Century of Public School Reform* (Cambridge, MA: Harvard University Press, 1995), esp. 60–109.

60. Clark, *Higher Education System*.

61. Burton R. Clark, "The Problem of Complexity in Modern Higher Education," in *The European and American University since 1800*, ed. Sheldon Rothblatt and Björn Wittrock (Cambridge: Cambridge University Press, 1993), 263–79.

62. William G. Tierney, *Curricular Landscapes, Democratic Vistas* (New York: Praeger, 1989); Patricia J. Gumport, "Curricula as Signposts of Cultural Change," *Review of Higher Education* 12 (1988): 49–62.

63. See, for example, Scott Frickel and Neil Gross, "A General Theory of Scientific/ Intellectual Movements," *American Sociological Review* 70 (2005): 204–32; Rojas, *Black Power to Black Studies*; Fabio Rojas, "Social Movement Tactics, Organizational Change, and the Spread of African-American Studies," *Social Forces* 84 (2006): 2147–66.

64. Sheila A. Slaughter, "The Political Economy of Curriculum-Making in the United States," in Brint, *Future of the City of Intellect*; Slaughter, "Class, Race, and Gender."

65. Dennis P. Jones and Peter Ewell, *The Effect of State Policy on Undergraduate Education* (Denver: National Center for Higher Education Management Systems, 1993); National Center for Public Policy and Higher Education, *Measuring Up 2008* (San Jose, CA: National Center for Public Policy and Higher Education, 2008).

66. Michael N. Bastedo, "The Making of an Activist Governing Board," *Review of Higher Education* 28 (2005): 551–70; Carol L. Colbeck, "State Policies to Improve Undergraduate Teaching: Administrator and Faculty Responses," *Journal of Higher Education* 73 (2002): 3–25.

67. Richard Arum and Josipa Roksa, *Academically Adrift: Limited Learning on College Campuses* (Chicago: University of Chicago Press, 2011).

# Chapter Four

# Harsh Realities

*The Professoriate in the Twenty-First Century*

Philip G. Altbach

The American academic profession finds itself in an era of largely deteriorating circumstances.[1] Financial cutbacks, enrollment uncertainties, pressures for accountability, and confusion about academic goals are among the challenges facing American colleges and universities in the early twenty-first century. The situation is in many ways paradoxical. The American academic model is seen as the most successful in the world, admired internationally for providing access to higher education to a mass clientele as well as for possessing some of the best universities in the world. Yet higher education has come under widespread criticism. Some argue that the academic system is wasteful and inefficient, and they place the professoriate at the heart of the problem.[2] Others urge that higher education reconsider its priorities and place more emphasis on teaching, reasoning that the core function of the university has been underemphasized as the professoriate has focused on research.[3]

Enrollment expansion, the Great Recession, changes in priorities in public spending, and other factors have created long-term financial problems for American higher education, and these have a significant impact on the academic profession. Further, many policy makers increasingly see higher education as a private good that does not deserve as much state support as it has had—and that the "users" (i.e., students and their families) should pay more of the cost. Many observers believe that higher education will not fully recover financially in the foreseeable future. It has been argued that higher education's golden age—the period of strong enrollment growth, increasing research budgets, and general public support—is over.[4] This means that the academic profession, as well as higher education in general, must adjust to new circumstances.

The American professoriate has been shaped by the social, political, and economic context of higher education. While academe enjoys relatively strong internal autonomy and considerable academic freedom, societal trends and public policy have affected both institutions of higher education and national and state policies concerning academe. There are many examples. In the 1860s, the Land Grant acts contributed to the expansion of public higher education and an emphasis on both service and research, while after World War II the GI Bill led to the greatest and most sustained period of growth in American higher education. Sputnik and the challenges of the Cold War contributed to increased support for research at the top universities. Court decisions relating to private higher education, race relations, affirmative action, the scope of unions on campus, and other issues have affected higher education policy and the professoriate. Education is a basic responsibility of the states, and the actions of the various state governments have ranged from support for the "Wisconsin idea" in the nineteenth century to the promulgation of the California "master plan" in the 1960s. State policies in the postwar period had a formative influence on postsecondary education and the professoriate.[5]

Precisely because the university is one of the central institutions of postindustrial society and the information age, the professoriate finds itself under pressure from many directions. Increasingly complicated evaluation procedures attempt to measure professorial productivity as part of the effort to increase accountability. The measurement of educational outcomes has become a major national concern, and efforts are being made to assess the effectiveness of teaching and the productivity of professors, as well as learning outcomes for students.[6] Calls for the professoriate to provide social relevance in the 1960s were replaced in the 1980s by student demands for vocationally oriented courses, and in the past decade for effective "workforce development."

A deteriorating academic job market has raised the standards for the award of tenure and increased the emphasis on research and publication. At the same time, there are demands for faculty to devote more time and attention to teaching. Further, only half of new appointments to the professoriate are on the traditional "tenure track"—leading to a career-length appointment after careful evaluation. The rest are either part-time lecturers or full-time contract teachers. These changes have created a profound shift in the nature of academic appointments and career prospects in the United States.

A constant tension exists between the traditional autonomy of the academic profession and external pressures—and in the past half-century autonomy has been steadily diminished as pressures from all directions have grown. The processes of academic hiring and promotion remain in professorial hands, but with significant changes: affirmative action requirements, tenure quotas in some institutions, the occasional intrusion of the courts into promotion and tenure decisions, and other constraints. The curriculum is still largely a responsibility of the faculty, but the debates over multicultural courses or over the number and scope of vocational courses, for example, affect curricular decisions. Governmental agencies influence the curriculum through grants and awards. The states engage in program reviews and approvals and, through these procedures, have gained some power in areas traditionally in the hands of the faculty.

The academic profession has largely failed to explain its centrality to society and to make the case for traditional academic values. Entrenched power, a complicated governance structure, and the weight of tradition have helped protect academic perquisites in a difficult period. But the professoriate itself has not articulated its own ethos.[7] The rise of academic unions helped to increase salaries during the 1970s, but it also contributed to an increasingly adversarial relationship between the faculty and administrators in some universities.[8]

We are in a period of profound change in American higher education, and it is likely that these changes will result in further weakening of the power and autonomy of the professoriate. This chapter considers the interplay of forces that have influenced the changing role of the American academic profession.

## A Diverse Profession

The American professoriate is large and highly differentiated, making generalizations difficult. There are more than 1.5 million full- and part-time faculty members in America's 4,700 institutions of postsecondary education. Almost 1,850 of these institutions grant baccalaureate or higher degrees, and 293 award doctoral degrees. More than a quarter of the total number of institutions are community colleges. A growing number of faculty are part-time or non-tenure-track academic staff, numbering more than half of the professoriate nationwide. The part-timers enjoy little or no job security and only tenuous ties with their employing institutions. The proportion of part-time staff has risen in recent years from 40.9 percent in 1995 to 48.7 percent in 2013, reflecting fiscal constraints.[9] Full-time but non-tenure-track appointees are a new and growing category of faculty. In 2013, 31.9 percent of all full-time faculty at all colleges and universities held a non-tenure-track position.[10] They usually hold limited-term positions that are generally focused on teaching. While they may be given multiple appointments, they are not eligible for tenure. Faculty are further divided by discipline and department—working conditions and salaries may vary considerably.

Although one may speak broadly of the American professoriate, the working life and culture of most academics is encapsulated in disciplinary and institutional frameworks. Variations among the different sectors within the academic system—research universities, community colleges, liberal arts institutions, and others—also shape the academic profession.[11] Vast differences exist in working styles, outlooks, remuneration, and responsibilities between a senior professor at Harvard University and a beginning assistant professor at a community college. Further distinctions reflect field and discipline; the outlook of medical school professors, for example, and that of scholars of medieval philosophy are quite dissimilar. Indeed, given the changing nature of the academic workforce, it is becoming more and more irrelevant to speak of a unified academic profession. One must focus on the increasingly differentiated segments of the professoriate.

In the 1950s, the academic profession was largely white, male, and Protestant. It has grown increasingly diverse. Since then, the proportion of women in academe has grown steadily; it is now 47 percent of the total and 48 percent of the new entrants to the profession.[12] However, women are concentrated at the lower academic ranks and suffer some salary discrimination. Salary inequalities based on gender persist—with women earning less in virtually all disciplines, institutional categories, and ranks than their male counterparts. Women are now a majority in many humanities fields and can increasingly be found at all academic ranks. Racial and ethnic minority participation has also increased, but while Asian Americans are well placed in the academic profession, African Americans and Latinos remain underrepresented. African Americans constitute around 6.7 percent of the total professoriate, while Hispanics represent 4.1 percent.[13] The substantial discrimination that once existed against Catholics and Jews in the professoriate has been largely overcome, and there has been a modest decline in the middle- and upper-middle-class domination of the professoriate.[14] Despite these demographic changes and expansion in higher education as well as significant progress in increasing diversity, the academic profession has retained considerable continuity in terms of its overall composition.

## The Historical Context

The academic profession is conditioned by a complex historical development. Universities have a long tradition, dating to medieval Europe, and the professoriate is the most visible repository of this tradition.[15] While national academic systems differ, all stem from common roots in Europe. The model of professorial authority that characterized the medieval University of Paris, the power of the dons at Oxford and Cambridge universities, and the centrality of the "chairs" in nineteenth-century German universities all contributed to the ideal of the American academic profession. Its medieval origins established the self-governing nature of the professorial community and the idea that universities are communities of scholars. The reforms in German higher education in the nineteenth century augmented the authority and prestige of the professoriate, while at the same time linking both the universities and the academic profession to the state.[16] Professors were civil servants, and the universities were expected to contribute to the development of Germany as a modern industrial nation.[17] Research, for the first time, became a key responsibility of universities. The role and status of the academic profession at Oxford and Cambridge in England also had an impact on the American professoriate, since the early American colleges were patterned on the British model, and the United States, for many years, was greatly influenced by intellectual trends from Britain.[18]

These models, plus academic and societal realities in the United States, helped to shape the American academic profession. To understand the profession in its contemporary form requires a look at its most crucial period of development, beginning with the rise of land-grant colleges following the Civil War and the establishment of innovative, research-oriented private universities in the last decade of the nineteenth century.[19] The commitment of the university to public service and to "relevance" meant that many academics became involved with societal issues, applied aspects of scholarship, and training for the emerging professions and for skilled occupations involving technology. The contribution of land-grant colleges to American agriculture was the first and best-known example. Following the German lead, the new and innovative private universities (Johns Hopkins, Chicago, Stanford, and Cornell), followed a little later by such public universities as Michigan, Wisconsin, and California, emphasized research and graduate training. A doctorate soon became a requirement for entry into at least the upper reaches of the academic profession; earlier, in the mid-nineteenth century, top American professors had obtained their doctorates in

Germany. The prestige of elite universities gradually came to dominate the academic system, and the ethos of research, graduate training, and professionalism spread throughout much of American academe. As these norms and values gradually permeated the American academic enterprise, they have come to form the base of professorial values.

The hallmark of the post–World War II period was massive growth in all sectors of American higher education through most of the last half of the 20th century. The academic profession tripled, and student numbers expanded even more rapidly. The number of institutions also grew, and many universities added graduate programs. Expansion characterized every sector, from community colleges to research universities. Growth was especially rapid in the decade of the 1960s.

This expansion ended in the early 1970s as a result of a combination of circumstances, including demographic shifts, inflation, and government fiscal deficits. Part of the problem in adjusting to conditions of diminished resources was the very fact that the previous period of unusual growth was a temporary phase.[20] From the 1980s to the present time, there has been increasing enrollment and an expansion of the professoriate—but the bulk of this growth has been among part-time teachers and non-tenure-track faculty.

Expansion shaped the vision of the academic profession for several decades, just as structural change and austerity affects perceptions in the second decade of the twenty-first century. Postwar growth introduced other changes, which came to be seen as permanent when, in fact, they were not. The academic job market became a seller's market, in which individual professors were able to increase their salaries and improve working conditions. Most fields had a shortage of teachers and researchers.[21] Average academic salaries improved significantly, and the American professor moved from a state of semipenury into the increasingly affluent middle class.[22] The image of Mr. Chips was replaced by the jet-set professor. University budgets increased, and research-oriented institutions at the top of the academic hierarchy enjoyed unprecedented access to research funds. The space program, the cold war, rapid advances in technology, and a fear in 1958 (after Sputnik) that the United States was "falling behind" educationally contributed to greater spending by the federal government for higher education. Expanding enrollments meant that the states also invested more in higher education and that private institutions prospered.

The academic profession benefited substantially. Those obtaining their doctorates found ready employment. Rapid career advancement could be expected, and interinstitutional mobility was fairly easy. This contributed to diminished institutional loyalty and commitment. To retain faculty, colleges and universities lessened teaching loads, and the average time spent in the classroom declined. Access to research funds from external sources expanded, not only in the sciences but also, to a lesser extent, in the social sciences and humanities. The availability of external research funds made academics in research universities less dependent on their institutions, and helped to create a national academic labor market, at least at the top of the profession.

The turmoil of the 1960s had an impact on higher education at the time and on the consciousness of the professoriate. A number of factors in the turbulent sixties contributed to emerging problems for higher education. The very success of the universities in moving to the center of society meant that they were taken more seriously. In the heady days of expansion, many in the academic community thought that higher education could solve the nation's social problems, from providing mobility to minorities to suggesting solutions to urban blight and deteriorating standards in the public schools. In this context, it is not surprising that colleges and universities became involved in the most traumatic social crises of the period—including the civil rights struggle and the antiwar movement triggered by the Vietnam War. The antiwar movement emerged from the campuses, where it was most powerful.[23] Student activism came to be seen by many, including government officials, as a social problem for which the universities were to be blamed. Many saw professors as contributing to student militancy.

The campus crisis of the 1960s went deeper than the antiwar movement. Its new and much larger generation of students, from more diverse backgrounds, seemed less committed to traditional academic values. Faculty members, especially in the research universities, turned their attention away from undergraduate education, abandoned *in loco parentis*, and allowed the undergraduate curriculum to fall into disarray. Overcrowded facilities were common. The overwhelming malaise caused by the Vietnam War, racial unrest, and related social problems produced a powerful sense of discontent among students. Many faculty members, unable to deal constructively with the crisis and feeling under attack from students, the public, and governmental authority, became demoralized. Faculty governance structures proved unable to bring the diverse interests of the academic community together. This period was one of considerable debate and intellectual liveliness on campus, with faculty taking part in teach-ins and a small number of professors becoming involved in the antiwar movement.

However, the lasting legacy of the 1960s for the professoriate was largely one of divisiveness and the politicization of the campus. Further, a large segment of the public turned against the universities, feeling that the quality of education was deteriorating and that the academic community was the source of social unrest. While the past several decades have been largely free of activism, either from professors or students, the "culture wars" of an earlier period have had some resonance.

## The Sociological and Organizational Context

Academics are, at the same time, both professionals and employees of large bureaucratic organizations. Their self-image as independent scholars dominating their working environment is increasingly at odds with the realities of the modern American university.[24] Indeed, the conflict between the traditional autonomy of the scholar and demands for accountability to a variety of internal and external constituencies is one of the central issues of contemporary American higher education. The rules of academic institutions, from stipulations concerning teaching loads to policies on the granting of tenure, govern the working lives of the professoriate. Despite the existence in most institutions of an infrastructure of collegial self-government, academics feel increasingly alienated from their institutions. In a 1990 survey, two-thirds described faculty morale as fair or poor, and 60 percent had negative feelings about the "sense of community" at their institutions.[25] Things have not improved since then, and recent surveys show similar results.[26]

Academics continue to exercise considerable autonomy over their basic working conditions, although even here pressures are evident, especially in mass-access colleges and universities. The classroom remains largely sacrosanct and beyond bureaucratic controls, although recent debates about "political correctness" have had some impact on teaching in a few disciplines, and emerging technologies are beginning to stimulate some changes in teaching styles. Professors retain a significant degree of autonomy over the use of their time outside of the classroom. They choose their own research topics and largely determine what and how much they publish, although research in some fields and on some topics requires substantial funding and therefore depends on external support. There are significant variations based on institutional type, with faculty at community colleges and at nonselective, teaching-oriented institutions subject to more constraints on their autonomy.[27] Non-tenure-track and part-time faculty also have much less autonomy than their tenured colleagues and, as noted earlier, these groups are an increasingly large part of the profession—half of all new appointments fall into these categories.

As colleges and universities have become more and more bureaucratized and demands for accountability have extended to professors, this autonomy has come under criticism. The trend toward decreased teaching loads for academics during the 1960s has been reversed, and now more emphasis is placed on teaching and, increasingly, on the quality of teaching. The movement to measure learning outcomes has brought additional pressure on professors to demonstrate their teaching effectiveness. Without question, there is now tension between the norm (some would say the myth) of professional autonomy and demands for accountability. There is little doubt that the academic profession will be subjected to increased controls as academic institutions seek to survive in an environment of financial difficulties and demands from government and the public for accountability. Professorial myths—of collegial decision making, individual autonomy, and the disinterested pursuit of knowledge—have come into conflict with the realities of complex organizational structures and bureaucracies. Important academic decisions are reviewed by a bewildering assortment of committees and administrators. These levels of authority have become more powerful as arbiters of academic decision making.

The American academic system is enmeshed in a series of complex hierarchies. These hierarchies, framed by discipline, institution, rank, and specialty, help to determine working conditions, prestige, and, in many ways, orientation to the profession. As David Riesman pointed out more than a half century ago, American higher education is a "meandering procession," dominated by the prestigious graduate schools and ebbing downward through other universities, four-year colleges, and, finally, to the community college system.[28] Most of the profession attempts to follow the norms, and the fads, of the prestigious research-oriented universities. Notable exceptions are the community colleges, which employ one-fourth of the academics in the United States, and some of the less-selective four-year schools. Generally, prestige is defined by how close an institution, or an individual professor's working life, comes to the norm of publication and research—a cosmopolitan orientation to the discipline and the national profession—rather than to local teaching and institutionally focused norms.[29] Even in periods of fiscal constraint, the hold of the traditional academic models remains strong indeed.

Within institutions, academics are also part of a hierarchical system, with the distinctions between tenured and untenured staff a key to this hierarchy. The dramatic increase in number of part-time instructors has added another layer at the bottom of the institutional hierarchy.[30] And the new category of full-time but non-tenure-track academics adds yet another layer. In general, these groups have little power in the patterns of governance in colleges and universities.

Disciplines and departments are also ranked into hierarchies, with the traditional academic specialties in the arts and sciences, along with medicine and, to some extent, law at the top. The hard sciences tend to have more prestige than the social sciences or humanities. Other applied fields, such as education and agriculture, are considerably lower on the scale. These hierarchies are very much part of the realities and perceptions of the academic profession.

Just as the conditions of expansion of the second half of the twentieth century shaped academic organizations—affecting salaries, prestige, and working conditions, and giving more power to the professoriate in the shared governance model of colleges and universities, current diminished circumstances also bring change. In an unheralded academic revolution, there has been an increase in the authority of administrators and unprecedented bureaucratic control over working conditions on campus. In general, professors have lost a significant part of their bargaining power, which was rooted in moral authority as well as traditional shared governance. As academic institutions adjust to a period of declining resources, there will be additional organizational shifts that will inevitably work to diminish the perquisites—and the authority—of the academic profession. Universities, as organizations, adjust to changing realities, and these adjustments will work against the professoriate.

## Legislation, Regulations, Guidelines, and the Courts

The academic profession has been directly affected in a number of areas by the decisions of external authorities. American higher education has always been subject to external decisions, from the Dartmouth College case in the period following the American Revolution to the Land Grant Act in the mid-nineteenth century and the GI Bill in the mid-twentieth century. Actions by the courts and legislative authority have profoundly affected higher education and the professoriate. In the contemporary period, governmental decisions continue to have an impact on American higher education and the academic profession. The financial challenges of higher education have already been discussed. However, academe's difficulties stem not only from new economic priorities, but also from quite deliberate policies by government at both the federal and state levels to change funding patterns for higher education and research. Other pressing social needs, combined with public reluctance to pay higher taxes, have worked to restrict higher education budget allocations. Cuts in research funding have been felt by both public and private institutions and their faculties.

Specific governmental policies have also had an impact on the profession. One area of controversy has been affirmative action, the effort to ensure that college and university faculties include women and members of underrepresented minorities, so as to reflect the national population.[31] A variety of specific regulations have been mandated by federal and state governments relating to hiring, promotion, and other aspects of faculty life to ensure that women and minorities have greater opportunities in the academic profession. Some professors have opposed these regulations, viewing them as an unwarranted intrusion on academic autonomy. These policies have, nonetheless, had an impact on academic life.

The legal system has had a significant influence on the academic profession in recent decades.[32] The courts have ruled on university hiring and promotion policies, as well as on specific personnel cases, and on other aspects of academic life. While the courts are generally reluctant to interfere in the internal workings of academic institutions, they have reviewed cases of gender or other discrimination, sometimes reversing academic decisions.[33] The US Supreme Court decision that compulsory retirement regulations are unconstitutional, which came into effect in 1994, has had an impact on the academic profession and has meant that many faculty are retiring later; as a result, fewer new positions open up.

These examples illustrate the significance and pervasiveness of governmental policies on the academic profession. In a few states, there is now legislation concerning faculty workloads. Other accountability measures have also been considered. Such laws, as well as those dealing with affirmative action, directly affect the professoriate. Shifts in public opinion are often reflected in governmental policies on higher education and the professoriate. The courts, through the cases they are called on to decide, also play a role. The cumulative impact of governmental policies, laws, and decisions of all kinds has profoundly influenced the professoriate.[34] In the post–World War II era, as higher education has become more central to society, government has involved itself to a greater extent with higher education, and this trend is likely to continue.

### The Realities of the Twenty-First Century

The past several decades have been problematic for the academic profession. During the 1990s, when university budgets were reasonably good, the academic profession did not expand much. During the Great Recession in

2008, budgets deteriorated significantly, with hiring and salary freezes. While the situation has somewhat improved, the immediate future does not offer the promise of a significant revival of either salaries or working conditions for the academic profession. Indeed, many states continue to cut higher education budgets. The following issues are likely to be central in the debates of the coming period.

TEACHING, RESEARCH, AND SERVICE

One of the main debates—the appropriate balance between teaching and research in academe—goes to the heart of the university as an institution and is crucial for the academic profession. Many outside of academe, and quite a few within it, have argued that there should be more emphasis on teaching in the American higher education system. For some time it has been generally agreed that research is overvalued and that, especially considering fiscal constraints and demands for accountability, professors should be more productive, mainly in teaching.[35] The reward system in academe has produced this imbalance. Critics charge that, outside of 200 major research universities, the quality and relevance of much academic research is questionable.

The issue of faculty productivity has produced action in several states and on a few campuses. Massachusetts, Nevada, New York, Arizona, and Wisconsin are among the states that have been involved in workload studies. The California State University System has compared the teaching loads of its faculty members with professors at other institutions. A few states require annual reports on workloads, and some have mandated minimum teaching loads: Hawaii and Florida, for example, require twelve hours of classroom instruction or the equivalent for faculty in four-year institutions.[36]

American professors seem to be working longer, not shorter, hours, and classroom responsibilities have not declined in recent years. In 1992, according to a study by the Carnegie Foundation for the Advancement of Teaching, full-time American professors spent a median 18.7 hours a week in activities relating to teaching (including preparation and student advisement).[37] On average, professors spent 13.1 hours per week in direct instructional activity: those in research universities teach 11.4 hours per week, and those in other four-year institutions, 13.8 hours.[38] Not surprisingly, professors in research universities produce more publications than do their colleagues in other institutions. For example, 61 percent of faculty in research universities reported publishing six or more journal articles in the previous three years, compared with 31 percent of faculty working elsewhere.[39] If anything, workloads and the pressure for publication and re-search have intensified in the past two decades.

With pressure for the professoriate to focus more on teaching and to spend more time in the classroom, there is likely to be more differentiation among sectors within the academic system, so that academics at the top research universities will teach significantly less than their colleagues in comprehensive colleges and universities. Indeed, like so much in American society in the early twenty-first century, higher education has seen unprecedented stratification, creating a small number of "haves"—mainly among the more generously endowed private research universities—and many institutions struggling for resources and experiencing deteriorating working conditions. Unsurprisingly, the academic profession is itself increasingly stratified.

As mentioned earlier, a shift in thinking has taken place about research and its role. External funding for research has declined in most fields, and competition for resources is intense. There is also an orientation toward more applied research, closer links between industry and universities, and more service to the private sector. These changes affect the kind of research that is conducted. As a result, there may well be less basic research in the future and more applied research linked to products, some of it funded by corporations eager for research results.

### DEMOGRAPHIC CHANGES AND THE DECLINE OF COMMUNITY

As discussed earlier, the "age bulge" has meant that the large cohort of academics who entered the profession in the 1960s and 1970s has taken up a disproportionate share of jobs. Although many have been retiring recently, their ranks have often been filled by part-time or full-time contract faculty—thus changing the nature and orientation of the profession. It is much harder for a midcareer academic to find another position if he or she becomes dissatisfied or desires a change in location. The safety valve of job mobility no longer functions as well. While many institutions have used early-retirement incentives to meet mandated budget cuts, this has not produced significant numbers of full-time academic jobs. As with much of American society, the current period remains a time of diminished expectations.

The academic job market for new entrants has deteriorated as well, although there are major variations by field and discipline. Smaller numbers of recent PhDs are being hired, and as it has become clear that the academic job market has contracted, enrollments in many fields at the graduate level have declined or leveled off, especially in the traditional arts and sciences disciplines. Bright undergraduates have gravitated to law school or management studies. Perhaps the greatest long-term implication is a missing generation of younger scholars, although there is also a generation of itinerant scholars who are relegated to part-time teaching with little chance of a full-time, tenure-track position. Further, a generation of fresh ideas has been lost. While there is currently a need for new PhDs to handle growing enrollments and take the place of retirees, there has been only a modest growth in full-time faculty positions, because part-timers and non-tenure-track appointees have been hired in large numbers.[40]

The size and increased diversity of the academic profession have made achieving a sense of community more difficult.[41] As institutions have grown to include well over a thousand academic staff, with elected senates and other, more bureaucratic governance arrangements taking the place of the traditional general faculty meeting, a sense of shared academic purpose has become elusive. Academic departments in larger American universities can number up to fifty. Committees have become ubiquitous, and the sense of participation in a common academic enterprise has declined. Increasing specialization in the disciplines contributed to this trend. Two-thirds of the American professoriate in the Carnegie study judged morale to be fair or poor on campus, and 60 percent felt similarly about the sense of community at their institution.[42]

## Tenure, Retrenchment, and Unions

The profession has seen its economic status eroded after a decade of significant gains in real income during the 1960s. Academic salaries began to decline in terms of purchasing power in the 1970s, although there was a leveling off in the 1980s and a modest improvement in the 1990s. During the recession of the late 1970s and early 1980s, faculty members in Massachusetts and California saw actual salary cuts, while many states, including New York and Maryland, froze salaries, sometimes for more than a year. The 2008 recession brought unprecedented salary freezes, mandatory furloughs, and other cost-cutting measures that have affected the professoriate. Professional prerogatives seemed less secure, and autonomy was threatened.

The tenure system came under attack in the 1970s and again in the 1990s. Some argued that the permanent appointments offered to professors once they had been evaluated and promoted from assistant to associate professor bred sloth among those with tenure, although there was little evidence to back up this claim. Tenure was also criticized because it interfered with the institution's ability to respond to fiscal problems or changes in program needs. Professors could not easily be replaced or fired. Originally intended to protect academic freedom, the tenure system expanded into a means of evaluating assistant professors, as well as a way to offer lifetime appointments. As fiscal problems grew and the job market deteriorated, it became more difficult for young assistant professors to be promoted. Tenure quotas were imposed at some institutions, and many raised their standards for awarding tenure. These measures added to the pressures felt by junior staff.

The tenure debates of the 1970s ended without any significant changes and with tenure intact. The renewed discussion in the 1990s, stimulated by many of the same concerns as in the earlier period, also resulted in little direct change.[43] Post-tenure review and other reforms have been widely implemented. As noted, there are also a growing number of academics who are not part of the tenure system, and these full-time, non-tenure-track staff are increasing in number as institutions try to maximize their flexibility.

Retrenchment—the firing of academic staff without regard to tenure—has always been one of the major fears of the professoriate.[44] During the first wave of fiscal crises in the 1970s, a number of universities attempted to solve their financial problems by firing professors, including some with tenure, following programmatic reviews and analyses of enrollment trends. The American Association of University Professors, several academic unions, and a number of individual professors sued the universities in the courts, claiming that such retrenchment was against the implied lifetime employment arrangement offered through the tenure system. The courts consistently ruled against the professors and unions, arguing that tenure protects academic freedom but does not prevent firings due to fiscal crisis. Universities that were especially hard hit, such as the City University of New York and the State University of New York System, declared fiscal emergencies, firing a small number of academic staff, including tenured professors, and closing several departments and programs. Many institutions found that the financial savings were not worth the legal challenges, decline in morale, and bad national publicity, and in later crises fewer tenured faculty were terminated. The fact is that tenure in American higher education does not fully protect lifetime employment, although, in general, commitments are honored by colleges and universities.[45] The retrenchments, and discussions and debates about retrenchment, left an imprint on the thinking of the academic profession, contributing to low morale and feelings of alienation.

The growth of academic unions in the 1970s was a direct reaction to the difficulties faced by the professoriate. Most professors turned to unions with some reluctance, and despite accelerating difficulties in the universities, the union movement has not become dominant. Indeed, the growth of unions slowed and even stopped in the late 1980s. In 1980, 682 campuses were represented by academic unions. Of this number, 254 were four-year institutions, and the numbers have only modestly increased since then. Very few research universities are unionized; only one of the members of the prestigious Association of American Universities is unionized, for example. Unions are concentrated in the community college sector and in the public lower and middle tiers of the system.[46] Relatively few private colleges and universities are unionized, in part because the US Supreme Court, in the *Yeshiva* case, made unionization in private institutions quite difficult. The court ruled that faculty members in private institutions were, by definition, part of "management" and could not be seen as "workers" in the traditional sense. However, further court rulings have made it easier for private college faculty to organize unions.

The growth of academic unions slowed in the 1990s and beyond, although expansion continues as working conditions continue to deteriorate. Unionization among part-time faculty, graduate teaching assistants, and non-tenure-track staff has also become more common as well. In addition, while unions brought significant increases in salaries in the first years of contractual arrangements, this advantage lessened in later contract periods. In normal times, many faculty have seen unions as opposed to the traditional values of academe, such as meritocratic evaluation. Often, unions are voted in following severe campus conflict between faculty and administration. Further, unions have been unable to save faculty from retrenchment or deterioration in working conditions. Both public university systems in New York State are unionized, but both have been hard hit by fiscal problems, and their faculty unions did not shield staff from retrenchment, salary freezes, and the like. Unions, however, were part of an effort in the 1970s to stop the erosion of faculty advantages. Unions were also an expression of the attempt by professors in institutions with only limited autonomy and weak faculty governance structures to assert faculty power. In both of these areas, unions had only limited success.

## ACCOUNTABILITY AND AUTONOMY

The academic profession has traditionally enjoyed a high degree of autonomy, particularly in the classroom and in research. While most academics may be only dimly aware of it, the move toward accountability affects their professional lives. This trend will intensify, not only due to fiscal constraints, but also because all public institutions have come under greater scrutiny—for example, in several states, politicians have proposed imposing minimum teaching hours for professors. Institutions, often impelled (in the case of public universities) by state budget offices, require an increasing amount of data concerning faculty work, research productivity, the expenditure of funds for ancillary support, and other aspects of academic life. What is more, criteria have been established for student-faculty ratios, levels of financial support for postsecondary education, and the productivity of academic staff. New sources of data permit fiscal authorities to monitor how institutions meet established criteria, so that adjustments in budgets can be quickly implemented. While most of these measures of accountability are only indirectly felt by most academics, they nonetheless have a considerable impact on the operation of universities and colleges, since resources are allocated on the basis of closely measured formulas. The basic outputs of academic institutions—quality of teaching and quality and impact of research—cannot be calculated through these efforts at accountability. Indeed, even the definitions of teaching quality and research productivity remain elusive.

If autonomy is the opposite side of the accountability coin, then one would expect academic autonomy to have significantly declined. But, at least on the surface, this has not occurred. Basic decisions concerning the curriculum, course and degree requirements, the process of teaching and learning, and indeed most of the matters traditionally the domain of the faculty have largely remained in the hands of departments and other parts of the faculty governance structure. Most academics retain the sense of autonomy that has characterized higher education for a century—although confidence is slipping. Autonomy remains relatively strong at the top-tier institutions. There have been few efforts to dismantle the basic structure of academic work in ways that would destroy the traditional arrangements.

Change is nonetheless taking place, which will continue to shift the balance increasingly from autonomy to accountability and erode the base of faculty power. Decisions concerning class size, the future of low-enrollment fields, the overall academic direction of the institution, and other issues have been shifted from the faculty to the administration, or even to systemwide agencies. Academic planning, traditionally far removed from the individual professor and seldom impinging on academic careers, has become more of a reality as institutions seek to streamline their operations and worry more about external measures of productivity.

## ACADEMIC FREEDOM

American professors at present enjoy a fairly high degree of academic freedom, although just half of the professoriate agrees that there are "no political or ideological restrictions on what a scholar may publish."[47] There are few demands for ensuring the political or intellectual conformity of professors, and the concept of academic freedom seems well entrenched. The AAUP has noted very few cases in which institutions have sought to violate the academic freedom of their staff, and there has been virtually no governmental pressure to limit academic freedom. The tensions of the McCarthy era seem far removed from the current period. The fact that the past decade or more has not experienced the major ideological and political unrest and activism that characterized some earlier periods, such as the Vietnam War era, certainly has contributed to the calm on campus; however, even during the Vietnam War, academic freedom remained relatively secure. This record was, however, not entirely spotless. A number of junior faculty were denied tenure during this period because of their political views.[48] In the aftermath of September 11, 2001, there have been a few incidents relating to the academic freedom of Muslim scholars.

Academic freedom nevertheless remains a contentious issue. One of the most visible academic debates in recent decades relates to "political correctness," an unfortunate shorthand term for a variety of disputes concerning the nature and organization of the undergraduate curriculum, interpretations of American culture, the perspectives of some disciplines in the humanities and social sciences, and what some conservatives claim is the infusion of ideology into academe. Some conservatives have argued that American higher education has been taken over by left-wing ideologists seeking to transform the curriculum through the infusion of multicultural approaches and the destruction of academe's traditional focus on Western values and civilization. Other conservative critics, including then secretary of education William Bennett, took up the call, and a major national debate ensued.[49] Some conservatives claim that the academic freedom of some conservative faculty is being violated, although there is no evidence that this is the case. The debate, however, has affected thinking about the curriculum and the role of multiculturalism on campus. While it has not touched on academic freedom directly, the politics of race, gender, and ethnicity has left a mark on academic life.[50] These social issues have entered into discussions of the curriculum, and some faculty have claimed that these issues have inappropriately influenced decision making. There have also been incidents of racial- or gender-based intolerance on some campuses.

Some analysts see threats to academic freedom from more indirect but, in some ways, just as dangerous sources. The increasing links between universities and industry in terms of research and other relationships have, in the view of some critics, created a certain amount of tension on campus regarding academic freedom. In some cases, corporations have made agreements with universities that restrict the publication of research results, and corporate influence, in general, is seen to constrain faculty members who may be in departments or schools with such corporate links. During the past few decades, while there have been occasional external pressures, and while issues such as political correctness on campuses have become controversial, academic freedom has been reasonably secure.

## STUDENTS

Students and faculty are, of course, the central elements of any college or university. These two groups are not often linked in analyses of higher education, although students have profoundly affected the academic profession throughout history. Before the rise of the research university at the end of the nineteenth century, American higher education was student oriented and interaction between faculty and students was substantial. Even in the postwar period, most colleges remained oriented to teaching although, with the decline of *in loco parentis* in the 1960s, faculty became less centrally involved in the lives of students.[51] Students affect faculty in many ways. Increases in student numbers have had the result of expanding the professoriate, and changes in patterns of enrollments also affect the academic profession. Student demands for social relevance in the 1960s had implications for the faculty, as did the later vocationalism of student interests. American higher education has traditionally responded to changing student curricular interests by expanding popular fields and departments or by cutting offerings in unpopular areas. Student consumerism is a central part of the ethos of American higher education.[52]

Student interests have also had some impact on academic policy and governance. In the 1960s, students demanded participation in academic governance, and many colleges and universities opened committees and other structures to them—occasionally even seats on boards of trustees. These changes were short-lived, but the student demands aroused considerable debate and tension on campus at the time.[53] Recently, students have shown little interest in participating in governance and have been only minimally involved in political activism, on campus or off, although there has been a recent increase in student volunteerism for social causes. Student interests and attitudes affect the classroom and enrollments in different fields of study. Students are themselves influenced by societal trends, government policies concerning the financial aspects of higher education, perceptions of the employment market, and many other factors. These student perceptions are brought to the campus and are translated into attitudes, choices, and orientations to higher education. Student opinions about the faculty and the academic enterprise have a significant influence on institutional culture and morale.[54]

TECHNOLOGY

Society, and of course higher education, is undergoing an unprecedented technological revolution, and technology is having a significant impact on academic life. Traditional academic publishing is affected by online journals and electronic publishing. The peer review system for evaluating scholarly work is threatened. Blogs and other informal knowledge-communication networks are widely used. Universities have not yet discovered how to adjust evaluation arrangements for faculty to the technological revolution. How do electronic publications "count" for promotion and tenure? How does evaluation take place in this new environment?

An increasing number of professors are teaching online courses. This has required acquiring new skills and new styles of teaching and evaluating students. Massive open online courses (MOOCs) are also part of the academic landscape—with additional teaching and curricular integration challenges for faculty. The ubiquitous use of e-mail as a way of communicating with students has also changed faculty roles to some extent—adding the necessity to respond quickly to student requests.

## Conclusion

The discussion presented in this chapter is not optimistic. The academic profession has been and continues to be under considerable pressure, and the basic conditions of academic work in America have deteriorated. Some of the gains made during the period of postwar expansion have been lost. The golden age of the American university is probably over. The essential structure of American higher education remains unaltered, and while it is unlikely to change fundamentally, the academic profession will be adversely affected by future trends.

The professoriate stands at the center of any academic institution and is, in some respects, buffered from direct interaction with many of higher education's external constituencies. Academics do not generally deal with trustees, legislators, or parents. Their concerns are with their own teaching and research and with their immediate academic surroundings, such as their departments. Yet external constituencies and realities increasingly affect academic life.

Some of the basic trends that have been discussed in this chapter, factors that are likely to continue to affect the academic profession in the coming period, can be summarized as follows:

- Increased competition for federal research funds made such funds more difficult to obtain in most fields.[55] Governmental commitment to basic research declined as well, and funding for the social sciences and humanities fell. With the end of the Cold War, the emphasis on military research has diminished somewhat.

- Changes in student curricular choices have been significant: from the social sciences in the 1960s to business, engineering, and law starting in the 1980s and continuing to the present, all with a strong vocational focus. Declines in enrollments in the traditional arts and sciences at the graduate level have also been notable.

- Demands from government for budgetary and programmatic accountability have affected higher education at every level.

- In this climate of increased accountability, academic administrators have gained power over their institutions and, inevitably, over the professoriate.

- Economic challenges in society have caused major financial difficulties for higher education, affecting the faculty directly in terms of salaries, resources, and teaching loads. The financial future of higher education, regardless of broader economic trends, is not favorable in the medium term.

- A modest decline in public esteem and support for higher education, triggered first by the unrest of the 1960s and enhanced by some questioning of the academic benefits of a college degree, has caused additional stress for the professoriate.

- The academic profession will become further differentiated. The full-time, tenure-track professoriate is already shrinking, and the numbers of part-timers and non-tenure-track teachers are growing.

In addition, terms and conditions of academic work in the different segments of the academic system will be more diverse and unequal.

- The shrinking academic employment market has meant that fewer younger scholars have been able to enter the profession, and it has limited the mobility of those currently in the profession. The increased use of part-time faculty has further restricted growth.

Given these factors, it is perhaps surprising that the basic working conditions of the American professoriate have remained relatively stable. The structure of postsecondary education remains essentially unchanged, but there have been important qualitative changes that, from the perspective of the professoriate, lead generally in a negative direction. Academic freedom and the tenure system remain largely intact, but there have been increased demands for accountability and fewer academics are on the tenure track. Academics retain basic control over the curriculum, and most institutions continue to be based on the department, which remains strongly influenced by the professoriate. Institutional governance, although increasingly impacted by administrators, remains unchanged.

The period of expansion and professorial power during the middle years of the twentieth century will not return. How, then, can academics face the challenges of the coming period? At one level, the academic profession needs to represent itself effectively to external constituencies. If academic unions could more effectively assimilate traditional academic norms, they might have the potential of representing the professoriate. Traditional academic governance structures are the most logical agencies to take responsibility for presenting the case for the academic profession to a wider audience, both to the public and to political leaders, probably in cooperation with university administrators.

The professoriate reacted to the challenges of the postwar period. It was glad to accept more responsibilities, move into research, and seek funding from external agencies. It relinquished much of its responsibility to students. The curriculum lost its coherence in the rush toward specialization. Now it is necessary to reestablish a sense of academic mission that emphasizes teaching and the curriculum. To a certain extent, this has occurred on many campuses, with the rebuilding of the undergraduate general education curriculum and the reestablishment of liberal education as a key curricular goal at some colleges and universities. The current emphasis on teaching is another important trend that may restore the credibility of the profession.

NOTES

1. See Jack H. Schuster and Martin J. Finkelstein, *The American Faculty: The Restructuring of Academic Work and Careers* (Baltimore: Johns Hopkins University Press, 2006) for a thorough analysis of recent changes in the academic profession.

2. See Allan Bloom, *The Closing of the American Mind: How Higher Education Has Failed Democracy and Impoverished the Souls of Today's Students* (New York: Simon and Schuster, 1987); Charles J. Sykes, *Profscam: Professors and the Demise of Higher Education* (Washington, DC: Regnery Gateway, 1988); Martin Anderson, *Imposters in the Temple* (New York: Simon and Schuster, 1992). For a more optimistic perspective, see Philip G. Altbach, Patricia J. Gumport, and D. Bruce Johnstone, eds., *In Defense of American Higher Education* (Baltimore: Johns Hopkins University Press, 2001).

3. Ernest L. Boyer, *Scholarship Reconsidered: Priorities of the Professoriate* (Princeton, NJ: Carnegie Foundation for the Advancement of Teaching, 1990).

4. Benjamin Ginsberg, *The Fall of the Faculty: The Rise of the All-Administrative University and Why It Matters* (New York: Oxford University Press, 2011).

5. Richard M. Freeland, *Academia's Golden Age: Universities in Massachusetts, 1945–1970* (New York: Oxford University Press, 1992).

6. Richard Arum and Josipa Roksa, *Academically Adrift: Limited Learning on College Campuses* (Chicago: University of Chicago Press, 2011).

7. Edward Shils, "The Academic Ethos under Strain," *Minerva* 13 (1975): 1–37. See also Henry Rosovsky, *The University: An Owner's Manual* (New York: Norton, 1990).

8. Robert Birnbaum, "Unionization and Faculty Compensation, Part II," *Educational Record* 57 (1976): 116–18.

9. National Center for Education Statistics, College and Career Tables Library, "Number of faculty in degree-granting postsecondary institutions, by employment status, sex, control, and level of institution: Selected years, fall 1970 through fall 2013," http://nces.ed.gov/programs/digest/d14/tables/dt14_315.10.asp [accessed July 13, 2015].

10. Steven Shulman, "Faculty and graduate student employment at US colleges and universities, 2013," https://s3.amazonaws.com/s3.chronmedia.com/workforce/FacultyEmploymentReport.pdf [accessed July 14, 2015].

11. Kenneth P. Ruscio, "Many Sectors, Many Professions," in *The Academic Profession: National, Disciplinary, and Institutional Settings*, ed. Burton R. Clark (Berkeley: University of California Press, 1987).

12. National Center for Education Statistics, College and Career Tables Library, "Table 7: Number and percentage of staff and new hires at Title IV institutions and administrative offices, by employment status, gender, and primary function/occupational activity: United States, fall 2009," http://nces.ed.gov/datalab/tableslibrary/viewtable.aspx?tableid=7097 [accessed July 14, 2015].

13. The most through analysis of the American academic profession is in Schuster and Finkelstein, *The American Faculty*. For statistics on race and ethnicity among the professoriate, see National Center for Education Statistics, College and Career Tables Library, "Table 12. Number of staff at Title IV institutions and administrative offices, by race/ethnicity, gender, and primary function/occupational activity: United States, fall

2009," http://nces.ed.gov/datalab/tableslibrary/viewtable.aspx?tableid=7107 [accessed July 14, 2015].

14. Jake Ryan and Charles Sackrey, *Strangers in Paradise: Academics from the Working Class* (Boston: South End, 1984).

15. Charles Homer Haskins, *The Rise of Universities* (Ithaca, NY: Cornell University Press, 1965).

16. Joseph Ben-David and Awraham Zloczower, "Universities and Academic Systems in Modern Societies," *European Journal of Sociology* 3 (1962): 45–84.

17. Fritz K. Ringer, *The Decline of the German Mandarins: The German Academic Community, 1890–1933* (Cambridge, MA: Harvard University Press, 1969).

18. Frederick Rudolph, *The American College and University: A History* (New York: Vintage, 1965 [1962]).

19. Laurence Veysey, *The Emergence of the American University* (Chicago: University of Chicago Press, 1965).

20. This theme is developed at greater length in David Henry, *Challenges Past, Challenges Present* (San Francisco: Jossey-Bass, 1975).

21. The academic job market of this period is captured in Theodore Caplow and Reece J. McGee, *The Academic Marketplace* (New York: Basic Books, 1958). See also Dolores L. Burke, *A New Academic Marketplace* (Westport, CT: Greenwood, 1988), a replication of the earlier Caplow and McGee study, and Schuster and Finkelstein *The American Faculty*.

22. See Logan Wilson, *American Academics: Then and Now* (New York: Oxford University Press, 1979).

23. Seymour Martin Lipset, *Rebellion in the University* (New Brunswick, NJ: Transaction, 1993).

24. Burton R. Clark, *The Academic Life* (Princeton, NJ: Carnegie Foundation for the Advancement of Teaching, 1987). For a structural discussion of American higher education, see Talcott Parsons and Gerald Platt, *The American University* (Cambridge, MA: Harvard University Press, 1973).

25. These figures come from a survey of the views of the American academic profession undertaken by the Carnegie Foundation for the Advancement of Teaching in 1992. See J. Eugene Haas, "The American Academic Profession," in *The International Academic Profession: Portraits of Fourteen Countries*, ed. Philip G. Altbach (Princeton, NJ: Carnegie Foundation for the Advancement of Teaching, 1997).

26. William K. Cummings and Martin J. Finkelstein, *Scholars in the Changing American Academy: New Contexts, New Rules, and New Roles* (Dordrecht, Netherlands: Springer, 2012).

27. See James S. Fairweather, *Faculty Work and Public Trust: Restoring the Value of Teaching and Public Service in American Academic Life* (Boston: Allyn and Bacon, 1996); Robert T. Blackburn and Janet H. Lawrence, *Faculty at Work: Motivation, Expectation, Satisfaction* (Baltimore: Johns Hopkins University Press, 1995).

28. David Riesman, *Constraint and Variety in American Education* (Garden City, NY: Doubleday, 1958), 25–65.

29. Alvin Gouldner, "Cosmopolitans and Locals: Toward an Analysis of Latent Social Roles, 1," *Administrative Science Quarterly* 2, no. 3 (Dec. 1957): 281–303; Alvin Gouldner,

"Cosmopolitans and Locals: Toward an Analysis of Latent Social Roles, 2," *Administrative Science Quarterly* 2, no. 4 (Mar. 1958): 445–67.

30. Judith M. Gappa and David W. Leslie, *The Invisible Faculty: Improving the Status of Part-Timers in Higher Education* (San Francisco: Jossey-Bass, 1993).

31. See, for example, Valora Washington and William Harvey, *Affirmative Rhetoric, Negative Action: African-American and Hispanic Faculty at Predominantly White Institutions* (Washington, DC: George Washington University, School of Education, 1989).

32. Michael Olivas, *Suing Alma Mater: Higher Education and the Courts* (Baltimore: Johns Hopkins University Press, 2013).

33. William A. Kaplin and Barbara A. Lee, *The Law of Higher Education: A Comprehensive Guide to Legal Implications of Administrative Decision Making* (San Francisco: Jossey-Bass, 1995).

34. Edward R. Hines and Leif S. Hartmark, *The Politics of Higher Education* (Washington, DC: American Association for Higher Education, 1980).

35. The most influential consideration of this topic is in Boyer, *Scholarship Reconsidered*. See also William F. Massy and Robert Zemsky, *Faculty Discretionary Time: Departments and the Academic Ratchet* (Philadelphia: Pew Higher Education Research Program, 1992).

36. Arthur Levine and Jana Nidiffer, "Faculty Productivity: A Re-Examination of Current Attitudes and Actions," unpublished manuscript, Institute of Educational Management, Harvard Graduate School of Education, 1993.

37. See Ernest L. Boyer, Philip G. Altbach, and Mary Jean Whitelaw, *The Academic Profession: An International Perspective* (Princeton, NJ: Carnegie Foundation for the Advancement of Teaching, 1994). Academics in other countries report that they teach the following amounts: Germany, 16.4 hours per week; Japan, 19.4; Sweden, 15.9; England, 21.3.

38. Haas, "American Academic Profession," 351.

39. Ibid.

40. William G. Bowen and Julie Ann Sosa, *Prospects for Faculty in the Arts and Sciences* (Princeton, NJ: Princeton University Press, 1989). Demographic projections, however, must be carefully evaluated, because they have frequently been wrong. See also Martin J. Finkelstein, Robert K. Seal, and Jack H. Schuster, *A New Academic Generation* (Baltimore: Johns Hopkins University Press, 1998).

41. Carnegie Foundation for the Advancement of Teaching, *Campus Life: In Search of Community* (Princeton, NJ: Carnegie Foundation for the Advancement of Teaching, 1990).

42. Haas, "American Academic Profession."

43. Matthew W. Finken, ed., *The Case for Tenure* (Ithaca, NY: Cornell University Press, 1996). See also Cathy A. Trower, *Tenure Snapshot* (Washington, DC: American Association for Higher Education, 1996); Richard P. Chait, ed., *The Questions of Tenure* (Cambridge, MA: Harvard University Press, 2002).

44. See Marjorie C. Mix, *Tenure and Termination in Financial Exigency* (Washington, DC: American Association for Higher Education, 1978).

45. Sheila A. Slaughter, "Retrenchment in the 1980s: The Politics of Prestige and Gender," *Journal of Higher Education* 64 (1993): 250–82. See also Patricia J. Gumport,

"The Contested Terrain of Academic Program Reduction," *Journal of Higher Education* 64 (1993): 283–311.

46. For example, in the sixty-four-campus State University of New York System, which is unionized, there is a bifurcation between the four research-oriented university centers, which have been reluctant to unionize, and the fourteen four-year colleges, which favor unionization. Since the four-year college faculty are in the majority, the union has prevailed.

47. Boyer, Altbach, and Whitelaw, *The Academic Profession*, 101. The United States falls at the lower end on this spectrum, with scholars in Russia, Sweden, Mexico, Germany, Japan, and other countries feeling more positive about their freedom to publish.

48. Joseph Fashing and Stephen F. Deutsch, *Academics in Retreat* (Albuquerque: University of New Mexico Press, 1971).

49. Among the numerous books on the topic, see Paul Berman, ed., *Debating P.C.: The Controversy over Political Correctness on College Campuses* (New York: Dell, 1992); Patricia Aufderheide, ed., *Beyond PC: Toward a Politics of Understanding* (Saint Paul, MN: Graywolf, 1992); Francis J. Beckwith and Michael E. Bauman, eds., *Are You Politically Correct? Debating America's Cultural Standards* (Buffalo, NY: Prometheus, 1993).

50. William A. Smith, Philip G. Altbach, and Kofi Lomotey, eds., *The Racial Crisis in American Higher Education* (Albany: State University of New York Press, 2002).

51. Helen Lefkowitz Horowitz, *Campus Life: Undergraduate Cultures from the End of the Eighteenth Century to the Present* (Chicago: University of Chicago Press, 1987).

52. Arthur Levine, *When Dreams and Heroes Died: A Portrait of Today's College Student* (San Francisco: Jossey-Bass, 1980).

53. Alexander W. Astin, Helen Astin, Alan Bayer, and Ann Bisconti, *The Power of Protest* (San Francisco: Jossey-Bass, 1975).

54. Alexander W. Astin, *What Matters in College: Four Critical Years Revisited* (San Francisco: Jossey-Bass, 1993).

55. See Roger L. Geiger, *Research and Relevant Knowledge: American Research Universities since World War II* (New York: Oxford University Press, 1993).

# Chapter Five

# Graduate Education and Research

*Interdependence and Strain*

Patricia J. Gumport

This chapter examines over a century of forces that have reshaped the content and conduct of graduate education in American research universities. I focus on the nexus between graduate education and research, showing the interdependence among doctoral education, academic research, and the federal government. Despite the long-standing and pervasive view that American graduate education is the best in the world, signs of strain have been evident on campuses and nationally. Most of the tensions arise from perennial challenges, albeit with some ebb and flow in the particulars, given changing economic conditions and differences across fields of study.

The contemporary scene reflects this clearly. In graduate admissions at many research universities, faculty lament the need to reduce the size of incoming doctoral cohorts due to funding constraints as well as to academic labor market projections for an oversupply of PhD recipients reminiscent of the early 1970s. Talented doctoral students consider abandoning tenure-track faculty career ambitions to pursue alternatives—whether within academia or in the business, government, or nonprofit sectors. Although their predecessors also anticipated years of long hours at low pay, this generation is concerned about disappearing tenure-track faculty jobs and feel pressured to develop publications while still in doctoral programs and postdoctoral positions. Regarding research training, increased competition for limited federal research funding has motivated faculty to generate more grant proposals to the federal government and industry, and to generate faster yet still novel research findings. Observers are concerned that this heightened competition along with intellectual property interests may diminish the free exchange of ideas and collegiality. As teaching assistants, graduate students are estimated to provide one-quarter of all undergraduate instruction nationally. Collective bargaining activities at close to fifty universities involve 40,000 graduate student "employees" working in teaching assistantships. While graduate school has long been characterized as an exercise in deferred gratification, reports reveal students' perceptions of unrelenting competition, pressures to produce, and uncertainty about career paths, all exacerbating mental health issues.[1] Concurrently, the enormous growth and proliferation of professional and master's programs and graduate certificates reflect increased interest in credentials for advanced skills in the knowledge economy. In a global context, with increasing graduate enrollments in other countries, the United States has begun to lose its market share of international students, which has been a longtime source of pride and affirmation.

Although some readers may be inclined to minimize these trends as selective or exaggerated, I make the case that several axes of persistent tension have been redefining the graduate education–research nexus, thereby compromising some long-held ideals. Most problematic are uncertainty in external funding for graduate education; increased competition for federal research funds that often include caps on tuition and stipends; commercialization of research; and students' concerns that academic positions are less available and academic careers less desirable. Viewed historically, the above tensions exemplify larger challenges for universities as they strive to preserve standards of excellence for teaching and research, while also managing the rising costs of a complex research infrastructure to attract talented faculty and students. Public universities in particular have additional constraints, especially in states where bleak economies and shifting priorities triggered sizable and successive cuts in public funding, and where an "industry logic" has gained traction and unprecedented legitimacy.[2] These signs of strain—and the wider contexts that exacerbate them—reshape the character of graduate education.

Against that backdrop, this chapter examines the historical development of graduate education and research; specifically, the intersections among doctoral education, academic research, and the federal government. This interdependence has strong roots in the expansion of research universities and disciplinary specialization. While the structural foundations of graduate programs reflect much continuity, the conduct of graduate programs in many fields has undeniably changed—directly in research training practices, and indirectly through changes in academic research and public expectations of what higher education should be and do. Historians have varying accounts of this interdependence between graduate education and research, set within the broader story of how well universities have adapted to external sponsors' agenda or have maintained their academic autonomy.[3] Nonetheless, some basic changes are undisputed.

As universities transformed into modern research complexes, the organizational character and rhythm of academic work changed to accommodate the increased centrality of externally sponsored research.[4] Research training of graduate students, most relevant to science and engineering, became oriented to the stark realities of ongoing quests for funding, especially from federal sources, namely uncertain funding levels, changing agenda of federal agencies, and increased competition.[5] The imperatives to seek external funding for university research have at times directly challenged ideals for graduate education: when knowledge transfer, patents, and financial gain become primary aims, instead of disinterested inquiry; when students must focus on topics and skills required to complete externally funded projects, rather than exploring what interests them; when faculty hire postdoctoral researchers instead of funding novice doctoral students. Each of these trends exemplifies how serving the educational and advising needs of graduate students can become a lower priority for faculty. It is a classic case for the caution not to let the urgent trump the important.

In the context of these tensions, university officials, faculty, and at times graduate students themselves have sought greater control in the conduct of academic affairs to protect their interests. Yet each is also well aware of interdependence with the others. University reputations are bolstered by retaining high-profile faculty and talented graduate students from around the world. Universities rely on their faculty's success in obtaining grants and producing valuable research both to balance budgets and to maintain prestige. Faculty rely on grants to support their research and recruit talented doctoral students. Graduate students need faculty mentoring and research training in their chosen specializations. Upon completing their PhDs, graduates may need postdoctoral research training, which has become a *de facto* requirement in ever more fields.

Although more visible in the sciences and engineering, some of these interdependencies also apply to the social sciences and humanities. As a prominent common denominator across academic fields, the expansion of undergraduate education has come to depend on graduate students to serve as teaching assistants (TAs). Talented TAs can be excellent instructors and inspiring role models for undergraduates, which benefits universities insofar as they can replace faculty time with lower-cost TAs. Although TAs gain valuable teaching experience, the role can be detrimental for graduate students if it is excessive and lengthens their time to degree completion. Inevitably, with these inextricable links, changes in one area affect the entire complex—a set of dynamics reviewed in this chapter.[6]

## Historical Overview

Major transformations in American higher education over the past century have had their effects in graduate education, as they have in other areas. The most prominent external force has been funding from the federal government. The varying forms and amounts of federal funding signal changes in the ways graduate education is expected to serve different societal needs. In the evolving relationship between universities and the federal government, graduate education has become intertwined in complex organizational symbioses with academic research, research funding, and undergraduate education. This historical overview traces continuity alongside change: expansion in higher education's structural foundations on the one hand, with significant qualitative changes in the academic work of faculty and graduate students on the other.

Although graduate education in the United States has been neither centrally planned nor standardized, its expansion during the twentieth century retained a fundamental structural consistency, especially at the doctoral level. In this second decade of the twenty-first century, by cross-national standards, the United States has the largest, most decentralized, and most highly differentiated arrangements for post-baccalaureate education—which spans more than 2,200 of the country's 4,600 colleges and universities, with graduate students accounting for 3 million of the 21 million students enrolled in higher education. In the United States over 750,000 master's degrees and over 170,000 doctorates (including MDs and DDSs), of which over 70,000 are research doctorates (i.e., PhDs), are awarded annually.[7]

This tremendous breadth of activity notwithstanding, decentralized organization with faculty authority at the department level has remained the basic model for doctoral education. After a few years of prescribed courses and examinations for advancement to degree candidacy, PhD students do original research with guidance from a faculty committee, culminating in a dissertation. The ideal, dating back to Wilhelm von Humboldt in the early nineteenth century, has been for students to engage in advanced study alongside research.[8] Research training has reflected distinct disciplinary patterns: in the sciences, where research is laboratory-intensive, students work under faculty supervision, with the dissertation as a piece of a faculty member's research projects; while in the humanities, students work independently, often with little faculty contact, unless they initiate it. These patterns of social relations are, in part, intrinsic to the disciplines and tied to professional norms, the nature of disciplinary inquiry, and the research technologies.[9]

In contrast to these structural continuities, the historical arc simultaneously reveals profound changes in the nature of student-faculty relationships. Nevitt Sanford assessed this with critical concern back in 1976, and it remains relevant even into the twenty-first century:

> The structure of graduate education seems to have changed hardly at all since the 1930s . . . What has changed are the purposes for which the structure is used and the spirit with which it is managed. The motives of professors and graduate students are less purely intellectual and more professional . . . The general climate of today is one of competitiveness among universities, between departments in a given university, and between subgroups and individuals within the same department. Students are regarded less as potential intellectual leaders and more as resources to be used in the struggle for a place in the sun.[10]

To the extent that this characterization is apt today, the research foundations of graduate education are central to an analysis of how this shift came about and what the consequences have been. Specifically, changes in the funding patterns for graduate education and university research have been a critical mediating force in this transformation.

Historically, graduate education has been financed primarily through externally sponsored research and secondarily through a variety of loan programs, as well as by state-funded and institutionally funded teaching assistantships and fellowships. Federal support for academic research has been concentrated in the top one hundred research universities, which have accounted for approximately 80 percent of federal research and development (R&D) expenditures. By the turn of the new century, the top one hundred produced nearly 50 percent of doctoral degrees and nearly 25 percent of all master's degrees. This increased concentration of resources and activity for graduate education has persisted to the present.[11] Sponsored university research has had the greatest effect in these universities and on the sciences and engineering fields within them. Still, it does have salience for others—if only by denying them funds.

Federal involvement in graduate education and university research can be traced back to the late nineteenth century, when the organizational structure of the modern research university emerged to accommodate scientific research and graduate programs. These activities expanded in scale, as faculty and administrators sought more external sponsorship. Although by the twenty-first century many universities have succeeded in raising endowed funds for professorships, fellowships, and selected research areas, the federal government has been the longest principal source of funds for most research-intensive universities, thereby playing the most pivotal role in supporting research training of graduate students. Three consequences have been most apparent: increased specialization in faculty research and administrative infrastructure; stratification, with heightened within-sector competition for fiscal and human resources; and a proliferation of organizational subunits for academic research to reflect the agenda of external sponsors. How these changes came about is the next piece of the story.

## Nineteenth-Century Beginnings

Graduate education achieved a stable American presence during the last two decades of the nineteenth century, when awarding PhD degrees became a laudable goal. The opening of Johns Hopkins University in 1876 is often cited to mark the establishment of graduate education in the United States. Johns Hopkins became known as the "prototype and propagator" of research as a major university function.[12] Coupled with its commitment to scientific research, Johns Hopkins offered merit-based graduate fellowships for full-time study, including state-of-the-art research training.

Both within and immediately surrounding higher education, interest in scientific research burgeoned from the mid-nineteenth century. With great frequency, scientists and those seeking advanced study traveled to Germany for the requisite exposure. Work in chemistry, even into the 1870s, required a trip to Germany. On the American front, after some initial resistance to the German idea of studying science for its own sake—and after conflicts between self-identified pure and applied scientists—scientific research gradually gained acceptance. It took on a distinctive meaning in the American context: science would be "a collective enterprise like those in business. Modern science needed labor, capital, and management."[13] Proclamations at Johns Hopkins reflected this change in scientific research from "a rare and peculiar opportunity for study and research, eagerly seized by men who had been hungering and thirsting for such a possibility" to an increasingly more prestigious endeavor, proclaimed by G. Stanley Hall, Clark University's first president, as "the very highest vocation of man—research."[14] Science became an increasingly specialized activity that professors could pursue autonomously—yet with security of support, personal advancement, and prominence as faculty within an academic institution.

Following Johns Hopkins' ideal of linking scientific research and graduate education, other graduate schools emerged in the 1890s, usually within larger universities whose undergraduate missions and size offered a broad and stable base of support in tuition and endowment. Some were established at the founding of a new university, so as to offer both undergraduate and graduate instruction at their inception, as at Stanford University (1891) and the University of Chicago (1892). Others added a graduate school onto an older, established, private college, such as Harvard University and Columbia University. Some state universities—Wisconsin, Michigan, and Illinois—evolved from land-grant institutions, dependent on government funds for agriculture and mechanical arts (through the Morrill Acts of 1862 and 1890) and for experimental agricultural stations (through the Hatch Act of 1887). By 1900, fourteen PhD-granting institutions awarded a total of three hundred doctorates in an expanding array of fields.[15]

In addition to taking on scientific research commitments, PhD programs came to be viewed as attractive for expanding and advancing an institution's competitive position in the growing higher education system. To confer prestige on their institutions, universities sought out faculty with research interests and sponsored research funds to build laboratories that would attract eminent scientists. Since faculty increasingly wanted to pursue basic research and train selectively chosen graduate students, universities were compelled to provide opportunities for research and advanced training and, hence, developed graduate programs across disciplines.

## Organizing Principles: Departmentalization and Disciplinary Specialization

The widespread adoption of graduate programs within universities was enhanced by the departmental organization that developed in the last quarter of the nineteenth century. Departments provided a flexible organizational structure for decentralizing and compartmentalizing graduate instruction. While PhD programs were organizationally integrated as a level separate from the liberal education of undergraduate colleges, they were also made part of departments responsible for undergraduate instruction in a discipline—a linking arrangement that has been remarkably stable over time and across universities. The drive to conform to this structure was so strong that Johns Hopkins added undergraduate education to its mission.

This organization allowed the same faculty to exercise authority over both undergraduate and graduate programs.[16] Courses and research training for each discipline could be designed and coordinated by each department's faculty. One functional by-product was that graduate programs maintained continuity and cohesion. Faculty propagated themselves and their field of study by training their professional successors, who became stewards of the discipline, and responsibility for their graduate students kept faculty attentive to their departments. Graduate programs kept research and teaching activities interlocked and the institution functionally integrated, at least at the department level, despite increased specialization.

This interdependence was crucial to the success of graduate study, perhaps most specifically in facilitating the doctoral student's transition from coursework to dissertation research—which, among the many hurdles for PhD students across the disciplines, emerged as the paramount challenge and persists as such to this day. Research training experiences have been central to a student's shift from consumer to producer of research and thus are integral to successful degree completion. In correspondence with established areas of knowledge, departments designed research apprenticeships appropriate to specialized training in each discipline.

Specialization in the disciplines—which the departments mirrored—represented professors' primary intellectual interests and aspirations. This was particularly apparent in newly established natural and social science departments, whose very existence was justified on the basis of specialized research. Beyond the campus level, as disciplines formed national professional associations, they came to serve as visible external referent groups that provided a semblance of standardization across graduate programs: "disciplines and departments had powerful reciprocal effects upon one another" in reinforcing the authority of departments on campuses and the professional judgments of faculty as peers nationally.[17]

Especially during the 1890s, the size and complexity of the graduate-education-and-research enterprise encouraged local coordination and control, which generated university administrative structures. Although departments served faculty interests for autonomy in research and instruction, hierarchies of academic rank within departments and competition for resources across departments created more incentives—and therefore more productivity in the form of research activity. As one observer has noted, "clearly it had become a necessity, from the administrator's point of view, to foster the prestigeful evidences of original inquiry."[18] The dual tasks of graduate education and research were institutionalized most easily in organizations that had greater resources, both financial and reputational. Those that succeeded in the competitive drive became a peer group of leading institutions. The prominence of this tier was reflected in its founding the Association of American Universities (AAU) in 1900. The AAU was ostensibly established to ensure uniformity of standards, yet it simultaneously functioned as an exclusive club.[19] The AAU signified an implicit systemwide division of labor in the United States, where the highest-prestige institutions differentiated themselves at the top of the hierarchy, which legitimately had the concentration of resources for research and graduate education. Although many universities have competed for faculty, graduate students, and philanthropic support, the persistent concentration of fiscal and status resources at the top of this sector became a distinctive feature of the US system, wherein success begets future success, an institutional version of Robert Merton's Matthew Effect.[20]

Termed "a new epoch of institutional empire-building," this period of American higher education was characterized by explicit aims for universities to accrue and retain status in an increasingly stratified system. This was seen in academic rivalry, such as bidding for faculty, and in emulating each other's highly regarded academic departments. While this system is not unique in its inclination toward stratification, the institutional drive for competitive advancement among research universities has been characterized by one American scholar as "almost an obsession."[21]

Thus the end of the nineteenth century saw the research university emerge as a new kind of social institution, devoted to scientific research as well as to graduate education. Pursuing this institutional ambition became pervasive. Across the country, homogeneity in proliferating graduate programs and faculty positions suggests that universities sought to acquire not only intellectual legitimacy, but also unprecedented economic and political legitimacy. These priorities have been at the forefront for a growing number of universities throughout the twentieth century and to the present day.

## Twentieth-Century Rise of Sponsored Academic Research

The expansion of graduate education in the modern university subsequently developed hand-in-hand with the expanding national system of sponsored research. Initially, external resources for academic science were amassed principally from philanthropic foundations, while industry played a minimal role. However, after World War II, foundations and industry were eclipsed by federal sponsorship, as government agencies became the major funder of academic research through the end of the twentieth century.

Looking back, the earliest sources of research sponsorship were wealthy benefactors and their philanthropic foundations. In the 1870s, philanthropic contributions to higher education averaged $6 million per year—mainly to individual scientists. By 1890, philanthropic support showed a more widespread and instrumental orientation, directing funds to emerging universities for their potential contributions to industrial growth, employment, and commercial endeavors. The funds supported a wide array of institutional activities, especially in the applied sciences—including equipment, overall plant expansion, and new professional schools. In some cases philanthropists provided large sums of money, such as John D. Rockefeller's $35 million endowment to the University of Chicago. Rockefeller and Andrew Carnegie established the two largest foundations supporting research: the Rockefeller Foundation, started in 1913 with an endowment of $182 million; and the Carnegie Corporation, created in 1911 with $125 million. However, in the early 1920s these foundations favored donations to separate research institutes, such as the Rockefeller Institute of Medicine and the Carnegie Institute of Washington.[22]

By the 1930s, universities could no longer depend on philanthropic foundations as a stable sponsor for academic science. While still essential, the foundations reoriented their allocations to project grants and postdoctoral fellowships, especially in medical research and in the natural sciences, and, to a lesser extent, the social sciences. In 1934, the Rockefeller Foundation's funding constituted 35 percent of overall foundation giving, comprising 64 percent of what went to the social sciences and 72 percent of gifts to the natural sciences.[23] Such voluntary contributions provided universities with resources essential to institutionalizing graduate education and scientific research as two interdependent functions.

The course was set. Universities and their faculties built their own rationales and adapted organizational structures to expand the scope of their research, while training the next generation of knowledge producers. Upholding university autonomy and academic freedom became important not only for the institution, but equally for individual faculty. The professionalization efforts of faculty during this era were, in part, an effort to buffer themselves from an array of powerful external interests, and not merely an outgrowth of the knowledge explosion, as is commonly cited.[24] In claiming expert authority, faculty established some distance for themselves from the agendas of prominent philanthropists.

Private industry entered the academic scene as an unexpected and unpredictable supplement.[25] As industry R&D expenditures rose in the 1920s, corporations conducted both applied and basic research in their own industrial laboratories, both in communications and in chemical technologies. Two prestigious research universities—the Massachusetts Institute of Technology and the California Institute of Technology—exemplified successful industry sponsorship of university research during this era. Overall, however, corporate R&D funds stayed in their industrial laboratories through the 1930s.

By the late 1930s, university research was genuinely flourishing, primarily in the nation's most visible universities. American universities also became a haven for preeminent scientists from Europe, which helped elevate the universities' scientific capability and reputation. This concentration of research activity was paralleled by a similar concentration of research training activity: in 1937, sixteen universities accounted for half of the total expenditures on university research and granted 58 percent of all doctorates.[26] The consolidation of research resources with doctoral-granting activity was a pattern that would persist even after the era of privately financed university research. This basic imprint for university research acquired a taken-for-granted status, along with its promise for self-reproduction: a concentration of external research resources, enabling talented faculty to provide research training for the next generation while yielding first-class academic research—all of which was viewed as valuable by external sponsors.

### Surge of Federal Investment

The government's sponsorship of research and research training evolved incrementally, rather than through a coordinated policy on science or graduate education, as has occurred in some countries. Beginning with the federal and state governments' role in land-grants through agricultural research, universities were increasingly regarded as a national resource for basic research and training that could assist economic growth, national security, and health care. Over time, including two world wars, the government became the major sponsor of scientific research and higher education.

Federal involvement in academic science began with organizational efforts to designate advisory boards for scientific research. Acknowledging both the value of modern science and a perceived need to oversee the country's research intentions, the first national organization, the National Academy of Sciences (NAS), was founded in 1863.[27] In 1919, the National Research Council (NRC) was established by NAS essentially to carry out the earlier congressional mandate. As the principal operating agency of both NAS and—after 1964—the National Academy of Engineering, the NRC was intended to bridge the interests of its constituents: the federal government, the public, and the community of scientists and engineers. Over time, the NRC became a principal organizational vehicle for overseeing national research efforts and for monitoring how federal funds were to be channeled into university research.

The NRC, along with the American Council of Learned Societies (also founded in 1919) and the Social Sciences Research Council (founded in 1923), relied on the resources of philanthropic foundations to assume a prominent role in facilitating and promoting university research. As channels for foundation funds, these organizations provided interested sponsors with access to scientists and scholars, as well as with administrative assistance in selecting recipients for small research grants and postdoctoral fellowships in the areas of mathematics, physics, and chemistry. By the 1920s American science was mobilized under "the guidance of the private elites," who "came together for the purpose of furthering science." The memberships of the NRC and NAS were constituted by "the same group of individuals [who] encountered one another, in slightly different combinations."[28]

The federal government's large-scale, multiagency funding system to support academic science expanded incrementally during and after each world war. In the late 1930s, annual federal expenditures for American science were estimated at $100 million; most of these funds went to applied research within federal bureaus, especially agriculture, meteorology, geology, and conservation. The shift to university-based research occurred when the expertise of academic researchers became valuable for national defense.[29] In World War I, for example, the government financed psychologists to construct intelligence tests and encouraged scientists to follow up on diagnostic physical examinations for nearly 4 million draftees. For such work, universities granted leaves to full-time life scientists and physical scientists, as well as to social scientists and historians. The government also allocated funds for researchers working from their own campuses. By World War II this type of funding spread. During the 1940s, the Office of Naval Research contracted with more than 200 universities to conduct about 1,200 research projects involving some 3,000 scientists and 2,500 graduate students. Between 1941 and 1945, the United States spent a total of $3 billion on

R&D—one-third of which went to university-based research aimed at winning the war and devising "new instruments of destruction and defense."[30]

The expansion of sponsored research within universities was coupled with doctoral training. Between World War I and World War II, the number of institutions awarding doctoral degrees doubled—from fifty in 1920 to one hundred in 1940; and the number of doctorates awarded increased fivefold—from 620 in 1920 to 3,300 in 1940.[31] In addition, enhancing the caliber of doctoral students became a priority; in the 1920s, the majority of graduate students had been "undistinguished," reflecting "uneven preparation, uncertain motivation, and unproven ability."[32]

By the end of World War II, the federal government viewed research universities as a precious public resource for research and research training, worthy of the government's investment and partnership—even during peacetime. The establishment of the National Science Foundation (NSF) in 1950 reflects this explicit federal agenda that science would indeed offer "an endless frontier," and that universities could be ideal settings for such research, as Vannevar Bush stated in his 1945 report to President Franklin Roosevelt: funding would go to scientists working in their home universities, rather than bringing them to the few existing government labs. In the 1950s, the federal research budget grew steadily, and the academic research enterprise expanded in the top tier of institutions. In 1953–54, the top twenty spent 66 percent of all federal research funds and awarded 52 percent of all doctorates—most in the life sciences, physical sciences, and engineering, the same fields receiving the most research funds.[33]

### Postwar Expansion of Funds for University Research and Doctoral Education

Spurred by the Soviet launch of Sputnik in 1957, the US government provided even more funds for basic research. Federal sponsorship of research increased every year from 1958 to 1968. That decade alone saw a fivefold expansion in annual federal funding for academic research. As this investment grew, so did universities' share of total basic research, from one-third to one-half during that decade.[34] The post–World War II period clearly established research as a separate operation, largely paid for by the government, wherein universities performed a large share of the nation's research effort. With higher education's increased legitimacy in this research role, enrollment rose from 3 million to 7 million students, and it doubled within doctorate-granting universities—up from 1.24 million to 2.5 million for undergraduates and graduates combined.

Annual PhD production in science and engineering rose from 5,800 in 1958 to 14,300 in 1968.[35]

The allocation of federal research funds followed two basic imperatives: multiagency support and competition among proposals for specified projects of limited terms. Federal sponsorship had a clear presidential directive—Executive Order 10521, in 1954—for multiagency support, such that no single agency within the government was to be given sole responsibility for distributing research funds. Rather, each agency was to sponsor research related to its mission, such as health, defense, and energy. In 1959, 96 percent of funding came from five agencies: the Department of Defense; the Department of Health, Education, and Welfare, largely through the National Institutes of Health (NIH); the Atomic Energy Commission; the NSF; and the Department of Agriculture. In the same year, nearly all of the $1.4 billion allocated for research was channeled into the life sciences, physical sciences, and engineering, leaving the social sciences, and particularly the humanities, virtually neglected.[36]

These funding allocations were determined through merit-based peer review by researchers in the scientific community. This competitive system was presumed to ensure that the best research would be performed and further excellence cultivated. The result was to reinforce the strength of the science fields in the leading tier of research universities—with the life sciences and physical sciences accounting for over half of the basic research budgets.

Federal support for doctoral education expanded as well, with the government's interest in having trained science and engineering personnel to meet national needs. Aside from short-term interests to advance science and technology, improving research capacity ("manpower training," as it was called) required a longer-term investment to develop "the pipeline." Mechanisms were established to attract talented students: direct student aid, such as fellowships; student aid channeled through institutions, as traineeships; and project grants to individual faculty that included salaries for graduate student research assistants. The precedent for this explicit twofold agenda—to ensure the strength of research and of the workforce—was clear in the National Cancer Act of 1937, which set up grant-in-aid funds to nongovernmental scientists and fellowships to students. By the 1950s, the NSF offered more than five hundred prestigious portable fellowships to students.

Similarly, the National Defense Education Act of 1958 conveyed a commitment to rebuilding the nation's research capability through "manpower training"; specifically, to support science education through a host of fellowship and traineeship programs from a variety of federal agencies—the NIH, the NSF, and the National Aeronautics and Space Administration (NASA). The National Research Service Awards (NRSA), administered through three federal agencies in the 1960s, had the same aim. These training programs were intended to attract talented students, offering them stipends for predoctoral and postdoctoral support, as well as to improve training on campuses through institutional allowances. Between 1961 and 1972, these programs assisted more than 30,000 graduate students and 27,000 postdoctoral scholars.[37]

While direct support of doctoral education—fellowships and traineeships—was allocated to students on a competitive basis, it ended up funding students at the leading research universities, which did the bulk of federally funded academic research. This concentration of resources for both research and doctoral education gave these institutions a doubly competitive edge in attracting high-quality students and faculty.

Post–World War II federal initiatives were even more instrumental in cementing the legitimacy of this interdependence: funding university research had short-term R&D value, and graduate education promoted "manpower training." Between the end of World War II and 1972, the government spent $200 billion cumulatively on R&D; the academic institutions' share of total R&D expenditures rose from 5 to 10 percent. More notably, their share of basic research expenditures went from one-quarter of all funds in 1953 to one-half in the early 1970s. By the end of that era, the surge of federal sponsorship resulted in a pattern that would persist over subsequent decades: about half of the country's basic research was done in universities; about two-thirds of university research expenditures came from the federal government; and about half the federal funds for basic academic research went to the top twenty-five research universities.

### Postwar Expansion of Graduate Education

The end of World War II marked a turning point. Within this context of funded research opportunities, the graduate education system grew at a constant rate during each decade.[38] More doctorates were granted in the 1950s than in all the preceding years; the number of doctorates granted increased from 6,000 in 1950 to 10,000 in 1960. The 1960s experienced an even more pronounced expansion: a threefold increase in one decade alone—from 10,000 to nearly 30,000 research doctorates, or PhDs. The number of master's degrees also increased dramatically, rising from about 25,000 in 1940 to a genuine flourishing in the decades following World War II—about 60,000 in 1950, 75,000 in 1960, and nearly 300,000 two decades later.

This proliferation of doctorates and master's degrees reflects both overall growth in degree production and expansion into more fields of study, especially in the sciences and professional fields. The physical sciences, life sciences, and engineering accounted for close to half of the doctorates awarded in 1965; two decades later they still predominated, although PhDs in the life sciences edged out the other two fields. Social science and psychology remained fairly constant, at about 20 percent; humanities dropped from 20 to 10 percent; and education increased from about 15 to 25 percent, reflecting an increasingly professional orientation in graduate study. The overall diversification of doctoral fields was marked—with more than 550 fields in 1960. Beyond additional areas of concentration, several dozen types of doctoral degrees developed besides the PhD, which remained the most common research doctorate, such as degrees in education (EdD), social work (DSW), and business administration (DBA).

A similar orientation to the demands of the marketplace is evident in the growth of master's degrees since 1965, especially in practitioner-oriented fields. By 1982–83, only 16 percent of master's degrees were conferred in research-oriented MA programs. Business master's degrees increased from 7 to 23 percent; engineering accounted for 10 percent; and the health professions (such as nursing) for about 6 percent. Education held the largest share of master's degrees, although it declined from 40 to 30 percent of the total.[39]

On the whole, in the decades following World War II, graduate education at the master's and doctoral levels developed into a vast enterprise in which the leading tier of research universities became the model for aspiring institutions to emulate, both in the United States and around the world. Less elite institutions had a smaller resource base in terms of the scale of their facilities, the amount of departmental funds, and a critical mass of sought-after faculty and students. Their approach was to invest in selected fields, although it was not until the 1970s that asserting a distinctive institutional mission become a clear strategy for gaining a competitive edge in specialized areas. At leading universities, the dynamic was different: able to cover many fields with depth, universities undertook even more sponsored research and expanded PhD enrollment and degree production. This is the modern research imperative—the vehicle whereby universities protect, if not advance, their institutional mobility. It became taken for granted that "the institution which is not steadily advancing is certainly falling behind."[40]

Thus, up to the contemporary period, graduate education and research in the leading universities were guided by opportunities funded by the government:

scientific research for national priorities in defense and economic development; the government's rising research budget for R&D, specifically in basic research; and a peer review system aiming to distribute resources to the best science. The fact that multiple funding agencies were supporting academic research reduced the universities' dependence on a single agency. However, during the last quarter of the twentieth century, shifts in organization and sponsorship brought uncertainty in the amounts and mechanisms of funding, posing new challenges for the research foundations of graduate education and a motive for research universities to further diversify their funding base.

## The Contemporary Era: Signs of Strain

While patterns that formed in the post–World War II period remained prominent, as the wider economic, social, and political conditions changed, university-government relations showed signs of strain. The early 1970s witnessed an economic crisis that threatened even the strong research-training link in the sciences, as well as the solid resource base of the most prominent research universities. An era of retrenchment—between 1969 and 1975—began with a tightening academic labor market and inflation in the wider economy. This era signaled an unanticipated fact: the federal government was an unstable base of financial support for university research and graduate education. Political support was also unpredictable, as Democratic and Republican administrations modified funding to reflect their distinctive priorities.

The dramatic expansion fueled by the post–World War II surge of federal support for university research and graduate education had appeared limitless. By the 1970s, research universities had extended their capital-intensive research infrastructures, securing their position as international centers of excellence for research and research training. US universities attracted a steady stream of international students, who earned 10 percent of PhDs by the late 1960s.

It became the norm for doctoral students to work as research assistants for faculty engaged in sponsored research projects. This need, and the scale of funding, became a major determinant of the size and types of graduate programs. In addition, on the teaching side, surging enrollments meant that more graduate students could serve as TAs for undergraduate courses. So, even while most applicants to graduate school sought to engage in advanced study and obtain advanced degrees, their contributions as research and teaching assistants became central to their learning experiences, while concurrently enabling universities to expand their institutional capacities for both research and undergraduate education. Government-funded traineeships and portable fellowships supported those fortunate graduate students, covering educational and living expenses. Such direct federal aid was limited to US citizens and permanent residents, which created challenges in funding students from other countries, most of whom held temporary visas.

The early 1970s also saw changes in the funding climate, with sharp declines in direct federal support for fellowships and the reorientation of basic research funds to more applied projects that prioritized economic competitiveness. Budget crises, in turn, fostered hopes that industry would become more involved in funding academic research. Joseph Ben-David characterized this new reality: a reduction of the massive federal support was "inevitable, but . . . the system was entirely unprepared for it when it came."[41] Graduate enrollments and degrees awarded reached unprecedented highs and then leveled off during this period, another indicator that expansion was not limitless. There was concern that supply had exceeded demand, as exemplified by "taxi-driving ABDs" (the acronym for students who had completed All But the Dissertation). How universities would manage to achieve stability in funding graduate education, let alone thrive, in a context of uncertain job prospects and volatile federal funds became an ongoing question, along with how to sustain an infrastructure for excellence in both research and research training. Indeed, the ongoing viability of graduate programs at several hundred campuses across the US has been remarkable, given these broad challenges.

As for funding changes in that era, between 1968 and 1971 the national basic research budget fell more than 10 percent in real terms.[42] Annual academic research expenditures contributed by the federal government declined from $5 billion in 1968 to $4.7 billion in 1974. The government's priority was for research that made scientific knowledge technologically relevant. As a result, physical resources—such as equipment and campus buildings—were neglected. In addition to declining funds for academic science, support for graduate students declined. Thus both research and research training became "victims of federal benign neglect."[43] The government abruptly withdrew the bulk of its direct fellowship support for graduate students, especially some of the larger programs funded by the NIH. By one count, the 57,000 federal fellowships and traineeships funded in 1968 shrank to 41,000 in 1970; another estimate is that federal fellowships fell from 51,000 in 1968 to 6,000 by 1981.[44] As graduate fellowships were "cut back too fast and too far," a series of national reports looked at graduate education financing.[45] They cited the destabilizing effects of "stop-and-go" federal funds and the disadvantages of smaller-scale fellowships. The decline left the bulk of doctoral students seeking direct support from loans, which tripled during one decade alone, from 15 percent of graduate enrollment in 1974 to 44 percent in 1984. It is estimated that by 1984, more than 600,000 students working toward graduate degrees had borrowed $2 billion from the federal government in Guaranteed Student Loans (later known as Stafford Loans).

The federal government's funding for doctoral education became more indirect, through research assistantships. In the 1980s, funds for graduate student research assistantships were embedded in $13 billion of federal academic R&D. However, aside from cuts in fellowships and traineeships in the early 1970s, the stipends for research assistantships were, in effect, reduced when the Tax Reform Act of 1986 reconfigured them as taxable pay for work (hence salaries) rather than tax-exempt educational subsidies. This initiative also taxed state-funded teaching assistantships, which were previously excluded from income taxes. Universities and their national representatives, with outspoken graduate students, worked to have this legislation amended.[46] The tax reform, which required technical changes in administering graduate student financial aid, marked a profound shift in how graduate students were viewed: as instrumentally valuable for their work, rather than as inherently worthy of direct support. Many saw this as "a big bite" out of "survival wages" and still consider it an unreasonable burden.

Nonetheless, doctoral degree production resumed its growth, and by the late 1980s universities had regained the numerical losses that had occurred in the mid-1970s; the number of doctoral degrees awarded annually stabilized at above 35,000, surpassing the 1973 peak. When examined cumulatively over the last three decades of the twentieth century, the overall growth is impressive: doctoral degrees awarded from 1969 to 1999 increased by 60 percent, with only brief periods of decline.[47]

International students account for some of that increase in doctorates. Over the last four decades of the twentieth century, the proportion of US doctorates awarded to international students rose from about 10 percent in the 1960s to 23 percent in the late 1990s. Even more notable, the proportion of international students earning doctorates in science and engineering tripled over this period, from 13 to 39 percent; engineering stood out, from 16 to 44 percent of the annual doctorates awarded in that field.[48]

Growth in doctoral degrees has also been attributed to increased participation of women. The proportion of doctoral degrees awarded to women in the fields of science, technology, engineering, and mathematics (STEM) fields increased from 1966 to 2006: in the biological sciences, from one-eighth to one-half of doctorates; in computer science, engineering, and physics, from less than 3 percent to about one-fifth. Despite progress, women still comprised less than 50 percent of graduates in all STEM fields in 2006, except for the biological sciences.[49]

Less progress has been made for underrepresented US minorities, especially in STEM fields, which have drawn high international enrollment. The proportion of STEM doctorates earned by underrepresented US minorities only increased from 4 percent in 1995 to 7 percent in 2007.[50] Increasing their participation is seen as a national necessity in order to maintain global competitiveness, in addition to addressing social justice concerns. Observers fear that if degree attainment rates of underrepresented minorities do not improve, the increasing diversity of the US population will *de facto* lead to a less highly trained workforce. Obviously this challenge extends beyond graduate education, as it occurs at each lower level of education up through faculty ranks. The federal government has funded "pipeline" programs for undergraduates as well as for graduate students (e.g., Ronald E. McNair Post-Baccalaureate Achievement Program, Louis Stokes Alliances for Minority Participation Program, Alliances for Graduate Education and the Professoriate). Some universities fund their own initiatives to advance diversity in graduate education, as well as to cultivate interest in and preparation for faculty careers.[51]

Nationally, a concentration of doctoral degree production in the same universities has persisted in recent decades, continuing its interdependence with sponsored research. In 1992, the top fifty universities granted 54 percent of all doctorates; and the top ten, 17 percent of the total. By 2007, the fifty biggest doctoral-producing universities granted over half the PhDs, while the top ten universities granted 15 percent. Looking at the particular universities, of the top fifty producers in 1992, all but six remained in the top fifty fifteen years later, supported by their concurrent research activity. Of those top fifty doctorate-granting universities in 2007, thirty-four were also in the top fifty for federally funded R&D expenditures; of the top twenty-five doctoral producers, all but one were also in the top fifty for federal R&D support, again showing the concentration of those activities in the same locales. The converse is also the case: of the top ten universities receiving federal R&D funds, seven were in the top twenty-five for doctorates awarded in 2007.[52] Of the universities in the top twenty-five for receiving federal R&D funds in 2012, all but seven were in the top twenty-five for doctoral granting in 2013.[53]

Disaggregated by field of study, however, doctoral degree trends suggest minor shifts: an increase in the life sciences and engineering, a marked decline in the humanities, and slightly less of a decline in the social sciences. The life sciences, the largest single field since 1990, continued to grant the most doctorates (over 11,000 of the 48,000 awarded) in 2008. In 2013, health sciences still led with just under 16 percent of the total, followed by engineering at 14.0 percent, but with education and social and behavioral sciences close behind—at 14 percent and 13 percent, respectively.[54] Federal research funds in science and engineering fields have continued to facilitate their doctoral degree production, although in recent years the funding has not kept up with inflation. Universities also have had to rely on their own funding as well as graduate students' self-support.

Postdoctoral researchers (commonly referred to as "postdocs") have become indispensable to the graduate education–research nexus for their contributions in research, grant writing, publications, and supervising and mentoring graduate students and undergraduates. In some science and engineering fields (especially the biosciences), several years as a postdoc is regarded as a necessary career step for new PhDs, and it has become more common in the social sciences. Educators are concerned that this extended time discourages PhDs from academic careers by prolonging their work in relatively low-status positions for low pay (a beginning postdoc salary or stipend has historically been about one-third of starting salary for faculty) as well as delaying the start of independent projects that are foundational to advancing in the faculty ranks. While skeptics point to this mass of postdocs, over 60,000 just in biomedical fields, as an "academic reserve army of unemployed PhDs," postdoctoral work is a key phase of professional development for research training and mentoring, as well as for generating publications with increasing autonomy.[55]

In the first decade of the twenty-first century, universities continued to perform over half the country's basic research (56% in 2006)—a significant proportion of the overall national R&D effort. Most R&D funds went to development ($206 billion in 2006, compared with $75 billion to applied research and $62 billion to basic research). Nationwide R&D activities doubled, from $171 billion in 1995 to $340 billion in 2006. Of that 2006 total, 28 percent was provided by the federal government and 66 percent by industry. Even though industry became a big performer in R&D, its support for academic research has remained relatively small, close to the level in the mid-1980s. In 2008, colleges and universities were still relying on governmental sources for R&D support, with 60 percent of academic R&D funded by the federal government (roughly the same as forty years previously), 6.5 percent by state and local governments, and 5.5 percent by industry. The most dramatic change was from the universities themselves, covering 20 percent of academic R&D with their own institutional funds.[56] Universities' share of federal basic research funding has remained steady in recent years, despite concern that funding has not kept pace with inflation, and with the prospect of agencies' cuts to existing and new grants, especially the NIH.[57]

The distribution of basic research funds among academic institutions reflects the ongoing concentration of research activity and sponsored research resources noted above. In dollars, by 2007 the top 100 institutions accounted for almost $40 billion—80 percent of all academic R&D expenditures; the top fifty, $27 billion (55%); the top ten, just under $9 billion (17%). Again, research funds have remained concentrated in a top tier of colleges and universities that has been relatively stable. Only five of the top one hundred institutions in 2008 were not on the list twenty years earlier. In FY 2012, the top twenty institutions accounted for over $12 billion of the $40 billion of R&D funding to universities: over 30 percent.[58]

The distribution of academic R&D across fields has also remained stable. Life sciences receives the bulk of R&D funding (60% in 2006, 57% in 2012), followed by engineering (15% in 2006, 16% in 2012), while funding to social sciences declined. Between 1996 and 2006, the life sciences and psychology saw an increased share of R&D funding; the physical sciences had modest increases; engineering decreased slightly, after increases between 1975 and 1996. The social sciences had the largest decrease between 1975 and 1996 (from 7.5% to 3.6% between 1975 and 2006), and decreased further to 2.3 percent in 2012.[59]

The patterns of federal support for doctoral students established at the end of the twentieth century remain largely unchanged today. Since 1971, the share of federal science and engineering funding used for fellowships, research traineeships, and training grants has declined, from a high point of 20 percent of all federal science and engineering funding in 1971 to less than 4 percent in the 2000s.[60] These changes in sources of support have been experienced by successive cohorts of doctoral students since the mid-1970s. Their graduate education became more labor-intensive (working in assistantships) and more reliant on university-funded fellowships and loans. Nearly half of the doctoral recipients in 2008 reported their primary source of financial support as teaching and research assistants; one-quarter relied on fellowships; and one-fifth used their own resources.[61] Variation across fields remains, with those in fields outside the sciences and engineering amassing the greatest education-related debt burdens: in the social sciences (32%), humanities (26%), education (29%), and other non-S&E fields (27%).[62]

The leading research universities, well aware of the uneven and unstable financial base in external sources, keep close tabs on what peer universities offer in financial aid (without violating federal antitrust requirements) to compete for doctoral students. To buffer themselves from changes in external funding sources, not only in financing graduate education but also in research funding, universities have launched their own major fundraising initiatives. Establishing endowed funds for professorships, research institutes, and fellowships in specific fields provides essential income. The scale of success in fundraising is impressive, with graduate fellowships often embedded in larger university campaigns. The University of California at Berkeley's success has been inspiring, generating $3.1 billion in a five-year campaign that concluded in 2014, during one of the worst economic periods since the Great Depression. Stanford University announced the launch of a $4.3 billion campaign in 2006, the largest to date in higher education. Its theme, "Seeking Solutions, Educating Leaders," succinctly depicts the interdependence of research and graduate education and, more significantly, the stark reality that even this top private research university had to turn to alumni and friends to support its core missions. That fundraising goal was exceeded early—with pledges—in 2009. In fact, even with the economic downturn of 2009, when charitable giving to colleges and universities nationwide dropped 12 percent, Stanford brought in $640 million, earning its ranking as the leading fundraising university for the fifth consecutive year.[63] That five-year fundraising campaign concluded with a total of $6.2 billion, far exceeding its goal. The capability of fundraising specifically for endowed graduate fellowships had been proven in Stanford's 1997 pioneering effort to raise $200 million for students in the sciences and engineering—as a buffer from the vagaries of federal funding. The goal was quickly met. By 2010, over 1,500 students had support from these multiyear fellowships, expending about $200 million, and the principal had more than doubled in value. Clearly, endowment payout has become a significant staple to fund graduate education for universities able to attract donors to invest in future academic generations.

## Organized Research Units

In their efforts to broaden their funding base, universities have created extradepartmental research units that reflect specialized areas of interdisciplinary and applied research. In the historical organization of departmental structures, faculty in the departments work both as investigators and as mentors to their advanced graduate students in the department's degree programs. The post–World War II period has given rise to the major exception to this mode of organization, known generically as "the organized research unit" (ORU). Before the twentieth century, ORUs were primarily observatories and museums, but the post–World War II expansion of academic research fueled their proliferation on campuses to meet new societal demands for research that did not correspond with the instructional areas of departments—especially for research projects that were disproportionate to departments in magnitude and expense. Funded by the national government, state governments, industry, and foundations, ORUs over subsequent decades enabled university research to expand into interdisciplinary, applied, and capital-intensive areas. They emerged in biotechnology, artificial intelligence, microelectronics, and materials science, and in fields explicitly aiming to solve social problems such as bioengineering, nanotechnology, neuroscience and imaging, photon science, and global climate and energy.[64]

ORUs have proven effective because they can be visible and highly adaptive. Flexibility is achieved by employing specialists as researchers and technicians on fixed-term appointments, in addition to attracting tenure-track faculty and graduate students. Some of the country's most competitive research universities have ORUs backed by external funding as well as their own institutional funds. By the end of the 1980s, estimates of the number of ORUs ranged from 2,000 to more than 10,000 across US universities. By 2000, estimates ranged from a few dozen to several hundred ORUs at any given university, located within or across schools.

Many universities have also used their own funds to support some of these cost-intensive research activities—including facilities and equipment—in addition to accelerating efforts to collaborate with industry.[65] Industrial sponsorship—whether arranged as ORUs, or as formal or informal collaboration—brings some inherent tensions, given the different norms from academia. Such differences may include the research process (for example, secrecy), the product (for example, negotiation over intellectual property), and exclusivity clauses against the formation of other alliances. These affect research activities, in terms of concerns about a potential blurring of boundaries—if not purposes—between academic researchers and external sponsors. When profit is likely and students are involved, other issues also emerge: while the quasi-exploitation of students for a faculty member's academic advancement is historically grounded in the university research system, it is another matter for a professor to profit financially from a student's work on a commercial venture.[66] That said, these collaborations can provide unique research opportunities for faculty and students alike, as well as facilitating the transfer of knowledge, and they are commonly seen as a win-win so long as these issues are well managed.

As sites of research training for doctoral students, ORUs can provide essential research training while addressing "real world needs and problems."[67] As such, they have proven to be an ideal organizational form for interdisciplinary inquiry. Practically, they may provide dissertation research support and stipends for graduate students. Often better research equipment is available. Finally, as an indirect benefit, they employ specialists—postdoctoral or nonfaculty researchers— in a home akin to that of a department.

This can evoke challenges, however, if it works at cross-purposes with departmental organization. In general, students and younger faculty want the opportunity to work with researchers and state-of-the-art equipment in such a setting. The fear is that ORUs may draw intellectual, organizational, and economic vitality away from department-based graduate programs as faculty and graduate students join these research groups. Research personnel may supervise graduate research assistants, but they do not have faculty status.[68] Graduate students in ORUs may become more distant from their "home" departments, which can also raise competing expectations from faculty in different locations. ORU budgets are typically overseen by different managers than those anchored in departments. This results in complex administrative arrangements for research and research training that fall outside of the department. Even if these concerns can be satisfactorily addressed, ORUs may meet resistance from faculty who advocate for students to have strong disciplinary training first. Thus far into the twenty-first century, enthusiasm for such extra-departmental research is pervasive, because it is seen as cutting edge, and it attracts faculty and students who want to pursue ideas beyond disciplinary boundaries. Participants acquire needed skills as the research unfolds, form collaborations as they see fit, and potentially gain recognition for path-breaking research that will help solve vexing problems. ORU pursuits range widely, from developing advanced energy technologies and finding cures for pervasive illnesses and spinal cord injuries, to addressing global challenges like climate change and cybersecurity.

Despite uncertainties and potential tensions, ORUs are a very effective organizational mechanism to assemble a critical mass of researchers for new projects, and to compete for funding that will support novel investigations that benefit researchers' careers and students' research training. The downside for universities is that, once established, ORUs that use cost-intensive equipment, facilities, and staff infrastructure must be fed by a stable flow of funds. They are also very difficult to close. Thus universities must assess the risks against the benefits, especially in fields with unclear trajectories and high costs. If the undertaking looks daunting for universities and, by their criteria, they cannot afford to do it, they may nonetheless conclude that they cannot afford *not to*— especially if they aim to remain competitive in attracting top faculty and students. Given state economic contexts, there is growing concern about public universities' capacity to keep pace with private universities in this regard. These decisions—just what business a university should be in and which organizational forms are best for pursuing new ideas—have implications for research, research training, degree specializations, and attracting highly sought-after faculty as well as the requisite funding.

### Indirect Costs

Universities recover some of the enormous costs incurred in research by charging external sponsors overhead for infrastructure expenses (such as lighting, heat, and libraries), as the indirect costs of research. Each university negotiates its indirect cost rate with the government to gain an additional percentage for every dollar of government funds; as a result, the rates vary from one campus to the next.[69] For decades, university administrators, faculty researchers, and federal agencies have struggled to reconcile conflicting interests in this arena, fueling internal tensions on campus between faculty, who want as much funding as possible for their research, and administrators, who want a higher indirect cost rate so they can recoup expenses for the infrastructure.

Underlying discussions over insufficient indirect cost recovery is a widespread perception by research university advocates that the instrumentation in university laboratories fares poorly when compared with that in government or commercial laboratories, along with the concern that this may result in a decline in the research productivity of academic scientists as well as in first-rate training opportunities for graduate students. In 2010, advocates for research universities asserted that they bore enormous unreimbursed indirect costs for federally sponsored research, with national estimates of the shortfall to be between $2.5 and $4 billion. In addition to the financial burden of cost-sharing expectations with grants, another concern is over faculty time spent administering research grants, estimated to have increased from 18 to 42 percent from 1990 to 2010.[70]

Public universities that are already stretched financially are clearly not well positioned to afford such unreimbursed costs, especially after budget cuts that forced staff layoffs. This strain jeopardizes the quality of research, research training, and financial support for graduate education. It suggests that, even in the near term, universities may become even more stratified in the quality and reputation of both their academic research and their doctoral education.

A related concern is that universities may miss cutting-edge opportunities if they are unable to provide resources for innovative interdisciplinary research and research training. The fear is that if universities do not have the support to make "some realistic accommodation . . . an increasingly large portion of basic research and academic activity which is necessary to the quality of [graduate] education . . . will move outside the university structure."[71] The long-term issue is that faculty may not have the resources to continue to advance the frontiers of knowledge and that the best researchers may move away from graduate students, thereby jeopardizing a foundational premise of the system—that "the best and the brightest" produce the best science and the best new generation of scientists, at universities regarded as centers of excellence.

### Consequences for Graduate Students

Over the past four decades, graduate education has become more expensive, and yet—as noted—its funding base has evolved in unanticipated ways. This has been most evident for PhD students in the sciences, at the heart of the research funding and federal government nexus. Uncertainties have deeply affected their research training experiences, principally while funded on research assistantships. Even more acutely, without federal support, PhD students in the humanities have had teaching assistantships as their major source of financial aid, especially on campuses without resources for fellowships. Uncertainty over funding is one among many factors known to impact PhD student attrition, estimated to be as high as 50 percent nationally, albeit with variation across fields and institutions.[72]

How graduate education is financed has obvious implications for time to degree completion. In 1983, the median time for doctoral recipients was 8.2 years, and it increased to 8.7 years a decade later. Yet in recent years the trend has moved in the opposite direction: 8.5 by 2003 and 7.7 in 2008. This could be due to more students in fields with faster times to degree, or in fields with more international students, who have strong incentives to finish more quickly (i.e., those on temporary visas are ineligible for direct federal aid and their spouses cannot work). The median time also obscures substantial differences across fields of study. In 2008, the field of education took the longest (a median of 12.7 years), and physical sciences and engineering had the least time (6.7 years).[73] Times to degree have held steady in the physical sciences and engineering to 2010.[74] Beyond factors intrinsic to differences in disciplinary research, an unstable and unequal funding base is clearly a major factor. In disciplines without research funds, such as the humanities, or with declining research support (education, social sciences), doctoral students rely on teaching assistantships and self-support. Their quest for funding is distinct from their research rather than advancing their progress to degree, as in the sciences.

High loan debt for graduate students has been a concern for decades, as noted above. Students acquire more loan debt the longer they defer employment, and they become discouraged from the loss of momentum. In an effort to speed up the process, some programs have reduced requirements for coursework, so that students begin working on their dissertations earlier. The University of Chicago instituted a reduced-coursework policy in 1982 to encourage students "to engage in their doctoral research as quickly, as clearly, and as self-consciously as possible," which would lead to "a healthier emphasis on the research stage of graduate student work."[75] The need for change has become especially pressing in the humanities, where adapting to knowledge change has tended to be cumulative—with more material to incorporate into graduate course work—while in the sciences, for example in physics and the biological sciences, the faculty revamp the curricula more often. Along similar lines, expectations for the dissertation may be revised, as seen thus far in the sciences and in economics, where a compilation of published or publishable research articles (usually with a framing introduction and conclusion) has become common.[76] Such changes help students make a smoother transition to a faculty position, with material ready for submission to a peer-reviewed journal, or a dissertation ready for a book contract in fields where that is the currency. Competitive pressures have ratcheted up expectations, to the point that students even at the leading universities ask themselves how they can compete. The tendency is to stay longer to do ever more.

Studies documenting the overproduction of doctorates in science and engineering supplement the already bleak picture for new PhDs in the humanities and social sciences, who are disheartened by an unfavorable academic labor market. Most recently, the legitimacy of doctoral study in humanities has been questioned with a sense of urgency, yielding recommendations to redesign degree requirements, expand preparation for teaching and other professional skills, and provide resources for careers beyond the academic workforce.[77] In the absence of projections for an academic hiring boom, some faculty across disciplines have begun working with doctoral students earlier in their programs to prepare them for alternatives to an academic career. Some programs have been more transparent in providing prospective students with PhD alumni career employment data. Nationally and institutionally, career pathways of PhDs have become a focus for study.[78] Some programs have reduced the number of PhD admits.

Many universities have replaced some tenure-track positions with "off-track" full-time and part-time positions, commonly referred to as "contingent" faculty. Borrowed from the discourse on labor, this term reflects concerns about job security for contingent workers, and about exploitation of these highly skilled individuals. Yet the trend is advantageous for the hiring organizations, giving them flexibility to adapt to changing student interests. From roughly 1975 to 2007, the percentage of tenure-track faculty declined from 57 to 31 percent, according to the American Association of University Professors. Current estimates are that more than two-thirds of new hires are not tenure track. The economic crisis that hit in 2009 left universities eliminating jobs or freezing faculty hiring: according to the *Chronicle of Higher Education*, at the end of 2012, 70 percent of faculty at colleges across the United States were off the tenure track.[79] The significance of this sea change can hardly be overstated; it alters the very nature of the enterprise.

Over decades of federal research sponsorship, an even less visible and yet potentially more profound transformation has occurred in the nature of student-faculty relationships during research training, especially for students in the sciences. While the historical ideal entailed a student working "at the bench" with a mentor, sponsored research became the central medium for supervision and collaboration. Concerns have been raised that faculty have become more like project managers and administrators than mentor-professors, and that students are supervised in a more directive manner—treated like employees and technicians rather than as apprentices. As one observer suggests, "the roles of faculty member (mentor) and principal investigator (employer) are becoming inconsistent, straining the incumbents. Principles and practices that the mentor would prefer are inconsistent with the needs of the scientist as employer."[80]

While the flow of federal research funds to the sciences and engineering may appear preferable to conditions in the humanities and social sciences, increased competition for research grants has squeezed professors into developing leaner budgets with tighter time constraints. This has dramatic consequences for graduate students, as they too face the exigencies of an increasingly competitive arena of research support. The schedules of short-term grants leave less leeway for mistakes; less available grant monies create competitive pressures to produce better results; sharing capital-intensive instrumentation means longer hours of work, often in other geographic locations; the increased size of research teams entails perfecting a technique on one part of a project, rather than completing an entire project from beginning to end; and time spent in research is valued over time spent teaching younger students—or time for family responsibilities, since nowadays more doctoral students are older and have families. The contemporary arrangements call for an unprecedented intensity for students and faculty alike.

One manifestation of this can be found in the organizing efforts of graduate students to gain bargaining status as employees.[81] Changes in the academic workplace, along with momentum from faculty collective-bargaining activities, strengthened the willingness and ability of graduate students to unionize. In the 1970s, dismal labor market prospects for emerging PhDs exacerbated graduate students' concerns about a longer time to degree. These concerns were amplified into the 1980s and 1990s, due to students' higher levels of financial debt, their perceptions of inadequate faculty advising, and the stark realization that benefits accrued to universities as a result of the institutions' leveraging faculty time through the "cheap labor" of graduate assistants. In 1989, graduate students founded the National Association of Graduate-Professional Students to advocate for improved living and working conditions. By the end of the 1990s, these factors contributed to a growing awareness of discrepancies between ideals and realities, and at the national level, fostered widespread discussions about the quality of doctoral education.[82]

In 2001, a key ruling by the National Labor Relations Board (NLRB) reversed precedent on the collective bargaining rights of graduate students. That decision found that graduate students who hold positions as teaching or research assistants, or similar titles, were eligible to unionize; other graduate students were not suited to making the case that they were employees. Estimates are that more than 40,000 graduate students at close to 50 universities have been involved in organizing drives or have formal collective bargaining representation (31 are officially recognized); more than 16,000 of these were members of the United Auto Workers (UAW).[83] However, graduate student unionization efforts were dealt a serious blow by a 2004 NLRB ruling that reversed the 2001 regional decision, stating that graduate students at private universities were not employees and thus lacked the right to collective bargaining.[84] While recognizing that state law permits collective bargaining at public universities, the NLRB chose to impose a single federal standard on the private universities under its jurisdiction. Graduate students continue to organize themselves, but private universities are under no legal obligation to negotiate. Yet, observers note the NLRB has "flip-flopped on the issue." And in 2015 it indicated interest in unionizing activity by TAs at Columbia University and the New School to see if they are sufficiently different from those at Brown in 2004, even if not reversing the Brown ruling.[85] To underscore the high stakes, the graduate dean of arts and sciences at New York University voiced a view widely held among academic leaders, expressing skepticism about the UAW's promises of what a graduate union could do there: "At heart, what matters in the university are academic values, and I am wary of any force that might corrode them."[86]

By the end of the first decade of the twenty-first century, the worst financial crisis since the Great Depression had widespread impacts on every part of higher education, and has had long-term repercussions for many. This is so despite a very short-term one-time gain from some of the federal government's $787 billion in stimulus funding.[87] Universities have used cost-saving measures such as budget cuts to core academic programs, enrollment reductions, hiring freezes, and layoffs and furloughs for full-time employees, including tenure-line faculty. Morale on campuses has been low, especially at public universities. The job outlook is bleak for students soon to complete their degrees, especially those seeking to launch academic careers. Finding a decent job—let alone a dream job—seems unattainable. Reminiscent of the 1970s, faculty and staff are helping doctoral students consider options for using their skills in nonacademic careers. These differ by field, of course: biotechnology expertise has applications in industry, whereas humanists may work in the private sector given their communication skills, and historians may turn to nonprofits to do public history—for example, in museums, libraries, foundations, and government agencies. This prompts universities to consider adjusting doctoral admissions to match fluctuations in demand, not only to adjust to changes in the flow of research funds.

As for American graduate education's standing worldwide, roughly one-third of US graduate enrollment is international, having risen since the decline that immediately followed the devastating terrorist attacks of September 11, 2001. By 2007, international students accounted for a significant proportion of the graduate degrees in science and engineering, receiving one in four master's degrees and one in three doctorates. The top countries of origin for international graduate students are China, India, South Korea, and Taiwan; together, they account for about 20 percent of doctorates awarded. Historically, the infusion of international talent has reached well beyond graduate education and university research, bringing significant innovations into the economy, especially in those areas that draw on engineering expertise. Indeed, the United States has grown so dependent on international talent that analysts are concerned that the United States is losing its market share in the global pool of mobile students, having already declined from 25 to 16 percent of the total in 2012.[88] Although some of that decline is attributed to an increase in sheer numbers, other countries have become more proactive in attracting talented students from abroad, and the United States lacks an overall strategy in this arena.[89]

As these varied changes and open questions reveal, continuity in the structures of graduate education and academic research are by no means assured. Yet despite the tensions inherent in these interdependencies and the frustrations expressed over a lack of progress on resolving some persistent issues, the continued success of the US arrangements remains undisputed. Visitors from around the world continue to regard ours as exemplary practices, because of our impressive track record of producing highly skilled and thoughtful leaders while making dramatic advances in knowledge and innovative technologies for the new economy.

## Master's Degree Programs and Graduate Certificates

Aside from the research foundations of graduate education, a distinct set of dynamics has propelled post-baccalaureate education in new directions. Student demand for career-oriented, skills-focused credentials has aligned with institutional interests to increase graduate enrollment. Post-baccalaureate education that is more applied, technical, or explicitly aligned with occupations is typically paid for by students themselves or by their employers. These programs may have few if any ties to traditional departments, faculty research, and doctoral education, and they are often administered separately. They may be offered primarily or entirely online, and at or through institutions of all types (public, private, for-profit). The forces behind this broad and varied activity are intertwined with the trends discussed thus far.

Nationally, the magnitude of interest and participation in master's degree programs on the part of students and employers has not often been foregrounded as a strength of US higher education, despite increased breadth and undisputed gains in their market value. As one indicator of expansion, the annual production of master's degrees more than doubled over two decades, from 290,000 in

1987 to 630,000 in 2007, and more recently to over 750,000.[90] Growth persisted over economic cycles, even as institutions orchestrated rounds of budget cuts and determined where to selectively reinvest. This growth became a major current in a larger pattern of academic restructuring that gained momentum from expectations in the wider society, reflecting an industry logic that prioritized higher education's role in advancing economic development and helping students cultivate specialized skills to align with workforce needs, even at the level of advanced study.[91] It reflects interest in career advancement, including among older students returning to school or starting second (or more) careers. As for-profits like the University of Phoenix grew, they cherry-picked lucrative master's degree programs in high demand, such as business, psychology, technology, and healthcare.[92]

Nationwide, as academic program offerings have adapted to market conditions, post-baccalaureate activities also took the form of short courses leading to graduate certificates, estimated at 35,000 granted per year in 2014, and appear to be gaining momentum rapidly, as they have at lower levels of higher education. In need of credentials that will increase their earnings, student-consumers are seeking more cost-effective learning opportunities. Prospective employers unquestionably value post-baccalaureate study, which has created a wide-open field for graduate certificates. Undergraduate degrees no longer mean as much as they once did: the greater the percentage of the general population that earns them, the more they became like high school diplomas. Even those already holding master's degrees have been attracted to further study, especially to short courses that grant graduate certificates, as a way to distinguish themselves in a competitive job market, while learning advanced skills quickly in applied, technical, and business areas. Topics range widely and include emerging areas such as digital media, data science, health management, global studies, and cybersecurity. In addition to the path to higher salaries, some graduate certificate programs have been regarded as a potential gateway to further graduate study, possibly to count later toward a degree program. Even Harvard offers professional graduate certificates through its Extension School, in areas such as bioinformatics, corporate finance, nanotechnology, sustainability, software engineering, and web technologies.[93]

The growing demand indicates that students are eager to study subjects that most directly improve their competitiveness, advance their careers, and boost their salaries. Broader, more flexible graduate offerings can also benefit any given college or university by generating revenue, allowing the hiring of instructors on a short-term basis, and providing supplemental pay for regular faculty. However, institutions should be wary of unanticipated costs, both financial and to their reputation. Some uniformity of expectations may be advisable, along with establishing the appropriate infrastructure. Those already offering extension courses or executive education programs may most easily adapt their infrastructure to coordinate the graduate certificate programs, and most likely have already learned that costs for distance learning are real and can be prohibitive. While master's degree programs have demonstrated their staying power, both feasible institutionally and beneficial to students, there's no verdict yet on graduate certificates—on how widely they will be perceived as valuable and whether they will retain their value into the future. Depending on one's vantage point, the swift proliferation of graduate certificate activities may be seen as enhancing graduate study—or diluting it into bite-sized commodities.

## Conclusion: Changing Conduct in Changing Contexts

The trajectory of historical development in the United States is clear: graduate education became so intertwined with sponsored research that the two emerged as the foremost raison d'être for universities in the top tier, as an increasingly noble aim for lower tiers to strive to achieve, and as an implicit professional imperative for research university faculty. Historical scholarship reveals that obtaining research funds from the federal government and other patrons has been a requirement for university expansion and competitive advancement. As universities aggressively vied for talented faculty and graduate students, they have sought to preserve their autonomy by stabilizing a funding base from a plurality of sources—including a range of external sponsors, philanthropic support, and internal revenue-generating activities. Over time, universities initiated fundraising to amass significant endowments, knowing that these would yield discretionary resources and thereby minimize the skewing of institutional priorities toward the incentives of short-term R&D sponsors, in addition to buffering them from the ebb and flow of external funding.

Nonetheless, in recent decades universities have been continually challenged by uncertainty, as federal funds have concentrated support for doctoral education in the physical and life sciences and in engineering, provided far less to the social sciences, and remain virtually nonexistent in the humanities. Over the past four decades, uncertainty became the norm in federally funded fellowships and traineeships, leaving individual students relying on university funds and loans. The bulk of federal support has become indirect—through research assistantships on short-term R&D projects that strain the ideals of the mentor-apprentice relationship. Academic ideals have been challenged by research training activities that create finer status distinctions among students to secure support from "the right" principal investigators on "cutting-edge" and well-funded research projects. To the extent that doctoral education functions as professional socialization, a distinctive portrait of very demanding and competitive professional work is the model for students in those fields. Research, and hence research training, has been defined by increased competition for peer-reviewed grants, a situation where faculty submit many more proposals than are awarded, where research is conducted on faster clocks with higher stakes, and where sponsors' agenda are magnets for faculty and student engagement that may or may not reflect their passionate interests nor advance them in their fields of study. This raises the question, for what career paths are graduate students being prepared?

The aim of this analysis has been to identify the structural foundations in the interdependence of graduate education and research, and to show some of the developments over recent decades and the effects therein. While the tone may not be optimistic, the long view of this enterprise clearly underscores the remarkable resilience demonstrated by universities, their faculty, and the generations of graduate students who have proceeded with ground-breaking research and research training despite fluctuating resources and uncertain futures. Of course, the future organization and sponsorship of graduate education requires careful collective deliberation. A host of issues must be addressed about the conduct and operation of the enterprise, beyond basic decisions as to which graduate degree programs a campus should offer. These include the adequacy of financial aid mechanisms, the demographics of incoming students, the adequacy of advising and mentoring for academic and nonacademic careers, the expectations for research and teaching assistantships across the disciplines, the factors contributing to attrition and long time to degree, the neglect of humanities and non-science fields by external funders, the appropriateness of industrial sponsorship that is explicitly for profit, and the ownership of intellectual property. The issues are not strictly about efficient means, but also about desirable ends.

Admittedly, to say that graduate education is paying a price for its links to the university research enterprise marks a distinctive shift in scholarly attention away from highlighting what accounts for the remarkable success of this world-renowned enterprise. Usually, among the inseparable interdependencies within universities, undergraduate education is often characterized as diminished, given all the time and resources focused on faculty research.[94] In truth, the argument can be made that each of these components is suffering. With greater frequency, scholars critically examine other costs and potential tradeoffs in academic science, with crucial consequences for the vitality of the academic profession.[95] Efforts to pursue these and related lines of inquiry in graduate education have been hampered by incomplete longitudinal data, and by work that may be in-depth but provides only a snapshot of one point in time. Over the past few decades, national data are collected more consistently and thus lend themselves to trend analyses.[96] However, such databases have substantial limitations for addressing qualitative concerns. Fortunately, some major foundations have supported initiatives that include interventions, in the hope of improving the quality of doctoral education and reducing attrition, as well as diversifying the pipeline for STEM fields.[97]

Moreover, posing perhaps a more formidable obstacle than data availability, deliberation on these high-stakes issues is undermined by the complex and problematic interdependence between graduate education and sponsored research at the national level. There is no clear leverage point for change. Analytically, we can see how the wider society's demands on the social functions of higher education have been changing: graduate education is immersed in an institutional enterprise that produces goods and services, determines expertise, distributes resources, and regulates the uses of and access to knowledge and power. At the center of this enterprise, faculty and their universities continue to carry out their multiple roles while preparing the next generation for the academic profession, among other careers, and conveying to them—either explicitly or implicitly—what is taken for granted about the tensions experienced daily. University faculty display exceptional resilience and ingenuity to stay the course, often creatively leveraging limited resources, including their own time and energy, over decades. Nonetheless it is clear that economic and political challenges will continue to fuel internal tensions in universities, and thus risk dismantling the longstanding humanistic ideals of knowledge creation for its own sake in favor of purposes that, at their worst, resemble a short-sighted opportunism. Too much is at stake in the years to come—the education of the next generation, the trajectory of faculty careers, the infrastructure of universities, the advancement of knowledge—for us to forego further analyses of these issues. Higher education researchers can play a central role in promoting such informed and thoughtful deliberation.

NOTES

1. Examples drawn from *Chronicle of Higher Education* archives, 2005–15. Despite more widespread activities, graduate student unions are officially recognized at only thirty-one US universities.

2. Patricia J. Gumport, "Built to Serve: The Enduring Legacy of Public Higher Education," in *In Defense of American Higher Education*, ed. P. Altbach, P. Gumport and B. Johnstone (Baltimore: Johns Hopkins University Press, 2001).

3. As to the question of universities retaining autonomy amid a plurality of sponsors, for celebratory and critical interpretations, respectively, see Roger L. Geiger, *To Advance Knowledge: The Growth of American Research Universities, 1900–1940* (New York: Oxford University Press, 1986); and David F. Noble, *America by Design: Science, Technology, and the Rise of Corporate Capitalism* (New York: Alfred Knopf, 1977). Scholars have separately documented the rise of modern American science—Robert V. Bruce, *The Launching of Modern American Science: 1846–1876* (New York: Alfred Knopf, 1987); the emergence of the American research university—Geiger, *To Advance Knowledge*, and Laurence Veysey, *The Emergence of the American University* (Chicago: University of Chicago Press, 1965); the emergence of graduate education—Richard J. Storr, *The Beginnings of Graduate Education in America* (Chicago: University of Chicago Press, 1953), and Bernard Berelson, *Graduate Education in the United States* (New York: McGraw-Hill, 1960); and postwar changes in federal support of academic science—John T. Wilson, *Academic Science, Higher Education, and the Federal Government, 1950–1983* (Chicago: University of Chicago Press, 1983).

4. The shift is evident beyond research universities; see Françoise A. Quéval, "The Evolution toward Research Orientation and Capability in Comprehensive Universities," PhD diss., University of California, Los Angeles, 1990.

5. Patricia J. Gumport, "Learning Academic Labor," *Comparative Social Research* 19 (2000): 1–23.

6. Little scholarly work has been done at the intersection of these arenas to examine their interrelationship. The major exceptions are Joseph Ben-David, *Centers of Learning: Britain, France, Germany, United States* (New York: McGraw-Hill, 1977); and Burton R. Clark, *Places of Inquiry* (Berkeley: University of California Press, 1995). For a review essay, see Gary D. Malaney, "Graduate Education as an Area of Research in the Field of Higher Education," in *Higher Education: Handbook of Theory and Research*, ed. John C. Smart (New York: Agathon, 1988), vol. 4, 397–454. Most research since then has focused on doctoral students, drawing on national data or retrospective accounts. See, for example, William G. Bowen and Neil L. Rudenstine, *In Pursuit of the PhD* (Princeton, NJ: Princeton University Press, 1992); Michael T. Nettles and Catherine M. Millet, *Three Magic Letters: Getting to PhD* (Baltimore: Johns Hopkins University Press, 2006); Barbara E. Lovitts, *Leaving the Ivory Tower: The Causes and Consequences of Departure from Doctoral Study* (Lanham, MD: Rowman and Littlefield, 2001); and George E. Walker, Chris M. Golde, Laura Jones, Andrea Conklin Bueschel, and Pat Hutchings, *The Formation of Scholars: Rethinking Doctoral Education for the Twenty-First Century* (San Francisco: Jossey-Bass, 2008); and longitudinal reports on PhD career paths and outcomes from the Center for Innovation and Research in Graduate Educaiton. The graduate education–research nexus is undertheorized, except as it is defined by the political economy; see Sheila A.

Slaughter and Gary Rhoades, *Academic Capitalism and the New Economy* (Baltimore: Johns Hopkins University Press, 2004).

7. Institutional data are from The Carnegie Classification of Institutions of Higher Education, *Summary Tables, Graduate Instructional Program Classification*, "Distribution of Institutions and enrollments by classification category," http://carnegieclassifications .iu.edu/summary/grad_prog.php [accessed Jan. 6, 2015]; The National Center for Educational Statistics, *Digest of Education Statistics*, table 318.20 (2013), http://nces.ed.gov /programs/digest/d13/tables/dt13_318.20.asp [accessed Dec. 19, 2014]; and Jeff Allum, "Graduate enrollment and degrees: 2003 to 2013," *Council of Graduate Schools* (Sept. 2014), http://www.cgsnet.org/ckfinder/userfiles/files/GED_report_2013.pdf [accessed Dec. 19, 2014]. R&D data is from the National Science Foundation (NSF), Division of Science Resource Statistics, *Academic Research and Development Expenditures: Fiscal Year 2007*, NSF 09-303, Mar. (Arlington, VA: National Science Foundation, 2008).

8. Clark, *Places of Inquiry*. The term "elbow learning" refers to students and faculty working side by side in labs, dating back to G. Stanley Hall, Clark University's first president and himself a well-regarded mentor; see Walker et al., *Formation of Scholars*, 117.

9. Charles P. Snow, *The Two Cultures* (New York: Cambridge University Press, 1959); Tony Becher, "The Cultural View," in *Perspectives on Higher Education: Eight Disciplinary and Comparative Views*, ed. Burton R. Clark (Berkeley: University of California Press, 1984), 165–98; Walter P. Metzger, "The Academic Profession in the United States," in *The Academic Profession: National, Disciplinary, and Institutional Settings*, ed. Burton R. Clark (Berkeley: University of California Press, 1987), 123–208.

10. Nevitt Sanford, "Graduate Education: Then and Now," in *Scholars in the Making*, ed. Joseph Katz and Rodney T. Harnett (Lexington, MA: Ballinger, 1976), 250–51.

11. NSF/SRS, *Academic Research & Development Expenditures: FY 2007*; NSF/SRS, *Academic Research & Development Expenditures: FY 2000*, NSF 02-308 (Arlington, VA: National Science Foundation, 2002); National Science Foundation, National Center for Science and Engineering Statistics, *Higher Education Research and Development Survey, Fiscal Year 2012*, table 5, http://ncsesdata.nsf.gov/herd/2012/html/HERD2012_DST_05 .html [accessed Jan. 4, 2015].

12. See Bruce, *The Launching of Modern American Science*, 335–338. The earliest signs of doctoral education in the United States were in 1861, when the first PhDs were awarded by Yale's Sheffield Scientific School. More significant were the incorporation of an explicit mission for graduate education in the opening of Johns Hopkins University in 1876 and the founding of Clark University in 1887 as the first all-graduate school in the United States; Christopher Jencks and David Riesman, *The Academic Revolution* (Chicago, IL: The University of Chicago Press, 1977, 2nd ed.), 13.

13. Dael Lee Wolfle, *The Home of Science: The Role of the University* (New York: McGraw-Hill, 1972), 4.

14. Veysey, *Emergence of the American University*, 149, 168, 318–19.

15. Richard Hofstadter and C. DeWitt Hardy, *The Development and Scope of Higher Education in the United States* (New York: Columbia University Press, 1952), 44–45; Berelson, *Graduate Education*, 33.

16. Lewis B. Mayhew, *Reform in Graduate Education*, SREB Research Monograph No. 18 (Atlanta: Southern Regional Education Board, 1972), 6; Ben-David, *Centers of*

*Learning*, 61. See also Burton R. Clark, *The Higher Education System* (Berkeley: University of California Press, 1983).

17. Geiger, *To Advance Knowledge*, 37; Ben-David, *Centers of Learning*, 61.

18. Veysey, *Emergence of the American University*, 177.

19. Geiger, *To Advance Knowledge*, 19.

20. Robert K. Merton, "The Matthew Effect in Science," *Science* 159 (Jan. 1968): 56–63.

21. Martin Trow, "The Analysis of Status," in Clark, *Perspectives on Higher Education*, 134; see also Veysey, *Emergence of the American University*, 312.

22. Bruce, *Launching of Modern American Science*, 329–34; Fredrick Rudolph, *The American College and University* (New York: Vintage/Random House, 1962), 425–27.

23. Berelson, *Graduate Education*; Geiger, *To Advance Knowledge*, esp. 166.

24. Undertaking applied research activity also became incorporated into the ideal of service, especially for faculty in public universities. See Noble, *America by Design*; Gary Rhoades and Sheila A. Slaughter, "The Public Interest and Professional Labor," in *Culture and Ideology in Higher Education*, ed. William G. Tierney (New York: Praeger, 1991).

25. Geiger, *To Advance Knowledge*, 174–225.

26. Ibid., 262.

27. Over the next decade, NAS became the site of severe conflicts over membership—limited to fifty—and mission, as American scientists from different fields vied for control of the scientific community; see Bruce, *The Launching of Modern American Science*, 301–5, 315–17.

28. Geiger, *To Advance Knowledge*, 13, 100, 165, 256.

29. Paul Starr, *The Social Transformation of American Medicine* (New York: Basic Books, 1982), 193.

30. Wolfle, *Home of Science*, 110; David Dickson, *The New Politics of Science* (Chicago: University of Chicago Press, 1984); Alice M. Rivlin, *The Role of the Federal Government in Financing Higher Education* (Washington, DC: Brookings Institution, 1961), 31.

31. Martin J. Finkelstein, *The American Academic Profession* (Columbus: Ohio State University Press, 1984), 24.

32. Geiger, *To Advance Knowledge*, 220.

33. Rivlin, *The Role of the Federal Government*, 47.

34. Dickson, *New Politics of Science*; Government-University-Industry Research Roundtable, *Science and Technology in the Academic Enterprise* (Washington, DC: National Academy Press, 1989).

35. Government-University-Industry Research Roundtable, *Science and Technology*; Ben-David, *Centers of Learning*, 119.

36. Douglas M. Knight, ed., *The Federal Government and Higher Education* (Englewood Cliffs, NJ: Prentice Hall, 1960), 135–37.

37. Estimate by Porter E. Coggeshall and Prudence W. Brown, *The Career Achievements of NIH Postdoctoral Trainees and Fellows*; NIH 85-2744 (Washington, DC: National Academy Press, 1984).

38. Berelson, *Graduate Education*; National Research Council [NRC], *Summary Report 1986: Doctorate Recipients from United States Universities* (Washington, DC: National Academy Press, 1987); US Department of Education, *Digest of Education Statistics 1989*

(Washington, DC: National Center for Education Statistics, 1989); Judith S. Glazer, *The Master's Degree: Tradition, Diversity, Innovation*, ASHE-ERIC Higher Education Report No. 6 (Washington, DC: Association for the Study of Higher Education, 1986).

39. NRC, *Summary Report 1986*; Berelson, *Graduate Education*, 35; Glazer, *Master's Degree*. Education and business remained the largest fields at 29 and 23 percent, respectively, in 2007–8; see Nathan E. Bell, *Graduate Enrollment and Degrees: 1998 to 2008* (Washington, DC: Council of Graduate Schools, 2009).

40. Rudolph, *American College and University*, 239; see also Patricia J. Gumport, "The Research Imperative," in Tierney, *Culture and Ideology*, 87–106.

41. Ben-David, *Centers of Learning*, 124.

42. Government-University-Industry Research Roundtable, *Science and Technology*.

43. Charles V. Kidd, "Graduate Education: The New Debate," *Change* 6 (May 1974): 43; Wolfle, *Home of Science*, 256; Frederick E. Balderston, "Organization, Funding, Incentives, and Initiatives for University Research," in *The Economics of American Universities*, ed. Stephen A. Hoenack and Eileen L. Collins (Albany: State University of New York Press, 1990), 40; Arthur M. Hauptman, *Students in Graduate and Professional Education* (Washington, DC: Association of American Universities, 1986); Sheila A. Slaughter, "The Official Ideology of Higher Education," in Tierney, *Culture and Ideology*, 59–86.

44. Balderston, "Organization, Funding, Incentives, and Initiatives," 40.

45. Kidd, "Graduate Education"; Hauptman, *Students in Graduate and Professional Education*.

46. They succeeded in an exemption for direct educational expenses—for tuition, books, materials, and equipment used in pursuit of an academic degree; see "Tax Law Shrinks Stipends," *Scientist*, 1, no. 23 (Oct. 18, 1987): 1.

47. Mark K. Feigener, *Numbers of US Doctorates Awarded Rise for Sixth Year, but Growth Slower*, Science Resource Statistics Info Brief, NSF 10-308, Nov. (Arlington, VA: National Science Foundation, 2009); NSF/SRS, *Doctorate Recipients from US Universities: Summary Report 1999*, SRS 01-339 (Chicago: National Opinion Research Center); NRC, *Summary Report 1986*.

48. "Survey of Earned Doctorates," reported in Lori Thurgood, Mary J. Golladay, and Susan Hill, *US Doctorates in the 20th Century*, NSF 06-319, June (Washington, DC: National Science Foundation, Division of Science Resource Statistics, 2006).

49. Catherine Hill, Christianne Corbett, and Andresse St. Rose, *Why So Few? Women in Science, Technology, Engineering, and Mathematics* (Washington, DC: American Association of University Women, 2010).

50. National Science Board [NSB], *Science and Engineering Indicators 2010*, NSB 10-01 (Arlington, VA: National Science Foundation, 2010).

51. Stanford University has two such doctoral fellowship programs: Diversifying Academia, Recruiting Excellence (DARE) for advanced PhD students, and Enhancing Diversity in Graduate Education (EDGE) for incoming PhD students. Each program provides funding; aims to increase students' knowledge, skills, and confidence; and fosters community through peer mentoring.

52. NSF/SRS, *Doctorate Recipients 2007–08*; NSF/SRS, *Academic Research & Development Expenditures: FY 2007*, NSF 09-303, Mar. (Arlington, VA: National Science Foundation, 2009).

53. NSF, *S&E Doctorates*, table 3.

54. Doctoral degree production figures between 1978 and 2008 show large increases in the share of doctorates earned in the life sciences, physical sciences, and engineering, while the relative share of doctorates in the humanities, social sciences, and education decreased. The last decade, from 2003 to 2013, has seen continuing increases in health sciences (7.7%), biological and agriculture sciences (2.8%), engineering (2.7%), and mathematics and computer sciences (2.7%); with minor increases in most other fields. CGS, Allum, *Graduate enrollment*, table 2.25, 49, table 3.7, 89.

55. Some national data on postdocs are estimates that understate the totals when they count only those with PhDs from US universities. Nonetheless, this total more than doubled, from 18,000 in 1981 to 39,000 in 1998; within that total, about 75 percent worked in educational institutions, 12 percent in government, and 11 percent in industry. By some counts, over half are foreign-born, most on temporary visas. See Thomas B. Hoffer, Karen Grigorian, and Eric Hedberg, *Postdoc Participation of Science, Engineering, and Health Doctorate Recipients*, Science Resource Statistics Info Brief, NSF 08-307, Mar. (Arlington, VA: National Science Foundation, 2008); and Committee on Science, Engineering, and Public Policy, *Enhancing the Postdoctoral Experience for Scientists and Engineers* (Washington, DC: National Academy Press, 2000). Nationally, up to three-quarters of these postdocs are estimated to be funded by federal grants, revealing their centrality to the research enterprise. Persistent dismay over the low beginning salaries of postdocs is evident in a significant report that urged NIH to increase its minimum annual stipend to $50,000: *The Postdoctoral Experience Revisited* (Washington, DC: National Academy Press, 2014), following up on the NIH Biomedical Workforce Report of 2012. For FY15 it was increased to only $42,840, citing limited funding.

56. Data from NSB, *Science and Engineering Indicators 2008*, 2 vols., NSB 08-01 (vol. 1) and NSB 08-01A (vol. 2: appendix tables), Jan. (Arlington, VA: National Science Foundation, 2008); Jaquelina C. Falkenheim and Mark K. Fiegnener, *2007 Records Fifth Consecutive Annual Increase in US Doctoral Awards*, Science Resource Statistics Info Brief, NSF 09-307, Nov. (Arlington, VA: National Science Foundation, 2008).

57. Michael Yamaner, "Federal Funding for Basic Research at Universities and Colleges Essentially Unchanged in FY 2012," *NSF 14-318* (Sept. 2014), http://www.nsf.gov/statistics/infbrief/nsf14318/[accessed Jan. 6, 2015].

58. NSF/NCSES, *HERD*, table 5. Interest in facilitating a wider geographic distribution of federal funds for academic research has been a recurring topic in Congress, exemplified by the 1978 authorization for the NSF to establish an Experimental Program to Stimulate Competitive Research, and it still exists in 2015. http://www.nsf.gov/od/iia/programs/epscor/nsf_oiia_epscor_index.jsp [accessed June 22, 2015].

59. NSF/SRS, *Academic Research & Development Expenditures: FY 2007*; NSB, *Science and Engineering Indicators 2008*; NSF/NCSES, *HERD*, table 3.

60. NSF/SRS, *Federal Science and Engineering Support to Universities, Colleges, and Nonprofit Institutions: FY 2007, NSF 09-315* (Arlington, VA: National Science Foundation, 2007).

61. Disaggregating the data by field of study reveals major differences in the experiences of graduate students. Assistantships (research or teaching) have been the most common form of support in the physical sciences (74%) and engineering (70%). In con-

trast, less than half of doctoral graduates in the life sciences (44%), social sciences (42%), and humanities (37%)—and even fewer in education (18%)—report assistantships as their primary source of support. Fellowships are most common in the life sciences (42%), humanities (38%), and social sciences (28%), followed by engineering (21%), physical sciences (19%), and education (11%). Personal sources (including loans) are the dominant form of support for education graduates (60%), and such sources are also relied upon by graduates in the humanities (23%) and social sciences (27%). NSF/SRS, *Doctorate Recipients 2007–08.*

62. NSF, *Doctorate Recipients from US Universities 2010, Survey of Earned Doctorates,* 8–9, http://www.nsf.gov/statistics/sed/digest/2010/nsf12305.pdf [accessed Jan. 8, 2015].

63. Council for Aid to Education, press release, Feb. 3, 2010.

64. Roger L. Geiger, "Organized Research Units: Their Role in the Development of University Research," *Journal of Higher Education* 61 (Jan./Feb. 1990): 1–19. See also Gerald J. Stahler and William R. Tash, "Centers and Institutes in the Research University," *Journal of Higher Education* 65 (Sept./Oct. 1994): 540–54.

65. ORUs were viewed as a way to replace federal support with industrial sponsorship. Federal initiatives were launched to encourage industry to fund campus-based, larger-scale operations. In the mid-1970s, NSF established the Industry-University Cooperative Research Projects. In the late 1980s, NSF promoted proposals for the university-based Engineering Research Centers, as well as the Science and Technology Centers. These programs were to be funded initially by congressional appropriations, and then to be gradually weaned from NSF funds to industry.

66. Martin Kenney, *Biotechnology: The University-Industrial Complex* (New Haven, CT: Yale University Press, 1986), 118–21.

67. Robert S. Friedman and Renee C. Friedman, "Organized Research Units in Academe Revisited," in *Managing High Technology: An Interdisciplinary Perspective,* ed. Brian W. Mar, William T. Newell, and Börje Saxberg (Amsterdam, Netherlands: Elsevier Science, 1985), 75–91.

68. See Clark Kerr, *The Uses of the University* (New York: Harper and Row, 1963). Estimates of nonfaculty researchers in universities ranged from 5,000 to over 30,000. See Charles V. Kidd, "New Academic Positions: The Outlook in Europe and North America," in *The Research System in the 1980s: Public Policy Issues,* ed. John M. Logsdon (Philadelphia: Franklin Institute Press, 1982), 83–96; Carlos E. Kruytbosch, "The Organization of Research in the University: The Case of Research Personnel," PhD diss., University of California, Berkeley, 1970; and Albert H. Teich, "Research Centers and Non-Faculty Researchers: A New Academic Role," in *Research in the Age of the Steady-State University,* ed. Don I. Phillips and Benjamin Shih Ping Shen, AAAS Selected Symposium Series No. 60 (Washington, DC: American Association for the Advancement of Science, 1982), 91–108.

69. Private universities have had slightly higher indirect cost rates than public universities for several decades, although the size of the gap has varied in recent decades. For a discussion of the rationale, see Roger G. Noll and William P. Rogerson, "The Economics of University Indirect Cost Reimbursement in Federal Research Grants," in *Challenges to Research Universities,* ed. Roger G. Noll (Washington, DC: Brookings Institute, 1998), 105–46.

70. Arthur Bienenstock, "Administrative Burdens Stifle Faculty and Erode University Resources," *American Physical Society Newsletter* 18, no. 7 (July 2009): 8, http://www.aps.org/publications/apsnews/20090/backpage.cfm [accessed Mar. 23, 2010].

71. Carol Frances, "1984: The Outlook for Higher Education," *AAHE Bulletin* 37, no. 6 (Feb. 1985): 3–7; Kenneth Hoving, "Interdisciplinary Programs, Centers, and Institutes: Academic and Administrative Issues" (paper presented at the Twenty-Seventh Annual Meeting of the Council of Graduate Schools, Washington, DC, Dec. 1–4, 1987); Bruce L. R. Smith, "Graduate Education in the United States," in *The State of Graduate Education*, ed. Bruce L. R. Smith (Washington, DC: Brookings Institution, 1985).

72. Daniel Denecke and Helen Frasier, "PhD Completion Project: Preliminary Results from Baseline Data," *Council of Graduate Schools Communicator* 38, no. 9 (Nov. 2005): 1–2, 7.

73. NSF/SRS, *Doctorate Recipients 2007–08*; Robert O. Simmons and Delores H. Thurgood, *Doctorate Recipients from US Universities: Summary Report 1994*, SRS 95-334 (Washington, DC: National Academy Press, 1995).

74. NSF, *Doctorate Recipients 2010*, 7.

75. University of Chicago, "Report of the Commission on Graduate Education," *University of Chicago Record* 16, no. 2 (May 3, 1982): 67–180. Two decades later, the university requires "continuous registration" for doctoral students, where they must be enrolled and pay the requisite tuition and fees, thereby creating a financial incentive that is thought to speed up time to degree.

76. Barbara E. Lovitts, *Making the Implicit Explicit* (Sterling, VA: Sylus, 2007); Brian Paltridge, "Thesis and Dissertation Writing," *English for Specific Purposes* 21 (2002): 125–43.

77. See *Report of the MLA Task Force on Doctoral Study in Modern Language and Literature*, May 2014, http://www.mla.org/pdf/taskforcedocstudy2014.pdf [accessed June 20, 2015]. This echoes concerns from preceding decades. See Joseph Berger, "Slow Pace toward Doctorates Prompts Fear of Unfilled Jobs," *New York Times*, May 3, 1989, A1. At that time, one study estimated a 22 percent overproduction of science and engineering doctorates—see William F. Massy and Charles A. Goldman, *The Production and Utilization of Science and Engineering Doctorates in the United States* (Stanford, CA: Stanford Institute for Higher Education Research, 1995)—but it was later critiqued for methodological flaws, another sign to be skeptical even of data-based forecasts.

78. J. R. Allum, J. D. Kent, and M. T. McCarthy, *Understanding PhD Career Pathways for Program Improvement: A CGS Report* (Washington, DC: Council of Graduate Schools, 2014).

79. Audrey Williams June, "Adjuncts Build Strength in Numbers," *The Chronicle of Higher Education* (Nov. 5, 2012), http://chronicle.com/article/Adjuncts-Build-Strength-in /135520/ [accessed Jan. 13, 2015].

80. Edward J. Hackett, "Science as a Vocation in the 1990s," *Journal of Higher Education* 61 (May/June 1990): 267. Stated more dramatically, the climate has been characterized as a factory floor—or a "quasi firm"—rather than a center of learning. See Henry Etzkowitz, "Entrepreneurial Scientists and Entrepreneurial Universities in American Academic Science," *Minerva* 21 (1983): 198–233.

81. However, structural and normative barriers are major obstacles, impeding the construction of a collective identity, and thus a basis for solidarity, among graduate stu-

dents. See Patricia J. Gumport and John Jennings, "Graduate Student Employees: Unresolved Challenges," *CUPA (College and University Personnel Association) Journal* 48, no. 3/4 (Fall/Winter 1997–98): 33–37. For a discussion of the contextual shift to a more corporate model of the academy, see Robert A. Rhoads and Gary Rhoades, "Graduate Employee Unionization as Symbol of and Challenge to the Corporatization of US Research Universities," *Journal of Higher Education* 76, no. 3 (2005): 243–75.

82. Chris M. Golde and Timothy M. Dore, *At Cross Purposes: What the Experiences of Doctoral Students Reveal about Doctoral Education* (Philadelphia: Pew Charitable Trusts, 2001); see also Patricia J. Gumport, "Learning Academic Labor."

83. Daniel J. Julius and Patricia J. Gumport, "Graduate Student Unionization: Catalysts and Consequences," *Review of Higher Education* 26 (Winter 2002): 187–216; see also Scott Smallwood, "United Auto (or Is that 'Academic'?) Workers," *Chronicle of Higher Education* (Jan. 17, 2003), http://chronicle.com/article/United-Auto-or-Is-That/5739 [accessed Jan. 13, 2015].

84. *Brown University v. NLRB*, 342 US 402, 483–500 (2004).

85. Scott Jaschik, "More Routes to T.A. Unions," *Inside Higher Ed* (Mar. 16, 2015).

86. Catharine Stimpson, "A Dean's Skepticism about a Graduate-Student Union," *Chronicle of Higher Education* (May 5, 2000), http://chronicle.com/article/A-Deans-Skepticism-About-a/4588/ [accessed Jan. 13, 2015].

87. The American Recovery and Reinvestment Act of 2009 included $10 billion for health research and the construction of NIH facilities, and $9 billion for scientific research, channeled (in part) as follows: $3 billion to the National Science Foundation, $2 billion to the US Department of Energy, and $1.3 billion for university research facilities. Another $50 billion went to a State Fiscal Stabilization Fund, with the stipulation that governors had to spend 80 percent on education, which includes higher education.

88. Ivana Kottasova, "US losing its appeal for foreign students," *CNN Money* (Dec. 1, 2014), http://money.cnn.com/2014/12/01/pf/college/international-students-education/index.html [accessed Jan. 15, 2015].

89. John Aubrey Douglass and Richard Edelstein, "Whither the Global Talent Pool?" *Change: The Magazine of Higher Learning* 41, no. 4 (July/Aug. 2009): 36–44. The international graduate student "stay rate" in the United States rose from 50 to 70 percent in the last decade of the twentieth century. It held steady in science and engineering in the first decade of this century, but dove after 2009 and recovered somewhat in other fields. NSF/SED, *Doctorate Recipients 2011*, http://www.nsf.gov/statistics/sed/digest/2011/nsf13301.pdf [accessed January 15, 2015].

90. National Center for Education Statistics, table 323.10, http://nces.ed.gov/programs/digest/d13/tables/dt13_323.10.asp [accessed June 22, 2015].

91. Gumport, "Built to Serve."

92. The University of Phoenix lists nineteen master's programs under nursing and healthcare alone. University of Phoenix, *Graduate Programs*, http://www.phoenix.edu/degrees/masters.html [accessed Jan. 4, 2015]. Not all such programs are explicitly tied to occupational skills. Stanford, for example, offers a master of liberal arts degree under continuing studies, a part-time degree program with evening classes.

93. Harvard Extension School, http://www.extension.harvard.edu/academics/professional-graduate-certificates [accessed June 20, 2015]. Stanford has programs such

as Ignite, a prestigious graduate certificate program from the Graduate School of Business that is offered all over the world. Stanford, *Graduate School of Business,* http://www.gsb.stanford.edu/programs/stanford-ignite [accessed Jan. 12, 2015].

94. Alexander Astin, "Moral Messages of the University," *Educational Record* 70 (Spring 1989): 22–25.

95. Sheila A. Slaughter, *The Higher Learning and High Technology* (Albany: State University of New York Press, 1990); Hackett, "Science as a Vocation"; Etzkowitz, "Entrepreneurial Scientists."

96. See NSF's *Survey of Earned Doctorates,* http://www.nsf.gov/statistics/srvydoctorates/, conducted by the National Opinion Research Center; the survey accumulates longitudinal data in the Doctorate Record File; see also the National Center for Education Statistics, *Integrated Postsecondary Education Data System,* http://nces.ed.gov/ipeds/, for institution-level data on enrollment and degrees awarded, as well as their *Digest of Educational Statistics,* http://nces.ed.gov/programs/digest/, for national trend data. See NSF's data on *Science and Engineering Indicators,* http://www.nsf.gov/statistics/seind/.

97. In 1991 the Andrew W. Mellon Foundation funded the ten-year Graduate Education Initiative, focused on the humanities and social sciences, at ten universities. In 2001 Atlantic Philanthropies, Inc., funded a five-year study by the Carnegie Foundation for the Advancement of Teaching to create local solutions to major challenges in doctoral education, working with eighty-four departments across six disciplines in forty-four universities. In 2004 the Ford Foundation and Pfizer, Inc., supported the Council of Graduate Schools' PhD Completion Project, focusing on science, engineering, and mathematics at more than twenty-nine universities. As for diversifying STEM fields, intervention programs by the federal and state governments, foundations, nonprofits, universities, and scholars have proliferated over the past three decades, but they often lack evaluation and measurable gains. As a sign of the magnitude of this investment, one estimate is that federal agencies alone spent close to $3 billion on over two hundred programs in fiscal year 2004; see Cheryl Leggon and Willie Pearson, Jr., "Assessing Programs to Improve Minority Participation in the STEM Fields," in *Doctoral Education and the Faculty of the Future,* ed. Ronald G. Ehrenberg and Charlotte V. Kuh (Ithaca, NY: Cornell University Press, 2009), 160–71.

# Chapter Six

# The Intersecting Authority of Boards, Presidents, and Faculty

*Toward Shared Leadership*

Peter D. Eckel and Adrianna Kezar

Think of complex orchestral scores: each musician must play her or his respective part, but as a whole they must work together. Soloists become part of a collective driving toward a common mission and purpose. Similarly, effective leadership in colleges and universities[1] requires orchestration among its key players—faculty, senior administrators, and trustees. Each group must lead independently in its primary spheres of work, but also lead collaboratively for the good of the institution. While each note on the score might seem easy to play, the collective execution of a complex passage can be difficult. Universities have different and competing sources of influence through which various stakeholders seek to exert leadership, unlike simpler organizational structures with clear lines of communication and sources of authority and control.[2] Leadership through governance is nuanced and complex.

This chapter explores the leadership dynamics of universities through the lens of governance and the three groups of actors that play dominant roles— trustees, presidents, and faculty.[3] While we recognize the important contributions of students or staff,[4] this chapter focuses on the three groups most consistently influential and that are part of the formal governance structure. In addition to describing the leadership of boards, presidents, and faculty, it explores the organizational and environmental contexts of leading in the academy, select theories of leadership that pertain to higher education, and the intersection of faculty, trustee, and administrative influence.

## Boards of Trustees

At the top of the formal university organizational hierarchy sits the board of trustees.[5] Boards of trustees, sometimes called boards of governors, and infrequently called boards of visitors (for example in Virginia), boards of overseers (Harvard), or boards of curators (in Missouri) are the legal authority of the institution. Boards have the final jurisdiction on all matters related to the policies of the university. The boards, in turn, delegate the authority to manage the day-to-day operations of the university to the president. In some instances, in addition to governing boards universities may have other types of boards, often called boards of visitors (just to confuse things), that serve in advisory rather than governance roles. The distinction is that these do not have the fiduciary responsibilities of governing boards. According to the Association of Governing Boards, there are an estimated 50,000 trustees in the United States. The overwhelming majority of them are volunteers; only trustees of for-profit universities tend to be compensated, although trustees abroad may be compensated similar to corporate trustees.

A *fiduciary* is the steward of public trust and is responsible for ensuring that the assets (financial, reputational, and physical) of the organization are safeguarded and held for the benefit of another; in the case of universities this refers to the trustees.[6] It is from this function that board leadership stems. The fiduciary role encompasses three duties:[7]

- *The duty of care* requires that trustees carry out their responsibilities in good faith, in the best interest of the university. The expectation is that a board member is actively engaged in the work of the board and knowledgeable about the university, and that she or he acts reasonably, competently, and prudently when making decisions as a steward of the institution. The duty of care assumes a degree of diligence and attention to one's work and the work of the board.
- *The duty of loyalty* requires board members to put the interests of the institution before all others and to act in ways consistent with the institution's public purposes. It prohibits a board member from acting out of self-interest and directly or indirectly benefitting personally. For instance, the board's conflict-of-interest policy provides guidance on how a conflicted board member can avoid putting personal interests first.
- *The duty of obedience* refers to the board member's obligation to advance the mission of the college or university consistent with its stated

purpose and within the boundaries of the law. Failure to fulfill this duty can result in a loss of public confidence in the institution.

Boards exert their influence through tasks they carry out, which can be distilled into five broad categories[8]:

1. Setting the organization's mission and overall strategy, and modifying either as necessary
2. Monitoring organizational performance and holding the administration accountable;
3. Selecting, evaluating, and supporting the president, and, if necessary, removing that individual from the position;
4. Developing and safeguarding the institution's financial and physical resources; and
5. Serving as a conduit between the institution and its environment, and advocating on its behalf.

The nature of college and university boards in the United States grew out of the historical tradition of lay or independent boards in which individuals who were not employees of the organization served as fiduciaries, a model first adopted in the colonies by Harvard University.[9] Therefore, the board's leadership is different from that of administrators and faculty. It is more distant and episodic as the board members are not formally involved in the daily workings of the institution they govern. This concept can even be inferred from Thomas Jefferson's labeling of the University of Virginia's governance body as "the Board of Visitors." That is, the board members visit but do not inhabit the university. The benefits of lay boards are that they "can help to form a fresh vision for the institution; focus attention on the most critical challenges; critique the prevailing wisdom from the vantage point of knowledgeable outsiders; bring new perspective, often from the business world; and illuminate old problems."[10] Board members provide an informed external view of the world and can add depth and perspective by tapping their outside expertise and experiences. Effective boards govern, but do not manage.

The goal of boards should be to add value. "A board can reach that destination only if it functions as a team," writes Nadler.[11] The authority of boards lies in the collective, not with individual trustees.[12] So boards should and need to act as a body. However, as Chait points out, some boards are often "orchestras of soloists,"[13] in which members try to exert their individual influence rather than working through the board. An extreme example of this is the governance break-down at the University of Virginia in 2012 that resulted in the termination and subsequent reinstatement of its president.[14]

Boards face many uphill battles when it comes to exercising their influence and being effective leaders.[15] Members must make their decisions collectively but they usually only come together periodically. They are volunteers who, while highly accomplished and influential individuals in their own professions, are not of the academy. They must forge and maintain a complex relationship with the president whom they both oversee and partner with strategically, and they have to address a long list of complex issues essential to the institution's well-being, typically without deep higher education backgrounds. Finally they need to keep their work at the policy level and not overreach into the tasks of manage-ment. "Effective governance entails influential participation in meaningful dis-cussions about consequential matters that lead to significant outcomes" writes Chait.[16] Board structure and composition make this calculus challenging as the discussions may not be salient, participation can be fluid, and many decisions put before boards by campus administrators or even board leadership may be of little consequence to the institution.

Chait, Ryan, and Taylor argue that even beyond these structural challenges, boards may underperform because the work often lacks purpose. "Many boards are ineffectual not because they are confused about their role but because they are dissatisfied with their role. They do not do their job well because their job does not strike them as worth doing well."[17] Trustees want to serve and give back to their institutions. For some there is tremendous prestige in the role. Thus they trudge on even when facing frustrations. That said, boards do develop processes, and, more importantly, cultures to be effectively influential.[18]

To be most consequential and purposeful, Chait, Ryan, and Taylor[19] argue, boards should focus their work in three distinct streams—fiduciary, strategic and generative, which combine like a triple helix to create governance as lead-ership. The first type of work, fiduciary, requires that boards live up to their stewardship role, are compliant with laws and regulations, work to advance the mission of the institution, and use resources appropriately. The strategic work focuses on advancing the institution's mission and priorities, and aligning the institution's strengthens and weaknesses with threats and opportunities. This is not to say boards develop the strategic plan outside of the traditions of academic governance. As Chait writes elsewhere, "The board can and should test whether plans are consistent, tactics are plausible, risks are reasonable, milestones are feasible, and metrics are sensible."[20] The final type of work, which the authors call "generative," involves using trustee knowledge and wisdom to meet the challenges and opportunities facing the university as it develops strategies, plans, and policies. It is the "grapple factor." This final type of engagement occurs when the work is still ambiguous and open to interpretation. Effectiveness in this domain requires a strong and effective partnership between the board and the campus, a foundation of trust, and an understanding that challenges can be ambiguous.[21] "Engaging the collective mind of everyone around the board table should lead to better deliberations and better decisions" argues Trower regarding generative governance.[22]

Studies of boards tend to be narrow in scope, focusing on structure, composition, and roles. However, Kezar offers a multidimensional model of public board effectiveness with six elements.[23] Based on interviews with over a hundred board members and staff, the model includes leadership/board agenda, culture, education, external relations, relationships, and structure. This model is important because most of the earlier work on boards has been conducted on private boards. Kezar's process-based model presumes and promotes interdependency among these characteristics, which often are considered individually or in isolation. Leadership is at the heart of public boards. The other elements (culture, education, external relations, relationships, and structure) help to support and advance leadership. The themes are prioritized in importance related to effectiveness. For example, after leadership, culture is the most often noted theme in the data, followed by education, external relations, relationships, and structure. Board leadership involves developing a common vision and purpose, creating a multiyear agenda, asking tough questions, and forging a strong relationship between the board chair, other members of the board, and the campus CEO. In terms of the culture, leaders build a professional and nonpartisan culture among the board. The tendency of boards to become mired in politics can be overcome through a careful attention to a professional culture. Effective boards have highly elaborated board orientations for new members, ongoing opportunities for education throughout the year, educational opportunities outside of board meetings, strong data from staff, and educational experiences that are based on a careful evaluation of the board's needs. In terms of external relations, effective boards coordinate with legislative and governor's strategic plans, have joint goal-setting meetings with external stakeholders, develop sophisticated communication vehicles across the various layers of governance, have access to the governor and other important state officials, and stick to their agenda even as governors turn over. In terms of relationships, the CEO and board chair have ongoing communication, board members engage university constituents actively, and the board meetings include a social aspect to develop trust among the members. Lastly, in terms of structure, the board works to clarify its role, develops needed ad hoc committees, have a clear board chair role, and engage in ongoing evaluation of their work.

The impact of board work is transmitted from the board to the campus via the president. "The working relationship between the president and the board is the essential alliance in bringing about positive change."[24] In a national survey of approximately 500 presidents, roughly 80 percent reported that their boards had had a positive impact, and a similar percentage were either satisfied or very satisfied overall with their boards.[25] However, the flip side is that one in five presidents reported that their boards did not have a positive impact. This is high percentage given the influence that boards can have, both positive and negative. Furthermore, almost a quarter of presidents in this study indicated that they were not confident in their board's abilities to address future institutional changes. On this point, key differences existed between the boards of public and independent institutions, with 80 percent of presidents from private institutions being confident or very confident about their boards' ability to govern into the future; only 60 percent of presidents from public universities felt this way. Together the data suggest that, although boards are highly influential, a sizable share of presidents are not confident that their boards can provide needed leadership over either the short or the long term.

In that same study, important differences emerged by presidential tenure and by type of institution. When long-term presidents (those serving ten or more years at a single or multiple institutions) were asked about the changing nature of governance, approximately two-thirds indicated that boards were more *important* today than when they first became presidents; one-third did not. A similar number reported that boards were more *effective* today than when they first took office. Only half of longstanding presidents from doctoral/research universities said boards were more essential today, and one in five reported boards being *less* effective today than when they began. Less than one-fifth of new presidents (three years or less) strongly agreed that their boards made a positive impact. By contrast, more than half of presidents in office twelve years or longer reported the same feeling. Almost one-third of newly hired presidents reported being not very satisfied or even dissatisfied with the board. This rate is twice that of their longer-serving colleagues with eight to twelve years in their posts and three times the rate of presidents who have served for more than twelve years. Furthermore, just over one in five newly hired presidents report not being on the same page as their boards regarding future institutional change and were unsure whether they and their boards were in sync about future challenges. One would expect the search process to clarify such goals, but clearly this did not happen, meaning new presidents were immediately in difficult positions with their boards regarding future institutional directions. New presidents may have different and possibly higher expectations for boards than longer-serving presidents or middle-term presidents. Regardless, boards matter and presidents believe their effects are more easily felt today than in the past.

## The President

The individual most likely identified as the leader of a university or college is the president, who also may be called chancellor, rector, or vice chancellor, depending on the continent and the system. As the Task Force on the State of the Presidency in American Higher Education of the Association of Governing Boards of Colleges and Universities noted in its statement, "no leader comes to personify an institution in the way a president does. A president must provide leadership in maintaining the institution's academic integrity and reputation. He or she must assimilate and tell the institution's story to build pride internally and support externally. The president has the primary responsibility for increasing public understanding and support for the institution . . . and must lead the institution as it confronts new external challenges."[26]

Boards charge presidents with leading the institution. Presidents are responsible for the wise use of scarce resources and are accountable for their institution's effectiveness. They coordinate institutional strategic direction, develop and put into action both master and strategic plans, and are accountable for the institution's future well-being. They support institutional work by making choices—for instance, regarding space and facilities, enrollments, and budgets. They liaise with critical external stakeholders, such as policy makers, alumni, and donors, and they hire and manage other key campus leaders. The attention they choose to give to certain activities, functions, and issues matters, both operationally and symbolically.[27] Further evidence of their importance is the sizable financial investment made by trustees in identifying and retaining talented presidents, with the highest salaries and benefits over $1 million per year (but still lagging behind football and basketball coaches). Successful presidents are essential to dynamic, relevant, and robust colleges and universities. Seen from the other direction, failed presidencies are costly in all-too-numerous ways. Regrettably, higher education is often reminded of these unfortunate costs.

Much of the president's time is spent away from the campus, with off-campus constituencies, and the external demands on the position are growing. In an ACE study of college presidents, 57 percent of long-serving presidents (those who have been in their positions for ten years or more) report that as new presidents, they spent the most time with constituents who were internal campus stakeholders. In contrast, only 14 percent report that, as experienced presidents, internal constituents still occupy the majority of their time. Instead, 39 percent spend more time with external constituents, and 47 percent spend time equally with external and internal constituents.[28] While new presidents are likely to invest time on campus establishing themselves as the new leader, the sizable difference experienced presidents have reported in the amount of time previously and currently spent on campus suggests that the nature and demands of the job today are also different. Much of the on-campus leadership is now delegated to the chief academic officer (CAO) or provost, who tends to be the campus number-two leader (behind the president) and reports spending little to moderate time on off-campus activities.[29]

The external work of campus leaders is tied to the growing importance of the need to secure more resources as expenses grow and public dollars do not keep pace, and institutions cannot raise tuition high enough to support their expenses.[30] Presidents find themselves as the lead entrepreneur.[31] Of the ten areas identified most frequently by long-serving presidents as taking more time today than these areas initially did during their tenure, half are directly related to securing or spending dollars (fund raising, capital improvement, budget and financial management, entrepreneurship, and operating costs) and three others are indirectly related to this (technology planning, strategic planning, and enrollment management). Furthermore, fund raising is the task all presidents, regardless of their time in office, most often identified as being the one they were underprepared to address when they began their position.[32] Presidents meet with potential donors to the institution, such as alumni and corporate leaders, and they are the key lobbyists interacting with public officials in the statehouse as well as in Washington, DC. They drive entrepreneurial agendas by building relationships with corporate leaders and seeking technology transfer and licensing agreements; sponsoring new business incubators; and seeking to capitalize on patents and intellectual property rights; and they are ultimately responsible for traditional and innovative auxiliary services (such as hospitals, residence halls, and athletics), investments, and endowment returns. These external demands tax the effectiveness of the president on campus and the role in shared governance. Presidents simply are absent from on-campus decision making.

Therefore, presidents influence campus through a variety of mechanisms, such as leveraging strategic plans and budgets, managing and evaluating senior staff, and promoting institutional goals. An essential mechanism is through engaging stakeholders. Clark Kerr, former the chancellor of the University of California system, described the difficulty presidents have with serving so many different stakeholders, from traditional ones such as faculty, students, and alumni to newer stakeholders such as business and industry, federal and state governments, local communities, and, over time, international communities.[33]

It is indirect not direct interactions through which presidents wield the most influence on campus. They serve in what is a highly symbolic role as campus heads and signal intent through the interpretations of their actions.[34] In his national study on presidential leadership, Birnbaum notes that "presidents, by virtue of their hierarchical positions and legitimacy, are believed by others to have a coherent sense of the institution and are therefore permitted, if not expected, to articulate institutional purposes."[35] From this perspective, "leadership influences people to focus their attention on specific stimuli and to interpret them in the ways intended by the leader . . . Good leadership is not defined by an ability to get subordinates to do something, but rather by a leader's effectiveness in making values and activities meaningful to others and developing a vocabulary to be used in communicating that meaning throughout the institution."[36] Shaping interpretation and meaning allows presidents influence across numerous stakeholders.

As part of his national study of presidents, Birnbaum grouped presidents into three categories: exemplary, modal, and failed. Exemplary presidents developed the skills and knowledge to "influence both the way their institutions are managed and the interpretations that define the reality of other organizational participants" and they "gave equal attention to tasks and relationships, and have a collaborative relationship with the faculty."[37] Modal presidents, he found, "manage institutional processes but have lost the ability to affect the interpretive life of the campus."[38] They no longer can affect relationships and meaning, and instead focus on management tasks. The research reinforces the idea that managers do not make exemplary leaders. The final group, failed presidents, develop an adversarial relationship with the faculty and lose the ability to shape meaning.

Birnbaum writes elsewhere about this phenomenon, paraphrasing an old song, "Old presidents never die; they just lose their faculties."[39]

The difficulty for many presidents is that the demands of the position, including off-campus and on-campus stakeholder expectations, require that they be able to effectively function equally well across a set of leadership contradictions. A roundtable focus group of contemporary presidents convened by ACE found that they need to simultaneously

- be visionary *and* pragmatic;
- have an on-campus presence *and* work externally off-campus;
- focus on immediate needs *and* keep an eye on the future;
- balance long-term patience with immediate intensity;
- appreciate and understand complexity of the job, the institution, and the environment *and* keep things simple; and
- exude confidence *and* have humility.[40]

Finding a way to accomplish all this when some tasks do not align with an individual's personal strengths is difficult. The complexities of the job and the real limits to leadership affect the extent to which presidents can be effective leaders regardless of how much people expect them to lead.

### Faculty Leaders

Faculty have historically exerted leadership through shared governance structures. While other structures exist such as councils or university-wide bodies, the faculty senate is the most widely utilized formal structure for faculty leadership, with 90 percent of institutions having such a structure.[41] Although there were senates created as early as 1890, most faculty senates emerged during and after World War II[42] and were part of the university movement, which established faculty as major power brokers on campus. By the 1960s, faculty senates were normative on most campuses.[43] Since World War II, faculty influence grew and faculty continued to professionalize, which resulted in more checks on governing boards and the administration than in any previous time period.[44] The reason for the growth of senates was the prevailing view that faculty were professional and that professionals should have direct input into overall organizational decisions, particularly their own working conditions.[45] However, it is also important to note that historically many senates emerged as a reaction to overreach by administrators in academic decision making, and an attempt by faculty to equalize influence.

Formal governance structures evolved as a means to create shared governance where it did not exist in spirit or action.[46] However, this structure was not sufficient on many public campuses, and unionization efforts throughout the 1970s led to faculty being involved in campus leadership through collective bargaining rather than through shared governance.[47]

The traditional view is that faculty inclusion in major university decision making is a way to protect faculty interest and ensure that institutions maintain fidelity to the academic mission.[48] It is important to note that tensions between faculty and administrators are historic as much as contemporary, grounded in the differing perspective, focus, and priorities of administrators and faculty. Of the many criticisms of faculty senates and the ability of faculty to participate in shared governance, almost none are empirically based. These critiques suggest faculty are too deliberative and slow, are too inclined toward consensus, cannot make hard decisions, and are too self-interested.[49] In one key study that examines this untested assumption, Eckel identified how faculty are willing and able to participate in a constructive way in institutional decision making, even in high-stakes decisions such as program closure, and that faculty are responsible agents in shared governance processes in ways that counter administrative common wisdom.[50]

Most research on senates examines and describes their structure and authority. One key difference that has been identified is the distinction between elite and non-elite institutions[51] and those more market sensitive.[52] At research universities, faculty experience greater levels of freedom and autonomy, but at less selective institutions faculty may experience greater restraints and less involvement in governance. So context can impact the ability of faculty to have an authentic leadership role. Other studies look at the representativeness of the faculty, voting rights, subcommittee structures, and purpose.[53] For example, having a sound executive committee or smaller committees has been identified with higher satisfaction among faculty involved.[54] Senates can also have vastly different power, with some being mostly advisory and others having significant delegated authority.[55] Faculty's leadership is more likely to be prominent in those institutions where they are delegated authority, which typically relates to academic issues, curriculum, and student-related matters. This grounding was codified in the 1966 joint statement on government by the American Association of University Professors (AAUP), with signatories by the American Council on Education (ACE) representing presidents and the Association of Governing Boards of Universities and Colleges (AGB) speaking for trustees, and outlined the responsibilities of senates. Faculty involvement in governance is a fundamental part of American higher education and embodies a central value on most campuses, although there is not universal agreement on the areas in which faculty should have authority or how widely construed their authority should be.

One important aspect of faculty governance is the way senates exert leadership potential. Three approaches are discussed: Birnbaum, Tierney and Minor. Birnbaum looked at the espoused and actual roles that senates play in university decision making. He uses four alternative organizational models—bureaucratic, collegial, political, and symbolic.[56] Birnbaum documents that senates are more likely to be inefficient and slow, and not politically representative, and are more likely to expose latent conflict than to increase a sense of community. But he suggests efficiency should not be as important as effectiveness and describes an effective senate as one where senate leaders and administration leaders meet regularly (formally as members of committees and cabinets and informally), communicate, cooperate on goals, and recognize and respect each body's scope of authority. Birnbaum takes a complex view of effectiveness by arguing that senates operate under different and sometimes multiple logic models—bureaucratic, political, and collegial.

Under Birnbaum's bureaucratic model, a faculty senate would clarify institutional purposes, specify program objectives, reallocate income resources, develop new income sources, and be involved in issues such as the management of academic operations, degree requirements, academic behavior, and program evaluation. A senate, in the model, might be considered effective to the extent that it efficiently considered institutional problems and, through rational processes, developed rules, regulations, and procedures that resolved them.

In Birnbaum's political model, the senate is a forum for the articulation of interests and as the setting in which decisions on institutional policies and goals are reached through compromise, negotiation, and forming coalitions. Senates provide a means for discussion and conflict resolution over the mission and operation of the institution. A senate, under the political system, might be considered effective to the extent that, perceived as fully representative of its constituencies, it formulates and clarifies goals and policies.

In Birnbaum's collegial model, the senate is a forum for achieving dynamic of consensus. A senate, in the collegial model, might be considered effective to the extent that, through interaction across key constituent groups, it develops shared values leading to consensus.

In Birnbaum's symbolic model, the senate is most important as a symbol about faculty voice, a reminder to the campus, including the board, that faculty perspective is important in decision making processes. In the symbolic frame the senate is effective if administrators and staff feel that decisions need to be run through the senate for input. From this perspective, the outcomes of decisions are less important than the search for consensus and the use of democratically-oriented forms of decision making.

In addition to these manifest functions, Birnbaum notes that latent functions of senates are also important and should be considered when thinking about ways faculty can contribute to leadership and decision making. In terms of latent functions, the senate can provide opportunities for socialization, congregation, discussion, professional screening, and the like. Senates can contribute to institutional stability in the potentially divided and changing environment of higher education. Thus leadership is exhibited in varying ways, and faculty who can operate across bureaucratic, political, and collegial approaches will be more effective.

Other organizing constructs exist to explain the work of senates. For example, Tierney categorizes the functions of the senate as directional (where the chair gives direction to the members, usually bounded by the senate doors), news related (where the chair or president or another administrator shares official campus news), ceremonial (emphasizing important events), confirmational (wherein the senate confirms a decision), and decisional.[57] The most important is the decisional function, which is where the bulk of the senate's work takes place. As important as the other functions may be, the main purpose or role of the senate is making decisions that affect the university; this is the function that should take up the most time and energy of the senate. Tierney suggests that successful faculty leaders optimize the decision function and not allow other roles to monopolize time.

Minor argues that there are four types of senates—functional, influential, ceremonial, and subverted—and that they have very different consequences for effective faculty leadership and decision making.[58] Functional senates have clearly designated authority, a traditional electoral, representative structure, and, like the Birnbaum model, serve the bureaucratic functions of setting goals and making decisions, mostly related to faculty-specific matters. Influential senates share some characteristics with functional senates in that they make decisions related to faculty specific issues, but in addition they create and frame their own agenda to promote policy changes within the institution that aim to promote the general welfare of the institution. Influential senates generally have collaborative, instead of confrontational, relationships with the administration. Ceremonial senates are fairly inactive, existing mainly in name only as symbolic artifacts that have little real interest in and influence on governance or institutional leadership. Subverted senates are ineffective because they have been subverted by other venues for faculty participation in governance such as an informal or ad hoc kitchen cabinet group of trusted faculty that the administration turns to for advice. Subverted senates may maintain authority in traditional areas of faculty concern such as curriculum, tenure, and instruction but usually clash with the administration.

Regardless of the typologies of senates, the focus on senate structures and roles is too narrow and does little to advance a deeper understanding.[59] A broader view of shared governance may be more constructive, including factors such as the relationships between faculty and president, and between faculty, presidents, and boards; how senates learn and change; and how senates fit into the larger governance ecology. For instance, a senate may be labeled as ceremonial because the institutional environment will not permit it any other role. However, the issue may change when a different lens of study is adopted. In considering the ways faculty leaders can be effective, these broader viewpoints are critical to understanding leadership among faculty.

There is great concern today about whether faculty can continue to play a role in campus leadership through governance.[60] Given the shrinking number of tenure-track professors, from 70 percent with tenure or on the tenure track in the 1970s to only 30 percent of faculty currently with tenure or on the tenure track, far fewer can feel free to speak up on governance issues without fearing retribution.[61] This leaves open questions about how authentic shared governance is today.

The 70 percent of faculty off the tenure track are generally not involved in governance, so a large majority of faculty no longer have any input into institutional decisions.[62] Those who are tenured and tenure-track faculty may not well represent the views and priorities of the whole professoriate. A recent report from the Association of Governing Boards highlights the lack of faculty input into todays' governance processes and questions whether a true shared governance approach exists to any meaningful extent.[63] The report also calls on boards to reengage and re-envision shared governance with a changing faculty.

Additionally, Minor has identified that the new generation of tenure track faculty are not interested in participating in governance, which represents another challenge to creating effective shared governance.[64] While the desire to participate is greater in bachelor's institutions, at doctoral institutions, where faculty tend to have the most influence, the interest in participating in governance is the lowest, with only 19 percent showing a strong interest in participating and 75 percent saying they do not have an interest. Minor's survey also highlighted the fact that faculty have authority over a narrow range of topics, which contributes to the perception that senates are not influential and cannot impact institutional operations in consequential ways. Given reports that administrators have centralized decision making in the last twenty years, it is not surprising that faculty are feeling a lack of involvement in important institutional decisions.[65] So the lack of a meaningful role that faculty perceive among senates feeds into the lack of interest into participation.

Kezar and Lester suggest that as a result of the decline of shared governance, faculty increasingly lead from outside formal structures.[66] In this grassroots leadership approach, faculty form informal groups and lead change, but not from within the formal structures. The research suggests that leadership is defined as bringing about important changes on campuses and that this is increasingly happening independently from institutional structures. Effect not structure matters most. For example, faculty are creating new majors, forming centers on environmentalism, advancing institutional policies related to environmental sustainability, helping foster environments of inclusion for students of color, and obtaining funding for new buildings and programs but from outside of senates and committee structures. If traditional structures are involved they may be so only at the end of the process and out of necessity. Thus, new directions for faculty leadership are being documented and may be more prominent in the future.

As faculty leadership faces various challenges not only internal to the institution but also externally, the future of shared governance remains fragile. For instance, state legislatures have put increased emphasis on linking institutional funding to certain performance-based outcomes, in an attempt to improve undergraduate teaching, to assess faculty performance, and to contribute to state economic development.[67] Anderson notes it is reasonable to have administrators deal with these issues because faculty do not have the time, expertise, nor inclination to do so and that administrators are better equipped to respond to these challenges.[68] As pressure increases and the challenges become more complicated, the future of shared faculty leadership via traditional governance structures does not look good.

## The Contexts Shaping Influence

Leadership in all three domains occurs within the context of the institution, which shapes how leaders act, the impact of those actions, and how others perceive the importance of those actions. For example, the literature on senates, cited above, documents how external contexts, campus environments, changes in the academic workforce, and other contextual features shape the nature of academic leadership. Writing about presidential leadership, Birnbaum notes that "presidential leadership is influenced by interacting webs of administrative routines, environmental pressures, and political processes that take place in the context of institutional history and culture."[69] Such webs influence boards and faculty as well. Colleges and universities, while having characteristics similar to other types of organizations, have a set of atypical organizational dynamics that mitigate the direct influence of any single group. This section explores three of the institution-specific contexts that shape leadership: dual sources of authority, loose coupling, and garbage-can decision making.

First, unlike more traditional hierarchical organizations, where authority is correlated with one's administrative position, colleges and universities are defined by their dual sources of authority—bureaucratic (or administrative) and professional (or academic).[70] As discussed above, colleges and universities evolved in ways that gave faculty priority over the curriculum and administrators responsibility over managerial elements. The result of this evolution is two sources of authority within a single organization. Bureaucratic authority is grounded in the organization's structure and arises from the legal rights of the board as delegated to senior administrators to set direction, control and monitor budgets, develop institution strategy, hire and terminate employees, develop and implement policies, and assess progress toward objectives and priorities. The second source of authority—professional authority—stems from the high degree of knowledge, expertise, and specialization required to perform the core functions of the institution (i.e., teaching and research). This authority provides the faculty with a different and often competing source of influence, in many ways akin to doctors in hospitals, lawyers in firms, and consultants in professional service consultancies. The effect is that authority is not consolidated in the hands of the organization's positional leaders. Instead, it is dispersed; some might suggest that authority is shared, but in reality there exist two types of authority. Depending on the topic and the context (such as budgeting and planning), administrative authority can be the stronger source. However, professional authority is dominant in decisions about faculty hiring, curricular offerings, and the research that is pursued. It even strongly shapes the overall strategy an institution pursues.[71]

This dynamic is captured in the 1966 "Statement on Government of Colleges and Universities," jointly formulated by the American Association of University Professors, the American Council on Education, and the Association of Governing Boards of Universities and Colleges. The Statement attempts to outline areas of responsibility for faculty, administrators, and trustees, as well as areas of shared authority. However, decisions are not easy to categorize, and a topic can easily overlap traditional areas of responsibility, leading to conflict between sources of authority. When Duke University sought to open a campus in China, administrators invoked administrative authority regarding planning, budgeting, and setting the strategic priority of the institution. Faculty, however, invoked professional authority focusing on the curriculum and the conferring of degrees. The result was a longstanding stalemate that needed continued negotiation between influence wielders.[72]

Second, the relationships between various units and the central administration and between the units and departments themselves can be described as "loosely coupled," which makes central coordination and oversight, and, by extension, the role of the president, difficult.[73] Loose coupling describes weak connections among organizational units. Both the relationship between units, and that between units and the center are weak. Information travels slowly and indirectly between these areas, and coordination among them is difficult and minimal. Long-time University of Chicago president Robert Hutchins's definition of a university serves as a pointed reminder of the nature of loose coupling in higher education: "The university is a collection of departments tied together by a common steam plant."[74] While it can be expected that loose coupling is most descriptive of large institutions, smaller colleges can also be defined by it.

While loosely coupled organizations create problems for central administrators seeking to coordinate organizational activities, these weak relationships also have some advantages.[75] First, loosely coupled systems are able to respond more sensitively to environmental changes. However, the likelihood is just as great that the unit will pay attention to external stimuli rather than requests from a president. The benefit here is that changes pertinent to one department, such as new professional standards in accounting, may affect the curriculum there, but these changes do not require a curricular overhaul throughout the institution. Second, loosely coupled organizations promote and encourage localized innovations and, at the same time, prevent poor adaptations from spreading to other parts of the organization. The curricular change described above does not require the consent of a busy president or consensus by other departments; instead, the individual department concerned can respond more quickly. Furthermore, poor ideas are not spread easily throughout the institution. Keeping bad decisions quarantined means that although presidents may not know about the adaptations occurring throughout the organization or may not be able coordinate those changes, they will probably not have to fix widespread damage caused by bad ideas. Third, loosely coupled organizations benefit from localized expertise. For instance, the president does not need to be an expert in all disciplines. Local decisions can be made by the people who know best. Lastly, loosely coupled organizations have few coordination and centralization costs. A large central bureaucracy is not required, allowing institutions to invest more resources locally rather than centrally.

Regardless of the organizational pluses of loose coupling, one drawback is that administrative leaders cannot easily create organizational efficiency because of weak central coordination. Instead, they struggle to disseminate helpful innovations widely, because communication between units occurs indirectly, sporadically, and unevenly.[76] Senior administrators often learn that units are working at odds with one another, and with the central administration, as they each scan their own environments and pursue local adaptations. Of course loose coupling empowers faculty leaders to be highly innovative in their own units. For example, one unit may be advancing its service-learning activities, while another is focusing on graduate education, and a third internationalizing its curricula. Aligning activities and priorities is a continual challenge for university leaders, what the Kellogg Commission on the Future of State and Land-Grant Universities called "institutional coherence."[77]

A final dynamic is garbage-can decision making that takes place in organizations labelled "organized anarchies."[78] Three additional organizational dynamics beyond the control even of presidents create these conditions. First, colleges and universities pursue a set of inconsistent, ambiguous, and uncertain goals, and these goals may conflict. For instance, institutions are concerned both with serving local students *and* with having a global effect; they seek the unfettered pursuit of knowledge *and* the leveraging of scientific breakthroughs for economic gain. Second, the ways in which they conduct their core functions—particularly teaching and learning—are complex. Most faculty do not really agree on how students learn best, nor do they understand the essential processes involved in creating civic-minded students or globally competent citizens. The result is that multiple informal theories of what should happen and how it should happen exist within the institution. Third, because time and attention are limited, participation in decisions is fluid as faculty and administrators choose among competing opportunities, based on their own preferences as to what is important. Although they are busy people, key decision makers cannot be in all places at all times. "Every entrance is an exit somewhere else . . . Participation stems from other demands on the participants' time."[79] Taken together, these three elements create situations Cohen and March label "organized anarchies."[80]

The effect of these organizational realities is that decision outcomes depend on the combined flow of (1) decision makers, (2) institutional problems, and (3) potential solutions that are present in the institution. In places where they are in contact, these three streams of people, problems, and solutions come together in a range of metaphoric garbage cans throughout the institution. Solutions are in search of problems as much as problems are in search of solutions, and decisions depend on the mix of people, problems, and solutions in the garbage can at any particular time.[81] Organizations are often thought to render decisions after leaders have defined the problem, explored potential outcomes, and selected a course of action to maximize the effect of the decision.[82] However, the dynamics of colleges and universities create a situation within organized anarchies—described as garbage-can decision making—in which the prototypical, rational approach to rendering decisions is only one way to actually reach a decision.[83]

In the garbage-can model, decision making takes place in one of three ways. Decisions can be made by *resolution*, in which participants make a concerted effort to apply solutions to recognized problems. Decisions can also be made by *flight*, when problems become attached to other unintended solutions or participants. For example, a suggested science or foreign language requirement can easily turn into conversations about faculty hiring, classroom space utilization, or the undue influence of accrediting agencies, different and seemingly unrelated sets of problems and solutions. Finally, decisions can be made by *oversight*. Key participants are too busy to participate in all decisions, so problems and solutions in another garbage can become coupled together with little attention and involvement from key campus leaders.

It is the mix of problems, solutions, and people in a decision opportunity that shape the outcome, not just the preferences of administrative leaders. To render their desired outcomes, presidents can (1) spend time on the problem, since people willing to invest time on any particular decision are likely to

different approaches and strategies to exert influence and are applicable to boards, senior administrators and faculty. Much of the empirical literature focuses on presidents, thus our examples below will highlight them more often than the leadership of boards or faculty, but these theories have shown promise across different types of leaders.

## Contingency Leadership

Perhaps the most insightful school of thought has focused on the *contingency of leadership*. Effective leaders understand the importance of the context in which they are operating, and they know that leadership varies by the institutional context, environmental conditions, campus culture, and organization dilemma being addressed (advancing a campus diversity versus a cost savings/efficiency program, for example).[87] As John Levin notes regarding presidents, "in all cases, institutional context is equally or more important than the perception of presidential influence in contributing to organizational actions and outcomes . . . Presidents who were perceived as the most influential are those who fit into the socially constructed story of the institution."[88] In other words, the organizational and environmental contexts vary so much that those seeking influence must modify their actions to make sense of and be effective within their specific campus context.

One very important contextual element that effective leaders pay attention to is the set of unique characteristics individual institutions possess.[89] As discussed above and throughout this volume, colleges and universities are characterized by certain features that distinguish them from other organizations and, in turn, affect their leadership. Some examples of these features are shared governance; academic freedom and autonomy; tenure; multiple and complex authority structures, with boards of trustees and faculty senates; and unique reward structures that are distributed between the disciplines and the institutions. Birnbaum noted that presidents in his studies were more successful when they worked within and acknowledged these various aspects of the academic culture.[90] Neumann noted that presidents who develop communication skills, style, and a strategy that is culturally appropriate are perceived as more effective by key constituencies.[91]

It is not the specific behaviors, styles, traits, or actions of leaders that make them effective, but the extent to which those elements are accepted and viewed as legitimate by key stakeholders. Underlying contingency theories of leadership is the notion that leaders need the support of different groups of individuals in an institution, groups that often have very different priorities, passions, and perspectives.[92] As Birnbaum notes, "good leadership is what its constituents believe it to be—and they don't always agree."[93] For faculty members, effectiveness may mean having significant autonomy and being included in key decision-making processes, while for trustees, it may mean defining an aggressive campus growth agenda or raising money to advance the institution's mission.

A third element in the contingency approach to effective leadership is temporal. Over the last forty years, the characterization of effective leaders has changed, reflecting shifts in society.[94] Forty years bounds the timeframe, because it is the period during which the college presidency has been more formally studied. Forty years ago, more hierarchical and authoritative images of college presidents were seen as being effective.[95] The characteristics noted for effective presidents were also often considered typical masculine traits, such as risk taking, task orientation, confidence, and the ability to work alone. Contemporary views of effective presidents focus more on relationship building, collaboration, and a quest for input, characteristics often associated with women and reflective of more contemporary social customs.[96] It is only more recently that women have moved into college presidencies in substantive proportions, and therefore these changing qualities may reflect alterations in expectations of what is deemed appropriate. In 1986, women held approximately 10 percent of all presidencies, while in 2011 their share more than doubled, to 25 percent.[97] For instance, James Fisher and James Koch, drawing largely on studies done in the 1980s, suggest that presidents should use more unilateral forms of power, and judiciously punish and reward; demonstrate expertise; maintain appropriate distance; and develop charisma and public presence.[98] Later studies, in contrast, focus on power and influence as a two-way process and show that effective leaders are negotiators, coalition builders, and facilitators.[99] The fact that presidents use power effectively has remained important throughout the decades, but the understanding of the concept of power and its dynamics is different.

Trait and Behavior Approach to Leadership

Although the most complex and nuanced approach to understanding leadership effectiveness is through contingency theories, there is a long tradition in higher education and in the broader leadership literature that focuses on the *traits and behaviors* of effective leaders. Bensimon, Neumann, and Birnbaum summarized much of this tradition that tried to identify certain traits that would make a leader effective.[100] Rather than actually testing whether certain traits were associated with more effectiveness, they argue that most of the studies seek characteristics of people who had been identified as effective presidents. The problem with this approach is that such studies strongly mirror expected characteristics, corresponding to the period of time in which each study was conducted.[101]

Studies that concentrate on behaviors, such as whether leaders should focus on goals, vision, planning, or motivating people to action, fall into similar traps. These studies reflect people's expectations or perceptions, rather than testing effective behavior by looking at how behavior affects certain outcomes. If expectations of traits and behaviors differ by campus climate and culture as well as time (as they often do), then the identified traits and behaviors of effective leaders will vary with individual expectations within the setting, but they may not be correlated with change or effectiveness.[102] The importance of qualities such as credibility and integrity suggests that presidents, faculty, and trustees must be clear about their values and act authentically; they will jeopardize their effectiveness if they are perceived as lacking these qualities. Overall, the search for universal traits and qualities has not proven to be particularly helpful. Instead, such studies tend to offer time- and contextual-specific insights. That said, certain themes do appear vital to understanding leadership effectiveness: honesty, integrity, and respect, for example, seem to transcend context, stakeholder, and institutional type. Research has generated further consensus regarding certain qualities that tend to be identified as important across any institutional setting, such as trustworthiness; fairness; honesty; respect, or treating people with dignity; caring; and credibility or integrity.[103]

### Transactional and Transformational Leadership

An ongoing debate in the literature is whether leaders should play a *transformational* or *transactional* leadership role.[104] Transactional leadership focuses on leader-follower exchange, such as allocating resources, rewards, or status; controlling budgetary processes; creating priorities; and establishing accountability and assessment structures. Transformational leadership, alternatively, involves leaders who interact with followers in ways that appeal to their higher needs and aspirations. They motivate others by connecting through higher moral purposes. Bensimon, Neumann, and Birnbaum argue that transactional leadership might be the more effective approach in higher education, given the relationships between presidents and faculty and the organizational contexts in which they must work (such as loose coupling), as a more directive influence by a president may not be effective.[105] They believe that presidents should rely on exchange, rather than a higher calling, and be influential through ongoing organizational activities such as the yearly budgetary process, the allocation of rewards, and accountability structures. Other studies, however, suggest that effective leaders can be transformational by creating an overarching vision for the campus, playing a role in its overall guidance and direction by motivating and inspiring, and demonstrating commitment for moving forward in a new direction.[106]

A middle ground exists, and recent studies demonstrate that effective leaders use both transactional and transformational approaches. For example, we examined college presidents who are successful in advancing campus-wide diversity agendas and found that such presidents articulate a preference for strategies that could be described as transformational, but that they were much more effective when they used both transactional and transformational approaches.[107] These presidents recognize that different stakeholders respond to different approaches, and that both are needed. They found that the appropriateness of certain approaches is often tied to the stage of the change efforts. For instance, when a campus is initially starting a concerted effort to advance campus diversity, strategies that inspire (transformational leadership) are necessary. As the campus advances in its efforts, more transactional leadership is necessary, using rewards and accountability structures. Our study also reinforces the importance of thinking about effectiveness as varying by stakeholder, phase of change, and cultural context—again reinforcing contingency approaches to leadership.

### Cognitive Theories of Leadership

While theories of transaction and transformation suggest that leadership is more than behavior or traits, *cognitive theories* of leadership focus specifically on the ways leaders make sense of and shape understanding within a campus. Cognitive theories examine the socially constructed world of organizations.[108] The premise of such approaches is that organizations consist of events and actions that are open to interpretation: Is opening a state-of-the-art student recreation center a good thing, for instance to create community, or a waste of precious institutional resources that should focus on academic priorities? It probably depends on whether the institution serves traditional-age, residential students or students who are only on campus for classes. Action and behavior thus proceed from cognition. Shaping and understanding the meaning and cognition associated with ambiguous and uncertain elements of campus life is the centerpiece of this approach.

One of the largest studies of university leadership focused on how presidents approach and view their organizations, and people's actions within them, through archetypes: bureaucratic, collegial, political, and symbolic.[109] Leaders using a bureaucratic frame observe their campuses through a lens of structure and organization, pay attention to goals and priorities, and invoke authority and control. Leaders using a collegial frame focus on people, relationships, team building, consensus, and loyalty. Leaders using a political frame see the inherent politics of organizations, build agendas, mobilize coalitions, and focus on negotiation and conflict. Lastly, presidents using a symbolic frame focus on mission, vision, values, symbols, stories, and the history of the institution. Regardless of how complex leaders strive to be (even ones with doctorates), Birnbaum's research suggests that most college and university presidents see the world through one or two sets of assumptions or frames.[110]

## Team-Based Leadership

Researchers furthermore have shifted the unit of analysis from an individual leader to a team of leaders to ensure greater cognitive complexity. A single individual rarely possesses all of the skills and knowledge required to be an effective leader. Leadership teams provide an avenue for creating greater presidential effectiveness by capitalizing on different people's strengths—some people might be good at working with others and developing relationships, different individuals can influence institutional politics, others can effectively examine data, while still others can communicate and translate information in effective ways to the campus community. Bensimon and Neumann propose that presidents can be much more effective if they work in "real" leadership teams (as opposed to illusionary teams), using examples such as working with the presidential cabinet and capitalizing on greater expertise throughout the institution.[111] They advocate moving beyond the image of leadership as being invested in a single individual and to conceptualize leadership as a group process. Their research demonstrates that teams can develop and leverage greater cognitive complexity and be more effective, but only if the teams act in what the authors call "authentic ways." Their study outlines many of the characteristics needed to develop real leadership teams, such as ensuring that criticism is embraced, building relationships among the team members so that people feel free to share information, guaranteeing that the president is truly open to sharing power and being challenged, and recognizing the importance of the collective sense leadership team members make together. They also note that real leadership teams fit into the unique culture and context of higher education that has traditionally been based on consensus, collaboration, and an intellectual environment.

As a set, these theories of leadership provide insight into leadership effectiveness in the academy and, used in combination, can help us better understand the complexities of what makes presidents, faculty and, to some extent, trustees influential. Leaders, regardless of formal position, must analyze and be fully aware of the multiple contexts and environments in which they operate. In a way they must become anthropologists. They must also balance tasks and relationship building. They need to examine and understand organizations, problems, and people in complex ways that lead to complex actions. And they need to build effective leadership teams, as well as distribute leadership by helping to identify and develop leaders throughout the campus. Given today's complex and contradictory environment, contingency approaches are particularly important, suggesting that what it takes to be an effective leader depends on stakeholder expectations, time period, and institutional context.

### Conclusion: Shared Influence, Shared Leadership

This chapter argues that within higher education are multiple spheres of leadership that interact through governance structures to shape institutional direction—trustees, presidents, faculty, and others not discussed here in depth, such as administrative staff and students. These multiple spheres can be catalyzed to create a shared notion of leadership that benefits the university. Today and into tomorrow, the effectiveness of academic leadership may well depend on how strongly a complex web of leadership exists—involving cabinet, external stakeholders, faculty, staff, and students.[112]

A shared leadership approach, albeit difficult to implement, may serve institutions well. While the idea of shared governance is common to the academic arena, shared *leadership* is not, and traditional forms of shared governance are not substitutes for shared leadership. Shared leadership involves the delegation of authority, and very little authority is delegated in shared governance; instead, it is often divided or limited to particular topics. See, for instance, how the 1966 Statement seeks to direct and divide areas of responsibility. In shared leadership, administrators and faculty are asked to approach challenges much more collaboratively, rather than sequentially with one group weighing in on the decisions of others. There are other key distinctions. For instance, shared leadership involves a great number of individuals while shared governance involves only officially voted or nominated individuals.

A shared leadership model has many advantages, but it is difficult to execute effectively. Shared leadership is particularly well adapted to addressing the organizational characteristics noted earlier, such as dual sources of authority, loose coupling, and garbage-can decision making. For example, within a shared leadership, presidents vest more power in leaders across campus, and they put accountability systems in place to monitor decision making and its effect. These new accountability structures might yield more decisions through resolution and less through oversight.

Shared leadership also can help better address challenges that leaders face in the external environment. The rate and pace of decision making has increased; a single individual is no longer capable of understanding the vast array of issues that face higher education, and leaders increasingly need to rely on a broad group of people with varying expertise to address all of these challenges. An overwhelming number of tasks vie for presidential attention. As leadership is shared with more individuals, formal leaders, such as presidents and vice presidents or elected faculty senate leaders, can delegate responsibility to others and ensure that they spend their own time only on the most critical issues. Second, a shared leadership model allows the institution to address a larger and more diverse agenda more effectively. Colleges and universities will have more priorities, rather than fewer. Shared leadership helps to ensure that an issue is being worked on by the campus, even though the president is not directly addressing this issue. Third, a shared leadership model expands the number of people who embody the values of the institution. Diversity, access and affordability, and quality are often values that are in conflict, and a shared leadership approach may be better able to cope with such disparate priorities. Finally, a shared leadership approach is a natural evolution for higher education, which has gone from relatively small institutions with a narrow mission to complex corporate structures with multiple missions and a vast array of stakeholders and external influences.

One of the reasons that shared leadership may seem more fiction than reality is because of the headlines generated when faculty, trustees, and administrators clash. Little is more contentious than when faculty vote "no confidence" in the president, which often call for boards to step in and take action. This is a drastic situation that reflects the potential contentiousness of both shared governance and shared leadership, so much so that it is often referred to colloquially as the "nuclear option." MacTaggart in his review of twenty cases of no-confidence votes in the past ten years made the following observations, although he notes that "the realities of a no-confidence vote are always more complex than any one of the parties may allege"[113]:

- Most calls of no confidence are grounded in faculty perceptions that presidents fail to engage, become arrogant, and issue top-down edicts (mirroring Birnbaum's findings).
- No-confidence votes tend to be tied to presidents trying to affect drastic change without engaging the faculty in expected ways.
- Conversely, faculty use these votes to express serious dismay with leaders' poor judgment or lack of progress on key institutional priorities.
- Ethical lapses such as excessive expenditures, disproportionate compensation, and moral turpitude are other causes of no-confidence votes. Presidents who overspend or have little accountability on their actions seem ripe for such actions by the faculty.

Such deep strife between the faculty and administration require boards to act but this can be difficult as the issues may not always be clear and boards need to consider carefully which side—faculty or the president—they will support. What might be shared leadership becomes leadership coalitions and conflicting interest groups. Boards need to respect faculty voices and not rush to judgment. Such situations put into direct conflict the leadership of the three key groups.

While shared leadership can be challenging based on the multiplicity of stakeholders, unclear lines of control and power, diffuse influence and authority, and difficult environmental circumstances, the evidence in support of a shared approach to leadership suggests it is worth the struggle. This chapter also argues for the importance of a robust shared governance approach as part of shared leadership. While higher education institutions have a long history of shared governance, AGB's recent report[114] suggests that shared governance has been in decline in the last two decades. Pressures to cut costs and respond to external challenges have led to trends of top-down decision making. We hope to encourage further examination of the need to view various stakeholders as shared stewards of the overall organization in difficult times.

As the opening metaphor of the orchestra suggests, many institutions may end up with an enterprise that soon sounds like a brass section only instead of the rich array of complex and rich music that has characterized higher education leadership. And while we often have not fulfilled the potential of a full orchestra, research tells us this is where we should be headed.

NOTES

1. We use the terms "institutions," "universities," and "colleges" interchangeably in this chapter.

2. Robert Birnbaum, *How Colleges Work: The Cybernetics of Academic Organization and Leadership* (San Francisco: Jossey-Bass, 1988); Henry Mintzberg, *Structures in Fives: Designing Effective Organizations* (Englewood Cliffs, NJ: Prentice Hall, 1983).

3. Robert Birnbaum, *How Academic Leadership Works: Understanding Success and Failure in the College Presidency* (San Francisco: Jossey-Bass, 1992).

4. Adrianna J. Kezar and Jaime Lester, *Enhancing Campus Capacity for Leadership: An Examination of Grassroots Leaders in Higher Education* (Palo Alto, CA: Stanford University Press, 2011).

5. Birnbaum, *How Colleges Work.*

6. Association of Governing Boards of Universities and Colleges (AGB), *Consequential Boards: Adding Value Where It Matters Most* (Washington, DC: AGB, 2014).

7. Ibid.

8. Richard P. Chait, William P. Ryan, and Barbara E. Taylor, *Governance as Leadership: Reframing the Work of Nonprofit Boards* (Hoboken, NJ: Wiley, 2004), 14.

9. Chait, Ryan, and Taylor, *Governance as Leadership;* Adrianna Kezar, "Rethinking Public Higher Education Governing Boards Performance: Results of a National Study of Governing Boards in the United States," *Journal of Higher Education* 77 no. 6 (Nov.–Dec. 2006): 969–1008.

10. Terrance MacTaggart, *Leading Change: How Boards and Presidents Build Exceptional Academic Institutions* (Washington, DC: Association of Governing Boards, 2011), 17.

11. David Nadler, "Building Better Boards," *Harvard Business Review* 82 no. 5 (May, 2004): 104.

12. AGB, *Consequential Boards.*

13. Richard Chait, "Why Boards Go Bad," *Trusteeship Magazine,* 14 no. 3 (May–June, 2006), 2.

14. Jack Stripling, "UVa's Painfully Public Lesson in Leadership," *The Chronicle of Higher Education* (July 2, 2012), http://chronicle.com/article/UVas-Painfully-Public-Lesson /132701/.

15. Kezar, "Rethinking Public Higher Education Governing Boards Performance."

16. Richard P. Chait, "Gremlins of Governance," *Trusteeship Magazine* (Jul.–Aug., 2009), 2–5, http://agb.org/trusteeship/2009/julyaugust/the-gremlins-of-governance.

17. Chait, Ryan, and Taylor, *Governance as Leadership,* 16.

18. Chait, "Gremlins of Governance." Jeffrey Sonnenfeld, "What Makes Great Boards Great," *Harvard Business Review* 80 no. 9 (Sept. 2002): 106–13.

19. Chait, Ryan, and Taylor, *Governance as Leadership.*

20. Chait, "Gremlins of Governance."

21. Cathy A. Trower, *The Practitioner's Guide to Governance as Leadership: Building High-Performing Nonprofit Boards* (San Francisco, CA: Jossey-Bass, 2012).

22. Ibid., 19.

23. Kezar, "Rethinking Public Higher Education Governing Boards Performance."

24. MacTaggart, *Leading Change,* 39.

25.  Peter D. Eckel, "What Presidents Really Think of Their Boards," *Trusteeship Magazine* (Nov.–Dec., 2013), 6–13.

26.  Association of Governing Boards of Colleges and Universities, "The Leadership Imperative: The Report of the AGB Task Force on the State of the Presidency in American Higher Education," ED 493 570 Association of Governing Boards of Colleges and Universities (2006), vi.

27.  Birnbaum, *How Academic Leadership Works*.

28.  American Council on Education (ACE), *The American College President: 2007 Edition* (Washington, DC: ACE, 2007).

29.  Peter D. Eckel, Brian J. Cook, and Jacqueline E. King, *The CAO Census: A National Profile of Chief Academic Officers* (Washington, DC: ACE, 2009).

30.  See, for example, Michael K. McLendon and Christine G. Mohker, "The Origins and Growth of State Policies that Privatize Public Higher Education," in *Privatizing the Public University: Perspectives from Across the Academy*, ed. Christopher C. Morphew and Peter D. Eckel (Baltimore: Johns Hopkins University Press, 2009), 7–32; Robert Toutkoushian, "An Economist's Perspective on the Privatization of Public Higher Education," in Morphew and Eckel, *Privatizing the Public University*, 60–86.

31.  James L. Fisher and James V. Koch, *The Entrepreneurial College President*, The ACE/Praeger Series on Higher Education (Westport, CT: Praeger, 2004).

32.  ACE, *American College President*.

33.  Clark Kerr, *The Uses of the University*, 5th ed. The Godkin Lectures on the Essentials of Free Government and the Duties of the Citizen 11 (Cambridge, MA: Harvard University Press, 2001).

34.  Robert Birnbaum and Peter D. Eckel, "The Dilemma of Presidential Leadership," in *American Higher Education in the Twenty-First Century: Social, Political, and Economic Challenges*, 2nd ed., ed. Philip G. Altbach, Robert O. Berdahl, and Patricia J. Gumport (Baltimore: Johns Hopkins University Press, 2002), 340–65.

35.  Birnbaum, *How Academic Leadership Works*, 154.

36.  Ibid., 55.

37.  Birnbaum, *How Academic Leadership Works*, 158–59.

38.  Ibid., 159.

39.  Ibid., 23.

40.  Peter D. Eckel and Matthew Hartley, *Presidential Leadership in an Age of Transition: Dynamic Responses for a Turbulent Time* (Washington, DC: ACE, 2011).

41.  James E. Gilmour, Jr., "Participative Governance Bodies in Higher Education: Report of a National Study," *New Directions for Higher Education*, 19 no. 3 (1991): 29–32.

42.  Roger L. Geiger, *Research and Relevant Knowledge: American Research Universitiessince World War II* (New York: Oxford University Press, 1993); Roger L. Geiger, *The American College in the Nineteenth Century* Vanderbilt Issues in Higher Education (Nashville: Vanderbilt University Press, 2000).

43.  Ibid.

44.  Christian K. Anderson, "The Creation of Faculty Senates in American Research Universities," PhD diss., Pennsylvania State University, 2007.

45.  Geiger, *The American College in the Nineteenth Century*.

46. Anderson, *The Creation of Faculty Senates in American Research Universities.*

47. Ibid.

48. Larry G. Gerber, "Inextricably Linked: Shared Governance and Academic Freedom," *Academe* 87 no. 3 (May–June, 2001): 22–24.

49. William G. Bowen and Eugene M. Tobin, *Locus of Authority: The Evolution of Faculty Roles in the Governance of Higher Education* (Princeton, NJ: Princeton University Press, 2015); Robert Birnbaum, "The End of Shared Governance: Looking Ahead or Looking Back," ED 482 064, Center for Higher Education Policy Analysis (2002).

50. Peter D. Eckel, "The Role of Shared Governance in Institutional Hard Decisions: Enabler or Antagonist?" *Review of Higher Education* 24 (2000): 15–39.

51. Gerber, "Inextricably Linked."

52. Birnbaum, "The End of Shared Governance."

53. Adrianna Kezar and Peter D. Eckel, "Meeting Today's Governance Challenges: A Synthesis of the Literature and Examination of a Future Research Agenda," *Journal of Higher Education* 75 no. 4 (2004): 372–99.

54. Anderson, *The Creation of Faculty Senates.*

55. James T. Minor, "Understanding Faculty Senates: Moving from Mystery to Models,"*Review of Higher Education* 27, no. 3 (2004): 343–63.

56. Birnbaum, *How Colleges Work.*

57. William G Tierney, "Governance by Conversation: An Essay on the Structure, Function, and Communicative Codes of a Faculty Senate," *Human Organization* 42, no. 2(1983): 172–77.

58. James T. Minor, "Understanding Faculty Senates: Moving from Mystery to Models,"*Review of Higher Education* 27, no. 3 (2004): 343–63.

59. Kezar and Eckel, "Meeting Today's Governance Challenges."

60. Bowen and Tobin, *Locus of Authority.*

61. Adrianna Kezar and Daniel Maxey, "Troubling Ethical Lapses: The Treatment of Contingent Faculty," *Change* 46 no. 4 (2014): 34–37.

62. Adrianna Kezar and Cecile Sam, *Non-Tenure-Track Faculty in Higher Education: Theories and Tensions,* ASHE Higher Education Report 36:5 (Hoboken, NJ: Jossey-Bass, 2011).

63. AGB, *Consequential Boards.*

64. James T. Minor, "Four Challenges Facing Faculty Senates," *Thought & Action* (Summer 2004): 125–40; William G. Tierney and James T. Minor, "*Challenges for Governance: A National Report* (Los Angles: University of Southern California, 2003).

65. Jack H. Schuster and Martin J. Finkelstein, *The American Faculty: The Restructuring of Academic Work and Careers* (Baltimore, MD: Johns Hopkins University Press, 2006).

66. Adrianna Kezar and Jamie Lester, *Enhancing Campus Capacity for Leadership.*

67. Anderson, *The Creation of Faculty Senates in American Research Universities.*

68. Ibid.

69. Birnbaum, *How Academic Leadership Works,* 146.

70. Birnbaum, *How Colleges Work;* Mintzberg, *Structures in Fives.*

71. Henry Mintzberg, *Tracking Strategies* (New York: Oxford University Press, 2007).

72. Ian Wilhelm, "Duke's China Plan Sparks Doubts on Campus," *The Chronicle of Higher Education* (May 25, 2011), http://m.chronicle.com/article/Dukes-China-Plan -Sparks/127640/.

73. Karl E. Weick, "Educational Organizations as Loosely Coupled Systems," *Administrative Science Quarterly* 21, no. 1 (1976): 1–19.

74. As cited in Robert Birnbaum, *Speaking of Higher Education* (Westport, CT: Praeger, 2004), 185.

75. Weick, "Educational Organizations."

76. Ibid.

77. Kellogg Commission on the Future of State and Land-Grant Universities, *Returning to Our Roots: Toward a Coherent Campus Culture* (Washington, DC: National Association of State Universities and Land-Grant Colleges, 2000), 41.

78. Michael D. Cohen and James G. March, *Leadership and Ambiguity: The American College President*, 2nd ed. (Cambridge, MA: Harvard Business Review Press, 1986), 82.

79. Ibid.

80. Ibid.

81. Ibid.

82. James G. March, *A Primer on Decision Making: How Decisions Happen* (New York: Free Press, 1994).

83. Cohen and March, *Leadership and Ambiguity*.

84. Birnbaum, *How Colleges Work*; Cohen and March, *Leadership and Ambiguity*.

85. Birnbaum, "Dilemma of Presidential Leadership."

86. Ibid., 330.

87. Birnbaum, *How Academic Leadership Works*.

88. John S. Levin, "Presidential Influence, Leadership Succession, and Multiple Interpretations of Organizational Change," *Review of Higher Education* 21, no. 4 (1998): 420.

89. Birnbaum, *How Academic Leadership Works*; Anna Neumann, "Context, Cognition, and Culture: A Case Analysis of Collegiate Leadership and Cultural Change," *American Educational Research Journal* 32, no. 2 (1995): 251–79.

90. Birnbaum, *How Academic Leadership Works*.

91. Anna Neumann, "Context, Cognition, and Culture."

92. Birnbaum, *How Academic Leadership Works*.

93. Ibid., 55.

94. Adrianna J. Kezar, Rozana Carducci, and Melissa Contreras-McGavin, *Rethinking the "L" Word in Higher Education: The Revolution of Research on Leadership*, ASHE Higher Education Report, vol. 31, no. 6 (San Francisco: Jossey-Bass, 2006).

95. Estela M. Bensimon, Anna Neumann, and Robert Birnbaum, *Making Sense of Administrative Leadership: The "L" Word in Higher Education*, ASHE-ERIC Higher Education Report, no. 1 (Washington, DC: George Washington University, School of Education and Human Development, 1989).

96. Kezar, Carducci, and Contreras-McGavin, *Rethinking the "L" Word*.

97. ACE, *American College President*.

98. James L. Fisher and James V. Koch, *Presidential Leadership: Making a Difference* (Phoenix: Oryx, 1996).

99. Vicki J. Rosser, Linda K. Johnsrud, and Ronald H. Heck, "Mapping the Domains of Effective Leadership" (presented at the annual meeting of the Association for the Study of Higher Education, Sacramento, CA, Nov. 2000).

100. Bensimon, Neumann, and Birnbaum, *Making Sense of Administrative Leadership*.

101. Kezar, Carducci, and Contreras-McGavin, *Rethinking the "L" Word*.

102. Ibid.

103. Ibid.

104. Ibid.

105. Bensimon, Neumann, and Birnbaum, *Making Sense of Administrative Leadership*.

106. See, for example, William G. Tierney, "Advancing Democracy: A Critical Interpretation of Leadership," *Peabody Journal of Higher Education* 66, no. 3 (1991): 157–75.

107. Adrianna J. Kezar and Peter D. Eckel, "Advancing Diversity Agendas on Campus: Examining Transactional and Transformational Presidential Leadership Styles," *International Journal of Leadership in Education* 11, no. 4 (2008): 379–405.

108. Bensimon, Neumann, and Birnbaum, *Making Sense of Administrative Leadership*; Karl L. Weick, *Sensemaking in Organizations*, Foundations for Organizational Science 3 (Thousand Oaks, CA: Sage, 1995).

109. Birnbaum, *How Academic Leadership Works*.

110. Ibid.

111. Estela M. Bensimon and Anna Neumann, *Redesigning Collegiate Leadership* (Baltimore, MD: Johns Hopkins University Press, 1993).

112. Adrianna Kezar, Peter Eckel, Melissa Contreras-McGavin, and Stephen John Quaye, "Creating a Web of Support: An Important Leadership Strategy for Advancing Campus Diversity," *Higher Education: The International Journal of Higher Education and Educational Planning* 55, no. 1 (2008): 69–92.

113. Terrance MacTaggart, "What Confidence Should Boards Give No-Confidence Votes?" *Trusteeship Magazine* (Dec. 2012).

114. AGB, *Consequential Boards*.

PART II / Macro Forces at Work

# Chapter Seven

# Patterns of Higher Education Development

## Philip G. Altbach

Universities are singular institutions. They have common historical roots yet are deeply embedded in their societies. Established in the medieval period to transmit knowledge and provide training for a few key professions, in the nineteenth century universities became creators of new knowledge through basic and applied research.[1] The contemporary university is the most important institution in the complex process of knowledge creation and distribution, serving as home not only to most of the basic sciences, but also to the complex system of journals, books, and databases that communicate knowledge worldwide.[2] Universities are key providers of training in an ever-growing number of specializations. Universities have also taken on a political and cultural function in society. At the same time, academe is faced with unprecedented challenges, stemming from several key trends globally—the advent of mass higher education in the twentieth century and its accompanying role as a central element for social mobility, the centrality of universities in the emerging global knowledge economy, a decline in resources to deal with these seismic shifts, and others.[3] The unwritten pact between society and higher education in which the state provided expanding resources in return for greater access for students, as well as research and service to society, has broken down, with significant implications for both higher education and society. These trends can be seen in the United States as well as in many other countries.

This chapter is concerned with the patterns of higher education development evident in the post–World War II period throughout the world, discussing some of the reasons for these trends, and pointing to likely directions for universities in the coming decades. Issues such as autonomy and accountability, research and teaching, reform and the curriculum, and the implications of the massive expansion of universities in most countries are among these concerns.

## A Common Heritage

There is only one common academic model worldwide. The basic European university model, established first in Italy and France at the end of the twelfth century, has been significantly modified but remains the universal pattern for higher education. The Paris model placed the professor at the center of the institution and enshrined autonomy as an important part of the academic ethos. It is significant that the major competing idea of the period, the student-dominated University of Bologna, did not gain a major foothold in Europe, although it had some impact in Spain and later in Latin America.[4] The university rapidly expanded to other parts of Europe—Oxford and Cambridge in England, Salamanca in Spain, Prague and Krakow in Central Europe and a variety of institutions in the German states were established in the following century.

Later, the European colonial powers brought universities to their colonies, along with other accoutrements of colonialism. The British, for example, exported their academic models first to the American colonies and later to India, Africa, and Southeast Asia.[5] The French implanted their model in Vietnam and West Africa, and the Spanish throughout Latin America.[6] Colonial universities were patterned directly on institutions in the metropole, but often without the traditions of autonomy and academic freedom in the mother country.

The university has by no means been a static institution; it has changed and adapted to new circumstances. With the rise of nationalism and the Protestant Reformation in Europe, the universal language of higher education, Latin, was replaced by national languages. Academic institutions became less international and more local in their student bodies and orientations and were affected by their national circumstances, Protestant Amsterdam differing, for example, from Catholic Salamanca. Harvard University, although patterned on British models, developed its own traditions and orientations, reflecting the realities of colonial North America.

Academic institutions have not always flourished. Oxford and Cambridge, strongly linked to the Church of England and the aristocracy, played only a minor role in the industrial revolution and the tremendous scientific expansion of late eighteenth and nineteenth century Britain.[7] In France, universities were abolished in 1793, after the initial phase of the French Revolution; gradually, they were reestablished, and the Napoleonic model became a powerful force not only in France but also in Spain and Latin America.[8] German universities, which were severely damaged during the Nazi period by the destruction of autonomy and the departure of many professors, lost the scientific preeminence they once had.[9]

For the purposes of this chapter, two more recent modifications of the Western academic model are especially relevant. In the early nineteenth century, a modernizing Prussia and then newly united Germany harnessed the university for nation building. Under the leadership of Wilhelm von Humboldt, German higher education was given significant resources by the state, took on the responsibility for research aimed at national development and industrialization, and played a key role in defining the ideology of the new German nation.[10] German universities also established graduate education and the doctoral degree. For the first time, research became an integral function of the university, and the university was reorganized as a hierarchy based on the newly emerging scientific disciplines. These ideas were profoundly influential in other modernizing nations, especially the United States, Japan, and Russia. American reformers further transformed higher education by stressing the relationship between the university and society, a new research mission, and the concept of service and direct links with industry and agriculture—these ideas were enshrined in the Land-Grant Act passed by Congress in the 1862. American universities also democratized the German chair system through the establishment of academic departments, and stressed both research and expanded access to higher education.[11] Thus, even institutions that seem deeply embedded in national soil have in fact been influenced by international ideas and models. Indeed, one can see the contemporary American university as a combination of two foreign ideas—the English collegiate model, and the German research university—and one American concept—the links between the university and society through both research and service.

Virtually without exception, the institutional pattern followed by the world's universities derives from these Western models. Significantly, in perhaps the only fully non-Western institutions, Al-Azhar University in Cairo, which focuses mainly on traditional Islamic law and theology, science faculties are now organized along European lines.[12] There are many variations of the Western model—open universities, two-year vocational institutions, teacher-training colleges, polytechnics—but while the functions of these institutions differ from those of traditional universities, their basic organization, pattern of governance, and ethos remain remarkably close to the Western academic ideal.[13]

## Networks of Knowledge and Higher Education

There are many explanations for the dominance of the Western academic model. The institutionalization of the study of science and, later, scientific research are central elements. The link between universities and the dominant world economic systems no doubt is an important reason for Western hegemony. In many parts of the world, academic institutions were imposed by colonizers, and there were few possibilities to develop independent alternatives. Indigenous institutional forms withered, as in nineteenth-century India with the British establishment of European patterns.[14] None of the formerly colonized nations have shifted from their basically European academic model; the contemporary Indian university, for example, resembles its pre-independence predecessor.

Japan, which was never colonized, recognized after 1868 that it had to develop scientific and industrial capacity and jettisoned its traditional academic institutions in favor of Western university traditions, importing ideas and models from Germany, the United States, and other countries. Other noncolonized nations, such as China and Thailand, also imported Western models and adapted them to local needs and conditions.

The harnessing of higher education to the broader needs of national economic and social development was perhaps the most important innovation of this era. Western universities were successful in providing advanced education, fostering research and scientific development, and assisting their societies in the increasingly complex task of development. Universities in both the United States and Germany fostered industrial and agricultural development. The ideas that higher education should be supported by public funds, that the university should participate in the creation as well as the transmission of knowledge, and that academic institutions should, at the same time, be permitted a degree of autonomy were behind much of the growth of universities in the nineteenth century. In twenty-first-century terms, these were the disruptive technologies and ideas of the nineteenth century and they both transformed higher education while at the same time showing that universities could adapt to new circumstances and needs. Further, Western universities were centers of knowledge networks that included research institutions, the means of knowledge dissemination (such as journals and scientific publishers), and an "invisible college" of scientists—just as today's universities host important websites and virtual networks. As science became more international, a common scientific language emerged, first German in the nineteenth century and then, since the mid-twentieth century, English. The Internet and internationalization have since enhanced the role of English.

The circulation of scholars and students worldwide—even the brain drain—is an element of the international knowledge system, helping to circulate ideas and also maintaining the research hegemony of the major host countries. At least five million students study outside their home countries—around 2 percent of the global total. The large majority of them come from developing and middle-income countries and study mainly in the English-speaking developed countries. The United States hosted close to 900,000 international students in 2013 from some 200 countries, and is by far the largest host nation—with perhaps 20 percent of the world total. China and India are the largest sending countries. International students contribute $27 billion to the American economy. Over half a million American students studied abroad—about 1 percent of the total student population.[15] While there are no accurate statistics relating to the numbers of foreign faculty hired by US universities or how many American faculty go abroad for research or teaching, these numbers are also significant.

Student and faculty mobility is a key element of twenty-first-century globalization—much is learned from sojourns abroad that contribute to a global consciousness. Further, the United States benefits considerably from global mobility, since it the most popular destination for students and faculty—research shows that a large majority of students who completed their doctorates in the United States from China and India, as well as some other countries, prefer to remain after completing their degrees.

While the brain drain still exists in the sense that many foreign students and scholars from the developing world and from emerging economies choose to remain in the United States and other developed nations, there are often significant relationships with the home country. These are made possible by the relative ease of communications, both physical and virtual.

The English language and the Internet have become key elements in the contemporary knowledge network. English is now the unquestioned medium of scientific research and communication—with the major journals published in English, and international conferences and websites conducted in English. This places English-speaking academic systems, such as those in the United States, in a privileged position. The Internet has also greatly impacted knowledge networks. More journals are now published electronically, and scientific communication is increasingly conducted virtually. Paradoxically, while the Internet has permitted most of the world's scientific communities to participate in the global network, it has, in some ways, strengthened the major academic systems (especially the United States), which are most influential on the web.

The knowledge network is complex and multifaceted; while its centers remain extraordinarily powerful, there is a movement toward greater equalization of research production and use. Japan, for example, already has a powerful and research-oriented university system, and some of the newly industrializing countries of East and Southeast Asia are building research capacity in their universities, with China playing a particularly important role.[16] But while hegemony may be slowly dissipating, inequality remains endemic in the world knowledge system, with the United States remaining the dominant center.

## Massification: Hallmark of the Postwar Era

Postsecondary education has expanded since World War II in virtually every country in the world. This growth has, in proportional terms, been more dramatic than that of primary and secondary education—there were more than 200 million students in postsecondary education in 2015, worldwide, up from approximately 150 million in 2009. Writing in 1975, Martin Trow spoke of the transition from *elite* to *mass* and then to *universal* higher education in the context of the industrialized nations.[17] The United States enrolled some 30 percent of the relevant age cohort (eighteen- to twenty-two-year-olds) in higher education in the immediate postwar period, while European nations generally maintained an elite higher education system, with fewer than 5 percent attending postsecondary institutions. By the 1960s, many European nations were educating 15 percent or more of this age group; in 1970, Sweden enrolled 24 percent, and France 17 percent. That year, the United States increased its proportion to more than 50 percent and was approaching universal access. By the end of the twentieth century, most Western European countries had increased their enrollment rates to about half, reaching close to what is considered "universal" access. Thus, while American patterns of access have stabilized, those in Europe and many newly industrializing countries continue to expand. A number of countries, including South Korea, Russia, and Finland, among others, now enroll more than 70 percent of the relevant age group.

In the developing and middle-income countries, expansion has been even more dramatic. Building on tiny and extraordinarily elitist universities, higher education expanded rapidly in the immediate post-independence period, with the largest numerical expansion taking place in these countries. Indeed, all continents except Africa have enrollment rates approaching half of the age group. In India, enrollment grew from approximately 100,000 at the time of independence, in 1947, to more than 20 million by 2014. India has the world's second largest number of students, although it only enrolls approximately 20 percent of the relevant age group. China, with 32 million students, has the largest enrollment—and it is predicted that more than half of the world's enrollment expansion in the coming decade will be in China and India. Other parts of the world have seen similar patterns of expansion. This massive expansion has resulted, not surprisingly, in a decline in per capita student expenditure, and this has contributed to a decline in academic overall standards.[18]

Regardless of political system, level of economic development, or educational ideology, the expansion of higher education has been the single most important trend worldwide. In 2013, the gross worldwide enrollment in tertiary education reached 32.9 percent, a statistic that has increased each decade since World War II.[19] Higher education expanded first in the United States, then in Europe, and later in the developing and middle-income countries. Women now constitute 51 percent of university enrollments worldwide, with considerable variation by country.[20] Generalized statistics concerning enrollments in postsecondary education mask many key differences. For example, industrialized nations have, in general, a higher proportion of students in technological and scientific fields than in social science and humanities subjects, which tend to predominate in many developing nations—although even here there are exceptions, such as China.

Without question, massification has been the dominating force in higher education in the past half-century or more. Not only has access been provided to students from a diverse population, but higher education systems have been significantly changed as well. Most countries now have academic systems that consist of research universities, mass access universities focusing on teaching, and the equivalents of community colleges. The United States pioneered diversified higher education—and many countries have followed the American model. It is likely that the overall quality of higher education has declined as a result of massification. Traditionally, small elite universities served a limited population base. Massification has created much more variety in quality as different populations are served.

There are many reasons for the expansion of higher education, a central one being the increasing complexity of modern societies and economies, which demands a more highly trained workforce. Postsecondary institutions have been called upon to provide the required training. Whole new fields, such as computer science, have come into existence and rely on universities as a source of research and training. Countries that have emerged into the industrial and post-industrial economies in the past half-century, such as South Korea, Taiwan, India, and of course China, depend on academic institutions to provide high-level training as well as research expertise.[21]

Not only do academic institutions provide training, they also test and provide certification for many occupations in contemporary society. These roles have been central to universities since the medieval period, but they have been vastly expanded in recent years. A university degree is a prerequisite for an increasing number of occupations in most societies. Tests to gain admission to higher education are rites of passage in many societies and are important determinants of future success.[22]

The role of the university as an examining body has expanded as well. Universities are seen as meritocratic institutions, which can be trusted to provide impartial tests to measure accomplishment and, therefore, to determine access to professional employment. Furthermore, entirely new fields have developed for which no sorting mechanisms exist, and academic institutions are frequently called upon to provide not only training, but also examination and certification.

Expansion has also occurred because growing segments of the population of modern societies demand it. The growing middle classes, seeing that academic qualifications are necessary for success, demand access to higher education, and governments generally respond by increasing enrollment. When governments do not move quickly enough, private initiative frequently establishes academic institutions to meet the demand. In countries such as India, the Philippines, and Bangladesh, as well as most Latin American nations, a majority of the students are educated in private colleges and universities.[23] Indeed, the private higher education sector, including for-profit institutions, is the fastest growing part of postsecondary education worldwide.

Higher education is increasingly seen as a private good—primarily benefiting the student—rather than a public good that benefits the broader society through the long-term productivity of graduates and other public contributions. This has meant that students are asked to pay more for higher education through increased tuition and other fees. The inability or unwillingness of governments to allocate appropriate resources to higher education has resulted in higher tuition—although some countries still maintain largely free public higher education institutions.[24]

## Change and Reform

The demands placed on institutions of higher education to accommodate larger numbers of students and expand their functions and orientations to meet the needs of the global knowledge economy has resulted in significant change and reform over the past half-century worldwide. Those who claim that universities are incapable of change are clearly wrong in light of the reforms that have taken place.

In the aftermath of the volatile decade of the 1960s, which featured both the beginnings of massification in much of the world, and significant student activism in some countries, a good deal of change took place.[25] In a few instances, students demanded far-reaching reforms in higher education, especially an end to the rigid, hierarchical organization of the traditional European university.[26] The chair system was modified or eliminated, and the responsibility for academic decision making, formerly a monopoly of full professors, was expanded—in some countries, even to include students. At the same time, interdisciplinary teaching and research became widespread.

Reform was most widespread in several traditional Western European academic systems. Sweden's universities were completely transformed: decision making was democratized, universities were decentralized, educational access was expanded to previously under-served parts of the country, interdisciplinary teaching and research was instituted, and the curriculum was expanded to include vocational courses.[27] Reforms also took place in France and the Netherlands, where reformers stressed interdisciplinary studies and the democratization of academic decision making. In Germany, the universities in states dominated by the Social Democratic Party were also reformed, with the traditional structures of the university giving way to more democratic governance patterns. It is, however, quite significant that most of the reforms enacted during this period, under pressure from student activists and during the early stages of massification in Europe, were later eliminated or modified, and more bureaucratic structures put into place. Student and faculty governance were limited as corporate management became more influential to meet the demands of accountability, expanding enrollments, and government demands.

In many other countries, structural change was modest. In the United States, for example, despite considerable debate during the 1960s, there was very limited change in the structure or governance of higher education.[28] Japan, where student unrest disrupted higher education and spawned a number of reports on university reform, experienced virtually no basic change in its higher education system, although several "new model" interdisciplinary institutions were established, such as the science-oriented Tsukuba University near Tokyo. Many of the structural reforms of the 1960s were abandoned after a decade of experimentation or were replaced by other administrative arrangements.

By the end of the twentieth century, a second wave of reforms ensued. These reforms can be characterized as a "managerial revolution" in higher education, where the overall goal was to ensure more accountability and efficiency in the management of academic institutions. These reforms generally increased the power of administrators and reduced faculty authority; students, too, had less power. The traditional authority of the senior faculty that had traditionally dominated European universities was weakened. Some have called these changes the "corporatization" of higher education—others, more favorable, refer to this and related trends as new public management. In Germany, for example, reforms in governance that gave students and junior staff a dominant position in some university functions were ruled unconstitutional by German courts.[29] Outside authorities, such as government (particularly in the public sector)—but also including business, industry, and labor organizations—came to play a more important role in academic governance. These changes were stimulated both by the growing size and complexity of many academic institutions and systems and by a desire to rein in expenditures. Efforts were made to privatize elements of public institutions and, in some countries, to stimulate the private sector in higher education. Curricular innovations, however, have proved more durable; interdisciplinary programs and initiatives and the introduction of new fields, such as gender studies, remain.

Vocationalization has been an important trend in the past two decades. Throughout the world, there is a conviction that the university curriculum must provide relevant training for a variety of increasingly complex jobs. Students, worried about obtaining remunerative employment, have pressed universities to focus more on job preparation. Employers have also demanded that the curriculum become more relevant to their needs. The term "workforce development" is commonly used to stress this trend. Enrollment in the social sciences and humanities, in many countries, has declined.

Curricular vocationalism is linked to another worldwide trend in higher education: the increasingly close relationship between universities and industry.[30] Industrial firms have sought to ensure that the skills they need are incorporated into the curriculum. This trend also has implications for academic research, since many university-industry relations are focused largely on research. Industries have established formal linkages and research partnerships with universities to obtain help with research of interest to them. In many European countries, representatives from industry have been added to the governing councils of higher education institutions. In the United States, formal contractual arrangements have been made between universities and major corporations to share research results and sometimes to collaborate on the development and use of research facilities. In many nations, corporations provide educational programs for their employees, sometimes with the assistance of universities.

Technical arrangements with regard to patents, the confidentiality of research findings, and other fiscal matters have assumed importance as university-industry relations have become crucial. Critics also point out that the nature of research in higher education may be altered by this relationship, as industrial firms are not usually interested in basic research. University-based research, which has traditionally been oriented toward basic research, may be increasingly skewed to applied and often profit-making topics. There has also been some discussion of research orientation in fields such as biotechnology, in which broader public policy matters may conflict with the needs of corporations. Specific funding arrangements have also been questioned. Pressure to serve the training and research requirements of industry has implications for the organization of the curriculum, the nature and scope of research, and the traditional relationship between the university and society.[31]

The traditional idea of academic governance stresses autonomy, and universities have tried to insulate themselves from direct control by external agencies. However, as universities expand and become more expensive, there is immense pressure by those providing funds for higher education—mainly governments—to expect accountability. The conflict between autonomy and accountability has been a flashpoint for controversy in recent years. Without exception, university autonomy has shrunk, and administrative structures have been put into place in such countries as Britain and the Netherlands to ensure greater accountability.[32] The issue takes on different implications in different parts of the world. In most developing and middle-income countries, traditions of autonomy have not been strong, and demands for accountability, both political and economic, often mean government domination of academe. In the industrialized nations, accountability pressures are usually more complex. Although government "steering" of academic systems and institutions has become more widespread and traditional autonomy significantly curtailed, the basic structures of universities have seldom been fundamentally altered. As Edward Shils has argued, the "academic ethos" has been under strain, and while in some ways it has been weakened, it has so far survived.[33]

## Twenty-First-Century Challenges

The university is a durable institution. The modern university retains key elements of the historical models from which it sprang, even while evolving to serve the needs of societies during a period of tremendous change.[34] There has been a global convergence of ideas and institutional patterns and practices in higher education worldwide and the dominance of the Western higher education model. The impact of massification and globalization, felt everywhere, have meant great pressure on higher education around the world. Responses have varied across the globe, but the challenges are similar. Some argue that the university has lost its soul.[35] Others claim that the university is irresponsible because it uses public funds without meeting the needs of industry and government. Governmental authorities, militant students, external constituencies, and others have all placed great strains on academic institutions.

The period since World War II has been one of unprecedented growth in universities, and higher education has assumed an increasingly central role in virtually all modern societies. While growth will continue, the dramatic expansion of recent decades, at least in the industrialized countries, is at an end since access rates are quite high. Growth will continue in developing and middle-income countries; in fact half the expansion worldwide up to 2050 is likely to be in just two countries—China and India—as they move toward educating more than half their youth in post-secondary education. The central role of higher education both in educating elites and in providing skills to the population generally is reasonably secure. The university's research role is more problematic because of the fiscal pressures of recent years. There is no other institution that can undertake basic research, but the consensus that has supported university-based basic research has weakened.[36]

The challenges facing universities are significant. The following issues are among those that will be of concern in the coming decades.

## ACCESS AND COMPLETION

Access remains a central issue in many countries—especially in developing and middle-income nations. Worldwide, higher education is in general readily available to wealthier segments of the population. With expansion, the demand has broadened, and providing access to lower-income groups is a challenge, especially in the context of fiscal constraints in higher education. Even in the United States, where access is relatively open regardless of social class, because of a highly differentiated higher education system and government-sponsored loan and grant programs, some racial and ethnic minorities remain underrepresented in the student population. Western European countries, Russia, and several other nations have provided access to more than half of the relevant age group—and in some cases to as much as 80 percent of the relevant population. Access rates are rapidly expanding elsewhere. For example, in much of Latin America close to half of the age group has access. However, access rates vary significantly depending on socioeconomic status or, in some countries, ethnic or racial groups. Women, at one time dramatically underrepresented, have achieved parity in much of the world. In most of Africa, access rates remain quite low.[37]

Access to post-secondary education is not the same as degree or certificate completion. In much of the world, significant proportions of students who enter higher education institutions do not complete their studies—or take significantly longer than the allocated time to degree. Dropout rates are especially high among students from lower socioeconomic and often from minority groups. Access and completion remain key issues in many countries.

## ADMINISTRATION, ACCOUNTABILITY, AND GOVERNANCE

As academic institutions become larger and more complex, there is increasing pressure for professional administration, as in the United States. At the same time, the traditional forms of academic governance are increasingly criticized for being unwieldy and, in large and bureaucratic institutions, inefficient. As the administration of higher education increasingly becomes a profession, an "administrative estate" has been established. Accountability to funders, the government, and the public is now characteristic in much of the world. This will cause academic institutions considerable difficulty. Worldwide, the rise of "managerialism" and ever-more-complex bureaucratic arrangements are part of the academic landscape. American patterns of state coordination of public higher education, referred to in Europe as "steering," are common worldwide.

These changes have profoundly altered the balance of authority in universities worldwide. Traditionally, the locus of power in most European universities resided with the senior faculty and a rector elected by the faculty. Increasingly, European universities have boards of management that are not dominated by the faculty and are more directly accountable to government authorities for funding. The tradition of shared governance has been weakened or eliminated in many countries. These profound administrative and governance changes have for the most part been created by massification and its implications.

### KNOWLEDGE CREATION AND DISSEMINATION

The world of academic research and knowledge dissemination has been profoundly changed by massification and the global knowledge economy. Higher education systems in most countries have become more differentiated so that the small number of research universities at the top of national academic systems are able to carry out increasingly sophisticated research missions—and at the same time compete better in the global rankings. Many countries have spent significant funds upgrading their research universities. Universities have also created interdisciplinary research centers and other new arrangements to stimulate cutting edge research.

At the same time, the production and dissemination of research has changed considerably, propelled in large part by information technology. Scholarly journals, and the peer review system that maintains quality in them, remain, although many are owned by multinational media companies rather than by academic societies or universities.[38] Many journals and books are distributed mainly or entirely electronically. The number of academic journals has proliferated, and it is a challenge to assess quality or impact, although sophisticated measures have been developed to judge impact.[39]

Globalization, the expanding numbers of research universities worldwide, increased competition among academic institutions and researchers, changing patterns of ownership and control of knowledge systems, and other factors have created new and complex systems of knowledge creation and distribution.

Major Western knowledge producers constitute a kind of cartel of information, dominating not only the creation of knowledge but also most of the major channels of distribution. Simply increasing the amount of research and creating new databases will not ensure a more equal and accessible knowledge system.

## THE ACADEMIC PROFESSION

In most countries, the professoriate has been under great pressure in recent years. Demands for accountability, the increased bureaucratization of institutions, fiscal constraints, and an increasingly diverse student body have all challenged the professoriate. In most industrialized nations, a combination of fiscal problems and demographic factors has led to a stagnating profession.[40]

Circumstances vary by region, but some factors are evident worldwide. Fiscal problems create multiple difficulties. Salaries have not kept up with either the cost of living or remuneration offered elsewhere in the economy, and it is difficult to lure the "best and brightest" to academe.[41] The terms of academic appointments have deteriorated in many places—tenure has been abolished in Britain, for example, and in many countries a larger proportion of the profession is part time. Traditional career ladders have been modified—generally in ways that have not benefited the professors. Class sizes have increased and academic autonomy has been limited. Pressures on the professoriate, especially in the research universities, not only to teach and do research but also to attract external grants, engage in consulting, and earn additional income for themselves and for their universities have grown. The difficulties faced by the academic profession in developing countries are perhaps the greatest—to maintain a viable academic culture under deteriorating conditions and without the protection of established norms.

## PRIVATE RESOURCES AND PUBLIC RESPONSIBILITY

In almost all countries there has been a growing emphasis on increasing the role of the private sector in higher education. As noted, private higher education is the most rapidly growing part of postsecondary education worldwide. Latin America, for example, over a half-century moved from mainly public provision of higher education—and in many countries free public higher education—to a majority of students in private institutions, many of which are for-profit. Private higher education is growing rapidly in much of sub-Saharan Africa and in parts of Asia. Only Western Europe remains largely public in provision of higher education. The United States, with its stable proportion of 80 percent of enrollments in public institutions, is now one of the more public-dominated countries. It is worth noting that only in the United States and Japan are there significant numbers of private nonprofit research universities—the private higher education sector in most of the world consists of low-quality institutions serving students from relatively modest socioeconomic populations. In this way, the higher-quality public universities are providing less expensive and better quality education to elite sections of the population who can gain access through competitive entrance examinations.

Public higher education is becoming more privatized, with the state providing a decreasing part of the budget, as tuition costs increase in some countries. The United States is one of the leaders in the privatization of public higher education, with many states providing a decreasing amount of financial support for public higher education. Other countries that at one time provided low tuition or even free higher education have imposed tuition and fees— although there are exceptions, such as Germany, where some of the states that had begun to impose tuition charges have recently moved back to providing free tuition.

Governments try to limit their expenditures on postsecondary education. Privatization has been the means of achieving this broad policy goal.[42] Inevitably, decisions concerning academic developments will move increasingly to the private sector, with the possibility that broader public goals may be ignored. Whether private interests will support the traditional functions of universities— including academic freedom, basic research, and a pattern of governance that leaves the professoriate in control—is unlikely.

### Diversification and Stratification

While diversification—establishing new postsecondary institutions to meet diverse needs—is not new, it is of primary importance and will continue to reshape the academic system. In recent years, the establishment of research institutions, community colleges, polytechnics, and other academic institutions designed to meet specialized needs and serve specific populations has been a primary characteristic of massification worldwide. At the same time, the academic system has become more stratified—individuals in one sector of the system find it difficult to move to a different sector. There is often a high correlation between social class (and other variables) and participation in a particular sector. To some extent, the reluctance of traditional universities to change is responsible for some of the diversification. Perhaps more important is the belief that limited-function institutions are more efficient and less expensive.

An element of diversification is the inclusion of larger numbers of women and other previously disenfranchised segments of the population. In many countries, students from lower socioeconomic groups and racial and ethnic minorities have entered postsecondary institutions in significant numbers.

## ECONOMIC AND OTHER DISPARITIES

The substantial inequalities among the world's universities and academic systems are likely to grow—this is true within countries and between countries. Major universities in industrialized nations generally have the resources to play a leading role in scientific research, in a context in which it is increasingly expensive to keep up with the expansion of knowledge. Universities in most developing countries, however, simply cannot cope with the increased enrollments and budgetary constraints. Universities in much of sub-Saharan Africa, for example, find it difficult to function effectively in the context of massification, not to mention improve quality and compete in the international knowledge system.[43] Academic institutions in the newly industrializing Asian countries, where significant academic progress has taken place, will continue to improve. Thus the economic prospects for postsecondary education worldwide are mixed.

Countries that have invested heavily in higher education, such as China, have experienced significant improvements in their research universities—and this is reflected by a larger number of Chinese universities scoring better in the international rankings.[44] Universities in a small number of countries that have not had high-quality institutions, such as Singapore, Hong Kong, South Korea, and Brazil, have seen significant improvement. However, overall, the traditional academic centers in the major English-speaking countries and Western Europe will continue to dominate the rankings and produce most global research.[45] Thus, by and large, the arrangement of global academic powers will remain fairly stable.

## GLOBALIZATION AND INTERNATIONALIZATION

Universities throughout the world are necessarily engaged in an ever-more-globalized environment. Student and faculty mobility, an increasingly global job market, the internationalization of science and scholarship, and global competition for status are all part of contemporary globalization. There are now more than four million globally mobile students—with the largest number, more than 886,000, studying in the United States. It is estimated that global mobility may increase to more than 7 million in the coming two decades. Hundreds of universities, in the United States and elsewhere, now sponsor branch campuses around the world. Franchise arrangements, twinning programs, and many other internationalization efforts continue to expand rapidly.[46] Internationalization is becoming increasingly commercialized—and produces significant income for many host countries. For instance, international students produce $27 billion annually for the United States.[47] At the same time, students everywhere need an international perspective to cope with the global knowledge economy. Initiatives such as the Bologna programs in Europe, and many others, are also important aspects of twenty-first-century internationalization. The United States, as the most powerful academic system, has significant advantages in the international brain race, but the challenges of the new globalized environment create new realities.[48]

## Conclusion

Universities worldwide share a common culture and a common reality. At the same time, there are significant national differences that will continue to affect the development of academic systems and institutions. Although many observers are convinced that the current model of universities worldwide cannot survive the pressures of the twenty-first century, it is unlikely that the basic structures of academic institutions will change fundamentally. But deep change is inevitable. Examples include continuing deterioration in the working conditions for the academic profession—and a resulting challenge to recruit the "best and brightest" to academe; increased corporatization of universities, including the professionalization of university management; continuing financial pressures that will result in the growing privatization of public higher education; the impact of e-learning, including MOOCS, and the delivery of online degrees; demographic pressures, including declines in the relevant age groups in some countries and dramatic increases in enrollments in others; and many more. Worldwide, the coming period is one of major challenges for higher education.

NOTES

1. For a historical perspective, see Charles Haskins, *The Rise of Universities* (Ithaca, NY: Cornell University Press, 1957).

2. Philip G. Altbach, *The Knowledge Context: Comparative Perspectives on the Distribution of Knowledge* (Albany: State University of New York Press, 1987).

3. Philip G. Altbach, Liz Reisberg, and Laura E. Rumbley, *Trends in Global Higher Education: Tracking an Academic Revolution* (Rotterdam, Netherlands: Sense, 2010).

4. For further discussion of this point, see Alan B. Cobban, *The Medieval Universities: Their Development and Organization* (London: Methuen, 1975).

5. The history of British higher education expansion in India and Africa is described in Eric Ashby, *Universities: British, Indian, African* (Cambridge, MA: Harvard University Press, 1976).

6. See Philip G. Altbach and Viswanathan Selvaratnam, eds., *From Dependence to Autonomy: The Development of Asian Universities* (Dordrecht, Netherlands: Kluwer, 1989).

7. For a broader consideration of these themes, see Lawrence Stone, ed., *The University in Society*, 2 vols. (Princeton, NJ: Princeton University Press, 1974).

8. Joseph Ben-David, *Centers of Learning: Britain, France, Germany, the United States* (New York: McGraw-Hill, 1977), 16–17.

9. Friedrich Lilge, *The Abuse of Learning: The Failure of the German University* (New York: Macmillan, 1948).

10. Charles E. McClelland, *State, Society, and University in Germany, 1700–1914* (Cambridge: Cambridge University Press, 1980). See also Joseph Ben-David and Awraham Zloczower, "Universities and Academic Systems in Modern Societies," *European Journal of Sociology* 3 (1962): 45–84.

11. In the German system, a full professor was appointed as head (chair) of each discipline, and all other academic staff served under his direction; the position was permanent. Many other countries, including Japan, Russia, and most of Eastern Europe, adopted this system. On developments in America, see Laurence Veysey, *The Emergence of the American University* (Chicago: University of Chicago Press, 1965).

12. For a discussion of the contemporary Islamic university, see Hamed H. Bilgrami and Syed A. Ashraf, *The Concept of an Islamic University* (London: Hodder and Stoughton, 1985).

13. Philip G. Altbach, "The American Academic Model in Comparative Perspective," in *Comparative Higher Education*, ed. Philip G. Altbach (Greenwich, CT: Ablex, 1998), 55–74.

14. See David Lelyveld, *Aligarh's First Generation: Muslim Solidarity in British India* (Princeton, NJ: Princeton University Press, 1978).

15. Christine A. Farrugia and Rajika Bhandari, *Open Doors: Report on International Student Mobility, 2014* (New York: Institute of International Education 2014).

16. Robert A. Rhoads, Xiaoyang Wang, Xiaoguang Shi, and Yongcai Chang, *China's Rising Research Universities: A New Era of Global Ambition* (Baltimore: Johns Hopkins University Press, 2014). See also Martin Carnoy et al., *University Expansion in a Changing Global Economy: Triumph of the BRICS?* (Stanford, CA: Stanford University Press, 2013).

17. Martin Trow, "Reflections on the Transition from Elite to Mass to Universal Access: Forms and Phases of Higher Education in Societies since WWII," in *International Handbook of Higher Education*, ed. James J. F. Forest and Philip G. Altbach (Dordrecht, Netherlands: Springer, 2006), 243–80.

18. See Task Force on Higher Education and Society, *Higher Education in Developing Countries: Peril and Promise* (Washington, DC: World Bank, 2000).

19. The World Bank, "School Enrollment, tertiary (% gross)," http://data.worldbank.org/indicator/SE.TER.ENRR/countries?display=graph [accessed July 9, 2015].

20. UNESCO Institute of Statistics, "Percentage of Female Enrollment by Level of Education," http://data.uis.unesco.org/?queryid=145 [accessed July 9, 2015].

21. Philip G. Altbach et al., *Scientific Development and Higher Education: The Case of Newly Industrializing Nations* (New York: Praeger, 1989). See also Philip G. Altbach, Liz Reisberg, Maria Yudkevich, Gregory Androushchak, and Yaroslav Kuzminov, eds., *The Global Future of Higher Education and the Academic Profession: The BRICs and the United States* (New York: Palgrave, 2013).

22. Max A. Eckstein and Harold J. Noah, "Forms and Functions of Secondary School Leaving Examinations," *Comparative Education Review* 33 (1989): 295–316.

23. Roger L. Geiger, *Private Sectors in Higher Education: Structure, Function, and Change in Eight Countries* (Ann Arbor: University of Michigan Press, 1986). For a focus on Latin America, see Daniel C. Levy, *Higher Education and the State in Latin America: Private Challenges to Public Dominance* (Chicago: University of Chicago Press, 1986). See also Philip G. Altbach, ed., *Private Prometheus: Private Higher Education and Development in the 21st Century* (Westport, CT: Greenwood, 1999).

24. Bruce D. Johnstone, *Sharing the Costs of Higher Education: Student Financial Assistance in the United Kingdom, the Federal Republic of Germany, France, Sweden, and the United States* (Washington, DC: College Board, 1986).

25. For broader considerations of the reforms of the 1960s, see Ulrich Teichler, *Changing Patterns of the Higher Education System* (London: Kingsley, 1989).

26. For an example of an influential student proposal for higher education reform, see Wolfgang Nitsch, Uta Gerhardt, Claus Offe, and Ulrich K. Preuss, *Hochschule in der Demokratie* (Berlin: Luchterhand, 1965).

27. Jan Erik Lane and Mac Murray, "The Significance of Decentralization in Swedish Education," *European Journal of Education* 20 (1985): 163–72.

28. See Alexander W. Astin, Helen Astin, Alan Bayer, and Ann Bisconti, *The Power of Protest* (San Francisco: Jossey-Bass, 1975), for an overview of the results of the ferment of the 1960s on American higher education.

29. For a critical viewpoint, see Hans Daalder and Edward Shils, eds., *Universities, Politicians, and Bureaucrats: Europe and the United States* (Cambridge: Cambridge University Press, 1982).

30. See, for example, Ladislav Cerych, "Collaboration between Higher Education and Industry: An Overview, " *European Journal of Education* 20, no. 1 (1985): 7–18.

31. Of course, this is not a new concern for higher education. See Thorstein Veblen, *The Higher Learning in America: A Memorandum on the Conduct of Universities by Business Men* (New York: Viking, 1918).

32. See Klaus Hufner, "Accountability," in *International Higher Education: An Encyclopaedia*, vol. 1, ed. Philip G. Altbach (New York: Garland, 1991), 47–58.

33. Edward Shils, *The Academic Ethic* (Chicago: University of Chicago Press, 1983).

34. See Ben-David and Zloczower, "Universities and Academic Systems."

35. See, for example, Robert Nisbet, *The Degradation of the Academic Dogma: The University in America, 1945–1970* (New York: Basic Books, 1971). Allan Bloom, in his *The Closing of the American Mind: How Higher Education Has Failed Democracy and Impoverished the Souls of Today's Students* (New York: Simon and Schuster, 1987), echoes many of Nisbet's sentiments.

36. In those countries that have located much of their research in nonuniversity institutions, such as the academies of sciences in Russia and some Central and Eastern

European nations, there has been some rethinking of this organizational model, and a sense that universities may be more effective locations for major research. Since the collapse of the Soviet Union, there have been some moves to abolish the academy model. See Alexander Vucinich, *Empire of Knowledge: The Academy of Sciences of the USSR, 1917–1970* (Berkeley: University of California Press, 1984).

37. Altbach, Reisberg, and Rumbley. *Trends in Global Higher Education.*

38. See Thomas W. Shaughnessy et al., "Scholarly Communication: The Need for an Agenda for Action—a Symposium," *Journal of Academic Librarianship* 15 (1989): 68–78. See also National Enquiry into Scholarly Communication and American Council of Learned Societies, *Scholarly Communication: The Report of the National Enquiry* (Baltimore: Johns Hopkins University Press, 1979).

39. These issues are discussed in Altbach, *Knowledge Context.* For a different perspective, see Irving Louis Horowitz, *Communicating Ideas: The Crisis of Publishing in a Post-Industrial Society* (New York: Oxford University Press, 1986).

40. For an American perspective, see Jack H. Schuster and Martin J. Finkelstein, *The American Faculty: The Restructuring of Academic Work and Careers* (Baltimore: Johns Hopkins University Press, 2006).

41. Philip G. Altbach, Liz Reisberg, Maria Yudkevich, Gregory Androushchak, and Iván F. Pacheco, eds. *Paying the Professoriate: A Global Comparison of Compensation and Contracts* (New York: Routledge, 2012). See also Maria Yudkevich, Philip G. Altbach, and Laura E. Rumbley, eds. *Young Faculty in the Twenty-First Century: International Perspectives* (Albany: State University of New York Press, 2015).

42. Levy, *Higher Education.* See also Geiger, *Private Sectors in Higher Education.*

43. Kirsten Majgaard and Alain Mingat, *Education in Sub-Saharan Africa: A Comparative Analysis* (Washington DC: World Bank, 2012), 68–81.

44. Rhoads et al., *China's Rising Research Universities.*

45. Ellen Hazelkorn, *Rankings and the Reshaping of Higher Education: The Battle for World-Class Excellence* (New York: Routledge, 2015).

46. Darla K. Deardorff, Hans de Wit, John D. Heyl, and Tony Adams, eds., *The SAGE Handbook of International Higher Education* (Thousand Oaks, CA: Sage, 2012).

47. Farrugia and Bhandari, *Open Doors.*

48. See Philip G. Altbach, *Global Perspectives on Higher Education* (Baltimore: Johns Hopkins University Press, 2016).

# Chapter Eight

# The Federal Government and Higher Education

Michael Mumper, Lawrence E. Gladieux, Jacqueline E. King, and Melanie E. Corrigan

The federal government, notwithstanding the primary role of the states in our federal system, has played an essential role in shaping the size, scope, and character of American higher education. Today, it provides nearly $190 billion annually to assist students in covering college costs, help institutions expand their capacity to serve disadvantaged students, and engage faculty in the types of scientific and medical research that advance the national interest.

Despite this huge investment, the federal government's role has always been secondary or supplementary. It is the states and the institutions that are the primary policy makers for higher education. In this chapter, we summarize the evolving role that the federal government has played in higher education, including a review of the major interventions that have influenced and shaped the course of America's colleges and universities. Then we describe, in some detail, several of the areas where the federal role has been most crucial. These include the provision of direct aid to college students, the allocation of tax deductions and credits to students and colleges, federal funding of research and development, the impact of federal regulations on colleges and universities, and the efforts of the federal government to rein in college prices. These are the areas both of the greatest federal expansion over the years and where the greatest tensions remain. Finally, we briefly outline some of the major issues facing the federal government in higher education today and the prospects for federal relations with higher education over the coming decades.

## The Evolving Federal Role in Higher Education

In the US Constitutional system, the states have primary responsibility for all levels of education. The Tenth Amendment reserves all powers not delegated to the central government to the states. Since education is not explicitly mentioned in the Constitution, the states have taken the lead in this area, with the federal government playing a secondary role. While most of the framers supported this division of responsibilities, a few, including George Washington and James Madison, advocated for the creation of a national university. However, all proposals to establish such a university have failed. As a result, the federal government does not directly sponsor specific institutions of higher education, apart from the military academies and a few institutions serving special populations.

While the role of the federal government has been secondary, it has certainly not been unimportant. It has played a critical part in promoting the development and expansion of the nation's system of higher education. This growth in the influence of the federal government, however, did not unfold in a steady or linear pattern. Instead, it has proceeded in a series of sequential expansions over many decades, with each new expansion advancing the federal role in new and often fundamental ways. At several critical points in the nation's history, these federal interventions proved to be the driving force in the growth and expansion of the American higher education system. For the most part, these new federal programs were offered as "grants" under the Constitutional power to "promote the general welfare." While states could turn down such grants, the political reality is that they were never rejected, and the federal role has accordingly increased.

The first significant federal intervention occurred in the 1860s, as part of a federal effort to encourage Americans to migrate west and develop the nation's public lands along the way. While the Morrill Land Grant Act of 1862 was aimed at encouraging this western expansion, the approach it used has had a profound impact on the nation's colleges and universities.[1] Rather than embracing the classical liberal arts curriculum, the Morrill Act encouraged the creation of new institutions focused on the study of disciplines critical to westward expansion, including agriculture, engineering, mechanics, and mining. Within a few years, thirty-seven institutions were designated as land-grant colleges. In some states, the legislature opted to graft new programs onto an existing college. Other states created wholly new institutions. The result of this federal expansion was the creation and development of what are now some of the nation's great universities, including the University of Wisconsin, the University of California, Pennsylvania State University, Texas A&M University, and parts of Cornell University.

The next significant intervention in American higher education driven by the federal government was the post–World War II enrollment boom resulting from the GI Bill. While the Servicemen's Readjustment Act of 1944, popularly known as the GI Bill of Rights, was not intended to be higher education policy, its impact on American colleges and universities is difficult to overstate. The GI Bill provided returning veterans with a wide range of benefits, but to the general public it became synonymous with tuition assistance in attending college.

The most obvious impact of the GI Bill was on college enrollment. In 1945, as the war was coming to an end, there were about 1.6 million students enrolled in higher education. Only about 88,000 of those were veterans. Just two years later, college enrollment had increased 45 percent, to 2.3 million, and more than 1 million of those students were veterans.[2] With the assistance of the GI Bill, hundreds of thousands of Americans who otherwise would not have attended college returned to enroll in institutions of higher education and earn degrees. One important feature of the GI Bill was that it provided its benefits to all veterans, regardless of gender, race, ethnic background, or income level. Although the armed forces remained segregated at the end of World War II, the benefits of the GI Bill were available to anyone who had been on active duty for at least ninety days and had not been dishonorably discharged. The benefits of the GI Bill allowed many black and Hispanic veterans to use their education to boost themselves and their families into the middle class.

The massive influx of veterans onto the nation's campuses resulted in substantial changes in their facilities and physical plants, admissions procedures, and even their curricula and pedagogies. New housing and classroom space needed to be built, methods needed to be developed to assess the college readiness of veterans, and curricular adjustments needed to be made for veterans who were anxious to become wage-earners as quickly as possible. All of this expansion, much of which remained after the initial wave of veterans had completed their education, was funded by the dollars provided by the federal government through the GI Bill.

Glen Altschuler and Stuart Blumin argue that the most important contribution of the GI Bill was that the academic achievements of the veterans "enhanced the prestige, practical value, and visibility of a college diploma."[3] It also helped to "forge a consensus that the number of college caliber candidates drawn from all socioeconomic and ethnic groups was far larger than previously thought.

Americans began to perceive undergraduate and graduate degrees as gateways to the professions, the new route to the American dream."[4]

Federal involvement and investment in higher education accelerated through the Cold War years of the 1950s, 1960s, and 1970s. This occurred primarily through a larger federal role in university-based research and in the development of financial aid to college students. In direct and immediate response to the launch of the Sputnik satellite by the Soviet Union in 1957, Congress sought to ensure the nation's economic and military hegemony by encouraging more students to pursue higher education and making substantial investments in programs to boost scientific research. As the Cold War unfolded, Congress sought to encourage more students to attend college and study in areas of national interest, such as science, engineering, and foreign languages. The Cold War also produced a strengthening of the research partnership between the federal government and the nation's universities that had developed so strongly during World War II. This partnership aimed at creating the technology to explore space and supporting the science necessary to maintain dominance over the Soviet Union.

The next real breakthrough in the expansion of the federal role in higher education came in 1965, as a part of President Lyndon Johnson's Great Society program.[5] This was an aggressive effort to achieve equal opportunity for all Americans, and a central part of that effort was ensuring that everyone had an equal opportunity to attend college. The logic behind the first equal opportunity programs was that by bringing higher education within the financial reach of all Americans, lower-income students would enroll in greater numbers. This would result in their finding better jobs, earning higher wages, and moving out of poverty. Based largely on this economic rationale, the federal government developed an elaborate new plan to provide financial aid to needy college students. As we will describe later, these federal programs have grown until today they offer billions of dollars in aid to more than 14 million students attending almost every accredited institution of higher education in the nation.[6]

In 2009, the federal government made a new and largely unexpected intervention that has had long-term implications for American higher education. As Barack Obama entered office in January 2009, the national and international economy was in an almost unprecedented decline. Credit markets were frozen, the unemployment rate was soaring, and federal and state tax revenues had slowed dramatically. In the face of this crisis, President Obama persuaded Congress to adopt the American Reinvestment and Recovery Act (ARRA). A major part of this multifaceted legislation was a massive infusion of federal funds to state governments, intended to prop up their budgets, which were staggering under the combination of declining tax revenues and increasing state and local demands for health care and social services.[7]

Since most states have constitutional requirements to maintain balanced budgets, their declining revenues would have left governors and state legislatures with no choice but to make devastating reductions in higher education funding. Public colleges and universities, in turn, would have been left to cope with those reductions by reducing staff, cutting operating budgets, and sharply increasing tuition and fees. While the states and public colleges were certainly hurt by the budget crisis and subsequent recession, the full potential of that impact was substantially reduced by the federal support provided by ARRA. Federal dollars flowed directly and quickly to the states to "backfill" for their lost tax revenues. This reduced the amount states were forced to cut, protected many public colleges from enormous reductions in state support, and lessened the impact those reductions had on their students.[8]

### The Scope of the Federal Role

In the nineteenth century, the states served as intermediaries in federal support for higher education, as this federal support flowed to institutions through state governments. Toward the beginning of the twentieth century, however, federal support increasingly bypassed the states and went directly to institutions. Today, nearly all federal support is directed to institutions (departments, research institutes, schools, or individual faculty members within institutions) or to individual students. For this reason, there is not really a federal-state partnership in either the direction or financing of higher education. In fact, there is very little conscious coordination of funding purposes and patterns between the two levels of government. Federal activity proceeds independently of state activity. Chester Finn observes that "with a few modest exceptions, federal postsecondary spending arrangements make no attempt to stimulate state spending or compensate for differences in state wealth or effort, or to give state governments money to allot as they see fit."[9]

Today, the federal government's activities affecting higher education are so decentralized and so intermixed with other policy objectives that trying to enumerate the programs and tally the total investment is problematic. The creation of the US Department of Education in 1979 consolidated only about one-fourth of the more than 400 programs that existed at the time, and less than one-third of the total federal expenditures for higher education. The remaining programs and funds are still scattered across a number of federal agencies, in-

*Table 8.1*    Estimated federal assistance to higher education by type, 2013

| Type of federal aid | Billions of dollars | Percentage of federal total |
| --- | --- | --- |
| Student assistance | 78.8 | 42.2 |
| Student financial assistance | 44.9 | |
| Federal Direct Student Loans | 16.2 | |
| Federal Family Education Loans | 2.3 | |
| Tuition assistance for military personnel | 12.2 | |
| Other scholarships/fellowships | 3.2 | |
| Research and development | 60.6 | 32.6 |
| Basic research | 30.2 | |
| Applied research and development | 30.4 | |
| Other federal expenditures | 7.2 | 4.2 |
| Service academies | 1.1 | |
| All other on-budget expenditures for higher education | 6.1 | |
| Tax expenditures for students and families | 33.1 | 17.7 |
| Tax credits for tuition for postsecondary education | 23.4 | |
| Deductions for student loan interest | 2.3 | |
| Exclusion of scholarship and fellowship income | 3.2 | |
| Other tax expenditures for families | 4.2 | |
| Tax expenditures for institutions | 6.3 | 6.3 |
| Deduction for charitable contributions | 6.3 | |
| Total federal assistance | 186 | 99.8 |

*Sources:* US Congress, Joint Committee on Taxation, *Estimates of Federal Tax Expenditures for Fiscal Years 2014–18, https://www.jct.gov/publications.html?func=startdown&id=4663*; National Science Foundation, *Federal Government Is Largest Source of University R&D Funding in S&E; Share Drops in FY 2013* (Washington, DC: National Science Foundation, 2009); National Center for Education Statistics, *Digest of Education Statistics 2014* (Washington, DC: US Department of Education, 2013).

   *Note:* Student financial assistance includes all Title IV programs, in addition to various scholarship programs where monies are awarded directly to the student (except National Health Service Corps scholarships). Tuition assistance for military personnel also includes the Senior Reserve Officer Training Corps. Veterans' tuition benefits also includes the Department of Education–related expenses. Research and development includes all federal obligations for research and development. Service academies also include the Merchant Marine Academy. Other federal expenditures include historically black colleges and universities (HBCUs), the Agricultural Extension Service, mineral leasing, federal aid to Washington, DC, and educational exchanges.

cluding the departments of Defense, Labor, Agriculture, Homeland Security, Transportation, Health and Human Services, Veterans Administration, the Agency for International Development, National Aeronautics and Space Administration, and the Smithsonian Institution.

Table 8.1 provides an overview of federal support for higher education. In 2014, the federal spending total on higher education, including tax expenditures, was $186 billion. Of that total, 42 percent went to programs providing direct aid to college students (including student loans), 33 percent went to university-based research, 18 percent to tax programs providing benefits for students and their families, and 3 percent to tax benefits affecting nonprofit institutions of higher education. In constant dollar terms, the overall federal investment in higher education has increased by 58 percent between 2008 and 2014.

### DIRECT FEDERAL AID TO COLLEGE STUDENTS

Since the mid-1960s, the area where the federal government has had the greatest impact on the nation's colleges and universities is in the provision of direct aid to college students. The federal legislation that provided the rationale for this involvement and laid out its programmatic structure was the Higher Education Act of 1965 (HEA). Passed in the flurry of Great Society legislation—including the Voting Rights Act, the Civil Rights Act, and the Elementary and Secondary Education Act, as well as expansions in the availability of health care coverage (including the creation of Medicare and Medicaid)—the HEA established a new federal role and purpose in higher education: promoting equal opportunity. For the first time, the federal government was going to set a goal of removing the barriers, especially price barriers, which keep low-income students out of higher education.

Title IV of the HEA created three types of federal student aid programs, and their basic structures more or less remain today. The centerpiece of the student aid system was a large, need-based grant program. Originally called the Educational Opportunity Grant, then the Basic Educational Opportunity Grant, the federal grant program was first designed to be administered by each campus. In 1972, the HEA was amended to centralize the administration and awarding of the program under a new name, Educational Opportunity Grant. The name was changed again to Pell Grant in 1980. These grants were intended to form the foundation of the federal student aid effort. Using a calculation based on a student's estimated family resources and the cost of the college to be attended, the student would receive a grant directly from the federal government to reduce his or her cost of attendance.[10] Pell grants were designed to target awards to students with the greatest financial need.

Second, for those students who had greater family resources but still needed additional federal support in attending college, the HEA created the Guaranteed Student Loan Program, which became the William D. Ford Direct Loan Program. Originally, students would be able to borrow from a private bank for their education and the federal government would facilitate those loans by providing the banks with subsidies and a guarantee of repayment. Today, these loans are made directly by the federal government, which has reduced the costs of subsidies and guarantees. This federal loan program was designed to provide secondary support for those students who did not qualify for the grant program, and it was expected to remain much smaller than the federal grant program.

Third, the federal government developed or redesigned a number of other programs that were intended to give campus financial aid offices resources that they could use to address the needs of individual students on a case-by-case basis. These campus-based programs included the Federal Work-Study Program, the Perkins Loan Program, and the Supplemental Educational Opportunity Grant Program.

## Rapid Expansion and Policy Drift

By the end of the 1970s, the federal student aid programs had all expanded rapidly and seemed to be well on their way to achieving their original purpose.[11] By 1980, as a result of the Title IV programs, lower-income families could make use of a wide range of federal resources in their efforts to pay for college. These included Pell grants and work-study aid. Students could also borrow directly from their school through the Perkins loan program or from a private lender through the federally guaranteed loan program. These resources combined to significantly reduce the net price of higher education facing low-income students. This expansion of federal student aid also improved the situation of most middle-income families during the 1970s. The changes to the HEA made in 1978 expanded eligibility for federally guaranteed and subsidized loans to all students, regardless of their family income. The resulting expansion of student loans allowed many middle-income families to shift the responsibilities of paying for college to their children.

By the early 1980s, the nation's economic and political circumstances changed in ways that made it difficult for policy makers to continue to pursue the original objectives of the Title IV programs. As these programs became more popular in the 1970s and 1980s, federal policy makers found themselves under tremendous pressure to spread their benefits out to a wider range of students. As college prices began to spiral upward and family incomes remained flat, parents demanded increased eligibility for federal grants and continued access to ever-larger federally subsidized loans. Similarly, policy makers were under pressure from for-profit and technical schools to broaden eligibility for the Title

IV programs from traditional colleges to the full universe of postsecondary education programs.

The eligibility of more students and more schools, in an environment of rising college prices, required the federal government to pump an ever-larger amount of funding into the Title IV programs in order to maintain their purchasing power for lower-income students.[12] Unlike his predecessors, President Reagan was determined to reduce federal expenditures and set out to cut federal spending in all areas except military defense. Reagan's efforts to cut the federal student aid programs were generally thwarted by a Congress that sought to continue their expansion. The result was a political stalemate, where policy makers continued to expand eligibility for the Title IV programs even when they did not appropriate the dollars to support their growth. This meant that during the 1980s, the purchasing power of Pell grants declined sharply relative to college prices. More students were receiving grants each year, but those grants were covering smaller and smaller portions of their educational expenses. Caught between rising prices and stable Pell grants, more lower- and middle-income students were forced to turn to the federal student loan programs.

As college prices continued to rise, and federal policy makers struggled with limited resources, the orientation of the federal programs changed in two fundamental ways. First, policy makers allowed the erosion of need-based allocation standards in order to provide at least some federal aid to a larger number of students. Second, by allowing the federal loan programs to grow much more rapidly than the grant programs, what had been a grant-centered system was transformed into a loan-centered system. Both of these changes resulted in shifting limited federal resources away from the neediest students and toward less-needy students.

The impact of this federal policy drift can be most clearly seen in table 8.2. In 1975, the full cost of attendance for one year at an average-priced public institution was $7,938 (in constant 2014 dollars). The maximum Pell grant would cover 77 percent of that cost. But a decade later, the cost of attendance had increased rapidly and Pell grants now only covered 58 percent of that cost. This decline was not the direct result of reductions in aggregate federal support. The number of students receiving Pell grants had actually increased by one-third over the decade, and total federal expenditures on the Pell grant program had increased to more than $8 billion dollars. More students were eligible for grants, but the value of those grants was falling rapidly.

*Table 8.2* Changes in size and purchasing power of Pell grants, 1974–75
to 2013–14, in constant 2014 dollars

|  | Total annual charges at public four-year institutions | Maximum Pell grant | Pell grant as a percentage of total charges | Number of Pell grant recipients (in $ millions) | Total federal expenditures on Pell grants (in $ billions) |
|---|---|---|---|---|---|
| 1974–75 | 7,938 | 6,160 | 77 | 1.9 | 6.2 |
| 1979–80 | 7,587 | 5,171 | 68 | 2.5 | 6.0 |
| 1984–85 | 8,427 | 4,620 | 58 | 2.6 | 7.9 |
| 1989–90 | 9,030 | 5252 | 58 | 4.0 | 10.5 |
| 1994–95 | 10,628 | 6,368 | 60 | 3.7 | 9.4 |
| 1999–2000 | 11,548 | 6,598 | 57 | 5.1 | 11.3 |
| 2004–05 | 14,310 | 5,227 | 36 | 5.5 | 16.5 |
| 2009–10 | 16,855 | 5,803 | 34 | 8.1 | 32.5 |
| 2013–14 | 18,943 | 5,645 | 30 | 9.1 | 33.7 |

*Sources:* College Board, *Trends in Student Aid 2014* and *Trends in College Prices 2014*, both at www.collegeboard
.com/html/trends/.

During the 1990s, the declining purchasing power of the Pell grant was reversed for a few years, but by the 2000s, that decline had returned and begun to accelerate. By 2014, federal spending on Pell grants had spiked to an all-time high of $33.7 billion, with 9.1 million students receiving awards. The value of the maximum grant now covered less than one-third of the cost of attendance, leaving many students with no choice but to borrow the difference from the federal loan programs.

As the number of students borrowing through the federal loan programs has grown, Congress has become increasingly concerned about the level of student debt.[13] Federal policy makers continue to argue that they want a better balance between grants and loans, but their policy choices have accelerated the drift in the opposite direction. In 1992, under great public pressure, Congress established a new unsubsidized version of the Stafford loan program that was not restricted by need. This made federal loans available to middle- and upper-income students who had previously been squeezed out of eligibility for regular student loans. This new program dramatically expanded the borrowing capacity of students and parents at all income levels, spurring a huge increase in borrowing through federal loan programs in the years after the law took effect.

*Table 8.3*    Number of borrowers and average loan amounts borrowed
through the federal Stafford loan program (subsidized and unsubsidized),
in constant 2014 dollars

|  | 1993–94 | 2003–4 | 2013–14 |
|---|---|---|---|
| Total borrowers (subsidized and unsubsidized) |  |  |  |
| Number of borrowers (in millions) | 4.1 | 6.5 | 9.3 |
| Average loan per borrower | $7,722 | $8,147 | $8,356 |
| Borrowers (subsidized) |  |  |  |
| Number of borrowers (in millions) | 3.6 | 5.5 | 6.9 |
| Average loan per borrower | $5,313 | $5,061 | $3,677 |
| Borrowers (unsubsidized) |  |  |  |
| Number of borrowers (in millions) | 1.8 | 3.9 | 7.9 |
| Average loan per borrower | $5,621 | $5,941 | $6,541 |

*Source:* College Board, "Types of Loans," in *Trends in Student Aid 2014.*
   *Note:* The number of total borrowers counts each borrower only once, but many students are
borrowing through both programs.

Not only did the number of federal borrowers grow even more rapidly than
the number of Pell grant recipients, the number of unsubsidized loans has expanded more rapidly than the number of subsidized borrowers. Table 8.3 shows
that between 2003–4 and 2013–14, the number of borrowers in the subsidized
loan program increased by about 25 percent. During that same time, the number
of unsubsidized borrowers more than doubled. Today, more than 1 million more
unsubsidized loans are made each year than subsidized loans.

As college prices have increased more rapidly than maximum federal loan
amounts, and as governments have tightened eligibility requirements for those
loans, a larger number of undergraduate and graduate students have turned to
private loans to cover their educational expenses. These loans are not guaranteed by the federal government and occur largely outside of government reporting requirements. In 2012, about 6 percent of undergraduates and 4 percent of
graduate students took out such a private loan. These private borrowers are more
heavily concentrated among students from low income families and those attending for-profit institutions.

Since 2010, Congress has implemented steps intended to reduce the number
of students borrowing and to lower the amount of their loans. As a result, after
two decades of steady growth, the total number of federal loan borrowers peaked
in 2012 at 10.3 million. By 2014, that number had declined by almost 10 percent
to 9.3 million. Similarly, the average amount borrowed was $18,550 in 2012, and

declined to $17,560 in 2014. While it is unclear that these declines will continue, the efforts of policy makers, coupled with the concerns about loan debt by students and families, have stabilized the borrowing rate.

## ACCESS TO WHAT?

Since the passage of the HEA, federal student aid policies have been directed primarily toward the goal of increasing access to higher education, especially among those students from the neediest families. Since the 1990s, a number of policy makers also sought to ensure that these programs are supporting access to academic and vocational programs. They question whether federal dollars are being directed effectively to those who really need the help and have a reasonable chance of benefiting from the education and training that is being subsidized. Are the programs attended by federal aid recipients of a reasonable quality? Do federal aid recipients complete their programs? Do they secure jobs in the fields for which they have been prepared? In short, are students and taxpayers getting their money's worth from their substantial investment in student aid?

For-profit trade schools have been a primary concern regarding quality and standards.[14] In the 1970s, Congress substituted the term "postsecondary" for "higher" in the student aid statutes and broadened their eligibility to include short-term vocational training provided by for-profit schools, as well as the traditional programs of public and private nonprofit institutions. In doing so, Congress embraced the view that students would "vote with their feet" and take their federal aid to those institutions that best served their educational and training needs. Unfortunately, the deregulation that followed did not address the critical questions of institutional quality and effectiveness. The result of this broadened eligibility was a burgeoning of the trade-school industry. Many for-profits emerged that were subsidized almost entirely by tax dollars. Some of these institutions even set their prices based on the federal aid packages available to their students. Even today, students attending many of these for-profit institutions report high levels of dissatisfaction with their programs and, in larger numbers, default on the loans they have taken out to cover their costs.

For quality control, the federal government has traditionally relied on a so-called triad of institutional accreditation, state reviews, and federal oversight. Federal responsibility, as carried out by the Department of Education, has included certifying accreditation agencies as well as ultimately approving institutions to participate in the federal programs. Over time, however, increasing numbers of observers have come to the conclusion that the triad arrangement is simply inadequate for the task.

Over the years, federal policy makers have tried to crack down on institutions with excessively high student-loan default rates. That effort has helped to reduce the overall level of defaults and eliminate schools that were clearly abusing the system. Some of the worst problems have been remedied. For example, the national default rate has dropped from a high of 22 percent in 1990 to less than 10 percent in 2014. However, there remain substantial differences in the loan default rate across institutional types. While students attending for-profit schools account for about 10 percent of all borrowers, they constitute 44 percent of all loan defaulters. Conversely, students attending public four-year institutions account for about 41 percent of all borrowers, but they constitute only 20 percent of loan defaulters.

In recent years, Congress has become concerned about whether institutions were serving as good stewards of federal student aid funds.[15] In particular, many members believe that colleges and universities were not paying sufficient attention to their low retention and graduation rates. To try to pressure institutions into focusing on improving these rates, Congress has enacted several changes that would reward or punish students who appear to be making insufficient progress toward their degrees or who have high failure or incomplete rates. The intrusiveness and complexity of implementing these changes has brought strong opposition from colleges and their representatives in Washington. However, as college prices continue to increase, and the resources available to fund student aid remain constrained, efforts to ensure that students and taxpayers are getting their money's worth are likely to continue.[16]

## Reforming the Delivery of Student Loans

In 1993, President Clinton proposed changing the way that student loans were originated, financed, serviced, and repaid. This would have been an entirely new system that would make loans directly to students rather than making use of traditional bank-based government guaranteed loans. The promise of direct loans was that they would streamline the lending process, better serve student borrowers, promote improvements in the bank-based system through competition, and save tax dollars by reducing subsidies to private lenders and guarantee agencies.[17] After a heated debate, Congress agreed to create the Direct Loan program, but rather than eliminating the bank-based system as Clinton had proposed, they decided to allow the two systems to operate as rival programs.

Institutions would be free to choose the program they decided would serve their students more effectively.

For nearly two decades, the two loan programs co-existed, with schools given the choice of which program to join. While banks continued to advocate for expansion of the loan guarantee program, the direct loan program remained popular with many schools. Then, in 2008, the widespread disruption of the credit markets resulting from the financial crisis caused many banks and private lenders to discontinue their participation in the bank-based program.[18] This drove an increasing number of schools to shift to direct loans. Finally, in 2010, President Obama persuaded Congress to eliminate the FFEL program. He argued that subsidies paid to private lenders under the program were unnecessary and that cost savings could be achieved if all federal student loans were made through the direct loan program. As of July 1, 2010, all new federal student loans have been made under the direct loan program. This change, which eliminated unnecessary subsidies to private lenders and other middlemen, was estimated by the Congressional Budget Office to save almost $69 billion in savings over the next ten years. These savings have been used to increase funding for the Pell Grant program.[19]

FEDERAL TAX POLICIES

In addition to direct funding of students and institutions, the federal government assists college students and their families, as well as colleges and universities, through a variety of tax policies. A number of exclusions, exemptions, credits, and deductions have been added to the federal tax code over the years to benefit education at all levels. Some of these provisions—for example, the personal exemption parents may claim for dependent students aged nineteen to twenty-four, as well as tax-advantaged savings plans, and tuition tax credits—affect the ability of individuals and families to save for and pay college costs. Other provisions affect the revenue and financing arrangements of colleges and universities—for example, their charitable 501(c)(3) status allows them to receive tax-deductible contributions. The monetary benefits of these tax expenditures to institutions and students are measured by the estimated amount of federal revenue that would be collected in the absence of such provisions. In 2014, the estimated annual federal tax expenditures for higher education (including for both students and institutions) totaled $21 billion.[20]

In 1997, the Clinton administration persuaded Congress to enact the Taxpayer Relief Act, which included a number of higher-education-related new tax breaks for students and families. Since that time, individual tax-based relief has become an important and expanding way for federal policy to address rising college prices. The challenge to policy makers was to promote affordability to middle-income families—the primary beneficiaries of these tax policies—without detracting from efforts to improve access for the neediest students through direct student aid. The scope of the Taxpayer Relief Act was dramatic. Indeed, it proved to be a watershed in the use of federal tax policy to address the burden of rising college prices on middle- and upper-income college students.

The Hope and Lifelong Learning tax credits were the largest of the tuition tax benefits incorporated into the law. The nonrefundable Hope tax credit provides a $1,500 credit per student per year for tuition expenses during the first two years of postsecondary education. Since it can only be claimed up to the amount of the taxpayer's liability, it effectively eliminates the eligibility of a large number of lower-income families. The Lifetime Learning tax credit provides up to one credit per household for up to $2,000, or 20 percent of tuition and related expenses. These credits represent a major shift away from targeted aid to low-income families and toward cost relief primarily benefiting middle- and upper-income families.[21]

The Taxpayer Relief Act also created several new vehicles for tax-advantaged savings for higher education expenses: Roth Individual Retirement Accounts (IRAs), Education IRAs (now called Coverdell Education Savings Accounts, or Coverdell ESAs), state prepaid tuition plans, and college savings plans (now generally called 529 plans after the provision in the tax code). These new instruments expanded and complicated the landscape for families saving for future college expenses.

The new tuition tax credits received broad and immediate public approval, and in 2001 Congress expanded their scope. The Economic Growth and Tax Reconciliation Act of 2002 raised the applicable income limits for Hope and Lifelong Learning credits, increased annual limits on contributions to educational IRAs, and eliminated interest earned under prepaid tuition programs and college savings plans. This new law further exacerbated the shifting of benefits from the neediest to middle- and upper-income families.[22] This is because lower-income families pay little or no federal tax and thus are not eligible to use these tax breaks. Along with educational IRAs and other tax-sheltered federal savings vehicles, which also primarily benefit upper- and middle-income families, these benefits were estimated to cost the federal treasury $17.7 billion in lost revenue in 2013.

Institutional tax-exempt status and the deduction of contributions from the taxable income of donors are the crucial tax policies benefiting institutions of higher education. The tax exemption predates most of the nation's colleges and universities and the federal tax code, so its long-standing precedent, and the political implications of change, have preserved the tax-exempt status of colleges and universities. However, institutions are required to pay a federal tax on unrelated business income for all activities that are not a part of their charitable purpose. As shown in table 8.1, the total cost in lost revenues of institutional tax expenditures is estimated to be $6.3 billion.

## FEDERAL SUPPORT FOR RESEARCH

Federal spending to support research and related activities goes back to 1883, when Congress first voted to support agricultural experiment stations. The federal investment in academic science remained fairly small until the demands of World War II caused spending for campus-based research to skyrocket. Guided by the newly created National Science Foundation (NSF), the boom in federally sponsored research continued through the 1950s and early 1960s. Today, the federal government remains the largest source of financing for campus-based research, supplying $61 billion in 2013.

Unlike student aid, federal research funding is highly concentrated on a relatively small number of institutions, most of them large research universities. According to the NSF, one hundred doctoral-degree-granting institutions receive

*Table 8.4*    Federal obligations for research, by agency, 1990–2014, in constant 2014 dollars (in millions)

|                                 | 1990   | 2000   | 2014   |
| ------------------------------- | ------ | ------ | ------ |
| Health & Human Services         | 12,472 | 24,626 | 31,427 |
| Defense                         | 5,972  | 6,763  | 6,668  |
| Energy                          | 4,349  | 5,565  | 7,706  |
| National Science Foundation     | 2,858  | 3,747  | 5,717  |
| Agriculture                     | 1,809  | 2,216  | 2,161  |
| NASA                            | 5,178  | 5,449  | 5,354  |
| Other                           | 3,783  | 4,447  | 5,166  |
| Total for all federal agencies  | 36,412 | 51,349 | 64,199 |

*Source:* National Science Foundation, Division of Science Resources Statistics, *Survey of Federal Funds for Research and Development: FY 2013–14,* www.nsf .gov/statistics/srvyfedfunds/.

more than 50 percent of all federal science and engineering obligations to academia.[23] This support flows from multiple federal agencies and is directed toward multiple policy objectives. While the NSF was originally conceived as a single agency having broad purview over federal research funding, this vision never came to be. Instead, there are diffuse priority-setting and allocation systems. Today more than a dozen mission-oriented agencies fund significant portions of academic science. These agencies serve multiple purposes and operate hundreds of competitive and noncompetitive sponsored-research programs.[24]

The large federal investment in scientific research has allowed a relatively small cadre of American research universities to achieve global pre-eminence in many fields. Further, the diffusion of funds into various agencies has prevented any single set of federal bureaucrats from setting the nation's entire research agenda. However, the growth of federally funded research has clearly influenced the priorities of research universities and, in the view of many observers, created an incentive structure that has led many universities to emphasize research over teaching, graduate over undergraduate education, and the sciences over the social sciences and humanities.[25]

Between 1970 and 2000, total research expenditures, from all sources, increased steadily. Federal research support grew, but research investments from industry, institutional funds, and other sources also increased during this period. In retrospect, this was an extraordinary time for investment in university-based research. The growth curve continued despite the end of the Cold War and the collapse of the Soviet Union. These events diminished public interest in military research and the "big science" projects that characterized this competition between the superpowers, and in large part the continued growth represented a shift toward medical research within federal funding priorities.

That long period of growth came to an end in the early 2000s. Federal research funding flattened out and has remained largely stable, as measured in constant dollars, for nearly two decades. The operating costs of the wars in Iraq and Afghanistan, as well as the reductions in federal revenue resulting from the great recession, left the federal government with very little budget flexibility. This pattern of flat funding has continued for more than a decade. In the absence of a common research goal, such as that provided first by Sputnik and later by the space race and the Cold War, it will be difficult to assemble the public and legislative support necessary to significantly increase federal spending on research and development. There are simply too many other priorities competing for limited discretionary federal dollars.

In addition to differences among policy makers on what goals federal research dollars should be directed toward, they are also divided over how those dollars should be awarded. Traditionally, federal campus-based research funds have been awarded via competitions involving a peer review process, where experts evaluated grant proposals in their field. Supporters of this peer review system argue that it ensures that the best research is funded. Opponents see it as an "old boy's network" that precludes many worthwhile projects because the researchers are not tied into the network, and that discriminates against younger faculty members, women, and minorities.[26]

For most of the 2000s, there was a rapid growth in the portion of federal research funding that was allocated through earmarking. In this process, which bypassed formal competition and peer review, Congress specifies the particular projects that will be funded. By 2010, earmarking has ballooned to almost $20 billion, sparking criticism that it is nothing more than "pork-barrel science" where elected officials are able to award research grants and contracts to campuses in their home districts.[27] In part, congressional earmarking was a reaction to the heavy concentration of research funding to relatively few institutions. Institutions outside of this select group could now go to their elected representatives directly to plead their case—often with the help of lobbyists and government-relations consultants. Earmarking was also a response to a long-term problem affecting virtually all research universities—the deterioration and obsolescence of scientific equipment and facilities. Only a small portion of federal research funds supports renovation, new construction, and the purchase of equipment. In the 1950s and 1960s, separate federal appropriations were made for these categories. More recently, the federal government has persisted in a policy of funding research activities at universities, but requiring those institutions to provide and maintain the research infrastructure. In reaction, some institutions have gone directly to the congressional appropriations committees to find funding for construction and renovation of particular facilities.

In 2010, new House Speaker John Boehner lead a move to ban congressional earmarking. This action was intended to make sure that lawmakers were making decisions that were best for the nation as a whole rather than for the more narrow interests of their constituents. But the federal government still needs to make decisions about where to award grants and contracts, which research programs to support, and which campus improvement projects to fund. Since 2010, these specific decisions are more likely to be made in the executive agencies than by the Congress as a whole. This does not mean that Congress no longer plays a role in these critical resource allocation decisions. Lawmakers now use letter writing and phone calls to bring pressure on executive agencies to take actions that reward their constituents. As such, earmarking did not really go away, it just moved from one branch of the federal government to another.[28] And it moved from a place where it could be easily seen and measured, to a more informal process where its impact can only be seen indirectly.

Whether funded by traditional competitions or by formal or informal earmarks, the nation's investment in science and technology must now compete directly with funding demands for health care, interstate highways, national parks, environmental protection, housing, and a host of other domestic needs. These are all vying for a smaller portion of the federal pie. Not only will budgets be tight for the foreseeable future, but questions surrounding the management and conduct of university research may have weakened the support for academic science. Since the end of World War I, the nation's substantial investment in science has been repaid many times over in both pathbreaking discoveries and practical applications. The computer, radar, the polio vaccine, and America's world leadership in agriculture can all be traced back to academic science. Yet controversy and skepticism have beset the university research community in recent years. Publicized cases of research fraud and other ethical breaches by federally sponsored researchers have triggered investigations and doubts about the integrity of scientific research.

All of these issues take on particular significance in light of the dependence of many universities on federal research dollars. While federal grants and contracts represent a small percent of total revenues to higher education, at some major research institutions federal dollars constitute 25 percent or more of their revenues. The decline in federal funding, coupled with budgetary problems faced by state governments and many private contributors, has placed many research universities in difficult financial situations. If the diminution of federal support continues, these institutions will be unable to afford to acquire the newest technologies, others will be unable to maintain and replace their existing research equipment, and most institutions will have difficulty in funding existing staff and operations.

## Federal Regulation

Federal regulation of higher education derives from two principal sources: (1) the requirements of accountability that accompany the receipt of federal funds, and (2) the dictates of social legislation, as well as the regulations, executive orders, and judicial decisions that stem from that legislation. In addition, the Civil War amendments to the Constitution have strengthened the role of the federal government in protecting civil rights. To the degree that government officials insist on accountability and congressional mandates addressing a range of social problems remain in place, there will be complexity and strain in the relationship between the federal government and higher education. Tensions are inevitable, given the traditions of institutional autonomy in higher education, the mandates of Congress, the missions of federal agencies, and the responsibilities of those agencies for the stewardship of taxpayer dollars.

One area where federal regulation has had an enormous impact on higher education is in the area of desegregation. From the 1890s until the 1960s, many states operated dual systems of higher education—one for black students and another for white students. Although desegregation of these systems was implied by the 1954 *Brown v. Board of Education* decision by the Supreme Court, meaningful steps toward that end did not take place until after the enactment of the Civil Rights Act of 1965. Since that time, through legislation and court decisions, the federal government has been involved with decisions about who colleges can (or must) admit, how they hire faculty and staff, and how they award scholarships. While these interventions represent a fundamental aspect of the federal government's role in higher education, the details of that role are discussed in Chapter 10, on the legal environment in higher education.

Federal regulation has rarely been welcomed by the nation's colleges. Indeed, the academic community has always been wary of entanglement with government. Still, despite their concerns, only a few, mainly independent, religiously affiliated institutions have been willing to refuse funds from Washington. The great majority of colleges have accepted federal patronage, even though it carries a high price in terms of compliance and external control. The federal government influences higher education through scores of statutes and regulations. Some mandates, such as the Americans with Disabilities Act or the regulations of the Environmental Protection Agency or the Occupational Safety and Health Administration, affect all types of organizations. Others, such as the Federal Educational Records Privacy Act and Title IX of the Education Amendments of 1972, which bars gender bias, are specific to higher education. Colleges have long argued that such regulations represent a burden that contributes to the rapidly rising price of higher education. They are seen as a series of "unfunded mandates" from Washington that impose regulatory requirements that leave institutions no choice but to pass those costs on to students in the form of higher prices.

While many in higher education support the broad goals of environmental and consumer protection, open records and meetings, and campus safety, they are concerned that the costs of compliance with the blizzard of federal regulations in these areas outweigh the benefits. One college president put it this way:

> We have a gazillion people working on compliance. The government requires us to do it. Is it reasonable? Do we do too much? At least from where I sit, it looks as though we have an excessive number of people working on this. But if we don't have them we would be in violation of the law.[29]

An often-cited example of such a federal mandate is the Jeanne Clery Disclosure of Campus Security and Policy and Campus Crime Statistics Act. This 1990 law requires all colleges and universities to disclose specific information about crime on their campuses and in the surrounding communities. The act, which is enforced by the US Department of Education, can result in severe penalties to institutions that do not comply. On the one hand, campus leaders can argue that it is precisely such federal mandates that drive up college prices, as gathering and reporting such data require substantial staff time. The Department of Education has a constantly changing manual of more than 200 pages on its website describing the actions campuses must take to comply with the law.[30] On the other hand, while such reporting requirements certainly have costs for institutions, there is little empirical evidence that such regulations have much of an impact on college tuition inflation.

Similarly, recent efforts by the federal government to ensure that Pell grant and student loan funds are spent effectively have generated a substantial regulatory burden on college financial aid offices. Ensuring that all students are taking only eligible courses, are not taking too many credits, and/or are making satisfactory academic progress toward their degrees every term, requires institutions to make large investments in the staff, training, and computer programming necessary to remain in compliance with increasingly complex Title IV regulations. These additional institutional costs may well be passed on to students in the form of higher tuition and fees. Thus, some federal efforts to control prices might actually exacerbate the tuition spiral they were implemented to control.

## Federal Policy and College Prices

Concern over the rising price of a college education has been one of the primary animating forces in federal policy at least since the late 1970s. The rapid tuition inflation that occurred after 2009 has only heightened federal concern over college prices. As tuitions spiral upward, so does the demand for increases in federal student aid. It was tuition inflation that finally brought enough public pressure to enact tuition tax credits, as well as the various educational savings programs and the 529 state savings plans. Similarly, the pressures for accountability and the resulting federal regulations sprang directly from concerns over rising prices.

In 1997 Congress established the National Commission on the Cost of Higher Education to determine what was driving tuition upward and what could be done about it. When the commission issued its report, however, it concluded that there is no single explanation for the tuition spiral.[31] The commission examined factors that may be driving up institutional costs—everything from faculty salaries, facilities, curriculum, technology, government regulation, and expectations of students (and their parents) about quality and amenities on campus. It concluded that "the available data on higher education expenditures and revenues make it difficult to ascertain direct relationships among the cost drivers and increases in the price of higher education. Institutions of higher education, even to most people in the academy, are financially opaque."[32]

In the end, the commission also decided that there was little that the federal government could, or should, do about tuition inflation. The commission admonished colleges to intensify their efforts to increase institutional productivity and inform the public about the actual price of postsecondary education, the returns on investment, and preparation for college. As for the federal role, the commission urged policy makers to do a better job of collecting and reporting standardized data on costs, prices, and subsidies in higher education and of analyzing the relationship between tuition and institutional expenditures—but not to impose any price controls.

Today, nearly two decades after the commission completed its work, the question of what actions the federal government can take to contain college prices continues to occupy federal policy makers. It should not be surprising, however, that all the debate has not led to any federal interventions in college pricing policies. It is not clear that the federal government has sufficient authority, or political will, to intervene in tuition pricing. While the federal government does provide the lion's share of direct student aid, it still supplies only 15 percent of college and university revenues. At least for now, federal policy makers have concluded that they are too far from the action and ought to leave cost containment and price setting to states, campuses, and market forces.

Instead of addressing college prices directly, federal policy makers have focused on ways to limit the availability of financial aid. In both the Pell grant and the federal loan programs, regulations have been implemented to force recipients to graduate more quickly. These limitations include lifetime grant caps, satisfactory academic progress standards, and the reduction of the maximum income for automatic eligibility. While these changes have indeed reduced the cost of the grant and loan programs, they have left more students without the resources they need to cover rising college costs.

## Prospects for the Federal Role in Higher Education

In summary, here are some of the issues that will influence the federal role in higher education as we move into the second decade of the twenty-first century:

- Even though state government revenues have generally returned to prerecession levels, state support for higher education still remains substantially below its 2007 levels. This has forced public colleges to continue to raise tuition, albeit at a lower rate than during the recession. These increases threaten to overwhelm the federal student aid system, as more and more students are borrowing ever-larger amounts to cover their rising costs.
- Despite significant new investments in the Pell grant in recent years, the purchasing power of the maximum grant continues to decline. In the face of rising tuitions, Congress will be forced to further tighten eligibility in order to target grants to the neediest students or to accept that grants will cover an ever smaller portion of college costs.
- Policy makers continue to worry about the consequences of growing student indebtedness for individuals and for society. As the policy drift toward a loan-based system seems likely to continue, policy makers will be under increasing pressure to find ways to address the debt burden on students. Issues of quality control, the price of education, and consumer protection will also continue to concern federal policy makers.
- There remain persistent concerns about research practices in academia. This, coupled with pressures to reduce federal spending, will bring federal research funding under further scrutiny. Many federal policy makers are calling for science and technology investments to be more

sharply focused on areas of national need and economic growth. Universities will be challenged to articulate more clearly how their research contributes to societal goals. Debates will also focus on the balance of funding between research and commercial applications, the need to upgrade the physical infrastructure of scientific research, and the adequacy of government support to train the country's next generation of top-flight scientists and engineers.

- Higher education will continue to press the federal government for regulatory relief. This may become the centerpiece of the next reauthorization of the Higher Education Act. Yet as long as government officials insist on accountability for taxpayer dollars and legislative mandates addressing a range of educational and social problems remain in force, the burden of rules and regulations will continue to be the price that universities must pay for federal support.

From the Morrill Act, to the GI Bill, to the Higher Education Act and its many reauthorizations, to the American Recovery and Reinvestment Act, the federal government has played a pivotal role in extending opportunities for higher education to a wider segment of American society. As the nation completes the second decade of the twenty-first century, the number of students entering college each year continues to grow. These new students are more diverse than ever. Given this reality, coupled with rising college prices and ballooning budget deficits, it is not clear whether the federal government will be able to sustain its historic commitment to assuring a fair chance of a college education for all citizens.

The federal government will undoubtedly continue to make important contributions to enhancing the academic enterprise and equalizing educational opportunities in America. As in the past, federal support will supplement the basic funding provided by states and private sources, and it will spring from objectives such as economic competitiveness, health, and the quality of life rather than on an interest in education for its own sake. Funds, along with regulatory controls, will continue to flow from a variety of agencies in Washington. Such support is untidy, piecemeal, and not without its headaches for institutions, students, and states. But the pattern serves a variety of national purposes and, in fact, ultimately may better serve to protect institutional diversity, a student's freedom of choice, and independent thought in American higher education than would an overarching federal policy.

NOTES

*This chapter was originally prepared by Lawrence E. Gladieux, Jacqueline E. King, and Melanie E. Corrigan for the first edition of* American Higher Education in the Twenty-First Century. *For this edition, Michael Mumper revised and updated the chapter. Any errors or mistakes in this version are his and not those of the previous authors.*

1. For two thoughtful discussions of the development of the federal role in higher education, see George N. Rainford, *Congress and Higher Education in the Nineteenth Century* (Knoxville: University of Tennessee Press, 1972); and John Thelin, "Higher Education and the Public Trough: A Historical Perspective," in *Public Funding of Higher Education: Changing Contexts and New Rationales,* ed. Edward St. Johns and Michael Parsons (Baltimore: Johns Hopkins University Press, 2004), 21–40.

2. Glenn C. Altschuler and Stuart Blumin, *The G.I. Bill: A New Deal for Veterans* (Oxford: Oxford University Press, 2009), 85.

3. Ibid., 87.

4. Ibid.

5. Francis Keppler, "The Higher Education Acts Contrasted, 1965 and 1986: Has Federal Policy Come of Age?" *Harvard Education Review* 57 (Spring 1987): 49–67.

6. College Board, *Trends in Student Aid 2014,* www.trends-collegeboard.com/student _aid/.

7. For an analysis of the impact of this act on state governments, see a report by the National Governors Association, *Education and Workforce* (Mar. 2, 2009), www.nga.org/Files /pdf/ARRAANALYSIS.PDF. For a review of the impact of the act on state colleges and universities, see Daniel Hurley, *Considerations for State Colleges and Universities in a Post-Recession America,* www.congressweb.com/aascu/docfiles/Considerations-AASCU11-09.pdf.

8. Daniel Hurley, "The Second Fiscal Crisis: Preparing for the Funding Cliff," *Public Purpose* (Sept./Oct. 2009): 2–3.

9. Chester Finn, Jr., "A Federal Policy for Higher Education?" *Alternative* (May 1975): 18–19.

10. For a detailed analysis of the creation of the Pell Grant program, see Lawrence E. Gladieux and Thomas R. Wolanin, *Congress and the Colleges: The National Politics of Higher Education* (Lexington, MA: Lexington Books, 1976).

11. Michael Mumper, "The Affordability of Public Higher Education: 1970–1990," *Review of Higher Education* 16, no. 2 (Winter 1993): 157–80.

12. James Hearn and Janet Holdsworth, "Federal Student Aid: The Shift from Grants to Loans," in St. Johns and Parsons, *Public Funding of Higher Education,* 21–40.

13. David Cho, "As College Costs Rise, Loans Become Harder to Get," *Washington Post,* Dec. 28, 2009, www.washingtonpost.com/wp-dyn/content/article/2009/12/27/ AR2009122702116.html.

14. A more complete discussion of the impact of the growth of the for-profit sector on federal student-aid policy can be found in Richard Apling, "Proprietary Schools and Their Students," *Journal of Higher Education* 64 (July/Aug. 1993): 379–415.

15. Stephen Burd, "Bush's Next Target?" *Chronicle of Higher Education,* July 11, 2003, http://chronicle.com/article/Bushs-Next-Target-/24767/.

16. Eric Kelderman, "Accountability Issues Persist under New Administration," *Chronicle of Higher Education* (Nov. 17, 2009), http://chronicle.com/article/Accountability -Issues-Persist/49190/.

17. General Accounting Office, *Direct Loans Could Save Billions in 5 Years with Proper Implementation* (Washington, DC: US Government Printing Office, Nov. 1993).

18. Gilbert Cruz, "Obama's Student Loan Plan: A Good Takeover?" *Time*, Sept. 16, 2009, www.time.com/time/politics/article/0,8599,1924128,00.html.

19. David Herszenhorn and Tamar Lewin, "Student Loan Overhaul Approved by Congress," *New York Times*, Mar. 25, 2010, http://www.nytimes.com/2010/03/26/us /politics/26loans.html/.

20. College Board, *Trends in Student Aid 2014*, www.trends-collegeboard.com/student _aid/.

21. Thomas Wolanin, *Rhetoric and Reality* (Washington, DC: Institute for Higher Education Policy, 2001).

22. Ibid.

23. Ronda Britt, "Federal Government Is Largest Source of University R&D Funding in S&E: Share Drops in FY 2008," *InfoBrief*, NSF 09-318 (Washington, DC: National Science Foundation, Sept. 2009).

24. Clark Kerr, *The Uses of the University* (Cambridge, MA: Harvard University Press, 1995).

25. Ibid.

26. General Accounting Office, Peer Review, *Reforms Needed to Ensure Fairness in Federal Agency Grant Selection*, GAO/PEMD-94-1 (Washington, DC: General Accounting Office, 1994).

27. Gail Russell Chaddock, "'Pig Book': Congressional 'Pork' Hits $19.6 Billion in 2009," *Christian Science Monitor*, Apr. 14, 2009, www.csmonitor.com/usa/politics/0414 /pig-book-congressional-pork-hits-196-billion-in-2009/.

28. Sarah Westwood, "Earmarks Never Went Away—They Changed Addresses," *Washington Examiner*, Sept. 26, 2014, www.washingtonexaminer.com/earmarks-never -went-away-they-just-changed-addresses.

29. John Immerwahr, Jean Johnson, and Paul Gasbarra, *The Iron Triangle: College Presidents Talk about Costs, Access, and Quality* (Washington, DC: National Center for Public Policy and Higher Education, Oct. 2008), 13.

30. Diana Ward and Janice Lee, *The Handbook for Campus Crime Reporting* (Washington, DC: US Department of Education, 2005), www.ed.gov/admins/lead/safety /handbook.pdf.

31. National Commission on the Cost of Higher Education, *Straight Talk about College Costs and Prices* (Phoenix: Oryx Press, 1998).

32. Ibid., 12.

# Chapter Nine

# The States and Higher Education

## Aims C. McGuinness, Jr.

The period of the early years of the twenty-first century is likely to be one of the most challenging in the history of the nation's higher education enterprise. Relations between state government and higher education have become especially strained because of four broad trends:

1. Escalating demands: These are driven not only by numbers, but also by higher expectations for what an increasingly diverse student population should know and be able to do as the result of a college education. The demands extend to virtually every dimension of higher education, including research and service. President Obama's call for the United States to regain global competitiveness and have the highest proportion of students graduating from college in the world by 2020 has intensified the challenge.

2. Severe economic constraints: Even with gradual economic recovery, it is unlikely that higher education will see significant improvements in funding, at least on a per student basis, within the next decade. The federal deficit, competing priorities for public funds, public anger about rising student costs, and severe competition for limited corporate and philanthropic funds will all contribute to the continuing financial constraints.

3. The academy's inherent resistance to change: As demands increase and resources dwindle, institutions are slowly recognizing that, if they

continue to do business as usual, their ability to educate students and continue their research and service missions will be seriously compromised. But translating this slow awareness into changes at the institutional core—in the curriculum, in modes of teaching and learning, and in faculty governance—will be a long-term, incremental process. The resulting public frustration with the academy's inability to respond to major societal needs only intensifies the danger of blunt governmental intervention.

4. Instability of state political leadership: The changes in political party control of governorships and state legislatures and the demands of political office are contributing to major changes in state leadership. This is especially pronounced in state legislatures. As each legislative session begins, the proportion of new members increases. The relative stability provided by the memory of long-term legislative leaders about state higher education policies is being lost. Other issues are dominating the agendas. The twenty-year trend toward larger and more dominant legislative staffs is accelerating.

These conditions are certain to exacerbate already frayed state relationships with higher education. Constructive resolution of these conflicts is essential both to the continued strength of American higher education and to its capacity to respond to major societal priorities. The purpose of this chapter is to present a framework and basic information about the state role as a beginning point for further reading and study.

### Autonomy and the Public Interest

For some within higher education, even the mention of state government conjures up negative images. There continues to be a widespread sense within the academy that virtually any state involvement, other than providing funding with no strings attached, is an infringement on legitimate institutional autonomy.

Historically, states have always provided the legal framework within which both public and private institutions operate. Following the principles established by the US Supreme Court's ruling in the Dartmouth College case (*Dartmouth College v. Woodward*) in 1819, states accorded both public and private institutions significant autonomy, especially on "substantive" decisions on whom to admit, what should be taught, and who should teach.[1]

For many within higher education, the relationships with states are viewed along a continuum: at one end, complete institutional autonomy is good; at the other end, state involvement is seen as bad. Frank Newman suggests a different, more constructive view. His point is that both institutional autonomy and state involvement are important. Governments have a legitimate interest in the responsiveness of the academy to major societal needs. At the same time, it is important for both society and the academy that higher education be able to pursue values and purposes that are different from and, in some cases, in conflict with the prevailing values and priorities of the state. "What becomes clear," Newman states, "is that the real need is not simply for more autonomy but for a relationship between the university and the state that is constructive for both, built up over a long period of time by careful attention on the part of all parties."[2]

Robert Berdahl makes a distinction between the concept of academic freedom, which is universal and absolute, and autonomy, which is "of necessity parochial and relative." He continues by emphasizing that "the real issue with respect to autonomy . . . is not whether there will be interference by the state but whether the inevitable interference will be confined to the proper topics and expressed through a suitably sensitive mechanism."[3] The key is for the higher education community to recognize that it has a stake, and even a responsibility, to engage actively with state political leaders in defining the nature of the relationship. This includes defining the major societal ends toward which the academy should direct its energies, and shaping the policies and other "suitably sensitive" mechanisms that will govern the relationships.

## Changing Relationships between Federal and State Policy

Clark Kerr observed in 1985 that state leadership in higher education has been the dominant pattern in US history except for brief periods of federal leadership: 1860–90 and 1955–85. Most of the early development of public universities came from the federal Morrill Act of 1862, which led to the establishment of land-grant universities in the 1860s and 1870s followed by the Morrill Act of 1890 supporting the establishment of historically black land-grant universities. Then, in the post–World War II period, the federal government became the predominant source of funding for research and development through the National Science Foundation and other federal research initiatives. The GI Bill stimulated the massive expansion of educational opportunity in the following two decades. Major federal initiatives including the National Defense Education Act of 1958, the Higher Education Facilities Act of 1963, the Higher Education Act of 1965, and finally the Education Amendments of 1972 have had a lasting impact on the shape of the nation's higher education system.

By the end of the 1970s, the pattern began to shift. Clark Kerr predicted in 1985 that the decade of the mid-1980s to mid-1990s (and perhaps beyond) would be one of state and private leadership in higher education. He further observed that as the effect of higher education on states' economies became more politically important, state governors would emerge as the most important political figures.[4]

Fulfilling Kerr's prediction, the states were the focus of higher education reform in the period from 1985 through the 1990s. Spurred by reports of national task forces and commissions sponsored by state-based organizations such as the Education Commission of the States and the National Governors Association, governors and state legislators made a fundamental change in the definition of accountability, and these changes continue to underlie many state policy initiatives.

In the early twenty-first century, however, a more mixed pattern is evolving, one of greater connection and interdependence between the federal and state roles in higher education. The more significant interrelationships relate to finance. Beyond the specific domain of higher education, federal budget and tax policies establish the fiscal framework for state finance. The declining percentage of state funding that is allocated to public institutions is the result, to a large extent, of the escalating costs of the federal Medicaid program. In 1994, expenditures for Medicaid were 14.2 percent of state general fund expenditures compared to 13.0 percent for higher education. In 2014, the share of expenditures for Medicaid had increased to 19.1 percent while the share for higher education had decreased to 9.4 percent. The shares of expenditures in other categories such as corrections and elementary and secondary education remained essentially unchanged. In other words, whether intended or not, the increase in Medicaid expenditures were directly offset by decreases in higher education funding. Within higher education policy, a long-standing link remains in the eligibility requirements for federal student financial aid and state licensure. In order to receive federal aid, an institution must be "authorized" or licensed by the state in which it is going to operate or deliver services. The rules governing not-for-profit institutions are generally based on federal, not state policy. Specifically within higher education, federal regulations related to the financing of research drive state and institutional decision making. State student financial aid programs commonly are tied to federal student aid policies, especially the methodology for determining eligibility for federal aid (the Federal Application Form for Student Financial Aid or FAFSA). Federal laws and regulations regarding privacy, civil rights, equal rights for women, environmental protection, and other issues have a far reaching impact on colleges and universities.

The Obama administration is pursuing an aggressive leadership stance on higher education with the president's stated goal of regaining the United States' status as a global leader in educational attainment, and the College Scorecard, free community colleges, and other initiatives related to affordability.

As noted later in this chapter, with the decreasing support from state governments and the increasing reliance of public institutions on tuition and fees, federal student aid policy will continue to grow in importance. In 2010–11, state and local governments provided approximately 35 percent of the revenue for public higher education. This state and local share compares with 18 percent from the federal government, 19 percent from student tuition and fees, and 32 percent from other sources (including endowments, private gifts, and grants).[5] The trend has been for the shares of financing from the students and the federal government to increase as share of state funding has decreased.

The state role differs distinctly from that of the federal government. Since the historic decision in the Education Amendments of 1972 to reject direct general-purpose aid to institutions, the federal government has emphasized aid to students, not to institutions. Federal funding to institutions is either through students, in the form of student financial assistance, or restricted funding for research and other purposes. The federal government is generally impartial about a particular provider's ownership and control (public, private, or proprietary), assuming other conditions for receiving a subsidy are met. The federal government thus tends to emphasize a strict separation between the government's role as "overseer of the public interest" and the institutional role of providing services.

In contrast to the federal government, states primarily finance higher education through the direct subsidy of public institutions. In this respect, states play a dual role of overseer of the public interest and provider of higher education services. States also provide aid to students, ranging from large programs in states such as New York to small programs in states such as Alabama.[6] However, only a few states (for example, Illinois, Maryland, Michigan, New Jersey, New York, and Pennsylvania) provide grants to private not-for-profit institutions for the purposes of general institutional subsidy;[7] in the recent fiscal crisis, several of these states discontinued or severely limited funding for these programs.

The increasing interdependence of state and federal policy will require fundamental changes in state-level capacity for policy leadership, as well as in the mechanisms for coordinating federal and state policy.

### Role of the State: Historical Perspective

The state role in higher education has evolved significantly over the nation's history. Higher education in the nineteenth century was primarily private. With only a few exceptions—such as the establishment of the University of Georgia in 1785, Ohio University in 1804, and the University of Virginia in 1819—states played a limited role in higher education. It was not until the end of the nineteenth century that the states began to play a more prominent role in higher education stimulated in part by the federal Morrill land-grant acts of 1862 and 1890. The evolution of the state role can be seen in roughly seven periods:[8]

- The enactment of the first Morrill Land-Grant Act in 1862 through the Progressive Era to the end of World War I
- The end of World War I to the end of World War II
- The end of World War II through to the late 1950s and the enactment of the National Defense Education Act of 1958.
- The late 1950s to early 1980s, including the massive expansion of the higher education
- The early 1980s through the mid-1990s
- The mid-1990s to 2008 on the eve of the Great Recession
- The Great Recession and continuing into the present

State policy did not evolve over these seven periods in a linear and uniform manner across all states. The time periods overlap. Periodically, especially during an economic crisis, states reverted to policies of an earlier time. Some of the structures and policies established in the earliest periods persist today. As emphasized later in this chapter, states' policies and structures differ significantly according to state history and culture.

The first period, from the enactment of the Morrill Land-Grant Act of 1862 through the Progressive Era to the end of World War I, saw the establishment of new state universities and the initial development of state normal schools to prepare teachers, schools that evolved into state colleges and universities by the mid-twentieth century. It was in this period that several states consolidated previously separately governed public institutions under single statewide governing boards such as the Iowa and South Dakota boards of regents.

The second period extended from the end of World War I to the end of World War II and included the years of the Great Depression and the mobilization of the nation's human, intellectual, and industrial capacity for war. In this period, states continued the trend toward consolidation of universities under single statewide boards in an effort to achieve economies-of-scale and to counter the political pressures arising from competing regional interests. As in the earlier period, the primary state role remained to provide state funding to relatively autonomous governing boards.[9]

The third period extended from the end of World War II through to the late 1950s and the enactment of the National Defense Education Act of 1958. It was in this period that higher education in the United States began the move from an elite system serving only a small fraction of the nation's population to a mass system. Stimulated by the GI Bill, enrollment increased 64 percent after the war from a pre-war level of 1.5 million to 2.4 million by 1949–50. In the following decade, enrollment continued to grow by another 49 percent to 3.6 million by 1959–60.[10] States in this period began to move from maintaining a limited number of public universities to developing public institutions with the goal of expanding opportunities for a broader spectrum of the state's population. In this context, New York established the State University of New York in 1948, making the state's first major commitment to public higher education.

The fourth period, from 1958 to the early 1980s, was one of dramatic expansion in which higher education in the United States moved decisively from an elite to a mass higher education system.[11] The states were a driving force behind this expansion: a 218 percent increase in enrollment from 3.2 million in 1959–60 to 11.6 million by 1979–80. In the same period, the number of institutions increased from 2,004 to 3,154.[12] The shape of state higher education systems changed dramatically from a limited number of public universities and normal schools to a complex and more diversified network of public institutions:

- *Multicampus universities* that had initially developed through an expansion of branch campuses of a major state university evolved into full-scale systems of separate institutions such as the University of California.[13]
- *Normal schools and teachers' colleges* expanded their missions to become state colleges and universities.
- *Community colleges* blossomed throughout the country and states established new community college systems.
- *Postsecondary technical schools* began to develop with support from the federal Vocational Education Act of 1963.

In this period, states' roles changed in fundamental ways from the relatively passive source of funding for institutions to actively ensuring student access and opportunity through the orderly development of new institutions. States established new statewide coordinating agencies charged with developing master plans, overseeing the development of new academic programs, institutions, and branch campuses, and developing methodologies for the rational allocation of resources among institutions. At the same time, state budget offices and legislatures expanded their analytic capacity utilizing new planning and budgeting tools.[14,15,16] The most famous statewide framework for coordination and governance in this period was the California Master Plan of 1960. The master plan established the three major systems (called "segments" in California), each encompassing multiple institutions: the University of California (UC), the California State University (CSU), and the California Community College System (CCCS). Each segment has a distinct mission with clear differences in admissions requirements and in the level of degree programs.

As noted earlier, it was in this fourth period that the federal government enacted landmark laws with provisions that required the states to establish new structures. The Higher Education Facilities Act of 1963 required states to establish state facilities commissions. Several provisions of the Higher Education Act of 1965 required the states to establish or designate state agencies and to strengthen state capacity for licensure or authorization of institutions. The Education Amendments of 1972 required the states to establish so-called 1202 state commissions in order to be eligible for federal assistance for comprehensive statewide planning and funding for expansion and improvement of community colleges and postsecondary occupational education.[17]

The fourth period ended with a leveling off of enrollment growth, economic stress, and concerns about the need for retrenchment and increased efficiency throughout the higher education system. The state agencies established to manage growth changed their focus toward cost-containment and increasing system and institutional efficiency.

The fifth period, from the early 1980s through the mid-1990s, witnessed another fundamental shift in the state role. As noted earlier, governors emerged as prominent leaders of state higher education reforms aimed at achieving a stronger alignment of higher education systems with the state's economic development. Up until the 1980s, states had primarily focused on issues of resource allocation and utilization and rarely became involved in basic questions about the outcomes of a college or university education. By the end of the 1980s, questions about outcomes (especially student learning outcomes) dominated states' agendas. More than any other force, it was state policies requiring institutions to assess student learning and provide information to the states and the public that stimulated higher education's attention to these issues. By the mid-1990s, the support for state assessment initiatives declined in part because of budget constraints but also in response to strong institutional opposition. Nevertheless, the state-led reforms had a lasting impact on expectations for higher education accountability embedded in regional accreditation standards and other requirements. During the 1980s, the states also led in developing new funding systems, such as competitive, incentive, and performance funding. The use of funding "on the margin" to support centers of excellence in research and technology and stimulate improvement in undergraduate education was widespread.[18]

Also in this fifth period, states countered the trend toward centralization and state regulation begun in the earlier period by enacting reforms to decentralize and deregulate their public higher education systems. Underlying many of these reforms was the interest of state leaders in "reinventing government," the growing impact of market forces on higher education, and interest in "new public management."[19,20,21,22]

The sixth period, from the mid-1990s to 2008 and the eve of the Great Recession, saw a continuation of themes from the previous period as well as a new state focus on developing a "public agenda." Public agenda reforms, led by major foundations and public advocacy organizations such as the National Center for Public Policy and Higher Education, stressed developing long-term state goals to narrow gaps in access, participation, and completion between the state's majority and minority populations, to maintain affordability, and to link higher education to the state's future environment for innovation and economic competitiveness.[23] Reforms included realigning the size and shape of the higher education system to meet these goals and reforming state financing policy through coordinated action on state appropriations, tuition policy, and student financial aid.

Prominent early examples of public agenda reforms include the Kentucky Postsecondary Reform Act of 1997, linking higher education reforms to a long-term goal of increasing the state's per capita income to the national average or above by 2020,[24] and the Texas Higher Education Coordinating Board's "Closing the Gaps" campaign to improve the state's higher education performance by 2015.[25] An increasing number of governors and state legislatures undertook initiatives to tie higher education reform to efforts to improve elementary and secondary education (P–20: preschool through higher education and lifelong learning), linking research and development to economic development and other efforts to strengthen states' global competitiveness. In the early 2000s, the publication of the national report card on state performance, *Measuring Up*; the creation of a collaborative state higher education project supported by the Pew Charitable Trusts, among others;[26] and national reports from the State Higher Education Executive Officers, the National Conference of State Legislatures, the National Governors Association, and the Education Commission of the States all gave greater impetus to state public agenda reforms.[27,28]

In a trend that began in the previous period (the late 1990s and early 2000s), states intensified their interest in linking state funding to performance. Joseph C. Burke and associates at the Rockefeller Institute of Government began tracking state policies linking accountability with funding in 1997 and continued these annual surveys until 2003. The initial surveys tracked two kinds of policies: performance funding and performance budgeting.[29] The "Seventh Annual Survey" added an additional but closely related policy—performance reporting. The number of states using performance funding and performance budgeting increased significantly during the late 1990s. The number peaked in 2000, at a time when state budgets were still robust. In 2000, eighteen states had performance funding and twenty-eight states had performance budgeting. The number of states with these policies dropped as the state fiscal crisis developed. In the 2003 survey, fifteen states indicated that they were using performance funding and twenty-one indicated that they were using performance budgeting. At the same time, the number of states indicating that they had policies of performance reporting increased significantly. Burke and associates attribute the upswing in performance reporting to the reality that this form of accountability is both less costly and less controversial than the other two forms, and to the effect of the national state-by-state report card on higher education, *Measuring Up*. The number of states with performance reporting increased from thirty-nine in 2001 to forty-six in 2003.[30]

The seventh and current period, beginning with the Great Recession and continuing into the present, represents a continuation of many of the themes of the previous period. What is different in the current period is the sense of urgency for fundamental reform. The economic crisis and concerns about restoring economic competitiveness prompted more states to adopt long-term public agenda goals. Driving this change is President Obama's goal that the United States should have the highest proportion of students graduating from college in the world by 2020.[31] The Lumina Foundation's "Big Goal" to increase the percentage of Americans with high-quality degrees and credentials to 60 percent by the year

2025 is also having an impact.[32] A survey conducted in 2014 found that twenty-six states had a statewide goal to increase the postsecondary education attainment of their citizens. Fourteen states reported that they did not have such a goal and ten reported that creating such a goal is "in progress."[33] The Bill and Melinda Gates Foundation is playing a prominent role as well, in promoting higher education reform through Complete College America and other initiatives.

In the long view, the seventh period may be seen as one of foundation-driven reform. Since the late 2000s, the Lumina Foundation and the Bill and Melinda Gates Foundation have been pursuing deliberate strategies to engage state policy

*Table 9.1*    Changing assumptions about the role of government in tertiary education

| A shift from: | To: |
| --- | --- |
| Rational planning for static institutional models | Strategic planning for dynamic market models |
| A focus on providers, primarily public institutions | A focus on clients: students/learners, employers, and governments |
| Service areas defined by geographic boundaries of the state and monopolistic markets | Service areas defined by the needs of clients without regard to geographic boundaries |
| Clients served by single providers (e.g., a public university) | Clients served by multiple providers (e.g., students enrolling simultaneously with two or more institutions) |
| A tendency toward centralized control and regulation through tightly defined institutional missions, financial accountability, and retrospective reporting | More decentralized governance and management using policy tools to stimulate a desired response (e.g., incentives, performance funding, consumer information) |
| Policies and regulation to limit competition and unnecessary duplication | Policies to "enter the market on behalf of the public" and to channel competitive forces toward public purposes |
| Quality defined primarily in terms of resources (inputs such as faculty credentials or library resources) as established within tertiary education | Quality defined in terms of outcomes, performance, and competence, which are defined by multiple clients (students/learners, employers, governments) |
| Policies and services developed and carried out primarily through public agencies and public institutions | Increased use of nongovernmental organizations and mixed public/private providers to meet public/client needs (e.g., developing curricula and learning modules, providing student services, assessing competencies, providing quality assurance) |

*Source:* Aims C. McGuinness, Jr., *A Conceptual and Analytic Framework for Review of National Regulatory Policies and Practices in Higher Education,* prepared for the Education Committee, OECD, Feb., EDU/EC (2006) 3 (Paris: Organisation for Economic Co-operation and Development, 2006).

makers in shaping a new generation of policies intended to improve educational attainment and college completion.[34] Similar efforts are also directed at shaping federal education policy. It is too early to evaluate the impact of these initiatives. If they remain primarily foundation-driven reforms, it is unlikely that they will be sustained over the longer term. Nevertheless, there appears to be growing consensus that without fundamental changes in the current configuration and cost-structure of the higher education system, the United States cannot reach the goals that the nation and states are setting in a way that is affordable to students and state taxpayers. In this view, what will be required to achieve the goals are fundamental changes in the performance and business model of existing institutions and new, more cost-effective modes of provision. To support and enable reforms significant changes will be needed in state structures for policy leadership and in finance policy involving far more strategic, coordinated decisions regarding state subsidy of institutions, tuition policy, and student financial aid. [35,36]

In summary, the changes in the state role, especially in the periods since the mid-1980s, reflect a subtle yet fundamental shift in basic assumptions about the role of government in higher education. These changes are summarized as shifts in policy assumptions (table 9.1).

## Differences among States

In addition to the obvious variations in size, population, and enrollment, the fifty states differ significantly in history, culture, and political and economic dynamics. These differences are further reflected in the overall performance of their higher education systems, as well as in their financing policies, governance, and state regulatory culture related to higher education. A particularly informative, yet controversial, way of thinking about state variations is presented by political science literature on state political "cultures." Daniel Elazar, for example, sets forth a theory of political subcultures and classifies states according to whether they are moralistic, individualistic, or traditionalistic; their culture and ethnicity; and whether their "ethos" is "public-regarding" or "private-regarding."[37]

The following sections of this chapter describe significant differences among the states in higher education structures, finance policy, and regulation and highlight some of the recent policy changes.

## State Structures for Higher Education

The basic patterns of state-level organization across the nation today were in place in the early 1970s. The year 1972 marked the culmination of more than a decade of development of state higher education agencies formed to coordinate the massive expansion in the late 1950s and 1960s, as described earlier in this chapter. By that year, forty-seven states had established either consolidated governing boards responsible for all senior institutions (and, in some cases, community colleges also) or coordinating boards responsible for statewide planning and coordination of two or more governing boards. Three small states with a limited number of institutions did not form a special statutory agency, but instead continued to handle statewide higher education issues through existing governing boards, informal coordination, and direct involvement of the governor and state legislature.

Each state has a unique state structure and relationship between government and higher education.[38] The differences among states reflect variations in their general governmental structure (for example, different legal responsibilities of the executive and legislative branches), political culture, and history. Most states have established an entity (for example, a state board of higher education, state board of regents, or higher education commission) explicitly charged with statewide policy for higher education.

Despite the complexity of the differences, the approaches taken by states can be understood in terms of the variations in the authority and responsibility of state higher education entities for key policy tools and processes—such as budget review and approval, review and approval of academic programs, and public accountability—and the extent to which these entities are directly involved in institutional operations (governance). The following is an overview of these variations.

The distinction between *governance* and *coordination* is fundamental for understanding state higher education structures and the assignment of responsibility for budgetary and financial decision making and for institutional financial management. Some structures are established to govern institutions, while others are established to coordinate the state postsecondary education system or sectors (for example, a system of locally governed community colleges).

The term "governance" has a particular meaning when applied to the authority and responsibility of governing boards of public colleges and universities. American postsecondary education has a strong historical and legal tradition of institutional autonomy—a high degree of freedom from external intervention and control. A basic responsibility of governing boards is to oversee the delicate balance between institutional autonomy and public accountability.

All states assign responsibility for governing public colleges and universities to one or more boards, which are most often composed of a majority of lay citizens representing the public interest. The names of these boards vary, but "board of trustees" and "board of regents" are the most common. The responsibilities of these boards are similar to those of boards of directors for nonprofit corporations. Public institution governing boards were modeled after the lay boards of private colleges and universities. Private college boards usually govern a single institution. In contrast, public institution boards most often govern several public institutions. In fact, more than 65 percent of the students in American public postsecondary education attend institutions whose governing boards cover multiple campuses.[39]

Common responsibilities of public governing boards include governing a single corporate entity, including all the rights and responsibilities of that corporation as defined by state law and, if it is a system board, encompassing all institutions within a system. Individual institutions within the board's jurisdiction usually do not have separate corporate status, although governing boards may have subsidiary corporations for hospitals, foundations, or other purposes. Other responsibilities include appointing, setting the compensation for, and evaluating both system and institutional chief executives; planning strategically, budgeting (operating and capital), and allocating resources between and among the institutions within the board's jurisdiction; ensuring public accountability for the effective and efficient use of resources to achieve institutional missions; maintaining the institution's assets (human, programmatic, and physical), and ensuring alignment of these assets with the institutional mission; developing and implementing policy on a wide range of institutional concerns (for example, academic and student affairs policies) that do not need the approval of external agencies or authorities; awarding academic degrees; advocating for the needs of the institutions under the board's jurisdiction to the legislature and governor; and establishing faculty and other personnel policies, including approving the awarding of tenure and serving as the final point of appeal on personnel grievances.

There are a number of ways to categorize public governing boards, but the approach suggested by Clark Kerr and Marian Gade in *The Guardians: Boards of Trustees of American Colleges and Universities* is particularly useful.[40] They categorize public governing boards in three ways. First, there are consolidated governance systems in which one board governs all public two- and four-year institutions, or one board covers all four-year campuses (with separate arrangements for two-year institutions). Second, there are segmental systems in which separate boards govern distinct types of campuses (for example, research universities, comprehensive colleges and universities, and community colleges; this may include separate boards for postsecondary technical institutes or colleges and for adult education, as well). Third, there are campus-level governing boards that have full, "autonomous" authority over a single campus that is not part of a consolidated governing board or multicampus system. Several states combine consolidated governance and campus-level boards. For example, in North Carolina and Utah campus-level boards have authority delegated by the central board and can make some decisions on their own. The State University of New York System, the University of Maine System, and the University System of Maryland also have campus boards, though they are largely advisory.

A number of states have established coordinating boards responsible for key aspects of the state's role in postsecondary education. Some coordinating boards have the responsibility for statewide coordination with a broad range of functions such as strategic planning and policy leadership, institutional mission approval, program review and approval, and budget development and resource allocation). Other coordinating boards are responsible for only a single sector, such as community colleges.

The important point is that coordinating boards do *not* govern institutions, in the sense defined above (for example, appointing institutional chief executives or setting faculty personnel policies). Specifically, coordinating boards appoint, set compensation for, and evaluate only the agency executive officer and staff, but not the institutional chief executives. In several states, the governor is the final appointing authority for the agency executive, although usually with recommendations from the coordinating board. Coordinating boards do not generally have corporate status independent of state government; they focus more on state and system needs and priorities than on advocating the interests of a particular institution or system of institutions, and they plan primarily for the state postsecondary education system as a whole. In most coordinating board states, this planning includes both public and private institutions and, in some states, for-profit institutions. Coordinating boards may or may not review and make recommendations on budgets for the state system as a whole, rather than only for one part of that system. A few coordinating agencies recommend consolidated budgets for the whole public system. Several are responsible for recommending the funding formulas, including outcome-based funding criteria, for allocating state appropriations among public institutions. Others simply make recommendations to the governor or legislature on individual institutional or segmental budgets. Most coordinating boards have a responsibility to implement budget policy only for funds appropriated specifically to the agency for operations and special initiatives, or for reallocations to the institutions for performance, incentives, or other purposes; they may or may not review or approve proposals for new academic programs and may or may not have authority to require institutions to review existing programs. They are not directly involved in setting or carrying out human resource or personnel policies, except to carry out legislative mandates for studies of issues such as faculty workload and productivity or tenure policy.

Twenty-one states have statewide coordinating boards with responsibility for strategic planning, carrying out state-level administrative functions, and, in most cases, providing advice to the governor and state legislature on budgets. In each of these states, the governance of public institutions is the responsibility of multiple system and/or institutional governing boards. Ten states and the District of Columbia and Puerto Rico have a single statewide governing board for all public institutions. The remaining nineteen states have multiple system and/or institutional governing boards but have no statewide entity with responsibility for system coordination and strategic planning for the higher education system as a whole. In many cases, one of these state boards is responsible for governing or coordinating community and technical colleges. In several of these states, the second board is a coordinating board for community and technical colleges. Fourteen of these states have higher education service and regulatory agencies with responsibility for functions such as administration of student financial aid programs and regulation of non-state institutions. None of these agencies has authority to coordinate the higher education system as a whole.[41]

## Changes in State Structures

Despite the apparent continuity in state structures over time, significant changes have taken place and continue to take place in the form and substance of state coordination and governance.[42] Changes in political leadership (for example, newly elected governors or changes in party control of the state legislature) are often the occasions for restructuring.[43] The forces behind the changes can be grouped into two broad categories: first, "perennial" issues that throughout the past have consistently spurred governors and legislators to make higher education reorganization proposals and, second, broader changes in state expectations and roles.

## PERENNIAL ISSUES

Perennial issues tend to be long-standing problems that may fester for years but then, especially at points of changes in political leadership or severe economic downturns, trigger debates, lead to special study commissions, and often eventually result in full-scale reorganization. The following are examples of several of the most common issues:

- *Access to high-cost graduate and professional programs:* In most states, regional economic, political, and cultural differences present serious challenges to state policy makers. These regional stresses are amplified and played out in conflicts within the states' postsecondary education systems. A common scenario begins with pressure from a growing urban area to have accessible graduate and professional programs. Subsequent local campaigns and state lobbying efforts seek to expand these initiatives from a few courses to full-scale programs, and then the new campuses lead to opposition from existing universities and other regions. The same scenario often plays out when isolated rural areas struggle to gain access to programs for place-bound adults. Local and regional end runs to the governor or legislature to get special attention either to advance or block such initiatives usually spark political struggles that inevitably lead to major restructuring proposals.

- *Conflict between the aspirations of two institutions (often under separate governing boards) in the same geographic area:* Again, conflicts tend to be over which institution should offer high-cost graduate and professional programs. Major reorganization proposals, usually mergers or consolidations, frequently occur after years of other efforts to achieve improved cooperation and coordination.

- *Political reaction to institutional lobbying:* As governors and legislators face politically difficult and unattractive choices to curtail rather than expand programs, intense lobbying by narrow, competing institutional interests can spark demands for restructuring. Political leaders seek to push such battles away from the immediate political process by increasing the authority of a state board, with the hope that the board will be able to resolve the conflicts before they get to the legislature. The reverse situation also occurs frequently, when a state board will act to curtail an institutional end run and then face a legislative proposal, frequently stimulated by the offending institution, to abolish the board. Short-term victories gained through end running the established coordinating structures usually lead to greater centralization.

- *Frustrations with barriers to student transfer and articulation:* Cumulative evidence that student transfers between institutions are difficult, or that the number of transfer credits is limited, often leads to proposals to create a "seamless" system. Before the mid-1990s, most of the reorganization proposals were limited to postsecondary education (for example, consolidating institutions under a single governing board), but an increasing number of states are debating proposals to create P–16 (primary through postsecondary education) structures.

- *Concerns about too many institutions with ill-defined or overlapping missions:* At issue may be small, isolated rural institutions or institutions with similar missions in close proximity to one another. Governance debates often emerge from proposals to merge, consolidate, or close institutions or to make radical changes in institutional missions. The intense lobbying and publicity raised by persons opposing these solutions will often lead to proposals for governance changes. In some cases, the proposals are to abolish the board that proposed the changes. In other cases, just the opposite is proposed—to increase the board's authority out of frustration with its inability to carry out a recommended closure or merger.

- *Lack of regional coordination among institutions (for example, community colleges, technical colleges, and branch campuses) offering one- and two-year vocational, technical, occupational, and transfer programs:* Many states have regions or communities where two or more public institutions, each responsible to a different state board or agency, are competing to offer similar one- and two-year programs. In the worst situations, this may involve a postsecondary technical institute, a community college, and two-year lower-division university branches competing for an overlapping market in the same region.

- *Concerns about the current state board's effectiveness or continuing relevance to state priorities:* Reorganizations often result from efforts to change leaders or leadership styles. As illustrated by the brief summary of changes over the past twenty-five years, state leaders tend to see the importance of statewide coordination in times of severe fiscal constraints, but when the economy is strong and these leaders face fewer difficult choices among competing priorities, the relevance of state agencies is less evident. Common triggers for change include a sense that a board, or its staff, is ineffective or lacks the political influence or judgment to address critical issues facing the state, which are often one or more of the other perennial issues. The board or staff may be perceived as unable to resolve problems before they become major political controversies, or they may have handled difficult issues poorly in the past. Another trigger is often a desire to change the leadership style or the underlying philosophy of the state role. This may be a reaction to aggressive, centralized leadership and an effort to shift to a more passive, consultative leadership approach—or the reverse. The change may be to move from a focus on or management issues internal to postsecondary education to a focus on policy leadership relative to a broader public agenda. Finally, state leaders also may propose reorganization not because the structure has problems, but simply to change the leadership or personalities involved in the process.

## Changes in the Context of Public Agenda Reforms

The National Center for Public Policy and Higher Education in 2005 called upon states to improve their capacities for dealing with the challenge of improving the states' educational attainment and for providing public policy leadership.[44] The center's core recommendation was that states must have a broad-based, independent, credible public entity with a clear charge to increase the state's educational attainment and to prepare citizens for the workforce. The specifics might differ across states, but whatever the organizational forms, effective, sustained policy leadership for higher education needed to include:

- The strength to counter inappropriate political, partisan, institutional, or parochial influences.
- The capacity and responsibility for articulating and monitoring state performance objectives for higher education that would be supported by the key leaders in the state, objectives that would be specific and measurable, including quantifiable goals for college preparation, access, participation, retention, graduation, and responsiveness to other state needs.
- The engagement of civic, business, and public school leaders beyond state government and higher education leaders.
- A recognition of distinctions between statewide policy—and the public entities and policies needed to accomplish it—and institutional

governance. The role of statewide policy leadership is distinct from the roles of institutional and segmental governing boards.

- The information-gathering and analytical capacity to inform the choice of state goals/priorities and to interpret and evaluate statewide and institutional performance in relation to these goals.
- The capacity to bring coherence and coordination in key policy areas, such as the relationship between institutional appropriations, tuition, and financial aid.
- The capacity to influence the direction of state resources to ensure accomplishment of these priorities.

The National Center acknowledged that establishing such an entity would require a substantial redesign of the organizations and agencies that are currently in place. They cautioned that if states failed to make these changes, "traditional decision-making entities, built for other times and other public purposes and based primarily on institutionally focused issues will crowd out attention to critical public priorities."[45]

Some coordinating boards are making a transition to the broader role called for by the National Center, but the political and budgetary context for these changes is problematic. Governors in several states have gained control of the previous independent coordinating agencies either by requiring that the executive officers be appointed and serve at the pleasure of the governor or in some cases tying the agency directly to the office of the governor. In the short term, these changes increase the chances that the governor will consider the coordinating agency's advice. Nevertheless, the agencies have lost a degree of their independence and their ability to provide objective analysis and advice to both the governor and the state legislature, and to maintain a trusting relationship with the state's higher education leadership. Because the agency's leadership will be replaced when a new governor is elected, its ability to attend to long-term goals and reforms is also weakened.

As agencies have attempted to decrease their regulatory role and avoid getting involved in institution-level governance and management issues, they have increasingly been assigned regulatory tasks that draw them back to their previous roles. Legislators' frustrations with decisions by institutional governing boards and presidents, reactions to institutional lobbying, and institution-level controversies lead to new mandates for the coordinating agency which further draw it into potential governance conflicts with institutional leaders.

In the budget crisis and the drive to reduce the number of state employees, higher education agency staffs were cut and, in at least one state (California), the governor eliminated the agency's funding from the state budget. Agencies in other states face the challenge of undertaking an increased regulatory burden with no additional staff. The staff capacity to undertake a more strategic leadership mission is simply not available.

Limitations on salaries of state employees constrain the ability of the higher education agency to compete with public universities for qualified staff, especially staff who have both academic credibility and public policy expertise.

The most important policy gap is the lack of connection between public agenda reforms and state finance policy. When state coordinating bodies were established in the 1960s and 1970s, they played a central role in the state budget process. The agencies provided an objective source of analysis and recommendations on budgets, funding formulas, and capital funding to the governor and state legislature. As the sophistication of governor's budget office and legislative fiscal staffs grew, the role of many coordinating boards in the budget process declined. Today, only a few state higher education agencies play such a role. As a consequence, states lack a venue where key state leaders come together to develop both long-term strategic goals for the performance and sustainability of the higher education system and a strategic financing plan to achieve those goals. There is no place where strategic decisions can be made about how to achieve the goals within the constraints of limited public funding and serious questions about affordability for students and families. As noted in the overview of state coordinating and governing structures, more than a third of the states have two or more large governing systems but do not have an overall system coordinating entity. These states are finding it more difficult to shape a public agenda for the state as a whole—across all sectors and institutions. Large, multi-institution governing systems will remain an important dimension of the US higher education landscape. These systems have the potential to play central roles in the realignment of the nation's higher education capacity to achieve long-term state and national goals and to create a policy environment for a highly diverse and sustainable network of institutions.[46] Large systems such as the State University of New York (SUNY) and comparatively small systems such as the University of Maine System are leading the way in shaping a new role for systems. These systems are enhancing the power of the system to serve the state by moving from a collection of individual institutions competing with each other for students and resources, to a coordinated, differentiated network of institutions in which the impact of the system is far greater than the sum of its parts (e.g., the "Power of SUNY: SUNY and the Entrepreneurial Century"[47] and the University of Maine System Plan for Strategic Integration and Financial Sustainability[48]). Nevertheless, systems that fail to undertake fundamental reforms can present several barriers to both the competiveness of component institutions and campuses as well as to the achievement of state goals.

## Finance Policy and Budget

### THE BUDGET PROCESS

The states differ greatly in the details of their budget processes and in the roles of the governor, the state legislature, and state higher education coordinating and governing bodies.[49] In all states, the state executive departments for finance and budget development and the legislative committees responsible for appropriations play a dominant role in determining the share of the state budget to be appropriated for higher education purposes and other finance policy oversight. Higher education regulations are often embedded within the budget and state appropriations to institutions. As depicted in figure 9.1, the flow of funds to support higher education is a complex process involving multiple sources and multiple decision points.

The key state or system-level decisions regarding financing public higher education relate to (1) state appropriations or grants to public institutions, (2) tuition and fees, (3) student financial aid, and (4) funding for capital development (facilities and equipment).The reality of the state-level policy process is that decisions on these four elements are often made by different entities and at different points in the policy process.

To complicate matters even further, state decisions on funding for research are often made in the process of considering state economic development priorities while decisions regarding funding of workforce training are made in still another arena.

States vary greatly in detail embedded in the budget and appropriations for higher education: from single line-item appropriations to detailed line-item appropriations including specifications regarding the number of state-funded positions. As noted in the following section of this chapter, the trend over the past half-century has been for states to grant public institutions increased autonomy regarding the expenditure of state appropriations.

The tuition-setting process commonly involves multiple levels of decision making. The variations across the fifty states defy easy generalizations. While the

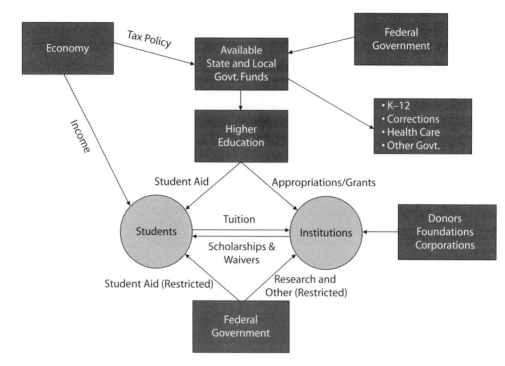

*Figure 9.1.* Elements of finance policy

*Source:* Dennis P. Jones, "Financing in Sync: Aligning Fiscal Policy with State Objectives," in *Financing in Sync: Appropriations, Tuition, and Financial Aid for Higher Education* (Boulder, CO: Western Interstate Commission for Higher Education, 2003), 7.

final authority to set tuition and fees may rest with a public university governing board, either for an individual university or for a governing system, the governor and state legislature commonly have a powerful influence on the final decision.

For example, in nine states, the state legislature has final decision-making authority for university-level tuition; in another sixteen states, the state legislature has an informal, consultative role. In practice, the political pressures to contain the rise in tuition for state residents dominate the decision-making process at all levels.

Many states also regulate the expenditure of revenue generated from tuition. In the most restrictive cases, the state constitution requires that all nonstate revenue generated by state agencies, including universities, be deposited in the state treasury and then expended only through action of the state legislature. Because tuition revenue is categorized as nonstate revenue, the legislatures in these states can—and often have—not only established a range of limits such as those mentioned above but also have, in the process of balancing the overall state budget, expended these funds for purposes outside of higher education, as described above.[50]

States also differ widely in the shares of funding for public institutions borne by state appropriations and tuition. Net tuition revenue (tuition minus institutionally funded student aid) as a percentage of total public institution educational funding (funding from state appropriations plus tuition revenue) averages 46.8 percent for the United States. Nevertheless, states range from 13.8 percent (Wyoming) to 84.5 percent (New Hampshire) in net tuition as a percentage of total general fund revenue. (figure 9.2).[51]

State financing of higher education has followed a roller coaster pattern over the decades, with periods of significant increases in state appropriations when economic times are good, followed by dramatic decreases in periods of economic downturn or recession. Because governors and state legislatures recognize that higher education has a revenue source (tuition and fees), in contrast to most other governmental services, higher education tends to be the "budget balancer." Consequently, in each period of economic downturn, tuition and fees have increased dramatically.

These trends in state funding have resulted in a major shift in funding of public higher education from state appropriations to student tuition. The shift from institutional subsidy to a greater reliance on tuition is taking place on a largely ad hoc basis, primarily without coordination with student aid policy and attention to the long-term implications for student access and opportunity.[52]

From 1988 to 2013, the share of funding per full-time student from state appropriations decreased from 76 percent to 53 percent, and the student share increased from 24 percent to 47 percent (figure 9.3). The share of financing borne by the student and the state have shifted dramatically over the same time period (figure 9.4).

State funding for student aid (student subsidies) to offset tuition increases is growing, but the trend is for this aid to be awarded largely on the basis of merit (academic performance and qualifications) rather than need. The National Association of State Student Grant and Aid Programs (NASSGAP) reported that in the 2012–13 academic year, states awarded about $11.2 billion in total state-funded student financial aid. The majority of state aid (85 percent) was in the form of grants. In 2012–13, almost 4.1 million grant awards were made, representing about $9.6 billion in need-based and non-need-based grant aid. Of the grant money awarded in 2012–13, 75 percent was need-based (up slightly from last

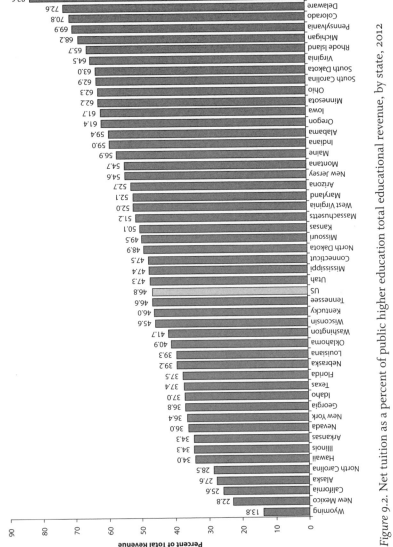

*Figure 9.2.* Net tuition as a percent of public higher education total educational revenue, by state, 2012

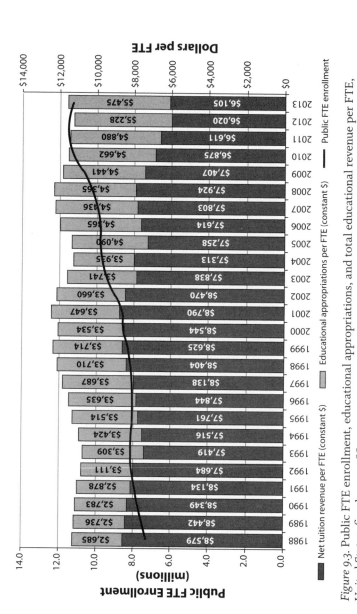

*Figure 9.3.* Public FTE enrollment, educational appropriations, and total educational revenue per FTE, United States, fiscal year 1988–2013

*Source:* State Higher Education Executive Officers, "Public FTE Enrollment, Educational Appropriations and Total Educational Revenue per FTE, United States—Fiscal Years 1988–2013," http://www.sheeo.org/resources/publications/shef-%E2%80%94-state-higher-education-finance-fy13.

*Note:* Constant 2013 dollars adjusted by SHEEO Higher Education Cost Adjustment. Educational appropriations include ARRA funds.

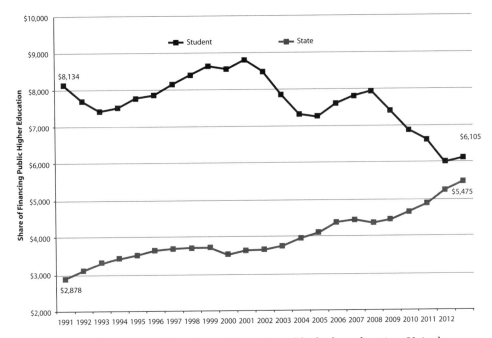

*Figure 9.4.* Change in student share of financing public higher education, United States, 1991–2013
*Source:* State Higher Education Executive Officers, "Public FTE Enrollment, Educational Appropriations and Total Educational Revenue per FTE, United States—Fiscal Years 1988–2013," http://www.sheeo.org/resources/publications/shef-%E2%80%94-state-higher-education-finance-fy13.
*Note:* Constant 2013 dollars adjusted by SHEEO Higher Education Cost Adjustment. Educational appropriations include ARRA funds.

year) and 25 percent was non-need-based. Eight states (California, New York, Texas, Pennsylvania, Illinois, New Jersey, Washington, and North Carolina) collectively awarded about $5 billion in undergraduate need-based grant aid, accounting for about 70 percent of all aid of this type. States also provided about $1.7 billion in nongrant student aid, including loans, loan assumptions, conditional grants, work-study, and tuition waivers.[53]

The dramatic cuts in state funding for higher education in the fiscal crises of the early 2000s and then again beginning in 2008 raised fundamental questions about the states' commitment to higher education as a public good and their future role in the oversight and funding of public higher education.[54,55] The crises reflected a long-term trend toward a decreasing share of revenue for higher education from public sources. Even when the economy began to recover, higher education still felt a squeeze in state funding. The reasons for the long-term decline in state support are more structural than the result of deliberate decisions about higher education per se. In many states, the demand for higher education is far outstripping the states' fiscal capacity—a consequence of conditions such as the faltering economy, mandated increases in funding for health care and K–12 education, and deliberate tax reductions.[56]

## CHANGES IN STATE FINANCE POLICY

A central theme of public agenda reforms is that states should align finance policy with long-term strategic goals.[57] Among other points, it could be expected that state finance policy would:

- Frame funding decisions by clear state goals.
- Ensure that the decisions regarding state appropriations, tuition and fees, and student financial aid are synchronized. For example, if an appropriations decrease required an increase in tuition and fees, the state would ensure that adequate funding for student finance aid be available so as to maintain the state's commitment to affordable access for low-income students.
- Recognize that both students and institutions need a degree of predictability in financing.

Predictability is important to both students and families as they plan to pay for tuition, living expenses, and other costs, as well as for institutions to carry out their teaching and research missions (e.g., academic programs and faculty must be in place as students begin the academic year). The reality, however, is that decisions regarding state appropriations, tuition and fees, and student financial aid are often made with no reference to state goals, are not synchronized, and, as noted earlier, are made by different policy makers on different schedules.[58]

As noted earlier, up until the 1980s, states had primarily focused on issues of resource allocation and utilization, and rarely became involved in basic questions about the outcomes of a college or university education and the contributions of higher education to the state's economic competitiveness. In period six, from the mid-1980s to 2008, there was renewed interest in performance funding and performance budgeting. However, as reported by Joseph Burke and Henrik Minassains, this development was difficult for states to sustain.[59]

With strong support from the Lumina Foundation and the Bill and Melinda Gates Foundation, the interest in performance funding, now renamed "outcome-based" funding, increased dramatically as the nation recovered from the Great Recession in 2010. By early 2015, the majority of states reported that they had either implemented or were developing outcome-based funding. The characteristics of these initiatives varied widely, however. Not surprisingly, the states with the most highly developed and carefully designed policies were those with many years of experience with performance funding and relatively complex funding formulas (Illinois, Indiana, Ohio, and Tennessee, are examples). These states linked outcome-based funding to long-term state goals and incorporated the new policies within a redesign of the state's core higher education financing.[60] At the other end of the spectrum, some states appeared to be adopting outcome-based funding as an add-on to existing finance policy with little consideration of the policy's relationship to state goals and did so without addressing the underlying dysfunction in existing policies.[61]

It remains to be seen how the drive for outcome-based funding will develop and what its long-term impact will be on the overall performance of the higher education system. As noted earlier, there appears to be a growing consensus that fundamental changes in the current configuration and cost structure of the higher education system are needed. A shift in financing policy toward outcomes is an important means to promote change. However, outcome-based funding is likely to have a limited impact if it is implemented as a one-off solution, disconnected from broader strategies for reform.[62]

### Regulation by Other Non-Higher Education State Agencies

Non-higher executive branch departments, especially in states in which public universities have a legal status as state agencies, regulate functions that are central to institutional governance and management. The most common regulations relate to:

- *Procurement:* requirements that purchases above certain minimum levels be approved by and be handled through the state government purchasing department;
- *Capital planning and construction:* requirements that all buildings constructed with state financing be managed through a central state department for all state government;
- *Human resources:* University staff (especially those funded with state appropriations) are state employees, are accorded civil service protections, and are included within the state's pension and health plans. The

state controls the number of state-funded positions and state agencies control other dimensions of university human resource policy.

The extent of regulation by non-higher education state agencies differs in relationship to the legal status accorded to public colleges and universities. The four levels of state control of institutions can be represented on a continuum from high to low (table 9.2).

The four categories of institutional legal status represent theoretical types. In practice, no state currently treats all of its public institutions as if they were in

*Table 9.2*    Levels of state control and institutional legal status

| Level | Type | Legal status |
|---|---|---|
| High regulatory control | A. Institution as state agency | Higher education institutions are treated in a manner similar to other state agencies, such as the transportation/highway department. |
| | B. State-controlled institution | The distinctiveness of higher education institutions from other state agencies is recognized, but most of the budget and financing policies applied to other state agencies are also applied to higher education. |
| | C. State-aided institution | Higher education institutions have a legal status according them substantial autonomy from state government. The state provides base, categorical, and capital funding, but with an expectation of substantial nonstate funding (tuition, private giving, etc.). |
| Low regulatory control | D. Corporate model for institutional governance | As in model C, institutions have a legal status (e.g., a public corporation) according them substantial autonomy. The expectation of state funding is less certain and may be allocated not in grants to the institution, but in the form of vouchers or grants to students to offset tuition charges. |

either of the two extremes: institution as a state agency or institution as an independent corporation.[63] There are three common patterns:

- Pattern 1: Different sectors are accorded different levels of independence from state procedural controls. For example, both the University of California and the California State University systems are treated as "state-aided" institutions, although each is subject to specific regulations that treat the institutions as "state controlled." The University of California System is established in the state constitution and has a higher level of independence from state procedural controls than the California State University System, which is established in state statutes and, until the early 1990s, was closely linked to state budget, personnel, and purchasing requirements. In contrast to the two university systems, the California Community Colleges are governed by extensive state statutory and regulatory policies and, in many respects, are treated as state-controlled institutions.

- Pattern 2: All public universities are established as public corporations (state aided) but are subject to detailed state oversight in specific areas, such as capital construction or personnel. North Dakota and Kentucky are examples of this pattern—the North Dakota University System as a single university system and Kentucky's system, where each university is a separate public corporation. In both cases, the institutions are subject to specific state procedural controls related to capital construction and other areas. As another example, the University of Wisconsin System is organized as a public corporation but is subject to detailed oversight by the Wisconsin State Department of Administration on all capital projects, and all classified (nonprofessional) personnel are included in the state civil service system.

- Pattern 3: Most public institutions are established as public corporations (state aided), but specific institutions are accorded greater independence from state procedural controls as a result of deliberate state actions to decentralize governance and diversify revenue sources. The University System of Maryland, for example, is accorded a degree of independence as a public corporation (state aided), but St. Mary's College of Maryland was granted increased autonomy in return for meeting specific accountability requirements.[64] The State of Colorado has implemented a similar policy through which institutions may enter into "compacts" with the state in return for increased autonomy.[65]

The pressures for increased institutional autonomy and management flexibility tend to intensify in periods of severe fiscal stress. As the fiscal crisis of the early 2000s hit the states and the percentage of public institutions' funding from states decreased precipitously, university leaders argued that increased flexibility was essential for their institutions to sustain access and quality and to compete in the global knowledge economy.[66] These calls for change coincided with other calls, especially from political conservatives, for fundamental shifts in the financing of higher education: from institutional subsidy to student subsidy or student vouchers.[67,68,69]

Deregulation initiatives adopted by states in recent years can be grouped as follows:

- *Changes related to the specific issue of tuition flexibility,* such as changes that grant institutions authority to increase tuition and, in many cases, to retain tuition revenue. In exchange, states have required universities to agree to allocate a percentage of the increased revenue to need-based student financial aid, to commit to ensuring access to in-state students, to improve graduation rates, and to agree to further performance requirements. Most cases of tuition deregulation have been accompanied by caps on the rate of increase (e.g., no more than $x$% over $y$ years) and a requirement that the institution obtain approval for any increases exceeding these limits.

- *Incremental changes related to other specific procedural/operational issues,* increasing authority in respect to issues related to human resource management (e.g., position controls), purchasing, construction contracts, information technology, or retirement plans offered as alternatives to the state retirement system. In some cases, these changes have involved deregulation of substantive issues such as academic program approval. In most cases, these changes provide for delegating to a public university the authority to carry out certain functions (e.g., purchasing or entering into and overseeing construction contracts) under the condition that the university abide by the basic requirements (e.g., competitive bidding) applicable to all other state agencies. In other words, the authority is delegated, not granted to the university by virtue of its legal status as an independent legal entity.

- *Systemwide deregulation,* including both tuition flexibility and procedural deregulation granted in exchange for greater performance and accountability through performance or management agreements with the state. Examples include the changes enacted through the 2005 Virginia Restructured Higher Education Financial and Administrative Operations Act[70] and the 2010 Louisiana Granting Resources and Autonomy for Diplomas Act (the "Grad Act").
- *Changes in the legal status of university systems,* thereby granting these entities authority to carry out procedural/operational functions independent of the direct oversight of state agencies. For example, legislation enacted in 1999 established the University System of Maryland as a public corporation. Nevertheless, the system remained accountable to the state for complying with some of the previous state procedural requirements, albeit with some increased independence, even under their new legal status.
- *Changes in the legal status of individual institutions to established "charter" colleges.* Examples of these changes (e.g., Saint Mary's College of Maryland) are limited and reflect unique circumstances that largely are not applicable to other state and institutional contexts.[71]

In order to bring about fundamental change, higher education systems and institutions will need the authority and management flexibility to achieve a significant realignment of human and physical resources. "Procedural" regulations by non-higher education agencies can be significant barriers to needed systemic reform. Nevertheless, the experience of past deregulation initiatives is that they must be accompanied by institutional accountability for serving public purposes. The changes in states with long traditions of centralized controls have taken place on a step-by-step basis over a number of years. Without careful planning and attention to the need for accountability, with a change in political leadership the state may revert to its historic regulatory role and reestablished centralized controls.

## Restructuring of Systems

The most controversial recent proposals for large-scale deregulation have been to restructure existing public university systems by increasing the autonomy of research universities within systems or even separating these institutions from their systems. Oregon, Wisconsin, and California are among the most debated examples of these proposals.[72] The Oregon debate led to changes. The California and Wisconsin proposals are likely to be raised in the future.

The variations among states in the degree of regulatory authority retained by the state government versus the authority of a consolidated system board affect these debates about increasing institutional autonomy. Oregon and Wisconsin remain among the states in which the state government retains significant regulatory control of higher education. In essence, these states continue to treat universities as state agencies, not as separate legal entities (e.g., a corporation organized to carry out public purposes) with a degree of autonomy from state financial and procedural regulation.[73]

The governance debate in Oregon extended back to the early 2000s and involved the state's multifaceted higher education governing and coordinating structures. Much of the national attention on Oregon within higher education circles focused on a controversial proposal by then-president of the University of Oregon, Richard W. Lariviere, to establish his institution as an independently governed university under a board of trustees outside the Oregon University System (OUS), as well as to establish a new financial model of a public endowment that would provide sustained support for the university largely independent of the state.[74]

While national attention focused on the University of Oregon proposal, state leaders were concerned with how to achieve the most ambitious goals in the country for increasing the educational attainment by the state's population. Oregon set a goal (the "40-40-20 goal") that by 2025 40 percent of the population would have at least a bachelor's degree, 40 percent would have an associate's degree or postsecondary education credential, and the remaining 20 percent would have attained a high school diploma.[75]

In 2011, the legislative assembly established a statewide coordinating entity, the Higher Education Coordinating Commission, charged with statewide planning and coordination of all postsecondary education, including OUS institutions and the community colleges. In subsequent legislation, enacted in 2013 and 2014, Oregon granted the Oregon State University, Portland State University, and the University of Oregon authority to establish their own governing boards, effective July 1, 2014. The legislation extended the same authority to all other Oregon public universities effective July 1, 2015. At the same time, the legislation strengthened the authority of the Higher Education Coordinating Commission to coordinate the increasingly decentralized higher education system.

In Wisconsin, the chancellor of the University of Wisconsin-Madison (UW-Madison), Carolyn "Biddy" Martin, proposed in 2010 a "New Badger Partnership" that would separate the campus from the system and grant it substantial autonomy from state government.[76] Governor Scott Walker introduced a similar idea as a provision of the 2011–13 biennial budget bill. It would have created UW-Madison as a public authority independent of the University of Wisconsin System (UW System) Board of Regents and governed by its own board of trustees. If adopted by the legislature, the governor's version of the budget bill would have granted UW-Madison substantial operational flexibility compared to current law.[77] The proposal to separate UW-Madison from the system was eventually rejected. At the same time, legislation was enacted granting both the system and UW-Madison increased flexibility in managing human resources. At the time this chapter was written, Wisconsin was embroiled in a wide-ranging debate about a new proposal by Governor Walker to establish the University of Wisconsin as a public authority with considerable procedural autonomy from state government. The proposal is accompanied by a $300 million budget cut over a two-year period and a two-year tuition freeze.[78] The outcome of this debate is far from clear at this point.

In early 2012, the Chancellor of the University of California, Berkeley, Robert Birgeneau, presented a proposal to the Board of Regents of the University of California (UC) system to create and delegate some responsibilities to campus boards.[79] In contrast to the proposals by the University of Oregon and the University of Wisconsin-Madison, the UC Berkeley chancellor did not recommend that Berkeley or any other campus be separated from the system. Rather, he recommended that the board of regents grant the campuses additional autonomy within the framework of a modernized statewide system. While the Oregon and Wisconsin debates have led to action by the states' political leaders and system governing boards, the California proposal is in the early stages of discussion as of this writing.

The cases of California, Oregon, and Wisconsin reflect an ongoing debate regarding the future of public research universities: their role within systems, their future funding, and their relationships to state government.[80,81] The cases also illustrate the growing tension between the missions and aspirations of public universities to be globally competitive and the imperative of states to ensure access and opportunity for the state's population in a manner that is affordable for both students and the state's taxpayers. These tensions are likely to continue to frame debates about the state role in higher education in the coming decade and beyond.

## Long-Term Impact of Reforms

It is unclear what the long-range impact of the current period of higher education reform will have on the overall system performance. Several efforts have been made to assess the impact of public agenda reforms implemented primarily in the sixth period, from the late 1990s to 2008. Perna and Finney undertook the most comprehensive assessment available to date of what they call "The Attainment Agenda."[82] Through case studies of five states—Georgia, Illinois, Maryland, Texas, and Washington—they examine state reforms in relationship to evidence regarding improvements in educational attainment. The case studies sought to address two questions:

- What is the performance of higher education in the selected states, where performance is measured by indicators of preparation, participation, completion, affordability, and equity across groups in these indicators?
- What is the role of public policy in explaining changes from the early 1990s until 2010 in higher education performance in the selected states?[83]

Based on the case studies, Perna and Finney proposed a conceptual model for understanding how state policy influences higher education performance. The model illustrates how the variables of state policy leadership and steering, strategic use of fiscal resources, preparation and movement of students, and optimization of system capacity contribute the goal of overall advancement and equity in education. The findings from the case studies show that well-intentioned reforms had mixed results. The authors attribute the limited impact to significant gaps in state-level capacity for sustained policy leadership and lack of alignment of other policies (especially finance policy) with the long-term goals. They outline a number of issues that should be the subject of further analysis in order to provide guidance to the next generation of policymakers.[84]

The findings of the Perna and Finney study underscore how difficult it is to bring about long-term improvements as envisioned in the current generation of public agenda reforms. As states emerged from the economic crisis and Great Recession, the trajectory of change in system governance was clear, but the extent and pace of change varied across the fifty states. There is growing concern, however, that the current state-level policy environment serves as a major barrier to the changes needed to achieve long-term goals and to reshape the public higher education enterprise to remain affordable and sustainable. The policymaking processes and structures for system governance and regulation established for an earlier time are not adequate for the future. The reality, however, is that getting support among state political leaders for the needed changes is a challenge. The state political scene is highly splintered, with serious divisions among opposing views about the role of government. Turnover in political leadership, term limits, and political divisions mean that short-term agendas drive steal attention from long-term reform. Understanding has been lost concerning the underlying rationale for higher education structures including basic values such as the need for autonomy and a degree of independence of system-level structures from political control. Lack of trust in government is a theme that cuts across the political spectrum.

In the economic crisis, states tightened controls in the budget process, in public employment, and in the expenditure of state funding. In this environment, there is little room for long-term strategy such as linking long-term strategic goals to strategic finance policy. No venue exists for this conversation. State budget offices and legislative appropriations committees are focused on balancing the state budget, controlling expenditure of state appropriations, and reducing or containing long-term liabilities in funding pensions and healthcare.

Despite these challenging conditions, a number of states are moving ahead with promising reforms and are drawing on the lessons of earlier efforts. The Lumina Foundation, the Bill and Melinda Gates Foundation, and others are investing significant resources in building the state leadership capacity to shape and sustain reforms and to develop a new generation of policy tools to stimulate and support essential reforms.

## Conclusion

Sustaining attention toward the public and societal purposes of higher education in the turbulent times of the next decade and beyond will require fundamental improvements in state-level capacity to lead change in the public interest. As summarized above, few states are prepared to meet the fundamental prerequisites for that leadership. Many of the state structures formed for other purposes in an earlier time cannot be expected to make the transition to new missions and modes of leadership. New thinking is needed about the ways states can shape decision-making structures and policies designed explicitly for new missions and functions. Crafting new alternatives must be a shared responsibility of both higher education and state leaders.

NOTES

1. Robert Berdahl makes an important distinction between "substantive" autonomy, meaning autonomy on matters of standards, curriculum, faculty appointments, and similar matters, and "procedural" autonomy, meaning autonomy from state procedural controls. See Robert O. Berdahl, *Statewide Coordination of Higher Education* (Washington, DC: American Council on Education, 1971).

2. Frank Newman, *Choosing Quality* (Denver: Education Commission of the States, 1987), xiii.

3. Berdahl, *Statewide Coordination*, 9.

4. Clark Kerr, "The States and Higher Education: Changes Ahead," *State Government* 58, no. 2 (1985): 45–50.

5. National Center for Education Statistics, *Digest of Education Statistics: 2012*, figure 17, Percentage distribution of total revenues of public degree-granting institutions, by source of funds: 2010–11, http://nces.ed.gov/programs/digest/d12/figures/fig_17.asp?referrer=figures.

6. National Association of State Scholarship and Grant Programs [NASSGAP] (2014), *44th Annual Survey Report for the 2012–13 Academic Year*, www.nassgap.org.

7. Education Commission of the States, *Preservation of Excellence in American Higher Education* (Denver, CO: Education Commission of the States, 1990).

8. Aims C. McGuinness, Jr., "The History and Evolution of Higher Education Systems in the United States," *Higher Education Systems 3.0: Harnessing Systemness, Delivering Performance*, SUNY Series, Critical Issues in Higher Education, ed. Jason E. Lane and D. Bruce Johnstone (Albany: State University of New York Press, 2013), 45–71.

9. Ibid., 50–51.

10. National Center for Education Statistics, "Table 301.2, Historical summary of faculty, enrollment, degrees, and finances in degree-granting postsecondary institutions: Selected years, 1869–70 through 2011–12," *Digest of Education Statistics: 2013*, http://nces.ed.gov/programs/digest/d13/tables/dt13_301.20.asp.

11. Martin Trow, *Problems in the Transition from Elite to Mass Higher Education* (Berkeley, CA: Carnegie Commission on Higher Education Berkeley, 1973).

12. National Center for Education Statistics, "Table 301.2."

13. Eugene C. Lee and Frank M. Bowen, *The Multicampus University* (New York: McGraw-Hill, 1971).

14. Lyman A. Glenny, *Autonomy of Public Colleges: The Challenges of Coordination* (New York: McGraw-Hill, 1959).

15. Robert O. Berdahl, *Statewide Coordination of Higher Education* (Washington, DC: American Council on Education, 1971).

16. Lyman A. Glenny, *State Budgeting for Higher Education* (Berkeley: Center for Research and Development in Higher Education, University of California, 1976).

17. Aims C. McGuinness, Jr., *Intergovernmental Relations in Postsecondary Education: The Case of the 1202 Commissions,* PhD diss., Maxwell Graduate School of Citizenship and Public Affairs, Syracuse University, 1979.

18. Peter T. Ewell and Dennis P. Jones, "Assessing and Reporting Student Progress: A Response to the "New Accountability,' " ED 337 112 (State Higher Education Executive Officers Association, 1991); Association of Governing Boards of Universities and Colleges, "Ten Public Policy Issues for Higher Education in 1994," *AGB Public Policy Series,* No. 94-1, January 1994, http://files.eric.ed.gov/fulltext/ED366236.pdf.

19. James Mingle and Rhonda E. Epper, "State Coordination and Planning in an Age of Entrepreneurship," in *Planning and Management for a Changing Environment,* ed. Marvin W. Peterson, David D. Dill, and Lisa A. Mets (San Francisco: Jossey-Bass, 1997), 45–65; Terrance MacTaggart, *Seeking Excellence through Independence* (San Francisco: Jossey-Bass, 1998).

20. James Mingle, ed. *Management Flexibility and State Regulation in Higher Education* (Atlanta, GA: Southern Regional Education Board, 1983).

21. Aims C. McGuinness, Jr., "Restructuring State Roles in Higher Education: A Case Study of the 1994 New Jersey Higher Education Restructuring Act," ED 394 457 (Denver: Education Commission of the States, 1995).

22. National Center for Public Policy and Higher Education, "State Capacity for Higher Education Policy Leadership," *National Crosstalk* supplement (San Jose, CA: National Center, July 2005); Gordon K. Davies, *Setting a Public Agenda for Higher Education in the States: Lessons Learned from the National Collaborative for Higher Education Policy* (San Jose, CA: National Center for Public Policy and Higher Education, Dec. 2006), http://www.highereducation.org/catreports/governance_state_policy_leadership.shtml.

23. National Center for Public Policy and Higher Education, "State Capacity for Higher Education Policy Leadership"; Davies, *Setting a Public Agenda for Higher Education in the States.*

24. Kentucky Council on Postsecondary Education, *Five Questions—One Mission: Better Lives for Kentucky's People: A Public Agenda for Postsecondary and Adult Education, 2005–2010* (Frankfort, KY: Kentucky Council on Postsecondary Education, 2005), http://cpe.ky.gov/planning/strategic/; Aims C. McGuinness, Jr., "Globally Competitive, Locally Engaged: The Case Study of Kentucky," *Higher Education Management and Policy* 20, no. 2 (2008): 74–89.

25. Texas Higher Education Coordinating Board, *Closing the Gaps: The Texas Higher Education Plan* (Austin: Texas Higher Education Coordinating Board, 1999).

26. Davies, *Setting a Public Agenda for Higher Education in the States.*

27. State Higher Education Executive Officers, *Accountability for Better Results: A National Imperative for Higher Education,* Report of the National Commission on Accountability in Higher Education (Boulder, CO: State Higher Education Executive Officers, 2005); National Conference of State Legislatures, *Transforming Higher Education: National Imperative—State Responsibility* (Denver, CO: National Conference of State Legislatures, 2006); National Governors Association, *A Compact for Postsecondary Education* (Washington, DC: National Governors Association, 2006).

28. Davies, *Setting a Public Agenda for Higher Education in the States.*

29. Joseph C. Burke and Henrik P. Minassians, "Performance Reporting: 'Real' Accountability or Accountability 'Lite,'" *Seventh Annual Survey*, ED 480 586 (Albany, NY: Nelson A. Rockefeller Institute of Government, 2003).

30. Ibid.

31. The White House, "Meeting the Nation's 2020 Goal: State Targets for Increasing the Number and Percentage of College Graduates with Degrees" (Washington, DC: The White House, 2011), https://www.whitehouse.gov/sites/default/files/completion_state_by _state.pdf.

32. Lumina Foundation, *Lumina's Strategic Direction: The Big Goal* (Indianapolis, IN: Lumina Foundation, 2012), http://www.luminafoundation.org/goal_2025/goal2.html.

33. National Center for Higher Education Management Systems (NCHEMS), *State Policies and Practices Consistent with the National Attainment Agenda* (Boulder, CO: Lumina Foundation, Sept. 2014), http://www.nchems.org/c2sp/.

34. See information on Complete College America, http://www.completecollege .org/.

35. Dennis P Jones, "The Unanswered Question: How Will We Pay for Aggressive Attainment Goals?" *Change Magazine* (July/Aug. 2014), 18.

36. Aims C. McGuinness, Jr. "System Regulation and Governance: Ireland and the International Context" (background paper prepared for 21st Century Universities: Performance and Sustainability symposium, Irish Universities Association, Dublin, Ireland, Sept. 29, 2014).

37. Daniel J. Elazar, *American Federalism: A View from the States* (New York: Thomas Y. Crowell, 1966).

38. For more detail on state structures, see National Center for Higher Education Management Systems (NCHEMS), *State Postsecondary Education Governance Database*, http://www.nchems.org/psgov/.

39. For more on multicampus systems see Jason E. Lane and D. Bruce Johnstone, eds., *Higher Education Systems 3.0: Harnessing Systemness Delivering Performance* (Albany: State University of New York Press, 2013); Eugene C. Lee and Frank M. Bowen, *The Multicampus University* (New York: McGraw-Hill, 1971); Aims C. McGuinness, Jr., "Perspectives on the Current Status and Emerging Policy Issues for Public Multi-Campus Higher Education Systems," AGB Occasional Paper No. 3 (Washington, DC: Association of Governing Boards of Universities and Colleges, 1991); Marian L. Gade, *Four Multicampus Systems: Some Policies and Practices that Work* (Washington, DC: Association of Governing Boards of Universities and Colleges, 1993); Gerald H. Gaither, ed., *The Multicampus System: Perspectives and Prospects* (Sterling, VA: Stylus, 1999); E. K. Fretwell, Jr., *More than Management: Guidelines for System Governing Boards and Their Chief Executives* (Washington, DC: Association of Governing Boards of Universities and Colleges, 2000).

40. Clark Kerr and Marian L. Gade, *The Guardians: Boards of Trustees of American Colleges and Universities: What They Do and How Well They Do It* (Washington, DC: Association of Governing Boards of Universities and Colleges, 1989).

41. More detail on state structures is available on the website of the National Center for Higher Education Management Systems (NCHEMS), http://www.nchems.org/psgov/.

42. Malcolm C. Moos and Francis E. Rourke, *The Campus and the State* (Baltimore: Johns Hopkins University Press, 1959); Lyman A. Glenny, *Autonomy of Public Colleges*

(New York: McGraw-Hill, 1959); Carnegie Commission on Higher Education, *The Capitol and the Campus: State Responsibility for Postsecondary Education* (New York: McGraw-Hill, 1971); Lyman A. Glenny, Robert O. Berdahl, Ernest G. Palola, and James G. Paltridge, *Coordinating Higher Education for the '70s* (Berkeley: University of California, Center for Research and Development in Higher Education, 1971); Education Commission of the States, *Challenge: Coordination and Governance in the 1980s* (Denver, CO: Education Commission of the States, 1980); John D. Millet, *Conflict in Higher Education: State Government versus Institutional Independence* (San Francisco: Jossey-Bass, 1982); Mingle and Epper, "State Coordination and Planning"; Richard C. Richardson, Jr., Kathy Reeves Bracco, Patrick M. Callan, and Joni E. Finney, *Designing State Higher Education Systems for a New Century* (Phoenix, AZ: Oryx Press, 1999); Paul E. Lingenfelter, "The 21st Century Challenge for State Planning and Policy for Higher Education, working paper (Boulder, CO: State Higher Education Executive Officers, 2007), http://archive.sheeo .org/About/paulpres/The%2021st%20Century%20Agenda%20for%20State%20 Planning%20and%20Policy.pdf; Aims C. McGuinness, Jr., "State Policy Leadership in the Public Interest: Is Anyone at Home?" in *Public Policy Challenges Facing Higher Education in the American West,* ed. Lester F. Goodchild, Richard W. Jonsen, Patty Limerick, and David A. Longanecker (New York: Palgrave Macmillan), 71.

43. See Michael McLendon, S. Deaton, and J. Hearn, "The Enactment of Reforms in State Governance of Higher Education: Testing the Political Instability Hypothesis," *The Journal of Higher Education,* 78, no. 6, Nov./Dec. 2007), 645–75.

44. National Center for Public Policy and Higher Education, "State Capacity for Higher Education Policy Leadership."

45. Ibid.

46. Lane and Johnstone, eds., *Higher Education Systems 3.0.*

47. State University of New York, *The Power of SUNY: Strategic Plan: 2010 and Beyond* (Albany: 2010), https://www.suny.edu/powerofsuny/.

48. University of Maine System, "Strategic Integration and Financial Sustainability," http://www.maine.edu/wp-content/uploads/2014/02/TAB-3.1-2014-Strategic-Outcomes.pdf.

49. National Association of State Budget Officers, *Budget Processes in the States* (Washington, DC: NASBO, 2008).

50. Andrew Carlson, *State Tuition, Fees, and Financial Aid Policies for Public Colleges and Universities* (Boulder, CO: SHEEO, 2013), http://www.sheeo.org/sites/default/files /publications/Tuition%20and%20Fees%20Policy%20Report%202013015.pdf.

51. For the latest information on state financing differences and trends, see State Higher Education Executive Officers [SHEEO] annual reports, *State Higher Education Finance,* http://www.sheeo.org/resources/publications/shef-%E2%80%94-state-higher -education-finance-fy13.

52. Dennis P. Jones, "Financing in Sync: Aligning Fiscal Policy with State Objectives," WICHE, *Financing in Sync,* 5–22. Patrick M. Callan and Joni E. Finney, eds., *Public Policy and Private Financing of Higher Education: Shaping Public Policy in the Future* (Phoenix, AZ: Oryx Press, 1997); NCPPHE, *The Challenge to States: Preserving College Access and Affordability in a Time of Change* (San Jose, CA: National Center for Public Policy and Higher Education, Mar. 2009), www.highereducation.org.

53. NASSGAP, *44th Annual Survey Report,* 3.

54. Katherine C. Lyle and Kathleen R. Sell, *The True Genius of America at Risk: Are We Losing Our Public Universities by De Facto Privatization?* Praeger Series on Higher Education (Westport, CT: American Council on Education, 2006).

55. AASCU Task Force on Making Public Higher Education a State Priority, *Creating a New Compact between States and Public Higher Education* (Washington, DC: American Association of State Colleges and Universities, 2013).

56. National Association of State Budget Officers (NASBO), *Improving Postsecondary Education through the Budget Process: Challenges & Opportunities: Challenges and Opportunities* (Washington, DC: NASBO, 2013).

57. Western Interstate Commission on Higher Education [WICHE], *Financing in Sync: Appropriations, Tuition, and Financial Aid* (Boulder, CO: WICHE, 2003), http://www.wiche.edu/info/publications/PoliciesInSync.pdf.

58. Dennis P. Jones, "Financing in Sync."

59. Joseph C. Burke and Henrik P. Minassians, "Performance Reporting: 'Real' Accountability or Accountability 'Lite.' "

60. Martha Snyder, *Driving Better Outcomes: Typology and Principles to Inform Outcomes-Based Funding Models* (Washington, DC: HCM Strategists, 2015).

61. Dennis P. Jones, "Performance Funding: From Idea to Action," paper prepared for Complete College America (Washington, DC: Complete College America, 2012), http://files.eric.ed.gov/fulltext/ED536832.pdf; Dennis P. Jones, "Outcome-Based Funding: Wave of Implementation," paper prepared for Complete College America (Washington, DC: Complete College America, 2013), http://completecollege.org/pdfs/Outcomes-Based-Funding-Report-Final.pdf.

62. Jones, "Outcome-Based Funding: Wave of Implementation."

63. Aims C. McGuinness, Jr., "A Conceptual and Analytic Framework for Review of National Regulatory Policies and Practices in Higher Education," prepared for the Organization for Economic Co-operation (OECD), Feb., 2006 (Paris: EDU/EC, 2006), 3.

64. Robert O. Berdahl, "Balancing Self-Interest and Accountability: St. Mary's College of Maryland," in *Seeking Excellence through Independence*, ed. Terrence J. MacTaggart (San Francisco: Jossey-Bass, 1998), 59–84.

65. Western Interstate Commission for Higher Education [WICHE], *An Evaluation of Colorado's College Opportunity Fund and Related Policies: A Report for the Colorado Department of Higher Education* (Boulder, CO: Western Interstate Commission for Higher Education, 2009).

66. Lyle and Sell, *True Genius of America*; Michael K. McLendon, "Setting the Governmental Agenda for State Decentralization of Higher Education," *Journal of Higher Education* 74, no. 5 (2003): 479–516.

67. Lara K. Couturier, *Checks and Balances at Work: The Restructuring of Virginia's Public Higher Education System* (San Jose, CA: National Center for Public Policy and Higher Education, 2006), www.highereducation.org/reports/checks_balances/.

68. WICHE, *Evaluation of Colorado's College Opportunity Fund.*

69. Michael K. McLendon, Donald E. Heller, and Steven P. Young, "State Postsecondary Education Policy Innovation: Politics, Competition, and the Interstate Migration of Policy Ideas," *Journal of Higher Education* 76, no. 4 (July/Aug. 2005): 343–400.

70. Couturier, *Checks and Balances at Work.*

71. McGuinness, "System Regulation and Governance."

72. Aims C. McGuinness, Jr., "Serving Public Purposes: Challenges for Systems in Changing State Context," in *Higher Education Systems 3.0: Harnessing Systemness, Delivering Performance*, SUNY Series, Critical Issues in Higher Education, ed. Jason E. Lane and D. Bruce Johnstone (Albany: State University of New York Press, 2013), 193–212.

73. Aims C. McGuinness, Jr., "A Conceptual and Analytic Framework for Review of National Regulatory Policies and Practices in Higher Education."

74. University of Oregon, *Preserving Our Public Mission through a New Partnership with the State* (Eugene, Oregon, 2010), http://newpartnership.uoregon.edu/blog/2010/05 /12/the-white-paper-introduction-and-oregons-public-responsibility-regarding-higher -education/index.html.

75. Oregon Rev. Statutes Ann. § 351.009 (2011).

76. C. A. Martin, "New Badger Partnership" (PowerPoint presentation, University of Wisconsin-Madison, Dec. 2010), http://www.uwsa.edu/news/2010/12-2010/New-Badger -Partnership.pdf.

77. Wisconsin Legislative Fiscal Bureau, *Create UW-Madison Authority* (Paper No. 690) (Madison, WI, 2010), http://www.mbo.wisc.edu/biennial/bienn1113/LFB690-Create%20UW -Madison%20Authority.pdf.

78. Wisconsin Legislative Fiscal Bureau, "2015–17 Summary of Governor's Budget Recommendations" (Madison, WI, Feb. 2015), http://legis.wisconsin.gov/lfb/publications /budget/2015-17%20Budget/Pages/Governor.aspx.

79. Robert Birgeneau, George Breslauer, Judson King, John Wilton, and Frank Yeary, *Modernizing Governance at the University of California: A Proposal that the Regents Create and Delegate Some Responsibilities to Campus Boards*, Research and Occasional Papers Series (Berkeley: Center for Studies in Higher Education, University of California, Apr. 2012), http://cshe.berkeley.edu/publications/docs/ROPS.Birgeneau%20et%20al .UC%20Gov.4.23.2012.pdf.

80. Katharine C. Lyall, "Reorganizing Higher Education Systems: By Drift or Design?" in *Higher Education Systems 3.0: Harnessing Systemness, Delivering Performance*, SUNY Series, Critical Issues in Higher Education, ed. Jason Lane and D. Bruce Johnstone (Albany: State University of New York Press, 2013), 127–47.

81. Matthew T. Lambert, *Privatization and the Public Good: Public Universities in the Balance* (Cambridge: Harvard University Press, 2014).

82. Laura W. Perna and Joni E. Finney, *The Attainment Agenda: State Policy Leadership in Higher Education* (Baltimore: Johns Hopkins University Press, 2014).

83. Ibid., 38.

84. Ibid., 200–39.

# Chapter Ten

# The Legal Environment

*The Implementation of Legal Change on Campus*

Joy Blanchard and Benjamin Baez

If Clark Kerr was correct that the idea of the university as a single community has given way to a conglomerate-like organization with many, often conflicting, communities—a multiversity[1]—then the law will have even more force in shaping its future. This does not mean, of course, that the law will support good practice, as Michael Olivas has pointed out,[2] but it will play a role in adjudicating conflicting claims between institutions of higher education and their increasingly varied constituents, internal and external. There can be no doubt that the rapid growth in the number and size of institutions, the increasing necessity of collegiate credentials for distinguishing job applicants, the mission creep characterizing public higher education (especially), the movement from elite to mass higher education since World War II, the increasing enrollment of nontraditional students, the pressure for various modes of delivering instruction, the commercialization of research and other forms of academic capitalism,[3] and the relentless demands of performance metrics in the funding of public institutions all bring with them the intrusion by courts into collegiate life. The idea of the "ivory tower," if it gave coherence to higher education in the past, certainly now seems rather more nostalgic than real.

Yet, from assigning grades to deciding tenure, courts historically have shown wide deference to the judgment of those associated with institutions of higher education. Courts recognize not only the unique place that colleges and universities occupy in American society but also the specialized expertise held by those who work within the industry. At the same time, however, American higher education is facing a continual climb in the amount of litigation, regulations, and oversight from governing bodies. This chapter will cover some, but certainly not all, of the ways in which courts are brought in to settle disputes involving students, faculty, and governing agencies.

### Legal Governance

Whether an institution is classified as private or public has significant governance implications as well as legal ones; of key distinction is the application of constitutional rights and contractual claims. Constituents at private colleges and universities are typically governed by the contracts they enter into with the institution. Those affiliated with public institutions, however, enjoy rights not only established via contract (e.g., in faculty handbooks, student codes of conduct, and housing manuals) but also rights guaranteed to all citizens dealing with an arm of the state.

The landmark civil rights-era case of *Dixon v. Alabama State Board of Education*[4] recognized college students as adults, no longer under the purview of *in loco parentis*,[5] and established their "property rights" in higher education (thus requiring due process before such rights are taken away). Courts today have expanded the application of such constitutional rights to numerous contexts. At public institutions, the Fourth Amendment of the Constitution protects students from unlawful searches. In *Piazzola v. Watkins*, the Fifth Circuit Court of Appeals confirmed that the dean of students could not aid campus police in searching a residence hall room for marijuana without consent or just cause.[6] Searches done for the health or safety concerns of the campus community, or those stipulated in the housing contract (e.g., plain-view searches for contraband), however, are permissible.

Another constitutional right afforded to students, faculty, staff, and even visitors to public campuses is that of the First Amendment. Whether it is related to speech, publications, or recognition of student organizations, courts have clearly set forth that any regulations must be content neutral and not done out of fear of potential disruption. In the case of *Bazaar v. Fortune*, the University of Mississippi attempted to stop the publication of a campus literary magazine because one story referenced interracial marriage and utilized what were referenced as four-letter obscenities. Members of the university review committee found some of the language objectionable, in poor taste, and that it could potentially cause public reaction. The university contended that because the literary magazine was advised by a member of the English department that its content would reflect poorly upon the institution. The appellate court held against the university and noted that the language contained in the objectionable story was not unlike what was heard on campus, printed in contemporary literature, or featured in film and other media.[7]

As with publications, fear of potential disruption does not constitutionally justify denying official recognition to student organizations. In the case of *Healy v. James,* administrators at Central Connecticut State College denied recognition to the local chapter of the Students for a Democratic Society based on the ostensibly disruptive reputation the national organization had garnered in protesting the Vietnam War on campuses across the country, even though the students of the local chapter testified to campus officials that they would not affiliate with the national organization. Though Justice Lewis Powell, writing for the majority of the court, did stipulate that institutions may regulate and punish organizations that violate campus rules and interfere with regular school functions, the burden was on the institution to articulate why it would not recognize the institution—and fear of disruption or disagreement with its ideals were not constitutionally justifiable.[8]

Officially recognizing student organizations often means that they gain access to campus facilities and campus student fees. Any decisions regarding such recognition must be done in a content-neutral manner. In *Rosenberger v. Rector and Visitors of the University of Virginia,* a campus Christian organization was denied funding for its publication because campus regulations prohibited the use of student funds for groups that were political or religious in nature. In a narrow five-to-four vote, the US Supreme Court found that such restrictions did not violate the establishment clause of the First Amendment but did, indeed, violate the free speech rights of the student organization:

> The University does not exclude religion as a subject matter but selects for disfavored treatment those student journalistic efforts with religious editorial viewpoints. Religion may be a vast area of inquiry, but it also provides, as it did here, a specific premise, a perspective, a standpoint from which a variety of subjects may be discussed and considered.[9]

Due process is another constitutional right afforded to those at public institutions. As first established in *Dixon* and later affirmed in *Goss v. Lopez* (a K–12 case related to long-term suspension), students have a legal interest in continuing their education and must be afforded appropriate procedural and substantive due process.[10] The students in *Dixon* faced expulsion, which would lead to a greater potential punishment and loss; therefore, the court ruled, the institution in such a case must provide more due process rights, such as allowing students to bring attorneys to judicial proceedings. Most jurisdictions, however, do not compel universities to allow legal counsel to partake in campus disciplinary proceedings (namely because such processes are viewed as educational, not punitive) but the proceedings must be patently fair. Students must still be allowed to present evidence in defense of the charges and must have the right to appeal any sanctions.

This discussion about due process applies only to public institutions, as private institutions are not subject to such requirements. The inception of this private-public dichotomy began not long after the establishment of the colonial colleges. Dartmouth College of New Hampshire was created in 1769 via a charter granted by King George III of England. By the early 1800s, the college's president had been removed by its trustees and, in an effort to regain order, the legislative body of the state of New Hampshire attempted to alter the original charter so that power to appoint trustees would be vested with the governor. (Unfortunately, political interference is common even today, as seen in the much publicized removal of University of Virginia president Teresa Sullivan by the university's board of visitors). The deposed trustees filed suit and the US Supreme Court upheld the contractual nature of the establishment of Dartmouth College— thus preserving its status as a private entity and rejecting the state's attempt to wrestle control.[11]

While private institutions enjoy the power of governance absent substantial governmental interference (subject mostly to the contractual rights they themselves grant), public institutions enjoy a different sort of legal protection: sovereign immunity. The Eleventh Amendment protects a state as defendant in federal court, unless it consents to jurisdiction.[12] State constitutions regulate the doctrine of immunity for state claims; the extent to which and for what the government may be sued varies among the fifty states. Individuals acting within the purview of their official governmental duties typically enjoy immunity, but Section 1983 of the Civil Rights Act states that any state actor who deprives an individual of constitutionally protected rights shall be held liable. The US Supreme Court established in *Harlow v. Fitzgerald* that a state official cannot assert immunity for actions for which the law had been clearly established and the defendant knew or should have known that those actions abridged a person or persons' rights.[13]

This discussion of sovereign immunity underscores an important point: While public institutions are subject to a greater array of laws than private institutions, they too are also shielded from many of these laws. Indeed, institutions of higher education are in a practical sense immune from lawsuits, since legal claims against them rarely proceed to trial, and when they do, the institutions usually win. In terms of legal outcomes, the private/public distinction has little practical meaning. Institutions of higher education can generally govern themselves without significant constraint related to litigation (though the mere threat of litigation can be a powerful factor in the ways they govern themselves).

## Faculty

The legal issues associated with faculty probably should not be completely set apart from those relating to employees generally. While there are key differences, current economic and political conditions require that one see those differences as not altogether meaningful. The economic conditions leading to an increase in part-time labor, as well as the political assault on unions, public employees, and on civil rights, affect the field of employment writ large. Academic freedom and the tenure that protects it do distinguish the academic from other employment settings, but economic, legal, and political forces are undermining tenure in more or less intentional ways, and if these trends continue, academic freedom and tenure will no longer be the distinguishing characteristics between academic and other kinds of employees. The issues associated with faculty are myriad, so here we limit our discussion to academic freedom, tenure, collective bargaining, intellectual property, and employment discrimination.

### Academic Freedom

While tenure is seen by the academic profession as necessary for the protection of academic freedom, the cases giving legal definitions to academic freedom and tenure are not often framed as if the loss of one leads to the loss of the other. Thus, in keeping with this questionable legal framework, we separate the discussions of academic freedom and tenure without intending to argue that tenure is unrelated to academic freedom.

The American version of academic freedom was first explicitly given expression in the American Association of University Professors' (AAUP) *1915 Declaration of Principles of Academic Freedom and Tenure*, in which academic freedom was deemed necessary for inquiry, teaching, and extramural activities.[14] But it is the *1940 Statement of Principles on Academic Freedom and Tenure* that has become the definitive understanding of the AAUP's stance on academic freedom. The *1940 Statement* is commonly mentioned in institutional policies, and courts often look to these policies in resolving conflicts over academic freedom, at least as evidence of academic custom.[15] The 1940 Statement reinforces the 1915 Principles' notion of academic freedom but also adopts certain responsibilities for the faculty member.[16] Thus, while professors should indeed enjoy the freedom of inquiry, they also should be honest in conducting research; while professors should have the freedom to teach their courses, they should stick to matters within their expertise; and while professors, as citizens of the larger public, should be able to talk about political issues important to them, they should be careful to dissociate themselves from their institutions when doing so.

This statement, of course, makes the resolution of conflicts sound simple, but reality is never as neat. The AAUP's distinction presupposes a tension between a professor engaging in controversial activities for the public's interest and an administration that would rather not deal with controversial matters at all. But conflicts arise not just between the faculty member and the administration; they also occur between the faculty member and students (the politics around the Academic Bill of Rights is illustrative of this),[17] and between a faculty member and the public at large (the examples of Ward Churchill at the University of Colorado and Sami Al-Arian at the University of South Florida come to mind).

The legal bases for academic freedom are constitutional law at public institutions, contract law at all institutions, and perhaps state law. The two key cases indicating, but not officially establishing, academic freedom as a constitutional right really do need to be read within the particular historical period of the Cold War: *Sweezy v. New Hampshire*,[18] involving a professor held in contempt for refusing to answer state officials' questions regarding a lecture he delivered at his university, and *Keyishian v. Board of Regents*,[19] involving professors who refused to sign what were in effect loyalty oaths. In *Keyishian*, the US Supreme Court indicated that academic freedom was a "special concern of the First Amendment."[20] Courts, however, are more likely to resort to such constitutional language when state officials seek to control the freedom of academics or their institutions. When the issues relate to disputes between academics and their institutions, the courts tend to balance the rights of public employees to exercise their freedom of speech with those of administrators to ensure the smooth operation of institutions.[21] Courts focus mostly on free-speech rights, and academic freedom becomes a kind of professional custom, offering faculty only a minor basis for claiming rights against their institutions.

As a general legal rule, the institution has extensive authority over what happens in the classroom, including course content, the relevancy of learning activities,[22] and whether faculty can express their political or religious views in the classroom.[23] Faculty have more say in terms of teaching strategies, but even here, if a professor is notified that a particular strategy is unacceptable, it can be restricted. Institutions also have leeway in dictating personal appearances and certain lifestyle decisions. Nevertheless, faculty at public institutions do have constitutional rights. The legal standard for determining the free-speech rights of faculty members at public institutions is whether their speech or activities (e.g., associations, political activities, etc.) relate to matters of "public concern." We must stress that this standard holds for all public employees.

The key US Supreme Court case here is *Pickering v. Board of Education*,[24] which supports the free-speech rights of faculty when they relate to matters of public concern. But these rights are counterbalanced by institutional rights to ensure employee harmony, effective classroom performance, or smooth institutional operations. In *Givhan v. Western Line Consolidated School District*, the court held that where the speech took place (on- or off-campus) is irrelevant in determining whether it relates to a matter of public concern.[25]

In *Mt. Healthy City School District v. Doyle*, the court held that employees can be disciplined, even for protected speech, if there are other justifiable reasons for the discipline.[26] In *Connick v. Myers*, the court held that matters related to personnel concerns are not protected speech, and that it is not only the content of the speech that must be considered when deciding whether or not to punish a public employee for speaking on a matter (public concern or personnel issue), but also the context (the facts surrounding the speech) and form (the manner in which it is spoken).[27] In *Waters v. Churchill*, a nurse at a public hospital was dismissed by her employer for making negative comments about her supervisors and department (she claimed she talked only about the hospital's cover-up of serious understaffing, talk which she contended was a matter of public concern and therefore protected by the First Amendment; her version was corroborated by other employees).[28] The court indicated that when there is disagreement over what was said, deference should be given to what the employer reasonably believed was said, and not necessarily to what was actually said. Here the court appears to have shifted the burden of proving illegal institutional motives to the employee, granting extensive deference to institutions. Finally, in *Garcetti v. Ceballos*, the court determined that employees speaking in their official versus private role may lose their right to free speech.[29] What faculty and other public employees have now, then, is a more theoretical than concrete right to speak on matters of public concern.

The cases just discussed apply to public institutions only, and only when free-speech rights are asserted. At private institutions, and for arguments about academic freedom as a professional imperative, legal rights must be located in contract law. And in this regard, an explicit incorporation of AAUP principles into institutional policies goes a long way toward establishing legal rights for faculty. These principles may provide evidence of academic custom and practice when contractual language is in dispute.

## TENURE

The primary legal basis for employee rights generally is contract law, although at public institutions employees may claim constitutional rights, as we indicated with regard to academic freedom as commonly understood. With regard to tenure, the constitutional rights generally relate to discrimination and due process (we will discuss discrimination later in this chapter). Tenured faculty are assumed to have due process rights when institutions seek to terminate their positions, but there is some dispute over what these rights actually entail. Do tenured faculty have the right to lose their jobs only for cause ("substantive" rights)? Or, do tenured faculty have only the right to the procedural processes indicated in their employment contracts ("procedural" rights)?

A court's decision in *Branham v. Thomas M. Cooley Law School* established a problematic precedent with regard to this question of whether tenure gives individuals substantive versus procedural rights. In this case, a law professor hired to teach criminal law with "the rank and title of professor of law" was assigned courses other than criminal law. In her second term, she refused to teach an assigned course and insisted on teaching a criminal law class; she was summarily dismissed by her dean with no hearing. A trial court ordered the law school to follow its procedures in having a hearing, and this process confirmed the dean's decision. The Sixth Circuit Court of Appeals determined that the faculty member had no other rights than those enumerated in the contract.[30] In other words, all tenure affords is the right to have the institution follow its own procedures in dismissing a faculty member.

The issue of tenure and the rights associated with it often raise the most concern when the institution wants to dismiss tenured faculty during times of retrenchment. Most institutions have adopted AAUP policies and procedures for dismissing faculty during times of "financial exigency" and "program elimination," which may or may not involve financial difficulties,[31] and courts have looked to these policies when faculty are dismissed for such reasons. In *AAUP v.*

*Bloomfield College*, a court required that the financial exigency be "bona fide" in reinstating fourteen dismissed faculty, and the contracts of the others altered, ostensibly for financial exigency.[32] This case notwithstanding, the courts generally defer to institutions, even if they do not declare financial exigency as required by AAUP policies (see *Krotkoff v. Goucher College*[33]), or the financial problem is only in one program (see *Scheuer v. Creighton University*[34]).

With regard to denials of tenure for nonfinancial or nonprogrammatic reasons, the courts are consistent in deferring to the institutions unless they do not follow their own procedures. When institutions do not follow their own procedures, faculty might in limited cases claim a violation of the due process clause of the Fourteenth Amendment for a denial of tenure at public institutions, but only if they can show either a property or a liberty interest. The property interest is created by state law or contracts with a public institution. Tenured faculty are in these cases deemed to have property interests, but are untenured faculty at public institutions entitled to due process? The US Supreme Court has indicated otherwise. In *Board of Regents v. Roth*, a faculty member who was not renewed was deemed to have no rights to due process.[35] But on the same day, in *Perry v. Sindermann*, the court ruled that tenure may be inferred when university policies and practices indicate an untenured faculty member has an expectation of continued employment.[36] We refer to *Perry* as giving a claim to *de facto* tenure. A liberty interest applies when a state action creates stigma or damage to one's reputation, thus preventing future employment. But the US Supreme Court has limited the situations for which one may claim such an interest: The action must lead to reputational damage; it must foreclose other employment; it relates to loss of job, not promotions; and the action must be publicly disclosed to a noninterested party.[37] The US Constitution thus appears to give few rights to faculty members denied tenure or renewal of their untenured contracts, so any rights relating to these issues must come from the employment contract and institutional policies incorporated or implied in that contract.

## COLLECTIVE BARGAINING

Conservative political forces undermining employee rights in general, whether in the form of attacks on civil liberties or on collective bargaining, have, paradoxically, made unionization the most important avenue for protecting faculty rights, at least at public institutions and perhaps at small private colleges. It appears that just over 350,000 faculty are part of collective bargaining agreements.[38] A key trend in the 1990s and early 2000s was the unionization of graduate students. Collective bargaining also may be the key to significant rights for adjuncts, who are making up an increasing number of the teaching staff in higher education, but who are poorly paid and have few of the rights full-time faculty take for granted (e.g., an office). Adjuncts can legitimately be called the "indentured servants of academia."[39]

Legal rights associated with collective bargaining require that we distinguish faculty at public institutions from those at private ones. The former are governed by state laws, but the latter are governed by the federal National Labor Relations Act of 1935. In all sectors, but mostly in the public one, attacks on collective bargaining have taken various forms, such as prohibiting payroll deductions for union dues by employers, requiring recertification of any union that falls below 50 percent membership, or passing right-to-work legislation. Right-to-work legislation in many states, especially those in the South, and more recent ones in the Midwest, will make it more difficult for faculty at public institutions to form unions. Such legislation usually prohibits what is commonly understood as a "union shops," or the requirements that all employees represented by the union join the union or pay dues.

Until 1980, in the private sector, and in private institutions, faculty were treated by labor relations boards like other employees, that is, with rights to collective bargaining. In 1980, the US Supreme Court handed down its infamous decision in *NLRB v. Yeshiva University*, holding that faculty at institutions like Yeshiva, or "mature universities," were "managerial" and thus expected to be aligned with the administration.[40] The court treated what before had been understood as the professional custom of shared governance as actually the work of the administration. What this now means is that private research universities are not required to recognize, and the National Relations Labor Board cannot authorize, a faculty union at such universities, but this decision has implications for institutions in which faculty had extensive rights to shared governance. This case, of course, must be understood in the context of concerted attempts to eliminate employee rights, and since this decision, the US Supreme Court has expanded employer rights by extending the definition of "employer" in order to undermine seriously the collective bargaining of professional employees.[41] As faculty become increasingly managed by the corporatization of the university, the political assaults on public and private collective bargaining become less irrelevant to faculty.

## INTELLECTUAL PROPERTY

The US Constitution grants Congress the power "to promote the Progress of Science and useful Arts, by securing for limited Times to Authors and Inventors the exclusive Right to their respective Writings and Discoveries."[42] Two such types of intellectual property rights apply to faculty work: copyright and patents. The former historically has not been a lucrative enterprise such that institutions generally have let academics assert claims to those work products with little resistance. The latter has greatly influenced academe within the past few decades, prompting the idea of "academic capitalism" denoting the market-driven activities in which institutions seek to generate alternate revenue streams from the creations produced by their academic employees.

With regard to copyrightable works, an interesting judicial carve-out has been made to recognize the unique and salubrious role research in American universities has in society at large. Though the "work for hire" doctrine[43] grants an employer ownership of works created by employees, courts recognize the public good created by the free dissemination of knowledge generated via university research. In *Williams v. Weisser*, a faculty member won his challenge against a company that sought to sell his lecture notes. In fact, UCLA, Williams' home institution, had a policy at the time that granted ownership of class and lecture notes to faculty; the court in this instance ruled that it could find little reason as to why an institution would want to do so otherwise.[44] Other cases in dicta (i.e., editorializing by judges) have agreed that faculty were entitled to a *de facto* "teacher exception" to the work for hire doctrine.[45]

Being that the teacher exception, like academic freedom, is more like court deference to institutional prerogatives, should it be legally tested, the landmark case of *Community for Creative Non-Violence v. Reid* would be most instructive.[46] In deciding whether a sculptor commissioned by an organization was the owner of a particular work, the US Supreme Court set forth a thirteen-prong test for determining whether or not someone is acting as an independent contractor or employee—which would control whether the work for hire doctrine would apply.

The first factor, and the most relevant to our discussion, pertains to the employers' right to control "the manner and means by which the product is accomplished."[47] According to the AAUP, "in the case of traditional academic works . . . the faculty member rather than the institution determines the subject matter, the intellectual approach and direction, and the conclusions. This is the very essence of academic freedom."[48] Additionally, faculty exert considerable freedom when deciding at what times and from where to write, in addition to deciding on what to write.[49] (However, the quality controls utilized in tenure decisions could be construed as supervision vis à vis an employer-employee relationship.) Some institutions have grappled with whether or not faculty should be given ownership to the online courses they create (notably at much cost to the institution). To head off litigation, many have begun to address the issue in faculty handbooks, and it generally appears that it should be a mandatorily negotiable item for institutions with a faculty union.[50]

When it comes to patents, institutions doggedly assert claims or, at the very least, profit sharing for marketable inventions produced by faculty and university researchers, especially since the passage of the Bayh-Dole Act of 1980 allowing institutions to claim ownership to inventions stemming from work funded by federal grants. Though there has been some litigation in the matter (typically involving professors' attempts to circumvent surreptitiously their institutions in order to gain more profit), what is most troubling in this matter is the effect the increasing reliance on patents for creating "soft money" has had on faculty work. Particularly in the sciences, the notion of academic freedom and freedom of inquiry as it was originally intended has been eroded as faculty employability and tenure rely on procuring grants to support faculty work as well as supplement institutional coffers. Knowledge for knowledge's sake has given way to pandering research agendas deemed most en vogue by those agencies with available funding.

## DISCRIMINATION

Litigation over racial, ethnic, and gender discrimination in employment constitutes a significant body of law, and as with such claims in general, faculty suing their institutions over illegal discrimination do not fare well in court. The most important laws regarding discrimination in employment are the Equal Protection Clause of the Fourteenth Amendment (for faculty at public institutions), Title VII of the Civil Rights Act of 1964, Title IX of the Educational Amendments of 1972, and the Equal Pay Act of 1963. We can dispense pretty quickly with the law associated with equal-protection claims in higher education. When alleging discrimination under the Fourteenth Amendment's Equal Protection Clause, the employee must prove intentional discrimination. In theory, courts should look to history and context, the sequence of events, the extent to which there was differential treatment, as well as overall patterns of employment practices. But for all practical purposes, the only cases won under the Fourteenth Amendment are obvious discrimination cases[51] and those challenging affirmative action, where race or gender is an obvious criterion for selection.

Title VII is the most important antidiscrimination law. This law prevents discrimination in employment on the basis of race, color, religion, gender, or national origin. These classifications, however, can be justified if they amount to a "bona fide occupational qualification." So, for example, religious affiliation is a legal criterion for employment in a religiously affiliated school, although it is unlikely that any religious discrimination is permissible in a public institution. There are two types of claims that can be brought under Title VII: (1) *disparate treatment* (i.e., when an employee claims he or she was treated less favorably than others); and (2) *disparate impact* (i.e., when apparently neutral practices have a discriminatory impact on certain groups of people).

In *McDonnell Douglas Corp. v. Green*, the court established a three-step process for proving disparate treatment discrimination under Title VII, and this case is important because it stands for the idea that intentional discrimination can be inferred if one does not have direct evidence of it.[52] First, the faculty member must establish a prima facie case inferring discrimination by, among other things, showing that she was qualified for, say, a promotion but was denied; second, the institution then offers a legitimate reason for the denying, say, the promotion (e.g., the faculty member did not have enough publications); and third, the faculty member must prove not only that the proffered reason was false, but that it was a pretext for discrimination. By adding this last step, the US Supreme Court ensured that only the most obvious types of discrimination can be proven. Most faculty members fail this last step.

For disparate impact, the plaintiff must show that neutral policies had a negative impact on certain groups of people. The important case here is *Griggs v. Duke Power Co.*, which invalidated the company's use of diploma and intelligence tests for jobs because it had a discriminatory impact on African Americans.[53] This type of claim under Title VII follows a three-step process similar to that of disparate treatment claims, except that inference of discrimination is usually done by offering statistical evidence of the disparate impact of institutional practices. And, as with disparate impact, the third step in proving illegal discrimination is the proof of pretext for discrimination, and thus most plaintiffs, faculty and otherwise, fail this last step.[54]

As an example of the kind of legal contortions necessary to justify what is essentially antagonism toward civil rights, one can offer the Supreme Court's decision in *Ricci v. DeStefano*, which seriously puts into question the disparate impact theory in discrimination law.[55] In *Ricci*, the city of New Haven eliminated the results of a promotion exam for firefighters because it had a disparate impact on racial minorities, but white plaintiffs who passed the exam and were not promoted sued under Title VII. The court decided that such a decision constituted a racially discriminatory action against those bringing the case. Thus, it appears that, as with affirmative action cases generally, a college or university's attempt to eliminate discrimination may itself constitute discrimination against white (or male) faculty.

In short, the legal context related to faculty is one in which the rights exist in theory but not in practice. Yes, faculty members have free-speech rights, but institutions have the upper hand in determining what those rights might be. Faculty members can still count on tenure, but apparently this means only that institutions must follow their own procedures before dismissing tenured faculty. Faculty members at public institutions and perhaps a few private ones may form a union, but that soon may be a thing a thing of the past if conservatives have their way. Faculty members have the right not to be discriminated against, but the legal barriers to such a claim means they are barely able to prove it.

## Students

As we indicated with regard to faculty, institutions of higher education also enjoy deference in courts when sued by students. But students might be more successful in court than faculty. For one, the nature of the institution-student relationship is not entirely governed by contract, although student handbooks and codes of conduct are often framed in contract language. While college students do not have a right to a collegiate education in the same way that children have the right to a public education, once they are admitted to an institution of higher education, courts do require some kind of due process at public institutions (or fundamental fairness at private ones) before they can suspend or punish students. As with faculty, the issues involving students are myriad, so here we limit ourselves to some of the key contemporary legal disputes associated with students: free speech, sexual harassment, tort liability (especially over campus safety), affirmative action, and collegiate athletics.

### Free Speech

Special interest groups, or what legal scholar Michael Olivas calls "purposive organizations," have begun to exert considerable leverage on courts' agendas.[56] Among the most active in recent years have been the Center for Law & Religious Freedom, along with the Alliance Defense Fund, in representing the Christian Legal Society (CLS) in several cases against infiltration by non-Christian and nonheterosexual students. In *Christian Legal Society v. Walker*, the Seventh Circuit Court of Appeals ruled in favor of CLS, finding that the dean of the law school at Southern Illinois had not established a compelling interest to quash the organization's constitutional right to expressive association when he declined to recognize the chapter as an official student organization after it refused to admit a gay member.[57] A similar case at Hastings Law School at the University of California-Berkeley, however, made its way to the highest court, and in a five-to-four split, the US Supreme Court found the law school's "'accept all comer's policy' to be a constitutionally valid, viewpoint-neutral policy aimed at diversifying and enriching the educational environment."[58]

Viewpoint neutrality, as previously mentioned, is an important principle pertaining not just to the recognition of student organizations but also in relation to such things as inviting speakers to campus and creating "free speech zones." Overall, the latter has effectually been ruled impermissible, and the Foundation for Individual Rights in Education (FIRE) has taken the lead in challenging these policies. In one such case, a federal court prohibited Texas Tech University from enforcing regulations that restricted free speech to a small gazebo on campus and required students to get approval to speak outside of that designated area.[59] Any restrictions to open forums must comport with a strict "time, place, manner" test, in which only speech-related activity that substantially interferes with instruction and normal functions of the university may be suppressed or regulated.

### Sexual Harassment and Assault

Though prior restraint (i.e., restrictions of speech before it happens) on speech often runs afoul of free-speech protections, institutions must balance the rights to free speech with the right to learn and work in an environment free of harassment. Title IX requires that campuses prohibit sexually hostile environments, including those allowing harassing speech. In 2012 Yale University entered into an agreement with the US Department of Education's Office of Civil Rights (OCR) after an investigation found that the university failed to respond adequately to a sexually hostile environment present on its campus, most notably after a highly publicized incident in which members of a Greek-letter fraternity chanted sexually explicit phrases outside of the campus women's center.[60]

Enforcement of Title IX is a priority now of the federal government and the US Department of Education, and with tightened and broader sweeping legislation enacted and more on the horizon, it promises to continue to be a high-level policy prerogative. The Obama Administration has furthered this initiative by commissioning reports with recommendations for practice (e.g., "Not Alone") and establishing social norming projects such as "It's On Us." As of August 2014, the OCR was investigating seventy-six institutions for failing to properly report and curb sexual assault and sexual harassment on their campuses.[61] That number is exponentially higher than in years prior, and the number of complaints being reported to the OCR has more than doubled in the past two years.[62]

Though the OCR has issued several "Dear Colleague" letters related to Title IX compliance, confusion still exists as to how to properly implement campus policies and conduct investigations. The OCR issued recommendations in 2013 after it conducted an in-depth investigation into thirty-three complaints it received within three years against the University of Montana and its procedures for handling sexual misconduct investigations. The OCR found that personnel handling the adjudication process had not been properly trained and that the process in place failed to protect complainants from retaliation. The investigation also discovered "inconsistent and inadequate" definitions of sexual harassment in the university's policies and that the appeals process disfavored victims' rights.[63]

Following the investigation, the OCR issued what has been coined the "Montana Blueprint": a model for other institutions to follow. It required the university to designate an "equity consultant" to revise and to disseminate effectively to the university community its policies on sexual misconduct and on reporting incidents, to provide Title IX training to all faculty and staff, to develop a better system to track all reports of sexual harassment and sexual assault, to create a "resource guide" for students, and to conduct annual focus groups and surveys to gauge the campus climate and students' familiarity with the reporting process.

In addition to enforcement, legislation aimed at mitigating the problem of campus sexual violence—or at least holding institutions accountable for curbing this problem—has recently been enacted. Regulations under the Violence Against Women Reauthorization Act of 2013 construe sexual misconduct to cover not just sexual assault but also dating violence, domestic violence, and stalking. This law requires institutions to provide annual security reports as well as information regarding prevention and awareness programs to incoming students and new employees. It also requires ongoing prevention and awareness campaigns for students and employees. Moreover, the White House has issued recommendations suggesting that the definition of "consent" be modified to recognize that "past consent does not imply future consent" and "consent can be withdrawn at any time."[64] In October 2014, California passed a law that requires institutions to utilize an "affirmative consent" standard when adjudicating sexual assault cases.[65]

While institutions can face regulatory penalties for failing to curb sexual violence on campus, there also have been stiff civil penalties. In 2014, the University of Connecticut announced a $1.3 million settlement with five women who brought forth claims that the institution failed to investigate adequately their reports of sexual assault.[66] In 2007, the University of Colorado settled with two female students over a similar suit: one received $2.5 million and the other $350,000.[67] In 1998 Kathy Redmond reached a $50,000 settlement with the University of Nebraska after she filed suit claiming that the institution was deliberately indifferent to her report of rape by a university football player.[68]

Perhaps the most costly and arguably most disturbing sexual assault case involving a university did not involve students but, instead, children who were abused repeatedly over many years by retired Penn State assistant football coach Jerry Sandusky. While Sandusky was convicted criminally on nearly fifty counts, Penn State settled with twenty-six victims for almost $60 million. Important to note about the settlement is that it ended any further claims against the institution or its employees. This is not to say that personal liability in similar cases is not on the horizon.

In 2006, in *Williams v. Board of Regents of the University System of Georgia*, the Eleventh Circuit ruled that a legal claim of liability for the sexual assault of students could be established (though the case was later settled out of court).[69] Williams, a female student at the university, had engaged in consensual sex in a residence hall with a student athlete but was later raped by two other student athletes who had been hiding in a closet. The court found enough evidence that would give rise to a finding of "deliberate indifference," a necessary element for a Title IX claim, particularly because the university waited a year before convening a judicial proceeding and because officials recruited one of the student athletes despite knowing of his past record of sexual assault.

## Tort Liability

The governmental regulations and legal cases associated with sexual assault should make it clear that risk management has become important to institutions for such misconduct and for other potential negligence-related charges—most notably those around campus safety. In April 2007 the Virginia Tech campus experienced the most deadly shooting in American history when a graduate student shot and killed thirty-two faculty and students while wounding another seventeen before killing himself. Seung-Hui Cho had been ordered by Virginia courts to receive mental health counseling, and, though some at the university were concerned about his mental health, confusion over FERPA prevented adequate information sharing.[70]

Following the Virginia Tech tragedy a presidential commission recommended several policy changes: reform of the inconsistency among state laws regarding mandatory reporting to the National Instant Criminal Background Check System; a campaign to end the stigma of mental illness to encourage reporting and referrals; strengthening of the access to community mental health systems; and an end to the confusion and ambiguity about what information can be shared between mental health practitioners, campus administrators, and law enforcement. (That commission also found that campus administrators and law enforcement mistakenly believed that they could be held personally liable for sharing certain believed-to-be protected information.)

While the majority of families of those killed in the shootings agreed to an $11 million settlement, the families of two of the victims filed a wrongful death lawsuit against the state and campus officials, among others. Though a jury verdict initially ruled in favor of the plaintiffs, the Virginia Supreme Court reversed that ruling.[71] On the morning of the incident, campus police discovered the first victim and investigated what it believed at the time was a domestic homicide. A campus-wide alert was issued, but police did not place the university on lockdown. Utilizing an "imminent probability of injury" test, the state's supreme court did not conclude that the university breached a duty to protect "against the criminal acts of a third party" because at the time of the mass shooting, campus police were conducting a good faith investigation into what it believed was an isolated incident. Despite the ruling in this case, it is certainly advisable that university officials review their crisis-management procedures to ensure they adequately deal with the threat of such tragedies.

One area of litigation that has been expanding is premise liability. Cornell University has notably been under scrutiny for the rise in suicides on its campus and any related responsibility the institution and the city have to make its campus environment less conducive to such acts. The institution is situated in an area with gorges and cliffs that have proved to be dangerous, both in relation to suicides and fatal accidents. In *King v. Cornell University*, the parents of a student who died after falling into a gorge filed suit claiming that the university should be held liable for not properly maintaining its premises.[72] Though the student was inebriated at the time, a court rejected Cornell's motion for summary judgment (i.e., dismissal of the case without a full trial), finding that an important fact to be determined is whether the trail from which the student had fallen had been properly maintained. In *Ginsburg v. City of Ithaca*, a court also did not grant summary judgment in a suit filed against Cornell (and the city), finding that a duty potentially existed to erect guards to prevent an area bridge from being used for carrying out a suicide.[73]

Litigation related to student life and student safety are not the only areas for which institutions must defend themselves in court, as they also have been increasingly sued for curricular decisions. One of the most interesting, if not entertaining, cases of this sort in recent years is *Tatro v. University of Minnesota*. There, a mortuary science student made postings on her Facebook page that university officials found to violate professional standards, such as assigning a nickname to a cadaver used in completing classroom assignments, threatening "to stab a certain someone in the throat with a trocar," and declaring that she would be "updating my 'Death List #5.'"[74] A campus disciplinary committee ordered that she receive a failing grade for the course and enroll in an ethics course. The state's supreme court upheld the sanctions on the basis that Tatro's actions violated professional standards. This ruling was a departure from the standard set by the US Supreme Court in *Hazelwood School District v. Kuhlmeier*, which justified restrictions on student speech as long as it served a curricular or pedagogical purpose.[75]

Litigation related to deceptive practices and misrepresentation of post-graduation employment statistics has increased, yet class action lawsuits involving such claims by former law students in New York[76] and Minnesota were dismissed. The Minnesota court relied on the theory of *caveat emptor*, or "buyer beware," when students alleged that employment statistics included work that did not require a law degree or statistics that did not factor in nonemployed students, both of which skewed the reported annual income of graduates.[77] Several for-profit universities have been investigated and fined in recent years for deceptive practices and inflated job-placement statistics, including Everest College ($6.5 million settlement with the attorney general of California) and Career Education Corporation ($10.25 million settlement with the attorney general of New York).

## Affirmative Action in Admissions

Affirmative action in higher education has a long history and, perhaps unlike many other issues, the controversy over it seems not to wane. Legally, however, affirmative action in college admissions can be framed as the *Bakke* era and the post-*Hopwood* era. *Regents of University of California v. Bakke* in 1978 was the first case in which the US Supreme Court handed down a decision on the legality of affirmative action in college admissions.[78] There, an applicant twice denied admissions to one of the medical schools of the University of California sued. The US Supreme Court, in a decision without a true majority, held that "strict scrutiny" governs how courts should view racial classifications in admissions, and under such a standard quotas (the medical school set aside sixteen seats for minority applicants) were illegal under the Fourteenth Amendment and Title VI of the Civil Rights Act of 1964 (under strict scrutiny, a policy must further a compelling governmental interest and be narrowly tailored to further that interest). But Justice Lewis Powell, whose opinion took the middle ground, indicated that because student-body diversity was a compelling state interest, institutions of higher education could consider race or ethnicity a "plus factor" in admissions decisions.[79]

The *Bakke* decision appeared to stabilize the legal concerns over this issue until *Hopwood v. Texas* in 1996.[80] In this case, the Fifth Circuit Court of Appeals invalidated a separate admissions process that gave preferences to African American and Mexican American applicants to the Austin Law School at the University of Texas. The court held that because Powell's opinion was not a majority opinion, it need not follow it. It also held that the affirmative action policies were unconstitutional because furthering diversity was not a compelling state interest. This case upended what had been accepted legal reasoning for affirmative action since *Bakke*, and it also introduced a new era in which the circuit courts issued conflicting opinions, forcing the US Supreme Court to settle the matter. It did so in two cases challenging the admissions policies at the University of Michigan.

In *Gratz v. Bollinger*[81] (involving undergraduate admissions) and *Grutter v. Bollinger*[82] (involving law school admissions) the US Supreme Court held that strict scrutiny would govern affirmative action in college admissions but that the University of Michigan was furthering a compelling state interest when it sought to promote the educational benefits of a diverse student body. The court thus affirmed Justice Powell's reasoning in *Bakke* (except that here, diversity is important for its own sake). The legal difference between the two University of Michigan cases hinged on the second prong of the strict-scrutiny standard, that is, whether the policies were narrowly tailored to achieve the compelling interest of furthering the educational benefits of diversity. In the *Gratz* case, the institution's use of a point system and separate admissions review was deemed illegal. In the *Grutter* case, the court approved an admission process in which race was considered in an individualized, holistic review of every applicant.

Despite these rulings, conservatives would not rest, of course, and it was not long after the University of Michigan cases were decided that *Fisher v. University of Texas* was given a fast track to the US Supreme Court. In the wake of the *Hopwood* decision, the Texas legislature adopted a "top-ten percentage plan" requiring that the top ten percent of all high school graduates will be admitted to the University of Texas. After the *Gratz* and *Grutter* cases, the University of Texas developed an admissions program that gave students a score that combined traditional academic measures ("AI") with other things, such as leadership, extracurricular activities, work experience, community service, and other special circumstances ("PAI"). The PAI score also considered the applicants' race or ethnicity. This practice was challenged as racially discriminatory. The US Supreme Court appeared to affirm that ensuring a diverse student body is a compelling interest, but then it put a great deal of emphasis on the strict scrutiny standard, suggesting that it was for a court, not the university, to decide whether a practice was "necessary" in order to be narrowly tailored to achieve the compelling governmental interest.[83] Previous decisions indicated that good faith efforts by institutions would be given some deference, and this case now seems to create a "necessity" standard that did not exist before, making it much more difficult to justify affirmative action in college admissions.

## ATHLETICS

Illegal payment to students. Betting on games. Highly-paid coaches. Cheating. Student-athletes who are academically ineligible. These were, and continue to be, some of the issues facing intercollegiate athletics since the early 1900s. Despite the problems associated with college sports, its popularity continues, primarily because of the lucrative payouts from television contracts and merchandising, as well as the strong constituency network it builds. However, changes in the NCAA's governance structure and potentially game-changing lawsuits (literally and figuratively) could substantially alter the system as we know it, or even dismantle it.

What could be the most significant challenge to NCAA authority came in 1984 with the *NCAA v. Board of Regents of the University of Oklahoma* case.[84] Probably no one at the time recognized the long-range effects this case would have, but the repercussions have irrevocably shaped the landscape of college sports. Before this case reached the US Supreme Court, the NCAA negotiated television contracts on behalf of its member institutions. It controlled how often and for how much college football teams could play on national television. Recognizing their power within that market, powerhouse teams such as the University of Oklahoma, the University of Georgia, and University of Notre Dame founded the College Football Association (CFA) in order to negotiate their own television contracts, separate from the NCAA. The NCAA responded by threatening to expel any member institution that played in contests against CFA members. The legal battle that ensued reached the nation's highest court, which found the NCAA's actions to be that of a cartel with regard to price fixing and suppressing competition.

Justice Byron White, a former college and professional football player himself, warned that permitting "a small number of colleges, even poplar ones, to have unlimited television appearances, would inevitably give them an insuperable advantage over all others and in the end defeat any efforts to maintain a system of athletic competition among amateurs who measure up to college scholastic requirements."[85] And that appears to be what has happened. Coaches and recruits are attracted to the teams with the most television and media coverage, the most money, and the best facilities. Between 1950 and 2005 the same five football programs finished the season ranked in the top eight 25 percent of the time; during that same period, the same four men's basketball teams accounted for 25 percent of Final Four appearances.[86] Coaches' salaries have risen 750 percent since the *Regents* ruling, while faculty salaries have only risen 32 percent.[87] NCAA-sponsored sports produce nearly twice the revenue that the National Football League does,[88] and the Southeastern Conference (SEC) has already broken the $2 billion mark.[89] All the while, student-athlete compensation has remained constant: tuition, room and board, and books.

The amount of an athletic scholarship can run $3,000 to $6,000 below the full cost of attendance at many institutions.[90] Two recent lawsuits, premised on vastly different legal theories, sought to bridge that financial gap. In 2014, a regional office of the National Labor Relations Board ruled that football players from Northwestern University could unionize in order to seek scholarships that cover full cost of attendance, assistance for degree completion, and improved medical treatment. Taking into account the commercial nature of college athletics[91] and the immense control[92] coaches exert over players' lives, the NLRB found that the football players functioned more like employees than students. This ruling currently is on appeal, but if it stands it could expand litigation to include for athletes other rights to workmen's compensation (for which student athletes currently are not eligible) and to Title VII sexual-harassment protections.[93]

In 2010, former UCLA basketball standout Ed O'Bannon commenced a case against the NCAA and others, challenging regulations requiring student athletes to sign away rights to their likenesses in perpetuity and prohibiting them from profiting from broadcasts and from video games. While EA Sports, the company that produces NCAA-related videogames, settled with the class of current and former student athletes for $40 million, the case against the NCAA went to trial in 2014. A district court ruled that although student athletes were not entitled to profits from live broadcasts and archival footage, restrictions prohibiting them from benefitting from the sale of videogames that used their likenesses violated antitrust law. The court stated, "Videogame developers do not need the intellectual property rights of both the NCAA and all of its conferences in order to produce a college sports videogame. If a sufficient number of schools and conferences were willing to license their intellectual property for use in videogames, a submarket for student athletes' group licenses would likely exist."[94] Such a submarket does exist, as EA Sports paid the NFL players union $35 million in royalties in 2010.[95] The court agreed that the NCAA's attempts to preserve amateurism could be achieved in a less restrictive manner, and the ruling allows institutions to utilize revenue from licensing agreements to increase athletic scholarships to cover the full cost of attendance and to put into trust funds to be utilized by student athletes after their eligibility expires.[96] In November 2014 the NCAA sought an appeal before the Ninth Circuit and that case is still pending.

In addition to the legal challenges brought by advocates of student athletes' rights, a 2014 change in the governance structure of the NCAA has paved the way for more student athletes to receive full-cost-of-attendance scholarships—but this new structure also may serve to perpetuate a caste system among athletic conferences. The five most resourced conferences (Atlantic Coast, the Big 12, the Big Ten, Pac-12, and Southeastern) now are able to enact rules that govern themselves exclusively. In January 2015 this group of conferences approved a measure that allows its member institutions to begin offering scholarships that cover the full cost of attendance, which is prohibited (for now) at other NCAA institutions. Though this is a positive development for the rights of student athletes, it invariably will affect recruiting and all but guarantee that the best recruits—and ostensibly best coaches—will continue to flock to these schools in these powerhouse conferences. Additionally, many fear that the costs associated with increasing scholarships may cause institutions to close smaller nonrevenue sports so as to divert money to men's basketball and football.

## Conclusion

We started this chapter by suggesting that the emergence of the multiversity has also meant the beginning of the end of the "ivory tower." The vast array of activities in which institutions of higher education engage brings them into conflict with all types of stakeholders, and in the United States conflicts are often resolved in court. Litigation, of course, shapes institutional policy, which in turn has served to make judicial courts key stakeholders in what we call "higher education." Still, colleges and universities enjoy considerable deference in the judicial system; they are usually only required to follow the policies that they themselves develop. With regard to faculty, in particular, institutions of higher education can control what faculty say, how they are promoted, rewarded, and assigned work, how they are evaluated (and what evidence they can provide—but need not prove—if sued for discrimination), and what they create with their research. The only obstacle to unfettered institutional prerogatives might be unionization, but conservative political movements have made the future of collective bargaining unclear.

The same deference applies in the case of students. Colleges and universities can control what students say, though students have more rights than faculty do in this regard, and paradoxically so, given the lip service paid to academic freedom by administrators—which seems to us most prevalent by administrators when their behavior is the focus of attention by politicians. It does appear, however, that institutional prerogatives will be given a bit less weight by courts when dealing with incidents in which students are harmed or in which white applicants allege racial discrimination (allegations of discrimination by white women and racial minorities are often unsuccessful unless the discrimination is obviously blatant). And we are seeing public pressure on universities to address the exploitation associated with collegiate athletics.

This last argument about public pressure raises one final point we would like to make in this chapter. Courts are not alone in shaping policy for higher education. Politicians, governing and accrediting bodies, and regulatory agencies also influence the higher education policy. At stake, of course, are the real and purported benefits of a higher education for the economy and for individuals. There still exists a sense that colleges and universities provide social and private goods, and the increasing importance of higher education means that what colleges and universities do is of keen interest to everyone. Institutions of higher education have done a good job of promoting the idea of their necessity, but this does not come without a cost to their autonomy. In a sense, the more necessary institutions of higher education become in determining our futures, the more necessary it may become that they not be governed by a logic characterizing an "ivory tower."

NOTES

1. Clark Kerr, *The Uses of the University*, 5th ed. (Cambridge, MA: Harvard University Press, 2001), 5.

2. See Michael Olivas, "Governing Badly: Theory and Practice of Bad Ideas in College Decision Making," *Indiana Law Journal* 87 (2012): 951–77.

3. See, generally, Sheila Slaughter and Gary Rhoades, *Academic Capitalism and the New Economy* (Baltimore: Johns Hopkins University Press, 2004).

4. *Dixon v. Ala. State Bd. of Educ.*, 294 F. 2d 150 (5th Cir. 1961).

5. *In loco parentis* is Latin for "in place of the parent." This term can be traced to the seventeenth century to describe the schoolmaster-pupil relationship in which the tutor was granted custodial authority by a student's father and served to insulate institutions from liability rather than recognize a legal duty to protect. See Robert D. Bickel & Peter F. Lake, "Reconceptualizing the University's Duty to Provide a Safe Learning Environment: A Criticism of the Doctrine of 'In Loco Parentis' and the Restatement (Second) of Torts," *Journal of College & University Law* 20 (1994): 261–93.

6. *Piazzola v. Watkins*, 442 F.2d 284 (5th Cir. 1971).

7. *Bazaar v. Fortune*, 476 F.2d 570 (5th Cir. 1973).

8. *Healy v. James*, 408 US 169 (1972).

9. *Rosenberger v. Rector and Visitors of the Univ. of Va.*, 515 US 819, 831 (1995).

10. *Goss v. Lopez*, 419 US 565 (1975).

11. *Dartmouth Coll. v. Woodward*, 17 US 518 (1819).

12. Based on the notion that the king could do no wrong, the rationale for sovereign immunity was solidified in 1793 in *Chisholm v. Georgia* (2 US 419) even prior to the amendment's passage.

13. *Harlow v. Fitzgerald*, 457 US 800 (1982). This ruling eliminated another prong, which had been established in *Wood v. Strickland* (420 US 308 (1975)), focusing on the subjective standard of whether the act was done with malice.

14. American Association of University Professors, "1915 Declaration of Principles of Academic Freedom and Tenure," in *Policy Documents & Reports*, 9th ed. (Washington, DC: American Association of University Professors and Johns Hopkins University Press, 2001), 291–301.

15. See, for example, *Island Trees Sch. Dist. v. Pico*, 457 US 853 (1982).

16. American Association of University Professors, "1940 Statement of Principles on Academic Freedom and Tenure (with 1970 Interpretive Comments)," in *Policy Documents & Reports*, 9th ed. (Washington, DC: American Association of University Professors and Johns Hopkins University Press, 2001), 3–10.

17. Michael Olivas, in a version of this chapter for prior editions of this book, laid out nicely the conflicts between faculty and students.

18. *Sweezy v. N.H.*, 354 US 234 (1957).

19. *Keyishian v. Bd. of Regents*, 385 US 589 (1967).

20. Ibid., 603.

21. See, for example, *Waters v. Churchill*, 511 US 661 (1994).

22. See, for example, *Hardy v. Jefferson Cmty. Coll.*, 260 F.3d 671 (6th Cir. 2001).

23. See, for example, *Bishop v. Aronov*, 926 F.2d 1066 (11th Cir. 1991).

24. *Pickering v. Bd. of Educ.*, 391 US 563 (1968).

25. *Givhan v. Western Line Consol. Sch. Dist.*, 439 US 410 (1979).

26. *Mt. Healthy City Sch. Dist. v. Doyle*, 429 US 274 (1977). Doyle's dispute with another teacher at the school had begun to be unwieldy for the school's principal.

27. *Connick v. Myers*, 461 US 138 (1983).

28. *Waters v. Churchill*, 511 US 661 (1994).

29. *Garcetti v. Ceballos*, 547 US 410 (2006).

30. *Branham v. Thomas M. Cooley Law School*, 689 F.3d 558 (6th Cir. 2012).

31. For a discussion of faculty dismissals because of declining enrollments, see Gwen Seaquist and Eileen Kelly, "Faculty Dismissal Because of Enrollment Declines," *Journal of Law and Education* 28 (1999): 193–207.

32. *AAUP v. Bloomfield Coll.*, 346 A.2d 615 (N.J. Super. Ct. App. Div. 1975).

33. *Krotkoff v. Goucher Coll.*, 585 F.2d 675 (4th Cir. 1978).

34. *Scheuer v. Creighton Univ.*, 260 N.W.2d 595 (Neb. 1977).

35. *Bd. of Regents v. Roth*, 408 US 564 (1972).

36. *Perry v. Sindermann*, 408 US 593 (1972).

37. *Roth*, pp. 573–75; see also *Bishop v. Wood*, 426 US 341 (1976).

38. See Joe Berry and Michelle Savaris, *Directory of U.S. Faculty Contracts and Bargaining Agents in Institutions of Higher Education* (New York: The National Center for the Study of Collective Bargaining in Higher Education and the Professions, 2012).

39. See, for example, John C. Duncan, "The Indentured Servants of Academia: The Adjunct Faculty Dilemma and Their Limited Legal Remedies," *Indiana Law Journal* 74 (1999): 513–86.

40. *NLRB v. Yeshiva Univ.*, 444 US 672 (1980).

41. Rita L. Lieberwitz, "Faculty in the Corporate University: Professional Identity, Law and Collective Action," *Cornell Journal of Law and Public Policy* 16 (2007): 263, 290–330.

42. US Const. art. 1, § 8, cl. 8.

43. This term is defined as (1) a work prepared by an employee within the scope of his or her employment; or (2) a work specially ordered or commissioned for use as a contribution to a collective work, as a part of a motion picture or other audiovisual work, as a translation, as a supplementary work, as a compilation, as an instructional text, as a test, as answer material for a test, or as an atlas. Copyright Act of 1976, 17 USC § 101 (2000).

44. *Williams v. Weisser*, 273 Cal.App.2d 726 (Cal. Ct. App. 1969).

45. See, for example, *Weinstein v. Univ. of Ill.*, 811 F.2d 1091 (7th Cir. 1987) and *Hays v. Sony Corp. of America*, 847 F.2d 412 (7th Cir. 1988).

46. *Cmty. for Creative Non-Violence v. Reid*, 90 US 730 (1989).

47. Ibid., 751.

48. American Association of University Professors, "Statement on Copyright" (1999), http://www.aaup.org/report/statement-copyright [accessed Apr. 25, 2015].

49. See generally, Sherri L. Burr, "A Critical Assessment of *Reid's* Work for Hire Framework and Its Potential Impact on the Marketplace for Scholarly Works," *Marshall Law Review* 24 (1990): 119–43.

50. See generally, Michael W. Klein and Joy Blanchard, "Are Intellectual Property Policies Subject to Collective Bargaining? A Case Study of New Jersey and Kansas, Revisited," *Texas Intellectual Property Law Journal* 20 (2012): 389–428.

51. See, for example, *Clark v. Claremont Univ. Ctr.*, 8 Cal. Rptr. 2d 151 (Cal. Ct. App. 1992). In this case, Clark overheard tenure-committee proceedings in which a faculty member said, "I don't know how I would feel working on a permanent base [sic] with a black man" (p. 157).

52. *McDonnell Douglas Corp. v. Green*, 411 US 792 (1973).

53. *Griggs v. Duke Power Co.*, 401 US 424 (1971).

54. See, for example, *Scott v. Univ. of Del.*, 455 F.Supp. 1102 (D. Del. 1978). In this case, the court ruled in favor of the university when Scott alleged that the requirement of a Ph.D. for faculty positions discriminated against racial minorities.

55. *Ricci v. DeStefano*, 557 US 557 (2009).

56. In his book, *Suing Alma Mater: Higher Education and the Courts* (Baltimore: Johns Hopkins University Press, 2013), Olivas focused on the positive policy changes such groups (e.g., NAACP Legal Defense Fund and Mexican American Legal Defense and Education Fund) have had on court rulings, as well as the role religious purposive organizations have had in pushing a pro-Christian agenda through the judicial system. He argued that these groups "will not be happy until its sectarian jihad is accomplished and evangelical Christians—as narrowly trademarked by their singular creed—have full access to all college resources and enjoy full financial and organizational resources from secular institutions, even while denying all apostates and sinners from membership in their many organizations" (p. 151).

57. *Christian Legal Soc'y v. Walker*, 453 F.3d 853 (7th Cir. 2006).

58. *Christian Legal Soc'y v. Martinez*, 561 US 661 (2010). The dissent in this countered that the ruling allowed "no freedom for expression that offends prevailing standards of political correctness" (p. 706).

59. *Roberts v. Haragan*, 346 F. Supp. 2d 853 (N.D. Tex. 2004).

60. Details of that agreement included designating a Title IX coordinator, making more public the institution's reporting procedures for Title IX infractions, increasing and improving training on campus, conducting semiannual reviews related to compliance, conducting campus climate surveys, and developing programming to establish appropriate social norms within student organizations. Voluntary Resolution Agreement Yale University, Complaint No. 01-11-2027 (2012), https://www2.ed.gov/about/offices/list/ocr/docs/investigations/01112027-b.pdf [accessed Apr. 25, 2015].

61. See Tyle Kingkade, "76 Colleges Are Now under Investigation for How They Handled Sex Assault Cases," *Huffington Post* (Aug. 13, 2014), http://www.huffingtonpost.com/2014/08/13/college-sex-assault-cases_n_5675564.html [accessed Sept. 1, 2014].

62. See Rachel Axon, "FSU under investigation for handling of Jameis Winston case," *USA Today*, Apr. 4, 2014, http://www.usatoday.com/story/sports/ncaaf/2014/04/03/jameis-winston-florida-state-rape-investigation-title-ix-civil-rights/7262359/ [accessed May 1, 2105].

63. Resolution Agreement, http://www2.ed.gov/documents/press-releases/montana-missoula-resolution-agreement.pdf [accessed Apr. 25, 2015].

64. White House, "Not Alone: The First Report of the White House Task Force to Protect Students from Sexual Assault," http://www.whitehouse.gov/sites/default/files/docs/report_o.pdf [accessed Aug. 27, 2015].

65. California Senate Bill No. 967 (2014). Some feel, however, that threshold will be impractical to enforce, considering the extemporaneous nature of such encounters.

66. Monica Vendituoli, "5 Plaintiffs Reach Agreement with UConn in Sexual-Assault Lawsuit," *Chronicle of Higher Education*, July 18, 2014, http://chronicle.com/article/5-Plaintiffs-Reach-Agreement/147815/ [accessed Apr. 25, 2015].

67. Libby Sander, "U. of Colorado at Boulder Settles Lawsuit over Alleged Rapes at Football Recruiting Party for $2.85 Million," *Chronicle of Higher Education*, Dec. 6, 2014, http://chronicle.com/article/U-of-Colorado-at-Boulder/286/ [accessed May 1, 2015].

68. She alleged that she had twice been raped in the residence hall. The accused had previously been arrested for unrelated sexual assaults. See Joy Blanchard, "Institutional Liability for the Sexual Crimes of Student-Athletes: A Review of Case Law and Policy Recommendations," *Journal for the Study of Sports and Athletes in Education* 1 (2007): 221–40.

69. *Williams v. Bd. of Regents of the Univ. Sys. of Ga.*, 441 F.3d 1287 (11th Cir. 2006).

70. See Joy Blanchard, "University Tort Liability and Student Suicide: Case Review and Implications for Practice," *Journal of Law and Education* 36 (2007): 461–77.

71. See *Commonwealth of Va. v. Peterson*, 749 S.E.2d 307 (Va. 2013). At trial the Commonwealth of Virginia was the only defendant. The initial award was $4 million to each family but was later reduced to $100,000 in accordance with state tort law.

72. *King v. Cornell Univ.*, 973 N.Y.S.2d 534 (N.Y. Sup. 2013).

73. *Ginsburg v. City of Ithaca*, 839 F.Supp.2d 537 (N.D.N.Y. 2012). Numerous suicides had occurred on that bridge in the prior decade. In 2014 the father of the deceased student accepted $100,000 to settle the suit.

74. *Tatro v. Univ. of Minn.*, 816 N.W.2d 509, 512 (Minn. 2012).

75. *Hazelwood Sch. Dist. v. Kuhlmeier*, 484 US 260 (1988).

76. See *Gomez–Jimenez v. N.Y. Law Sch.*, 956 N.Y.S.2d 54 (N.Y. App. Div. 2012).

77. *Macdonald v. Thomas M. Cooley Law Sch.*, 880 F. Supp. 2d 785 (W. D. Mich. 2012).

78. *Bd. of Regents of Univ. of Calif. v. Bakke*, 438 US 265 (1978).

79. To be clear, Justice Powell used the logic of academic freedom in justifying such diversity, rather than diversity as important in itself.

80. *Hopwood v. Tex.*, 78 F.3d 932 (5th Cir. 1996).

81. *Gratz v. Bollinger*, 539 US 244 (2003).

82. *Grutter v. Bollinger*, 539 US 306 (2003).

83. *Fisher v. Univ. of Tex.*, 133 S. Ct. 2411 (2013).

84. *NCAA v. Bd. of Regents of the Univ. of Okla.*, 468 US 85 (1984).

85. See Brian L. Porto, *The Supreme Court and the NCAA: The Case for Less Commercialization and More Due Process in College Sports* (Ann Arbor: University of Michigan Press, 2012) 81.

86. Marc Edelman, "The Future of Amateurism After Antitrust Scrutiny: Why a Win for the Plaintiffs in the NCAA Student-Athlete Name & Likeness Licensing Litigation Will Not Lead to the Demise of College Sports," *Oregon Law Review* 92 (2014): 19–55.

87. Taylor Branch, "The Shame of College Sports," *The Atlantic* (October 2011), http://www.theatlantic.com/magazine/archive/2011/10/the-shame-of-college-sports/308643/ [accessed Ap. 25, 2015].

88. James Monks, "Revenue Shares and Monopsonistic Behavior in Intercollegiate Athletics," Cornell Higher Education Research Institute, 2013, https://www.ilr.cornell.edu/sites/ilr.cornell.edu/files/WP155.pdf [accessed May 1, 2015].

89. Christian Dennie, "Changing the Game: The Litigation That May Be the Catalyst for Change in Intercollegiate Athletics," *Syracuse Law Review* 62 (2012): 15–51.

90. Nicholas Fram and T. Ward Frampton, "A Union of Amateurs: A Legal Blueprint to Reshape Big-Time College Athletics," *Buffalo Law Review* 60 (2012): 1003–78.

91. The court here analogized the state of intercollegiate athletics to a 1970 case involving librarians at Cornell University. In that ruling the court found a commercial aspect existed because the institution made $4,890 from selling microfilms and the "Germanic and Romanic Reviews" and $21,150 from radio and television broadcast rights to football games; see *Cornell Univ.*, 183 N.L.R.B. 329, 336 (1970).

92. The board found that coaches regulated student-athletes' social media pages, off-campus apartment leases, and course schedules. Though NCAA regulations state that student-athletes must only participate in a maximum of twenty hours per week of athletic-related activities, during the season football players spent fifty to sixty hours traveling for games, participating in mandatory workouts, and attending team meetings.

93. The standard by which an institution can be held liable for an employee's sexual assault is much looser than that of Title IX, which requires a finding of actual notice and of deliberate indifference to known harassment.

94. *O'Bannon v. Nat'l Collegiate Athletic Ass'n*, 7 F.Supp.3d 955, 965 (N.D. Calif. 2014). EA Sports testified that if not for the challenged rules they would have still sought to acquire individual rights to student-athletes' likenesses.

95. See Branch, "The Shame of College Sports."

96. The court stipulated that institutions must set aside no less than $5,000 for every year that each student-athlete is academically eligible for competition. This ruling, by the way, only applies to Division I Football Bowl Subdivision institutions, as they are the only ones that have obtained revenue from videogames. As such, student-athletes at other institution types will probably not benefit from this ruling.

# Chapter Eleven

# Financing American Higher Education

*Reconciling Institutional Financial Viability
and Student Affordability*

D. Bruce Johnstone

Higher education in America, as nearly everywhere, is beset with financial problems that challenge institutional financial viability as well as student affordability, access, and success. At the heart of these problems lies the seemingly inexorable rise in college and university costs, fueled by the increasing cost of faculty and staff compensation (in spite of a more than decade-long stagnation in wages and salaries), by the surging costs of technology, and by the rising costs associated with recruiting, enrolling, and retaining a student body that meets the academic, demographic, diversity, and revenue-producing targets of the institution. At the same time, the price of higher education to students and their families—consisting most visibly of tuition and fees, but also including instructional equipment, food and lodging, transportation, and other expenses such as clothing, entertainment, and mobile telephones—continues to rise, becoming for many students either unaffordable altogether or affordable only with increasingly unmanageable debts.

This chapter first elaborates on the complex and sometimes countervailing perceptions of cost, price, and the appropriate shares of instructional costs to be borne by parents, students, taxpayers, and philanthropists. It examines the basis for the underlying cost increases and the seeming limits both to ever-increasing tax revenue in the public sector and to annual increases in net (i.e., after discounts) tuitions in the private sector. It examines possible solutions to higher education's financial austerity, beginning with actions on the revenue side, especially tuition and fee increases and their inevitable clash with the goals of enhancing access and completion as well as the realities of demographics and increasing price resistance, particularly for private colleges and universities lacking deep and affluent applicant pools. It examines a frequently advocated but highly controversial policy solution for public higher education sometimes referred to as "high tuition–high aid." The chapter then examines solutions to financial austerity on the cost side: by cutting expenditures, which is painful and always controversial, or by increasing efficiency, or added output per dollar, which is especially complex and equally controversial due to the absence of consensus on higher education's multiple and hard-to-measure outputs.

The chapter concludes with speculations about higher education's financial future and the underlying conflicts among:

- the financial needs of institutions—which appear to require continuously increasing (but problematic) contributions from taxpayers and parents as well as students;

- the social and political pressures for expanded access and completion—which are compromised by continuously increasing tuitions and debt loads and by resistance to the ever-increasing needs for financial aid and tuition discounts;

- the political and demographic realities, which seem, as of 2015, to portend continuing austerity for most US colleges and universities, public and private alike (albeit for different reasons), a widening of financial fortunes among institutions (depending mainly on differences in wealth and selectivity), and slow progress in expanding student access, completion, and success.

## Problems, Perceptions, and Issues

Financial austerity in higher education has been around for decades—perhaps forever—quite apart from the impact of any slowdown, recession, or turbulence in the general economy or in state or federal politics.[1] This austerity is a function not simply of higher education's high costs, but of the annually increasing trajectory of these costs, and therefore of annually increasing college and university revenue needs. These increasing revenue needs will in most years outpace the prevailing rates of inflation, and will almost certainly exceed the likely trajectory of available revenues, especially from the state governments—many of which have been disinvesting in their public universities for years and all of which have been shifting more of the burden of support onto parents and students as well as donors.

The juxtaposition of the declining financial condition of higher education institutions in spite of rising tuitions, together with the declining affordability of higher education, in large part because of increasing tuitions, has raised many issues for students, their families, educational leaders, politicians, and the general citizenry. At the heart of these financial issues—some of them political and ideological, and intertwined with even larger issues such as income inequality and racial divisions—are critical and long-standing perceptions of the financial condition of America's colleges and universities. These perceptions, most with substantial elements of truth, but all with varying applicability to the enormous diversity of America's colleges and universities, and most with complex explanations that defy simple policy solutions, include many or all of the following charges:

- The operating costs of colleges and universities are excessive, and becoming more so.
- The prices of colleges and universities, public as well as private—that is, tuitions—are if anything, even more excessive.
- Contributing to these excessive costs—at least in so-called elite and want-to-be-elite institutions—is a kind of prestige arms race, driven by academic leaders, faculty and governing boards alike, to move up in the national and international scholarly rankings.
- Also contributing to generally high and rising costs is the reluctance and difficulty of faculty and academic leaders to reallocate resources, to accept labor-saving instructional innovations such as online learning, or to reduce faculty and staff numbers (frequently attributed to a combination of shared governance, tenure, absence of clear performance metrics, and unionization).
- These excessive and surging tuitions—whether caused by institutional inefficiencies or by state budget cuts—are putting higher education beyond the financial reach of more and more families, in response to which many students are incurring debts they are unlikely to be able to repay or are being forced to select the lowest-cost higher educational option rather than the institution that is right for them.

These problems and perceptions raise a number of public and institutional policy questions that are informed, if not always definitively answered, by economic and financial perspectives. For example, how, if at all, can costs—especially to the taxpayer and the student—be substantially lowered (more than they have already been in very many colleges) without damage to academic quality or to principles of access and completion? What are appropriate ratios of students to faculty and to professional and administrative staff at various kinds of institutions? What are reasonable conceptions and expectations of higher educational productivity—and what are the appropriate outputs, or products, and how are they to be measured?

And perhaps the ultimate question, which this chapter will explore but will not be able to answer is whether the prevailing trajectory of per-student costs rising annually at rates in excess of the prevailing rates of inflation—which many economists have thought to be more-or-less normal in higher education (as in other labor-intensive, productivity-resistant sectors of the economy)—sustainable in the long run? And if not, what sort of profound changes in American higher education and the instructional practices of colleges and universities are realistically likely? Such changes, for example, might include (1) a greater differentiation of university faculty workloads; (2) a large-scale shedding of noninstructional staff and related costs in such sectors as athletics, public relations, student activities, and general administration; (3) the adoption of three-year bachelor's degrees, perhaps in conjunction with an expansion of college-level learning in high school; or (4) a large-scale acceptance of e-learning and credit-by-examination.[2]

The contemplation of such profound solutions leads to other questions: Will the relatively small number of colleges and universities with large endowments and deep and affluent applicant pools continue on their historical cost trajectories and leave such profound, difficult, and controversial changes to the many less fortunate and less selective public and private colleges and universities? Or, will public colleges and universities for the most part simply cope with ever-increasing revenue needs and declining state appropriations by continuing to cut faculty and staff positions, deferring maintenance, shifting ever more of the cost burden onto parents and students, and hoping that generous state appropriations will someday return? And will private colleges and universities continue with the same cost-cutting practices as in the past and hope that creative enrollment management, new market niches, advanced marketing strategies, more aggressive philanthropy, and a continuing influx of tuition-paying Asian students will maintain enrollments and net revenue?

The issue of affordability and the related issues of access, persistence, and completion lead to still other questions: How can enrollment management, or

selective price discounting, be used to attract students with qualities or characteristics sought by the institution and still maximize net tuition revenue? Are
taxpayer dollars in the public sector best used to cover even more than the government's share of underlying instructional cost increases, thus holding down the
need for tuition—that is, for the parent's and student's shares—to increase at all?
Or, in recognition of the fact that relatively modest tuition increases in public
colleges and universities have little or no effect on access or continuation except
for students from low-income families, should state governments allow tuition to
rise in accord with the rising costs of instruction and use governmental revenue
to strengthen need-based financial aid where the dollars will make a greater difference in accessibility?[3] Are public aid dollars—limited as they are—best used
for grants or for loan subsidies? Should public aid be based on academic promise
and performance as well as upon family financial need? And what is the appropriate response by institutions and governments to the pervasive condition of
austerity in higher education, whether brought on by declining enrollments, declining state tax assistance, allegations of runaway costs, or—still evident as this
chapter is being written in 2015—remnants of the severe economic downturn of
2008–10 that ravaged endowments, state budgets, current giving, and the ability
of many families to cover the high and still rising costs of a college education?[4]

## Economic, Social, and Political Context

All of these problems, issues, and proposed policy solutions are influenced by
perceptions, which may diverge in some cases from reality. For example, perceptions of the financial conditions, troubles, and the appropriate policy solutions
for America's colleges and universities may depend on whether the object of the
perception is one's own collegiate experience or the experience of a recent child,
or is a kind of abstraction, like one's view of government in general, or of public
schools, or of health care—all of which (along with many other institutions)
seem, in the middle of the second decade of the century, to be suffering from
declining civic approval. Perceptions may differ depending on whether the reference is to public or private higher education, to elite and selective schools, or to
affordable and open-access colleges.

Perceptions of higher education's financial troubles may also differ according
to one's underlying political persuasion, although where one is positioned on a
conventional political/ideological continuum, ranging from extreme conservative to extreme progressive/liberal may not predict how one will perceive the
problems of American higher education or the appropriate policy solutions. For

example, affluent Americans—themselves likely to be graduates of elite institutions, both public and private, and likely to identify with the political right or center-right—may be critical of what they may perceive to be excessive state taxpayer subsidization of public higher education, but be less critical of the level of the underlying instructional costs themselves, which they may believe ought to be covered by higher tuitions and fewer frills like the costly quest for greater diversity or indulgent, curiosity-driven research.

Those who identify with the left or the center-left may be more accommodating to higher taxes (especially if these are to fall on the wealthy or on businesses) and to place a high priority on the expansion of access, which calls for the support of need-based financial assistance and the full state funding of public higher education to forestall higher tuitions. On the other hand, middle and lower socioeconomic class Americans may especially resent the rise in public tuitions, which they may attribute in part to politically conservative tax-cutting, but also to too many frills. And middle and upper-middle class Americans alike may resent the costliness of higher education generally, which they see as putting many colleges and universities out of their financial reach and/or burdening their children with excessive debt.

Politicians and the general citizenry may be critical of the well-publicized high tuitions of elite private colleges and universities but may not recognize that the net tuition fee after institutional and governmental financial assistance is generally far lower. Or they may be unswayed in their criticism by the fact that those students and families paying the full price are expressing a private value in the way that value is revealed in any competitive market (not unlike the purchase of an expensive luxury car) and that there is undoubtedly an abundance of lower-priced but still high-quality colleges they could have chosen instead. Similarly, those who criticize public colleges and universities for raising tuitions at rates higher even than the rate of increase of their instructional costs may not realize (or may choose to not recognize) that the increase may have been forced upon the public institution by state governors and legislatures who have chosen to cut taxes or invest in other public goods and services knowing that another compensating tuition increase will be the end result (even if they decry the increased fees for their political purposes).

Fundamental to the economic, social, and political context is the fact that higher education is recognized both as an engine of economic growth and as a gatekeeper to individual positions of high remuneration and status. Advanced education—particularly in high technology, information processing, sophisticated management, and financial analysis—is thought to be essential to maintaining America's economic position in the increasingly competitive global economy. It follows that most jobs of high remuneration and status will require an advanced education, frequently beyond a bachelor's degree. And it also follows that youth lacking postsecondary education will probably have lower incomes and marginal status.

These propositions, however, do not mean that advanced education necessarily makes individuals more productive or that all recipients of advanced education will find remunerative, high-status employment. Higher education can make individuals more productive, but it can also simply screen, or select, for the kinds of intellectual, social, and personal characteristics required for the high-remuneration, high-status jobs that may be available. In short, higher education is essential for most good jobs, and the absence of education beyond high school will be an increasingly formidable barrier to obtaining them, but the mere possession of an advanced degree will guarantee neither good, nor lasting, employment.

Complicating the links between higher education, income, and status is the fact that American society is increasingly polarized by class, race, and ethnicity. More and more children grow up in poverty, both rural and urban. The dilemma presented by higher education's gatekeeper function is that access to, and especially success in, college and university remains highly correlated with socioeconomic class. This correlation has not significantly diminished in recent years, even though American higher education is more accessible than the higher education systems of other countries. Thus, with the increasing disparities of income in the decades ending the twentieth and beginning the twenty-first centuries, and with the increasing correlation of economic success in life to success in college, there is reason to be alarmed at the degree to which our colleges and universities perpetuate, and even accelerate, the intergenerational transmission of wealth and status.

As to the political context, American society, or at least the voting electorate, has become increasingly polarized and conservative. As this chapter is being written shortly after the 2014 capture of both branches of the Congress, and most of the state governorships, by substantial conservative majorities, there exists a growing resistance to the notion of a benign government, to the expansion of social welfare programs (including affordable health insurance), and to transfer payments to the poor (including an expansion of Pell grants). Insofar as there is to be a governmental agenda for higher education, conservatives in 2015 would have it advanced through private, or at least market-oriented, mechanisms such as performance budgeting, tuition tax credits, tuition caps on public colleges and universities (principally to incentivize further institutional efficiencies), merit aid, a continued shift of federal financial assistance from need-based grants to loans, and a disinclination to accept ethnic or racial preferences (i.e., affirmative action) in admissions or in the awarding of financial assistance.

These economic, social, and political themes, for all their complexity, provide a context for consideration of the three broad areas of questions regarding higher education finance in America (or for that matter in any country):

- *The size of the America's publicly funded higher educational enterprise (including the publicly funded portion of the private sector)*: that is, how much publicly supported higher education do we need or will we choose to afford, measured either in total expenditures or as a percentage of our gross domestic product?

- *The efficiency and productivity of this enterprise*: that is, what should higher education, particularly public higher education, cost per unit (whether the *unit* is to be students enrolled, degrees granted, scholarship produced, service rendered, or combinations thereof)?

- *The sources of revenue to support this enterprise*: that is, who pays (or who should pay) for the costs of higher education—government or taxpayers, parents, students, or philanthropists?

### The Size of the Enterprise

The American higher education enterprise is enormous—in number of institutions (especially if the for-profit, non-degree-granting institutions are counted), in enrollments, and in expenditures, even controlling for our great wealth and population. For example, the number of degree-granting postsecondary institutions in 2012–13 (the latest count from the National Center for Education Statistics as of early 2015) was 4,726, including 689 public four-year, 934 public two-year, 1,555 private nonprofit four-year, and 97 private nonprofit two-year colleges.[5]

These institutions enrolled some 19.5 million full- and part-time students in 2013, according to the Census Bureau's household survey data reported in September 2014. This total included 10.5 million undergraduates in four-year colleges and universities (public, private nonprofit, and private for-profit), 3.7 million in graduate and advanced professional schools, and 5.3 million in two-year colleges. This was down by some 463,000 from previous year and down by 930,000 from 2011.[6]

*Table 11.1*    Numbers of US degree-granting postsecondary
institutions and enrollments

|  | Number of institutions 2012–13 | Number of students fall 2011 |
|---|---|---|
| Public 4-year | 689 | 8,047,729 |
| Public 2-year | 934 | 7,062,467 |
| Private non-profit 4-year | 1,555 | 3,887,322 |
| Private non-profit 2-year | 97 | 39,864 |
| Private for-profit 4-year | 782 | 559,080 |
| Private for-profit 2-year | 669 | 397,651 |
| Totals | 4,726 | 20,994,113 |

*Source:* NCES, *Digest of Education Statistics 2013*, tables 317.10 and 223.

The US Department of Education's National Center for Education Statistics (NCES), which reports data originating from the institutions of higher education rather than from the household census surveys, reported a fall 2011 total enrollment of 20,894,113 full- and part-time students in all degree-granting institutions. This preliminary total was down slightly from the fall of 2010, but higher than any other previous year.[7] The numbers of institutions by control and level, together with the NCES-reported enrollment data, are shown in table 11.1.

Of course, the large numbers enrolled are to a considerable degree a function of America's large population. A better international comparative measure, controlling for differences in total population, would be the percentage of some age cohort—say, age 25–34—that has attained some level of postsecondary education. By such a comparison, the United States, at 33 percent of its 25–34 age cohort having attained a bachelor's degree or the equivalent, is above the average for highly industrialized nations of the Organization for Economic Cooperation and Development (OECD) at 29.5 percent, as well as the percentages for Canada (31.1%), France (27%), Germany (18.3%), Spain (26.2%), and Ireland (31.1%), but is behind Australia (35%), Japan (34.9%), Korea (38.9%), Finland (37.8%), and Norway (45.7%).[8]

Although the numbers in the traditional college-age youth cohort will flatten or decline in the years between 2011 and 2022, enrollments were projected by the NCES in 2014 to increase at a modest rate through at least 2022.[9] Absent increasing numbers of college-age youth, the enrollment growth from 2015 to 2020 and beyond will be fed by immigration and students from abroad, increasing

*Table 11.2*     Projection of US post-secondary enrollments to 2020

| | 2005 | 2010 | 2015 | 2020 | % increase 2010–2020 |
|---|---|---|---|---|---|
| Public 4-year | 6,838 | 7,925 | 8,395 | 8,896 | 12.2 |
| Public 2-year | 6,184 | 7,218 | 7,326 | 7,855 | 8.8 |
| Private 4-year | 4,162 | 5,410 | 5,684 | 6,073 | 12.3 |
| Private 2-year | 304 | 463 | 450 | 484 | 4.5 |
| Total | 17,487 | 21,016 | 21,805 | 23,309 | 10.9 |

*Source:* NCES, *Projections of Education Statistics to 2022*, tables 22–26, pp. 60–64.

graduate and advanced professional enrollments, a continuation of adults returning to complete studies once abandoned, and a hoped-for increase in high school and college completion, which are two of the more salient reform movements at the local, state, and federal levels in the middle of the twenty-first century's second decade. Table 11.2 shows the NCES projections from 2014 by public and private institutions (combining nonprofit and proprietary, and two- and four-year levels).

Total expenditures for all degree-granting colleges and universities in America were reported by the NCES to be some $488 billion in 2011–12. This very large and inevitably approximate number was composed of expenditures at all public postsecondary institutions totaling $306 billion, expenditures at all private nonprofit institutions totaling $160 billion, and $23 billion for the private for-profit sector.[10] However, such expenditure data, aside from being dated by the time of compilation and publication, is difficult to portray in any meaningful sense, especially to compare institutional expenditures against some norm. Part of the difficulty, of course, is that college and university expenditures vary greatly by level, or mission, especially as to the role to be played by research and graduate-level training, and by various practices and institutional outputs other than undergraduate instruction. Research universities, for example, tend to pay higher salaries and to require student-faculty ratios that can accommodate research expectations and lower course loads in addition to expensive libraries, laboratories, computational power, and other research-related expenditures. Thus, research universities would normally be expected to spend more per student or per faculty member than would two-year or bachelor's degree colleges.

A second source of institutional expenditure variation arises from the very great institutional variations in wealth—especially in endowments and continuing fund-raising productivity—in part reflecting the affluence of an institution's alumni—as well as its ability to set and annually increase tuition (which in turn is largely a function of the depth and relative affluence of the institution's applicant pool). This expenditure variation reflects Howard Bowen's famous revenue theory of cost, which postulates that colleges and universities raise as much revenue as they can and spend all that they raise—seemingly purposefully and for purposes appropriate to their mission.[11]

Still another source of variation in institutional expenditures is the inclusion in some reported expenditure data of amounts spent on activities such as hospitals, auxiliary enterprises (i.e., institutionally provided food and lodging), and sponsored research, all of which bring dedicated revenue that is not able to be reallocated to instruction or other purposes. Thus, any search for institutional comparisons or for normative expenditure data generally limits the expenditures that are reported to college and university accounting categories such as instruction, academic support, and student services, and omits such categories as hospitals, auxiliary enterprises, and sponsored research.

A more useful and at least somewhat comparable portrayal of American college and university expenditure data from the NCES *Digest of Education Statistics* would show expenditure categories that at least approximate the instructional costs per full-time equivalent student in the NCES reporting categories of instruction, academic support, and student services—omitting expenditure categories such as research, hospitals, auxiliary enterprises, and operation and maintenance of the physical plant, as shown in table 11.3 (bearing in mind that the NCES reporting category of four-year institution in both the public and the

*Table 11.3*    Selected institutional expenditures per student by institutional level and control, 2012–13 (in dollars)

| | Public 4-year | Public 2-year | Private non-profit 4-year | Private non-profit 2-year |
|---|---|---|---|---|
| Instruction | 9,398 | 4,500 | 16,111 | 6,371 |
| Academic support | 2,514 | 800 | 4,379 | 1,605 |
| Student services | 1,455 | 1,091 | 3,964 | 2,671 |
| Total | 13,367 | 6,391 | 24,454 | 10,547 |

*Source:* NCES, *Digest of Education Statistics 2013*, tables 334.10, 334.30, and 334.50.

private nonprofit sectors combines and averages data from small bachelor's degree-granting colleges and large comprehensive research universities).

## Revenues and the Sharing of Higher Educational Costs

Total revenues in support of America's higher educational enterprise, as reported by institutions and as compiled and reported by the NCES, were more than $500 billion in the latest reporting year (2011–12).[12] They would be well in excess of that amount by the middle of the second decade of the century in spite of serious cuts in state appropriations to public colleges and universities in the aftermath of the 2008 recession (much of which was recovered by increases in tuitions and by federal stimulus funds) and in spite of a considerable, if only temporary, decline in endowments and annual giving. However, revenues in any sort of national aggregate are difficult to report with any precision or interpretive value because of differences in institutional reporting and in the accounts themselves. For example, just as the reporting above on aggregate expenditures omitted such essentially "break even" categories of expenditures as auxiliary enterprises, hospitals, and sponsored research, the reporting of revenues from these categories of operation vary so greatly among institutions even in the same sectors that such data would add little understanding about the financial state of a single institution, much less US higher education in general.

Revenues in support of higher education come from:

- tuitions and mandatory fees (with the difference between what is called a tuition and what is called a mandatory fee quite immaterial to the family);
- payments for institutionally provided food, lodging;
- services such as parking or Internet provision that could have been—and in many colleges and universities are—privatized, or provided by private providers;
- state appropriations to public institutions of higher education (with counties and other local units of taxing authority providing some revenues to community colleges in some states);
- state student assistance (including both need- and merit-based aid);
- federal student assistance (including various grant and loan programs that are mainly need-based and fully portable);
- federal support directly to institutions and programs (principally serving low-income students or minority-serving institutions);

- federal support of research (mainly through universities, both public and private, and generally covering the indirect as well as the direct costs of research);
- returns on institutional investments (including both true endowments that are restricted as to use by donors as well as unrestricted funds from operating surpluses and unrestricted gifts that are invested along with endowment); and
- unrestricted gifts to college and university operations that are budgeted solicited, collected, and spent in a fiscal year.

An analytically useful perspective on higher educational revenue is to view the costs of higher education as being borne, or shared, by four principal parties: (1) *parents*, who finance portions of their children's higher educational expenses from current income, savings, or future income via borrowing (as in Federal Direct PLUS loans or home equity loans); (2) *students*, who finance their share from savings, summer earnings, term-time earnings, and future earnings via a variety of governmental and private loans; (3) *government, or taxpayers*, at the state level for the (partial) funding of public colleges and universities and some student financial assistance, and at the federal level for the student financial assistance and research; and (4) *donors, or philanthropists*, including individuals, corporations, and foundations financing certain higher education expenditures through either endowments or current giving.[13,14]

The sharing and shifting among these parties can be a zero-sum game in which a lessening of the burden upon, or revenue from, one party must be compensated either by a reduction of underlying college or university expenditures or through a shift of the burden to another party. Thus, if state taxpayers' share of higher education costs is to be lessened—or even fail to keep up with rising costs—that reduced share must either lead to reduced institutional expenditures or be shifted, probably to students and parents via higher tuition. But if parents cannot pay or have enough political power to limit, by statute or regulation, a higher expected parental contribution (as happened when voter pressure forced Congress to eliminate home equity from the assets considered in determining need for the purpose of awarding federal Pell grants), the burden would shift to students, principally through higher debt loads. This scenario—lower taxpayer contributions, reduced institutional budgets, higher tuitions, level parental contributions, and much higher debt burdens—is exactly what has happened throughout most of the last decades of the twentieth century and first decades of the twenty-first century.[15]

A number of policy questions regarding tuitions and financial assistance are sharpened by this cost-sharing perspective. For example, what is the appropriate amount that should be expected from parents to cover the higher educational costs of their children? Or, should undergraduate students in the United States, as in the Nordic countries, be considered financially independent (even if generally impecunious) young adults rather than as financially dependent children? Assuming that the expected parental contribution is to be maintained for both financial and equity reasons, is this share to be a function only of current income, to be met by family belt tightening? Or are parents also expected to have saved from the past or to borrow against the future? Are family assets to be figured in the calculation of need? How long should parental financial responsibility continue—that is, through undergraduate years only, or until the age of, say, twenty-four or twenty-five? And what is the expected contribution from a noncustodial parent? These are important questions that must be answered in the myriad laws and regulations underlying the federal and state financial assistance programs. But their complexity belies the notion that federal financial assistance is vastly complex and needs only to be simplified to be fixed.

## TUITION AND MANDATORY FEES

Tuition and mandatory fees in America are high, especially in elite, or highly selective, private nonprofit colleges and universities. Tuitions are also high in public research universities, especially compared to what they were before the turn of the last century and compared to tuition fees in almost all other highly industrialized nations.[16] But what has attracted attention and controversy in both the public and private sectors has not been actual tuitions—even for those at the top of the range—but the yearly increases in tuitions, and especially the fact that these increases have in most years and for most institutions, both public and private, so substantially exceeded the prevailing rates of inflation, and in recent years exceeded the average annual increases in household incomes. For example, average tuitions and mandatory fees for all private, nonprofit, four-year institutions (which does not reveal the great range within this category) in 2014–15 was $31,231—up from 2004–05 by almost 24 percent in inflation-adjusted dollars. Public-sector tuitions have risen even faster: the average four-year public institution—which, like the average four-year private institution, includes a great range of tuitions and tuition increases—rose from an inflation-adjusted $6,448 in 2004–05 to $9,139 in 2014–15 for a ten-year inflation-adjusted increase of some 41.7 percent.[17]

Tuitions at private institutions are set by governing boards (in the case of non-profit institutions and by owners in the case of for-profit institutions) on the basis of market demand within a particular institution's market niche and marketing strategy. For example, most colleges want to be priced close to their competitor's prices: higher tuition could lose them price-conscious families and students; tuitions set too low might suggest either low quality or some reason for losing market share.

A deep and affluent applicant pool not only invites higher tuition, but allows more tuition discounting in order to enroll a more desirable class—whether the desirability sought is academic brilliance, diversity, athletic ability, or some other special talent. A consequence of the great variations in institutional wealth, reputation, and depth of applicant pools is a great variation in private-sector tuitions. According to the College Board, the median tuition for private, nonprofit colleges and universities in 2014–15 was $32,340. But nearly 17 percent charged tuitions in excess of $45,000 (before any discounting) and more than 10 percent were able (or forced by the market) to charge less than $12,000.[18]

Public-sector tuitions have also become greatly differentiated as they have been increased in recent decades throughout the fifty states. Public-sector tuition has generally been higher in the Northeast—presumably because of the prevalence (or even dominance) of private colleges and universities and a consequently high tuition expectation among families and politicians alike. The highest public university tuitions are in New Hampshire and Vermont. The median public four-year college tuition in 2014–15 was $9,390 a year. But 17 percent of all students in public four-year colleges and universities are in institutions that charge tuitions of $15,000 or higher.[19] In short, it is no longer necessarily the case, as it was in the 1970s and 80s, that most public four-year colleges and universities are accessible to students from very low-income families as long as they apply for all of the available need-based grants, work part-time during college terms, save something in the summer, and are willing to assume some manageable debt.

Tuitions, mandatory fees, and room and board charges for 2014–15 are shown in table 11.4 by public and private, nonprofit, two- and four-year institutions and for two-year for-profit colleges. Average institutionally posted room and board charges are also shown, providing average total charges for these sectors in 2014–15. The actual student and family-borne expenses, of course, may be considerably higher than these charges when costs of transportation, clothing, entertainment, and incidentals are added. However, these additional expenses are exceedingly variable and may be more appropriately considered costs of living than the expenses of being a student (even though the student and his or her family may see little difference in the distinction). Even within the average total charges by sector, as in table 11.4, there is great variation, especially in tuition and fees within the four-year institutions as among the so-called Carnegie classifications of doctoral, master's, and bachelor's degree-granting institutions. These variations are shown in table 11.5.

*Table 11.4*    Tuition, fees, and room and board average published charges 2014–15 (in dollars)

|  | Public 4-year in state | Public 2-year | Public 4-year out-of-state | Private nonprofit 4-year | Private for-profit |
|---|---|---|---|---|---|
| Tuition and fees 2014–15 | 9,139 | 3,347 | 22,958 | 31,231 | 15,230 |
| Room and board | 9,804 | 7,705 | 9,804 | 11,188 | - |
| Total charges | 18,943 | 11,052 | 32,762 | 42,419 | - |

*Source:* College Board, *Trends in College Pricing 2014*, table 1b, 11.

*Table 11.5*    Tuition, fees, and room and board charges: Four-year doctoral, master's, and bachelor's institutions

|  | Public | | | Private Nonprofit | | |
|---|---|---|---|---|---|---|
|  | Doctoral | Master's | Bachelor's | Doctoral | Master's | Bachelor's |
| Tuition & fees | $10,075 | $7,968 | $7,142 | $39,008 | $27,594 | $29,404 |
| % increase from 2013–14 | 2.8% | 2.9% | 3.6% | 4.2% | 3.4% | 3.4% |
| Room & board | $10,208 | $9,109 | $9,472 | $12,979 | $10,824 | $10,165 |
| % increase from 2013–14 | 3.3% | 3.3% | 3.3% | 3.0% | 3.4% | 3.6% |
| Total institutional charges | $20,283 | $17,077 | $16,614 | $51,987 | $38,418 | $39,569 |
| % increase from 2013–14 | 3.0% | 3.0% | 3.4% | 3.9% | 3.4% | 3.4% |

*Source:* College Board, *Trends in College Pricing 2014*, table 1b, p. 11.

## STATE APPROPRIATIONS

State appropriations to public colleges and universities have been declining for years, especially those amounts for annual operations (i.e., excluding capital and special appropriations) and controlling for increasing enrollments and inflation. The College Board reported that state appropriations to public institutions of higher education declined by 16 percent in constant 2012–13 dollars from 2007–08 to 2012–13: from $90.5 billion to $76.2 billion. Much of this was due to the 2008 Great Recession, which devastated state revenues. Although some of this loss was recovered through short-term federal stimulus funds, there were many competing calls for these federal funds—and state governments, unlike the federal government, cannot make up for a sudden loss in revenue through borrowing. However, as devastating as the recession may have been on state higher education appropriations, the decline in support in most states—particularly the failure of appropriations to keep pace with higher education's inflation index—had been going on for decades, and continues as this chapter is being written in 2015.

State appropriations to programs of financial assistance have also been declining, along with appropriations to state institutions. Also significant to the issue of static or even declining accessibility has been the shifting in many states of what may have been predominately need-based aid to forms of merit assistance. The inclusion of merit as a criterion in the disposition of state grants is politically popular, although most analysts believe that it does little to alter student behavior (other than instilling some pride) and may take away from the forms of student assistance that recognize financial need and are more likely to make a difference in accessibility, completion, and choice of college to attend.

State government is still an important, albeit proportionately declining, source of revenue for public colleges and universities in the early decades of the twenty-first century. However, some public research universities, in the face of this declining state tax support and their increasing reliance on tuition, federal research overhead, and philanthropy to make up for the declining state support, have claimed (partly for rhetorical effect) to be no longer state supported, or even state aided, but reduced to the status of merely state located. A few have even considered asking the state to set them entirely free to be a private corporation (nonprofit), requiring no further annual appropriations—but for the state to hand over to the new corporation the physical plant, equipment, land, and other assets of the university, as well as the authority to establish (that is, to raise) tuitions and to execute contracts like any other private nonprofit university.

The supposed attraction to the state, especially to some fiscally conservative politicians, is the possibility of further privatization and reduced high educational appropriations (which, in spite of some disinvestment still consume considerable portions of most state operating budgets). The attraction to a few state university leaders—particularly leaders of elite public research universities with very robust and generally affluent applicant pools, including many international and nonresident applicants—is the possibility of charging and annually increasing tuition fees to levels comparable to elite private universities—in addition to being rid of all of the other restrictions and politics that accompany state status. Encouraging this wish for greater independence from state and public system authority is the view that the state support has already dwindled and that the prospect of getting back on the track of state appropriations increasing annually at least at the rate of higher education's underlying rate of inflation is, at least at the time this chapter is being written in 2015, increasingly dim.

However, the numbers of state colleges and universities with sufficiently deep and affluent applicant pools to match their elite private counterpart tuitions is small. Furthermore, given the increasing political and civic opposition to high tuitions, the accompanying rise in concern over unmanageable student debt loads, and the pressure for greater socioeconomic inclusiveness even at highly selective public colleges and universities, those politicians favorable to the privatization of public universities in theory may be reluctant to convert their universities to private corporations. In addition, although the elite public universities have greatly increased their philanthropic successes in recent decades, replacing annual state appropriations, in addition to matching private tuition fees, would require significantly enlarging their fund raising—which they have been working at for years, but which probably cannot be significantly enhanced if potential donors believe that their contributions are going not to enhance their university but to facilitate even further state budget cuts. Even so, it will be difficult to match the annual and capital fund raising records of the elite private universities. (In 2013, the average fund-raising totals of the ten most successful universities—all of them elite private universities—was $586 million.[20])

Finally, even with the admittedly declining annual appropriations to public higher education in most states, state support continues to constitute an important—however dwindling—source of unrestricted revenue. Instituting very large increases in tuition and aiming for similarly large increases in annual giving—even if the privatization were to be granted—may be unlikely to replace fully these unrestricted state funds. And public research universities that point to a very small and declining portion of total revenue coming from the state some-times arrive at that ratio because of a very large volume of non-state revenue from hospital and sponsored research that is neither fungible nor assured into the future. At the same time, many public research universities, along with some public comprehensive colleges that have similarly deep and generally affluent ap-plicant pools, are likely to continue to view higher tuitions and greater autonomy from both the state and the public multicampus system as solutions to the deep-ening austerity brought on by continuing state budget cuts.

## Solutions on the Cost Side

If the climate of austerity that continues to pervade much of US higher educa-tion cannot be solved entirely on the revenue side by ever higher tuitions and waiting for the return of generous state appropriations, colleges and universities, both public and private, will continue to search for solutions on the cost side by increasing the efficiency and productivity of the enterprise. The concepts of effi-ciency and productivity look at both costs, or expenditures, and at benefits, or outputs. These concepts deal with costs *per*, whether per student (which, of course, is not really an output, but which has the advantage of being easily and unam-biguously measured), or per unit of research (which is difficult to specify or mea-sure), or per unit of learning (also difficult to measure), or per unit of learning added by the institution. Because the real outputs of the university—the discov-ery, transmission, and promulgation of knowledge—are both multiple and dif-ficult to measure, and because revenue, at least for the support of instructional expenditures, generally tracks student enrollment in both the public and the pri-vate sectors, the expenditure per student inevitably dominates approaches to questions of productivity and efficiency. But we ought never to forget that enrollment—however measured and however sensitive to fields of study, levels of higher education, or methods of instruction—is still merely a proxy for the hard-to-measure real output, which is student learning.

### Variation in Unit Costs

In the production of goods, there are usually multiple ways of combining pro-ductive inputs—mainly different combinations of labor, capital, materials, and managerial effectiveness—to produce a unit of output. The most efficient combi-nation of inputs is determined by the alternative manufacturing technologies and the relative costs of the inputs. Given a set of input costs and a set of tech-nologies for combining inputs into desired outputs, there generally is an unambiguously most efficient way: that is, a lowest cost per unit. The efficiency, then, of any alternative producer or production process can be measured by how that producer or that process compares to that most efficient way.

Higher education is not as fortunate as these goods-producing enterprises. The technology of a university, whether it is producing student learning or scholarly research, is unclear and highly idiosyncratic to the institution, the course, and the individual professor. We know that per-student costs vary greatly. For example, higher education is generally assumed to be more costly at research universities than at undergraduate colleges due to the higher salaries, lower teaching loads, and more extensive academic support (e.g., libraries and computer facilities) accorded the faculty of the research university. However, the direct instructional costs (especially at the margin) at least of freshmen and sophomores at a typical public research university can be rather low due to the prevalence of low-cost teaching assistants and very large lecture courses—in contrast to the typical public four-year college, where most instruction will be carried out by regular faculty in moderate-sized classes, albeit with heavier average teaching loads. In the end, it is probably appropriate to assert that per-student costs even for undergraduates are higher at most research universities than at most four-year colleges. But it must not be forgotten that this is so at least partly because of certain assumptions and cost allocations that, while reasonable, are nonetheless at least in part because things have always been done that way, and may sometimes be questionable.

Among like institutions, most interinstitutional variation in per-student costs can be attributed to differences either in the amenities provided to the students (recreational and cultural facilities, for example, or academic and student services support staff) or in the costs of faculty. Differential faculty costs, in turn, reflect differences not only in salaries—which are low for part-time faculty, who provide much of the teaching at low-cost colleges, and high for the full-time senior professoriate at prestigious private universities and colleges—but also in that other major faculty expense, which is time—which translates into light teaching loads at wealthy colleges and heavy teaching loads at low-cost "access" colleges.

Howard Bowen, in his classic 1980 study of higher education costs, found great variation in costs among seemingly similar institutions with seemingly similar outcomes. Among a sample of research and doctoral-granting universities arranged from lowest to highest in per-student expenditures, the average university in the third quartile spent twice as much per student as the average in the second quartile, and the highest-spending university in the sample spent almost seven and one-half times as much as the first quartile average. Variation among colleges was less, but the colleges in the third quartile of per student costs still spent about 50 percent more than the colleges in the second quartile.[21] While Bowen's data are old, these cost disparities have continued and probably accelerated, as shown in table 11.3.

But even if the definition and measure of cost that we use to calculate undergraduate productivity at Harvard were the same as what we might use at, say, neighboring Wheelock College or at UMass, Boston, we still cannot say unambiguously that Wheelock and UMass, Boston, are more efficient or more productive than Harvard. They may be less expensive per student, to be sure, but whether they are more efficient requires a measure of output that we do not have and that we probably could not agree upon. And if Harvard were to contest its possible characterization as inefficient or unproductive, it would probably point to the extraordinary knowledge and competence of its graduates, or to the lifetime of added benefits that Harvard presumably helped to produce, or the value to society (uncaptured by private lifetime income streams) that Harvard at least in part produced.

In short, without better agreement on the proper outputs of higher education, not to mention how to weight and how to measure them, we are left with cost per student (or full-time equivalent student) as best as we can measure it, as the dominant metric of higher educational productivity—and as a measure that should presumably get lower (or cheaper) in response to the demands of students, parents, and taxpayers that higher education become less costly.

### Inflation in Unit Costs

The problem of unit costs and efficiency (or inefficiency) in higher education is less a function of high unit costs per se and more a function of the seemingly inexorable increase of such costs—and of the resulting tuition increases—at rates considerably in excess of the prevailing rates of inflation. This is the "cost disease" described by William Baumol and William Bowen as characteristic of the so-called productivity-immune sectors of the economy, which are generally labor intensive, with few opportunities for the substitution of capital or of new production technologies for labor. (Among such sectors, for example, would be live theater, symphony orchestras, social welfare agencies, and education.[22]) Unit costs in such sectors generally track their increases in compensation. Because workers in such enterprises (e.g., faculty) typically get the same wage and salary increases as those in the productivity-sensitive, goods-producing sectors of the economy, in which constant infusions of capital and technology produce real productivity gains and allow unit cost increases to be less than compensation increases, the unit costs in the productivity-resistant sectors will inevitably exceed those in goods-producing sectors. Thus, unit-cost increases in higher education will be "above average." And since the rate of inflation is nothing more than a weighted average of many price increases, it is inevitable that unit costs—and thus tuition—in higher education will rise in normal years faster than the rate of inflation.

This phenomenon of rising relative costs and prices has been thought by many economists and higher education policy analysts to be the normal, or default, condition in higher education: unit costs that essentially track increases in overall compensation, which in most years increases at a rate slightly in excess of the prevailing rate of inflation. Tuitions, however, tend to increase at even higher rates, often substantially exceeding the prevailing rates of inflation—and even exceeding the rates of growth in median family incomes. This extra boost in can be attributed to:

- State governments that continue year after year to shift the cost burden from taxpayers to students and families through lower appropriations and higher tuitions;
- More technology, more course and program opportunities, more costly physical plants, and more amenities that are thought to be essential in order to differentiate a particular college from less costly public or private competitors and that by some measures may lead to a better— but virtually never a cheaper—education;
- Private colleges that year after year have to put more of their marginal tuition dollars back into student aid or tuition discounts, thus requiring even larger tuition increases to keep up with rising costs;
- Compensation increases for faculty and administrative staff that do not merely track compensations increases in the larger economy, but occasionally exceed them;
- For the most selective and sought-after colleges and universities, both private and public, the opportunity to raise prices in a highly supply-constrained market that exhibits considerable price inelasticity (see endnote 3).

Thus, the natural trajectory of unit costs in higher education, as described above, is inexorably upward, usually at rates in excess of prevailing rates of inflation. The corresponding rate of increase of anticipated revenues is substantially flatter, if not downward, being dampened in the public sector by the aforementioned cuts in state appropriations and in the private sector by a growing price resistance from middle and upper-middle income parents—manifested by a shift in demand to increasingly selective public universities as well as by aggressive bargain hunting for more affordable, if still private, alternatives—and in a flattening of federal research dollars and lower returns on most invested funds. The net overall effect is one of diverging trajectories of costs and revenues: costs continuing to rise even as most institutions of higher education have been cutting operating costs and deferring maintenance, and as most traditional sources of revenue fail to keep pace.

All of these factors have been at work for most of the past several decades. The result has been a thirty-year (1984–85 to 2014) average published tuition increase at private nonprofit four-year colleges and universities of some 146 percent in constant, or inflation-adjusted, dollars. Over the same period, tuitions at four-year public institutions rose in inflation-adjusted dollars by some 225 percent (of course from a much lower base). And although public two-year colleges remain the most affordable alternative, similar factors have worked to increase their average inflation-adjusted tuitions over this thirty-year period by some 150 percent.[23]

## High Tuition–High Aid

For many years, proposals have been made that direct state funding of public colleges and universities, at least for the support of instruction, be drastically reduced or eliminated altogether, with public-sector tuitions raised to full or near full cost and eliminating or greatly reducing what the proponents of this view call the subsidy to the students and families of students attending public colleges and universities. In place of direct state revenue, which currently supports anywhere from 50 to 90 percent of public four-year undergraduate instructional costs, proponents of the high tuition–high aid model would substitute a much expanded program of need-based grants that would diminish as parental or student incomes rose. The grants would phase out entirely for families and students whose income was deemed sufficient to pay the full cost of tuition in addition to other expenses.[24]

The high tuition–high aid model is based on claims of efficiency and equity. The efficiency claim begins with the tenet of public finance theory that any public subsidy of a good or a service that consumers are likely to purchase anyway in the absence or diminution of the subsidy is an inefficient use of public tax dollars. The tax dollars released, if public-sector tuitions were allowed to rise (or forced to be raised) would supposedly go toward public needs of greater priority: more need-based student aid, health care, public infrastructure, tax cuts, or public deficit reduction. And if the demand for public higher education should decline as a result of lower subsidies and higher prices, this too might be a move in the direction of a more efficient use of the nation's resources. Subsidies can generate overproduction of a good or service, and higher priced public higher education might discourage ambivalent, ill-prepared students whom some advocates of high tuition and high aid assume are taking up space and wasting precious resources in our public colleges and universities.

A corollary of the efficiency claim is that there exists, at least in some states, underutilized capacity in the private higher education sector that could be filled at relatively low marginal cost. A shift of tax dollars from the direct support of public colleges and universities to need-based student aid, portable to the private sector, would presumably shift enrollments there and enable the socially optimal level of enrollments to be supported more in the private sector, but at a lower additional net cost to the taxpayer.

The equity argument in favor of high tuition–high aid is based on two assumptions: first, that public higher education is actually partaken of disproportionately by students from middle, upper-middle, and high income families; and second, that the state taxes used to support public higher education tend to be proportionate or even regressive and thus are paid by many lower-middle income and poor families who are unlikely to benefit. Thus, the high tuition–high aid model of public higher education finance is claimed to be more equitable than across-the-board low tuition because it targets all public subsidy only on the needy and imposes full costs on students or families affluent enough to pay.

The case against the high tuition–high aid model rests partly on the oversimplification and political naïveté of the case made on its behalf, summarized above, and partly on the case to be made for the very existence of a public higher education sector. The case against high tuition, high aid may be summarized by four points.[25]

First, a tuition that would recover the full cost of instruction would lead to a full cost of attendance of $40,000 to $50,000 or more for a full-time year at a public college or university—even with the prospect of generous financial aid or a lower tuition for those in need. This would almost certainly discourage many from even aspiring to higher education. The total costs to students and parents of a year of full-time study at a public four-year college or university, as shown in table 11.4, make many public colleges and universities even today a relatively heavy financial burden for most families and for nearly all independent students. This fact alone does not fully negate the more theoretical arguments of efficiency and equity presented on behalf of full-cost or near-full-cost pricing for public higher education, as summarized above. But even with financial aid, costs at a public college are daunting to many students and their parents, especially to students from low-income or otherwise disadvantaged families.

Second, a high tuition–high aid policy would lessen the quality of public colleges and universities. The purpose of high tuition–high aid plans is to reduce state tax revenues currently going to public colleges and universities, even though some proponents claim that this revenue loss would be made up by increased revenue from the much higher tuitions paid by the more well-to-do. Private-sector proponents of high tuition–high aid, however, make no secret of their aim to shift enrollments and tuition dollars of middle and upper-middle income students (or at least the most attractive and able ones) from the public sector to the private sector. With little or no price advantage left in the public sector; with the resource advantage of large endowments, wealthy alumni, and the tradition of philanthropic support in the private sector; with the patina of elitism and selectivity associated with private colleges and universities (especially in the Northeast); and with greater constraints and burdens remaining on the public sector, many of the nation's nearly seven hundred public four-year colleges and universities would become places for students whom the private colleges, now priced the same as public colleges, would not accept. Such erosion in the relative status and quality of public colleges and universities does not seem to be in the nation's public interest.

A third element in the case against high tuition–high aid is that high tuition in of itself does not guarantee high aid. Governors, legislators, and voters, continually pressed by public needs exceeding available resources, are likely to support that part of the public sector in which they perceive that they or their children have a stake. They are much less likely to maintain the financial aid, or tuition discount, portion of the public higher educational budget when it is devoted almost exclusively to the poor. The not-unlikely consequences of a policy of high tuition–high aid, rather than the purported enhancements of efficiency and equity, are higher tuition, lower taxes, inadequate aid, diminished access, and deteriorating public colleges and universities.

Fourth and fundamentally, the high tuition–high aid model is a denial of the appropriateness of higher education as a public good. The nation's public colleges and universities have been built and supported over the last century and a half not merely to provide a subsidized education to those who might not otherwise have an opportunity for higher education. Rather, voters and elected officials wanted public colleges and universities that would attract and hold the best and brightest students and scholars, serve society, aid the economy, and be a signal of the state's culture. The high tuition–high aid model essentially denies most of these public purposes to public higher education and substitutes only a public subsidy for those who are too poor to afford what would become an otherwise unsubsidized, expensive, and essentially privatized product. States need to consider whether these continue to be important reasons for supporting public higher education or whether they mainly want to get needy students into some college, in which case high tuition–high aid is almost certainly, as public finance theory correctly states, less expensive to the taxpayer.

## Summary and Conclusions

The financial fortunes of American colleges and universities vary greatly by institutional characteristics. Those relatively few private institutions with large endowments, traditions of generous alumni giving, top scholarly reputations (especially in such fields as biomedical sciences), and deep applicant pools of desirable students will continue to do well. They will experience the pressures of rising costs—especially for administrative and academic computing, faculty and staff compensation and benefits, the rising costs of libraries and scientific equipment, and the need for scholarship funds critical to attracting, enrolling, and maintaining students with the desired attributes. And they will remain vulnerable to adverse demographics and to occasional downturns in the national economy that may diminish endowments and charitable giving. But they will continue to do well financially.

Public institutions that are similarly situated with deep and affluent applicant pools, with established traditions of philanthropic support, and with research strengths in areas of continuing public investment (e.g., biomedical and applied sciences) may suffer temporary state revenue cutbacks, but will continue to prosper and may gain some market share from the troubles of the less financially fortunate institutions.

Some of the less selective and less endowed private institutions, particularly in small towns or rural areas, may be able to find a specialized market niche, either vocational (e.g., health-related professions) or cultural/ideological (e.g., conservative Christian) and with good management and low faculty costs may also prosper. Many private nonprofit colleges and universities, however, will experience a fierce revenue squeeze, primarily driven by demographics: that is, a lack of growth in the number of upper-middle-class parents able or willing to pay high tuitions and in the number of students willing to take on increasing levels of debt. They will experience most of the unavoidable cost pressures of their more well-known and better endowed counterparts, but will also experience the added cost pressure (or revenue losses) of the deep discounts required to enroll and maintain a class. Some will alter their historic missions and characters altogether: as in changing from a residential Roman Catholic liberal arts college for women to a co-educational college featuring professional training with large numbers of commuters and part-time adult students. Some will experiment with online education—although they will find that new entrants with investment capital and without all the costly baggage of a failing traditional college can probably do that better. And a few will explore mergers—but most that do will come to realize that most financially successful mergers are actually takeovers and that a merger of two financially faltering colleges—each trying to preserve as much of its history, mission, and staff as possible—will be unable to shed enough costly staff and outmoded programs to attract the new students it needs.

Most public colleges and less research-intensive universities will continue to experience flat or declining state tax support, forcing higher tuitions, more program closures, and an increasing reliance on part-time and adjunct faculty. Some will attract students who might formerly have chosen a more expensive private college. Some will try to stem declining enrollments with aggressive out-of-state and international recruiting. Many will add advanced professional programs. All will adopt new measures to enhance persistence and completion. And more than a few will close programs and shed staff—even reaching into tenured ranks.

As more and more colleges and universities reach a ceiling on enhancing non-state revenue through ever-higher tuition fees and enhanced fund raising, and as they exhaust the obvious cost-side measures for increasing productivity such as cutting staff and closing under-enrolled programs, interest may turn more seriously than it has in the past to increasing higher educational productivity on the learning side. Expressed another way, the major remaining productivity problem in higher education may lie less in excessive cost than in insufficient output—that is, insufficient learning. This could be a function of redundant learning; aimless academic exploration; excessive nonlearning time in the academic day, week, and year; insufficient use of self-paced learning; and insufficient realization of the potential of college-level learning in high school. Enhancing the productivity of learning, then, would reduce vacation time and other time spent in other-than-learning activities; provide better advising and incentives to lessen aimless curricular exploration; enhance opportunities for self-paced learning (especially e-learning); minimize curricular redundancy; and maximize the potential of college-level learning during the high school years.[26]

Technology, particularly the Internet, e-mail, super computers, and cloud data storage has already profoundly affected the way research university faculty and advanced students conduct, collaborate in, and communicate research. In a more uneven but still profound way, advances in instructional technology such as the electronic conveyance of readings and lectures, massive open online courses (MOOCs), the so-called tipped classroom, combining online lectures with regular seated classes, and other forms of e-learning will enrich teaching and learning in virtually all colleges and universities, but in more financially secure institutions will generally lead to better—but no less costly—student learning. However, such technologies may profoundly alter instructional methodology in learning venues such as proprietary institutions, professional certification and recertification programs in all colleges and universities, and in the less selective private nonprofit institutions that will be under the greatest pressure to slash costs and find new, nontraditional market niches.

The shift in cost burden from taxpayers to students will lead to even more students having to seek part-time (and even full-time) employment and incurring more debt—which will stymie efforts to shorten the time to degree. Students and families will more aggressively shop for lower cost collegiate options, pushing back on tuition increases in both private and public sectors, but also encouraging such expense-saving arrangements as taking the first two years of a bachelor's degree at a less expensive community college, and electing combined bachelor's and advanced professional programs to shorten the total time (and the debt) required for advanced professional degrees in fields such as law, education, management, and medicine. Marketing will become even more frenzied.

State and federal politicians, including US presidents and state governors, will continue to make well-publicized efforts to solve the problem—generally meaning somehow fixing the problems of high tuitions, excessive college and university costs, prolonged time to degrees, and/or insufficient graduate job readiness. The federal government, lacking constitutional authority over education, including public colleges and universities, lacks the necessary authority to alter the underlying instructional paradigms even of public—much less of private—higher education. So there will mainly be more federal studies, national commissions, and Congressional exhortations to reduce expenditures, lower tuitions, and produce more job-ready graduates.

But the federal government does have considerable leverage over higher education, public and private, through its ownership and funding of federal financial assistance programs. Federal efforts to rein in certain practices, mainly at proprietary and community colleges that lead to excessive borrowing and student loan defaults, have proven to be politically controversial, but remain very much on the table in the second decade of the century. Efforts to expand the income-contingent and other income-based repayment options in an effort to increase the manageability of student debts will also continue, as will efforts to simplify and consolidate the myriad of student aid and loan programs.

State solutions such as tuition prepayment and tax-exempt savings plans as well as various merit aid programs that have been around since the turn of the century, while still politically popular, have generally failed either to alter institutional practices or to increase student access or retention—and have sometimes proven excessively costly. Most state higher education budgets will be flat or smaller, but this reduction will be accompanied in most states by greater flexibility together with performance criteria and incentives, such as premiums to institutions that improve retention and completion rates.

Most institutions have been shaping their missions for years to adjust to more low-income, minority, older, part-time, and place-bound students. Many have been moving in the direction of more applied and vocational programs as well as trimming or eliminating those that are not excellent, popular, or central to the institution's mission. In short, much of the vaunted restructuring that management consultants and observers of higher education have been calling for as a solution to the continuing financial austerity of US higher education may not be a solution to the remaining financial problems—for the simple reason that it has been going on for years. Most of the smaller and comprehensive colleges have reallocated resources and altered their programs and faculty profiles dramatically; many have changed mission altogether. Some small, nonselective, nonendowed private colleges may close their doors; most will continue to reduce costs and seek new markets.

Also in some financial jeopardy may be those universities, both public and private, largely regional, and with minimal or uneven scholarly reputations, that continue to pursue the research university model but are unlikely to penetrate the top ranks, measured by the scholarly prestige of their faculty or their graduate programs. Here, pressures to control costs are likely to focus on an increasing separation of funding for instruction and research, much as has occurred in the United Kingdom. If these measures are successful, the result could be less indirect public subsidization of faculty scholarship, a widening difference in faculty workloads, and a reduced administration overhead on federal research grants.

As to the widely touted goal of expanding higher educational accessibility and opportunity, and although the United States probably does more than any other nation to provide postsecondary opportunities to those from low socioeconomic backgrounds, the larger American society, at least as this chapter is being written in 2015, is becoming not only more unequal, but less willing and less able, at either the state or the federal levels, to craft politically acceptable governmental solutions to higher education's financial problems. America's colleges and universities will thus continue, as they have been, to seek new markets, students, and revenues and to trim costs where they can. And financial austerity and attempts to reconcile institutional financial viability and student affordability will continue to be a dominant theme for policy at both institutional and governmental levels.

## NOTES

1. An early and influential report on higher education's austerity was Earl Cheit's *The New Depression in Higher Education: A Study of Financial Conditions at 41 Colleges and Universities* (Hightstown, NJ: McGraw-Hill, 1971), one of the first reports of the Carnegie Commission on Higher Education. The higher education literature is full of reports on college and university austerity, including, for example, David W. Breneman, *Liberal Arts Colleges: Thriving, Surviving, or Endangered?* (Washington, DC: The Brookings Institution, 1994); D. Bruce Johnstone, "Those 'Out of Control' Costs," in *In Defense of the American Public University*, ed. Philip G. Altbach, D. Bruce Johnstone, and Patricia J. Gumport (Baltimore: Johns Hopkins University Press, 2001); and William Zumeta, David W. Breneman, Patrick M. Callan, and Joni E. Finney, *Financing American Higher Education in an Era of Globalization* (Cambridge, MA: Harvard University Press, 2012).

2. D. Bruce Johnstone, "Public Universities in an Era of Continuing Austerity: More of the Same or Profound Change?" *Faculty Senate Bulletin: A Publication of the State University of New York University Faculty Senate* (Fall/Winter, 2013–14): 11–14, http://www.gse.buffalo.edu/org/IntHigherEdFinance.

3. Economists employ the term "price elasticity" to refer to the increase or decrease in total demand and net revenue in response to an increase or decrease in the price of a commodity. Thus, oranges in the market may be quite price elastic, referring to demand being quite responsive to changes in the price, while milk or bread may be said to be generally price inelastic. In the example in the text, public higher education at a relatively modest tuition is thought to be generally price inelastic to most students and

families—meaning little or no enrollment decline in response to an increase in tuition— although low-income (or ambivalent) students may exhibit tuition price elasticity and fail to enroll or drop put because of a tuition increase.

4. D. Bruce Johnstone, "The Impact of the 2008 Great Recession on College and University Contributions to State and Regional Economic Growth," in *Colleges and Universities as Economic Drivers*, ed. Jason E. Lane and D. Bruce Johnstone (Albany: SUNY Press, 2012).

5. National Center for Education Statistics (NCES), *Digest of Education Statistics*, table 317.10, http://nces.ed.gov/programs/digest/current_tables.asp [accessed Feb. 2015].

6. US Census Bureau, "College Enrollment Declines," http://www.census.gov/news room/press-releases/2014/cb14-177.html [accessed Feb. 2015].

7. National Center for Education Statistics (NCES), *Digest of Education Statistics*, table 223, http://nces.ed.gov/pubs2014/2014015_3.pdf [accessed October 2015].

8. National Center for Education Statistics (NCES), *Digest of Education Statistics*, table 603.30, http://nces.ed.gov/programs/digest/d13/tables/dt13_603.30.asp [accessed October 2015].

9. William J. Hussar and Tabitha M. Bailey, *Projections of Education Statistics to 2022* (Washington, DC: NCES, February, 2014), 19, http://nces.ed.gov/pubs2014/2014051.pdf [accessed Feb. 2015].

10. NCES "Fast Facts: Postsecondary Enrollments," https://nces.ed.gov/fastfacts /display.asp?id=75 [accessed Feb. 2015].

11. Howard R. Bowen, *The Costs of Higher Education: How Much Do Colleges and Universities Spend Per Student, and How Much Should They Spend?* (San Francisco: Jossey-Bass, 1980).

12. NCES, "Postsecondary Revenues by Source," *Conditions of Education*, http://nces .ed.gov/programs/coe/indicator_cud.asp [accessed Feb. 2015].

13. Some consider business a possible fifth party to bear a share of the costs. However, grants from businesses to higher education are better viewed as either (1) the purchase of a service, in which case the grant should cover the full costs of the added service but would not be expected to bear a share of core instructional costs; (2) a voluntary contribution coming out of owner or stockholder profits, in which case it would fall under "philanthropy"; or (3) a contribution considered part of the cost of doing business to be included in the price of the products and paid for by the general consumer, like a sales or consumption tax—in which case the incidence, or burden, is much like that of other taxes and may be included, at least conceptually, with the "taxpayer" party.

14. For the theory of cost-sharing, which has been used mainly in a comparative examination of higher education costs, see, D. Bruce Johnstone and Pamela Marcucci, *Financing Higher Education Worldwide: Who Pays? Who Should Pay?* (Baltimore: Johns Hopkins University Press, 2010); D. Bruce Johnstone, *Sharing the Costs of Higher Education: Student Financial Assistance in the United Kingdom, the Federal Republic of Germany, France, Sweden, and the United States* (New York: College Entrance Examination Board, 1986); and D. Bruce Johnstone, "The Economics and Politics of Cost Sharing in Higher Education: Comparative Perspectives," *Economics of Education Review* 20, no. 4 (2004): 403–10.

15. Ronald G. Ehrenberg, ed., *What's Happening to Public Higher Education? The Shifting Financial Burden* (Baltimore: Johns Hopkins University Press, 2006); Katherine Lyall and Kathleen R. Sell, *The True Genius of America at Risk: Are We Losing Our Public Universities to De Facto Privatization?* ACE-Praeger Series on Higher Education (Westport, CT: Praeger, 2006).

16. Tuition in publically financed universities in England as of 2014 was comparable to, or higher than, tuitions in top US public research universities. Tuitions in Japanese and some Canadian provincial universities are also roughly comparable. But universities in the Nordic countries remain free, and most of the rest of Europe features public university tuitions that Americans would consider only nominal. See Johnstone and Marcucci, *Financing Higher Education Worldwide*.

17. College Board, *Trends in College Pricing 2014*, 17, table 2A, https://secure-media .collegeboard.org/digitalServices/misc/trends/2014-trends-college-pricing-report-final .pdf [accessed Mar. 2015].

18. College Board, figure 2, *Trends in College Pricing 2014*, 13.

19. College Board, figure 3, *Trends in College Pricing 2014*, 14.

20. Don Troop, "Gifts to College Reached $333.8 Billion in 2013, Topping Pre-Recession Levels," *Chronicle of Higher Education* (Feb. 21, 2014): A10.

21. Howard R. Bowen, *The Costs of Higher Education*, 116–19.

22. William J. Baumol and William G. Bowen, *Performing Arts: The Economic Dilemma* (New York: Twentieth Century Fund, 1966); also, William G. Bowen, *The Economics of the Major Private Universities* (Berkeley, CA: Carnegie Commission on the Future of Higher Education, 1968).

23. College Board, *Trends in College Pricing 2014*, 16.

24. The case for high tuition–high aid was popularized in W. Lee Hansen and Burton A. Weisbrod, *Benefits, Costs, and Finance of Public Higher Education* (Chicago: Markham, 1969). See also Carnegie Commission on Higher Education, *Higher Education: Who Pays? Who Benefits? Who Should Pay?* (New York: McGraw-Hill, 1973); Frederick J. Fischer, "State Financing of Higher Education: A New Look at an Old Problem," *Change* (Jan./Feb., 1990).

25. D. Bruce Johnstone, *The High-Tuition–High-Aid Model of Public Higher Education Finance: The Case Against* (Albany: State University of New York Office of the Chancellor, for National Association of System Heads, 1990).

26. For more on the concept of learning productivity see D. Bruce Johnstone, "The Productivity of Learning," *Journal for Higher Education Management* (Summer/Fall, 1995): 11–17; D. Bruce Johnstone and Patricia Maloney, "Enhancing the Productivity of Learning: Curricular Implications," in *Enhancing Productivity: Administrative, Instructional, and Technological Strategies*, ed. James E. Groccia and Judith E. Miller, New Directions for Higher Education #103 (San Francisco: Jossey-Bass, 1998); and Richard Arum and Josipa Boska, *Academically Adrift: Limited Learning on College Campuses* (Chicago: University of Chicago Press, 2011).

PART III / Frontiers of Rapid Change

# Chapter Twelve

# Extending Opportunity, Perpetuating Privilege

*Institutional Stratification amid Educational Expansion*

## Lauren T. Schudde and Sara Goldrick-Rab

The American ethos positions education as a powerful mechanism through which young people achieve status based on their own merits, unconstrained by family origins. Yet family background, such as income, wealth, and parental educational and occupational attainment, predicts educational outcomes, and the strength of its influence appears to be growing.[1] At the same time, those who persist to earn a bachelor's degree are better equipped to overcome socioeconomic origins.[2] How can we interpret trends—racial and socioeconomic inequality in postsecondary attainment despite increased college access—in an era when college is increasingly deemed "for all"?

Educational expansion, in which more Americans are attending college than in the past, is well documented.[3] Changing student composition is one of the most fundamental shifts in American higher education over the last half-century. While in the past college-goers constituted a highly elite group, today's undergraduates often resemble the "average" American.[4]

Yet many students from groups that were historically underrepresented in higher education, including racial minorities and students from low-income families, are concentrated in less selective colleges. The American higher education system is structured as a "pyramid of institutions," in which the tip is comprised of a few select and prestigious colleges and the base consists of the most inclusive institutions.[5] The polarization of the most selective and least selective institutions appears to be growing—white students are increasingly concentrated in the nation's 468 most well-funded and selective four-year colleges, while blacks and Hispanics are concentrated in the 3,250 least-funded and broad-access two- and four-year colleges.[6] While improved access to higher education theoretically reduces inequality, this is not true if that access is limited to colleges with low degree completion and limited labor market value. College may offer the "possibility of getting ahead" but, for those who enter institutions at the pyramid's base, it also increases "the probability of not getting ahead very far."[7]

In this chapter, we examine shifts in the demography of college attendees, as well as shifts in the structure of American higher education. We explore variation in student composition across college types and consider the implications of "institutional stratification"—in which institutions vary in their mission, selectivity, and rates of degree attainment—for students who enter college in hopes of improving their life chances.[8] If extending opportunity through increased postsecondary access aims to offset existing social and economic inequality, how does this play out in a hierarchical system in which access and returns to different institutional tiers is unequal?

## Educational Expansion: Extending Opportunity through College Access

Higher education in the United States has changed substantially over time to serve more citizens; that move was accompanied by shifts in the composition of both students and schools. In this section we describe those trends, emphasizing that as the student body grew more diverse, so did the kinds of colleges and universities serving it. Opportunities both expanded in number and became more distinct and disparate, reflecting and preserving key aspects of the inequality of opportunity and outcomes.

### WIDENING PARTICIPATION

College is a progressively more common part of American life; as such, the characteristics of undergraduates are far different than they once were. Sixty percent of high school seniors expect to graduate from a four-year college, up from 48 percent in 1990.[9] Fully 95 percent of high school seniors expect to gain some college education. There is relatively little variation in those expectations based on race or gender, and expectations are quite high (90 percent) even among children of low-income families.[10] At the same time, routes to and through college vary greatly.

Many people realize their educational expectations through at least some form of college attendance. In 1970, there were 6.3 million undergraduates in the

United States, and the number of participants increased by more than one-third over the next ten years to over 9 million. Between 1980 and 2000, undergraduate enrollment continued to enlarge by 26 percent. During the Great Recession, college enrollment swelled, reaching an all-time high in 2011, when 16.6 million Americans enrolled in some form of undergraduate education. The numbers appear to have leveled off in the face of recovery, with just under 16 million undergraduates in 2013.[11]

The increase in overall enrollment rates is partly attributable to population growth. Between 2000 and 2010, the number of eighteen- to twenty-four-year-olds increased from 27.3 million to 30.7 million (an increase of 12 percent), contributing, along with increasing educational aspirations, to the 15 percent increase in college enrollment during the same timeframe.[12] In addition, high school graduation rates expanded, affecting the percentage of young adults receiving at least basic preparation for college entrance. In 1970, only 52 percent of adults aged twenty-five or over completed a high school education. By 2013, that number had reached 88 percent.[13]

Changes in the American labor market also prompted many people to pursue a college education as the country transitioned from manufacturing to a knowledge-based economy. Between 1986 and 2006, the share of high-skill jobs (those requiring a bachelor's degree or more) grew, while the share of low-skill jobs (requiring a high school diploma or less) saw a decline.[14] The Bureau of Labor Statistics estimates that in 2012, almost a quarter of all job openings required at least a bachelor's degree.[15]

## Compositional Change: Students

While absolute growth in the college-going population shaped today's higher education structure, compositional changes also impacted the college experience, turning "college" into a set of highly diverse institutions and experiences that lead to very different outcomes. Today's students are heterogeneous in many dimensions, including race and ethnicity, academic ability, precollege achievement, effort level, study skills, ambitions, and religious background.[16]

### Changes in Undergraduate Population

The undergraduate population in the United States has altered in numerous respects since 1970. For example, it has become increasingly diverse in terms of race, gender, and social class. The proportion of white students steadily declined (dropping from 83 percent of enrollees in 1976 to 60 percent in 2010), while the proportion of Hispanic and Asian students nearly quadrupled and the proportion of black students grew by almost 40 percent.[17] As barriers to college entry for women diminished, women became a dominant presence in higher education. In 1970, 42 percent of undergraduates were female compared to 57 percent in 2010.[18]

There have also been notable changes in the age distribution of students. While the average age of undergraduates has increased, that change was primarily driven by shifts in the proportion of students aged nineteen and under (which declined from 46 percent in 1970 to 27 percent in 2013) and the proportion aged twenty-five and older (which increased from 12 percent in 1970 to nearly 27 percent in 2013).[19]

While many policies and practices have attempted to diminish the extent to which family background predicts college access, the link between parental education, family income, and college attendance is increasing.[20] For example, as more citizens earn college degrees, access to college for the next generation is increasingly linked to parents' educational attainment. Among college attendees in the National Longitudinal Study of 1972 (NLS: 72), 28 percent had a father and 16 percent had a mother holding a bachelor's degree.[21] In contrast, among college attendees in the National Educational Longitudinal Study of 1988 (NELS:88), fully 35 percent had that paternal educational advantage and 30 percent had a mother with a bachelor's degree.[22] Estimates from the National Postsecondary Student Aid Study suggest that 41 percent of all undergraduates in 2012 have at least one parent with at least a bachelor's degree and 65 percent of all undergraduates come from a household in which parents had at least some college.[23]

There have also been shifts in the income distribution of college students, although these are more difficult to document because colleges and universities rarely collect family income information on all students. According to estimates comparing the NLS and NELS studies, the proportions of undergraduates from the lowest and highest family-income brackets have increased over time, while the proportion from middle-income families declined somewhat. The number of Pell grant recipients—students who apply for and receive federal need-based financial aid—nearly tripled, and their representation among all undergraduates has grown (increasing from 14 percent to 23 percent from 1976 to 2008).[24]

One of the most-derided changes to American higher education is the declining academic preparation of its students. That shift is at least partly a function of widening participation: as more students from a variety of backgrounds entered college, the average levels of academic preparation had to decline (similarly, as

SAT test taking has become more common, the average score has declined). Comparisons over time are hard to document, as they are complicated by factors such as grade inflation. According to one measure—tested math ability—the proportion of college-goers in the bottom quartile of the distribution increased from 11 to 16 percent between 1970 and 1990, while the representation of students with scores in the top quartile decreased from 41 to 33 percent.[25] Taking these changes into account, it should come as no surprise that 40 percent of college students require at least one remedial course. More than one-fifth of college freshmen take remedial math coursework.[26] Rates of remediation are the highest among the groups that have most dramatically increased their representation in higher education over time—for example, 63 percent of students who come from families in the bottom socioeconomic quintile need remediation, typically in reading.[27] Their growing presence in postsecondary education therefore represents great strides in the nation's goals for an inclusionary postsecondary system, and brings with it the need to rethink the particular goals of "higher" education.

### Changes in College-Going Rates

Even though many policies endeavor to promote equality of educational opportunity, college attendance rates for high school graduates remain highly stratified by family background. Consider, for instance, trends by family income. In 1975, about one-third of high school completers from the poorest families entered college the fall after high school graduation. Over the next thirty-five years the proportion of low-income students entering college immediately after high school rose dramatically, reaching 45 percent in 1990 and 52 percent in 2012. Despite increases among low-income students, which were driven by policy efforts to diminish inequality, the college enrollment gaps across family income remain large and persistent. The enrollment gap between low-income and high-income students was 18 percent in 1975 and 16 percent in 2010.[28] This is largely due to comparably large gains in college attendance rates among middle- and high-income high school graduates.

Disparities based on parental educational attainment also threaten equity in postsecondary outcomes. The rates of college attendance among the children of parents without a bachelor's degree has not increased since 1992, but grew 5 percentage points among those with at least one parent holding a BA. The difference in college-going rates between the children of BA-educated parents and those of parents with "some college" widened from 14 to 21 percentage points.[29] As a result, the gap between those from the most educated families and the least educated homes is 35 percentage points.

While higher education has become more diverse in terms of race and ethnicity, racial inequality in college-going rates has not diminished much since 1975. Even though the black college-going rate among high school graduates swelled to nearly 66 percent (up from 43 percent in 1975), the white college-going rate also grew substantially, with 71 percent of white high school completers immediately enrolling in college (up from 51 percent). Because college-going rates of Hispanics have not changed much since the 1970s, a Hispanic-white gap grew as more whites entered college, producing an 11 percentage-point gap in college-going between white and Hispanic high school graduates in 2010.[30]

## COMPOSITIONAL CHANGE: INSTITUTIONS

With the compositional transformation of the college-going population, postsecondary institutions evolved, giving rise to new institutions and prompting changes in existing colleges. Like students, colleges are more varied than ever.

In 1870 there were 563 institutions of higher education in the United States. By the turn of the twentieth century there were 977; by the turn of the twenty-first century there were 4,182. Between 1976 and 2012, the number of public institutions grew by 25 percent for four-year universities and nearly 4 percent for two-year colleges. Private not-for-profit institutions experienced very different changes. Over the same period, the number of four-year institutions in that sector rose by almost 15 percent, but two-year institutions experienced a dramatic decline of 48 percent (in 1976 there were 188 institutions of this type, but in 2012 only 97 remained).[31]

At the same time, the representation of private for-profit institutions increased dramatically. In 1976, there were only 55 for-profit institutions in the United States. Forty of these colleges served students seeking associate's degrees and short-term certificates, and only fifteen offered bachelor's degrees. By 2012, underfunded public institutions were unable to absorb the growing demand for college education, and the number of for-profit colleges swelled to 533 two-year and 782 four-year institutions. In 1976 these institutions accounted for just 2 percent of all postsecondary institutions; today almost one in four colleges and universities is private for-profit.[32] The private for-profit sector is growing rapidly, with particularly large enrollment gains during the recession, when it increased its enrollment by approximately 15 percent from the 2008–2009 to the 2009–2010 academic year alone.[33]

Public two-year (also referred to as community colleges throughout this chapter) and proprietary (another term for "for-profit" colleges) institutions represent very different educational options for college students. While both proprietary schools and community colleges traditionally provide career-focused education (though both also offer other pathways), there are many differences between the two types of institutions, including mission, governance, size, cost, and market orientation. They vary in their recruitment techniques, approaches to student services such as job placement, and in how they set tuition and leverage financial aid dollars. Compared with students at public two-year colleges, students at for-profit institutions are disproportionately women, African American or Hispanic, and single parents.[34] Students may be attracted to these institutions because they benefit from a higher level of support and guidance compared with students enrolled at community colleges. Proprietary colleges also have far fewer options in terms of programs and electives, compared with community colleges. The curricula at proprietary colleges tend to be more standardized, presumably to allow faculty with varying experience levels to provide consistent instruction to students.

During the 1990s, proprietary colleges were forced to become more similar to community colleges, due to tighter accreditation standards and federal financial aid policies. While still maintaining their focus on preparing students for careers, these colleges now require general education courses as part of their degree requirements, as well as offering developmental education courses and classes for English-language learners.[35] Their rapid growth and market orientation may have lasting implications for American higher education.

Other changes also shape undergraduate education. For example, the student-faculty ratio has also increased by nearly ten (to 39 to 1), and expenditures per student have declined—changes that most likely stem from the swells in undergraduate enrollment and persistent efforts to contain costs. According to one estimate, today's productivity in the nation's public colleges and universities (as measured by the ratio of degrees to expenditures) is less than half of what it was forty years ago.[36]

## Shifting Enrollment Patterns in the Context of Institutional Stratification

Today's students also change colleges frequently (sometimes called "swirling").[37] For example, according to one study, within eight years of high school graduation, one-third of the students who began their college education at a four-year school transferred at least once: nearly one-fifth transferred to another four-year institution, and 15 percent transferred to a two-year college. Among the group that transferred from a four-year to a two-year college (referred to as "reverse transfer"), 41 percent eventually transferred back into a four-year college or university.[38] In addition to transfer, college "stop out" is prevalent, with at least one-fourth of the students taking time off before returning to school.[39]

These shifts in enrollment behavior are at least partly attributable to the increase in educational options available to students. Not only are there a greater number and variety of institutions from which to choose, but the types of programs and their delivery methods create additional options.[40] At the same time, evidence indicates that students are not entirely free to choose their college pathways. There is a correlation between students' social class and their attendance patterns, and that relationship holds after taking high school preparation into account. For example, students from families in the lowest socioeconomic quintile are over four times more likely than students from advantaged socioeconomic backgrounds to either stop out of college or stop out before transferring to another institution. Students in the bottom socioeconomic quintile are half as likely as those in the top quintile to transfer between four-year colleges, yet they are three times more likely than their more privileged peers to reverse transfer. Reverse transfer is significantly less common among students whose parents are well educated, and this appears to be related to their greater tendency to achieve higher college grade point averages.[41]

Given those inequalities, it is especially troubling that the rates of bachelor's degree attainment are lower among students who change colleges. In one study, the average BA attainment rate among four-year starters who did not transfer was 78 percent, compared with 69 percent among students who transferred to another four-year school, and only 22 percent among reverse transfers.[42]

Rapidly shifting patterns of enrollment among students is likely due to the variety of institutional and programmatic choice, paired with the lack of guidance in college pathways. Even among swirling students, institutional stratification has important implications. It is important to note that, for simplicity's sake, we focus primarily on students' initial institutional type, although movement between colleges and across sectors is increasingly common.

Throughout the remainder of this chapter, we describe trends across institution types, particularly private not-for-profit four-year, public four-year, public two-year, and private for-profit colleges.[43] While the private nonprofit sector includes elite colleges (i.e., the Ivy League and selective liberal arts colleges), it is a heterogeneous group, including less-selective, but often expensive, private colleges that serve students with broader academic preparation and from narrower geographic regions. Likewise, public four-year colleges consist of flagship state colleges, often more selective in admission, and regional comprehensive colleges. While we acknowledge the heterogeneity within each institutional type, we describe trends for each of these broad categories. Even with these crude distinctions, there is still substantial variation across institutional level and control.

## The Implications of Institutional Stratification in the Context of Educational Expansion

Research suggests that increasing educational access benefits all citizens, ultimately reducing inequality. Findings from a cross-national study indicate that, as access to higher education expands, all social classes experience additional educational attainment.[44] The results hold true even in postsecondary educational contexts with privatization (there are private colleges in addition to the public) and differentiation (institutions are stratified by prestige, resources, and selectivity of both faculty and students), both of which are present in the United States.

According to the study, which includes data from fifteen countries, the share of citizens participating in higher education is larger in the presence of diversified postsecondary systems, like the United States, than in other systems. This is because students who might otherwise not have attended college are now able to do so, even if entry to selective postsecondary institutions is still reserved for the most affluent.[45] In countries where the most advantaged already have significant postsecondary access, educational expansion provides the socioeconomically disadvantaged with the largest opportunity gains in access.

Indeed, research suggests increasing postsecondary opportunities through broader access results in greater equity in college attendance in an American context. Attewell and Lavin tracked women who entered the City University of New York (CUNY) between 1970 and 1972 under its open admissions policy.[46] Under the policy, every high school student in the city was guaranteed a seat in the CUNY system, which includes two- and four-year colleges and, at the time, offered free tuition. Admitting students who are otherwise unlikely to attend college has important implications for their life outcomes. Students who are least likely to attend college appear to benefit more from degree attainment than their peers.[47] Women admitted only under CUNY's open-door policy gained more from college, thirty years after enrollment, than those who would have met previous selection criteria, showing a larger boost in earnings and homeownership.

The admissions policy also improved the rate of their children's college-going by 5 percent.[48] Unfortunately, the open door policy and free tuition were discontinued in 1976 due to fiscal constraints of the city of New York.[49]

While postsecondary educational access in the United States has dramatically increased, the gains have mostly occurred in the public two-year and private for-profit sectors—the bottom tiers of the pyramid. Access to selective colleges, which yield the greatest returns, is still "profoundly and persistently unequal."[50] The differentiation of postsecondary institutions "creates a structure in which [colleges] are formally equal but functionally quite different; where institutions that are most accessible provide the least social benefit, and those that are least accessible open the most doors."[51]

Broad-access colleges, like community colleges and proprietary colleges, increase educational access, but they also "effectively maintain" inequality, creating an illusion of increased opportunity while preserving the top tier of postsecondary education (elite four-year colleges).[52] As larger shares of high school graduates reached some form of higher education, socioeconomic class differences in access to selective colleges in the United States grew.[53] As we demonstrate below, affluent youth are more likely to attend four-year institutions, while the less privileged increasingly attend lower prestige institutions, including two-year colleges.[54] To further understand how institutional stratification impacts college degree attainment in the US, we examine patterns of access and completion across the institutional sectors.

### Variation in Access

Due to variation in degree completion and returns to college education, patterns of enrollment across the different types of postsecondary institutions have important implications. Approximately three quarters of college-goers attend public institutions (about 34 percent of all college-goers attend public four-year and 39 percent public two-year colleges), while 15 percent attend private, not-for profit colleges (almost all of which are four-year institutions) and nearly 10 percent attend private, for-profit colleges (with 9 percent of all college-goers attending for-profit four-year and 2.4 percent attending for-profit two-year colleges).[55] To consider how institutional stratification may influence inequality, we begin by illustrating that there is substantial variation in the institutions attended by students from different racial and socioeconomic subgroups and, as such, that student composition varies across institution type (we consider both level—two-year versus four-year—and control—public, private not-for-profit, or private for-profit).[56]

### Variation in Colleges Attended by Different Subgroups

While a growing number of Americans attend some form of postsecondary institution, educational expansion occurred largely at the bottom tiers of the postsecondary institutional hierarchy. Here, we move to study how different subgroups of college-goers are dispersed among the institutional types.

Low-income students and racial minorities are concentrated in low prestige colleges, which generally have lower rates of program completion. Figure 12.1 shows the distribution in enrollment across institutional type for each racial subgroup available in the NPSAS. Black and Hispanic students—both groups at higher risk of low college persistence—are among the least likely to attend four-year public and private not-for-profit colleges. The modal college type for both black and Hispanic college students is community college, with 40 percent of blacks and 51 percent of Hispanics attending public two-year institutions. A disproportionately high percentage of blacks and American Indians attend private for-profit colleges compared to other racial subgroups. Approximately half of Asian and white college students are enrolled at public and private not-for-profit four-year colleges.

Figure 12.2 and figure 12.3 demonstrate that there is substantial stratification by socioeconomic status. Figure 12.2 plots the distribution of dependent college students (those financially dependent on parents for financial aid purposes) from different income brackets and figure 12.3 plots the distribution of students within different levels of parental education. Students from low-income households appear more likely to attend broad-access institutions, with 50 percent of those from family incomes of under $50,000 enrolled at community colleges or proprietary colleges. Likewise, college attendees whose parents' highest level of education was high school are strikingly more likely to attend broad-access institutions, though this appears to be driven by enrollment in private for-profit colleges (one-fifth of first-generation college-goers attend a proprietary college), rather than community colleges. The percentage of students attending public four-year and private not-for-profit four-year colleges steadily increases with each step up the income and parental education ladders.

### Student Composition: Which Students
### do Different Institution Types Serve?

Another way to think about institutional stratification is to consider which type of students institutions serve, comparing the composition of their student

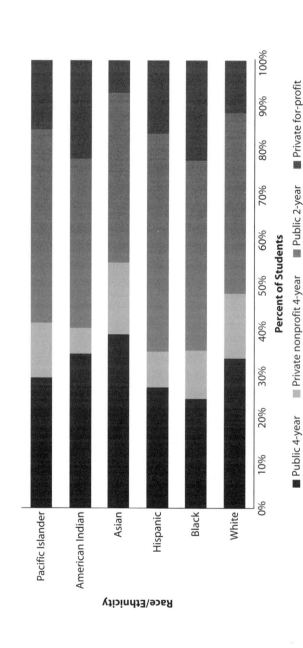

*Figure 12.1.* Racial stratification in enrollment across college type
*Source:* National Postsecondary Student Aid Study, 2012.

**Race/Ethnicity**

**Percent of Students**

■ Public 4-year   ■ Private nonprofit 4-year   ■ Public 2-year   ■ Private for-profit

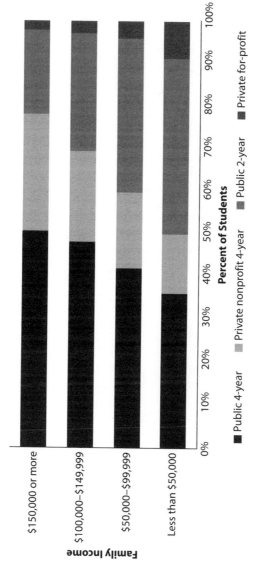

*Figure 12.2.* Family income stratification in enrollment across college type
*Source:* National Postsecondary Student Aid Study, 2012.

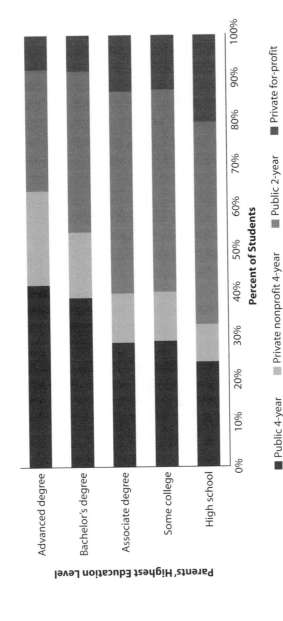

*Figure 12.3.* Parent education stratification in enrollment across college type
*Source:* National Postsecondary Student Aid Study, 2012.

populations. Because four-year public and private not-for-profit colleges tend to have greater selectivity (they evaluate applicants for admission, rather than broadly admitting students), they tend to serve a more privileged group of students. We describe the make-up of students who attend public four-year, private nonprofit four year, public two-year, and private for-profit colleges below.

Figure 12.4 offers a glimpse of this variation. Over two-thirds of the students attending private nonprofit colleges are white, while the next most represented group are black students (almost 14 percent), Hispanics (11 percent), and Asians (7 percent). Public four-year colleges are only modestly more diverse, with 64 percent of the student body identifying as white, 13 percent as black, 14 percent as Hispanic, 7 percent Asian, and 1 percent as American Indian or Native Alaskan. Private for-profit colleges serve a much higher proportion of racial minority students, comparatively. Only 50 percent of their students are white. Over a quarter are black and one-fifth are Hispanic. Public two-year colleges serve a student body that is largely white (58 percent), but with high representation among blacks and Hispanics (17 percent and 19 percent respectively).

Figures 12.5 and 12.6 present student composition within each institution type broken down by income and parents' highest level of education, respectively. Private not-for-profit colleges serve a much larger proportion of students from highly educated parents and high-income families. The average family income of students attending private not-for-profit colleges is the highest ($95,675 among dependent students), while the average income is over $10,000 lower among students attending public four-year colleges ($85,418 for dependents). The average income at public two-year and private for-profit colleges is drastically lower. A large proportion of students at broad access institutions are the first in their family to attend college (41 percent at public two-year and 53 percent at private for-profit colleges).

Institutions also vary in terms of student composition in gender, age, and receipt of federal need-based financial aid. Community colleges and for-profit colleges serve older students than those at public or private nonprofit four-year institutions.[57] Private for-profit colleges also disproportionately serve women, who comprise almost two-thirds of their students.[58] Finally, a point of controversy over the private for-profit sector is the high proportion of students receiving federal need-based aid. In 2012, 64 percent of for-profit students received a Pell grant (estimates from the prior academic year were even larger, at 73 percent[59]), compared to less than 40 percent of students attending public and private not-for-profit colleges.

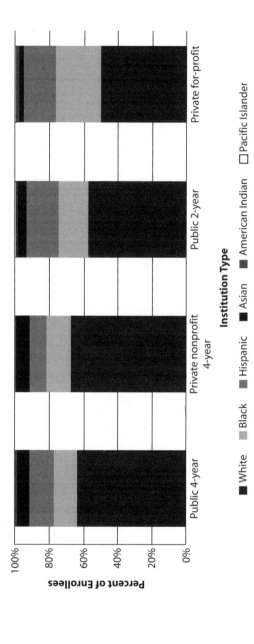

*Figure 12.4.* Student composition: Race and ethnicity
*Source:* National Postsecondary Student Aid Study, 2012.

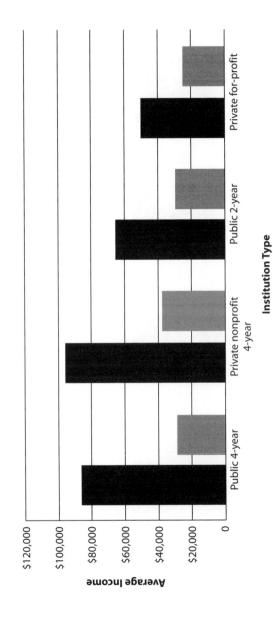

*Figure 12.5.* Student composition: Income by dependency status
*Source:* National Postsecondary Student Aid Study, 2012.

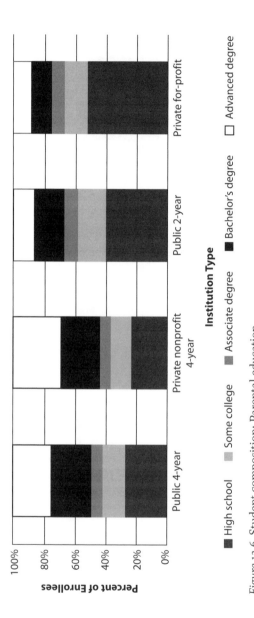

*Figure 12.6.* Student composition: Parental education
*Source:* National Postsecondary Student Aid Study, 2012.

An important caveat to our discussion of student composition is that it only represents students who gained admittance and enrolled, which overlooks an important component of inequality. Because students vary in their access to information, as well as preferences and constraints, regarding college choice, there is variation in the types of colleges to which students apply, gain admission, can afford, and, ultimately, attend.

Research on college access seeks to understand the observed subgroup stratification in institution type attended. A common explanation for the high concentration of low-income and racial minority students in broad-access institutions emphasizes prior achievement and academic preparation, arguing that the limited access to elite colleges is largely due to thresholds for admission (i.e., we see fewer disadvantaged students because they were concentrated in low-performing secondary schools and, thus, do not meet admission standards).[60] Other theories focus on information constraints—the idea that students from disadvantaged backgrounds do not have the information available to encourage their application to "reach" schools and selective colleges. Research on the small, but concerning group of high-achieving, low-income students who "undermatch" (i.e., attend a college that is less selective than their prior achievement and test scores suggest they could attend) has resulted in controversy over how much emphasis should be placed on ensuring that high-achieving low-income students gain access to selective and elite colleges.[61] Still, research on understanding gaps in access to four-year colleges suggests that socioeconomic and racial gaps in enrollment rates are not fully explained by prior achievement.[62] Other evidence suggests that the largest factor influencing college choice for students who attend broad-access colleges is proximity to home.[63]

The distributions reported here support recent research arguing that the structure of the American higher education system privileges students who already have several advantages—those who are white, from a higher income household, and with highly educated parents. Black and Hispanic students, students from families in which they are the first to attend college, and students from low-income households are concentrated in community colleges and private for-profit colleges. The sorting of students into different institution types has important implications for their educational attainment and the gains they can expect from attending college. Next we turn to variation in several outcomes across institutional types.

## Variation in Outcomes

Increased college access does not always translate into success. Students from low-income and racial minority backgrounds are much more likely than their peers to leave college without a degree. For example, college entrants from the highest income quartile are more than twice as likely to earn a bachelor's degree as those from the lowest quartile.[64] The family income gap in bachelor's degree attainment among those who entered college has grown since 1970, largely due to increasing attainment rates for students from the top family income quartile paired with stagnation among those from the bottom quartile. Since 1970, the family income gap in bachelor's attainment among college-goers by age twenty-four increased from 33 percentage points to 78 percentages points.[65]

Subgroup stratification across institution type has serious implications for individual status attainment as well as the reproduction of inequality across generations. Closing racial and socioeconomic gaps in college outcomes ultimately stands to reduce poverty and improve economic growth, essential to the long-term economic well-being of the nation.[66] As we demonstrate below, there is variation in the college outcomes and returns across institutional level and control.

**Degree Attainment**

Degree completion rates vary dramatically between and within the types of institutions students first attend. The differential completion rates across institution types grew with the increase in institutional stratification. In 1972, graduation rates were comparable (64 percent) for students attending four-year public and four-year private institutions, although bachelor's degree completion varied greatly based on the selectivity of the institutions within each category. The graduation rate at flagship public schools was 74 percent, compared with 62 percent at nonflagship public colleges.[67] The gap was even wider in the private four-year sector, with 80 percent of students at highly selective colleges earning a bachelor's degree, compared with 58 percent at less-selective private colleges. Only one-fifth of community college students in that cohort completed a bachelor's degree within eight years of high school graduation.

As more students entered college, college graduation rates flattened or, in some cases, decreased.[68] Only 59 percent of public and 64 percent of private non-profit four-year students who were first-time college entrants in 2004 earned a bachelor's degree within six years.[69] Within and between these sectors, there is still a great degree of variation based on selectivity. At the most selective public four-year colleges, 75 percent of students earn a bachelor's degree within six years. At comparable private four-year colleges, 81 percent do. The bachelor's degree attainment rate at minimally selective public four-year colleges is almost 25 percentage points lower than at the most selective publics. Among private nonprofits, the difference across selectivity is even larger (30 percentage points). In the four-year sector, private for-profits have, by far, the lowest bachelor's degree attainment—only 15 percent of students earn a degree within six years.

Among the two-year sector, we also see a great deal of variation in degree attainment. Approximately 14 percent of community college entrants earned an associate's degree within six years and 12 percent earned a bachelor's degree. Private for-profit two-year colleges produced a higher rate of associate's degree attainment—with 20 percent of entrants earning one within six years—but did not offer the same transfer pathway to a bachelor's degree (less than 1 percent).

Within each institution type, there are significant gaps in degree attainment across race and family income. For instance, only 40 percent of public four-year students from the lowest income quartile earned a bachelor's degree in six years compared to 75 percent of those from the top quartile. Private nonprofit colleges show a similarly sized attainment gap of 34 percentage points. At private for-profit four-years, the enrollment distribution is so skewed toward low-income families that we cannot produce a reliable estimate of variation in completion, but their dismal degree attainment rates speak for themselves. The racial gaps are just as jarring: 61 percent of white college entrants at public, 70 percent at private not-for-profit, and 17 percent at private for-profit four-year colleges earned a bachelor's degree, compared to 46, 44, and 8 percent of black and 48, 43, and 12 percent of Hispanic entrants, respectively.

Even at community colleges, students from low-income families are at a disadvantage, but mostly in terms of navigating their way to a four-year college in order to earn a bachelor's degree (12 percent of students from the lowest income quartile earn an associate's degree, but only 7 percent of entrants move on to earn a bachelor's degree, compared to 19 percent and 18 percent among their top quartile community college counterparts). The racial gaps at public two-years are also persistent. Sixteen percent of white entrants earn an associate's degree compared to 10 percent of blacks and 11 percent of Hispanics.

This demonstrates that, even within each sector, the rates are lowest for students who stand to benefit the most from a college degree. At the same time, there is substantial variation in the degree attainment rate across college type, which also has important implications for inequality, given the differential sorting in college enrollment.

While the patterns we display here are merely descriptive, large bodies of research have grown to investigate the role of institutional types on college completion. For instance, a great deal of research evaluates the impact of initial enrollment at a community college on bachelor's degree attainment. Some suggests a negative impact of community college attendance on achieving aspirations of attaining a bachelor's degree.[70] More recently, research finds that the negative "community college effect" is concentrated among students who otherwise would have attended four-year colleges.[71] Yet the majority of community college students would not have attended college without access to a public two-year. As such, community college has a modest positive impact on bachelor's degree attainment when comparing community college entrants to students who did not enroll in college within one year of completing high school.[72] Other work also touts the benefits of community colleges, arguing that they serve as a "safety net" for students who fail to persist at four-year colleges, offering another road to a credential.[73]

The community college effect has been of great interest to scholars over the past several decades. More recently, work has started to consider how for-profit colleges compare to peer institutions, particularly community colleges, but most of this work focuses on college choice, with a particular interest in recruitment practices and the logic of students' enrollment decisions, and persistence, highlighting structural features of the for-profit sector that help students navigate college pathways. More evidence is necessary to understand how they compare to the other sectors in terms of degree attainment, controlling for student background.[74]

### Debt

Institution types also differ in the financial burden students are left to carry after college. Among students earning associate's degrees from public two-year colleges in 2011–2012, 41 percent graduated with some level of student loan debt. In comparison, 88 percent of students receiving associate's degrees from private for-profit institutions incurred debt.[75] For students earning an associate's degree from a community college, 5 percent had student loan debt between $20,000 and $30,000 and 4 percent owed $30,000 or more. Among students earning their associate's degree from a proprietary college, over one-quarter owed between $20,000 and $30,000 and 28 percent carried student loan debt in excess of $30,000.[76] These statistics only refer to students who earned an associate's degree—they left with a diploma in hand—but, as we've seen, many students fail to earn a credential at private for-profit and public two-year colleges, making the accumulation of debt all the more troubling.

Students who attend proprietary schools have similar federal student loan balances to those of students at nonselective four-year colleges, but many for-profit students shoulder debt that covered just one- or two-year programs.[77] Undergraduates at for-profits are also more likely to default on their loans. For instance, the default rate for students who attend for-profit two-year institutions is 27 percent four years after borrowers enter repayment (students at private for-profit four-year colleges show similar rates), compared to 17 percent for students who attend public two-year institutions.[78]

While students at private for-profit colleges are disproportionately saddled with debt per year of education, student debt is a growing problem across all college types. Much of the debt burden may be due to the soaring college costs paired with stagnant need-based financial aid. In 2012, college costs were 2.3 times higher than in 1975, but the maximum Pell grant was 95 percent of what it was in 1975 (when converted to 2012 dollars).[79] The percent of college costs covered by Pell grants fell from its 1975 high of 67 percent to covering, on average, only 27 percent of college costs in 2012.[80] For all institution types, Pell recipients carry more debt after college than their non-Pell peers, which suggests that federal need-based aid is not enough to offset the growing costs of a college education.[81]

**Labor Market Outcomes**

The value of a college education is reflected in the differential wages for bachelor's degree holders compared with individuals with less education. In 2010, earnings for those with a high school diploma hovered around a median of $30,000, and for those with less than a high school diploma, the median was $20,000 or less.[82] College education offers a bump in pay, but all "college education" is not created equal. Those who attend college but leave without a degree have a median income of $33,401, compared to $37,773 among associate's degree holders and $47,435 among bachelor's degree holders.[83] Such numbers suggest a lifetime penalty for individuals who forego higher education, which may compel many Americans to enroll in college. At the same time, they also demonstrate the limited benefit of college attendance when it is not coupled with degree completion.

Among degree holders, there is significant variation in earnings based on college type and program. An audit study simulating the job search process for recent bachelor's degree earners found that employers respond, on average, 6 percent more frequently to applications from graduates of very selective private nonprofit four-year colleges than from very selective public four-year colleges.[84] Another audit study found that callback rates for positions requiring a bachelor's degree were higher for job applicants with degrees from both minimally selective and selective public four-year colleges than from for-profit four-year colleges (although a bachelor's degree from a for-profit does appear to increase the callback rate slightly for positions that do not require a bachelor's degree, compared to applicants with an associate's degree).[85] Of course, audit studies like these only capture employers' perceptions of applicant and credential quality, rather than telling us if there are different payoffs in terms of earnings across degrees from different institution types.

However, research also indicates a positive association between college selectivity and earnings of graduates. Among bachelor's degree recipients, institutional selectivity positively impacts earnings, with the greatest impact on earnings occurring later in graduates' careers; and the relationship between selectivity and earnings appears to be growing over time.[86] However, controlling for student characteristics that predict attendance at selective colleges diminishes the effect of selectivity on early career earnings, though positive effects remain for certain subgroups, like blacks and Hispanics.[87] Even among broader access institutions, there may also be variation in earnings among degree recipients based on perceived college quality. Students with an associate's degree from a community college earn a larger boost from their degree than those with the same credential from a for-profit college.[88]

## IMPLICATIONS AND CONCLUSIONS

The trends described in this chapter illustrate that American higher education in the twenty-first century serves a much more heterogeneous undergraduate population than ever before. Students vary not only in their family backgrounds and demographic characteristics, but also their approaches to college enrollment (e.g., where, how, and under what conditions they attend) and pathways through college (e.g., their attendance patterns and degree completion).

Concurrently, our higher education system has grown increasingly complex, with diversification in the mission, selectivity, and programs of postsecondary institutions and the value of their credentials. Institutional stratification has important implications for social inequality in the United States, both due to differential sorting into colleges and differential degree attainment between and within institutions. To improve outcomes in the context of our diversified post-secondary education system, some scholars argue that we need to improve the presence of disadvantaged students in the top tier. This is the crux of the debate over the need to "nudge" high-achieving, low-income students to apply to selective private nonprofit colleges.[89] But this approach merely highlights the strength of elite four-year colleges in getting students across the finish line, and ignores the fact that the majority of Americans are not high-achieving high school graduates.

Regional and broad-access colleges will continue to educate the majority of Americans. For that reason, other scholars call for an array of changes to the higher education system, including creating stronger pathways to degree completion in public, broad-access colleges to help students meet the demands of college-level coursework and more easily navigate degree programs; increasing the capacity of public colleges to education the masses by restoring government funding (thus enabling public colleges to meet the growing demand for college, rather than relying on for-profit colleges to take on more students); reducing the impact of financial constraints for students from low-income families by improving the buying power of the Pell Grant; and making the first two years of college free.[90]

The complexity of our higher education system produces a difficult set of problems for researchers, policymakers, and practitioners interested in ameliorating inequality through postsecondary education. We not only need to concern ourselves with how students sort into colleges, but also with how to improve degree attainment among students where they are.

NOTES

1. Michael Hout, "Social and Economic Returns to College Education in the United States," *Annual Review of Sociology* 38 (2012): 379–400; Sean F. Reardon, "The Widening Academic Achievement Gap between the Rich and the Poor: New Evidence and Possible Explanations," in *Whither Opportunity? Rising Inequality, Schools, and Children's Life Chances,* ed. Greg Duncan and Richard Murnane (New York: Russell Sage, 2011), 91–116.

2. Florencia Torche, "Is a College Degree Still the Great Equalizer? Intergenerational Mobility across Levels of Schooling in the United States," *American Journal of Sociology* 117 (2011): 763–807.

3. Claudia Goldin and Lawrence F. Katz, *The Race between Education and Technology* (Cambridge, MA: Harvard University Press, 2010); Patricia Gumport, Maria Iannozzi, Susan Shaman, and Robert Zemsky, *Trends in United States Higher Education from Massification to Post Massification* (Stanford, CA: National Center for Postsecondary Improvement, 1997).

4. Sarah E. Igo, *The Averaged American* (Cambridge, MA: Harvard University Press, 2007).

5. David Labaree, "A System without a Plan: Emergence of an American System of Higher Education in the Twentieth Century," *Bildungsgeschichte: International Journal for the Historiography of Education* 3, no. 1 (2013): 46–59.

6. Anthony P. Carnevale and Jeff Strohl, *Separate & Unequal: How Higher Education Reinforces the Intergenerational Reproduction of White Racial Privilege* (Washington, DC: Georgetown Public Policy Institute Center on Education and the Workforce, July 2013).

7. Labaree, "A System without a Plan."

8. Michael Bastedo and Patricia Gumport, "Access to What? Mission Differentiation and Academic Stratification in US Public Higher Education," *Higher Education* 46, no. 3 (2003): 341–59; Julie Posselt, Ozan Jaquette, Rob Bielby, and Michael N. Bastedo, "Access without Equity: Longitudinal Analyses of Institutional Stratification by Race and Ethnicity, 1972–2004," *American Educational Research Journal* 49, no. 6 (2012): 1074–111.

9. National Center for Education Statistics (NCES), *The Condition of Education 2012* (Washington, DC: National Center for Education Statistics, 2006), table A-35-1.

10. NCES, *The Condition of Education 2006* (Washington, DC: National Center for Education Statistics, 2006), table 23-1.

11. US Census Bureau, "Table A-7: College Enrollment of Students 14 Years Old and Over, by Type of College, Attendance Status, Age, and Gender; October 1970 to 2013," *Current Population Survey*, www.census.gov/hhes/school/data/cps/historical/.

12. Thomas D. Snyder and Sally A. Dillow, *Digest of Education Statistics 2011* (Washington, DC: National Center for Education Statistics, 2012), 279.

13. US Census Bureau, "Table A-2: Percent of People 25 Years and Over Who Have Completed High School of College, by Race, Hispanic Origin and Sex: Selected Years 1940 to 2013," *Current Population Survey*, www.census.gov/hhes/socdemo/education/data/cps/historical.

14. Harry J. Holzer and Robert I. Lerman, Brief #41, *The Future of Middle-Skill Jobs* (Washington, DC: Brookings Center on Children and Families, Feb. 2009).

15. Bureau of Labor Statistics, *Education and Training Outlook for Occupations, 2012–22* (Washington, DC: BLS, 2013), www.bls.gov/emp/ep_edtrain_outlook.pdf.

16. Jeffrey A. Smith, "Heterogeneity and Higher Education," in *Succeeding in College: What It Means and How to Make It Happen*, ed. Michael S. McPherson and Morton Owen Schapiro (New York: College Board, 2008).

17. Snyder and Dillow, *Digest of Education Statistics 2011*, table 237.

18. Ibid., table 214.

19. US Census Bureau, "Table A-7: College Enrollment."

20. Robert Haveman and Timothy Smeeding, "The Role of Higher Education in Social Mobility," *Future of Children* 16, no. 2 (2006), 1225–150.

21. Authors' calculations using National Longitudinal Study: 1972.

22. Authors' calculations using National Educational Longitudinal Study: 1988.

23. Authors' calculations using National Postsecondary Student Aid Study: 2012.

24. Postsecondary Education Opportunity, *Pell Grant Recipient Data by State, 1976–77 to 2007–08* (Aug. 2009), www.postsecondary.org.

25. The NCES Math Test figures are for NLS-72 and NELS:88 college-goers, obtained from John Bound, Michael Lovenheim, and Sarah Turner, "Why Have College Completion Rates Declined? An Analysis of Changing Student Preparation and Collegiate Resources," NBER Working Paper No. 15566, National Bureau of Economic Research (Dec. 2009), www.nber.org/papers/w15566 [accessed Feb. 5, 2010].

26. Postsecondary Education Opportunity, *Academic Preparation for College, 1983 to 2002* (Feb. 2003), www.postsecondary.org.

27. NCES, *The Condition of Education 2004* (Washington, DC: National Center for Education Statistics, 2004), table 18-1.

28. NCES, *The Condition of Education 2012*, table A-34-1.

29. NCES, *The Condition of Education 2011*, table A-20-2.

30. NCES, *The Condition of Education 2012*, table A-34-2.

31. Thomas D. Snyder and Sally A. Dillow, *Digest of Education Statistics 2012* (Washington, DC: NCES, 2013), table 317.10.

32. Ibid.

33. Snyder and Dillow, *Digest of Education Statistics 2011*, table 230.

34. Sandra Staklis, Vera Bersudskaya, and Laura Horn, *Students Attending For-Profit Postsecondary Institutions: Demographics, Enrollment Characteristics, and 6-Year Outcomes* (Washington, DC: NCES, 2012).

35. Thomas Bailey, Norena Badway, and Patricia Gumport, *For-Profit Higher Education and Community Colleges* (Stanford, CA: National Center for Postsecondary Improvement, 2003).

36. Douglas Harris and Sara Goldrick-Rab, *The (Un)Productivity of American Colleges: From "Cost Disease" to Cost-Effectiveness* (Indianapolis, IN: Lumina Foundation, 2009).

37. Sara Goldrick-Rab and Fabian T. Pfeffer, "Beyond Access: Explaining Socioeconomic Differences in College Transfer," *Sociology of Education* 82 (2009): 101–25.

38. Ibid.

39. Lutz Berkner, *Descriptive Summary of 1995–1996 Beginning Postsecondary Students: Six Years Later* (Washington, DC: NCES, 2002).

40. Thomas R. Bailey, Shanna Smith Jaggars, and Davis Jenkins, *Redesigning America's Community Colleges: A Clearer Path to Student Success* (Cambridge, MA: Harvard University Press, 2015); Sara Goldrick-Rab, "Following Their Every Move: An Investigation of Social-Class Differences in College Pathways," *Sociology of Education* 79 (2006), 61–79.

41. Goldrick-Rab and Pfeffer, "Beyond Access."

42. Ibid.

43. When describing trends in the distribution of students into institution types and the composition of attendees, we group two- and four-year for-profit colleges together because there is little variation between the two levels in terms of racial and socioeconomic subgroup enrollment. In our discussion of outcomes, we distinguish between the two levels because they offer different credentials.

44. Richard Arum, Adam Gamoran, and Yossi Shavit, "More Inclusion than Diversion: Expansion, Differentiation, and Market Structure in Higher Education," in *Stratification in Higher Education: A Comparative Study*, ed. Yossi Shavit, Richard Arum, and Adam Gamoran (Stanford, CA: Stanford University Press, 2007).

45. Ibid., 29.

46. Paul Attewell and David Lavin, *Passing the Torch: Does Higher Education for the Disadvantaged Pay off Across the Generations?* (New York: Russell Sage, 2007).

47. Ibid.; Jennie Brand and Yu Xie, "Who Benefits Most from College? Evidence for Negative Selection in Heterogeneous Economic Returns to Higher Education," *American Sociological Review* 75, no. 2 (2010): 273–302.

48. Attewell and Lavin, *Passing the Torch.*

49. "When Tuition at CUNY Was Free, Sort Of," *CUNY Matters* (Oct. 12, 2011), http://www1.cuny.edu/mu/forum/2011/10/12/when-tuition-at-cuny-was-free-sort-of/ [accessed Feb. 3, 2015].

50. Michael Bastedo and Ozan Jaquette, "Running in Place: Low-Income Students and the Dynamics of Higher Education Stratification," *Educational Evaluation and Policy Analysis* 33, no. 3 (2011): 318–39; Hout, "Social and Economic Returns to College."

51. Labaree, "System without a Plan," 49.

52. Samuel Lucas, "Effectively Maintained Inequality: Education Transitions, Track Mobility, and Social Background Effects," *American Journal of Sociology* 106, no. 6 (2001): 1642–1690; Lauren Schudde and Sara Goldrick-Rab, "On Second Chances and Stratification: How Sociologists Think about Community Colleges," *Community College Review* 43, no. 1 (2015): 27–45.

53. Sigal Alon, "The Evolution of Class Inequality in Higher Education: Competition, Exclusion, and Adaptation," *American Sociological Review* 74, no. 5 (2009): 731–55.

54. Ibid.

55. NCES, *The Condition of Education 2012* (Washington, DC: NCES, 2012), table A-10-1; Snyder and Dillow, *Digest of Education Statistics 2011*, table 230.

56. We highlight trends in college attendance among the 26 million undergraduates enrolled in postsecondary education in the 2011–2012 academic year using data from the most recent National Postsecondary Student Aid Study: 2012 (NPSAS). All calculations from the NPSAS were obtained using Powerstats (http://nces.ed.gov/datalab/powerstats). Later, to understand the implications of the distribution of students into different types of institutions, we use data from the Beginning Postsecondary Students (BPS) Longitudinal Study, which is representative of first-time college students who started college in 2004, to illustrate trends in degree attainment across the different college types.

57. The average age of a community college student in the 2011–2012 academic year was twenty-eight, and at proprietary colleges was thirty. This stands in comparison to an average age of approximately twenty-four at public four-year and private not-for-profit four-year colleges.

58. Sixty-four percent of students attending proprietary colleges are female, compared to approximately 55 percent of students attending public four-year, private nonprofit four-year, and community colleges.

59. Estimate for 2012 obtained from the NPSAS. Previous year estimate obtained from NCES, *Condition of Education 2012*, table A-41-1.

60. Research suggests that the academic preparation of low-socioeconomic status (SES) students has increased over time, as has the "match" between these students and the selectivity of their postsecondary institution. However, the academic preparation and postsecondary match concurrently increased among high-SES students, preventing

any notable shift in the representation of low-SES students at selective institutions. See Michael Bastedo and Ozan Jaquette, "Running in Place."

61. Michael Bastedo and Allyson Flaster, "Conceptual and Methodological Problems in Research on College Undermatch," *Educational Researcher* 43, no. 2 (2014) 93–99; Caroline Hoxby and Christopher Avery, "The Missing 'One-Offs': The Hidden Supply of High-Achieving, Low-income Students," *Brookings Papers on Economic Activity* 46, no. 1 (2013); Caroline Hoxby and Sarah Turner, *Expanding College Opportunities for High-Achieving, Low Income Students*, SIEPR Discussion Paper No. 12-014 (Stanford, CA: Stanford Institute for Economic Policy Research, 2013).

62. Martha Bailey and Susan Dynarski, "Gains and Gaps: Changing Inequality in US College Entry and Completion," in *Whither Opportunity? Rising Inequality, Schools, and Children's Life Chances*, ed. Greg Duncan and Richard Murnane (New York: Russell Sage, 2011); Charles T. Clotfelter, Ronald G. Ehrenberg, Malcolm Getz, and John J. Siegfried, *Economic Challenges in Higher Education* (Chicago: University of Chicago Press, 1991).

63. Ben Backes and Erin Dunlop Velez, "Community College Transfer Students: How Do They Choose Four-Year Colleges and Does It Matter?" (presented at the Association for Education Finance and Policy annual meeting, San Antonio, TX: 2014).

64. Author's calculations using BPS: 2004/2009.

65. Margaret Cahalan and Laura Perna, *Indicators of Higher Education Equity in the United States: 45-Year Trend Report* (Washington, DC: Pell Institute, 2015), 32.

66. Lane Kenworthy, *Egalitarian Capitalism: Jobs, Incomes, and Growth in Affluent Countries* (New York: Russell Sage, 2004).

67. Jennifer Engle and Vincent Tinto, *Moving beyond Access: College Success for Low-Income, First-Generation Students* (Washington, DC: Pell Institute, 2008), www .pellinstitute.org/files/COE_MovingBeyondReport_Final.pdf [accessed Jan. 31, 2010]. Note: These are based on *US News and World Report* rankings. In the original text, "top 50" and "non-top 50" designations were used instead of "flagship" and "nonflagship."

68. Based on estimates obtained using data from the BPS: 2004/2009.

69. Authors' calculations using BPS: 2004/2009.

70. Bridget Terry Long and Michal Kurlaender, "Do Community Colleges Provide a Viable Pathway to a Baccalaureate Degree?" *Educational Evaluation and Policy Analysis* 31, no. 1 (2009): 30–53.

71. Jennie E. Brand, Fabian T. Pfeffer, and Sara Goldrick-Rab, "The Community College Effect Revisited: The Importance of Attending to Heterogeneity and Complex Counterfactuals," *Sociological Science* 1 (2014): 448–65.

72. Ibid.

73. Demetra Kalogrides and Eric Grodsky, "Something to Fall Back On: Community Colleges as a Safety Net," *Social Forces* 89, no. 3 (2011): 853–77.

74. David Deming, Claudia Goldin, and Lawrence Katz, "For-Profit Colleges," *The Future of Children* 23, no. 1 (2013): 137–63; Constance Iloh and William G. Tierney, "Understanding For-Profit College and Community College Choice through Rational Choice," *Teachers College Record* 116 (2014): 1–34; James Rosenbaum, Regina Deil-Amen, and Ann E. Person, *After Admission: From College Access to College Success* (New York: Russell Sage, 2007).

75. College Board, Community Colleges, *Trends in Higher Education*, 2014, http://trends
.collegeboard.org/sites/default/files/2014-trends-student-aid-final-web.pdf.

76. Ibid.

77. Deming, Goldin, and Katz, "For-Profit Colleges."

78. US Government Accountability Office analysis of 2004 cohort data from the National Student Loan Data System (NSLDS), provided by the Department of Education, for two-year, three-year, and four-year default rates by sector, using December 2007 student loan data, in US Government Accountability Office, *Proprietary Schools: Stronger Department of Education Oversight Needed to Help Ensure Only Eligible Students Receive Federal Student Aid*, GAO-09-600 (Washington, DC: US Government Accountability Office, 2009).

79. Margaret Cahalan and Laura Perna, *Indicators of Higher Education Equity*, 19.

80. Ibid., 20.

81. Ibid., 29.

82. US Census Bureau, "PINC-03: Educational Attainment—People 25 Years Old and Over, by Total Money Earnings in 2010, Work Experiences in 2010, Age, Race, Hispanic origin, and Sex," *Current Population Survey*, Annual Social and Economic Supplement, http://www.census.gov/hhes/www/cpstables/032011/perinc/new03_262.htm.

83. Ibid.

84. S. Michael Gaddis, "Discrimination in the Credential Society: An Audit Study of Race and College Selectivity in the Labor Market," *Social Forces* 93, no. 4 (2014): 1451–79. The author refers to these two categories as "elite" versus "less selective" colleges in the paper, but the colleges he compares would all qualify as "very selective." For instance, he often compares very selective, private, nonprofit colleges (e.g., Harvard) to very selective, public, four-year colleges in the same region (e.g., UMass-Amherst, the flagship college of the University of Massachusetts system).

85. David Deming et al., "The Value of Postsecondary Credentials in the Labor Market: An Experimental Study," A CAPSEE Working Paper, Center for Analysis of Postsecondary Education and Employment (Oct. 2014).

86. Mark C. Long, "Changes in the Returns to Education and College Quality," *Economics of Education Review* 29 (2010): 338–47.

87. Stacy Dale and Alan B. Krueger, "Estimating the Return to College Selectivity of the Career Using Administrative Earning Data," *Journal of Human Resources* 49, no. 2 (2014): 323–58.

88. Deming, Goldin, and Katz, "For-Profit Colleges."

89. Hoxby and Turner, "Expanding College Opportunities."

90. Bailey, Jaggars, and Jenkins, *Redesigning America's Community Colleges*; Margaret Cahalan and Laura Perna, *Indicators of Higher Education Equity*; Sara Goldrick-Rab and Nancy Kendall, *Redefining College Affordability: Securing America's Future with a Free Two Year College Option* (Madison, WI: The EduOptimists, 2014).

# Chapter Thirteen

# The Diversity Imperative

*Moving to the Next Generation*

Daryl G. Smith

Diversity represents one of the most dramatic societal changes in the twenty-first century, with significant implications for American higher education.[1] It is shaping not only higher education, but also higher education's role in society. Today, diversity is no longer a projection—it is a reality. The challenge, however, is that while the historic issues of diversity, which have occupied many in US higher education over the last fifty years, have grown in their urgency, new issues are developing. Indeed, the breadth of concerns related to diversity on campuses throughout the United States include not only race, ethnicity, gender, and class, but religion, sexual orientation, gender identity, and disability, among others. The combination of shifting demographics and the increasing visibility of issues related to numerous identity groups indicates that the context for diversity is expanding. The growing context suggests that higher education's role in achieving the promise of democracy—developing a pluralistic society that works—could emerge as even more central than when the Truman Commission or the GI Bill articulated the link between higher education and a healthy democracy.

This chapter will briefly look at the status and the evolution of diversity efforts. It will then explore how diversity is being reframed, building on decades of research in a number of domains. The final section will examine some of the key themes from research and practice.

## The Status of Diversity

It is not possible, in this limited space, to provide an adequate overview of the development of diversity in higher education over time, nor of the current status of diversity, given its many dimensions. There are many resources available for those who want to take a more in-depth look.[2] A quick overview, however, is necessary to provide a context for the rest of the chapter and for understanding the roots of diversity, along with its future.

### DEMOGRAPHICS

The changing demographic context, from a racial and ethnic point of view, not only anchors the work on diversity in higher education, but it increasingly frames the context for the nation as well. These changes tell a powerful story, creating conditions for change that have not been seen before. Most projections suggest that by 2050 the United States will be a majority minority nation. Higher education's overall enrollment, which is now one-third "minority" (13% black, 12% Latino, 7% Asian American / Pacific Islander, 1% American Indian / Alaska Native) and 3 percent international, will, as early as 2018, be only about 59 percent white (non-Hispanic). Historically underrepresented minorities (URM—black, Latino, American Indian / Alaska Native) will comprise about 30 percent, and Asian Americans (and Pacific Islanders) about 8 percent. Significantly, while the *percentages* of white students will continue to decline, the increases in enrollment overall in higher education mean that the *numbers* of white students, as well as the numbers for every other racial and ethnic group, have and will continue to increase.[3]

While higher education will necessarily continue to address historically underrepresented groups of African American, Latino, American Indian, and low-income students, the dramatic shifts in immigration mean that other ethnicities are also emerging as underrepresented. Vietnamese and Hmong students are just two groups for whom access will be an issue. Class—often an invisible category, or one with limited data—is reappearing as critically important. Campuses now are more likely to attend to family income using Pell grants as a metric, to deduce first-generation or to look at levels of financial aid to understand the intersection of class with race and gender.

The shifting demographics of undergraduates, in particular, are not synonymous with the deep overall changes that many scholars suggest will be needed to build capacity for diversity: in leadership, faculty, centrality to the institution's core mission, research contributions, the graduate population, and the reduction of continuing gaps in student achievement. Indeed, scholars have expressed concern that diversity in undergraduate enrollments may camouflage the lack of diversity elsewhere on campus.

Faculty diversity, for example, has grown only marginally in the last twenty years. Since 1993, the percentage of full-time faculty black, Latino, and American Indian faculty combined has gone from 5 percent to 10 percent nationally. Asian American faculty has gone from 5 percent to 9 percent. International faculty has more than doubled as a percentage (from 2% to 4%). As with enrollment, even as the percentage of white faculty has declined, the numbers of white faculty, both male and female, continue to grow, with the largest expansion occurring among white women. This is in part because full-time and tenured or tenure-track faculty have grown significantly in size during this period.

Indeed, higher education has been in the midst of hiring the next generation of faculty. On a large number of campuses, that hiring has been robust. Many campuses have already replaced more than one-half of their faculty.[4] At this rate, the next generation will have been hired in the near future. However, a change in the nature of academic appointments, more part-time staff, more nontenure-track full-time faculty, and pressures on salaries are creating further problems.

Nevertheless, despite new hiring patterns that are slightly more diverse than the faculty composition overall, turnover rates now indicate that retention of faculty is slowing the rate of change. On some campuses, 60 percent of new hires go to replace people who leave, rather than enlarging the existing faculty.[5] On other campuses this percentage is even higher. Also, because federal data now make it possible to separate domestic numbers from international, we can see that the international component of faculty has grown faster than any racial and ethnic group since 1993. This suggests that campuses may understand the need to globalize their faculty for the sake of their own legitimacy more than they sense the urgency of increasing their faculty to include more members from historically underrepresented groups.

## THE EVOLUTION OF DIVERSITY

The central work of diversity, especially with respect to historically URM and white women in STEM fields (science, technology, engineering, and math), began over fifty years ago. The struggle for access focused not only on student admissions, but also on hiring. Legislation, legal challenges, and executive orders, along with campus activism, pushed higher education institutions to change.

Economic access has been a factor from early on. For example, the Higher Education Act of 1965 established need-based financial aid for the first time and created programs designed to support students from disadvantaged backgrounds. Through the early 1970s, other important steps were taken to address access: the establishment of Pell grants, a long-overdue fulfillment of the Truman Commission's report of 1947, and the passage of Title IX in 1972, mandating access for women.

While early research and policy work focused on access, the next generation recognized that opening doors would not be enough, and that student success would also need to be examined. Research done in the 1970s and 1980s began to focus on the institution, and explored whether institutions were prepared to educate a diversity of students for success. This period represents an important shift by not only addressing pipeline concerns, but also by considering the climate, culture, curriculum, research, and institutional ethos of higher education institutions more generally. During that time, important intellectual and academic developments, along with student and faculty activism, led to the creation of ethnic studies and women's studies programs. These efforts were largely compensatory, showing what was missing in the traditional curriculum. But at their core they represented fundamental critiques of generic approaches to knowledge and how knowledge, rather than being neutral and objective, reflected existing power and social structures.[6]

Historically, the primary domain of diversity has been directed to underrepresented communities and white women, although legislation and academic work has also addressed disability rights and struggles concerning equity and access for all communities of color, including Asian Americans, as well as LGBTQ (lesbian, gay, bisexual, transgender, and questioning) and working-class communities. Within each of these efforts, there have been calls for institutional change and attempts to make diversity central to that change. While one could argue that change has occurred—and somewhat dramatically—making diversity central has challenged practitioners and researchers alike.

Since the 1980s, the legal challenges to affirmative action have occupied a central place in the diversity literature. Important court battles, from *Bakke* in 1978 to the University of Michigan cases in 2002, and to *Fisher* in 2008, have succeeded in narrowing the use of race and gender in admissions criteria, especially in public institutions. In addition, several public initiatives, such as Proposition 209 in California and Proposition 2 in Michigan, have curtailed the explicit use of race and gender not only in admissions, but presumably in other domains as well. The challenges to affirmative action have centered on definitions of merit and whether race and gender should be considered a compelling national interest that would warrant different admissions and hiring criteria. In most of the litigation involving student challenges, merit has been defined as test scores, and the affirmative action disputes have relied on differences in test scores. Another argument posits that admitting students to selective institutions under affirmative action did not serve them well.[7] While the resulting court decisions have suggested that race, in particular, could be one of many factors to be considered, these decisions have virtually eliminated parallel admissions processes.

The impact of these rulings, by basically doing away with higher education's parallel access systems, have, in some respects, forced institutions to return to basic principles about the role of diversity in their educational and institutional missions. Redefining excellence in ways that consider diversity is now emerging as being critically important. Furthermore, while legal challenges remain, the communication challenge of educating the public, as well as constituencies within higher education, about the role of diversity in the well-being of society is beginning to shift conversations to higher education's role in creating the capacity needed for a pluralistic society.[8] Educational disparities—in graduation rates, teacher production, workforce capacity, and diversity in STEM fields—and health-related disparities, for example, are placing pressure on higher education to increase quality and reduce these differentiations. In addition, the research that documented the limited ability and effectiveness of standardized tests to identify talent, especially in "nontraditional" groups, has prompted institutions to consider other ways to identify talent and merit.

A great deal of work continues on access, student success and support, campus climate, curricular and pedagogical transformation, and the diversification of faculty and staff. The intellectual agenda begun over forty years ago is more likely to be reflected in the contemporary curriculum, and (though not without its challenges) it is also part of many, though not all, mainstream academic disciplines. Thus, even with all the legal and other challenges to affirmative action and diversity, it is reasonably clear that diversity is becoming more central to core institutional processes.

At the same time, the domains of diversity have increased to address the differences within the major ethnic categories; the intersections of race, class, gender, sexuality, and disability; and growing immigrant populations. Globalization presents an interesting case in point. It is clear that on many campuses,

internationalization has achieved a kind of centrality not always seen with domestic areas of diversity. And, for many, international diversity is clearly seen as
part of diversity. The increasing interest in globalization could develop in ways
that are compatible with diversity efforts, or in ways that overshadow issues of
equity dealing with race, class, and gender from a domestic perspective. Current
data suggest that international diversity may, to some degree, be being substituted for domestic diversity. International issues, while clearly bringing "diverse"
perspectives that challenge a US-centric approach, may well need to be tracked
separately, especially in terms of graduate education and faculty hiring.

## Reframing Diversity: The Research Base for the Future

The next generation of work on diversity is being built on decades of significant research. There are at least eight bodies of research that are critically important to building higher education's capacity for diversity, and, while they have
been well described in depth elsewhere, they are briefly summarized here.[9]

### EFFECTIVE EDUCATIONAL PRACTICES

Research looking at effective educational practices for URM students and for
white women in STEM fields provides a strong and growing body of knowledge
about what works and about the conditions under which students succeed. In
addition, the findings on student success more generally, and on what can be
learned in particular from special-purpose institutions such as historically black
colleges and universities, tribal colleges, and women's colleges, lays an important
foundation for the institutional elements that facilitate or hinder student success. Research suggests that good educational practices matter, and the following are just some of the themes that have emerged: the capacity of an institution
to place student learning and student success at the center of its culture, with
high expectations and the necessary support; faculty-student engagement in educationally purposeful activities; the creation of clear pathways to success; as-
surances that gateway courses are not barriers to a discipline; and attention to
advising, mentoring, and pedagogy.

### EXPERIENCING HIGHER EDUCATION

There is a rich body of literature that addresses diversity in higher education
from a number of perspectives, including historical, organizational, legal, developmental, and cultural ones. Some of the literature focuses on students and their
experiences. Other segments more broadly discuss the experience of Latinos,

African Americans, American Indians, Asian Americans, undocumented immigrants, LGBTQ peoples, those with disabilities, religious minorities, women, and the increasing diversity within each of these communities. Each of these literatures illuminates the ways in which institutional cultures inhibit diversity and change. While it is hard to summarize it adequately, this body of literature not only highlights the saliency of identity in institutional cultures and groups, but also underscores the diversity within groups (such as race, class, and sexual orientation).

## EDUCATIONAL BENEFITS OF DIVERSITY

The research on the educational benefits of diversity for all students has provided both legal and educational grounds for the positive implications of building diversity into educational programs. As that body of research has developed, it has become clearer that to achieve optimum results, appropriate conditions must also be created. Significantly, research has demonstrated the benefits of diversity to learning (such as cognitive complexity), to retention, and to satisfaction. This body of research has also explored the powerful role that identity groups play on campus; while this aspect is quite complex, there are a few conclusions that may be drawn. In the context of an institutional ethos committed to diversity and community, identity groups can play a positive role in student success. Furthermore, in contrast to the literature that challenged the balkanization of campuses because of ethnic identity groups, the research is reasonably clear that, on predominantly white campuses, it is the white student who is likely to be segregated. This body of research demonstrates the positive impact of experiencing a diverse curriculum and diversity programs.

## FACULTY DIVERSITY

This literature focuses both on the hiring and retention of a diverse faculty, and on the difference that a diverse faculty makes in terms of research and teaching. The hiring and retention literature stresses the barriers to hiring, including the myths given for limited hiring, the passive nature of searches, biases in how excellence is defined and sought, and embedded cultures that privilege existing norms over change. This research also records a similar set of challenges for the retention and success of diverse faculty. The research on the impact of a diverse faculty documents contributions not only in terms of teaching and learning, but also in terms of scholarship, community engagement, and leadership at all institutional levels.

## Emerging Conceptualizations of Identity

A large body of literature underscores the complexity of identity. While identity research is often introduced in higher education studies in the context of student development theory, this literature has important implications for the study of institutions as well. The new research facilitates the ways in which diversity must be understood as inclusive and differentiated. Three important concepts about identity have appeared in the literature: the multiplicity of identity, the ways in which identity intersects, and the contextual factors that underline how identity emerges in individuals, groups, and institutions. While this might suggest that any single identity is less important, or that studying identity at all is too complex, the literature strongly emphasizes that the significant role of identity in historical and social contexts is critically important in order to build institutions and societies that can function, creating the conditions for people to interact across boundaries.

Focusing on the ways in which identity is not about a single salient factor, but instead is inevitably about multiple characteristics (of individuals or institutions), creates conditions in which diversity within and across groups can be addressed. Furthermore, the robust body of scholarship that underscores how these intersect provides a more adequate approach to identity. More recent research on college students demonstrates how important it can be to look at race, class, and gender together, rather than singly. While it is appealing to examine one identity group at a time, the resulting picture is not adequate. If we study women and minority faculty separately, for example, the data on women will inevitably be about white women, just as the data on minorities will hide patterns concerning gender.

## Intergroup Research

In addition, there is a core group of studies in the organizational literature that demonstrates that simply bringing diverse groups together does not automatically create healthy institutional or educational environments, especially for those who are in the minority. This research highlights the important role played by the design of interventions and the culture of institutions, which impact the ways in which people participate. Asymmetry in intergroup relations is a consistent theme in the literature on diversity in groups and on intergroup dynamics, particularly in organizational and societal contexts. For example, the literature in social psychology dealing with ethnic conflict throughout the world and intergroup relations demonstrates that intergroup teamwork can be experienced quite differently, depending on the position of and the context for individuals. Indeed, this research suggests that for groups in less-powerful positions, trying to downplay identity will only enhance its significance. The management literature also suggests that placing diversity at the center of an institution's mission will be crucial in establishing the conditions in which diversity is positive.

Asymmetry in power and position and the role of institutional commitment are just two of the concepts that are important in understanding intergroup relations. The research literature is rather clear, however, in noting that this is not a function of the people who represent diversity, but rather of the capacity of institutions to create healthy conditions *for* diversity. While much of the intergroup research in higher education has focused on students, there is a large group of studies that looks at institutional capacity and conditions that create positive environments for all participants.

### Educational Competencies for a Global Society

There is increasing attention to the educational implications of a pluralistic society and a very interconnected world. A number of scholarly domains have paid attention to these educational implications in terms of outcomes and competencies. Some of this work emerges out of the intercultural literature that examined cultural knowledge and the ways in which students will need to build their competencies to cross cultures. Another body primarily focuses on the competencies required for addressing the inequity and power issues that emerge more from structural concerns than cultural ones. Recent work has attempted to provide frameworks that bring these two domains together, so that the outcomes of education enable students to cross boundaries of both culture and power.

### Levers for Change

Finally, there is an emerging literature that has begun to illuminate the levers for change in higher education, both broadly and for those dealing with diversity. When combined with other literature in the social sciences on change, this has produced increasing knowledge about the transformational process and the means by which capacity can be built. Emerging themes include the significance of institutional mission and culture, intentionality, commitment, leadership at all levels, change agents, critical incidents, social movements, and the role of outside agencies.

## Reframing Diversity to Include Building Capacity

Some important directions for the next generation begin to emerge from the efforts to date. One of the important shifts appears to be the question of diversity's relationship to the institution. Conceptualizing diversity, and the identities associated with it, as not only being about individuals and groups, but also as embedded in institutions, is emerging as central. In other words, diversity is being framed *institutionally*, not only in the ways institutions educate a diverse group of students, but also in the ways that institutions do or do not create healthy pluralistic communities and fulfill their mission for a pluralistic society.

Building both on the work that has come before and on dramatic changes in demography, it is reasonably clear that diversity, as with technology before it, is likely to be central to higher education's mission and excellence in the twenty-first century. While legal challenges to efforts that seem to target particular groups will probably persist, the overwhelming shifts in demography and the need to appear equitable will increase the pressures on institutions to "diversify." How this will be done, and which institutions will reflect the most change, will need to be studied in the coming years. This, however, does represent a shift from having to defend diversity as if it were optional. While the *value* of diversity may need to be demonstrated for communications purposes or in response to legal challenges, the *reality* of diversity is likely to become embedded in at least some parts of institutional practice. Diversity will have implications for how to build the capacity of institutions to be effective and high performing in an increasingly pluralistic society, forming an arena in which diversity thrives and also where conditions are created to make sure diversity works. Some of these changes may emerge from the necessity of appealing to diverse groups, or from incidents that require institutions to act, or from political pressures.

### THE TECHNOLOGY ANALOGY

Reframing diversity as addressing institutional capacity, and locating diversity as central to the institution, is not an easy transition conceptually. Understanding the notion of "building capacity" requires a clear picture of the stakes for *institutions* concerning diversity. Here I want to suggest a useful parallel, aligning diversity with campus efforts to build capacity for technology.

Several decades ago, as technological shifts began, campuses all across the country understood that their viability as institutions would rest on building capacity for technology. Technology was understood to be central, not marginal, to teaching and research. Most critically, technology was also seen as central to the viability of every institution—that is, central to how the institution communicated, built infrastructure, spent money, and went about hiring. The absence of technology was seen as a threat to the attractiveness of campuses and their ability to function. Moreover, because technology is continually changing, institutions, almost without question, adapted as new technologies were introduced. A redesign of all institutional domains—from the curriculum to hiring to infrastructure—has occurred. Technology, being at its core, is now a part of everyday life and of every corner of institutional life. And, on many campuses, a position has been created for a chief information officer whose task is to develop strategies for the future, for allocating resources, and for coordinating campus efforts.

Building technological capacity has required that institutions develop the human, physical, fiscal, knowledge, and cultural resources to respond effectively in a technological society. The technology imperative has required institutions to change in order to be excellent; it was not about changing just so students would be competent. Significantly, there was and has been skepticism, and even hostility, regarding the impact of technology on society and institutions. While many of the fears that were generated have not come to pass, it was also true that no one waited for the skeptics to be satisfied. Rather, technology was understood to be a given, and institutions realized that engaging technology was imperative for their viability.

### HIGHER EDUCATION AND DIVERSITY TODAY

We are now at a time when diversity, like technology, is a powerful presence. Current work suggests that increasing numbers of institutions will need to address diversity to be credible or, indeed, viable. An understanding of the role of diversity for institutional viability and vitality is emerging in business and other sectors of society. It is already fundamental to urban planning and the language of community building. Reframing diversity as central to institutional effectiveness, excellence, and viability will no doubt be a requisite for higher education. For example, enrollment-dependent institutions in the Midwest are already working to become more attractive to Latino and Asian communities in the Southwest.

One way to think about diversity in the twenty-first century is to begin with a scan of many compelling issues in society that are linked to diversity and higher education. Changing demographics, increasing demands for equity from many groups, immigration, health disparities, educational disparities, inequities, civil rights, nation states and ethnic identity, the strengthening of indigenous communities, acknowledgment of histories of injustice, equity in the workplace, and the business interest of appealing to diverse markets are among the larger topics with implications for higher education and diversity.

A fundamental question emerging in the literature is how society goes about building its capacity to harness the talent and full participation of its citizens in order to address the compelling challenges it faces. Indeed, almost every report that explores the political and economic future of society begins by discussing education and its role. For example, in its 2005 report, *Now Is the Time*, the American Association of State Colleges and Universities and the National Association of State Universities and Land-Grant Colleges declared that "the promise of a truly just and truly multicultural democracy made possible through a more diverse academy cannot wait for another generation. The challenge for change within higher education must be taken up and addressed boldly. And it must be addressed today."[10]

What, then, is higher education's role? The tendency in much of the literature is to imagine education as a linear path in which higher education is the elite end of the pipeline, with K–12 as the place to begin. At one point, the notion was that if K–12 were fixed, the problem would be fixed. Increasingly, however, higher education is understood as crucial to educational reform. Teacher training, workforce development, knowledge creation, and student success are just a few of the mandates linked to higher education. Yet, despite improvements in the pipeline, there is evidence that higher education is not prepared to educate the diverse students who come to its institutions. More critically, it is not well-enough prepared to identify talent and excellence in students, in staff, or in faculty to take full advantage of the talent and excellence that currently exists.

In this next generation of diversity work, student success is a necessary but not always sufficient indicator of institutional effectiveness. Judging from the literature, the next generation will need to take a systems approach to diversity, focusing on building capacity in all sectors: identifying talent, expanding the knowledge and research base, and even engaging in difficult dialogues. The literature strongly suggests that developing capacity for diversity will require, among other things, engaging more deeply with mission, including being able to link diversity with excellence; framing diversity in ways that are both inclusive and differentiated; building human capacity; and mounting an intentional effort to monitor progress.[11]

## Mission

The role of institutional mission is emerging as central to much of the writing and research on diversity seen from an institutional perspective. It has become clear that a key lever for change is the degree to which diversity is understood to be an imperative for the institution—an imperative that goes beyond simply serving students. A mission that places diversity at its center has implications for student success, for creating inclusive environments, and for fostering the benefits of diversity.

On many campuses, diversity efforts focus on undergraduate students and on admissions criteria. As important as these are, they are issues for only a small set of institutions. Even as diversity in admissions has been a central topic for selective institutions, increasing numbers of campuses are beginning to ask how and in what ways diversity is relevant to a university's *research* mission. Why is diversity in STEM fields important—not only at the undergraduate level, but at the field level? Why is diversity vital to a high-quality medical education in the twenty-first century? When the technology version of these questions were posed, the answers helped instigate fundamental changes in institutions. The same now applies to diversity. Framing diversity as central, rather than parallel, to the core mission of a campus or a field requires a deep understanding of the institution, its history, its position, and the imperatives that motivate it.

## Operationalizing Diversity as Inclusive and Differentiated

The definition of "diversity" is a challenging one these days. Indeed, on many campuses, diversity committees begin with the question, how will we define diversity? The subtext asks, are we to be inclusive or should we focus only on the historic issues of racial (or gender) inequities on campus? The reality is that there is a growing list of questions to be considered, with a growing set of projects and programs designed to provide support and promote institutional change. Historic and largely unfinished efforts related to race, class, and gender are being addressed. Other concerns—applying to disability, sexual orientation, gender identity, immigration, and religion, among others—are also pressing topics. This has led to strong criticism of many diversity efforts, seeing them as losing a crucial focus on historic issues of inequity in favor of a laundry list of concerns. At the same time, how can a campus choose among legitimate concerns expressed by diverse groups?

The evolution of diversity, as described earlier, shows how it can be understood to be both inclusive and differentiated. With careful articulation, it would seem possible to move forward on multiple fronts. In this conceptualization, access and the success of historically underrepresented populations remain the legacy and the soul of diversity. Moreover, the research on both diversity and identity makes it clear that intersections of identities and the multiplicity of identities will need to be addressed, even for traditionally underrepresented populations; these are places where gender and class, as well as other identities, are gaining in significance. Linking diversity to this multiplicity of identities, to the intersections of identities, and to their institutional and societal contexts is conceptually and analytically important.

Figure 13.1 presents a conceptual framework to reflect one way of capturing diversity across four institutional dimensions. Each engages different aspects of the university and encompasses much of the diversity work that is occurring. Each dimension is also clearly connected to the others. Together, they frame a way to think about an operational approach to diversity that is both inclusive and differentiated. While this figure was designed to foster thought about diversity institutionally, these four dimensions may also be useful in thinking about the larger task of systemic change. Moreover, because institutions (either within or outside of higher education) are centers for much of this effort, the institutional and societal connections are important and, hence, are reflected in the figure. Finally, if we think of the framework as holistically reflecting the mission and domains of an institution of higher education, it is not difficult to see how diversity efforts and excellence are linked.

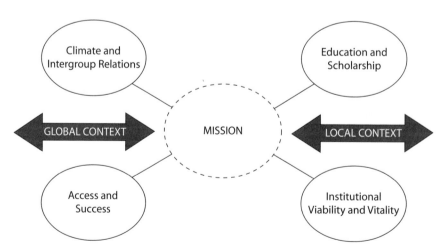

*Figure 13.1.* Framework for diversity

The *institutional viability and vitality* domain, in particular, addresses institutional-level concerns about capacity. How does the mission engage diversity? How are the core indicators of excellence and the priorities for strategic planning directly linked to diversity? For example, if we were to read a strategic plan for a research university, is diversity central in that document? This domain also includes how the institution is viewed from the perspective of diverse communities: whether it is seen as having a commitment to diversity, and whether it has the leadership capacity with the requisite expertise to meet the demands of diversity. Moreover, because institutions are also employers and organizations, excellence will include understanding whether the institution is inclusive, and whether it creates an environment in which all of its members can thrive.

The second domain for diversity reflects what diversity is in the academic core of higher education—*education and scholarship*. What is the knowledge that *all* students (including graduate and professional students) and professionals need to have in a pluralistic society, and what is the capacity of faculty to provide the necessary research and curricular base? In a research university, this dimension might also emphasize graduate education and scholarly contributions. In a community college, attention to success with respect to developmental education is important. This domain focuses not only on what is offered and what students take, but also on what students learn. Thus the educational domain goes directly to learning outcomes, so central to higher education today. What are the core competencies essential to a twenty-first-century education? Do these competencies address both global and domestic sets of issues? Excellence, then, as a twenty-first-century mandate, would be connected to how research, scholarship, teaching, and learning all relate to diversity.

The third dimension focuses on *climate and intergroup relations* on the campus as they apply to students, staff, and faculty. What is the climate, culture, and ultimate attractiveness of the institution, or what is it in a given area, such as STEM? This dimension is often the focus of concern for groups that have experienced marginalization. For all communities of color on predominantly white campuses, campus climate emerges as an essential topic. Climate has also been an important point of departure with respect to women's issues, as well as to those regarding sexual orientation and gender identity. In the years following 9/11, climate has been a concern for Muslim faculty, staff, and students, along with curricular concerns about whether enough is done to educate all about Islam. Some of the research today suggests that if campuses and departments don't deal with the issue of climate, and don't examine their attractiveness and capacity for people to thrive, pipeline efforts will reach a dead end. Excellence, then, would rest on whether an inclusive environment for diverse groups of faculty, staff, and students has been established.

This dimension also includes a concern for intergroup relationships. How do groups engage across differences? While higher education has begun to address, quite formally, intergroup relationships among students, there has been less engagement of intergroup relationships among faculty and staff. Indeed, the higher education literature has focused on the conditions for bringing students together in order to realize the benefits of diversity, applying what has been learned to creating the conditions necessary for bringing people from diverse backgrounds together at every level on a campus—from the president's cabinet, to decision-making bodies, to administrative units, to women's studies departments—is becoming increasingly important.

The literature clearly suggests that one area in which too few institutions have capacity is in that of engaging difficult issues. Even diversity task forces are challenged to talk through the topic of how to be both inclusive and differentiated with regard to diversity. The lack of capacity for such engagement is a powerful and negative model for students, and it also makes campuses increasingly vulnerable to incidents when such issues explode. Moreover, an inability to have difficult dialogues makes it hard to truly use all of the talent available to address the critical challenges of society. A Ford Foundation program identified this area as one of the most urgent ones on increasingly diverse campuses.[12] Significantly, the concerns expressed were not just about students. They touched on dealing with conflict in the classroom, decision making on the campus, and community relations.

The last of the four dimensions is really the soul and heritage of diversity in higher education—*access and success of historically underrepresented students*. Here one is asking not just about admissions (who has access?), but also about who succeeds. While graduation rates are often the starting point, increasingly campuses are asking how different groups are thriving. The movement out of STEM fields by many white women and underrepresented groups is taking center stage in current discussions about the human capital needs in STEM and the health professions. Of those who begin with an interest in science, which groups persist and why? For whom is higher education not successful, and what should be done about it?

Indeed, if we map much of the diversity work to date onto these dimensions, we would see that the bulk of it has been focused on improvement in the access and success dimension. Inevitably, however, institutional changes in each of the other dimensions emerge—climate, curriculum, faculty diversity, and so forth. Fortunately, the results of research and the evolution of promising practices in each of these domains are fairly well aligned. Moreover, because of the lack of adequate institutional capacity, focused efforts to support historically underrepresented groups so they can succeed will likely remain a critical priority, requiring strategic programmatic approaches. Excellence will be very much connected to the institution's success in educating diverse populations. This requirement is increasingly central to emerging accreditation practices, as well as federal and state discussions of effectiveness.

### Developing Human Capacity: The Rationale for Leadership Diversity

The important role of leadership at all institutional levels in building capacity for diversity is discussed in virtually all of the research and field work in higher education. It focuses not only on the critical role of leaders who may be presidents, but also on faculty, staff, administrators, and even students. While virtually all diversity work emphasizes diversity in leadership, the rationale is often implicit. As such, it deserves some elaboration here. These rationales apply to all the identities reflected in diversity efforts. However, because most of the attention in the leadership arena has been on the continuing inadequate representation of communities of color, they are the focus here.

In the literature on faculty diversity, for example, the rationale for diversity in hiring has relied on an assumption (one that has merit) that student success will be impacted by faculty diversity. The mismatch here is that faculty hiring is rarely determined by student demographics. Thus, while changing institutions for the sake of students is compelling to some, it is but one of the reasons that make diversity compelling for institutional success and excellence.

From both an institutional perspective and the perspective of the field, the central question is, what expertise and talent will be needed for institutions, in order for them to be credible, effective, and viable in a pluralistic society? When technology became central, this was clearly described. What, then, are the reasons that can be identified for diversity in leadership?

- Diversity in leadership represents values concerning equity in both hiring and retention. Any institution that simultaneously describes itself as open and committed to diversity, yet has the faculty or leadership demographic common today, could be seen as disingenuous and hypocritical.

- Diversity is also a central component in the academy's ability to develop newer forms of knowledge. The consistent findings from numerous studies demonstrate the role of diverse faculty in bringing diversity themes to scholarship, in increasing diversity in the curriculum, and in introducing more and different patterns of pedagogy, including upping the engagement of students in the community. The likelihood of framing new questions and approaches is greater when diversity is increased. The result for the institution is better knowledge and more credible applications of it.

- Another way in which leadership diversity contributes is in developing vital relationships with diverse communities. There are few campuses in the United States that have not begun to formulate relationships with communities off campus, many of which are very diverse. Moreover, some funding agencies are requiring campuses to demonstrate relationships with such communities for clinical purposes or educational efforts. At such times, campuses look to demonstrate their capacity with respect to diversity by highlighting key people on campus who can bring legitimacy to those community relationships. Community connections and credibility are compromised without diversity in leadership.

- Faculty and staff from diverse racial and ethnic backgrounds are also essential to the capacity of institutions and policy groups to make fully informed decisions at all levels—what has been called the demography of decision making. Such participation not only increases the likelihood of more informed perspectives, but also increases the credibility of decision making.

- These rationales are implicitly understood with respect to globalization (or technology, for that matter)—where an interest in furthering internationalization as part of an institution's mission almost inevitably involves hiring international faculty who bring educational and scholarly expertise. Moreover, it is clear that having people from international backgrounds represented on the faculty will enhance an institution's credibility and its ability to connect to an increasingly globalized society. While these arguments commonly inform global discussions, they are not always applied when hiring faculty from diverse domestic racial and ethnic backgrounds.

- Faculty and staff diversity is also essential for creating an environment that will be attractive to persons from diverse backgrounds as a good place to work and to develop. Increasing numbers of faculty and administrators (of all backgrounds) are basing their decisions about where to work on the diversity of students and the diversity of faculty and staff on the campus. Until there is sufficient diversity in campus departments and divisions, members of underrepresented groups will struggle to be seen as individuals, rather than as tokens. Environmental appeal appears to be well understood as a critical factor for white women in science. It remains underappreciated as it pertains to URM faculty and students, where the pipeline explanations are dominant.

- Perhaps the most overlooked rationale is the relationship between the current demographics of faculty and staff and the future leadership pipeline. Since most academic administrators come from faculty ranks, a relatively homogenous faculty clearly limits the future development of diversity in leadership—something that is cause for great concern in a number of sectors in higher education.

- Finally, the most frequently mentioned rationale is to provide role models for all. While the empirical literature is mixed, it seems reasonably clear that seeing individuals from diverse backgrounds function in faculty and other leadership roles in all areas provides ways of envisioning oneself (whether as an undergraduate, graduate, or faculty member) in that role or experiencing others there. While less often mentioned or studied, it is likely that the *absence* of diversity in so many departments and fields is what sends strong signals about what is possible and about the degree to which talent from diverse groups is valued. Consistent research in STEM fields highlights the number of 0s and 1s in the count of URM and white women in many science and medical school departments.[13]

These reasons are both broad and deep in their implications for diversifying leadership—the core strategy for building capacity. A review of current research and emerging literature on promising practices suggest that higher education will have to "interrupt the usual" to build its potential to identify talent and excellence in hiring and promotion.

## Monitoring Progress

A number of different initiatives have all concluded that monitoring progress will be essential for change.[14] The reality on many campuses is that perceptions of progress toward diversity are very much influenced by individual perspectives. Leaders often need to highlight positive changes, even as many in the institution see little or no change in other domains. Talking past one another is common, but it is an impediment to change.

The literature also recognizes that using data for decision making, especially in higher education, is difficult. This is not about compliance. Indeed, most of this literature frames its emphasis on the role of data in terms of organizational learning—that is, using data to assist in making decisions or evaluating progress. On too many campuses, diversity task forces are spinning their wheels or generating programs that the same few people have to oversee. Moreover, because creating programs does not require *addressing* institutional change, the proliferation of programs is leading to "projectitis" rather than change.[15] The guiding question now is, how can an institution know if it is making progress, and in what areas, so that resources can be strategically applied?

While the following paragraphs focus on key indicators that are often quantitative, qualitative assessments are also important. The quantitative indicators, however, serve as ways of seeing directions for change from an institutional or unit perspective. In fact, key indicators associated with each of the dimensions of diversity in figure 13.1 are beginning to be identified.

To date, the most common of these have to do with the access and success demographics of underrepresented students, disaggregated by race intersected with gender. Because patterns for African American, Latino, and American Indian men and women often differ, today's disaggregation among URM as well as Asian groups is providing more complete data. In addition, more attention is being paid to first generation students and the intersection with race and gender. Work in the access and success dimension is now focusing on indicators of success and institutional practices that facilitate success. Persistence and graduation rates are the most common, again disaggregated at least by race and gender. While graduation rates have been controversial—because of differences in institutional selectivity, federal reliance just on statistics for full-time students, and the fact that the information only reveals the graduation rate from a particular institution—these data provide powerful descriptions of an institution's success with the students it admits. Indeed, the cost of dropouts, both to society and to fields such as science and health, is now being documented. On campuses with high graduation rates, another key indicator being proposed is the diversity in STEM graduates or honors graduates. Moreover, there are data that suggest that many URM students enter higher education interested in STEM fields but leave during their undergraduate years, indicating that an emphasis merely on the pipeline may not be altogether appropriate.

Key indicators emerging in the viability and vitality dimension are faculty, staff, and board diversity. Because faculty diversity that moves beyond token representation is connected to every element of capacity building—research, clinical practice, teaching, decision making, external credibility, and so forth—it is located in the dimension related to institutional viability. Historically, the diversity of the graduate and professional school population was considered part of the analysis of student demographics. It is becoming increasingly clear that graduate student and professional school diversity instead needs to be linked to the pipeline for faculty. Indeed, on many campuses the graduate students are not much more diverse than the faculty. Higher education produces its own labor market, so concerns about faculty diversity involve monitoring graduate student populations as well.

What might indicators in the educational and scholarship domain be—at least, indicators that can be monitored?[16] For example, in medicine, to what degree does a medical education include cultural competency? Who is exposed to such a curriculum? What about the content of continuing education for physicians? Where and how much research is addressing diversity in health care, medicine, pharmacology, and the like? In the study of higher education, to what degree does the literature on organizational culture or leadership deeply engage the ways in which diversity influences and informs both theory and practice? A review of these areas suggests that a deep engagement with diversity is largely absent from the classical study of leadership and organizational culture, while there is a rich literature on that topic emanating from the study of diversity in higher education.

In the climate domain, there are a number of key indicators that are used. A powerful one for campuses has been the perception of an institution's commitment to diversity, disaggregated by constituency and identity groups. Single questions on overall satisfaction, and whether one would choose the institution (or field) again, can be very illuminating when disaggregated. While invisible forms of identity have often rendered some communities "silent" in official data, more and more campuses are asking about the campus climate for the LGBTQ community as well.

## Implications for Higher Education as a Field of Study

Just as diversity has often functioned parallel to core institutional domains, parallelism is also true in some areas in the study of higher education. While there is a substantial body of literature on college students that addresses diversity, less has been done on how diversity perspectives impact the study of organizations, especially in the context of higher education. Moreover, where diversity and organizational theory and practice are linked, the research and theory are often located in a larger body of literature connected to diversity, rather than to the study of higher education organizations.

Adrianna Kezar, Rozana Carducci, and Melissa Contreras-McGavin note that while literatures exist that do study, for example, leadership in cross-cultural contexts, little of that has impacted the core study of leadership in higher education.[17] Though there is considerable research on institutional change, Anthony Antonio and Marcela Muñiz suggest that work on the intersection of diversity and transformation has only begun.[18] Further, many scholars of color have observed that observations on how institutions are racialized or gendered are largely absent from the study of organizations within or outside of higher education.[19] Marta Calás and Linda Smircich describe it this way:

> The organizational literature that supposedly considers gender has been labeled women-in-management literature. The . . . label reveals that gender is important to organizational theorizing only because the biological entities—women—suddenly arrived in management, changing the nature of the situation. Prior to the entrance of women, there was (apparently) no "gender" in management.[20]

The significance of this quotation is that diversity, and the identities associated with diversity, are not only about individuals and groups. Rather, they are embedded in institutions—and, indeed, in the study of institutions—in ways that are more often ignored than addressed. While the literature on organizational culture often includes some reference to diversity, it is the literature on diversity that highlights the ways in which culture reflects the stratification and values of higher education and society. It is in that literature where what is often described generically as "institutional culture" is uncovered to show the ways in which culture is racialized, gendered, classed, and so on. If the study of culture is to be robust, the processes of how culture is shaped and changed by the dynamics of power and the asymmetry of power in institutions will need to be engaged.[21]

Indeed, Frances Maher and Mary Kay Tetrault, in their study of three universities in transition, found that an important element in institutional transformation, and therefore in the study of institutions, consisted of taking into account forms of privilege that are embedded in institutional norms and practices—forms of privilege that may be invisible to some, but are certainly very visible to those on the margins of that experience.[22] White privilege. Class privilege. Gender privilege. Heterosexual privilege. Additionally, Robert Merton's concept of cumulative advantage is applicable to the study of higher education, as an aid to understanding how privilege accrues in institutions.[23]

Just as the scholarship in ethnic studies and women's studies has ultimately informed many of the disciplines, the field of organizational studies in higher education is now positioned to benefit from decades of conceptual, theoretical, and practical work on diversity in higher education.

## Conclusion

Diversity as transformation has been apparent in the literature for decades. However, a changing societal context in the United States creates the likelihood that diversity, like technology, will take its place as more of an imperative, one that may lead to greater institutional change. And the pressure for change, as in the past, will most likely come from a variety of external entities. By framing diversity as central to the institution and to society, and emphasizing it as an imperative, campuses may be positioned to positively address contemporary challenges.

The emerging research suggests some important elements for building capacity: establishing links to mission and excellence; framing diversity as inclusive and differentiated; increasing diversity in leadership; and monitoring progress. It is clear from the literature that building institutional capacity so that individuals and groups can thrive will not be easy, but it is a critical component. Intentionality, rather than myths and excuses to explain a lack of progress, and the fostering of synergy among the many creative efforts and talented people already working in the area both appear to provide proactive and inclusive ways to create change. Finally, identifying key indicators and monitoring progress on a regular basis, with some form of accountability, is emerging in the literature as vital for institutions, in order to see where progress is being made and where more work is needed.

Higher education's crucial role in building a thriving pluralistic and equitable society is now being established. Reorienting diversity to an institutional level will be necessary if real progress is to be made. Diversity is no longer an option. Calls for accountability, and concerns about society, will make this agenda more and more urgent, and they are likely to determine higher education's role as a public good for a healthy democracy.

NOTES

1. For a more complete and extensive analysis see Daryl G. Smith, *Diversity's Promise for Higher Education: Making It Work*, 2nd ed. (Baltimore: Johns Hopkins University Press, 2015).

2. See, for example, Bryan J. Cook and Diana. I. Córdova, *Minorities in Higher Education: Twenty-Second Annual Status Report* (Washington, DC: American Council on Education, 2006); Michael J. Cuyjet, "African American College Men," in *African American Men in College*, ed. Michael J. Cuyjet (San Francisco: Jossey-Bass, 2006), 3–23; Catherine E. Freeman, *Trends in Educational Equity of Girls and Women: 2004*, NCES 2005-016 (Washington, DC: US Department of Education, Institute of Education Sciences, 2005); Jacqueline E. King, *Gender Equity in Higher Education: 2006* (Washington, DC: American Council on Education, Center for Policy Analysis, 2006); National Research Council, *Hispanics and the Future of America* (Washington, DC: National Academy Press, 2006).

3. National Center for Educational Statistics (NCES), *Projections of Education Statistics to 2018* (2009), Table 22, http://nces.ed.gov/pubsearch/pubsinfo.asp?pubid=2009062.

4. José F. Moreno, Daryl G. Smith, Alma R. Clayton-Pedersen, Sharon Parker, and Daniel H. Teraguchi, *The Revolving Door for Underrepresented Minority Faculty in Higher Education* (San Francisco: James Irvine Foundation, 2006), www.irvine.org/assets/pdf/pubs/education/insight_Revolving_Door.pdf; see also Smith, *Diversity's Promise*.

5. Alma R. Clayton-Pedersen, Sharon Parker, Daryl G. Smith, José. F. Moreno, and Daniel H. Teraguchi, *Making a Real Difference with Diversity: A Guide to Institutional Change* (Washington, DC: Association of American Colleges and Universities, 2007); see also Moreno et al., *Revolving Door*; Smith, *Diversity's Promise*.

6. See, for example, Elizabeth K. Minnich, *Transforming Knowledge*, 2nd ed. (Philadelphia: Temple University Press, 2005); Fabio Rojas, *From Black Power to Black Studies: How a Radical Social Movement Became an Academic Discipline* (Baltimore: Johns Hopkins University Press, 2007); Linda T. Smith, *Decolonizing Methodologies: Research and Indigenous Peoples* (London: Zed Books, 1999).

7. Carl Cohen and James P. Sterba, *Affirmative Action and Racial Preference: A Debate* (New York: Oxford University Press, 2003); Shelby Steele, *A Dream Deferred* (New York: HarperCollins, 1999); Richard H. Sander, "A Systemic Analysis of Affirmative Action in American Law Schools," *Stanford Law Review* 57, no. 2 (2004): 367–484; Mark A. Chesler,

Amanda E. Lewis, and James E. Crowfoot, *Challenging Racism in Higher Education: Promoting Justice* (Oxford: Rowman and Littlefield, 2005).

8. There is a tendency to assume that only the public external to higher education needs to be engaged. Instead, several of the movements against affirmative action in higher education began with internal constituencies of faculty and/or alumni.

9. Smith, *Diversity's Promise*.

10. American Association of State Colleges and Universities and National Association of State Universities and Land-Grant Colleges, *Now Is the Time: Meeting the Challenge for a Diverse Academy* (Washington, DC: American Association of State Colleges and Universities and National Association of State Universities and Land-Grant Colleges, 2005), 3.

11. See, for example, Estela M. Bensimon, "The Diversity Scorecard: A Learning Approach to Institutional Change," *Change* 36, no. 1 (2004): 45–52; Clayton-Pedersen et al., *Making a Real Difference*; Smith, *Diversity's Promise*.

12. Ford Foundation, *Difficult Dialogues: Promoting Pluralism and Academic Freedom*, http://fordfound.org/news/more/dialogues/05_difficult_dialogues_letter.pdf [accessed June 20, 2005].

13. Donna J. Nelson and Diana C. Rogers, *A National Analysis of Diversity in Science and Engineering Faculties at Research Universities*, www.now.org/issues/diverse/diversity _report.pdf [accessed June 15, 2007].

14. See, for example, Susan P. Sturm, "The Architecture of Inclusion: Advancing Workplace Equity in Higher Education," Columbia Public Law Research Paper No. 06-114 and *Harvard Journal of Law & Gender* 29, no. 2 (June 2006), http://ssrn.com/abstract =901992; Clayton-Pedersen et al., *Making a Real Difference*; Peter D. Eckel, Madeleine F. Green, and Barbara Hill, *On Change V: Riding the Waves of Change; Insights from Transforming Institutions* (Washington, DC: American Council on Education, 2001); Adrianna J. Kezar and Peter D. Eckel, *Leadership Strategies for Advancing Campus Diversity: Advice from Experienced Presidents* (Washington, DC: American Council on Education, 2005). Also see note 11.

15. Robert Shireman, "10 Questions College Officials Should Ask about Diversity," *Chronicle Review* (Aug. 15, 2003), http://chronicle.com/article/10-Questions-College-Offici /22781/.

16. More information about key indicators can be found in Smith, *Diversity's Promise*.

17. Adrianna J. Kezar, Rozana Carducci, and Melissa Contreras-McGavin, *Rethinking the "L" Word in Higher Education*, ASHE Higher Education Report, vol. 31, no 6 (San Francisco: Jossey-Bass, 2006).

18. Anthony L. Antonio and Marcela M. Muñiz, "The Sociology of Diversity," in *Sociology of Higher Education: Contributions and Their Context*, ed. Patricia J. Gumport (Baltimore: Johns Hopkins University Press, 2007), 266–94.

19. See, for example, Stella M. Nkomo and Taylor Cox, Jr., "Diverse Identities in Organizations," in *Handbook of Organization Studies*, ed. Stewart Clegg, Cynthia Hardy, and Walter R. Nord (Thousand Oaks, CA: Sage, 1996), 338–56.

20. Marta B. Calás and Linda Smircich, "Re-Writing Gender into Organizational Theorizing: Directions from Feminist Perspectives," in *Rethinking Organization: New*

*Directions in Organization Theory and Analysis*, ed. Michael I. Reed and Michael Hughes (London: Sage, 1992), 229.

21.  See, for example, Regina D. Langhout, Francine Rosselli, and Jonathan Feinstein, "Assessing Classism in Academic Settings," *Review of Higher Education* 30, no. 2 (2006): 145–84.

22.  Frances A. Maher and Mary Kay Tetrault, *Privilege and Diversity in the Academy* (New York: Routledge, 2007).

23.  Robert K. Merton, "The Matthew Effect in Science, II: Cumulative Advantage and the Symbolism of Intellectual Property," *ISIS* 79 (1988): 606–23.

# Chapter Fourteen

# Homing in on Learning and Teaching

*Current Approaches and Future Directions*
*for Higher Education Policy*

Anna Neumann and Corbin M. Campbell

O n viewing an active and busy college class these days, we are prompted to ask, are these students learning in full and rich ways—and does the teaching they experience in this classroom support such learning? To address these linked questions, we could invite a well-prepared observer to walk into the classroom, take a seat, and listen closely to what students and instructor say to each other about the topic they are studying—be that the logic of the periodic table in a chemistry class, meanings of culture in an anthropology class, or the concept of point of view in a literature class. We would ask that, at base, the observer understand the topic being taught deeply and flexibly enough to be able to trace changes in students' thinking about it over time and at levels signifying deep understanding. We would also want the observer to be skilled in examining what the instructor says and does to probe students' thinking and to help them work with ideas in ways that are new to them.

In contrast to this up-close narrative that a prepared observer could provide, contemporary teaching and learning assessments typically rely on more distanced and strategic views—for example, summary test results, student survey findings, teaching load reports, results of students' evaluations of teaching, and learning outcomes. Policy makers and institutional decision makers value such data, aggregated institutionally and beyond, since they contribute to high-level policy discourses and campus-level strategizing toward educational improvement. Assessments that produce such data have brought the "education" of higher education squarely into policy makers'—and the public's—view. Conceptions of educational quality growing out of such assessment data are now a centerpiece of policy discourses in American higher education. In fact, since the 1980s, a veritable assessment industry has arisen in response to policy needs and related institutional leadership.[1] Reaching still further into American homes, questions about educational quality matter increasingly to future students, their families, and their employers.

Given growing public and policy interests in educational quality, and in assessments of it, knowledge about both could be improved. The quality movement, including related assessment interests, call on policy makers to better understand what goes on in college classrooms in the name of academic learning, and of teaching defined as practices for advancing learning. Though useful in providing an institutional view, current assessment methods elide the richness of teaching and learning that only a front-row view—like that of the prepared observer—can provide.

In this chapter, we suggest that it will soon be possible to couple the current assessment movement's notable strengths—to "sum up" data toward an institutional view—with two newer developments: deepened research-based understandings of what it means personally for students to learn academic content and for instructors to teach toward such learning (the "front row" view), and new study designs and methods for collecting and analyzing data about these processes. We suggest that to support policy makers' efforts to "see" what goes on in classrooms—and on a scale far larger than a single observer can provide—we need new theories of teaching and learning, and new methods for putting those theories to work. Echoing the leading higher education researcher Robert Birnbaum, and before him, the eminent social psychologist Kurt Lewin, we are guided by the maxim that for persons seeking to improve large-scale organizational processes—like teaching and learning—"there is nothing as useful as a good theory."[2] We would add to that the need for good methods of assessing what those theories let us see.

Fortunately, we do now have access to new theory drawn from research on human cognition and the learning sciences on what it means to learn, and what it means to teach in ways that support learning.[3] These new perspectives—termed "cognitively responsive"—promise to inform public policy makers', college leaders', and instructors' understandings of learning and teaching and efforts to improve them.[4] They also promise to guide improvement of educational assessment, policy, and practice.

In this chapter, we lay out key facets of learning and teaching—focusing first on *what is learned*, then on *who is learning*, and finally, on what counts as *success in learning*—and alternating between a cognitively responsive view and one derived from extant policy uses (largely driven through attention to assessment of student learning outcomes). In doing so, we discuss current policy-anchored approaches to conceptualizing and assessing learning and teaching in higher education. Drawing on this analysis, we point out strengths and areas ripe for improvement. We conclude with directions for change in extant conceptualizations of higher education learning and teaching, and their assessment.

## Learning What? Learning of Academic Content

Below we present two views of students' academic learning: cognitively responsive and policy-driven.

### Cognitively Responsive View

From a cognitively responsive perspective, the question "What does it mean to learn?" can be further broken down into "What does it mean for a college student to encounter a subject-matter idea that is new to her, especially if it differs from what she might expect? And when she does, what happens in her thinking? Does she absorb the new idea easily even if it clashes with her personal knowledge of the world and herself? Does she resist it, and if so, how, and with what results? Or does she examine it openly? Further, what kind of teaching might inspire and support a student's willingness to do this?" These questions highlight an important feature of classroom-based instruction: It involves simultaneous consideration of four factors—learner (student), instructor (person who teaches), content (that which is learned), and contexts (multiple spaces of time and place in which academic learning happens). Understanding learning-teaching requires consideration of how these four features interact in any moment and over time.[5] Analysis of any one of the four factors requires attention to how the other three influence it.

A key component of learning in college, and in all schooling, is content. Learning implies learning something, and that something is content.[6] But the word "content" is overly broad since students learn many things, academic and nonacademic, in college. "Academic learning," as we use this term, targets students' learning, specifically, of disciplinary subject-matter content (e.g., chemistry, mathematics, history, literature, sociology, etc.). Foundational courses typically focus on students' learning of core disciplinary ideas. A core disciplinary idea is one around which other disciplinary ideas form. For example, in statistics, the mean—as a way to represent the middle of a frequency distribution—is a core idea around which other more advanced statistical ideas form—for example, variance and correlation. In organizational psychology, the concept of systems—open and closed—often is core to researchers' elaborated representations of organizations, leadership, and strategy. These more complex ideas build on the core concept of the "open system."[7] In English literature, the concept of the symbol underpins multiple figures of speech highlighting meaning beyond the literal, immediate, or conventional.[8] Examples of literary tools that use symbolism include metaphor, simile, synecdoche, and allegory. All these assume an understanding of the core concept of symbol.

Core ideas like these are foundational to understanding a particular discipline or field. But sometimes students enter a class with partial understandings of a core idea, or with understandings that elide a field's distinctive brand of knowledge—a distinctiveness they will need to grasp in order to build out from the core idea. For example, asked to define the concept of "mean" (average), a college student enrolled in an introductory statistics class may offer a formulaic or procedural representation: that the mean is the sum of the values of a set of items divided then by the number of items. An alternative, conceptually anchored view is that the mean is the middle of the collective value of that set, or its balance point. The concept of mean or average, taught conceptually, can feel new, even be eye-opening, to students who enter class with deeply engrained formulaic knowledge of the term. This is especially true for core ideas that reach—often surprisingly—from the classroom into students' personal, familial, and community lives, sometimes shaking up firm life-long beliefs.[9]

Other examples of such core ideas include evolution in the sciences, social control in the social sciences, and uncertainty in the humanities. Students must understand such core ideas deeply and flexibly in order to access still more complex concepts growing out of them, or in response to them. Thus core ideas open up paths for students' expanded learning in larger fields of study. As foundational building blocks, core disciplinary ideas may also help students apply their learning, for example, by using them to reframe social problems and possibly, to invent solutions. Learning core ideas, alongside other ideas that build out from them, is central to a learner's development of deep and flexible subject-matter (disciplinary) understanding.[10]

A key feature of the cognitively responsive view is that it "drills down" to what goes on in students' minds as they work at learning a core disciplinary idea.

Different students may do this in different ways. The "drilled down" view is critical. In addition to focusing on students' dynamics of mind, it considers the specifics of "what is learned"—which subject matter, how that subject unfolds in class, what students see and experience of its unique contours. An example of this view appears in Anna Neumann's study of teaching and learning in an urban undergraduate philosophy class at Meritage University (pseudonym).[11] Neumann observed first-year students' encounter with the core philosophical concept of Cartesian doubt, an orientation and method for questioning the veracity of one's own experiences, including one's long-held beliefs and senses. Judging from most of the students' initial responses, "Cartesian doubt" struck at their core sensibilities. Meritage undergraduates are highly diverse in terms of race and ethnicity, country of birth, and likely, religious/spiritual background; the majority are first-generation college students. Many are of traditional age and they commute, thus returning daily to their families and local communities. The philosophy class stood out as a microcosm of Meritage.

In reading the assigned course text, Rene Descartes' *Meditations on First Philosophy*, students encounter Descartes' core question, one that throws him into crisis: "Do I truly exist?" Descartes asks, "And what if I do not?" He wonders further, "What if I am a figment of some greater being's mind? What if all I know is made up?" These questions, presented here in words close to those used in class, collided with ideas—and ways of being in the world—that students held to deeply in their personal lives. Translated into the language of a cognitively responsive view and the learning sciences broadly, the new core subject-matter idea, Cartesian doubt, clashed with students' personal and cultural prior knowledge, personal ideas that framed their lives and their sense of the world. Many were palpably uncomfortable with Descartes' expression of doubt about his own existence. Yet to understand later on in the semester how Descartes' idea evolved historically—for example, through later writers' responses to it—and also how doubt, as method, could be made to apply to one's life beyond college—students would do well to learn it.

While we will follow shortly with discussion of what happens in this philosophy class as students encounter the concept of Cartesian doubt, it is worth pausing to draw out what this brief stage-setting scenario highlights about college students' learning: We are in a classroom of racially and ethnically, and possibly linguistically, religiously, and otherwise diverse first-generation college students. Their attention—and ours—is riveted by an event: the instructor's offering, to students, of a new—and to many—strange (possibly radical) idea about doubt.

Doubt—here, Cartesian doubt—is core to study in this class and in the discipline of philosophy. It has the power to frame students' learning later in the term, and possibly in classes beyond. Their participation in such learning, later, may well depend on how deeply and thoroughly they come to understand doubt in this class. Learning the concept of doubt requires that students travel through its under-pinning logics, much as expert philosophers do—and much as Descartes did initially—all while addressing questions that their own prior beliefs surface as well. More, of course, will follow from this scene. We can predict, for example, that some students will struggle with doubt—understanding it, but resisting too the challenges it poses to their previously well-learned personal beliefs.

We will return shortly to this narrative, appreciating, for now, the complexity of the core subject-matter concept, doubt, that has, quite literally, fallen into the center of the classroom. Students are to examine it, engage with it, and explore it deeply, much as did Descartes. Doing so poses multiple challenges well beyond the discomfort that some may feel. For one thing, to learn about doubt, as a core idea, is unlike learning a different core idea in a different discipline or field. This is because the content of a core idea is unique to its discipline. It reflects a sub-stantive interest and logics for working through it unlike those of other disci-plines (given their unique interests/logics). Thus, learning a core idea in any one discipline is different from learning a core idea in a different discipline. For ex-ample, learning a core idea in history (e.g., grasping the concept of protracted conflict) differs from learning a core idea in chemistry (e.g., understanding fu-sion), and these differ from learning a core idea in philosophy (e.g., Cartesian doubt). Learning these core disciplinary ideas in history, chemistry, and philoso-phy differs further from learning a core idea in biology (e.g., understanding what it means for something to be alive). Just as an historian, chemist, philosopher, and biologist think through ideas in history, chemistry, philosophy, and biology in ways unique to the content and form—or knowledge landscape—of each of these disciplines, so must students learn to do this.[12]

Learning deeply in a discipline requires students to probe disciplinary ideas in unique disciplinary terms. This involves students following, mindfully, the unique contours of disciplinary thinking.[13] In each discipline, the mind travels along different lanes of knowledge set within differing knowledge topographies. The road curves differently in each field and is paved in different ways. Learning entails developing expertise in navigating those curves competently while glean-ing meaning from the vistas they offer. Focusing, for now, only on the cognitive demand—setting aside students' challenges in working through conflicts with long-held personal beliefs—we offer the following claim toward a definition of students' academic learning in college:

> *Claim 1:* To learn is to *learn something* and to engage with that *something*—a disciplinary idea—on its own terms, thus following the contours of the disciplinary thinking that defines it. Learning within any one discipline is likely to differ from learning in another.[14]

In this view, learning requires a teacher who thoughtfully orchestrates study materials and other learning resources, assignments, teacher-with-student interaction, student-with-student discussion, and other class activities, all toward sharing disciplinary knowledge including core subject-matter ideas. An expert teacher knows that to share a core subject-matter idea, she must understand it deeply and from many different angles. This will likely help her glimpse the byways that students, each uniquely, travel as they approach an idea, and make their way through it. A teacher who is able to hear how a student makes sense of a core idea that is new to him positions herself, as teacher, to join that student in thinking it through. Joining the student, the teacher can raise questions fit to the student's thinking and she may then be able to open doors to more fruitful possibilities. To do this, a teacher must know a subject-matter idea thoroughly and flexibly enough to recognize when students' talk or writing about it is flawed, when it is partial, when it is stuck, and when it moves along in promising ways. The teacher also must *want* to do this, and have the requisite skills. Much more, of course, can be said about implications for teaching of the learning claim above.[15] This view of teaching emphasizes whether—and how—instructors understand their students' sense making of the subject-matter ideas being taught, and what they do then with the resources at their disposal, to advance students' learning further.

## POLICY VIEW

With the preceding definition of academic learning in hand, we now consider how, largely, the higher education policy community and institutional leaders understand college students' learning—notably through the learning outcomes assessment movement, and within this movement, through the lenses of student engagement and students' generalized competencies as indicators of learning. These two representations of student learning are widely used in national assessments, large-scale policy efforts, and institutional discourses.[16] Although higher education scholars, practitioners, and policy makers have considered college students' learning from multiple points of view, we focus here on just these two due to their significant influence in the field.

### Student Engagement

Student engagement—as conceptualized by many higher education researchers and institutional leaders—speaks to students' involvement in their college education, along with implications for how institutions can encourage and scaffold such involvement.[17] Researchers associated with the National Survey of Student Engagement (NSSE) have created engagement indicators to highlight student practices deemed beneficial to students' learning—for example, the number of papers students write, how often students collaborate with peers in coursework, how often students interact with faculty members.[18] An impetus for the NSSE was the hope that it would provide improved representations of college quality—in contrast to methods, like the ranking system of *US News and World Reports*, that focus primarily on resources and reputation. In contrast, the NSSE could be "a new source of evidence about college quality, based upon what students . . . say about their college experience."[19]

The concept of student engagement grew out of three bodies of literature reflecting three distinctive emphases.[20] First, student engagement builds on the concept of "quality of effort"—that greater frequency of engagement will result in increased learning and development.[21] Second, student engagement builds on a theory of involvement—that the more physical and psychological energy students devote to their studies in college, the more they are likely to learn.[22] Finally, student engagement relies on indicators of "good practice" in undergraduate education—thus emphasizing what institutions, faculty, and staff can do to facilitate college student learning (e.g., implementing active learning, setting high expectations, intensifying student-faculty interaction).[23] Carini, Kuh, and Klein sum up the student engagement movement as follows: "The premise is deceptively simple, perhaps self-evident: The more students study or practice a subject, the more they tend to learn about it."[24]

Student engagement, positioned as an indicator of learning, has had a broad reach in the higher education community. Findings from student engagement research have been used to frame and argue for institutional-level actions for improving educational practices, research on students' educational experiences (including learning) in college, and importantly, efforts to enhance public understanding of student experiences in higher education. To date, more than 1,500 colleges and universities have participated in the NSSE survey, an assessment of educational quality at the institutional level, based on students' responses to survey questions about what they do toward learning in college.[25] The participating institutions typically use NSSE results toward accreditation for accountability, and a growing number of institutions also use the NSSE also to guide improvement of educational practices at the institution level. The National Institute of Learning Outcomes Assessment (NILOA) reports that most institutions (80%) use national surveys, such as the NSSE, to report on student learning outcomes to accreditors.[26] Scholars of college student learning have also used the student engagement framework to examine students' educational experiences in a variety of college contexts, for example, in distance education,[27] women's colleges,[28] and liberal arts colleges.[29] Scholars also have relied on the NSSE to examine the experiences of various student groups, including first-year college students,[30] African American students,[31] members of Greek-letter organizations,[32] and first-generation college students.[33] The NSSE is very widely used in US higher education today; it has played a powerful role in shaping how policy and institutional leaders, and many higher education researchers, think about student learning.

### Generalized Competencies

In the early 2000s, a second conceptualization of college student learning appeared on the policy landscape, quickly capturing the attention of the American public which was, at the time, becoming increasingly concerned about the value of a college education during challenging economic times. With rising costs to consumers for a variety of social services, including education, and increasing calls for higher education to respond to a challenged economy and to individuals' career needs, policy makers cast their eyes on college graduates' competencies, asking: What do college graduates need to know and be able to do as workers in a global economy? And what do they need to know and be able to do to enact their roles competently as members of a democratic citizenry? In asking these questions, policy makers considered a list of what we term "generalized competencies."

Generalized competencies, as the term is used here, encompass multiple skills and multiple forms of knowledge cast as desirable for all college students' learning, regardless of students' backgrounds, academic preparation, preferences and interests, personal goals, and so on. Examples of generalized competencies include critical thinking, quantitative reasoning, and written communication, though clearly others have been proffered via higher education assessments and other teaching/learning improvement efforts.[34] As such, generalized competencies should be viewed as broadly composed and broadly applicable—targeting all college students, subject matters and fields, and institutions. Paralleling policy makers' questions around such generalized competencies were those raised by the media which, in turn, channeled questions about higher education's responsiveness back to an increasingly watchful American public.[35] Thus, paralleling the rapid spread among institutional leaders of assessments via student engagement concepts, we also have seen, over the past fifteen to twenty years, a swell of interest in competency-based assessments growing out of policy makers' and the public's concerns about the value of a college degree. Cast as vital to the twenty-first-century workforce and for democracy, generalized competences articulate "forms of learning and accomplishment that [a college] degree should represent."[36]

Following in the spirit of the generalized competencies movement, the Spellings Commission in 2005 considered promoting use of the Collegiate Learning Assessment (CLA), a standardized test of critical thinking skills, to assess college student learning, notably at the institutional level. As portrayed by the CLA, critical thinking is a competency that generalizes (or transfers) across multiple subjects, learners, majors, levels, and so on. It is viewed as a desirable outcome for all college graduates. In, quite possibly, this era's most widely read book on college students' learning in college, *Academically Adrift: Limited Learning on College Campuses*, Arum and Roksa use cross-sectional CLA data, collected in students' freshman and senior years, to assert, in generalizing ways, that the critical thinking skills of college students participating in their study did not improve (or that they improved but slightly) over four years of college.[37] Although *Academically Adrift* was lauded broadly in key higher education news outlets[38] and equally by the public media,[39] scholars of teaching and learning in higher education and K–12 education questioned whether measures of students' critical thinking via a single standardized test like the CLA could indeed capture the full breadth and depth of students' learning in college.[40] Despite such reservations, media response to *Academically Adrift* was strong, with headlines featuring the "tough news" that college students are learning far less than they, their families, and employers might expect and desire.[41] "If the purpose of a college education is for students to learn," said one higher education writer, "academe is failing."[42]

Development and use of assessments concerned with college students' acquisition of generalized competencies—for example, the CLA—have proliferated over the past several years. Another recent effort, also seeking to assess college graduates' generalized competencies, but more broadly, is the Essential Learning Outcomes (ELO) framework of the American Association of Colleges and Universities (AAC&U). The aim of the ELO framework is to describe what college students should know and be able to do as a result of study toward a bachelor's degree (generalized competencies stated as college learning outcomes), and to assess institutions in terms of their students' achievement on these outcomes. The framework was developed by the AAC&U through systematic consultation with hundreds of institutions (leaders and faculty), accreditors, and higher education stakeholders.[43]

According to the AAC&U, learning outcomes targeted by the ELO framework encompass four broad areas: (1) knowledge of human cultures and the physical and natural world (e.g., studies in sciences, humanities, histories that engage in enduring questions); (2) intellectual and practical skills (e.g., inquiry and analysis, critical thinking, quantitative literacy, teamwork); (3) personal and social responsibility (e.g., civic knowledge, ethical reasoning); and (4) integrative and applied learning (e.g., synthesis and application of knowledge).[44] The AAC&U developed accompanying Valid Assessment of Learning in Undergraduate Education (VALUE) rubrics to guide evaluation of student learning evidenced through mastery of the essential learning outcomes.[45] AAC&U staff are currently piloting the rubrics for formative use (i.e., evaluation directed at institutional and classroom improvement) and for summative assessment (i.e., comparing student learning on these measures across institutions at the level of state systems). Given its attention to content, albeit in compounded—or generalized—form, the AAC&U model appears to line up with the cognitively responsive approach on the following assumption: that in college, *learning* demands *learning something*, namely academic content. The AAC&U model portrays such academic content via its stated ELOs. Yet as may be obvious, the approach does not "drill down" to the individual subject matters that comprise the aggregated competencies reflected in the ELOs or to individual learners (like Adina for example).

## Emergent Views of Learning Academic Content

Like proponents of a cognitively responsive view, higher education policy leaders and researchers have grappled strenuously with how best to portray academic learning. But the two groups have worked, largely, on different tracks. If one group—namely, researchers in the learning sciences—is, indeed, to be characterized as "cognitively responsive" in their treatment of students' academic learning, the other group—policy researchers and leaders—might be cast as aspiring to an ethos of "public responsiveness." The work of the latter group reflects policy makers' and policy researchers' heightened attentiveness to public concerns about the value of a college degree. Distinctions—between cognitive and public responsiveness—are, of course, imprecise, highlighting each group's overall emphasis yet masking interesting (and promising) overlaps—like NSSE's increased attention to students' experiences in learning and the AAC&U's attention to what students learn via the ELOs (reflecting concern for subject-matter learning). Later in this chapter, we take up the significance of such overlaps for future work in higher education assessment and policy. For now, we focus on current states of practice, first from the policy view.

The higher education policy movement, focused on understanding the quality of higher education in terms of what students, aggregated institutionally, know and can do—and stated as learning outcomes—has made significant strides toward focusing the public's eye on the contribution of a college degree toward learning. This movement, articulated heavily via measures of engagement and generalized competencies, responds to public critiques about rising college costs and relevance—assertions that higher education is overly expensive, and that colleges and universities have not done a good job of explaining what a college degree offers toward students' learning and development.[46] Prior to this movement, the public had relied largely on corporate rankings emphasizing resources and reputation.[47] However, these ranking systems, powerful in shaping the public mind, said (and even now, continue to say) very little about teaching and learning. Prior to the engagement and generalized competencies initiatives, little more was available to the public and to policy makers for a vast range of high-salience decisions—from where to send one's child to college, to how to think about state and federal funding to higher education amid scarcity. Both the engagement initiative and the generalized competencies approaches have made substantial strides in shifting public and policy mindsets from, heavily, reputational and resource-based considerations, such as those promoted by rankings, to caring about educational quality and students' learning in college.

Yet viewed through a cognitively responsive lens—about how learning materializes in classrooms and how it varies by subject area—it is evident that current policy efforts could be further strengthened. A cognitively responsive analysis suggests that efforts to generalize learning across disciplines (e.g., assuming a single vision of critical thinking applicable to all fields) misses valuable information. A specific example can drive this home: Deep understanding of a core idea in biochemistry would likely yield a very different substantive critique (thus a different vision of what it means to think critically) than would one in political science, though both could possibly be applied—but differentially—toward analysis of significant problems in the world today—for example, water pollution and a variety of other environmental problems. Calls for critical thinking beg the question of "Critical thinking *about what?* and *through what?*"

Proponents of a cognitively responsive view might add one more twist to this argument, noting that critical thinking (or any kind of thinking) learned deeply in one disciplinary context does not transfer easily to another, requiring as much effort, for transfer, as does the original field-based learning.[48] However, much policy-attuned work portrays students' learning as transferring (overly readily in our view) across disciplines and subject areas, courses and curricula, learners, institutions, and institutional locations. Many extant assessment efforts overlook the challenges of transfer in learning. For example, within the ELO approach, the same VALUE rubric (generalized competencies approach) might be used to rate a paper from a first-year English course and a paper from a culminating course in applied engineering, and thereby to offer evidence of comparable learning, by students, via their achieved competencies in "ethical reasoning." Since ethical reasoning is likely to manifest uniquely as students "think through the subject matters of engineering" in comparison to their "thinking through the subject matters of English literature," different assessment rubrics, reflective of the distinctive knowledge being thought about, might be beneficial, as might use of different assessors—each with deep subject-matter knowledge of the field at issue. Such distinctions provide fodder for thought about the future of assessment in higher education.

## Who's Learning: Students as Academic Learners

While in the preceding section we focused on the "what"—or content—of learning, in this section, we consider learning's "who"—the student. Again we rely on cognitive responsiveness and policy views to guide analysis.

### Cognitively Responsive View

A cognitively responsive view highlights the power of students' prior personal, cultural, and academic knowledge in learning. Prior knowledge plays a formative role in students' learning as it mingles with new content.[49] It therefore matters too for teaching practices.

A cognitively responsive view assumes that it takes two kinds of knowledge for a person to learn: (1) the knowledge of a discipline "new" to students (core subject-matter ideas and other subject-matter ideas building on/around them as discussed above), and (2) students' prior knowledge, including cultural knowledge, personal knowledge, and school-based knowledge, all of which students draw on in encounters with new ideas.[50] Learning happens at the intersection of a discipline's subject-matter knowledge and a student's prior knowledge, shaped further by what a teacher offers pedagogically and by familial, community, organizational, and other social, economic, and cultural forces.

Prior knowledge is highly influential in students' efforts to learn new subject-matter ideas, including core disciplinary ideas that pave students' paths into further learning.[51] Confronted with disciplinary content for learning, a student may surface related prior knowledge drawn from her life that facilitates the "newer" learning, or in some cases, gets in its way.[52] Thus, students' prior knowledge may be "in tune" with the disciplinary ideas that a teacher presents in class,[53] or not.[54] In the latter case, learning depends on a student's willingness to surface and examine prior knowledge—including cultural and personal knowledge—that she may take for granted as accurate, true, and meaningful.[55] This may be knowledge to which the student is deeply attached.

We have already witnessed the earliest moments—the stage setting—of just such an encounter, between students' prior knowledge and a new core idea, Cartesian doubt, in Neumann's study of an undergraduate philosophy class.[56] To appreciate the power of students' prior knowledge in their academic learning, we return to that class to listen in on students' first encounter with Cartesian doubt,[57] a core idea in the study of philosophy:

> Faced with Descartes' questions—Do I exist? Or am I a figment of some greater being's mind, thus unreal? Am I a dream? Can I count on my senses to tell me what's real?—students in the philosophy class expressed surprise. Some questioned Descartes' sensibilities. Openly or silently, some resisted connecting to his crisis of thought—to the logic that took him there—and thus, too, to the logic that slowly and painfully he developed toward working his way out.
>
> One student, Adina (pseudonym), stood out. Through thirty minutes of the one-hour class session, Adina veered between acknowledging the rationality of Descartes' questions ("He makes sense," she said) and dismissive critique ("It is just not working for me"). Sharply observant and reflective, Adina expressed what it felt like for her to engage with the new academic idea, Cartesian doubt: "It's like . . . you've been knowing all this stuff [i.e., prior contrary

beliefs] since, like, forever. And then, like, you're gonna doubt it . . . Like, I can't follow along with him [Descartes] because I don't believe in that personally—"

The scenario gives one pause: Given Adina's personal and cultural anchors in ideas that she feels are quite at odds with Descartes', will it be possible for her to entertain the core philosophical idea—doubt—that he proposes? To understand Descartes' *Meditations* requires understanding his conception of doubt, and his experience, too, of coming to this idea—in effect, learning it. Adina's encounter with Cartesian doubt would go nowhere if she did not, first, acknowledge it as different from her own long-held views, and if she did not then examine her own prior beliefs while examining, too, the new idea. Were Adina to resist taking Descartes seriously—for example, by attending to the reading assignment just long enough to get through the class—she would miss out on the lesson in self-reflection and logical argumentation that reading Descartes can spur. Adina's experience brings to light another distinctive feature of academic learning:

> Claim 2: To learn is to surface and examine one's prior knowledge bearing on a disciplinary idea posed for learning.[58]

In a cognitively responsive view, students surface their prior beliefs and assumptions as part of their learning. Students' prior knowledge mediates their learning of new ideas. Caught in an encounter, like Adina's, between two seemingly incommensurate forms of knowledge, students may feel challenged, cognitively and emotionally. How then might teaching proceed? This view calls for instructors skilled in creating and orchestrating classroom conversations that support students talking through—or otherwise representing—what they know already, personally, that may in some way bear on the subject-matter idea being taught. While we have not revealed here the full picture of Adina's learning experience, suffice it to say she was fortunate. Her philosophy instructor, Sofia (pseudonym), closely followed Adina's struggle—between her simultaneous attraction to and skepticism of Descartes' logic. Descartes' speculation—that a greater being manipulates his own and all persons' sensibilities, and thus that what we claim to know may be contrived—appears to brush up against Adina's personal metaphysical assumptions. Sofia stepped in firmly, encouraging Adina to persist in considering the two sides of her thinking, each sharply at odds with the other. Sofia also acknowledged how hard it is, emotionally, for Adina to do this, and she never left her side. Sofia modeled what a teacher can offer as a student surfaces prior knowledge that conflicts with core subject matter ideas—respect and care.

## POLICY VIEW

Cognitively responsive views emphasize students as central in considerations of academic learning. Policy discourses concur. It is, in fact, striking how much attention higher education policy researchers give to students. While teaching and learning could potentially be measured in many ways—for example, relative to what faculty do or think toward helping students learn (via surveys or observations of faculty), how classroom cultures work (via observations), or how curriculum is constructed (via analysis of syllabi)—the learning outcomes movement, instantiated via engagement and general competencies efforts, hones in on students via surveys eliciting their self-reports, tests of students' competencies, analysis of student work, and the like. Researchers who use the engagement framework focus on students, cast as learners, as they measure the amount of time that students spend on activities deemed to contribute to learning—for example, interacting with faculty, working collaboratively on class projects, writing papers, and so on.[59] The generalized competencies view focuses on students as learners as it zooms in on student achievement (by testing, as with the CLA, or by analyzing student work, for example, via VALUE) toward understanding college quality.[60]

## EMERGENT VIEWS OF COLLEGE STUDENTS AS ACADEMIC LEARNERS

Both the cognitively responsive view, derived from the learning sciences, and the higher education policy view, portray students as learners of academic content. But the two views lead analysts down different tracks toward very different representations of learning and learners.

For one thing, and as the narrative about Adina's classroom experience illustrates, proponents of a cognitively responsive view highlight students' prior knowledge as mediating, substantively, their academic learning.[61] This view portrays individual students as undergoing learning uniquely—depending on how they filter subject-matter ideas through their earlier educational experiences, cultural knowledge, family expectations, classroom cultures, and other contextual forces. Thus, the learner—interacting with a teacher, academic knowledge, and layered contexts—undergoes a learning process unique to who she is, what she values, and what and how she understands.

Likewise, the two higher education policy movements—engagement and generalized competencies—and the learning outcomes movement broadly emphasize students. But they cast those students as collectivities—portraying them in the aggregate—rather than as individuals. Thus outcomes measure the products, collectively, of a group's members' learning—for example, for a certain college's freshman class. Those aggregated outcomes are then taken as indicators (signs, markers) of key institutional products or outputs—namely, the learning that one or more institutions of higher education contribute to the larger society (community, state, nation) they are charged to serve. This learning outputs/outcomes formulation is highly responsive to the kinds of questions that policy makers ask, given their mandate to advance, direct, and improve higher education as a vehicle for advancing learning as a societal goal. It also is highly responsive to the kinds of information seeking in which the public engages—toward increased understanding of the quality of the higher education in which they invest.

It is at this point, however, that another significant difference between the two views—policy and cognitive responsiveness—must be laid out: The learning outcomes view, central to policy making, articulates the *eventual results* of students' extended learning in college. Its succinctly aggregated packaging, indicative of the learning of one or more student populations, renders it helpful to policy makers. But the learning outcomes view does not—and in current form, cannot—speak to differences in the experiences of students toward getting there. In an era of rapid student diversification, learners bring an ever-expanding array of prior knowledge to class. Given its focus on eventual results, the outcomes movement misses what students bring to class. It therefore misses how students experience the learning of ideas that, at best, link nicely to what they know already, or at worst conflict with or elide what they know from their lives.

For example, proponents of the learning outcomes movement do not have the tools to see—and therefore cannot acknowledge—that for students like Adina learning means first seeing, and then working through intellectually complex encounters between new subject-matter knowledge and prior personal and/or cultural knowledge that does not easily align with the new. Other students, whose personal and cultural prior knowledge more closely links to the new, may work through such encounters more directly. New academic knowledge may make more sense, personally and culturally, to them. It may even be more intuitive to them. Getting to outcomes may be less of an intellectual and personal struggle for them.

Little of this is reflected in assessments that feature student outcomes, nor does it guide policy work today. Yet distinctions such as these do merit attention, especially in considerations of students' success in learning as a matter of high consequence for policy. We turn next to this topic.

## Success in Learning

Both the learning sciences community and the higher education policy community attend to students' academic learning. Both value content. Both construe students as learners of academic content. Yet traveling on different tracks, these communities see different learning landscapes. Academic content materializes differently for each, as do students as learners. The learning sciences travel the route of students' minds (featuring cognition, hence cognitive responsiveness). The higher education policy community pursues learning, largely, on a broader organizational and social plane (featuring learning, expressed as outcomes, as a whole-institutional or societal product and also as information for the public, policy makers, and institutional leaders). Though differing in what they "see" and emphasize, each view offers its users something of value toward consideration of college student learning. Each view also misses some of what the other view more readily accesses: Whereas the policy view misses defining nuances around what students' academic learning experiences entail, the cognitively responsive view overlooks learning as an organizational output that, in aggregated form, matters greatly for policy. In discussions of higher education policy, the institution (a college or university) stands as a primary unit of analysis; modern-day policy builds on this.

We turn next to the topic of success in learning, a topic of high consequence for policy makers who strive to support effective education delivered, in fact, through colleges and universities as organizations established and supported for this purpose. Again, both views—cognitively responsive and policy—inform our analysis of what success in learning entails.

### Cognitively Responsive View

In a cognitively responsive view, a student comes to know something new through an encounter between an idea she knows well and probably holds closely (possibly dearly) and a new idea that may or may not align with it. What does success in learning look like from the standpoint of cognitive responsiveness, and what kind of teaching supports it? The case of Adina offers promising insights. What is successful learning for Adina, and for other learners who, like her, stand at the crossroads of long-held personal beliefs and new academic knowledge that, at times, elides the old, or outrightly conflicts with it? To address this question, we return to Adina:

> Reading about Descartes' doubting of his own existence, Adina registers his point. We have heard her say so far that indeed, "he makes sense." Yet as Adina follows Descartes further into doubts about his existence—and thus others' existence as well—she projects further: She imagines herself doubting her own. But to doubt her own existence means doubting too all she knows and holds dear. Waking up to this surprising thought, Adina veers toward doubting Descartes' doubt, an idea she needs to master to fully grasp other philosophers' ideas and debates addressed later in the class.
>
> Amid the back and forth in her mind, Adina—listening also to related questions posed by her classmates—begins to discern a way to accept Descartes' doubt, but without surrendering the personal knowledge, linked to her life, that she draws out at the same time: Descartes' open doubting—his thinking in doubting ways—suggests to Adina that he is "a thinking thing." In being a "thinking thing"—in doubting—he exists. Thus Descartes' enactment of doubt explains his existence. In knowing that he exists, Descartes need not doubt his existence further.
>
> Adina can surmise this as well: She, like Descartes, can think in doubting ways, a sign that she too exists. "I've got it," says Adina. "It's, like, your beliefs [are] what makes us, us."

The case of Adina as a learner of core philosophical ideas spotlights the third claim about students' academic learning:

*Claim 3:* Learning occurs when a student acknowledges and works through differences between her prior knowledge and new subject-matter ideas. When old and new knowledge run parallel, even roughly, to one another, the old may serve as a bridge to the new. When old and new knowledge clash or otherwise fail to align, learning may falter, or be more challenging.[62]

Adina bridges her old and new knowledge, different as they are. In class, she does quickly grasp the concept of Cartesian doubt. But surfacing her personal beliefs, she resists it. Initially, she sees her personal beliefs and the new idea as inconsistent and mutually exclusive. Learning, for Adina, seems to involve envisioning a novel way for the two to co-exist in her mind—for example, by formulating a way of relating one to the other. Acknowledging the reasonableness of

Descartes' questioning of his existence (Does he exist? And how does he—and we—know this?), she points out that in doubting, he exists—indeed as a "doubting thing."

It is important to point out that encounters between students' prior knowledge and new subject-matter knowledge can occur more quickly and synergistically, for example, as students use familiar knowledge to bridge toward the new. Milagros Castillo-Montoya offers compelling examples of students surfacing and using their prior knowledge to support their learning of the core sociological concept, social stratification.[63] Keenly aware of their positioning near the base of the US social and economic structure, some students in Castillo-Montoya's study understood the core sociological concept of stratification long before they entered college. It resonated with their sense of their own positioning in the social world. Even if they were unfamiliar with the term, it no doubt felt familiar to them as a feature of the social world. Learning for these students involved tying stratification as a feature of social life to examples of it in their lives. Learning also involved students' deepening their understanding of stratification as a concept (e.g., considering its dynamics, its multiple forms). Not least, learning involved students' realizing that an experience long familiar to them has a sociological name. It is both a personal and academic idea. In such situations, instructors can support students' learning initially by drawing out their prior knowledge and by linking it to other examples to illustrate variation in the core idea being taught. They may then turn to further explanations in texts. Instructors play a prominent role in learning wherein students' prior knowledge advances, synergistically, their academic learning.

Instructors matter too for students who, like Adina, face a more challenging crossroad—wherein students' prior personal understandings and new academic ideas appear, on first encounter, as incommensurate. In class, Adina's teacher, Sofia, carefully follows Adina and her classmates. Sofia listens closely. She questions, sympathizes, draws out, orchestrates, and at times, corrects students' responses to questions, Adina's included. She stands by encouragingly in that instance when Adina, in a flash, glimpses a way to link the new academic idea, doubt, and her own prior thoughts—letting them co-exist sensibly in her life. Openly repeating Adina's realization, Sofia validates Adina's new thought: Descartes is a "thinking thing." In being a thing that thinks, he exists, much as does Adina. In situations like Adina's, instructors can support students' learning by giving them space—and resources, including pathways of thought—for working through the cognitive and emotional aspects of encounters between their prior knowledge and new subject-matter ideas.

Fully engaged in her learning, Adina is nonetheless challenged, but not because she fails to understand the core philosophical idea of doubt. She understands Cartesian doubt deeply enough to appreciate that it rubs against her own committed beliefs. Rather, Adina is challenged to figure out something still more complex: how to navigate between the new philosophical idea that she has just discerned—Cartesian doubt—and her prior beliefs which, on first look, appear in conflict. She seems to search for ways to hold to both, logically and faithfully. Success, for Adina, involves doing that, and thus we see her starting to craft an argument toward this end. At the point that Adina does succeed in getting this base of understanding firmly in place, she is positioned to use doubt as a stepping-off point for continued study in philosophy and related fields.

## Policy View

Having offered an analysis of success in learning from the perspective of cognitive responsiveness, we turn now to images of successful learning in higher education policy discourses. Both engagement and generalized competencies frameworks consider data on students in the aggregate (e.g., what a subpopulation of students—like a college's freshman class or senior class—know and can do) as evidence of quality learning at an institutional level. It is instructive to note that this aggregated representation of students' learning, rooted in the learning outcomes assessment movement, holds historical significance in its departure from earlier perspectives that defined learning success via individual students' GPAs. Due to a variety of measurement differences across institutions, courses, and students, data about student learning derived in the earlier approach were not comparable; nor were grades reflective of value-added or change in student knowledge resulting from the course.[64] As such, the earlier approach was of negligible use to policy makers interested in making cross-institutional comparisons. Current movements, offering common measures and means of assessment, offer significant technical improvements.

The engagement framework emphasizes how much effort students expend via practices deemed necessary for learning to happen[65]—for example, students' involvement in active or cooperative learning practices. Student effort, summarized as the frequency with which students engage in "effective" practices like these, is thereby positioned to indicate pursuit of a college degree of quality. For example, the NSSE, which reports engagement indicators for participating colleges and universities, features the average level (i.e., frequency) of engagement by an institution's students in meaningful practices such as quantitative reasoning, collaborative learning, and interacting with faculty.[66] It is relevant that these reports lay out data for each participating institution, thus yielding institutional profiles on the indicated measures. As previously noted, the engagement work was a noteworthy departure from the ranking movement (e.g., the *US News and World Report* ranking) which interpreted quality in terms of resources and reputation. It significantly boosted US higher education's efforts to focus policy discourses onto more substantive concerns, such as how often students engage in activities deemed central to learning.

Similarly, the generalized competencies approach emphasizes learning outcomes deemed desirable for all college graduates regardless of their background. The AAC&U's ELO framework is a case in point. The ELO framework defines, in generalized categories, what a college student ideally should have achieved at the point of being awarded a college degree. Another example is the CLA, which offers "badges" to students who pass the CLA test at a particular level of achievement.[67] Undergirding this practice is the belief, stated by proponents of the CLA, that employers want to know that the students they hire have achieved, minimally, a threshold of common ability in critical thinking viewed as a vital competency. The belief that a key aim of higher education is to prepare a competent and knowledgeable global workforce streams through prevailing policy efforts and equally through employers' views and public opinion.[68] In this view, higher education is called upon to bring every student up to a prespecified standard—as demonstrated competencies believed to result from preparation (e.g., ELOs, CLA). Much like the engagement work, the generalized competencies movement focuses on students (in terms of their achievement of generalized competencies) in its representations of educational quality and thus of success in higher education.

## Emergent Views of Success in Learning

Analysts subscribing to either of the two views described above travel on distinctive tracks, thus "seeing" different landscapes of teaching and learning. Not surprisingly, they conceive of success in learning also in different ways.

Analysts on the cognitive responsiveness track associate success with individual students' efforts to bridge toward understanding of core disciplinary ideas, new to them, via their prior knowledge. They use the older knowledge as a stepping-off point for thinking through the new, sometimes adjusting (e.g., correcting, revising) the old along the way. They appreciate the Adinas of the world, and also the Sofias—the teachers who orchestrate and support students' thinking at the crossroads of prior knowledge and new academic ideas. In a cognitively responsive view, academic learning is internal, tailored to individuals' past experiences and prior knowledge. Though about something substantively new, it nonetheless reflects prior learning, by individuals, in unique places, times, and lives.

In contrast, analysts on the policy track envision success through students' self-reports of engagement in learning and also through their achievement of generalized competencies, both stated as outcomes. Aggregated institutionally, the outcomes summarize the extent of student learning. Analysts on this track seek to convey how involved students are in activities deemed central to learning (engagement) as well as what they know and can do relative to standards set for all students' achievement (general competencies). Although the two views— cognitive responsiveness and policy—diverge in their portrayals of success in learning, the idea that students' academic learning is central to higher education runs through both.

Yet as noted earlier, the two views differ in what they let observers access toward appraisals of success in learning. We might ask how analysts working in the policy tradition would know success in learning if they saw it, compared to how analysts, steeped in images of cognitive responsiveness, would recognize it. Proponents of a policy view would likely search for signs of large-scale student involvement in activities deemed to yield learning. They might, for example, ask if students in a particular college regularly study collaboratively, meet with faculty, and so on, or they might look at reports on the quality of student work evaluated through rubrics laying out achievement criteria on particular learning outcomes (for example, as specified in the ELOs). They would seek a summary view of activity deemed to lead to learning. What they would not see—and would not be prompted to look for—are signs of learning, literally, going live. Proponents of a cognitively responsive view would probably try to establish at least three things: (1) whether students are grappling (or have grappled) with core disciplinary concepts; (2) whether students have surfaced prior personal, cultural, and academic knowledge bearing on those concepts; and (3) whether students have worked through differences or elaborated connections between the prior and new ideas. But proponents of this view would have no way to envision what these experiences look like or what they might mean on an institutional scale attuned to policy and public interests. Without tools to scale toward institutional views, their contributions would likely elide policy.

## Conclusion

Are college students, indeed, learning in full and rich ways? And does their classroom teaching support their learning, in depth, of core substantive ideas? Although these questions can be asked—and addressed—on a case-by-case basis by instructors and others working on the "ground floor" of academe (e.g., case of Adina), they are posed increasingly by the policy community. Interested in good teaching for all classrooms, policy makers seek to advance institutional practices that, used in tandem with local instructional practices, can improve college students' learning. Some proponents of a policy view have worried that college students today are not developing adequately in their critical thinking or in other generalized competencies.[69] However, it may be that the policy view itself could benefit from further development—for example, by considering what students experience and how they respond as their academic learning and their prior cultural learning interact. Dowd, Sawatzky, and Korn make this point succinctly in stating that the concept of "student effort"—decoupled from considerations of "intercultural effort"—offers but a partial look at student learning.[70] Without anchoring in a perspective that responds to students' cultural knowledge—treating that as central to their academic learning—critics may be unable to discern the full value of a college degree. Without a cognitively responsive view of learning—one that is purposefully culturally inclusive—we simply cannot determine whether today's college students are, indeed, learning in full and rich ways.

Given distinctions between the cognitively responsive view offering insights on teaching as it unfolds "on the ground," and the strategic institutional views that policy makers and college leaders seek, we see needs for interconnection—namely, ways to forge synergies among governmental policies, broad-scale institutional practices, and local classroom practices of teaching and learning. In working toward such synergies, policy makers, administrators, and faculty will need to remember that neither policy, nor institutional practice, nor classroom-based practices can "say it all." Work at each of these three levels has something of value to contribute to the building of synergies directed at educational improvement.

We know, for example, that cognitively responsive approaches align well with expert instructors' ingrained "wisdom of teaching practice" gained through attentive and in-depth learning on the job.[71] We should then be able to draw from such instructors' expert knowledge about what works in classrooms toward the forging of broader institutional practices and public policies with potential to make an educational difference. In their turn, policy views—including extant engagement and general competencies efforts and the outcomes movement overall—have effectively developed assessment criteria, tests of generalized competencies, and other tools for signaling student achievement. Such measures are typically summed to create institutional profiles amenable to policy makers' and institutional leaders' strategic educational improvement efforts. We should be able to apply aspects of this toolkit to support the development of new measures around classroom learning and teaching, scaled to reflect institutional performance.

Might the two overarching views—cognitively responsive and policy—be positioned to work in tandem? Might each view inform the other? Might they intertwine in ways that will advance educational improvement at large? With this possibility in mind, we suggest a three-pronged process.

1. *Infuse current tools known to work well—notably, engagement, general competencies, and other outcome-anchored rubrics—with new content derived from research-based theories of learning and teaching currently being developed in the learning sciences.* This approach would enrich and expand current efforts, widely in use, with improved data on what and how students learn in class. It is encouraging to see that such effort was made in NSSE's 2014 student surveys, which, among other questions, probed aspects of students' prior knowledge.[72]

2. *Create brand-new tools—new assessment designs, data collection methods, and data analytic strategies—that are grounded in cognitively responsive conceptions of teaching and learning and that are, simultaneously, geared to yield broad-scale institutional and cross-institutional views.* Such creations would—from the "get go"—meld the best of the two views we have laid out in this chapter: the substantive insights of the cognitively responsive view and the methodological strengths of the institutional-spanning policy view. We see progress in this direction in some researchers' efforts to refine generalized representations of "teaching methods" (e.g., lecture, discussion) by highlighting, among other things, the cognitive demands that instructors make of students as they implement such methods.[73] Other researchers are developing methods of "quantitative observation" implemented within multisite designs to examine teaching in terms of cognitive responsiveness—thus as seeking, explicitly, to

advance students' substantive learning via linkages to their prior knowledge.[74] Recent efforts include aggregating data on teaching in 50 to 100 classrooms per institutional site across nine campuses of varying levels of prestige.[75]

3. *Support theoretical development of cognitively responsive teaching and learning in higher education, as materializing amid the unique goals, contexts, and cultures of postsecondary education.* Such work should be designed to inform and otherwise support the two preceding efforts. It also should guide formulation of related initiatives—including development of new content for professional development programs directed at instructors, teaching and learning support staff, and university leaders. Rooted strongly in the learning sciences yet wholly attentive to the uniqueness of higher education, such efforts have been made via analyses of subject-matter teaching and learning practices,[76] comparative case analyses of teaching in classrooms, much like the one where Adina first encountered Cartesian doubt,[77] and research on new strategies for faculty professional development.[78]

We believe that a multipronged strategy like this will do two things: It will strengthen and advance extant teaching, learning, assessment, and policymaking practices in higher education. It also will make space for brand new practices to arise at the crossroads of public and cognitive responsiveness.

ACKNOWLEDGMENTS

*Special thanks to Mike Bastedo for thoughtful feedback, and to Dianne Delima and Marisol Jimenez for valuable research assistance.*

NOTES

1. Peter T. Ewell, "An Emerging Scholarship: A Brief History of Assessment," in *Building a Scholarship of Assessment*, ed. Trudy W. Banta and Associates (San Francisco: Jossey-Bass, 2002), 3–25; Peter T. Ewell, "Assessment and Accountability in America Today: Background and Context," *New Directions for Institutional Research* no. S1 (2008): 7–17; George D. Kuh, Natasha Jankowski, Stanley O. Ikenberry, and Jillian Kinzie, *Knowing What Students Know and Can Do: The Current State of Student Learning Outcomes Assessment in US Colleges and Universities* (Urbana: University of Illinois and Indiana University, National Institute for Learning Outcomes Assessment [NILOA], 2014).

2. Robert Birnbaum, *How Colleges Work: The Cybernetics of Academic Organization and Leadership* (San Francisco: Jossey-Bass, 1988), xvi.

3. John D. Bransford, Ann L. Brown, and Rodney R. Cocking, eds., *How People Learn: Brain, Mind, Experience, and School* (Washington, DC: National Academy Press, 2000). The volume summarizes an extensive body of cognition research.

4. To refer to these emergent perspectives, including the research and theory from which they are derived, we use the concept of cognitive responsiveness developed by Anna Neumann and Aaron Pallas in *College Teaching Reconsidered: Repairing the Heart of a College Education* (Baltimore: Johns Hopkins University Press, forthcoming). Neumann and Pallas explain cognitively responsive teaching in higher education and discuss implications for the faculty's professional development and key institutional practices.

5. Joseph J. Schwab, "The Practical 3: Translation into Curriculum," *School Review* 81 (1973): 501–22.

6. Anna Neumann, *Professing to Learn: Creating Tenured Lives and Careers in the American Research University* (Baltimore: Johns Hopkins University Press, 2009).

7. Anna Neumann, "Organizational Cognition in Higher Education," in *The Organization of Higher Education: Managing Colleges for a New Era*, ed. Michael N. Bastedo (Baltimore: Johns Hopkins University Press, 2012), 304–31.

8. For an example, see Carol D. Lee, *Culture, Literacy, and Learning: Taking Bloom in the Midst of the Whirlwind* (New York City: Teachers College Press, 2007).

9. We are grateful to Aaron Pallas for this insight about the meaning of "average" drawn from his teaching of statistics. For additional discussion of academic learning that may reach into students' personal lives, see Zelda F. Gamson, *Liberating Education* (San Francisco: Jossey-Bass, 1984); also Lee S. Shulman, *Teaching as Community Property: Essays on Higher Education* (San Francisco: Jossey-Bass, 2004).

10. Bransford, Brown, and Cocking, *How People Learn*.

11. The case example of the cognitively responsive pedagogy that follows below (about Adina's learning and Sofia's teaching) is a revised version of a previously published article by Anna Neumann. Copyright © 2014, Association for the Study of Higher Education. This article, Neumann's presidential address to the Association for the Study of Higher Education (November 2012), first appeared in *The Review of Higher Education* 37, no. 2 (Winter 2014): 249–67. Included here with permission of the publisher, Johns Hopkins University Press.

12. Shulman, *Teaching as Community Property*; Lee S. Shulman, *The Wisdom of Practice: Essays on Teaching, Learning, and Learning to Teach* (San Francisco: Jossey-Bass, 2004).

13. Joseph J. Schwab, "The Practical 4: Something for Curriculum Professors to Do," *Curriculum Inquiry* 13 (1983): 239–65; Shulman, *Teaching as Community Property*; Shulman, *The Wisdom of Practice*; Lee S. Shulman, "Those Who Understand: Knowledge Growth in Teaching," *Educational Researcher* 15 (1986): 4–14.

14. From Neumann, "Staking a Claim." For specific discussion, see Bransford, Brown, and Cocking, *How People Learn*; Schwab, "The Practical 3"; Shulman, *Teaching as Community* and *The Wisdom of Practice*; John Dewey, "The Child and the Curriculum" in *On Education*, ed. Reginald D. Archambault (Chicago: University of Chicago Press, 1902), 339–58; John Dewey, "The Nature of Subject Matter," in *On Education*, ed. Reginald D. Archambault (Chicago: University of Chicago Press, 1964), 359–72.

15. Shulman, *Teaching as Community Property*; Shulman, *The Wisdom of Practice*; Neumann and Pallas, *College Teaching Reconsidered*.

16. Association of American Colleges and Universities (AAC&U), *College Learning for the New Global Century* (Washington, DC: Association of American Colleges and Universities, 2007); Richard Arum and Josipa Roksa, *Academically Adrift: Limited Learning on College Campuses* (Chicago: University of Chicago Press, 2011); Corbin M. Campbell, "Serving a Different Master: Assessing College Educational Quality for the Public," in *Higher Education: Handbook of Theory and Research*, vol. 30, ed. Michael B. Paulsen (New York: Springer, 2015), 525–79; George D. Kuh, "The National Survey of Student Engagement: Conceptual and Empirical Foundations," *New Directions for Institutional Research* 141 (2009): 5–20; Christine M. Keller and John M. Hammang, "The Voluntary System of Accountability for Accountability and Institutional Assessment," *New Directions for Institutional Research* no. 1 (Fall 2008): 39–48; National Survey of Student Engagement (NSSE), *Bringing the Institution into Focus: Annual Results 2014* (Bloomington: Indiana University Center for Postsecondary Research, 2014).

17. George D. Kuh, "Assessing What Really Matters to Student Learning: Inside the National Survey of Student Engagement," *Change* 33 (2001): 10–17, 66; Lisa Wolf-Wendel, Kelly Ward, and Jillian Kinzie, "A Tangled Web of Terms: The Overlap and Unique Contribution of Involvement, Engagement, and Integration to Understanding College Student Success," *Journal of College Student Development* 50, no. 4 (2009): 407–28.

18. NSSE, *Bringing the Institution*.

19. NSSE, *Assessment for Improvement: Tracking Student Engagement Over Time– Annual Results 2009* (Bloomington: Indiana University Center for Postsecondary Research, 2009), 3.

20. Wolf-Wendel, Ward, and Kinzie, "A Tangled Web."

21. Nevitt Sanford, *Where Colleges Fail: A Study of the Student as a Person* (San Francisco: Jossey-Bass, 1967); C. Robert Pace, "Measuring the Quality of Student Effort," in *Improving Teaching and Institutional Quality, Current Issues in Higher Education* no. 1 (Washington, DC: American Association for Higher Education, 1980).

22. Alexander W. Astin, "Involvement: The Cornerstone of Excellence," *Change* 17, no. 4 (1985): 35–39.

23. Arthur W. Chickering and Zelda F. Gamson, "Seven Principles for Good Practice in Undergraduate Education," *AAHE Bulletin* 39 (1987): 3–7.

24. Robert M. Carini, George D. Kuh, and Stephen P. Klein, "Student Engagement and Student Learning: Testing the Linkages," *Research in Higher Education* 47, no. 1 (2006): 2.

25. NSSE, *Bringing the Institution*.

26. Kuh, Ikenberry, and Kinzie, *Knowing What Students Know*.

27. Pu-Shih Daniel Chen, Robert Gonyea, and George D. Kuh, "Learning at a Distance: Engaged or Not?" *Innovate: Journal of Online Education* 4, no. 3 (2008), http://www.innovateonline.info.

28. Jillian L. Kinzie et al., "Women Students at Coeducational and Women's Colleges: How do Their Experiences Compare?" *Journal of College Student Development* 48, no. 2 (2007): 145–65.

29. George D. Kuh, "Built to Engage: Liberal Arts Colleges and Effective Educational Practice," in *Liberal Arts Colleges in American Higher Education*, ed. Francis Oakely (New York: American Council of Learned Societies, 2007), 122–50.

30. James S. Cole and Ali Korkmaz, "Using Longitudinal Data to Improve the Experiences and Engagement of First-year Students," *New Directions for Institutional Research* (Assessment Supplement) no. 2 (2010): 43–51.

31. Shaun R. Harper, Robert M. Carini, Brian K. Bridges, and John C. Hayek, "Gender Differences in Student Engagement among African American Undergraduates at Historically Black Colleges and Universities," *Journal of College Student Development* 45, no. 3 (2004): 271–84.

32. John C. Hayek, Robert M. Carini, Patrick T. O'Day, and George D. Kuh, "Triumph or Tragedy: Comparing Student Engagement Levels of Members of Greek-letter Organizations and Other Students," *Journal of College Student Development* 43, no. 5 (2002): 643–63.

33. Gary R. Pike and George D. Kuh, "First- and Second-Generation College Students: A Comparison of Their Engagement and Intellectual Development," *The Journal of Higher Education* 76, no. 3 (2005): 276–300.

34. Terrel L. Rhodes, *Assessing Outcomes and Improving Achievement: Tips and Tools for Using Rubrics* (Washington, DC: Association of American Colleges and Universities, 2010).

35. For example, see Arum and Roksa, *Academically Adrift*.

36. AAC&U, *College Learning*, 2.

37. Arum and Roksa, *Academically Adrift*.

38. Scott Jaschik, "'Academically Adrift,'" *Inside Higher Education* (Jan. 18, 2011), http://www.insidehighered.com/news/2011/01/18/study_finds_large_numbers_of_college_students_don_t_learn_much.

39. C. Kent McGuire et al., "Does College Make You Smarter?" *The New York Times*, Jan. 24, 2011.

40. Trudy Banta, "Editor's Notes: Trying to Clothe the Emperor," *Assessment Update* 20, no. 2 (2008): 3–4, 15–16; Philip Garcia, "The Collegiate Learning Assessment: Using Cross-sectional Indicators as Proxies for Longitudinal Outcomes" (presentation at the Association for Institutional Research Forum, Seattle, WA, May 24–28, 2008); Ou Lydia Liu, Brent Bridgeman, and Rachel M. Adler, "Measuring Learning Outcomes in Higher Education: Motivation Matters," *Educational Researcher* 41, no. 9 (2012): 352–62; Aaron M. Pallas, "Assessing the Future of Higher Education," *Society* 3 (2011): 213–15; Mark D. Shermis, "The Collegiate Learning Assessment: A Critical Perspective," *Assessment Update* 20, no. 2 (2008): 10–12.

41. Tamar Lewin, "Most College Students Don't Earn a Degree in 4 Years," *New York Times*, Dec. 1, 2014; Kevin Carey, "'Academically Adrift': The News Gets Worse and Worse," *The Chronicle of Higher Education* (Feb. 12, 2012), http://chronicle.com/article/Academically-Adrift-The/130743/.

42. Jaschik, "'Academically Adrift.'"

43. AAC&U, *College Learning*.

44. Ibid.

45. Rhodes, *Assessing Outcomes*.

46. Ewell, "An Emerging Scholarship"; Alicia C. Dowd and Vincent P. Tong, "Accountability, Assessment, and the Scholarship of 'Best Practice,'" in *Handbook of Higher Education*, vol. 22, ed. John C. Smart (New York: Springer, 2007), 57–119.

47. Campbell, "Serving a Different Master."

48. Bransford, Brown, and Cocking, *How People Learn.*

49. Ibid.

50. See Gloria Ladson-Billings, "Toward a Theory of Culturally Relevant Pedagogy," *American Educational Research Journal* 32, no. 3 (1995): 465–91; Lee, *Culture, Literacy, and Learning.*

51. Bransford, Brown, and Cocking, *How People Learn.*

52. Ibid.

53. Shulman, *Teaching as Community Property*; Shulman, *The Wisdom of Practice*; Shulman, "Those Who Understand."

54. Patricia Hill Collins, "Learning from the Outsider Within: The Sociological Significance of Black Feminist Thought," *Social Problems* 33, no. 6 (1986): 14–32; Sandra Harding, "What Is Feminist Epistemology?" in *Whose Science? Whose Knowledge?: Thinking from Women's Lives* (Ithaca, NY: Cornell University Press, 1987), 105–37.

55. See Shulman, *Teaching as Community Property*; Shulman, *The Wisdom of Practice*; Shulman, "Those Who Understand."

56. See Neumann, "Staking a Claim."

57. Ibid. Scenario, related claims, and discussion are rewritten for this chapter, but draw directly from the content of the original research.

58. Ibid. For specific discussion, see Bransford, Brown, and Cocking, *How People Learn*; Dewey, "The Child and the Curriculum"; Shulman, *Teaching as Community Property*; Shulman, *The Wisdom of Practice*; Kris. D. Gutierrez and Barbara Rogoff, "Cultural Ways of Learning: Individual Traits or Repertoires of Practice," *Educational Researcher* 32, no. 5 (2003): 19–25; Ladson-Billings, "Toward a Theory"; Gloria Ladson-Billings, "Yes, but How Do We Do It?": Practicing Culturally Relevant Pedagogy," in *White Teachers/Diverse Classrooms: A Guide to Building Inclusive Schools, Promoting High Expectations, and Eliminating Racism*, ed. Julie Landsman and Chance W. Lewis (Sterling, VA: Stylus, 2006), 29–42; Lee, *Culture, Literacy, and Learning*; Anna Neumann and Penelope L. Peterson, eds., *Learning from Our Lives: Women, Research, and Autobiography in Education* (New York: Teachers College Press, 1997); Loukia K. Sarroub, *All American Yemeni Girls: Being Muslim in a Public School* (Philadelphia: University of Pennsylvania Press, 2005).

59. NSSE, *Bringing the Institution.*

60. Rhodes, *Assessing Outcomes.*

61. Bransford, Brown, and Cocking, *How People Learn.*

62. From Neumann, "Staking a Claim"; for a specific discussion, see Bransford, Brown, and Cocking, *How People Learn*; Lee, *Culture, Literacy, and Learning*; Norma González, Luis C. Moll, and Cathy Amanti, eds., *Funds of Knowledge: Theorizing Practices in Households, Communities, and Classrooms* (Mahwah, NJ: Lawrence Erlbaum Associates, 2005); Shulman, *Teaching as Community Property*; Shulman, *The Wisdom of Practice.*

63. Milagros Castillo-Montoya, "A Study of First-Generation African American and Latino Undergraduates Developing Sociopolitical Consciousness in Introductory Sociology Classes," EdD diss., Teachers College, Columbia University, 2013.

64. Ewell, "An Emerging Scholarship"; Keller and Hammang, "The Voluntary System."

65. Chickering and Gamson, "Seven Principles."

66. NSSE, *Bringing the Institution.*

67. "CLA+ References," CLA References, http://cae.org/participating-institutions/cla -references [accessed June 21, 2015].

68. AAC&U, *College Learning.*

69. Arum and Roksa, *Academically Adrift*; Earnest T. Pascarella, Charles Blaich, Georgianna L. Martin, and Jana M. Hanson, "How Robust are the Findings of Academically Adrift? Evidence from the Wabash National Study," *Change: The Magazine of Higher Learning*, 43, no. 3 (2011): 20–24. doi: 10.1080/00091383.2011.568898.

70. Alicia C. Dowd, Misty Sawatzky, and Randi Korn, "Theoretical Foundations and a Research Agenda to Validate Measures of Intercultural Effect," *The Review of Higher Education* 35, no. 1 (2011): 17–44.

71. Lee S. Shulman, "Knowledge and Teaching: Foundations of the New Reform," *Harvard Educational Review*, 57, no. 1 (1987): 1–21.

72. NSSE, *NSSE 2014 Engagement Indicators* (Bloomington: Indiana University Center for Postsecondary Research, 2014).

73. Matthew T. Hora, Amanda Oleson, and Joseph J. Ferrare, *Teaching Dimensions Observation Protocol (TDOP) User's Manual* (Madison: Wisconsin Center for Education Research, University of Wisconsin-Madison, 2013), http://tdop.wceruw.org/Document /TDOP-Users-Guide.pdf.

74. Corbin M. Campbell, Marisol Jimenez, and Christine Arlene N. Arrozol, "The Mirage of Prestige: The Educational Quality of Courses in Prestigious and Non-Prestigious Institutions." Presentation at the Annual Meeting of the Association for the Study of Higher Education, Denver, CO, November Nov. 5–7, 2015.

75. Campbell, "Serving a Different Master."

76. Neumann, *Professing to Learn*; Vilma Mesa, Sergio Celis, and Elaine Lande, "Teaching Approaches of Community College Mathematics Faculty: Do They Relate to Classroom Practices?" *American Educational Research Journal*, 51, no. (2014): 117–51; Lisa R. Lattuca, "Faculty Work as Learning: Insights from Theories of Cognition," *New Directions for Teaching and Learning*, 2005, no. 102 (2005): 13–21; Matt T. Hora and Craig Anderson, "Perceived Norms for Interactive Teaching and their Relationship to Instructional Decision-Making: A Mixed Methods Study," *Higher Education*, 64, no. 4 (2012): 573–92.

77. Neumann, "Staking a Claim"; Anna Neumann et al., "Defining 'Good Teaching': Pedagogical Practices for Advancing Diverse Students' Liberal Learning in Three Urban College Classrooms" (presentation at the Association for the Study of Higher Education, Washington, DC, Nov. 19–22, 2014).

78. "MetroCITI: Metropolitan Colleges Institute for Teaching Improvement," http://metrociti.pressible.org [accessed June 21, 2015]. MetroCITI employs a cognitively responsive approach to frame the content of a multi-campus institute for faculty professional development focused on teaching improvement.

# Chapter Fifteen

# Technology

*The Solution to Higher Education's Pressing Problems?*

Laura W. Perna and Roman Ruiz

No book designed to inform understanding of how higher education is influenced by and responds to societal changes, demands, and progress would be complete without a chapter on technology. Defined as "the application of scientific knowledge to the practical aims of human life," technology is a fundamental element of any society.[1] Technology is more than cutting-edge, advanced, "high-tech" innovations and is not limited to "technology sectors" like aerospace, nanotechnology, and robotics. Rather, the term "technology" refers to the tools that are available in the society in which we live and work, and that may be applied and leveraged to achieve various goals and purposes.

The relationship between technology and higher education is complex and ever changing. Higher education institutions are deeply intertwined with and linked to the societies they serve. Higher education is challenged to spur societal change and progress by encouraging the development of new technologies and, at the same time, to respond to demands created by technology. This chapter begins by describing the multiple roles of technology in three core functions of higher education: producing research, enrolling and supporting students, and teaching and encouraging learning. The chapter then considers the vexing question, *can technology solve the pressing problems facing higher education?* More specifically, *can technology enable higher education to increase access and attainment while also reducing costs and maintaining quality?* The final section of the chapter considers the barriers that limit the extent to which technology can productively address these challenges and transform higher education.

## Technology and Higher Education

With the ubiquity of high-speed Internet and the proliferation of mobile devices, information and communication technologies influence countless aspects of daily life and, consequently, numerous dimensions of higher education.[2] Current and prospective students, faculty, and administrators routinely use digital technologies and expect that a "modern" college or university will have state-of-the art Wi-Fi access, campus computing and technology laboratories, and web-based course management and student information systems. This section highlights the multifaceted role of technology in conducting research, enrolling and supporting students, and teaching and encouraging learning.

### The Role of Technology in Research

The connection between technology and research production is multidirectional. Higher education advances the creation and application of new technologies through the production of original research. At the same time, technology also influences the ways that higher education produces research and advances knowledge across fields and disciplines.

With the goal of encouraging higher education to develop, apply, and test new technologies, federal and state governments, philanthropic organizations, businesses, and other entities annually award considerable financial resources to higher education institutions. The federal government is the largest single provider of research funding for higher education, accounting for 61 percent of the total $65.8 billion university research and development expenditures in FY2012.[3]

One recent example of the federal government's efforts to stimulate technological innovation by higher education institutions is the First in the World (FITW) Program, a competition designed to encourage the development and use of innovative technologies to improve college student outcomes and affordability. Administered by the US Department of Education's Fund for the Improvement of Postsecondary Education (FIPSE), this program awarded grants in FY2014 ranging from $1.65 million to $4 million ($75 million total) to twenty-four higher education institutions. Of the twenty-four pilot projects that received funding, six focused on using technology to improve students' educational outcomes. Examples include the Georgia Institute of Technology's Center for

Accessible Materials Innovation project, which expands access to digital instructional content for students with print-related disabilities and Northeastern University's Lowell Institution Innovation Incubator project designed to increase student engagement and motivation in online STEM courses.[4]

Research institutions can be drivers of economic and technological advancement in their regions by encouraging the creation of technology parks and technology firms (e.g., Silicon Valley in Northern California and the Research Triangle in North Carolina) and engaging in partnerships with technology firms.[5] A number of US research universities have created technology transfer offices (or similarly named units) to facilitate (and monetize) the transfer of university-generated technologies into the private sector. Technology transfer offices are typically charged with advising university researchers on how to identify, patent, and market "commercially viable technologies" to potential licensees.[6]

According to a 2013 survey of more than 200 US research institutions, technologies created by university researchers contributed to the development of 719 new commercial products by companies licensing the technologies in FY2013.[7] Association of University Technology Managers (AUTM) member institutions also self-reported that "more than 10,000 patented products currently being sold originated in academic research laboratories."[8] The engagement of higher education institutions and faculty in market activities like patenting and licensing new technologies is consistent with the theory of academic capitalism as advanced and updated by Sheila Slaughter and Gary Rhoades.[9]

In addition to contributing to the development of new technologies, higher education has also incorporated and applied new technologies to change the process of knowledge production. Higher education researchers now operate within the context of a "cyberinfrastructure"[10] that includes the "distributed computer, information, and communication technologies combined with the personnel and integrating components that provide a long-term platform to empower the modern scientific research endeavor."[11] Low-cost information and communication technologies enable teams of researchers to collaborate in all aspects of a research project, from developing research grants, collecting and analyzing data, and authoring publications and other research products, regardless of where team members are physically located. With e-mail, Skype, FaceTime, and other web-based applications, researchers across the globe are now part of an interconnected "global grid of investigation and inquiry."[12] Low-cost software and enhanced data storage capacity also enable researchers to analyze larger databases using increasingly sophisticated analytic methods.

The knowledge production process has also been changed by Internet technologies that provide easy and broad access to research products and materials. Digital libraries and repositories (e.g., JSTOR, Artstor) make scholarly publications and resources electronically accessible anytime to researchers across the globe. For instance, JSTOR, a not-for-profit organization established in 1995, provides shared digital access to current and historical issues of over 2,000 academic journals for scholars at more than 9,200 institutions in more than 170 nations.[13] Accessing these digital collections may create additional costs for higher education institutions (as JSTOR and other repositories typically charge a fee to member institutions) but may also reduce the costs associated with storing and maintaining paper copies of materials in an institution's own library.

With the availability of Internet technologies and interest in low-cost methods of distributing academic research worldwide has also come open access publishing, defined as "unrestricted online access to articles published in scholarly journals."[14] As of December 2014, the Directory of Open Access Journals (doaj .org), an online index of peer-reviewed open access (OA) journals, cataloged 1.8 million articles from 10,200 journals from 136 countries. Suggesting widespread support of OA, 89 percent of more than 38,000 researchers with peer-reviewed publications who responded to a 2010 international survey reported that OA publishing is or would be beneficial to their field.[15]

Federal agencies and nonprofit organizations in the US have encouraged the advancement of OA publishing. Since 2009 the National Institutes of Health (NIH) has required that grant recipients submit accepted publications to its own PubMed Central, a free digital archive, within twelve months of official publication.[16] In 2013 the federal Office of Science and Technology Policy directed all federal agencies with more than $100 million in research and development expenditures to adopt OA policies similar to NIH.[17] Beginning in 2015, the Bill & Melinda Gates Foundation has required that all new foundation-funded research be freely available online with immediate access and reuse rights.[18]

## The Role of Technology in Enrolling and Supporting Students

The relationship between technology and students is also multifaceted. Students, parents, employers, governments, and other stakeholders expect that higher education will both produce graduates with the knowledge and skills required in a technologically driven, knowledge-based economy[19] and use current technologies to recruit and support students. Technology influences the characteristics of both the "product" that higher education is expected to produce and the expectations of individuals enrolling in higher education, a primary "input" into higher education.

Today's knowledge-based economy requires highly skilled workers who are able to use new technologies.[20] Some argue that increasing the supply of highly skilled workers is critical to not only ensuring the nation's future international competitiveness but also to reducing economic inequality.[21] In their examination of "the race between education and technology," Goldin and Katz observe that, in the first part of the twentieth century, increases in educational attainment kept pace with "skill-biased technological change."[22] Employers' demand for highly skilled workers—defined during this time period as workers with a high school diploma—was met with the available supply. During the last quarter of the twentieth century, however, growth in educational attainment slowed, and the demand for highly skilled workers—now defined as workers with a college degree—exceeded the supply.[23] Goldin and Katz conclude that the growth in economic inequality that occurred in the United States during the last quarter of the twentieth century is explained not by growing demand for the skills created by "the era of computerization," but rather by an insufficient increase in the supply of workers with the skills to use the new technologies.[24]

Increasingly the jobs that are available today—and the jobs that are projected to be available in the future—require workers to have information-processing, academic, and technical skills.[25] Suggesting the importance of technological skills, the Organisation for Economic Co-operation and Development now defines "adult basic skills" not only by measures of literacy and numeracy, but also by indicators of the ability to read digital texts and solve problems in environments that rely on information and communication technology.[26] Employers appear to reward technological expertise, as average earnings are higher for individuals who use computers than for those who do not, regardless of educational attainment level.[27]

Higher education institutions are expected to not only produce graduates with the skills required for available jobs in a technologically driven, knowledge-based economy, but also utilize practices that recognize the changing technological expectations and habits of entering students. The use of personal computers and the Internet is commonplace, especially for individuals born after 1980.[28] Today virtually all teens (ages twelve to seventeen) and young adults (ages eighteen to twenty-nine) use the Internet, and most teens own or have access to a desktop or laptop computer in their home (93%) and own a cell phone (78%).[29]

Known as "digital natives," today's traditional-age (ages eighteen to twenty-four) college students are assumed to be tech savvy and fluent with new technologies, learn in fundamentally different ways than previous generations, and be enthusiastic about gaming and virtual simulations.[30]

Virtually all (89%) eighteen- to twenty-nine-year-olds who use the Internet report using social media.[31] Among college-bound seniors in 2014, 75 percent reported using Facebook, 73 percent used YouTube, and 40 percent used Twitter.[32] Recognizing that social media usage among traditional college-aged students is now near universal,[33] the 2014 *NMC Horizon Report*—an annual publication in which an international panel of technology experts predicts key technology trends—identified the "growing ubiquity of social media" as one of the "fast trends" that is influencing higher education.[34] Although some faculty and administrators continue to worry about the privacy implications of social media, technology experts point to the potential benefits of social media in creating a venue where "anyone in the social networks can engage with content."[35] Social media is a collaborative arena that permits the transmission and consumption of user-generated content, including text, photos, audio, and video. Like other web-based technologies, social media transcends physical boundaries and connects users from around the globe.

Given these statistics, it is not surprising that prospective students (and their parents) are utilizing computers and mobile devices to obtain college-related information. In a March 2014 poll, both college-bound seniors and their parents ranked the institutional website as the most influential and reliable resource used in the college search process.[36] Nearly two-thirds (61%) of college-bound seniors and half (51%) of parents reported preferring to learn about college using web-based resources. Students are accessing college websites via both computers and mobile devices. Ninety-one percent of college-bound high school seniors reported having access to a mobile device (typically a smartphone) and 71 percent reported having looked at a college website on a mobile device.[37]

These characteristics compel higher education institutions to ensure that they are providing information and services in the form and with the functionality that students and their families need and want. Colleges and universities appear to be responding to these expectations, as more than 90 percent of the public and private two-year institutions responding to a 2006 survey reported that they were offering, or were planning to offer within two years, the following online services: course registration, financial aid and admission applications, digital course catalogs, student access to class schedules, and online courses.[38]

About 83 percent of campuses responding to a 2014 survey reported having implemented, or were planning to implement within the academic year, mobile apps, up from 78 percent of campuses in 2013 and just 60 percent in 2012.[39]

Digital technologies are also being developed to help students, especially students who are the first in their families to attend college and those enrolled at under-resourced high schools, to navigate the college enrollment process. For example, in partnership with Rossier School of Education researchers, USC's Game Innovation Lab has developed *Mission: Admission*, a free-to-play game available through Facebook.[40] In the game, students assume the avatar of a high school senior and spend their finite energy supply completing activities that make them eligible for college admission such as studying in the library, completing the FAFSA on time, and requesting letters of recommendation from teachers. Researchers designed the game to develop students' resilience and grit by confronting them with real-world obstacles that demand strategy and perseverance to accomplish challenges analogous to those they will encounter in the college application process. Another computer game developed by the lab, *Graduation Strike Force*, is modeled after a traditional action game and requires students to battle mutants and monsters as they learn how to overcome the seemingly insurmountable college affordability problem.[41]

Mobile phone apps are also being created with the goal of providing high school students with better college-related information in the context of the high student-to-counselor ratios in most high schools. College Summit, a nonprofit organization with the mission of increasing college enrollment among low-income students, created the virtual *College App Map* to organize apps by high school grade level and intended purpose (e.g., college selection, career exploration).[42]

Colleges and universities may be able to capitalize on emerging technologies to create low-cost mechanisms for promoting college enrollment and persistence.[43] For instance, using a multisite experimental design, Castleman and Page found that students who received a set of automated and personalized text messages had lower likelihood of "summer melt," defined as the failure of high school graduates who intend to enroll in college to actually matriculate in the fall semester.[44] The text messages provided reminders to students and their parents about such key tasks as "register for orientation and placements tests" and "complete housing forms" and links to information and resources (e.g., FAFSA completion, advising). The text messages were particularly effective for promoting enrollment at two-year colleges and for students from low-income families, those who had less access to college planning supports, and those who had not completed the FAFSA at the time of intervention.

Some colleges and universities are using technology with the goal of delivering more effective and efficient academic advising.[45] One example is Arizona State University's eAdvisor system. With more than 73,000 students in the fall of 2012,[46] Arizona State University and other large universities may be especially motivated to identify effective, technology-driven, low-cost innovations. The electronic advising system is expected to increase the time advisors have available to provide face-to-face counseling and mentoring for students most at-risk for academic failure. Implemented in 2007, the web-accessible, automated eAdvisor system enables undergraduates, at any time or place, to explore potential majors, identify optimal course sequences, and map out curricular scenarios associated with particular major field choices. By integrating information across several institutional databases, the online system may also enable advisors to better track students' progress toward an intended degree and identify early students who are not making adequate academic progress.[47]

Some institutions are using asynchronous technology (e.g., e-mail, web portals) and synchronous technology (e.g., instant messaging) to deliver career services. Examples include Old Dominion University's online career workshops and seminars and Emerson College's podcasts featuring alumni and other professionals working in career fields of interest.[48]

Student demand for tools that better meet their information needs is further signaled by the initiative some students have taken to develop their own mechanisms for leveraging available technologies.[49] For example, a Rutgers University student built an app that monitors enrollment of the university's most in-demand courses and notifies users when an opening becomes available. Two students at the University of California at Berkeley created a website that integrates course scheduling information, professor ratings, and required textbook listings in one location. Berkeley brokered a financial deal with the students to use the website; the site now serves students at four universities within the University of California system.[50]

These last examples are consistent with another trend identified in the 2014 *NMC Horizon Report*: the shifting role of students from consumers to creators.[51] Understanding the tech-savvy nature of traditional college-aged students, some universities provide technology laboratories for students and sponsor campus-wide initiatives designed to encourage student entrepreneurship. Examples of university-sponsored innovation initiatives include the University of Pennsylvania's

AppItUP challenge, in which UPenn students compete to win investor funding to develop a mobile application, and the Harvard College Innovation Challenge (also called "i3"), in which students compete for grant funding, consulting services, and workspace in order to develop their own startup company.[52]

## THE ROLE OF TECHNOLOGY IN TEACHING AND LEARNING

The relationship between technology and teaching and learning is also complex. Higher education has both incorporated new technologies into pedagogical practices and contributed to the development of new technologies for teaching and learning. That being said, however, technology has had relatively little impact on instructional approaches at most colleges and universities. Technology hypothetically allows for the reconfiguration of the traditional face-to-face, lecture-based instructional model that has historically been the norm in higher education. Yet most observers concur that, although technology has created many changes for higher education research, technology has largely been used to enhance traditional approaches to delivering higher education without fundamentally changing the nature of teaching and learning.[53]

Since the creation of early online course delivery systems in the late 1990s, the availability of higher education over the Internet has increased considerably.[54] The 2014 *NMC Horizon Report* identifies the incorporation of online, hybrid, and collaborative learning into face-to-face classroom instruction as one of the "fast trends" in higher education technology.[55] Using data from the Integrated Postsecondary Education Data System (IPEDS), the Babson Survey Research Group reports that the majority (71%) of degree-granting higher education institutions offered at least one online course in 2013.[56] More than 90 percent of public two-year and public four-year institutions reported offering online courses, compared with about two-thirds of private not-for-profit four-year and private for-profit four-year institutions. The availability of online courses generally increases with institutional size, as only 48 percent of institutions with fewer than 1,000 students had distance course offerings in the fall of 2013, compared with more than 95 percent of institutions with at least 5,000 students.[57] Online courses may also be more common "in subjects where mastery can be evaluated in response to questions with demonstrably right or wrong answers" (e.g., math and business rather than social science), as well as in professional rather than undergraduate education programs.[58]

Student participation in online courses has increased in recent years.[59] According to IPEDS, in the fall of 2012, 11 percent of undergraduate degree-seeking students enrolled exclusively in distance education courses, while another 15 percent enrolled in some but not all distance education courses. About 26 percent of all students (including undergraduate, graduate, and nondegree-seeking undergraduate students) were enrolled in at least one distance education course in the fall of 2012.[60]

One challenge for understanding the role of "online learning" is continued inconsistency in the definition and use of the term.[61] The range of approaches to online learning limits identification of "a set of mutually exclusive 'boxes' into which various approaches to online learning can be put."[62] Despite this caveat, one category involves using technology to "replicate traditional models of instruction" by offering course content "purely online" or with a "hybrid" approach. A "rare" but different approach, what Bacow and colleagues label "interactive learning online," utilizes "increasingly sophisticated forms of artificial intelligence, drawing on usage data collected from hundreds of thousands of students, to deliver customized instruction tailored to an individual student's specific needs."[63] Whereas purely online and blended/hybrid learning approaches are instructor-guided, interactive learning online is "machine-guided."[64]

Although not transforming the underlying teaching paradigm,[65] technology has been incorporated into various instructional practices. Course management systems (CMS), like Blackboard, are now commonly used by higher education faculty to share course information, document student grades, and converse with students.[66] Used by colleges and universities as well as other organizations providing education and training, a learning management system "is a software application that automates the administration, tracking, and reporting" of courses, and collects and provides access to content and learning materials for individual users.[67]

Reflecting the increasing use of social media among college-age students, a growing share of faculty is incorporating social media into the courses that they teach.[68] The most common social media platforms that faculty report using in course assignments are blogs and wikis, followed by podcasts. Some social media platforms require greater student engagement than others. For instance, blogs and wikis require students to create content or add original comments, whereas podcasts merely require students to listen.

Some educators and researchers have identified the potential benefits of incorporating the positive elements of games and gaming into the higher education learning context.[69] Observing the many hours that individuals of all ages across the globe devote to computers, mobile phones, and video games, Jane

McGonigal, the director of game research and development at the Institute for the Future, argues that games can be a powerful mechanism for encouraging "extreme effort," "reward[ing] hard work," and promoting "cooperation and collaboration."[70] Among other attributes, games focus on accomplishing a particular goal, have rules for achieving the goal, provide feedback on progress toward goal attainment, and assure "that intentionally stressful and challenging work is experienced as safe and pleasurable activity."[71] Identified as an emerging education technology development in the 2014 *NMC Horizon Report*, gamification is "the notion that gaming mechanics can be applied to routine activities," including learning.[72] By creating "positive emotions, positive activity, positive experiences, and positive strengths,"[73] games may promote engagement in course content, especially for digital natives. Gameful learning is not a prescribed, didactic experience. Instead, gameful learning is assumed to engender voluntary acquisition of knowledge and encourage a self-initiated process of discovery.[74] Adapting the hallmarks of games into the higher education teaching-learning process has the potential to enhance educational outcomes such as critical thinking, problem solving, and teamwork.[75] Nonetheless, although gaming practices may be more scalable than traditional pedagogical practices,[76] relatively few faculty have taken the steps required to "gamify" their courses.[77]

Another emerging innovation is the application of technology to competency-based education. With attention to measuring learning rather than seat-time,[78] competency-based education promises "a flexible way for students to get credit for what they know, build on their knowledge and skills by learning more at their own pace, and earn high quality degrees, certificates, and other credentials."[79] Competency-based educational practices do not necessarily incorporate technology, but technology is integral to some competency-based education reforms, such as interactive self-paced courses that are delivered online. In January 2015 the US Department of Education signaled its interest in competency-based education and prior learning assessment by granting at least forty higher education institutions waivers from some of the federal financial aid regulations that have limited related experimentation.[80] With a grant from Lumina Foundation, in March 2014 Public Agenda launched the Competency-Based Education Network (C-BEN), an entity intended to improve understanding of effective models for and approaches to competency-based education. As of January 2015, C-BEN counted eighteen higher education institutions and two public systems (the Kentucky Community & Technical College System and University of Wisconsin-Extension) as members.

Among the higher education institutions utilizing technology to advance competency-based education are Capella University, Southern New Hampshire University, University of Maryland University College, and Western Governors University (WGU). Founded in 1997 with initial $100,000 investments from governors of nineteen US states, WGU, a nonprofit completely online university, seeks to deliver a competency-based education at a lower cost than its for-profit competitors. In 2013 WGU enrolled 33,000 undergraduate and 10,000 graduate students from all fifty states. WGU serves high numbers of adult students, as the average age of all students is thirty-seven, and high numbers of students from low-income families, as 40 percent of undergraduate students receive a Pell grant.[81] WGU awards academic credit for students' previously held knowledge and allows students to work at their own pace, advancing in their degree program when they demonstrate course mastery. The average time to bachelor's degree completion at WGU is thirty-four months.[82] The model appears to be effective at controlling costs, as tuition at WGU is $5,800 per twelve-month year for most academic programs and has not increased since 2008.[83] WGU receives no state funding; funding comes from tuition revenue and financial contributions from partner organizations, including the Bill & Melinda Gates Foundation, Lumina Foundation, and Google.[84] Some observers[85] argue that the WGU model offers an effective approach for using technology to reconceptualize key dimensions of higher education, including whom it serves, how it delivers instruction, and how it is financed.

## The Role of Technology in Solving Higher Education's Most Pressing Problems

Higher education has encouraged the development of new technologies and changed its practices to incorporate evolving technologies. Higher education has also been called to use technology to solve the pressing problems facing higher education. One current challenge is to better meet the growing need for college-educated workers,[86] while also reducing costs and ensuring high-quality learning outcomes.[87] Because of the labor-intensive nature of the traditional college model, some academics have diagnosed higher education as suffering from "cost disease."[88] Identifying effective strategies for reducing costs is paramount, given recent declines in state funding for public higher education, concerns about continued increases in tuition and fees and growth in student borrowing, and growing competition from for-profit and other nontraditional higher education providers.[89]

New technologies, including those that focus on online instructional delivery, offer the promise of increasing the production of higher education while also reducing costs and enhancing or at least maintaining quality.[90] Online courses would also seem to address constraints on the physical space available to deliver face-to-face instruction and the scheduling restrictions that often limit course enrollment for nontraditional students.[91] Recent excitement about massive open online courses (MOOCs) illustrates both the extent to which some observers are seeking a technology-based solution to improving the productivity of higher education and the challenges of utilizing new technologies to achieve this goal. Although not fundamentally changing the nature of teaching and learning, analytics, another emergent technology trend, offers a potentially effective mechanism for improving student outcomes and reducing costs.

### MOOCs

Defined as full-length courses delivered over the Internet to large numbers of students at little or no charge, MOOCs build on a history of other approaches to delivering higher education at a distance.[92] Although originally conceived by Stephen Downes, George Siemens, and Dave Cormier as taking the form of an interactive seminar (the connectivist or cMOOC), recent attention in the national and higher education media has focused on the lecture-style xMOOC first launched in the fall of 2011 by Stanford University's Sebastian Thrun and Peter Norvig and advanced by such MOOC providers as Udacity, Coursera, and edX.

MOOCs offer the promise of both providing access to a high-quality education to students regardless of geographic location or ability to pay and improving productivity by teaching large numbers of learners at a fraction of the cost of traditional face-to-face instruction. Suggesting the appeal of this approach, twenty-two of the top twenty-five "best" national universities as ranked by *US News and World Report* offered at least one MOOC in 2013.[93] The *New York Times* proclaimed 2012 "the year of the MOOC."[94] MOOCs have attracted large numbers; Harvard University and MIT counted 1 million unique participants and 1.7 million total participants with 1.1 billion logged events in sixty-eight MOOCs offered between July 2012 and September 2014.[95]

MOOCs clearly represent a new "learning opportunity."[96] Regardless of their potential contributions as standalone courses, MOOCs are also a mechanism for "disseminating course tools, pedagogical innovations, and teaching modules" that may improve residential courses.[97]

Whether MOOCs create meaningful improvements in productivity and access to high-quality education will likely require greater attention to questions about low completion rates, as well as concerns about educational quality, credentialing, and financial sustainability.[98] Studies show that only between 5 percent and 12 percent of all participants complete a MOOC.[99] Completion rates have been found to be somewhat higher in the Harvard and MIT courses for those who indicated an intention to complete than for those who did not (24% versus 8%). But, suggesting that MOOCs (in their current form) have not dramatically expanded access to higher education, most (two-thirds) participants in the Harvard and MIT MOOCs already had at least a bachelor's degree.[100]

Beyond some selective colleges and universities, in 2014 only a very small fraction of the 2,800 colleges and universities responding to an annual online education survey reported having a MOOC (8%) or planning to offer a MOOC (6%).[101] Moreover, although the percentage of institutions offering a MOOC increased between 2012 and 2015 (from 3% to 8%), the share of academic leaders who agreed that MOOCs were a sustainable approach to delivering online courses declined from 28 percent in 2012 to 16 percent in 2014.[102] Further suggesting skepticism about the future role of MOOCs, the share of senior information technology officers at two-year and four-year institutions nationwide who agreed that "MOOCs offer a viable model for the effective delivery of online instruction" declined from 53 percent in the fall of 2013 to 38 percent in the fall of 2014.[103]

Despite these findings, exploration of the potential of MOOCs to deliver accessible, low-cost, high-quality credit-bearing higher education is continuing.[104] As of May 2015, a few institutions had announced plans to partner with MOOC providers like Coursera, Udacity, and edX to use MOOCs to deliver master's degree programs in business (University of Illinois at Urbana-Champaign) and computer science (Georgia Institute of Technology), as well as the first year of a bachelor's degree program (Arizona State University).[105] These endeavors have created additional questions for policy makers and campus leaders, including whether students can use financial aid to pay for these programs, the distribution of revenues to MOOC providers, mechanisms to assess content mastery in courses with "massive" enrollments, and ways to effectively engage students to promote learning.[106]

Kevin Carey, the director of education policy at the New America Foundation, projects that digital learning environments will continue to evolve so as to transform traditional higher education into the "University of Everywhere." In his vision, the University of Everywhere will enable individuals around the globe to receive the education that they need and want throughout their lifetime at a low/affordable price; completed education will be more commonly signaled by "open credentials" (e.g., badges) than by a "traditional college degree."[107] He also predicts that high-quality digital learning environments will transform the nature of academic work (with fewer people producing more and better education) and the higher education industry (with institutions that fail to evolve being driven out of the market).

In a thoughtful critique, Don Heller, dean of the College of Education at Michigan State University, outlines the negative implications that may come with an incomplete achievement of Carey's vision. Particularly worrisome is the possibility that policymakers react to Carey's vision by reducing appropriations to higher education institutions and reducing funding for student financial aid. As Heller notes, these actions would likely further stratify higher education opportunity and outcomes, with students from low-income families concentrated in "open credential" digital learning environments and students from high-income families representing even greater shares of students enrolled in four-year degree-granting institutions.[108]

### ANALYTICS

An emerging development in education technology with the potential to both improve student outcomes and reduce higher education costs is data analytics. Originated in the business sector,[109] analytics is "the use of data, statistical analysis, and explanatory and predictive models to gain insights and act on complex issues."[110]

Through analytics, higher education institutions can harness commonly collected data to answer strategic questions and improve the effectiveness of institutional practices. In a 2012 survey, 41 percent of responding institutional researchers and technology officers identified analytics as an important initiative at the department or unit level and 28 percent deemed analytics a major institutional priority.[111] Most respondents agreed that analytics were more important now than two years ago (84%) and would be even more important in the next two years (86%). To date, greater attention has been devoted to using analytics to improve student recruitment, learning, and persistence, rather than to reduce costs, optimize resource use, or improve administrative services.[112]

"Learning analytics," the educational application of data analytics, involves harnessing captured student data to "deliver personalized learning, enable adaptive pedagogies and practices, and identify learning issues in time for them to be solved."[113] Although tracing its roots to the 1990s, much of the development of learning analytics has occurred more recently. Learning analytics was not a featured technology in the annual *NMC Horizon Report* until 2011, the year the first International Conference on Learning Analytics and Knowledge convened. The first issue of the peer-reviewed *Journal of Learning Analytics* was published in 2013.[114] In 2014, the Learning Analytics Workgroup (LAW) at Stanford University released a foundational document on how to conceptualize, build, and maintain the emergent field of learning analytics.[115]

Learning analytics has been enabled by the growth of online courses and programs, hybrid courses, and MOOCs, and by the increasing sophistication of web-tracking tools. These technologies allow for the accumulation of vast data, potentially recording every interaction that a student has with online course content or a learning management system. Captured data may range from the general (such as time spent on a particular task) to more "nuanced information that can provide evidence of critical thinking, synthesis, and the depth of retention of concepts over time."[116] By mapping the learning process, learning analytics offers the potential to pinpoint precisely when a student experiences difficulties. Learning analytics may also be used to identify best practices for improving learning outcomes, particularly for learners with different characteristics and learning needs. Realizing the potential benefits of analytics will require higher education institutions to not only collect "big data," but also design data collection protocols that provide the types of data needed to inform understanding of effective instructional practices.[117]

The Predictive Analytics Reporting (PAR) Framework, a nonprofit collaborative overseen by the Western Interstate Commission for Higher Education (WICHE), is one example of a potentially productive application of analytics. According to its website, as of January 2015, the PAR Framework had accumulated 1.7 million de-identified student records and 18 million course-level records from thirty-three higher education institutions and systems. The PAR Framework is designed to mine these large-scale data to provide member institutions with performance benchmarks and predictors of academic risk and student success. Member institutions are expected to be able to use this information to develop appropriate and targeted intervention services that improve student outcomes.

## Barriers that Influence the Adoption of New Technologies

Perhaps because higher education is in the business of knowledge creation, stakeholders assume that higher education will use the most current technologies in core operations and functions. The Spellings Commission on the Future of Higher Education clearly articulated this assumption when it recommended that "America's colleges and universities embrace a culture of continuous innovation and quality improvement. We urge these institutions to develop new pedagogies, curricula and technologies to improve learning, particularly in the areas of science and mathematics."[118]

Technological innovation is occurring. But, even when associated with positive desired outcomes, higher education has experienced challenges bringing innovations to scale.[119] For example, one well-regarded approach to leveraging information technology to enhance student-learning outcomes and reduce the cost of higher education is the program and course redesign developed by the independent, not-for-profit, National Center for Academic Transformation (NCAT).[120] With $8.8 million in support from the Pew Charitable Trusts, NCAT developed the Program in Course Redesign (PCR). In the PCR project, NCAT worked with thirty colleges and universities from 1999 to 2004 to use instructional technology to deliver courses at lower cost and with at least comparable student learning and retention outcomes. Key components of the PCR model included "online tutorials, Web-based discussion groups, on-demand support and group activities, and automated assessment of class exercises, quizzes, and tests."[121] NCAT reports positive outcomes at all thirty of the original partner institutions, with cost savings ranging from 20 percent to 77 percent or a total savings of $3 million. NCAT has built on these initial efforts with funding from the Fund for the Improvement of Postsecondary Education (FIPSE), Bill & Melinda Gates Foundation, and several state systems of higher education (e.g., Arizona Board of Regents, State University of New York, University System of Maryland) to redesign other courses. NCAT reports that, of the 156 redesign projects completed to date, 72 percent have demonstrated improved student learning outcomes (with the remainder demonstrating comparable outcomes) and all have reduced instructional costs (with reductions ranging from 5% to 81%). NCAT also self-reports other positive outcomes, including higher course completion and program retention rates as well as student and faculty satisfaction.[122]

These improvements in instructional productivity have occurred largely at the level of the individual course, rather than at the department, university, or system levels.[123] Course-level improvements in instructional productivity tend to reflect an "incremental" approach to change[124] or a "sustaining innovation,"[125] as opposed to a "disruptive innovation."[126]

Unlike other innovations, disruptive innovation changes "the underlying structure of higher education" and involves more than just "simply operating within a tightened budget."[127] Christensen and colleagues define disruptive innovation as "the process by which a sector that has previously served only a limited few because its products and services were complicated, expensive, and inaccessible, is transformed into one whose products and services are simple, affordable, and convenient and serves many no matter their wealth or expertise."[128]

A sustaining innovation may improve an organization's performance and enhance the quality of products or services produced, but a disrupting innovation changes the nature of the product or service and attracts "a new population of customers."[129] A disruptive innovation is associated with fundamental changes in higher education—"its processes, where it happens, what its goals are."[130] Disruptive technologies typically begin at the margins, are initially expensive to produce, and are slow in gaining widespread appeal.[131]

Many forces restrict the widespread adoption and use of online learning and other technological innovation.[132] Although potentially creating many benefits, disruptive innovation often has economic and noneconomic costs. Some of the noneconomic costs are cultural, as disruptive innovation "threatens our security and challenges our traditions."[133] Other forces are structural, including constraints imposed by federal regulations, accreditation requirements, and internal institutional course approval processes.[134] Disruptive innovation may also be resisted because of potentially worrisome implications of technological innovation for access, cost, quality of education produced, and faculty, as well as for the well-being of both individual higher education institutions and the nation's higher education system as a whole.

### Can Technological Innovation Reduce Costs?

The implications of technology for higher education costs are ambiguous. Some assert that online learning and other technological innovation can create considerable reductions in instructional costs.[135] Others suggest that by enabling institutions to expand into previously untapped markets, online instruction may provide a new source of revenue.[136]

At the same time, others argue that online instructional delivery costs more, not less, than traditional face-to-face education.[137] Offering instruction online is more complex than simply uploading materials into a course management system.[138] Developing and delivering online learning may also generate new costs.[139] The initial financial resources required to develop online courses and provide the necessary technological infrastructure (e.g., a learning management system) may be sizeable, but decrease over time as more online courses are replicated.[140]

More than half of chief academic officers believe that it is likely (36%) or very likely (25%) that online courses will be substantially less expensive than face-to-face courses. Yet technological innovation—including both use of technology in instructional delivery and data analytics—has start-up as well as long-term and ongoing costs. Faculty and staff will likely regularly require assistance and training. IT staff will be required to provide ongoing system maintenance and technical assistance, and student support staff will be needed to manage online enrollment and troubleshoot technology-related difficulties.[141] Rapidly changing technologies will likely require regular hardware and software license upgrades as well.[142]

### Can Technological Innovation Maintain or Improve Quality?

One force limiting the growth of online education is continued uncertainty about educational quality and student learning outcomes. Over time, perceptions about the quality of online education have improved. About 74 percent of academic leaders responding to the 2015 Babson Survey Research Group's annual survey rated learning outcomes in online courses as the same or superior to learning outcomes in face-to-face courses. By comparison, when the survey began in 2002, 43 percent of chief academic officers believed that learning outcomes in online education were inferior to face-to-face education.[143]

Particularly important to the future of online education are the views of faculty. Only 9 percent of faculty responding to a fall 2014 survey strongly agreed (and only an additional 26 percent agreed) that online courses could produce student learning outcomes that were at least as good as those produced in face-to-face instruction.[144] Responding faculty were especially skeptical about whether online courses could provide high-quality interaction between faculty and students inside and outside of the courses, attention to at-risk students, and answers to student questions.[145] Only 28 percent of chief academic officers responding to the Babson Group's fall 2014 survey reported believing that their faculty "accept the value and legitimacy of online education."[146] Although the percentage has fluctuated somewhat over time, this percentage is virtually the same as it was in the fall of 2002 (27.6%).

Available research comparing learning outcomes for online and face-to-face instruction shows mixed results. Much of the research comparing outcomes for students in traditional face-to-face courses, online courses, and blended courses has noteworthy methodological limitations.[147] With funding from the US Department of Education, Barbara Means and colleagues conducted a comprehensive meta-analysis of 46 studies that used experimental or quasi-experimental research designs to compare student-learning outcomes in online and face-to-face instruction in courses from pre-college through graduate school. Defining online education as "learning that takes place partially or entirely over the Internet," the authors found that, on average, both blended learning and purely online learning models produced better student learning outcomes than face-to-face instructional models; average outcomes were highest for blended learning.[148] But some individual studies showed face-to-face instruction as producing better student learning outcomes. In a more recent review of 30 studies of online learning at higher education institutions, Lack concluded that results were inconclusive, noting that there is "little, if any, evidence to suggest that online or hybrid learning, on average, is more or less effective than face-to-face learning."[149] Lack, however, used less rigorous criteria for identifying included studies than did Means and colleagues.

### WILL TECHNOLOGICAL INNOVATION BE EMBRACED BY FACULTY?

Technological innovation will not increase degree production, reduce higher education costs, or enhance quality if faculty do not embrace and adopt the innovation. Online education has tended to expand in an ad hoc manner based on intrepid faculty members' interests rather than based on centralized administrative planning.[150] Faculty tend to "teach as they were taught,"[151] and may believe that online learning will limit interactions with students and/or enable institutions to cut faculty jobs.[152]

Institutional leadership and strategic campus planning will likely be required to counter faculty apathy (at best) and faculty resistance (at worst) to new technologies and thereby maximize any potential benefits.[153] Faculty resistance is one force that has limited the more widespread adoption of MOOCs on some campuses, including San Jose State and Amherst College.[154] The potential benefits of analytics also depend on faculty; the insights produced by analytics will not be incorporated into higher education practices if faculty (and administrators) mistrust institutional data and analysis or do not understand how data can be used to inform decisions.[155]

Providing training and ongoing assistance to faculty and staff is one strategy for encouraging faculty to use new technologies.[156] Reports from both faculty as well as senior technology officers indicate that many institutions now provide limited technology-related training to faculty.[157] Only a minority (28%) of senior information technology officers at two-year and four-year colleges nationwide reported in the fall of 2014 that current IT training for faculty was "excellent."[158] Most respondents (81%) reported that assisting faculty with the integration of information technology into instruction would be a high priority in the next two to three years.[159]

Another potential approach is to incentivize faculty and staff to engage in the training and adoption of new technologies.[160] Prevailing faculty reward structures tend to emphasize research productivity, providing little incentive for faculty to expend time and effort learning and incorporating new teaching practices.[161] Only 1 percent of faculty responding to a fall 2014 survey reported that their institution rewarded teaching with technology in tenure and promotion decisions.[162]

Faculty may also resist technological innovation that is perceived to threaten their autonomy or limit their ability to design a course, customize course materials, and determine course sequencing.[163] Online courses tend to be developed and implemented not by an individual faculty member working independently (as in a traditional face-to-face course) but by an instructional team that includes the faculty member as well as instructional designers and IT professionals. In short, online instruction tends to recast the traditional workflow model into a more horizontal, collaborative model.[164] This expansion of personnel has implications for faculty autonomy, as well as other complex and often contentious issues like intellectual property rights, shared governance, and compensation.[165]

### Concluding Note

Technology is an ever-present and ever-changing societal force that both influences and is influenced by higher education. Higher education will certainly continue to change in response to technological innovation. Whether these changes create more than incremental improvements in access, cost, and quality—and fundamentally increase access to high-quality higher education at lower cost—is yet to be seen.[166] Higher education institutions must not only be willing to change, but must also supply the leadership, financial resources, training, and incentives necessary for technological innovation to stimulate institution-wide reform and reduce the economic and non-economic costs of the reform.

Technology is a set of tools; higher education faculty, administrators, and policy-makers will determine whether and how available tools are used to advance higher education productivity and improve other valued outcomes.

NOTES

1. Editors of Encyclopædia Britannica, "Technology," Encyclopædia Britannica (2014) http://www.britannica.com/EBchecked/topic/585418/technology [accessed Feb. 1, 2015].

2. Pew Research Internet Project, 2014, *Social Networking Fact Sheet*, http://www.pewinternet.org/fact-sheets/social-networking-fact-sheet/.

3. National Science Foundation, *Higher Education Research and Development Survey: Fiscal Year 2012*, table 1 (Arlington, VA: National Science Foundation, National Center for Science and Engineering Statistics, 2014), http://ncsesdata.nsf.gov/herd/2012/.

4. U.S. Department of Education, "First in the World," 2014, http://www2.ed.gov/programs/fitw/awards.html.

5. William Zumeta, David W. Breneman, Patrick M. Callan, and Joni Finney, *Financing American Higher Education in the Era of Globalization* (Cambridge, MA: Harvard Education Press, 2012).

6. Association of University Technology Managers, *Highlights of AUTMS's US Licensing Activity Survey FY2013*, 2014, http://www.autm.net/AM/Template.cfm?Section=FY_2013_Licensing_Activity_Survey&Template=/CM/ContentDisplay.cfm&ContentID=13870.

7. Association of University Technology Managers, *Highlights*.

8. Ibid., 5.

9. Sheila Slaughter and Gary Rhoades, *Academic Capitalism and the New Economy: Markets, State, and Higher Education* (Baltimore: Johns Hopkins University Press, 2009).

10. John Willinsky, Gustavo Fischman, and Amy S. Metcalfe, "The Digital Technologies of Learning and Research," in *American Higher Education in the Twenty-first Century: Social, Political, and Economic Challenges*, 3rd ed., ed. Philip G. Altbach, Patricia J. Gumport, and Robert O. Berdahl (Baltimore, MD: Johns Hopkins University Press), 341–364.

11. Roy Pea, *The Learning Analytics Workgroup: A Report on Building the Field of Learning Analytics for Personalized Learning to Scale* (Stanford, CA: Stanford University, 2014), 18, https://ed.stanford.edu/sites/default/files/law_report_complete_09-02-2014.pdf.

12. Willinsky, Fischman, and Metcalfe, "The Digital Technologies," 346.

13. JSTOR, "New to JSTOR? Learn More About Us," http://about.jstor.org/10things.

14. Mikael Laakso, Patrik Welling, Helena Bukvova, Linus Nyman, Bo-Christer Bjork, Turid Hedlund, "The Development of the Open Access Journal Publishing from 1993 to 2009," *PLoS ONE* 6 (2011): e02961, para. 5, http://journals.plos.org/plosone/article?id=10.1371/journal.pone.0020961.

15. Suenje Dallmeier-Tiessen, Robert Darby, Bettina Goerner, Jenni Hyppoelae, Peter Igo-Kemenes, Deborah Kahn, Simon Labert, Anja Lengenfelder, Chris Leonard,

Salvatore Mele, Malgorzata Nowicka, Panayiota Polydoratou, David Ross, Sergio Ruiz-Perez, Ralf Schimmer, Mark Swaisland, and Wim van der Stelt, *Highlights from the SOAP Project Survey: What Scientists Think about Open Access Publishing*, 2011, http://arxiv.org /pdf/1101.5260v2.pdf.

16. National Institutes of Health, "NIH Public Access Policy Details," 2014, http:// publicaccess.nih.gov/policy.htm.

17. Michael Stebbins, "Expanding Public Access to the Results of Federally Funded Research." *White House Office of Science and Technology Policy Blog*, February 22, 2013, http://www.whitehouse.gov/blog/2013/02/22/expanding-public-access-results-federally -funded-research.

18. Carl Straumsheim, "Gates Goes Open," *Inside Higher Ed*, November 24, 2014, https://www.insidehighered.com/news/2014/11/24/gates-foundation-announces-open -access-policy-all-grant-recipients.

19. Laura W. Perna, ed., *Preparing Today's Students for Tomorrow's Jobs in Metropolitan America: The Policy, Practice, and Research Issues* (Philadelphia, PA: University of Pennsylvania Press, 2012).

20. Anthony W. Bates and Albert Sangrà, *Managing Technology in Higher Education: Strategies for Transforming Teaching and Learning* (San Francisco, CA: Jossey-Bass, 2011); Claudia Goldin and Lawrence F. Katz, *The Race between Education and Technology* (Cambridge, MA: Harvard University Press, 2008); Lynn A. Karoly and Constantijn Panis, *The 21st Century at Work: Forces Shaping the Future Workforce and Workplace in the United States* (Santa Monica, CA: RAND Corporation, 2004).

21. Goldin and Katz, *The Race.*

22. Ibid.

23. Ibid.

24. Ibid.

25. Anthony P. Carnevale, Nicole Smith, and Jeff Strohl, *Help Wanted: Projections of Jobs and Education Requirements through 2018* (Washington, DC: Georgetown University Center on Education and the Workforce, 2010), https://georgetown.app.box.com/s /ursjbxaym2npiv8mgrv7.

26. Louis Soares and Laura W. Perna, *Readiness for the Learning Economy: Insights from the OECD's Survey of Adult Skills on Workforce Readiness and Preparation* (Washington, DC: American Council on Education, 2014).

27. Carnevale, Smith, and Strohl, *Help Wanted.*

28. Erika E Smith, "The Digital Native Debate in Higher Education: A Comparative Analysis of Recent Literature," *Canadian Journal of Learning and Technology* 38 (2012): 1–18.

29. Pew Research Internet Project, *Social Networking Fact Sheet.*

30. Smith, "The Digital Native."

31. Pew Research Internet Project, *Social Networking Fact Sheet.*

32. Noel-Levitz, *2014 E-expectations Report: The Online Preferences of College-Bound High School Seniors and Their Parents*, 2014, https://www.noellevitz.com/documents/gated /Papers_and_Research/2014/2014_E-Expectations_Report.pdf?code=1321721065201469.

33. Jeanna Mastrodicasa and Paul Metellus, "The Impact of Social Media on College Students," *Journal of College and Character* 14 (2013): 21–29.

34. L. Johnson, S. Adams Becker, V. Estrada, and A. Freeman, *NMC Horizon Report: 2014 Higher Education Edition* (Austin, TX: The New Media Consortium, 2014), http://cdn.nmc.org/media/2014-nmc-horizon-report-he-EN-SC.pdf.

35. Johnson et al., *NMC Horizon Report*, 9.

36. Noel-Levitz, *2014 E-expectations Report.*

37. Ibid.

38. William Erickson, Sharon Trerise, Camille Lee, Sara VanLooy, and Susanne Bruyère, *Web-based Student Processes at Community Colleges: Removing Barriers to Access* (Ithaca, NY: Cornell University, 2007).

39. The Campus Computing Project, *The 2014 National Survey of Computing and Information Technology in US Higher Education*, 2014, http://www.campuscomputing.net/item/campus-computing-2014.

40. Adolfo Guzman-Lopez, "Winning This Game May Just Mean You Get Into the College of Your Choice," Pass/Fail (blog), March 14, 2014, http://www.scpr.org/blogs/education/2014/03/14/16085/winning-this-game-may-just-mean-you-get-into-the-c/.

41. Guzman-Lopez, "Winning."

42. Caralee Adams, "Students Teach School Counselors to Use College Access Apps" *Education Week*, October 14, 2014, http://blogs.edweek.org/edweek/college_bound/2014/10/students_teach_counselors_to_use_college_access_apps.html.

43. Benjamin L. Castleman and Lindsay C. Page, "Summer Nudging: Can Personalized Text Messages and Peer Mentor Outreach Increase College Going Among Low-Income High School Graduates?" *Journal of Economic Behavior and Organization*, forthcoming; J. Frankfort, R. E. O'Hara, R. E., and K. Salim, "Behavioral Nudges for College Success," in *Decision Making for Student Success: Behavioral Insights to Improve College Access and Persistence*, ed. B. L. Castleman, S. Schwartz, and S. Baum (New York, NY: Routledge, 2015), 143–159.

44. Castleman and Page, "Summer Nudging."

45. Bates and Sangrà, *Managing Technology.*

46. National Center for Education Statistics, *Digest of Education Statistics 2013*, table 310 (Washington, DC: National Center for Education Statistics, 2013).

47. Elizabeth D. Phillips, "Improving Advising Using Technology and Data Analytics," *Change: The Magazine of Higher Learning* 45 (2013): 48–55.

48. Melissa A. Venable, "Using Technology to Deliver Career Development Services: Supporting Today's Students in Higher Education," *Career Development Quarterly* 59 (2010): 87–96.

49. Ariel Kaminer, "Student-built Apps Teach Colleges a Thing or Two," *The New York Times*, August 27, 2014, http://www.nytimes.com/2014/08/28/nyregion/students-inventing-programs-to-streamline-their-colleges-data.html?_r=0.

50. Kaminer, "Student-built Apps."

51. Johnson et al., *NMC Horizon Report.*

52. Harvard University, "Harvard College Innovation Challenge: Overview and Eligibility," http://harvardi3.org/overview-eligibility; University of Pennsylvania, "AppitUP," http://www.appitupchallenge.com.

53. Bates and Sangrà, *Managing Technology*; Dominic J. Brewer and William G. Tierney, "Barriers to Innovation in US Higher Education," in *Reinventing Higher Education: The*

*Promise of Innovation,* ed. Ben Wildavsky, Andrew P. Kelly, and Kevin Carey (Cambridge, MA: Harvard Education Press, 2012), 11–4; Robert Zemsky, *Making Reform Work: The Case for Transforming American Higher Education* (New Brunswick, NJ: Rutgers University Press, 2009).

54. I. Elaine Allen and Jeff Seaman, *Changing Course: Ten Years of Tracking Online Education in the United States* (Babson College, MA: The Sloan Consortium, 2013), http://www.onlinelearningsurvey.com/reports/changingcourse.pdf; Phil Hill, "Online Educational Delivery Models: A Descriptive View," *EDUCAUSE Review* 47 (2012): 84–97.

55. Johnson et al., *NMC Horizon Report.*

56. I. Elaine Allen and Jeff Seaman, *Grade Level: Tracking Online Education in the United States* (Babson College, MA: The Sloan Consortium, 2015), http://online learningconsortium.org/read/survey-reports-2014/.

57. Allen and Seaman, *Grade Level.*

58. Lawrence S. Bacow, William G. Bowen, Kevin M. Guthrie, Kelly A. Lack, and Matthew P. Long, *Barriers to the Adoption of Online Learning Systems in US Higher Education* (New York: Ithaka S+R, 2012), 8, http://www.sr.ithaka.org/sites/default/files/reports /barriers-to-adoption-of-online-learning-systems-in-us-higher-education.pdf.

59. I. Elaine Allen and Jeff Seaman, *Grade Change: Tracking Online Education in the United States* (Babson College, MA: The Sloan Consortium, 2014), http://www .onlinelearningsurvey.com/reports/gradechange.pdf. Babson Survey Research Group has annually collected data from institutions about online education since 2003. For its 2015 report, it uses data from IPEDS to describe the availability of and participation in online courses. Likely reflecting differences in the definition of "online," in its 2014 report Babson Research Group found a somewhat higher rate of participation in online courses than reported by IPEDS. IPEDS first collected data on students enrolled in courses in which instructional content was delivered exclusively via distance education methods in fall 2012 (National Center for Education Statistics [NCES], 2014). IPEDS defines distance education as "education that uses one or more technologies to deliver instruction to students who are separated from the instructor and to support regular and substantive interaction between the students and the instructor synchronously or asynchronously" (NCES, 2014, p. 1).

60. National Center for Education Statistics, *Enrollment in Distance Education Courses, by State: Fall 2012,* NCES 2014-023 (Washington, DC: U.S. Department of Education, 2014), http://nces.ed.gov/pubs2014/2014023.pdf.

61. Allen and Seaman, *Grade Level*; Bacow et al., *Barriers*; Barbara Means, Marianne Bakia, and Robert Murphy, *Learning Online: What Research Tells Us About Whether, When and How* (New York, NY: Routledge, 2014).

62. Bacow et al., *Barriers*, 8.

63. Ibid., 6–7.

64. Ibid., 8.

65. Bates and Sangrà, *Managing Technology.*

66. Scott Jaschik and Doug Lederman, *2014 Survey of Faculty Attitudes on Technology* (Washington, DC: *Inside Higher Ed* and Gallup, 2014).

67. Ryann K. Ellis, *A Field Guide to Learning Management Systems* (Alexandria, VA: American Society for Training and Development, 2009), https://www.td.org/~/media /Files/Publications/LMS_fieldguide_20091.

68. Jeff Seaman and Hester Tinti-Kane, *Social Media for Teaching and Learning* (Boston: Pearson Learning Solutions and Babson Survey Research Group, 2013); George Siemens, Dragan Gašević, and Shane Dawson, *Preparing for the Digital University: A Review of the History and Current State of Distance, Blended, and On-line Learning* (2015), http://www.elearnspace.org/blog/2015/04/30/preparing-for-the -digital-university/.

69. Kevin Bell, "Online 3.0: The Rise of the Gamer Educator (The Potential Role of Gamification in Online Education)," PhD diss., University of Pennsylvania, 2014; Tracy Fullerton, "What Games Do Well: Mastering Concepts in Play," in *Postsecondary Play: The Role of Games and Social Media in Higher Education*, ed. William G. Tierney, Zoe B. Corwin, Tracy Fullerton, and Gisele Ragusa (Baltimore, MD: Johns Hopkins University Press, 2014), 125–45.

70. Jane McGonigal, *Reality Is Broken: How Games Make Us Better and How They Can Change the World* (New York: Penguin Books, 2011), 13.

71. McGonigal, *Reality Is Broken*, 21.

72. Johnson et al., *NMC Horizon Report*.

73. McGonigal, *Reality Is Broken*, 354.

74. Fullerton, "What Games Do Well."

75. Johnson et al., *NMC Horizon Report*.

76. Fullerton, "What Games Do Well."

77. Bell, "Online 3.0."

78. Robert Mendenhall, "What Is Competency-based Education?" *The Blog*, September 5, 2012, http://www.huffingtonpost.com/dr-robert-mendenhall/competency-based -learning-_b_1855374.html.

79. Competency-Based Education Network, "A National Consortium for Designing, Developing, and Scaling New Models for Student Learning," http://www.cbenetwork .org/competency-based-education/.

80. Paul Fain, "Experimenting with Competency," *Inside Higher Ed,* January 13, 2015, https://www.insidehighered.com/news/2015/01/13/feds-move-ahead-experimental-sites -competency-based-education.

81. Western Governors University, *2013 Annual Report*, 2014, http://www.wgu.edu /sites/wgu.edu/files/WGU_AnnualReport_2013_0.pdf.

82. Ibid.

83. Ibid.

84. Western Governors University, *University Governance*, 2014, http://www.wgu .edu/about_WGU/governors_industry.

85. Zumeta et al., *Financing American Higher Education*.

86. Carnevale, Smith, and Strohl, *Help Wanted*.

87. Patricia J. Gumport and Marc Chun, "Technology and Higher Education: Opportunities and Challenges for the New Era," in *American Higher Education in the 21st Century: Social, Political and Economic Challenges*, 2nd ed., ed. Philip Altbach, Robert

Berdahl, and Patricia J. Gumport (Baltimore, MD: Johns Hopkins University Press, 2005), 393–423.

88. William G. Bowen, *Higher Education in the Digital Age* (Princeton, New Jersey: Princeton University Press, 2013); Means, Bakia, and Murphy, *Learning Online.*

89. Scott A Bass, "Simple Solutions to Complex Problems—MOOCs as a Panacea?" *The Journal of General Education* 63(2014): 256–268; Deanna Marcum, *Technology to the Rescue: Can Technology-enhanced Education Help Public Flagship Universities Meet Their Challenges?* (New York: Ithaka S+R, 2014), http://www.sr.ithaka.org/sites/default/files /files/SR_BriefingPaper_Marcum_20140421.pdf; William F. Massy, "Creative Paths to Boosting Academic Productivity," in *Reinventing Higher Education: The Promise of Innovation,* ed. B. Wildavsky, A. P. Kelly, and K. Carey (Cambridge, MA: Harvard Education Press, 2012), 73–100; William F. Massy, *Stretching the Higher Education Dollar: Initiatives for Containing the Cost of Higher Education* (Washington, DC: American Enterprise Institute, 2013), http://www.aei.org/wp-content/uploads/2013/04/-initiatives-for-containing -the-cost-of-higher-education_164922677149.pdf; Zumeta et al., *Financing American Higher Education.*

90. Bowen, *Higher Education in the Digital Age.*

91. Bacow et al., *Barriers.*

92. Hill, "Online Educational Delivery Models"; Laura W. Perna, Alan Ruby, Robert Boruch, Nicole Wang, Janie Scull, Seher Ahmad, and Chad Evans, "Moving Through MOOCs: Understanding the Progression of Users in MOOCs," *Educational Researcher* 43 (2014): 421–32.

93. Brian D. Voss, *Massive Open Online Courses (MOOCs): A Primer for University and College Board Members* (White Paper) (Washington, DC: Association of Governing Boards of Universities and Colleges, 2013).

94. Laura Pappano, "The Year of the MOOC," *The New York Times,* November 2, 2012, http://www.nytimes.com.

95. Andrew Dean Ho, Isaac Chuang, Justin Reich, Cody Austun Coleman, Jacob Whitehill, Curtis G. Northcutt, Joseph Jay Williams, John D. Hansen, Glenn Lopez, and Rebecca Petersen, "Harvard and MITx: Two Years of Open Online Courses Fall 2012–Summer 2014" (Harvard Working Paper No. 10), 2015, http://ssrn.com/abstract =2586847.

96. Siemens Gašević and Dawson, *Preparing,* 6.

97. Ho et al., "Harvard and MITx."

98. Bass, "Simple Solutions"; Perna et al., "Moving Through MOOCs"; Voss, *Massive Open Online Courses.*

99. Ho et al., "Harvard and MITx"; Perna et al., "Moving Through MOOCs."

100. Ho et al., "Harvard and MITx."

101. Allen and Seaman, *Grade Level.*

102. Ibid.

103. Campus Computing Project, *The 2014 National Survey.*

104. Carl Straumsheim, "MOOCs for (a Year's) Credit," *Inside Higher Ed,* April 23, 2015, https://www.insidehighered.com/news/2015/04/23/arizona-state-edx-team-offer -freshman-year-online-through-moocs; Jeffrey R. Young, "U. of Illinois to Offer a Low-

cost M.B.A. Thanks to MOOCs," *Chronicle of Higher Education*, May 4, 2015, http://chronicle.com/article/U-of-Illinois-to-Offer-a/229921/.

105. Young, "U. of Illinois to Offer."

106. Straumsheim, "MOOCs for (a Year's) Credit"; Young, "U. of Illinois to Offer."

107. Kevin Carey, *The End of College: Creating the Future of Learning and the University of Everywhere* (New York, NY: Riverhead Books, 2015), 246.

108. Donald E. Heller, "The End of College? Not so Fast." *Chronicle of Higher Education*, March 30, 2015, http://chronicle.com/article/The-End-of-College-Not-So/228937/.

109. See Don Peck, "They're Watching You at Work: What Happens When Big Data Meets Human Resources?" *The Atlantic*, December 2013, http://www.theatlantic.com/magazine/archive/2013/12/theyre-watching-you-at-work/354681/; Johnson et al., *NMC Horizon Report*.

110. Jacqueline Bischel, *Analytics in Higher Education: Benefits, Barriers, Progress, and Recommendations* (Louisville, CO: EDUCAUSE Center for Applied Research, 2012), 6.

111. Bischel, *Analytics*.

112. Ibid.

113. Johnson et al., *NMC Horizon Report*, 38.

114. Pea, *The Learning Analytics Workgroup*.

115. Ibid.

116. Johnson et al., *NMC Horizon Report*, 39.

117. Perna et al., "Moving Through MOOCs."

118. Spellings Commission on the Future of Higher Education, *A Test of Leadership* (Washington, DC, 2006), 5.

119. Ben Wildavsky, Andrew P. Kelly, and Kevin Carey, "Conclusion," in *Reinventing Higher Education: The Promise of Innovation*, ed. Ben Wildavsky, Andrew P. Kelly, and Kevin Carey (Cambridge, MA: Harvard Education Press, 2012), 239–46.

120. National Center for Academic Transformation, "A Summary of NCAT Program Outcomes," http://www.thencat.org/Program_Outcomes_Summary.html; Zumeta et al., *Financing American Higher Education*.

121. Zumeta et al., *Financing American Higher Education*, 149.

122. National Center for Academic Transformation, "A Summary of NCAT Program Outcomes."

123. Massy, *Reinventing Higher Education*.

124. Marcum, *Technology to the Rescue*, 4.

125. Clayton M. Christensen, Michael B. Horn, Louis Caldera, and Louis Soares, *Disrupting College: How Disruptive Innovation Can Deliver Quality and Affordability to Postsecondary Education* (Washington, DC: Center for American Progress, 2011).

126. Massy, *Reinventing Higher Education*.

127. Bass, "Simple Solutions," 257.

128. Christensen et al., *Disrupting College*, 2.

129. Christensen et al., *Disrupting College*.

130. Ibid., 4.

131. William G. Tierney, "The Disruptive Future of Higher Education," in *Postsecondary Play: The Role of Games and Social Media in Higher Education*, ed. William G. Tierney,

Zoe B. Corwin, Tracy Fullerton, and Gisele Ragusa (Baltimore: Johns Hopkins University Press, 2014), 21–44.

132. Peter Stokes, "What Online Learning Can Teach Us about Higher Education," in *Reinventing Higher Education: The Promise of Innovation,* ed. B. Wildavsky, Andrew P. Kelly, and Kevin Carey (Cambridge, MA: Harvard Education Press, 2012), 197–224.

133. Stokes, "What Online Learning Can Teach Us," 222.

134. Bacow et al., *Barriers*; Mark J. Smith and William J. Bramble, "Funding of Distance and Online Learning in the United States," in *Economics of Distance and Online Learning: Theory, Practice, and Research,* ed. W. J. Bramble and S. Panda (New York: Routledge, 2008), 88–106; Wildavsky, Kelly, and Carey, "Conclusion."

135. See, e.g., Bowen, *Higher Education in the Digital Age*; National Center for Academic Transformation, "A Summary of NCAT Program Outcomes."

136. Bacow et al., *Barriers*; Marcum, *Technology to the Rescue*; Massy, *Stretching*.

137. See, e.g., Sarah Guri-Rosenblit, "Eight Paradoxes in the Implementation Process of E-learning in Higher Education," *Higher Education Policy* 18 (2005): 5–29; Rita Kirshstein and Jane Wellman, "Technology and the Broken Higher Education Cost Model: Insights from the Delta Cost Project," *EDUCAUSE Review* 47 (2012): 12–14.

138. National Research Council, Panel on the Impact of Information Technology on the Research University, *Preparing for the Revolution: Information Technology and the Future of the Research University* (Washington, DC: National Academies Press, 2002).

139. Bates and Sangrà, *Managing Technology*; Bowen, *Higher Education in the Digital Age*; Kirshstein and Wellman, "Technology."

140. Bowen, *Higher Education in the Digital Age*.

141. Deirdre A. Folkers, "Competing in the Marketplace: Incorporating Online Education into Higher Education: An Organizational Perspective," in *Emerging Information Resource Management and Technology,* ed. Mehdi Khosrow-Pour (Hershey, PA: Idea Group Publishing, 2007), 67–88.

142. Guri-Rosenblit, "Eight Paradoxes."

143. Allen and Seaman, *Grade Level*.

144. Jaschik and Lederman, *2014 Survey*.

145. Ibid.

146. Allen and Seaman, *Grade Level*, 54.

147. Robert M. Bernard, Eugene Borokhovski, R. F. Schmid, Rana M. Tamim, and Philip C. Abrami, "A Meta-analysis of Blended Learning and Technology Use in Higher Education: From the General to the Applied," *Journal of Computing in Higher Education* 26 (2014): 87–122, doi:10.1007/s12528-013-9077-3.

148. Barbara Means, Yukie Toyama, Robert Murphy, Marianne Bakia, and Karla Jones, *Evaluation of Evidence-based Practices in Online Learning: A Meta-analysis and Review of Online Learning Studies* (Washington, DC: US Department of Education, Office of Planning, Evaluation, and Policy Development, 2009), http://files.eric.ed.gov/fulltext/ED505824.pdf.

149. Kelly A. Lack, *Current Status of Research on Online Learning in Postsecondary Education* (New York: Ithaka S+R, 2013), http://www.sr.ithaka.org/sites/default/files/reports/ithaka-sr-online-learning-postsecondary-education-may2012.pdf, 18.

150. Hill, "Online Educational Delivery Models."

151. Bacow et al., *Barriers*, 19.

152. Bacow et al., *Barriers*; Steve Kolowich, "Faculty Backlash Grows Against Online Partnerships," *The Chronicle of Higher Education*, May 6, 2013, http://chronicle.com /article/Faculty-Backlash-Grows-Against/139049/.

153. Bowen, *Higher Education in the Digital Age*; Marcum, *Technology to the Rescue*; Zemsky, *Making Reform Work*.

154. Kolowich, "Faculty Backlash."

155. Bischel, *Analytics*.

156. Bacow et al., *Barriers*; Bates and Sangrà, *Managing Technology*; Bischel, *Analytics*.

157. Campus Computing Project, *The 2014 National Survey*; Jaschik and Lederman, *2014 Survey*.

158. Campus Computing Project, *The 2014 National Survey*.

159. Ibid.

160. National Research Council, *Preparing for the Revolution*.

161. Marcum, *Technology to the Rescue*; Stokes, "What Online Learning Can Teach Us"; Tierney, "The Disruptive Future of Higher Education."

162. Jaschik and Lederman, *2014 Survey*.

163. Bacow et al., *Barriers*; Stokes, "What Online Learning Can Teach Us."

164. Bacow et al., *Barriers*; Hill, "Online Educational Delivery Models."

165. Folkers, "Competing in the Marketplace"; Marcum, *Technology to the Rescue*.

166. Massy, *Stretching*; Zemsky, *Making Reform Work*.

# Chapter Sixteen

# Community Colleges

Peter Riley Bahr and Jillian Leigh Gross

lthough a casual review of the research and policy literature might lead one
to draw a different conclusion, in fact there is no such thing as *the community college.*" As the name suggests, community colleges were established to
respond to the needs of their local communities, although the scope of their
charge has grown considerably over the years.[1] Just as communities vary greatly,
the 1,123 postsecondary institutions in the United States that describe themselves as community colleges also are highly varied, differing across the states,
and even within a given state, in terms of size, geographic location, student
populations served, institutional culture, governance structure, funding sources,
programmatic focus, credentials awarded, and the like.[2,3] Even the moniker
"community college" is not universal among these institutions, with some retaining the historical "junior college," others describing themselves as "technical
colleges," and still others positioning themselves simply as "colleges."

Developing an understanding of community colleges must begin with an
acknowledgement of the great diversity of these institutions. To illustrate, though
every state in the union has at least one community college, they range in size
from fewer than 350 students (e.g., Rainy River Community College in Minnesota) to more than 165,000 students (e.g., Miami Dade College in Florida).[4,5]
Many of the largest community colleges in fact are multi-college systems with
numerous campuses spread over a broad area (e.g., Houston Community College
in Texas; Ivy Tech Community College in Indiana). Furthermore, community

colleges are distributed widely across geographic locales. About one-third (31%) of public community colleges are located in cities, two-fifths (20%) in suburbs, one-quarter (23%) in towns, and the remaining one-quarter (25%) in rural areas.[6] In fact, 95 percent of the US population lives within commuting distance of a community college,[7] leading to the frequent characterization of community colleges as being exclusively "commuter institutions," even though one-quarter (24%) offer on-campus housing.[8]

On-campus housing aside, community colleges typically have a fairly limited geographic service area, and, as a result, student populations vary greatly across institutions.[9] For instance, although public community colleges as a sector serve a disproportionately large segment of the population of black and Hispanic undergraduates in the United States,[10] about one-fifth (21%) of community colleges serve a student population in which 2 percent or less of students are black, and about one-quarter (23%) serve a student population in which 2 percent or less of students are Hispanic.[11] On the other hand, one-quarter (25%) of community colleges serve a student population in which 20 percent or more of students are black, and one-quarter (25%) serve a student population in which 20 percent or more are Hispanic.[12]

In part as a result of this institutional heterogeneity in size, geography, student population, and so forth, which itself results from heterogeneity in the communities that these institutions serve, the role of community colleges in American higher education is highly contested.[13] An important perspective highlighted throughout this chapter concerns the challenges associated with being a nonselective, low-cost college focused on meeting the diverse needs of the local community in which the institution is located.[14] With these social commitments as their backbone, community colleges have become a primary portal to higher education for first generation students, low-income students, underprepared students, underrepresented minority students, and students of nontraditional age and circumstances.[15] As such, community colleges, perhaps more than any other institution, highlight the complicated relationship between democratic, political, and social expectations and public and private goods that are served through higher education.[16] Recognizing the highly varied needs of community college students who are caught in the middle of a system that "promotes equality and adapts to inequality,"[17] scholars often regard the central tension for community colleges to be balancing broad access to postsecondary education with equity, where equity can be defined in terms of postsecondary outcomes,[18] quality of education,[19] and/or social and economic mobility.[20]

A second, related tension that is highlighted in this chapter concerns mission complexity. Community colleges have developed diverse constituencies and have been positioned as responsible to a wide range of stakeholders, including students pursuing many different types of educational and personal goals, local residents and businesses, regional industries, state organizations, systems of secondary and postsecondary education, and various federal agencies, among others.[21] The frequently competing demands of stakeholders are readily evident in the complex and sometimes conflicting curricular functions undertaken by community colleges. Balancing these curricular "missions" in the face of limited resources is a persistent tension to which any circumspect discussion of these institutions must attend. Moreover, individual community colleges, each operating at an intersection of particular social, economic, and political environments, respond and adapt differently to the challenge of mission complexity, adding substantially to their heterogeneity.[22]

In the sections that follow, we first discuss the origin and history of community colleges in order to locate the institutions, as we understand them today, in the rich historical context from which they arose. We then discuss the five principles that have developed over time as the mainstay of modern community colleges, namely, open access, comprehensiveness, lifelong learning, community centeredness, and teaching focus. Finally, we return to and elaborate the unresolved tensions that we have mentioned here, which frame much of the current discourse on community colleges.

## A Brief History of Community Colleges

Not to know what happened before you were born is to be a child forever.

MARCUS TULLIUS CICERO (106 BC TO 43 BC)[23]

### 1900–1920

Community colleges were born at the turn of the twentieth century. This newly minted educational form developed amid a wide field of private nonprofit and for-profit organizations, and a small handful of public organizations, offering diverse sub-baccalaureate education, including technical institutes, teacher preparation in normal schools, and women's colleges.[24] At the time, the country's population was swelling through tides of immigration, women were developing increased educational expectations, and K–12 education was expanding rapidly due to legislation that promoted compulsory secondary education. These conditions created a shortage of K–12 teachers, a growing number of high school graduates seeking further education with its promise of upward mobility, and rising enrollments in postsecondary education, which began to stress the capacity of existing colleges and universities.[25]

In this context, a brain trust of university leaders developed a plan for community colleges (referred to as "junior colleges" at the time) to offer the first two years of baccalaureate education, focusing on liberal arts education and preparation for transfer to "senior" (four-year) institutions.[26] Community colleges also offered terminal occupational coursework, and, contrary to popular belief today, they were engaged from the very beginning in remedial education to better prepare students for the rigors of college-level coursework, due largely to uneven quality in secondary education. As Tillery and Deegan explain, "remediation [of skill deficiencies] was as much a function of the early colleges as it was during later periods of great growth."[27]

Although university leaders led the early movement, many community colleges were conceived as extensions of secondary education, were physically housed in high schools, were governed by local school boards, and recruited secondary teachers to fill faculty positions.[28] Joliet Junior College, a vanguard of the community college movement, remains the oldest public two-year college operating in the United States today. It was established in 1901 at Joliet Township High School by Superintendent J. Stanley Brown and the University of Chicago's president, William Rainey Harper.[29]

Regardless of the varied retrospective critiques of the motivations underlying the birth of the community college movement,[30] it is clear that progressive social and academic leaders used these colleges as a testing ground for the development of a rational and efficient system of education, promoting their growth through a frame of democracy and equal opportunity.[31] By 1920, the explosive growth of community colleges was well underway, with 207 public (26%) and private nonprofit (74%) two-year colleges established throughout the country, an increase of 133 from just five years earlier.[32]

## 1920–1940

During the next two decades, leaders of the community college movement, including a newly formed professional association, the American Association of Junior Colleges (AAJC),[33] as well as administrators, university elites, and state and local government officials began to promote terminal occupational education in community colleges, but the primary focus remained on academic education and preparation for transfer to four-year institutions.[34] Although transfer remained the focus of community college curricula and the professed goal of the majority of students and parents,[35] it was becoming evident that most students (75%) ended their collegiate education without transferring and without preparing successfully for a career.[36] Brint and Karabel argue that, to address this discrepancy between stated and realized aims and to reduce the stigma attached to occupational pursuits, community college leaders developed an ideology of democratic vocationalism, countering the elitist academic ideology suffusing higher education.[37] By 1940, "it had come to be taken for granted by policy makers that terminal vocational programs were—despite the lack of much popular demand for them—at the very center of what the junior college was about."[38]

The 1920s and 1930s were a period of continued rapid expansion of community colleges, growing from 325 colleges in 1925 to 575 in 1939.[39] Additionally, control of the colleges began to shift from private firms and religious organizations to local public entities with an associated increase in expectations of responsiveness to local community needs.[40] This transition was made possible by the organization of local school districts, which often developed networks of community colleges.[41] As the shift to public control took hold, efforts toward centralization began. Statewide systems soon followed, beginning with California in 1921. Even within these state systems, however, local control and funding remained a "cornerstone" of community colleges.[42]

### 1940–1960

In the wake of the great depression and World War II, community colleges were well-positioned to serve as a site for national healing, democratic citizenship education, and the promise of upward mobility for veterans returning from war and for those recovering from years of unemployment.[43] The GI Bill (1944) funded increased access to higher education, and the 1947 President's Commission on Higher Education for American Democracy promoted the establishment of a nationwide system of tuition-free colleges that would "serve as cultural centers for the community, offer continuing education for adults, emphasize civic responsibilities, be comprehensive, offer technical and general education, be locally controlled, and blend into statewide systems of higher education, while at the same time coordinating their efforts with the high schools."[44]

President Harry Truman's vision laid the groundwork for the modern system of comprehensive community colleges. In addition, the commission's report explicitly called for the end of racial discrimination in higher education,[45] forecasting the important role that community colleges would come to play as a point of access to higher education for underrepresented students. This commission was chaired by an influential AAJC member and used a rhetorical strategy of shifting attention from *junior* colleges to *community* colleges to align the colleges with the "democratic tradition of American educational thought."[46] After the release of the Truman report, community college leaders began promoting community education as a primary function of the colleges (while still maintaining the academic and occupational curricula)[47] and positioning community colleges "as a catalyst for community change."[48] As Ratcliff explains, "increasingly, the very character of the two-year college was recast around the notion that community service was not just another function, it was intrinsic to the philosophy of the comprehensive community college."[49]

The number of community colleges continued to grow steadily between 1939 and 1957 from 575 to 652,[50] capturing an increasing proportion of student enrollment in higher education. Organizationally, public community colleges began to outnumber private community colleges.[51] By 1950, almost half the states had created formal community college systems.[52] However, many community colleges continued to be associated with public secondary education rather than higher education.[53] Clearly, the road toward recognition of community colleges as a legitimate part of higher education was a long one.[54]

It was also during this time that states began to establish enrollment-driven funding formulas to support the growth and functioning of community colleges,[55] eventually evolving into what would become known as the "enrollment economy."[56] Additionally, the faculty composition of colleges began to shift away from a predominance of high school teachers to individuals educated in specialized academic fields, entering teaching directly after university training.[57]

### 1960–1980

Considered by many to be the "boom years" of community colleges,[58] the next two decades saw abundant financial resources for higher education, and the number of community colleges nearly doubled, rising to 1,231 by 1980. In 1960, the California Master Plan for Higher Education became a bellwether for higher education with its statewide coordination and formal stratification of educational opportunities,[59] situating community colleges as the "lowest rung" on the higher education ladder.[60] During the following two decades, numerous states replicated and adapted California's plan, to accommodate specific state contexts, transition funding from a primarily local endeavor to a state priority, and manage the growing complexity of public higher education.[61] Of note, in 1979,

Tennessee was the first state to initiate higher education funding based on institutional performance, which would become widespread and have far-reaching implications for community colleges in the decades to come.[62]

With increasing support among community college leaders, legislation promoting vocational education was passed, and, with the Higher Education Act of 1972, federal funding for career and technical education outstripped federal funding to open new colleges or expand existing ones.[63] With the economic downturn of the early 1970s, student enrollment in vocational programs surpassed enrollment in liberal arts programs for the first time.[64] Given this evolving economic and policy context, it is not surprising that liberal arts curricula and rates of student transfer to four-year institutions declined in community colleges, while occupational education increased dramatically throughout these decades.[65] As a growing proportion of students pursued occupational fields of study, the applied baccalaureate was established in the 1970s, providing transfer pathways for students in occupational and vocational programs and further blurring the line between the academic and occupational functions of the curriculum.[66]

Simultaneously, the place held by remediation in community college curricula grew in importance, owing to increasing demand for postsecondary education among swelling numbers of high school graduates.[67] Community college faculty often expressed frustration about the limited academic preparation of incoming students but remained "committed to the open door mission."[68] Nascent research on teaching and learning in community colleges reflected a perceived drop in standards, as students increasingly entered college underprepared for college-level coursework.[69] However, this phenomenon was not isolated to community colleges; rather, it plagued higher education generally.[70]

To serve students who previously had been unable to pursue higher education for myriad reasons, the federal government initiated financial aid programs targeting low-income students with the Higher Education Act of 1965 and its amendments in 1972.[71] Federal financial aid policies aligned with the recommendations of the Carnegie Commission's 1970 report *The Open Door Colleges*, which promoted access for underserved students, explicitly encouraged a comprehensive mission for community colleges, and reiterated the sentiment of the Truman Commission that community colleges should be established within a reasonable commuting distance of 95 percent of the population.[72]

With growing fervor for community colleges at the local, state, and national level, their meteoric rise seemed almost unstoppable. However, a growing body of scholars began to criticize the community college movement as an instrument of the capitalist state in the reproduction of social inequality through vocational[73] and remedial education,[74] as a protector of university selectivity by "cooling out" transfer ambitions among students,[75] and as a "safety valve,"[76] diverting students from gaining access to elite higher education.[77] Summarizing this conflicted view of the community college movement, Cross asserts that, by the end of this era, "[t]he old ideals that sparked enthusiasm and the sense of common purpose in community colleges [had] receded, and new ideals [had] not yet emerged to take their place."[78]

### 1980s–2000

Although the growth in the number of community colleges began to level off during this period, the growth in student enrollment in community colleges continued, reaching 43 percent of all undergraduates, both public and private, by 2000.[79,80] Despite grave concerns in the previous era about "vocationalism" in community college curricula, academic and occupational coursework returned to near parity in both course offerings and student enrollment during these decades.[81] Additionally, policy makers and practitioners began to re-elevate the priority of the transfer function with its promise of access to a baccalaureate degree, which critics continued to believe was being threatened by the growth of career and technical education.[82] However, transfer was no longer a strict dichotomy between academic and occupational coursework[83] due to increased emphasis on general education requirements across the curriculum and growth in applied baccalaureate programs.[84]

State governments began promoting workforce and economic development priorities heavily,[85] and the 1990 Perkins Vocational Education Act required integration of academic and vocational coursework in order to better prepare students for the complex world of work in which technical skills alone were now seen as insufficient.[86] However, new efforts in this realm sometimes fell outside the traditional curriculum to focus on revenue generation for colleges (e.g., non-credit education and contract training), which added to the growing mission complexity faced by community colleges.[87]

Postsecondary accrediting organizations supported the push toward education for employability, requiring increased activity in both general and remedial education, though regional variation in accreditation standards contributed to differences in organizational adaptations.[88] Professional organizations also exerted an influence to align the curriculum with preparation for industry certification and licensing exams.[89] Some scholars contend that this shift reflects the neoliberal policies and market ideology that became pervasive in the discourse on higher education during this time.[90]

The strengthening of the transfer mission occurred in an educational context in which up to 80 percent of community college students in some colleges needed remedial assistance at the time of enrollment,[91] with the prevalence of remedial need being inversely correlated with the wealth of local school districts.[92] In keeping with other legislative initiatives to expand the educational responsibilities of community colleges, and in conjunction with the rising need for remediation across higher education, some state and system actors began moving to designate remedial education as the sole responsibility of community colleges.[93] At the practical level, community colleges often responded by separating remedial education from mainstream college-level coursework,[94] leading some to contend that remedial education is an "ideological battle" between policy makers and practitioners related to protecting the standards of four-year colleges and universities while maintaining open access to higher education.[95]

Against this backdrop, the American Association of Junior and Community Colleges (formerly the AAJC) promoted the idea of "Opportunity with Excellence" to address growing concerns about standards of quality and the reproduction of inequality through community colleges.[96] Yet, juxtaposed against Bragg's assertion that community colleges had become the primary vehicle for higher education among historically disenfranchised students,[97] Dowd notes that, in the 1990s, "financial aid policies shifted toward merit aid at the state level and tax credits at the federal level, both of which disproportionately favor wealthier students."[98] This change in policy, coupled with changing student demographics (e.g., growing participation in higher education among racial/ethnic minority, low-income, and underprepared students) and decreased state and federal funding, exacerbated the challenges facing all of higher education, intensifying concerns over access and equity.[99]

### 2000–Present

By the turn of the twenty-first century, responding to internal and external pressures to meet the social, educational, and economic needs of diverse constituents, all under one metaphorical roof, most community colleges took a comprehensive approach to education, implementing four primary curricular missions: academic, occupational, remedial, and community education. Against the backdrop of growing complexity, the period of 2000 to 2020 undoubtedly will be known as the era of performance accountability and competition for community colleges.[100] Enrollment in for-profit colleges and universities, which serve some of the same student populations as do community colleges, was growing rapidly.[101,102] Furthermore, by the mid-2000s, almost every state had adopted some form of performance reporting or performance funding for community colleges, increasingly tied to student outcomes as opposed to the historical focus on the institutional "input" of (growing) student enrollment.[103] This change reflects the re-envisioning of *access* to higher education as including student *success* in terms of both educational outcomes (e.g., learning, credential completion) and post-college labor market outcomes (e.g., job placement, earnings).[104]

As institutional efficiency takes center stage in this national discourse,[105] however, it has never been more evident that there is no universal way to assess community colleges when they implement curricular missions in such diverse ways.[106] Uniform performance accountability standards, such as the new national College Scorecard or the various state-level performance funding initiatives, rarely are responsive to the highly variable local contexts of community colleges.[107] Moreover, the assumptions common to research and assessment in four-year institutions about the relative uniformity of students' goals and students' timely, uninterrupted, linear flow through postsecondary education often do not apply to community college students (or, for that matter, to all students in four-year institutions).[108] These assumptions are based in part on values that idealize the baccalaureate degree as an educational outcome and do not account for differences in culture, goals, and priorities at the organizational and student levels.[109] Yet, these assumptions persist in research on community colleges and, consequently, in efforts to measure their performance.

## Principles of Community Colleges

Rooted in their historical development, contemporary community colleges are knit together by five interrelated principles. These principles are open access, comprehensiveness, lifelong learning, community centeredness, and teaching focus.[110] Though none of these principles individually is unique to community colleges, and though the emphasis placed on each principle varies across this diverse array of institutions, nevertheless it is the intersection of these five principles that defines and distinguishes community colleges in the larger landscape of postsecondary education and that orients them to the broader society.

## Open Access

The open access principle of community colleges is the most widely known, even defining, feature of these institutions. With a few exceptions, community colleges admit nearly any student who stands to benefit from the educational services of the institutions, rather than admitting students selectively based on their academic qualifications.[111] At the lower end of the spectrum of academic preparation, open access encompasses the "ability to benefit" standard applied in federal policies regarding the provision of student financial aid. Historically, this standard has been inclusive of students who have not completed a high school diploma or comparable credential, conditional on achieving a satisfactory score on a general skills test or completing successfully a small number of credits of college coursework.

More broadly, the "open admissions" policies of community colleges are inclusive of individuals who have been away from school for a time, those who are *not* seeking postsecondary credentials, those who already hold postsecondary degrees, and "traditional age" credential-seeking students who recently graduated from high school or transferred from another postsecondary institution. They include students who can attend full-time and continuously, and students who can attend only part-time and intermittently. They include individuals who lack college-level competency in basic subjects (e.g., math, reading, writing), advanced high school students who wish to enroll concurrently in college coursework, and students at four-year institutions who enroll in a community college during the summer to fulfill lower division program requirements at their primary institution.[112] Open admissions policies are inclusive of many other combinations of student needs and circumstances as well, and it is impossible to understand community colleges without first acknowledging the exceptionally wide range of academic backgrounds, and equally wide range of academic goals, represented in the population of students who are served by these institutions.

In addition to open admissions policies, the open access principle is expressed in other ways, most notably in the low cost of attendance, minimal admissions application requirements, and frequently flexible course scheduling options.[113] As illustrated in figure 16.1, community colleges are among the least expensive postsecondary options for students, with a full-time course load at public community colleges being, on average, roughly one-third (38%) of the cost of a comparable course load at a public four-year institution.[114]

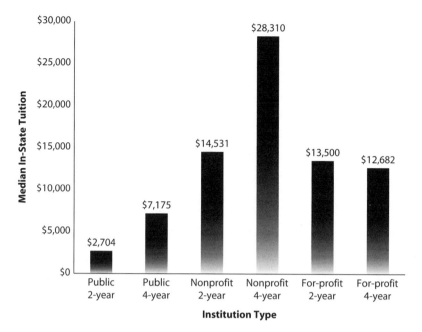

*Figure 16.1.* Median in-state tuition and fees in 2011–2012 for full-time students in degree-granting postsecondary institutions, by control and level of institution
*Source:* Snyder and Dillow, *Digest of Education Statistics 2012*, table 383.

Importantly, though, community colleges also receive less state financial support than do public four-year institutions. The combination of less state support, lower tuition revenue, less philanthropic support, and the absence of a significant funding stream from research results in community colleges operating on substantially less funding per student than do public four-year institutions. Overall, community colleges operate on one-third (33%) of the funding per full-time equivalent student of public four-year institutions.[115]

On one hand, this funding disparity may be framed in a positive light, insofar as the cost to taxpayers of community colleges may be as little as one-fifth (19%) that of public four-year institutions.[116] On the other hand, community colleges serve a disproportionate fraction of underrepresented students, first-generation students, and students who have the greatest educational needs. Thus, one might interpret the substantially lower public investment in community colleges as a reflection of a broad societal undervaluation of the talent and potential contributions of the students who are most likely to attend community colleges. Unfortunately,

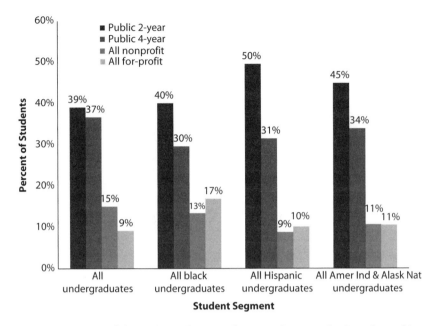

*Figure 16.2.* Share of the undergraduate student population and selected racial/ethnic segments of the undergraduate population served by each sector of postsecondary education in the fall of 2011
Source: Snyder and Dillow, *Digest of Education Statistics 2012*, table 268.

these are the very same students who face the greatest obstacles to accessing and progressing in higher education.

Owing to the open access principle, the population of students in community colleges is highly diverse.[117] For example, one observes in figure 16.2 that about two-fifths (39%) of all undergraduate students (across all sectors of higher education), and slightly more than half (52%) of undergraduate students in public institutions, enroll in public community colleges.[118] However, public community colleges enroll half (50%) of all Hispanic undergraduates across all sectors of higher education and more than three-fifths (61%) of Hispanic undergraduates in public institutions. Although public community colleges enroll a proportionate 40 percent of all black undergraduates across all sectors of higher education, they enroll a disproportionate 57 percent of all black undergraduates in public institutions.[119] Stated more succinctly, the public community college sector enrolls 7 percent more undergraduates than does the public four-year sector, but 57 percent more Hispanic undergraduates and 35 percent more black undergraduates.

With respect to other student characteristics, public community colleges enroll 48 percent of all undergraduates over the age of twenty-four across all sectors of higher education, and 67 percent of such students in public postsecondary institutions.[120] They enroll 64 percent of all part-time undergraduates across all sectors of higher education and 74 percent of all part-time undergraduates in public institutions.[121] In other words, more than twice as many undergraduates over the age of twenty-four, and nearly three times as many part-time undergraduates, enrolled in public community colleges as enrolled in public four-year institutions. In addition, more than one-third (36%) of community college students are first-generation students (i.e., the first in their respective families to attend college), one in six (17%) are single parents, and one in eight (12%) are students with a disability.[122]

Prominent in the current discourse on community colleges is the diversity of the student population with respect to academic preparation. The troubling reality is that the majority of community college students are not fully prepared for college-level coursework, whether with respect to skills in math, reading, writing, or some combination of these. Most community colleges have attempted to address this problem through remedial coursework—sequences of courses in basic subjects intended to help students advance their skills up to the level expected of a new college student.[123]

More than two-thirds (68%) of students who begin college at a public two-year institution enroll in at least one remedial course within six years of college entry, as compared with about two-fifths (39%) of students who begin at a public four-year institution.[124] That said, research indicates that a meaningful fraction of community college students who are placed into remedial coursework at college entry never enroll in these courses.[125] Thus, the need for remedial assistance among community colleges students likely is greater even than these statistics indicate.

The high level of need for remedial assistance among community colleges students generally is more pronounced among historically disadvantaged groups and others who face significant obstacles in their educational pursuits.[126] For example, approximately 75 percent of Hispanic students and 88 percent of black students who begin college at a public two-year institution enroll in at least one remedial course, as compared with 64 percent of white students.[127] Likewise, 73 percent of public two-year students whose incomes place them below the federal poverty level enroll in remedial coursework, as compared with 64 percent of students whose incomes are 200 percent or more of the federal poverty level.[128]

Thus, there is much riding on the success of the remedial intervention with respect to the promise of access to higher education embodied by community colleges.[129]

Unfortunately, research indicates that comparatively few students who begin a sequence of remedial coursework in a community college ultimately complete it and advance to college-level coursework.[130] Consequently, a central concern of community college stakeholders has been developing and testing improvements and alternative strategies for the delivery of remedial instruction, the support structures available to skill-deficient students, and the methods of placing students in coursework to avoid unnecessary remedial courses.[131] In this regard, several new initiatives show promise. One of these is the Accelerated Study in Associate Programs (ASAP), which provides a coordinated suite of services and additional financial support to community college students to help them complete an associate's degree within three years of initial enrollment. Evidence indicates that ASAP improves educational outcomes for students who have minimal to moderate skill deficiencies.[132] However, the program is expensive to operate and requires students to attend full-time, which limits its applicability and scope to a fraction of all community college students.

A very different initiative is multiple measures assessment, which focuses on more accurate placement of students in coursework to minimize unnecessary remediation.[133] In many community colleges, students are placed in coursework almost exclusively based on scores on standardized placement tests. Multiple measures assessment supplements these "high stakes" tests with additional measures that have predictive value regarding performance in coursework, such as high school grade point average or highest math or English course completed in high school. Some evidence suggests that, for recent high school graduates, placement tests could be replaced entirely with measures of high school performance with no loss (and some gain) in the accuracy of students' placement in the math and English curriculum.[134]

Still other initiatives focus on streamlining and contextualizing the material addressed in the developmental coursework. The most well-known of these—Quantway and Statway[135]—pertain to remedial math, which is the subject in which the lowest rates of advancement to college-level coursework are observed.[136] Such contextualization of remedial coursework sometimes is implemented as part of larger initiatives to streamline and simplify the dizzying array of choices that students must make early in their college careers in order to develop a coherent academic plan. These efforts to provide "guided pathways" to students at college entry are gaining momentum nationally.[137]

More broadly, the low overall success in helping underprepared students to acquire necessary competencies in basic subjects and to progress and succeed in college has drawn attention to a fundamental question about the principle of open access. Is the principle of open access a commitment solely to enroll students without regard to academic preparation or life circumstances or, much more than that, a commitment to provide education that meets students' highly diverse needs and helps them to achieve their evolving goals? Most succinctly, does the promise of access end on the first day of class, or does it continue to graduation and even beyond? While the reasonable answer to this question undoubtedly lies somewhere in the middle, it is the latter perspective that has driven much of the inquiry and innovation around remedial education, contributing to some of the most interesting developments for community colleges in many years.

### COMPREHENSIVENESS

The phrase "open access" has become virtually synonymous with community colleges, but the question "access to what?" is ever present in scholarly and policy discourse on these institutions. Although not the intent at the outset of the movement, contemporary community colleges largely have evolved to be comprehensive in their curricular missions, referring here to the widely varying programmatic offerings at the heart of the operations of community colleges.[138] While institutions vary in how they enact these missions, most community colleges provide educational opportunities in the following four areas: academic, occupational, remedial, and community education.[139]

*Academic education* in the liberal arts and sciences has been a primary focus of community colleges from the beginning, with the goal of preparing students to transfer to a four-year institution to earn a baccalaureate degree. In this regard, community colleges typically offer a full complement of lower-division coursework and associate degrees in traditional academic fields, including mathematics, the life, physical, and social sciences, the humanities, and the fine arts. While research suggests that earning an associate's degree in route to a four-year institution increases the likelihood that a student will complete a baccalaureate degree, many students transfer without completing a community college credential.[140]

A second curricular mission is *occupational education,* frequently described as career and technical education (CTE) or vocational education. In its early instantiations, occupational education was geared toward terminal (non-transfer) educational objectives to secure employment directly after leaving the institution, and, therefore, was considered distinct from academic education.[141] However, as noted earlier, the line between occupational education and transfer goals has become increasingly blurred.[142] For example, coursework in business, criminal justice, computer science, nursing, and other applied fields may prepare a student either for immediate employment or for transfer into a baccalaureate program, and students seeking occupational degrees take academic courses to fulfill general education requirements just as do students seeking academic degrees.[143]

*Remedial education* in reading, writing, and mathematics, sometimes referred to as developmental education or basic skills education, is the third curricular mission. As with the line between occupational education and transfer goals, the line between remedial and college-level coursework is not always clear. Courses that fulfill requirements for a postsecondary credential at a given community college may or may not be considered college-level courses at a nearby four-year institution. To illustrate, in 2007, California, which accounts for about one-quarter of all community college students in the nation,[144] raised the minimum English and math requirements for an associate's degree to first-semester college composition and intermediate algebra, respectively. The former fulfills the minimum English requirement for a baccalaureate degree from the California State University (CSU) system, but the latter is insufficient to fulfill the corresponding math requirement for a baccalaureate degree. Intermediate algebra is, in effect, a remedial course in the CSU system but a college-level course in the California Community College (CCC) system.

While there is no universal definition of *community education*—the last of the four curricular missions—the phrase often is used interchangeably with "noncredit education" and "continuing education."[145] It encompasses a wide range of typically noncredit educational activities, such as workforce development, contract training for local employers, English as a second language courses, basic skills offerings, and recreational courses, among others.[146]

What distinguishes community education from academic, occupational, and remedial education often lies more in its funding and organizational structures than its content. Community education frequently provides an alternative source of revenue for colleges and is less regulated at the state level, allowing for more flexibility in its implementation.[147] Furthermore, despite the overlap in content, there is little structural overlap between community education and the other three curricular missions; faculty and students engaged in community education rarely share classes with faculty and students engaged in academic, occupational, or remedial education.

Much of the research on community education focuses on its expression as an entrepreneurial activity, particularly as it relates to the dramatic growth in contract training,[148] which is education offered by community colleges to private companies or governmental entities on a contract basis.[149] In a broader sense, however, research on community education remains limited,[150] which is surprising given that noncredit education now accounts for 40 percent of community college enrollment,[151] and noncredit courses account for approximately 16 percent of the curriculum.[152]

More broadly, across the four curricular missions discussed here, community colleges must negotiate competing pressures arising from particular political, fiscal, and demographic realities. There is scant evidence to confirm that "simplification" of curricular missions would remedy the situation[153] or that colleges cannot pursue one mission without detracting from another. In fact, specialization in one curricular mission to the exclusion or marginalization of others appears to be possible only through regulatory action.[154]

Operating from the assumption that integration of missions is beneficial educationally and fiscally, Grubb and Perin both conclude that only an organizational commitment to teaching will overcome the numerous barriers to integration.[155] Complementary research portrays community colleges that have successfully integrated one or all curricular missions as having competent administrative leadership,[156] a unified, highly collaborative (full-time) faculty,[157] a supportive regulatory environment that promotes substantive rather than symbolic activity,[158] and stable funding.[159] Convergence on a redefinition of education as a "moral imperative" that views "all learning as developmental,"[160] coupled with active strategies to socialize faculty to work in multiple mission areas, appears to be essential for successful integration across curricular missions.[161]

### Lifelong Learning

The principle of lifelong learning is tied closely to the principles of open access and comprehensiveness. In offering open admissions, a college implicitly acknowledges that students may begin college at any point in their lives at which they discover that they have need for education, whether for professional or personal reasons. Furthermore, they may return to college as often as they need throughout their lives. This principle is exemplified in the recent discourse on skills-builder students[162] and stackable credentials.[163] Skills builders, who may comprise 10 percent or more of the student population of community colleges in states like California, enroll in a community college to acquire, refresh, or advance job skills, which itself is not an unusual use of the institution.[164] They are distinct from other segments of the student population in that they tend to enroll in just a few classes, typically CTE classes, to excel in these classes, and then to depart college without completing a credential and without transferring to a four-year institution; they also tend to be substantially older than traditional age, with the average age of skills builders being in the mid to late thirties.[165] Importantly, evidence suggests that skills builders often forgo the pursuit of a community college credential in order to focus on completing a state license or industry certification (i.e., a third-party credential) that has greater labor market value in their respective fields of employment than does a community college credential.[166] In other words, skills builders are highly successful noncompleters, contradicting widely held assumptions about the exchangeability of the terms "success" and "completion" in the community college context.[167]

Stackable credentials, on the other hand, are "sequence[s] of credentials that can be accumulated over time to build up an individual's qualifications and help them to move along a career pathway or up a career ladder to different and potentially higher-paying job."[168] Ganzglass describes several ways in which community colleges have implemented models of stackable credentials, such as (1) the modularization of longer-term associate degree programs into shorter-term certificates programs "to create manageable stepping stones to good jobs, further education, and career advancement"[169] and (2) embedding third-party certifications into existing postsecondary credential programs.[170]

The bodies of research on skills builders and stackable credentials both recognize that students engage with community colleges, pursue goals, and organize their educational pursuits in ways that contradict notions about traditional, linear, degree-focused educational pathways.[171] The ability to pursue skills building and stackable credentials, among other educational activities, is accommodated and supported through the principle of lifelong learning at the heart of these institutions. In this respect, community colleges provide an avenue for continuing workforce, civic, and personal development that, at present, cannot be met on the same broad scale by any other sector of higher education.

Still, given variation in needs across a community, the demands for lifelong learning placed on any community college are understandably diverse. Meeting these demands intensifies organizational complexity and often has implications for equity arising from the balancing of priorities and limited resources.

### COMMUNITY CENTEREDNESS

Although every postsecondary institution is located in a community of sorts, community colleges, much more than most four-year institutions, fundamentally are manifestations of the local community of which they are a part.[172] The central concern of community colleges is meeting the educational needs of the local community and surrounding service area. This *community centered* quality is expressed in a variety of ways, such as attentiveness and specialization with respect to the educational and training needs of local businesses and industries, the provision of adult basic education and instruction in English as a second language, coordination of activities with local social service agencies, the development of cooperative articulation agreements with nearby four-year institutions,[173] short-term course offerings (often under a noncredit framework) to meet community demand, and service as a hub for local cultural activities.

Community centeredness is reinforced in many states by the mechanisms used to fund community colleges. Unlike most public four-year institutions, community colleges often receive a meaningful portion of their funding through local taxation[174] and are overseen by boards that are elected locally or appointed,[175] which makes these institutions directly accountable to the local population. Although figures vary from state to state depending upon the higher education funding structure,[176] public two-year colleges receive an average of 16 percent of their total revenue from local taxation, as compared with 0.2 percent among public four-year colleges.[177] Additionally, four-fifths (79%) of community colleges engage in contract training agreements, serving local industry and governmental initiatives, a providing a sometimes substantial funding stream that further knits these institutions to their local communities.[178]

Importantly, this focus on the local community explains much of the observed variation in community colleges. As Bahr explains, "each community college is shaped by the needs and demands of its host community, resulting in a unique mix and expression of the multifaceted mission,"[179] with correspondingly unique challenges related to mission complexity and equity for students.

## TEACHING FOCUS

Lastly, community colleges are teaching-focused institutions. Community college faculty devote the lion's share (78%) of their time to instruction, as opposed to research or administration, more so than in any other sector of postsecondary education.[180] To illustrate, as of 2003, 58 percent of full-time faculty in public two-year institutions taught at least fifteen hours per week, compared with 15 percent of full-time faculty in public four-year comprehensive institutions, 10 percent in public doctoral institutions, and 6 percent in public research institutions.[181] Of note, however, due largely to the lower level of funding mentioned earlier, community colleges have come to rely heavily on part-time faculty.[182] As of 2003, two-thirds (67%) of faculty in public community colleges were part-time, as compared with about one-quarter of faculty (27%) in public four-year institutions.[183]

The consequences of a heavy reliance on part-time faculty for instructional outcomes and student success remains a point of debate among scholars, policy makers, and other stakeholders, and it is unquestionably a multidimensional issue.[184] On one hand, students in career and technical education programs may benefit greatly from instruction provided by industry professionals who hold part-time faculty roles.[185] Moreover, drawing a portion of instructional faculty from the local community can reinforce the relationship between the institution and the community.

On the other hand, many community college students interact and engage with the college almost exclusively through their course faculty, and research suggests that institutional reliance on part-time faculty has negative effects on students' outcomes.[186] Moreover, part-time faculty, who often receive comparatively little institutional support,[187] are more likely than are full-time faculty to teach remedial courses, where many of the students requiring the greatest amount of support are found.[188]

While some have concluded that the quality of instruction among part-time faculty is the cause of differences in student outcomes, others contend that it is inequitable institutional policies and a lack of institutional support for part-time faculty that are to blame. That is, the marginalized role of part-time faculty may hinder their capacity to provide the extracurricular support that community college students often need.[189]

In sum, embracing the five core principles of open access, comprehensiveness, lifelong learning, community centeredness, and teaching focus results in persistent and interdependent tensions related to mission complexity and equity. The expectation to be all things to all people is a vexing challenge that has resulted simultaneously in harsh criticism and ebullient praise for community colleges.

## Recurrent Themes and Debates

### MISSION COMPLEXITY

As evident in the brief history of community colleges discussed in this chapter, the multiple curricular missions of community colleges arose from evolving political and fiscal pressures and the demands of an increasing number of constituencies. The environments in which community colleges operate today are more complex and varied than at any time in the history of these institutions, and it is the variation in these environments across states and regions that shapes the balance and implementation of curricular missions from one college to the next.[190]

A comparatively recent development in the curricular missions of community colleges is the community college baccalaureate degree (CCB). As of 2015, twenty-three states had granted permission to their community colleges to award baccalaureate degrees, of which West Virginia was the earliest contemporary adopter, authorizing the CCB in 1989.[191] Currently, in twenty-one of the twenty-three states, four or fewer institutions offer CCB programs, and the majority (78%) of those colleges administer fewer than seven such programs.[192]

The motivations behind policy changes of this magnitude are rarely simple or entirely transparent. Levin argues that pressures from the government, professions, and global marketplace have provided much of the impetus for the development of the CCB.[193] State governments are interested in the economic benefits of a highly skilled workforce, while evolving professions increase the educational requirements of entry-level positions, and the expectations of working in a globalized economy demand both the technical and "soft" skills promised by a college education. Advocates of the CCB suggest that these programs allow community colleges to respond to local economic needs, to increase accessibility to baccalaureate education for place-bound students (who are more likely to be underrepresented or historically disadvantaged students), and to rectify capacity constraints at four-year institutions.[194] Thus, it is not surprising that the majority of CCB degrees are occupationally oriented,[195] which aligns with the vocational trajectory of the curriculum in community colleges[196] and higher education more broadly.[197]

Critics of the CCB contend that it will increase selectivity at community colleges and, thereby, threaten the open-access foundation of these institutions,[198] while also reducing focus on sub-baccalaureate occupational education.[199] More generally, though, some argue that the progression toward the CCB is a natural evolution of the principles and curricular missions of community colleges, while others view it as evidence of mission creep,[200] which itself is premised on the assumption that community colleges cannot pursue multiple missions well because fiscal and personnel resources present a zero-sum constraint on the focus of the colleges.

Concern about the evolving complexity of the curricular missions of community colleges is a recurrent theme in the history of these institutions. More than three decades ago, against the backdrop of changing student demography and decreased funding, Breneman and Nelson acknowledged that "community colleges face a fluid future, with important choices to be made regarding which programs to stress and which people to serve."[201] While the Carnegie Commission of 1970 advocated for the comprehensive approach to curricular missions,[202] others suggested that community colleges were being spread too thin and should refocus on a primary mission, though there was little agreement about what the focus should be, whether transfer, education-to-employment pathways, community education, or something else.[203] Beach summarizes the lack of coherence well, stating, "Scholars have never been able to completely agree on the mission of the community college, and therefore, have never been able to adequately determine what it is the community is supposed to do, nor how it is supposed to do it."[204]

More recently, scholars have sought to explain community college comprehensiveness and the general lack of coordination between curricular missions.[205] Contrary to prevailing wisdom that promotes "simplification" for productivity and efficiency, maintaining separate missions may help maximize external resources and minimize internal conflict, even though curricula often are duplicated across programs.[206] Given a complex resource environment dominated by decreased state funding, increased regulation and accountability, and competing demands of stakeholders, Bailey and Morest note that "by shedding programs in search of more focus, colleges risk alienating constituencies and ultimately reducing the overall resources available to the institution."[207]

In fact, not only are community college not shedding programs, some aggressively pursue both horizontal and vertical expansion initiatives that reinforce a "resilient" comprehensive model.[208] In addition to the CCB, community colleges are pursuing internationalization efforts both domestically and abroad, growing online education programs, and establishing or expanding honors colleges, on-campus residences, and programs for high school students. Generally, these expansion projects satisfy different constituencies, making complexity (rather than simplification) a rational choice for colleges in order to maximize support of stakeholders.[209] Often unexplored, though, are the implications of increasing complexity for access and equity. One might ask, what activities of the college, if any, are deprioritized to support these new initiatives? As a practical matter, which students have access to these programs, and which are excluded as a consequence of social or financial barriers? Such questions must be addressed as community colleges evolve to fill new roles in the higher education ecosystem.

## ACCESS AND EQUITY

The tension of maintaining access while also ensuring equity is a theme in much of the historical and contemporary discourse on community colleges and an important lens through which to understand the difficult task that community colleges face. This theme often is framed as a question of whether community colleges primarily are a force for democratization by distributing access to postsecondary education more widely and evenly across the citizenry[210] or a force for diversion by redirecting students from baccalaureate (or higher) aspirations into pathways leading to lower-level credentials and lower-status jobs.[211] Sometimes, this debate is framed as a question of whether community colleges primarily "cool out" or "warm up" students' educational aspirations and, therefore, their socioeconomic opportunities.[212] Inescapable in this debate is the fact that community colleges disproportionately serve low-income and historically disadvantaged students. Thus, the question of whether community colleges are a force for democratization (and warming up) or diversion (and cooling out) in fact is a question about the authenticity of the promise of meritocracy and upward mobility through education that is a bedrock of US society.

Early on, scholars recognized that the open admissions policy of community colleges guaranteed that many students would enroll in college with the desire to earn a baccalaureate degree but, being underprepared for college level coursework, would not succeed in achieving their goal.[213] Community colleges were positioned to bear primary responsibility to prepare these students for employment through terminal occupational programs, reflecting the reality of skill-deficient students' limited academic and socioeconomic opportunities.[214] In a well-known and often cited study, Clark drew on Goffman's concept of cooling out to describe the processes by which community colleges, as a matter of necessity, quietly and systematically sorted students between transfer and terminal curricula based on perceived potential.[215]

Other scholars, however, viewed the growth of occupational education in community colleges as evidence of the "false promise" of upward mobility[216] and a strategy to reinforce capitalist market structures through an educational system mirroring social class and labor-market relationships.[217] That is, critics reframed Clark's "cooling out" thesis from a "possible compromise, perhaps even a necessary one"[218] to a mechanism for social elites to maintain class differentiation.[219]

Building on the work of Brint and Karabel,[220] Dougherty offers an excellent synthesis of the competing arguments regarding the role and purpose of community colleges.[221] In one camp, functionalists view community colleges as fulfilling critical functions for society as a whole, including "providing social mobility, job training [for middle-level workers], and protection for high-quality universities."[222] In the other camp, instrumentalists assert that the true purpose of community colleges in society is to preserve elite interests and "reproduce the class inequalities of capitalist society."[223] Somewhere between these two very different perspectives, institutionalists suggest that the primary role of community colleges is "to finesse the contradictions between conflicting values in American society,"[224] providing an efficient method for managing students' ambitions,[225] sorting them more or less peacefully into an occupational structure in which the distribution of wealth, power, and privilege is intrinsically unequal. Highlighting the crucial role of self-interested government officials in the process, Dougherty concludes that community colleges developed as a hybrid institution offering multiple curricular missions to meet the needs of diverse stakeholders in a way that has "sown contradiction" rather than synergy.[226]

This debate about whether community colleges are primarily a force for democratization or diversion continues unabated and largely unresolved in the scholarly literature and national discourse today. In terms of the occupational mission of community colleges, scholars have reinitiated an effort begun some years ago to measure the labor market returns to community college credentials,[227] asking whether students receive equitable economic returns on their investment of time, effort, and money.[228] Although findings vary across studies, the accumulating evidence suggests that earning a community college credential in a CTE (occupational) field significantly improves students' earnings and employment prospects. In fact, in some CTE fields, completing the coursework alone, even without the credential, is sufficient to realize labor market returns,[229] which speaks to the important role that community colleges play outside of traditional "completion" pathways in training and retraining individuals for work.

Closer to the heart of the historical debate about the diversionary influence of community colleges, much of the current research concerns whether students who report baccalaureate ambitions and begin at a community college suffer a "community college penalty," completing baccalaureate degrees at a lower rate than do comparable students who begin at a four-year institution.[230] The fundamental challenge of this line of inquiry is differentiating the effect on students' outcomes of attending a community college (as opposed to a four-year institution) from the effects of individual characteristics that predispose a student to attend a community college in the first place, such as the need to work while attending college, being a first-generation college student, being older than traditional college age, having relatively lower academic performance in high school, having significant family or personal obligations, and so on. Although studies vary in their methodological nuances, the most important distinction in this class of research is whether students who begin at a four-year institution are compared with (1) similar baccalaureate-aspiring students who begin at a community college *and* transfer to a four-year institution, or (2) similar baccalaureate-aspiring students who begin at a community college *regardless* of whether they ultimately transfer to a four-year institution. The former tend to indicate no community college penalty, while the latter often reach the opposite conclusion,[231] which suggests that the primary challenge faced by baccalaureate-aspiring community college students lies in transferring to the four-year institution, rather than in succeeding in the four-year institution once they arrive. Whether the main obstacles to transferring to the four-year institution reside in community colleges, in the transfer policies of four-year institutions, or in some combination of the two remains to be determined.

That said, with few exceptions, current research on the question of democratization versus diversion tends to focus on a "small set of highly prized student outcomes linked to educational and economic attainment," ignoring the complex nature of student success and the many noneconomic (e.g., social, political, and health) benefits that accrue to students and their communities from participation in higher education.[232] It perhaps is not surprising that this research often idealizes the completion of degrees, when (we) scholars who conduct the research work in institutions that are in the business of providing degrees. However, a circumspect view of the many roles that community colleges fulfill in their communities and in the lives of local community members demands a much more expansive definition of success. Only then can researchers, policy makers, practitioners, and citizens critically and holistically assess the functioning of community colleges with respect to providing access with equity.

## Conclusion

This chapter describes the five principles that bind community colleges together. Perhaps more importantly, however, it illuminates the often-overlooked diversity of these institutions, which, in fact, is the result of adherence to these five principles. Given that community colleges serve half of all undergraduates in higher education, and millions more in noncredit education, acknowledging and attending to this institutional diversity is crucial. The sheer scale of potential positive social change that rests with community colleges demands that scholars and policy makers understand and study these institutions in the unique roles in which they exist in their host communities and in larger society, rather than casting them as something that they are not, namely four-year institutions. It has never been more important to reassess the assumptions of community college scholarship, policy, and practice, and to re-imagine the definition of student and organizational success in a way that accounts for the complexity of community college missions and the multifaceted nature of access with equity. This is not an easy task, as it will require stakeholders to grapple with difficult social and organizational questions and to relinquish the deficit perspective of community colleges (e.g., "scarce resources," "underprepared students," "low graduation rates") that plagues the field. Still, it remains one of the most significant and far-reaching objectives for higher education today.

NOTES

1. Arthur M. Cohen and Florence B. Brawer, *The American Community College* (San Francisco: Jossey-Bass, 2008).

2. American Association of Community Colleges (AACC), "Fast Facts from Our Fact Sheet," *American Association of Community Colleges* (May 14, 2015), http://www.aacc.nche .edu/AboutCC/Pages/fastfactsfactsheet.aspx; Stephen Provasnik and Michael Planty, *Community Colleges: Special Supplement to the Condition of Education 2008, Statistical Analysis Report, NCES 2008-033* (Washington, DC: National Center for Education Statistics, 2008).

3. The figure of 1,123 community colleges is based on data drawn from the institutional membership database maintained by the AACC. The figure includes 992 public community colleges, 96 independent community colleges, and 36 tribally controlled community colleges. A modestly different figure is provided by the National Center for Education Statistics (NCES), which reported that, as of 2011, there were 967 public two-

year degree-granting institutions and 100 private nonprofit two-year degree-granting institutions in the United States (Snyder and Dillow 2013, table 306). At that time, there also were nineteen tribally controlled two-year degree-granting institutions, sixteen of which were public institutions, while the rest were private nonprofit institutions (Snyder and Dillow 2013, table 280); Thomas D. Snyder and Sally A. Dillow, *Digest of Education Statistics 2012* (Washington, DC: National Center for Education Statistics, Institute of Education Sciences, US Department of Education, 2013).

4. National Center for Educational Statistics, *Integrated Postsecondary Education Data System* (IPEDS), www.nces.ed.gov/ipeds.

5. The figures from IPEDS provided here and elsewhere are based on the authors' analysis of data for the 935 institutions designated by IPEDS as public, two-year, degree-granting institutions in the United States that do not provide programs solely via distance education. These data were obtained May 22, 2015, from http://nces.ed.gov/ipeds/datacenter.

6. Ibid.

7. Arthur M. Cohen, "Community Colleges in the United States," in *Community College Models*, ed. Rosalind Latiner Raby and Edward Valeau (Dordrecht, Netherlands: Springer, 2009), 39–48.

8. IPEDS.

9. See, for example, AACC, "Fast Facts"; Mary Martinez-Wenzl and Rigoberto Marquez, *Unrealized Promises: Unequal Access, Affordability, and Excellence at Community Colleges in Southern California* (Los Angeles: The Civil Rights Project, 2012), http://civilrightsproject.ucla.edu/.

10. Snyder and Dillow, *Digest of Education Statistics 2012*.

11. IPEDS.

12. Ibid.

13. Linda Serra Hagedorn, "The Pursuit of Student Success: The Directions and Challenges Facing Community Colleges," in *Higher Education: Handbook of Theory and Research*, ed. John C. Smart (Dordrecht, Netherlands: Springer, 2010), 181–218.

14. Peter Riley Bahr, "Classifying Community Colleges Based on Students' Patterns of Use," *Research in Higher Education* 54, no. 4 (2013): 433–60; Cohen and Brawer, *The American Community College*; Vanessa Smith Morest, "From Access to Opportunity: The Evolving Social Roles of Community Colleges," *The American Sociologist* 44, no. 4 (2013): 319–28.

15. Hagedorn, "Pursuit of Student Success."

16. David F. Labaree, "Public Goods, Private Goods: The American Struggle over Educational Goals," *American Educational Research Journal* 34, no. 1 (1997): 39–81.

17. Ibid., 4.

18. See, for example, Alicia C. Dowd, "From Access to Outcome Equity: Revitalizing the Democratic Mission of the Community College," *The Annals of the American Academy of Political and Social Science* 586, no. 1 (2003): 92–119; John S. Levin, *Globalizing the Community College: Strategies for Change in the Twenty-First Century* (New York: Palgrave, 2001).

19. See, for example, Debra D. Bragg, "Community College Access, Mission, and Outcomes: Considering Intriguing Intersections and Challenges," *Peabody Journal of*

*Education* 76, no. 1 (2001): 93–116; Arthur M. Cohen, *Transfer Education in American Community Colleges*, ED 255 250, Los Angeles: Center for the Study of Community Colleges (1985); W. Norton Grubb, *Working in the Middle: Strengthening Education and Training for the Mid-Skilled Labor Force* (San Francisco: Jossey-Bass, 1996); Dennis McGrath and Martin B. Spear, *The Academic Crisis of the Community College* (New York, NY: SUNY Press, 1991); Dolores Perin, "Can Community Colleges Protect Both Access and Standards? The Problem of Remediation," *The Teachers College Record* 108, no. 3 (2006): 339–73.

20. See, for example, Steven Brint and Jerome Karabel, *The Diverted Dream: Community Colleges and the Promise of Educational Opportunity in America, 1900–1985* (New York: Oxford University Press, 1989); Kevin J. Dougherty, *The Contradictory College: The Conflicting Origins, Impacts, and Futures of the Community College* (New York: SUNY Press, 1994); David F. Labaree, *How to Succeed in School Without Really Learning: The Credentials Race in American Education* (New Haven: Yale University Press, 1997).

21. Peter Riley Bahr, "The Bird's Eye View of Community Colleges: A Behavioral Typology of First-Time Students Based on Cluster Analytic Classification," *Research in Higher Education* 51, no. 8 (2010): 724–49; Josh M. Beach, *Gateway to Opportunity: A History of the Community College in the United States* (Sterling, VA: Stylus, 2011), 1.

22. Jillian Leigh Gross, "Understanding Why Community Colleges Do What They Do: An Institutional Logics Perspective" (presentation, Annual Conference of the Association for the Study of Higher Education, Washington, DC, Nov. 20–22, 2014).

23. http://en.wikiquote.org/wiki/Cicero.

24. James L. Ratcliff, "Seven Streams in the Historical Development of the Modern American Community College," in *A Handbook on the Community College in America: Its History, Mission, and Management*, ed. George Baker III (Westport, CT: Greenwood Press, 1994): 3–16; Cohen and Brawer, *The American Community College*.

25. Ibid.; Cohen, *Transfer Education*.

26. Thomas Diener, ed., *Growth of an American Invention: A Documentary History of the Junior and Community College Movement*, vol. 16 (New York: Greenwood, 1985).

27. Dale Tillery and William L. Deegan, "The Evolution of Two-Year Colleges Through Four Generations," in *Renewing the American Community College: Priorities and Strategies for Effective Leadership*, ed. Dale Tillery and William L. Deegan (San Francisco: Jossey-Bass, 1985): 3–33.

28. Ibid.; Cohen, *Transfer Education*.

29. Dave Bartlett, "Colleges, Junior and Community," *Encyclopedia of Chicago*, 26 May 2015, http://www.encyclopedia.chicagohistory.org/pages/312.htmlhttp://www.encyclopedia.chicagohistory.org/pages/312.html; Joliet Junior College, "History," *Joliet Junior College*, 12 May 2015, http://www.jjc.edu/college-info/Pages/history.aspx.

30. See, for example, Samuel Bowles and Herbert Gintis, *Schooling in Capitalist America: Educational Reform and the Contradictions of Economic Life* (New York: Haymarket Books, 1976); Brint and Karabel, *The Diverted Dream*; Dougherty, *The Contradictory College*; Jerome Karabel, "Community Colleges and Social Stratification," *Harvard Educational Review* 42, no. 4 (1972): 521–62; Fred L. Pincus, "The False Promises of Community Colleges: Class Conflict and Vocational Education," *Harvard Educational Review* 50,

no. 3 (1980): 332–61; Steven L. Zwerling, *Second Best: The Crisis of the Community College* (New York: McGraw-Hill, 1976).

31. Beach, *Gateway to Opportunity.*

32. Cohen and Brawer, *The American Community College*, 17.

33. The American Association of Junior Colleges was established in 1920. Later, it was renamed the American Association of Junior and Community Colleges, and then the American Association of Community Colleges, which is the name that it retains today.

34. Brint and Karabel, *The Diverted Dream.*

35. Beach, *Gateway to Opportunity.*

36. Eells, *The Junior College.*

37. Brint and Karabel, *The Diverted Dream.*

38. Ibid., 42.

39. Cohen and Brawer, *The American Community College*, 17.

40. Tillery and Deegan, "Evolution of Two-Year Colleges."

41. The transition from private to public was further bolstered by post–World War II public investment in higher education that resulted in increased support for lower-cost institutions, magnified by the response of students to increasingly enroll in these new, more affordable colleges (Grubb and Lazerson, 2005b, 6); W. Norton Grubb and Marvin Lazerson, "Vocationalism in Higher Education: The Triumph of the Education Gospel," *The Journal of Higher Education* 76, no. 1 (2005), 1–25.

42. Ibid., 10.

43. Tod Treat and Thomas C. Barnard, "Seeking Legitimacy: The Community College Mission and the Honors College," *Community College Journal of Research and Practice* 36, no. 9 (2012): 695–712.

44. George B. Vaughan, *The Community College in America: A Short History. Revised* (Washington, DC: American Association of Community and Junior Colleges, 1985).

45. George F. Zook, *Higher Education for American Democracy: A Report of the President's Commission on Higher Education* (New York: Harper & Brothers, 1947).

46. Brint and Karabel, *The Diverted Dream*, 70.

47. Tillery and Deegan, "Evolution of Two-Year Colleges."

48. Vaughan, *Community College in America*, 17.

49. Ratcliff, "Seven Streams," 14.

50. Cohen and Brawer, *The American Community College.*

51. Cohen, *Transfer Education.*

52. Bruce Keith, "The Context of Educational Opportunity: States and the Legislative Organization of Community College Systems," *American Journal of Education* 105, no. 1 (1996): 67–101.

53. Terrence A. Tollefson, "The Evolving Community College Mission in the Context of State Governance," ED 417 776 (East Tennessee State University, 1998).

54. Brint and Karabel, *The Diverted Dream.*

55. Dowd, "Access to Outcomes Equity."

56. Burton R. Clark, "Organizational Adaptation and Precarious Values: A Case Study," *American Sociological Review* 21, no. 3 (1956): 332.

57. Cohen, *Transfer Education*, 155.

58. Vaughan, *Community College in America*.

59. W. Norton Grubb and Marvin Lazerson, *The Education Gospel* (Cambridge, MA: Harvard University Press, 2005a).

60. Brint and Karabel, *The Diverted Dream*.

61. Keith, "Context of Educational Opportunity"; Vaughan, *Community College in America*; Tillery and Deegan, "Evolution of Two-Year Colleges."

62. Kevin J. Dougherty, Sosanya M. Jones, Rebecca Spiro Natow, Hana Elizabeth Lahr, Lara Elaine Pheatt, and Vikash T. Reddy, *Envisioning Performance Funding Impacts: The Espoused Theories of Action for State Higher Education Performance Funding in Three States* (New York: Teachers College, Columbia University, Community College Research Center, 2014).

63. Karabel, "Social Stratification."

64. Brint and Karabel, *The Diverted Dream*, 341.

65. Brint and Karabel, *The Diverted Dream*; Dougherty, *The Contradictory College*.

66. Barbara K. Townsend, Debra D. Bragg, and Collin M. Ruud, *The Adult Learner and the Applied Baccalaureate: National and State-by-State Inventory* (Urbana-Champaign, IL: Office of Community College Research and Leadership, 2008).

67. McGrath and Spear, *Academic Crisis*; Cohen, "Transfer Education," 156.

68. Tillery and Deegan, "Evolution of Two-Year Colleges," 13.

69. Cohen, *Transfer Education*, 156.

70. Cohen and Brawer, *The American Community College*; Labaree, *Credentials Race*.

71. Vaughan, *Community College in America*.

72. Carnegie Commission on Higher Education, *The Open-Door Colleges: Policies for Community Colleges* (New York: McGraw-Hill, 1970).

73. Bowles and Gintis, *Schooling in Capitalist America*; Karabel, "Social Stratification"; Pincus, "False Promises"; Zwerling, *Second Best*.

74. McGrath and Spear, *Academic Crisis*.

75. Burton R. Clark, "The 'Cooling-Out' Function in Higher Education," *American Journal of Sociology* 65, no. 6 (1960): 569–76.

76. Christopher Jencks and David Riseman, *The Academic Revolution* (Garden City, NJ: Doubleday, 1968).

77. Karabel, "Social Stratification."

78. K. Patricia Cross, "Community Colleges on the Plateau," *The Journal of Higher Education* 52, no. 2 (1981): 113.

79. This figure excludes students who enrolled exclusively in noncredit coursework.

80. Snyder and Dillow, *Digest of Education Statistics 2012*, table 240.

81. Gwyer Schuyler, "A Historical and Contemporary View of the Community College Curriculum," *New Directions for Community Colleges,* no. 108 (1999): 3–15.

82. W. Norton Grubb, "The Decline of Community College Transfer Rates: Evidence from National Longitudinal Surveys," *The Journal of Higher Education* 62, no. 2 (1991): 194–222.

83. Ibid.; Jenny Castruita Striplin, "A Review of Community College Curriculum Trends" (UCLA: ERIC Clearinghouse for Community Colleges, 2000).

84. Cohen and Brawer, *The American Community College*.

85. Levin, *Globalizing the Community College.*

86. Grubb, *Working in the Middle,* 270.

87. Morest, "Double Vision."

88. Howard L. Simmons, "Accreditation and Curricular Change," *New Directions for Community Colleges,* no. 64 (1988): 61–69.

89. Cohen and Brawer, *The American Community College.*

90. For a thoughtful review of this argument see Adrianna J. Kezar, "Obtaining Integrity? Reviewing and Examining the Charter Between Higher Education and Society," *The Review of Higher Education* 27, no. 4 (2004): 429–59; Labaree, *Credentials Race;* Levin, *Globalizing the Community College.*

91. Bragg, "Community College Access," 100.

92. Martinez-Wenzl and Marquez, *Unrealized Promises.*

93. Grubb, "Community College Transfer Rates"; Keith, "Context of Educational Opportunity."

94. Carol A. Kozeracki and J. Bryan Brooks, "Emerging Institutional Support for Developmental Education," *New Directions for Community Colleges,* no. 136 (2006): 63–73; Kathleen M. Shaw, "Remedial Education as Ideological Battleground: Emerging Remedial Education Policies in the Community College," *Educational Evaluation and Policy Analysis* 19, no. 3 (1997): 284–96.

95. Shaw, "Remedial Education," 284. See also Delores Perin and Kerry Charron, "Lights Just Click on Every Day," in *Defending the Community College Equity Agenda,* ed. Thomas Bailey and Vanessa Smith Morest (Baltimore: Johns Hopkins University Press, 2006), 155–94.

96. Quoted in Vaughan, *Community College in America,* 26.

97. Bragg, "Community College Access," 108.

98. Dowd, "Access to Outcome Equity," 106.

99. Thomas R. Bailey and Irina E. Averianova, *Multiple Missions of Community Colleges: Conflicting or Complementary?* (New York: Teachers College, Columbia University, Community College Research Center, 1998).

100. Peter T. Ewell, "Accountability and Institutional Effectiveness in the Community College," *New Directions for Community Colleges,* no. 153 (2011): 23–36.

101. David J. Deming, Claudia Goldin, and Lawrence F. Katz, *The For-Profit Postsecondary School Sector: Nimble Critters or Agile Predators?* No. w17710 (Washington DC: National Bureau of Economic Research, 2011).

102. Of note, both for-profit institutions and community colleges have experienced a decline in enrollment as of 2015. See, for example, Ashley A. Smith, "Enrollments Fall," *Inside Higher Ed,* May 2015, http://www.insidehighered.com/news/2015/05/14/improved-economy-leads-enrollment-dips-among-two-year-and-profit-colleges.

103. Dougherty et al., *Envisioning Performance Funding Impacts.*

104. Peter Riley Bahr, *The Labor Market Return in Earnings to Community College Credits and Credentials in California* (Ann Arbor: Center for the Study of Higher and Postsecondary Education, University of Michigan, 2014), http://www.soe.umich.edu/people/profile/peter_riley_bahr/; Peter Riley Bahr, Susan Dynarski, Brian Jacob, Daniel Kreisman, Alfredo Sosa, and Mark Wiederspan, "Labor Market Returns to Community College awards: Evidence from Michigan," Center for Analysis of Postsecondary Education

and Employment, Teachers College, Columbia University (2015),http://capseecenter.org /labor-market-returns-michigan/; Christopher Aaron Baldwin, "From Student Access to Student Success: Exploring Presidential Views of the Evolving Community College Mission," PhD diss., University of Michigan, 2013.

105.  Clive Belfield, "Measuring Efficiency in the Community College Sector," Teachers College, Columbia University, Community College Research Center (2012), http:// ccrc.tc.columbia.edu/media/k2/attachments/measuring-efficiency-community-college .pdf.

106.  Bahr, "Classifying Community Colleges"; Dougherty et al., *Envisioning Performance Funding Impacts.*

107.  Joseph C. Burke and Henrik P. Minassians, "Implications of State Performance Indicators for Community College Assessment," *New Directions for Community Colleges,* no. 126 (2004): 53–64; Kathryn Baron, "Community Colleges to Release Scorecard Rivaling the President's," *EdSource* (Feb. 14, 2013), http://edsource.org/today/2013/community -colleges-to-release-scorecard-rivaling-the-presidents/27136#.

108.  Peter Riley Bahr, "The Deconstructive Approach to Understanding Community College Students' Pathways and Outcomes," *Community College Review* 41, no. 2 (2013): 137–53; Peter Riley Bahr, "Student Flow between Community Colleges: Investigating Lateral Transfer," *Research in Higher Education* 53, no. 1 (2012): 94–121.

109.  Beach, *Gateway to Opportunity*; Bragg, "Community College Access"; Regina Deil-Amen and James E. Rosenbaum, "The Unintended Consequences of Stigma-Free Remediation," *Sociology of Education* (2002): 249–68; Robert A. Rhoads and James R. Valadez, *Democracy, Multiculturalism, and the Community College: A Critical Perspective,* Critical Edition Practice Series (New York: Routledge, 1996).

110.  George B. Vaughan, *The Community College Story,* 3rd ed. (Washington, DC: American Association of Community and Junior Colleges, 2006).

111.  Bahr, "Deconstructive Approach"; Morest, "From Access to Opportunity"; Provasnik and Planty, *Community Colleges: Special Supplement.*

112.  Arthur M. Cohen, "Contemporary Issues in Community Colleges: A Synopsis," ED 281 907, Los Angeles: ERIC Clearinghouse for Junior Colleges (1987); Christopher M. Mullin, *Rebalancing the Mission: The Community College Completion Challenge,* AACC Policy Brief 2010-02PBL (Washington, DC: American Association of Community Colleges, 2010a).

113.  Morest, "From Access to Opportunity"; Vaughan, *The Community College Story.*

114.  Snyder and Dillow, *Digest of Education Statistics 2012,* table 383.

115.  Ibid., table 401.

116.  Mullin, *Rebalancing the Mission.*

117.  Morest, "From Access to Opportunity."

118.  Public community colleges accounted for 94% of all student enrollment in two-year institutions (public and private, nonprofit, and for-profit, but excluding the small number of two-year tribal institutions) in the fall term of 2011. See Snyder and Dillow, *Digest of Education Statistics 2012,* table 268.

119.  Ibid.

120.  Ibid., table 226.

121.  Ibid.

122. AACC, "Fast Facts."

123. Peter Riley Bahr. "Deconstructing Remediation in Community Colleges: Exploring Associations between Course-Taking Patterns, Course Outcomes, and Attrition from the Remedial Math and Remedial Writing Sequences," *Research in Higher Education* 53, no. 6 (2012): 661–93.

124. The figures reported here are based on the authors' analysis of data collected in the NCES 2004/09 Beginning Postsecondary Students Longitudinal Study (http://nces .ed.gov/pubs2012/2012246_1.pdf), using the NCES QuickStats website (http://nces.ed .gov/datalab/quickstats/createtable.aspx).

125. Thomas Bailey, Dong Wook Jeong, and Sung-Woo Cho, "Referral, Enrollment, and Completion in Developmental Education Sequences in Community Colleges," *Economics of Education Review* 29, no. 2 (2010): 255–70.

126. See, for example, Paul Attewell, David Lavin, Thurston Domina, and Tania Levey, "New Evidence on College Remediation," *Journal of Higher Education* 77, no. 5 (2006): 886–924.

127. NCES, *QuickStats*.

128. Ibid.

129. Alicia C. Dowd, "Community Colleges as Gateways and Gatekeepers: Moving Beyond the Access Saga toward Outcome Equity," *Harvard Educational Review* 77, no. 4 (2007): 407–19.

130. Thomas Bailey, "Challenge and Opportunity: Rethinking the Role and Function of Developmental Education in Community College," *New Directions for Community Colleges,* no. 145 (2009): 11–30.

131. Janet C. Quint, Shanna S. Jaggars, D. Byndloss, and Asya Magazinnik, *Bringing Developmental Education to Scale: Lessons from the Developmental Education Initiative* (Oakland, CA: MDRC, 2013).

132. Susan Scrivener, Michael J. Weiss, Alyssa Ratledge, Timothy Rudd, Colleen Sommo, and Hannah Fresques, *Doubling Graduation Rates: Three-Year Effects of CUNY's Accelerated Study in Associate Programs (ASAP) for Developmental Education Students* (New York: MDRC, 2015), http://www.mdrc.org/publication/doubling-graduation-rates.

133. Multiple Measures in Assessment Task Force 2013–14, *Multiple Measures in Assessment: The Requirement and Challenges of Multiple Measures in the California Community Colleges* (Sacramento: The Academic Senate for California Community Colleges, 2014), http://www.asccc.org/sites/default/files/Multiple%20Measures%20in%20Assessment_0.pdf; Judith E. Scott-Clayton, *Do High-Stakes Placement Exams Predict College Success?* (New York: Teachers College, Columbia University, 2012), http://ccrc.tc .columbia.edu/media/k2/attachments/high-stakes-predict-success.pdf.

134. Peter Riley Bahr, *Replacing the Compass Placement Test in Michigan's Community Colleges* (Ann Arbor: Center for the Study of Higher and Postsecondary Education, University of Michigan, 2015).

135. Scott Strother and Nicole Sowers, *Community College Pathways: A Descriptive Report of Summative Assessments and Student Learning* (Washington, DC: Carnegie Foundation for the Advancement of Teaching, 2014), http://cdn.carnegiefoundation.org/wp -content/uploads/2014/09/CCP_Assessment_Report.pdf.

136. Bahr, "Deconstructing Remediation."

137. Community College Research Center, *What We Know about Guided Pathways* (New York: Teachers College, Columbia University, 2015), http://ccrc.tc.columbia.edu /media/k2/attachments/What-We-Know-Guided-Pathways.pdf.

138. Kevin J. Dougherty and Barbara K. Townsend, "Community College Missions: A Theoretical and Historical Perspective," *New Directions for Community Colleges*, no. 136 (2006): 5–13; Morest, "From Access to Opportunity."

139. Steven Brint, "Few Remaining Dreams: Community Colleges since 1985," *The Annals of the American Academy of Political and Social Science* 586, no. 1 (2003): 16–37; Cohen and Brawer, *The American Community College*; Dougherty and Townsend, "Community College Missions"; Hagedorn, "Student Success."

140. Peter Michael Crosta and Elizabeth Mary Kopko, *Should Community College Students Earn an Associate Degree Before Transferring to a Four-Year Institution?* (New York: Teachers College, Columbia University, Community College Research Center, 2014); Jason L. Taylor and Debra D. Bragg, *Optimizing Reverse Transfer Policies and Processes: Lessons from Twelve CWID States* (Urbana-Champaign: University of Illinois, 2015).

141. Brint and Karabel, *Diverted Dream*; Walter Crosby Eells, *The Junior College* (Boston: Houghton Mifflin, 1931).

142. Alexander C. McCormick and Rebecca D. Cox, "Classifying Two-Year Colleges: Purposes, Possibilities, and Pitfalls," *New Directions for Community Colleges*, no. 122 (2003): 7–15.

143. Morest, "From Access to Opportunity."

144. Foundation for California Community Colleges, "Facts and Figures," *Foundation for California Community Colleges*, May 2015, http://www.foundationccc.org/About -Us/About-the-Colleges/Facts-and-Figures.

145. See, for example, Michael Miller, Kenda S. Grover, and Kit Kacirek, "The Organization and Structure of Community Education Offerings in Community Colleges," *Community College Journal of Research and Practice* 38, no. 2–3 (2014): 242–49; Thomas R. Bailey and Vanessa Smith Morest, *The Organizational Efficiency of Multiple Missions for Community Colleges* (New York: Teachers College, Columbia University, 2004).

146. Cohen, "US Community Colleges."

147. Bailey and Morest, *Organizational Efficiency*; Cohen, "US Community Colleges"; W. Norton Grubb, Norena Badway, Denise Bell, Debra Bragg, and Maxine Russman, "Workforce, Economic, and Community Development: The Changing Landscape of the Entrepreneurial Community College," ED 413 033, Washington DC: Office of Vocational and Adult Education (1997); Vanessa S. Morest, "Double Vision: How the Attempt to Balance Multiple Missions is Shaping the Future of Community Colleges," in *Defending the Community College Equity Agenda*, ed. Thomas Bailey and Vanessa Smith Morest (Baltimore: Johns Hopkins University Press, 2006), 28–50; Michelle Van Noy, James Jacobs, Suzanne Korey, Thomas Bailey, and Katherine L. Hughes, *Noncredit Enrollment in Workforce Education: State Policies and Community College Practices* (Washington, DC: American Association of Community Colleges, 2008).

148. Vickie Choitz, *Getting What We Pay for: State Community College Funding Strategies that Benefit Low-Income, Lower-Skilled Students* (Washington, DC: Center for Law and

Social Policy, 2010); Kevin J. Dougherty and Marianne Bakia, "Community Colleges and Contract Training: Content, Origins and Impact," *The Teachers College Record* 102, no. 1 (2000): 197–243; W. Norton Grubb, Norena Badway, and Denise Bell, "Community Colleges and the Equity Agenda: The Potential of Noncredit Education," *The Annals of the American Academy of Political and Social Science* 586, no. 1 (2003): 218–40; Grubb et al., *Entrepreneurial Community College*.

149. Robert Lynch, James Palmer, and W. Norton Grubb, "Community College Involvement in Contract Training and Other Economic Development Activities," ED 339 434, Macomb: National Center for Research in Vocational Education (1991).

150. Miller et al., "Community Education Offerings."

151. AACC, "Fast Facts."

152. Richard A. Voorhees and John H. Milam, *The Hidden College: Noncredit Education in the United States* (Charlottesville, VA: Curry School of Education, 2005).

153. Bailey and Morest, *Organizational Efficiency*.

154. Rhoads and Valadez, *Democracy, Multiculturalism*; Shaw, "Remedial Education."

155. Grubb, *Working in the Middle*; Dolores Perin, "The Location of Developmental Education in Community Colleges: A Discussion of the Merits of Mainstreaming vs. Centralization," *Community College Review* 30, no. 1 (2002): 27–44.

156. Bailey and Morest, *Organizational Efficiency*; Kozeracki and Brooks, "Developmental Education"; Rhoads and Valadez, *Democracy, Multiculturalism*; Shaw, "Remedial Education."

157. Grubb, *Working in the Middle*; W. Norton Grubb and Robert Gabriner, *Basic Skills Education in Community Colleges: Inside and Outside of Classrooms* (New York: Routledge, 2013); Perin, "Location of Developmental Education."

158. Ewell, "Accountability and Institutional Effectiveness"; Kozeracki and Brooks, "Developmental Education."

159. Van Noy et al., *Noncredit Enrollment*.

160. Grubb, *Quandaries of Basic Skills*; Grubb and Gabriner, *Basic Skills*; Perin, "Developmental Education"; Rhoads and Valadez, *Democracy, Multiculturalism*.

161. Dougherty and Bakia, "Contract Training"; Grubb, *Working in the Middle*; Grubb and Gabriner, *Basic Skills*; Perin, "Developmental Education."

162. Peter Riley Bahr and Kathy Booth, *What's Completion Got to Do with It? Using Course-Taking Behavior to Understand Community College Success* (Berkeley, CA: Research and Planning Group for California Community Colleges, 2012), http://www .learningworksca.org/whats-completion-got-to-do-with-it-using-course-taking-behavior -to-understand-community-college-success/.

163. James T. Austin, Gail O. Mellow, Mitch Rosin, and Marlene Seltzer, *Portable, Stackable Credentials: A New Education Model for Industry-Specific Career Pathways* (New York: McGraw-Hill, 2012), http://www.jff.org/sites/default/files/publications/materials /Portable%20Stackable%20Credentials.pdf.

164. Peter Riley Bahr and Kathy Booth, "What Gets to Count?: Constructing a Skills Builder Success Metric," presentation delivered at semi-annual conference of the California Community College Association for Occupational Education, San Francisco, CA, Mar. 26, 2015.

165. Kathy Booth and Peter Riley Bahr, *The Missing Piece: Quantifying Non-Completion Pathways to Success* (Oakland, CA: LearningWorks, 2013), http://www.learningworksca .org/the-missing-piece/.

166. Kathy Booth, *The Ones that Got Away: Why Completing a College Degree Is Not the Only Way to Succeed* (Oakland, CA: LearningWorks, 2014), http://www.learningworksca .org/the-one-that-got-away-why-completing-a-college-degree-is-not-the-only-way-to -succeed/.

167. Bahr, *Labor Market Returns California.*

168. US Department of Labor, *Training and Employment Guidance Letter 15-10*, Attachment 2 (Washington, DC: US Department of Labor, 2010), http://wdr.doleta.gov/directives /attach/TEGL15-10.pdf, 6.

169. Evelyn Ganzglass, *Scaling "Stackable Credentials": Implications for Implementation and Policy* (Washington, DC: Center for Postsecondary and Economic Success, 2014), http://www.clasp.org/resources-and-publications/files/2014-03-21-Stackable-Credentials -Paper-FINAL.pdf, 4.

170. Ibid.

171. Bahr, "Deconstructive Approach"; Cohen, *Contemporary Issues.*

172. Bahr, "Classifying Community Colleges"; Vaughan, *The Community College Story.*

173. Articulation is the mechanism used to guarantee credit transfer between institutions of higher education.

174. AACC, "Fast Facts"; Choitz, *Community College Funding Strategies.*

175. Cohen, "US Community Colleges."

176. Choitz, *Community College Funding Strategies.*

177. Snyder and Dillow, *Digest of Education Statistics 2012*, table 401.

178. Dougherty and Bakia, "Contract Training"; Grubb et al., "Entrepreneurial Community College"; US General Accounting Office, *Public Community Colleges and Technical Schools: Most Schools Use Both Credit and Noncredit Programs for Workforce Development* (Washington, DC: General Accounting, Office, 2004), GAO-05-4.

179. Bahr, "Classifying Community Colleges," 434.

180. Snyder and Dillow, *Digest of Education Statistics 2012*, table 292.

181. Ibid.

182. Morest, "From Access to Opportunity"; Provasnik and Planty, *Community Colleges: Special Supplement.*

183. Snyder and Dillow, *Digest of Education Statistics 2012*, table 294.

184. Kathryn Quinn Thirolf, "Community College Faculty Identities," PhD diss., Ann Arbor, MI: University of Michigan, 2015.

185. Maureen Murphy Nutting, "Part-Time Faculty: Why Should We Care?" *New Directions for Higher Education*, no. 123 (2003): 33–39.

186. Kevin M. Eagan Jr. and Audrey J. Jaeger, "Effects of Exposure to Part-Time Faculty on Community College Transfer," *Research in Higher Education* 50, no. 2 (2009): 168–88; Daniel Jacoby, "Effects of Part-Time Faculty Employment on Community College Graduation Rates," *Journal of Higher Education* 77, no. 6 (2006): 1081–103; Paul D. Umbach, "How Effective Are They? Exploring the Impact of Contin-

gent Faculty on Undergraduate Education," *The Review of Higher Education* 30, no. 2 (2007): 91–123.

187. Chad Christensen, "The Employment of Part-Time Faculty at Community Colleges," *New Directions for Higher Education*, no. 143 (2008): 29–36.

188. Center for Community College Student Engagement, *Contingent Commitments: Bringing Part-Time Faculty Into Focus* (Austin: University of Texas at Austin, Program in Higher Education Leadership, 2014), http://www.ccsse.org/docs/PTF_Special_Report .pdf.

189. Adrianna J. Kezar and Cecile Sam. "Institutionalizing Equitable Policies and Practices for Contingent Faculty," *The Journal of Higher Education* 84, no. 1 (2013): 56–87; Thirolf, "Community College Faculty Identities."

190. Bailey and Averianova, *Multiple Missions*; Cohen, *Contemporary Issues.*

191. Mary Fulton, "Community Colleges Expanded Role into Awarding Bachelor's Degrees" (Denver: Education Commission of the States, 2015), 1–2.

192. Mary Fulton, "Community Colleges Expanded Role"; Lyle McKinney, Michael Scicchitano, and Tracy Johns, "A National Survey of Community College Baccalaureate Institutions," *Community College Journal of Research and Practice* 37, no. 1 (2013): 54–63.

193. John S. Levin, "The Community College as a Baccalaureate-Granting Institution," *Review of Higher Education* 28, no. 1 (2004): 1–22.

194. Deborah L. Floyd and Kenneth P. Walker, "The Community College Baccalaureate: Putting the Pieces Together," *Community College Journal of Research and Practice* 33, no. 2 (2008): 90–124; Lyle McKinney and Phillip A. Morris, "Examining an Evolution: A Case Study of Organizational Change accompanying the Community College Baccalaureate," *Community College Review* 37, no. 3 (2010): 187–208; McKinney, Scicchitano and Johns, "National Survey."

195. Debra D. Bragg and Collin M. Ruud, *The Adult Learner and the Applied Baccalaureate: Lessons from Six States* (Urbana-Champaign: Office of Community College Research and Leadership, 2011); Deborah L. Floyd, "Achieving the Baccalaureate Through the Community College," *New Directions for Community Colleges*, no. 135 (2006): 59–72; Levin, "Baccalaureate-Granting Institution."

196. W. Norton Grubb and E. Kraskouskas, *A Time to Every Purpose: Integrating Occupational and Academic Instruction in Community Colleges and Technical Institutes*, ED 350 405, Berkeley: National Center for Research in Vocational Education, University of California at Berkeley (1992).

197. Grubb and Lazerson, *The Education Gospel*; David F. Labaree, "Mutual Subversion: A Short History of the Liberal and the Professional in American Higher Education," *History of Education Quarterly* 46, no. 1 (2006): 1–15.

198. Bailey and Morest, *Organizational Efficiency*; Dougherty and Townsend, "Community College Missions."

199. Bailey and Morest, *Organizational Efficiency*; Morest, "Double Vision."

200. Bailey and Morest, *Organizational Efficiency*; Dougherty and Townsend, "Community College Missions."

201. David W. Breneman and Susan C. Nelson, *Financing Community Colleges: An Economic Perspective* (Washington, DC: Brookings Institution Press, 1981), viii.

202. Carnegie Commission on Higher Education, *The Open-Door Colleges.*

203. See, for example, Cohen and Brawer, *The American Community College;* Commission on the Future of Community Colleges, *Building Communities: A Vision for a New Century* (Washington, DC: American Association of Community and Junior Colleges, 1988); Dougherty, *The Contradictory College;* Judith S. Eaton, *Strengthening Collegiate Education in Community Colleges* (San Francisco: Jossey-Bass, 1994); Grubb, *Working in the Middle,* 50.

204. Beach, *Gateway to Opportunity,* xx.

205. Bailey and Averianova, *Multiple Missions;* Bailey and Morest, *Organizational Efficiency;* Morest, "Double Vision."

206. Morest, "Double Vision."

207. Bailey and Morest, *Organizational Efficiency,* 35.

208. Morest, "Double Vision."

209. Bailey and Morest, *Organizational Efficiency.*

210. See, for example, Cohen and Brawer, *The American Community College;* Grubb, *Working in the Middle.*

211. See, for example, Brint and Karabel, *The Diverted Dream;* Dougherty, *The Contradictory College.*

212. See, for example, Peter Riley Bahr, "Cooling Out in the Community College: What Is the Effect of Academic Advising on Students' Chances of Success?" *Research in Higher Education* 49, no. 8 (2008): 704–32; Clark, "Cooling Out"; Karl Alexander, Robert Bozick, and Doris Entwisle, "Warming Up, Cooling Out, or Holding Steady? Persistence and Change in Educational Expectations after High School," *Sociology of Education* 81, no. 4 (2008): 371–96.

213. Clyde E. Blocker, Robert H. Plummer, and Richard C. Richardson, *The Two-Year College: A Social Synthesis* (Prentice Hall, 1965); Clark, "Cooling Out"; Leland L. Medsker, *The Junior College: Progress and Prospect* (New York: McGraw-Hill, 1960).

214. Medsker, *The Junior College.*

215. Clark, "Cooling Out"; Blocker, Plummer, and Richardson, *The Two-Year College;* Erving Goffman, "Cooling the Mark Out: Some Aspects of Adaptation to Failure," *Psychiatry* 15 (1952), 451–63.

216. Pincus, "False Promises."

217. Bowles and Gintis, *Capitalist America;* Karabel, "Social Stratification"; Pincus, "False Promises"; Zwerling, *Second Best.*

218. Burton R. Clark, "The 'Cooling Out' Function Revisited," *New Directions for Community Colleges,* no. 32 (1980): 15–31.

219. Dougherty, *The Contradictory College.*

220. Brint and Karabel, *The Diverted Dream.*

221. Dougherty, *The Contradictory College.*

222. Ibid., 18.

223. Ibid., 23.

224. Ibid., 20.

225. Brint and Karabel, *The Diverted Dream.*

226. Dougherty, *The Contradictory College,* 8.

227. W. Norton Grubb, "Postsecondary Education and the Sub-Baccalaureate Labor Market: Corrections and Extensions," *Economics of Education Review* 14, no. 3 (1995):

285–99; Thomas J. Kane and Cecilia Elena Rouse, "Labor-Market Returns to Two- and Four-Year College," *The American Economic Review* (1995): 600–14; Duane E. Leigh and Andrew M. Gill, "Labor Market Returns to Community Colleges: Evidence for Returning Adults," *Journal of Human Resources* (1997): 334–53; Dave E. Marcotte, Thomas Bailey, Carey Borkoski, and Greg S. Kienzl, "The Returns of a Community College Education: Evidence from the National Education Longitudinal Survey," *Educational Evaluation and Policy Analysis* 27, no. 2 (2005): 157–75.

228. Bahr, *Labor Market Returns California*; Bahr et al., *Labor Market Returns Michigan*; Clive R. Belfield and Thomas Bailey, "The Benefits of Attending Community College: A Review of the Evidence," *Community College Review* 39, no. 1 (2011): 46–68; Mina Dadgar and Madeline Joy Trimble, "Labor Market Returns to Sub-Baccalaureate Credentials: How Much Does a Community College Degree or Certificate Pay?," *Educational Evaluation and Policy Analysis* (2014); Christopher Jepsen, Kenneth Troske, and Paul Coomes, "The Labor-Market Returns to Community College Degrees, Diplomas, and Certificates," *Journal of Labor Economics* 32, no. 1 (2014): 95–121; Vivian YT Liu, Clive R. Belfield, and Madeline J. Trimble, "The Medium-Term Labor Market Returns to Community College Awards: Evidence from North Carolina," *Economics of Education Review* 44 (2015): 42–55; A. Stevens, Michael Kurlaender, and M. Grosz, "Career Technical Education and Labor Market Outcomes: Evidence from California Community Colleges" (presentation, Annual Conference of the Association for Education Finance and Policy, San Antonio, TX, Mar. 14, 2014), http://www.aefpweb.org/conferences/39th; Di Xu and Madeline Joy Trimble. *What about Certificates? Evidence on the Labor Market Returns to Non-Degree Community College Awards in Two States. A CAPSEE Working Paper* (Center for Analysis of Postsecondary Education and Employment, Teachers College, Columbia University, 2014), http://capseecenter.org/labor-market-returns-non-degree-community-college-awards-two-states/.

229. Bahr, *Labor Market Returns California*.

230. See, for example, Mariana Alfonso, "The Impact of Community College Attendance on Baccalaureate Attainment," *Research in Higher Education* 47, no. 8 (2006): 873–903; Peter Riley Bahr, Christie Toth, Kathryn Thirolf, and Johanna C. Massé, "A Review and Critique of the Literature on Community College Students' Transition Processes and Outcomes in Four-Year Institutions," in *Higher Education: Handbook of Theory and Research*, ed. Michael B. Paulsen (Dordrecht, Netherlands: Springer, 2013), 459–511; Cecile C. Dietrich and Eric J. Lichtenberger, "Using Propensity Score Matching to Test the Community College Penalty Assumption," *Review of Higher Education* 38, no. 2 (2015): 193–219; Bridget Terry Long and Michal Kurlaender, "Do Community Colleges Provide a Viable Pathway to a Baccalaureate Degree?" *Educational Evaluation and Policy Analysis* 31, no. 1 (2009): 30–53; Tatiana Melguizo and Alicia C. Dowd, "Baccalaureate Success of Transfers and Rising 4-Year College Juniors," *Teachers College Record* 111, no. 1 (2009): 55–89; Tatiana Melguizo, Gregory S. Kienzl, and Mariana Alfonso, "Comparing the Educational Attainment of Community College Transfer Students and Four-Year College Rising Juniors Using Propensity Score Matching Methods," *Journal of Higher Education* 82, no. 3 (2011): 265–91; Jonathan Sandy, Arturo Gonzalez, and Michael J. Hilmer, "Alternative Paths to College Completion: Effect of Attending a 2-Year School on the Probability of Completing a 4-Year Degree," *Economics of Education Review* 25, no. 5

(2006): 463–71; C. Lockwood Reynolds and Stephen L. DesJardins, "The Use of Matching Methods in Higher Education Research: Answering Whether Attendance at a 2-Year Institution Results in Differences in Educational Attainment," in *Higher Education: Handbook of Theory and Research* vol. 24, ed. John C. Smart (Dordrecht, Netherlands: Springer, 2009), 47–97.

231. Bahr et al., "Transition Processes and Outcomes."
232. Bragg, "Community College Access," 110.

# Chapter Seventeen

# State and Markets in Higher Education

*Trends in Academic Capitalism*

## Sheila Slaughter and Gary Rhoades

A cademic capitalism is more than an economic pattern of revenue-seeking colleges and universities, it is a knowledge/learning regime embedded in a range of intersecting public policies and private practices. Political developments over the past two cycles of presidential campaigns and midterm elections have both heightened and modified patterns of *academic capitalism* in higher education, reflecting emergent contradictions in that *knowledge/learning regime*. With the Great Recession of 2008 came heightened concern about college affordability and student debt (and default), which has sharpened the political critique of higher education institutions. With the new federal administration in 2009 came a push to increase Pell grants and then to make the first two years of college free, as well as a systematic attack on various institutional practices in the for-profit sector of higher education. Yet even as federal policy has challenged some elements of academic capitalism in higher education, it has substantially advanced other policies that have deeply extended this knowledge/learning regime's framing of higher education as optimized by greater intersection with the private sector, as a private good.

At the organizational level, academic capitalism is characterized by the increasingly embedded market logic and market practices in colleges and universities.[1] On the administrative side, commercialism pervades growing numbers of offices and services, ranging from enrollment management offices in student personnel services that market institutions to student consumers, to fund development offices within student services that solicit external funds and creative products offices that manage faculty copyrights in intellectual property departments. Despite a recurrent discourse of austerity, the noninstructional, administrative share of institutional expenditures in higher education has continued to increase in a pattern like that which in the private economy has been termed a "revenge of the managers."

On the academic side, commercialization spreads across the curriculum from science and engineering, where discoveries are patented and marketed, to a variety of other fields that market courseware and other instructional materials. The last decade has seen increased cuts in the humanities and other fields perceived as distant from private sector markets, and an increased concentration of research activities in realms intersecting with the business sectors of university board members.[2] The entrepreneurial initiatives do not benefit all students or fields or segments of business and society equally, nor do they necessarily generate large amounts of external revenue for institutions, although they sometimes cause them to incur serious costs. Commercialization is instituted by many actors, internal and external to colleges and universities, who seek to take advantage of the new opportunities created by the neoliberal state.

Numerous federal and state initiatives provide a policy framework for what we call an academic capitalist knowledge-learning regime. Among these initiatives are competitiveness-coalition legislation such as the America COMPETES Act (2007), which provides new and generous funding to science, technology, engineering, and mathematics fields to enhance economic development, innovation, and the United States' ability to compete in the global economy.[3] More recently, the Obama administration has also undertaken initiatives, such as the Race to the Top for College Affordability and Completion, that emphasize an accountability regime aimed at increasing efficiency without increasing funding.

In this chapter, we focus on three broad federal initiatives: a federal student financial aid policy that gives money to students rather than institutions (student as consumer); patent law and policies that marketize segments of the sciences and engineering; and copyright law and policies, along with information technology law and policies, that provide opportunities for colleges and universities to market curricula. We also pay particular attention to the realm of federal policy making in relation to for-profit higher education, which changed substantially with the administration of President Obama. The period in which the academic capitalist knowledge-learning regime developed is approximately from 1980 to 2000. It continues to accelerate in the twenty-first century, though in distinctive and sometimes contradictory directions in the last decade.

Within sections, we first describe the federal policy sets that we see as supporting academic capitalism, and then examine the way institutions intersect these initiatives. The presentation of laws and policies is followed by selected examples that illustrate the academic capitalist knowledge-learning regime. We conclude each section by looking at various data sets that allow us to use financial indicators (tuition, income from patents, income from distance education) to track changes. On the whole, we see the academic capitalism knowledge-learning regime as intensifying in the 2000s, even as we note some challenges to this regime in the last decade.

Although we begin with the federal government, we do not see the federal government as the sole policy driver for the academic capitalist knowledge-learning regime. Federal and state laws and policies, as well as institutional rules and policies, interact in complex ways to produce knowledge-learning regimes.[4] States have an array of initiatives that promote economic development. Many of these initiatives, ranging from preparing students for the workforce to fostering industries that contribute to the states' economic base, feature the participation of colleges and universities.[5] Indeed, several states frequently devise innovative solutions to pressing national problems before the federal government does (although they often also develop policies to tap into monies that are incentivized to states).[6] Moreover, colleges and universities are not simply acted upon, or *corporatized*. Actors within colleges and universities participate in creating new knowledge-learning regimes by networking and partnering with an array of external actors. Segments of the administration and the faculty work to shape the political/legal climate that fosters an academic capitalist knowledge-learning regime, and segments of the faculty and administration actively and ardently engage in commercialization. They are reinforced by judicial decisions, administrative law, executive orders, bureaucratic procedures, and institutional policies at both the state and federal levels.

Because this chapter focuses on policy, we want to clarify the theory of the state that informs our work. We see the academic capitalist knowledge-learning regime and the three policy sets on which we focus as tied to the rise of the *neoliberal state*.[7] The neoliberal state focuses not on social welfare for the citizenry as a whole, but on enabling individuals and corporations (which, in the United States, are legally considered as individual persons who are economic actors). The neoliberal state concentrates its funding in state agencies that contribute to economic growth and in leveraging states to foster economic development—for example, research funding for corporations and academic fields that produce exploitable intellectual property. It similarly seeks to incentivize such an orientation to economic development among public institutions, such as colleges and universities. The neoliberal state works to build the "new" economy, which is a knowledge, or information, economy. The neoliberal state attempts to articulate national economies with global economies. To provide funds to reshape the economy, the neoliberal state often institutes processes of deregulation, commercialization, and austerity in relation to the public sector even as it promotes privatization, reregulating in order to create a state that no longer provides "entitlements" such as welfare. Instead, the neoliberal state often restructures and reduces general services such as health care, social security and education in an austerity and accountability agenda. The benefits of the neoliberal state tend be distributed somewhat differently from those of the welfare state. They do not accrue to the citizenry as a whole; instead, they are acquired unevenly by various groups, often by the upper middle class closely associated with the growth of the new economy, and by the rich. Because higher education is simultaneously a welfare function of the state and a contributor to economic growth, the policy process often plays out in ironic, contradictory, and perhaps unintended ways, which we describe below.

### Student Financial Aid

Despite the rhetoric of student as consumer, which implies that all students are able to make informed choices among the many US institutions of higher education, federal student financial aid legislation segments the student markets in higher education, directing different types of aid to very different kinds of students. Some programs and appropriation patterns encourage upper-middle-class as well as knowledgeable, able students from other social strata to attend costly elite, (increasingly) private institutions.[8] Other programs and appropriation patterns encourage large numbers of adult learners to upgrade their education to master skills appropriate to the new economy through two-year and four-year programs, sometimes with substantial distance-education components, and increasingly through for-profit higher education institutions.

The two terms of the Obama administration have seen a continuation of the these patterns in some regards and yet some dramatic examples of counter-directional policies that have re-emphasized the importance of grants versus loans, that have featured college affordability and student debt as problems that have to be solved, and that have involved challenging the legitimacy and legality of financial aid and marketing practices of some major players in for-profit higher education. As shall be discussed, each of the latter three trends undermines the neoliberal approach to education that defines college as a private good, the costs (and risks) of which should be borne by the individual.

In the early 1970s, federal legislation shifted from institutional to student aid, making students consumers.[9] The Committee on Economic Development, together with a number of foundations, particularly the Carnegie Foundation for the Advancement of Teaching, worked assiduously for the *marketization* of higher education. The mechanism of marketization was federal financial aid placed in the hands of students. When students were able to spend their grants at the institution of their choice, proponents of what was perhaps the first educational voucher program argued that they were introducing market discipline to institutions of higher education, forcing colleges and universities to provide better services at lower costs to attract students. The Committee on Economic Development and Carnegie also pushed strongly for all postsecondary students, whether enrolled in public or private institutions, to pay for one-third to one-half of the costs of their education, a not unrealistic expectation in what was then a low-tuition era.[10]

Student choice in this context preferred the private colleges and universities, because the (public) grants for students attending private nonprofit schools were larger than those for students attending public institutions. In other words, students received a greater amount of government assistance to attend more costly private institutions, while students who attended public institutions had to pay more out of their own pockets as the cost of tuition gradually rose to one-third to one-half of the total cost of an education. The market model of higher education encouraged competition, but it did not reduce costs, a phenomenon that was in keeping with the philosophy of the neoliberal state, which sought to reduce programs for all citizens and shift costs to users. Of course, increasing tuition so that students bore a greater share of the cost of public higher education reduced the cost to the state, always an interest of taxpaying businesses. By the 1980s and 1990s, higher education was construed less as a necessary public or social good and more as an individual or private good, justifying "user pays" policies.[11]

Federal policy supported quasi-market competition for students among institutions of higher education, on the grounds of greater efficiencies that would lead to cost reductions. Ironically, as the market model became entrenched, costs escalated.[12] Although costs went up in all market segments, niche markets developed in which a relatively small number of (largely upper- and upper-middle-class) students competed nationally for ever-more-expensive places at a relatively small number of (elite and increasingly private) institutions. Federal loan programs enabled middle- and upper-middle-class students, especially those attending high-cost elite private institutions, to meet higher tuition costs. In effect, federal loans subsidized markets for students by providing some students with the funds to choose high-tuition institutions.[13]

As the shift from grants to loans benefited those families and students with the ability to repay the loans, so some programs in the Taxpayer Relief Act of 1997 benefited families with money to protect. The Taxpayer Relief Act included several programs: Hope scholarships, penalty-free individual retirement account (IRA) withdrawals for college expenses, tax-sheltered college savings accounts, and a tax credit for lifelong learning. Hope scholarships provided a $1,500 non-refundable tax credit for the first two years of college, which phased out for individuals earning $40,000–$50,000 per year or couples earning $80,000–$100,000 per year. Penalty-free IRA withdrawals would not count as gross income, so long as they paid for college expenses. Additionally, families could shelter up to $500 per year for each child in the same way as contributions to an IRA; these savings would be taxed as an IRA, so long as the funds were spent on college expenses. This program was capped for families earning $150,000–$160,000 per year. The subsidies provided by tax credits are not trivial. "The package of tax credits and tax deductions has been estimated to cost $39 billion in the first five years [of the Taxpayer Relief Act], making it slightly larger than the Pell Grant program, the primary federal grant program for low-income youth."[14] The increased ability of these well-to-do or market-knowledgeable and academically able students to pay for their postsecondary education makes them preferred customers for elite institutions.

Although the 1997 Taxpayer Relief Act applied primarily to nonprofit institutions of higher education, whether public or private, some programs within the act benefited working adults seeking further education to better compete in the new economy. The tax credit for lifelong learning offered a nonrefundable tax credit for undergraduate and graduate education that was worth up to 29 percent of up to $5,000 per year spent on tuition and fees through 2002, and 20 percent of up to $10,000 per year after that, with the same income caps as the Hope scholarships. The tax credit for lifelong learning expanded markets for for-profits, such as the University of Phoenix, which for a number of years required its attending students to have jobs. The tax credit also created opportunities for increasing numbers of public institutions, such as the University of Maryland

University College, that emulated for-profits by serving working adults retooling for the new economy. As all students paid a greater share of the cost of their tuition and fees, the costs to working adults who returned to school to improve their position in the new economy were normalized, even though those students paid a greater share of their income for tuition than did well-to-do, traditional-age students.[15]

The 1998 Higher Education Act further contributed to marketization, through new provisions that encouraged profit taking in higher education by creating a number of special provisions to aid for-profit postsecondary education. The law made it easier for for-profit higher education to appeal federal penalties stemming from their students' defaults on loans. Given that for-profits have an excessively high default rate, this was an important provision. Additionally, the law no longer required unannounced accreditation visits, allowing for-profit postsecondary educational institutions to prepare for inspections, making sure students were in class. Most importantly, the law no longer treated for-profits as a separate category; they were redefined as institutions of higher education. This allowed for-profits to share in federal aid. Their students were twice as likely to receive federal aid as students at nonprofits, and at the two-year level, their students received more federal aid than comparable students in public institutions. The 1998 Higher Education Act further signaled federal governmental support for for-profits by creating a special liaison within the US Department of Education for proprietary schools, a privilege previously held only by historically black tertiary educational institutions and community colleges.[16]

Changes in student aid legislation over the past thirty years contributed to the academic capitalist knowledge-learning regime by marketizing higher education. The legislation made students (partially) state-subsidized consumers in quasi markets for higher education.[17] According to the rhetoric surrounding marketization, markets empowered students by making them consumers, allowing them to use their grant or loan to discipline markets to better serve them. However, markets in higher education seem to work like all other markets. Far from being perfectly competitive, offering goods and services at the lowest price to any buyer, (deregulated and reregulated) markets tend to favor the middle and upper middle class.[18] Just as housing markets prefer middle-class customers with high credit ratings who are unlikely to be loan risks, and then indirectly subsidize them through mortgage tax deductions, so markets in higher education prefer students (and families) who are confident they can repay loans and are indirectly subsidized through parental tax relief and the higher grant or loan aid attached to private institutions. Ironically, market legislation, which defined higher education as a private benefit captured by individuals, prefers the middle and upper middle classes.

Student aid legislation also contributed to market segmentation. While middle- and upper-middle-class students became preferred customers, lower-middle-class students and working adults entered two-year colleges, four-year college programs with substantial distance-education components, and for-profit institutions of higher education. Given that many do not complete a degree at two-year colleges, they receive just-in-time education that channels them, with only a modicum of skills, into entry-level jobs in the new economy. Working adults in four-year programs often receive college degrees for what amounts to retraining or professional development, allowing them to upgrade their skills to better serve the needs of the new-economy corporations where they are already employed. Although these students do not receive dramatic returns on their investment in human capital, they are often satisfied with their education, because they do better than if they had not acquired some college education or a degree.

Since the early 1980s, the cost of college has risen steadily. In constant (1996) dollars, the average tuition at US four-year public institutions increased by nearly 128 percent between 1980 and 2002. Private four-year institutions' tuitions increased more rapidly, over 130 percent in constant dollars over this twenty-two-year period.[19] In 2002, tuition and fees at four-year private institutions averaged $18,273 and room and board averaged $6,779; when tuition and fees and room and board are combined, the average cost of attending a private college or university was $25,052. For a four-year public college or university, the average 2002 costs were $4,081 for tuition and fees and $5,327 for room and board; combined, the average cost was $9,408.[20] According to the College Board, by 2009–10, before discounts based on individual student characteristics, the average costs for tuition, room, board, and books were as follows: for public universities, $19,388, up 5.8 percent from the previous year; and for private universities, $39,028, up 4.4 percent from the previous year.[21] Although tuition at community colleges is much lower, with an average published cost of $2,544 in 2009–10, federal student financial aid is often difficult for students to secure.[22] Nearly one in ten community college students is unable to apply for student federal financial aid, because their schools do not participate in the program. This forces many community college students—who are more likely to be first generation, non-white, and women—to drop out, take fewer classes, work more hours for pay, or turn to more expensive private loans.[23]

As the costs of higher education increased, federal financial aid in the form of grants lagged behind, and the share of family income required to pay for college tuition increased for most families. The percentage of family income, after financial aid, needed to pay for public four-year schools has risen in all but two states since 2000. In 2008, "on average, students from working and poor families must pay 40 percent of family income to enroll in public four-year colleges. Students from middle-income families and upper-income families must pay 25 percent and 13 percent of family income, respectively, to enroll in public four-year colleges."[24] However, federal grants to pay students' tuition have decreased since the early 1980s, while loans have increased. In 1981, loans accounted for 45 percent of student federal financial aid, and grants for 52 percent. In 2000, loans represented 58 percent of federal student financial aid, and grants 41 percent.[25] This change, which accelerated dramatically in the 1990s, shifted costs from the state to the student. At the same time, student debt rose rapidly. The "average debt levels for graduating seniors with student loans rose to $23,200 in 2008—a 24 percent increase from $18,650 in 2004." For public universities, the average debt was $20,200, 20 percent higher than in 2004. At private nonprofit universities, it was $27,650, 29 percent higher than in 2004. For graduating seniors with Pell grants, 87 percent had student loans, with an average debt load of $24,800—almost $2,000 more than the average for all seniors graduating with loans.[26]

Market practices are increasingly incorporated into the recruitment of students at four-year nonprofit institutions. It is not just highly able students that colleges and universities are targeting, but well-to-do students whose parents can afford to pay full tuition with no financial aid. As Michael McPherson and Morton Shapiro put it with regard to private colleges and universities, "the simplest way to describe the change over the past decade in the way private colleges and universities approach student aid is to say that, rather than viewing student aid as a kind of charitable operation the college runs on the side, most private colleges and universities—and increasing numbers of public institutions—now regard student aid as a vital revenue management and enrollment management tool."[27]

As one commentator has suggested, "in some ways, American colleges and universities have become like airlines and hotels, practicing 'yield management' to try to maximize the revenue generated by every seat or bed. But in most cases, unlike hotels and airlines, colleges also care about who is in those seats and beds."[28] To that end, institutions develop early-decision admissions policies, no-test admission policies, and on-site admissions policies, all of which are aimed at increasing their *yield rates*, or the ratio of students who apply to those that accept. The higher the ratio, the higher the institution's rating in publications such as *US News and World Report*, and, hence, the higher the market value of the institution.

Early-decision admissions processes are employed by highly selective private colleges and universities. Students commit to enrolling in an institution if they are accepted, in return for which they are notified earlier than those who apply to the regular process. Such a practice increases the institution's yield rate, ensuring an almost one-to-one ratio of admitted students to those who will enroll. That enables the institution to increase its yield, and thereby enhance its market position. Yet early-decision programs may not serve the interests of prospective students, or of society. In forcing earlier and earlier decisions that may not be freely informed by a range of options, these programs represent a case of inherent market inefficiency, what Alvin Roth and Xiaolin Xing have referred to as "unraveling."[29] Such a system may tend to disadvantage students who have less access to good counseling and less knowledge of the admissions process, characteristics that disproportionately describe students from lower socioeconomic backgrounds. Indeed, these programs tend to undermine efforts to enhance the demographic diversity of entering classes, a fact that led the University of North Carolina, Chapel Hill, to eliminate its program, and Richard Levin, president of Yale, to call for the collective abandonment of such programs among selective institutions. This call, issued in 2001, has gone unheeded at Yale, though Harvard and Princeton dropped their early admissions programs in 2006.[30]

A second example of institutions seeking to manipulate their selectivity scores in ways that do not serve consumer interests is the practice of making SAT scores optional for applicants at several selective colleges. The strategy's effectiveness has been documented by Marcia Yablon in an article entitled "Test Flight: The Scam behind SAT Bashing."[31] The aim is to enhance a school's acceptance rate and average SAT score by not requiring these scores for admission. Less-qualified students are encouraged to apply, but only high-scoring students are likely to submit their test scores to these institutions, raising the overall selectivity profile of the institution.

"Snap apps" are another marketing tool of enrollment management offices seeking to achieve high yields, in which on-site admissions are an in-person, instant-admissions-decision program, often made during a prospective student's campus visit. In contrast to the early-decision process, these decisions are not binding; the student may later choose not to attend the institution. Advocates of the process see it as "a service to students and a savvy marketing tool."[32] Instant admissions benefit students, reducing the paperwork, time, and anxiety of the admissions process, as well as humanizing it. However, this type of admissions program is more typically found at less-selective institutions (for example, at the California State University System versus the University of California System, at Virginia Tech and Radford University versus the University of Virginia, and at many community colleges). By employing this process, such institutions are more likely to gain access to higher-achieving students, who are more likely to apply for instant admissions. Therein lies part of the problem, say critics of snap apps. Accelerated admissions encourage students to make decisions on the spur of the moment. Making the choice easier and more immediate for prospective students in some sense restricts their choice (though not in a legal sense), as it reduces their likelihood of shopping for colleges and exploring options that might prove to be a better fit. On-site admissions can be seen as a hard-sell approach to recruiting students, leading students to make their decisions during their campus visit, rather than encouraging them to reflect on and deliberate about their options over time.

Although the majority of for-profits do not compete directly with two- and four-year nonprofit institutions of higher education for the "market" in students, the rapid increase in for-profit higher education is a marker of the commercialization of higher education, and in the last decade has gained market share relative to four-year not-for-profit higher education. At the same time that nonprofit higher education institutions raised their tuition, targeting student niche markets, for-profit institutions multiplied, the number of students enrolled in them rose, and their costs went up. Between 1989 and 1999, enrollment in for-profit, degree-granting institutions increased 59 percent, totaling about 365,000 students.[33] For 2009–10, the cost of private universities rose to $39,028, and for-profit colleges saw the largest recent increase in the proportion of their students graduating with debt. In 2008, the average student debt at for-profit universities was $33,050, 23 percent higher than 2004, and substantially higher than the debt load at public and private nonprofit universities.[34] For-profit schools also have the highest federal student loan default rate. For the cohort who entered repayment in 2007, 400,000 had defaulted by 2009, representing 12 percent of all students who had entered repayment in that year. Nearly half of these borrowers (44%) attended for-profits, even though only one in fourteen students (7%) overall attends such schools.[35]

The federal student aid legislation was the first federal legislation to explicitly use market discourse. In some ways the market rhetoric was a trope for partial privatization, in that the neoliberal state effectively moved to a high tuition–low aid policy.[36] In other ways, the market rhetoric masked the continued and rising contribution by the state. Although federal financial aid has shifted from grants to loans, the amount of grant money available (although not the amount of the grant per individual) has risen every year, and many loans are publicly subsidized. At the state level, support for higher education increased 13 percent (in constant dollars) from 1980 to 1998, but tuition increased far faster. In other words, at one and the same time, the student markets for nonprofits and for-profits are heavily subsidized at both the state and federal levels, and the proportional shares of higher education costs have completely shifted from the state to the individual consumer.

Up until the administration of President Obama, then, federal and state student financial aid policy thus followed in a bipartisan and largely unquestioned path the general direction of neoliberal policy, moving away from treating public benefits as social goods for the citizenry as a whole and toward requiring the user to pay more. Public funds were shifted toward production functions by making aid available for working adults re-educating themselves for knowledge-economy jobs. That well-to-do users paid (relatively) less than other users also reflected trends characteristic of the new economy and the neoliberal state.

Yet the pace of change in that direction changed substantially in 2009, and in some regards even began a reversal of sorts. Most basically, the idea of higher education as a public good has been re-advanced, though in a neoliberal, competitive discourse that itself advances an academic capitalist view of higher education's project, as being fundamentally not just an economic one, but one of global corporate competitiveness. Nevertheless, within the first few years of the new administration, several national entities (including prominent foundations in higher education public policy such as the Lumina Foundation) had adopted a goal of substantially increasing the proportion of Americans with a college education. The goal was reduced and in significant regards watered down to include completion of some college, and to count short-cycle, vocational education and workforce development coursework in that goal. Still, the national charge was to dramatically increase college access and attainment to 60 percent of Americans, in order to put the country back at the top of the global hierarchy and realize dominance in the new economy. And it was a charge that was opposed by many policy makers on the other side of the aisle, who saw no value in college for all (equating 60% with all), and instead supported a more substantial segmentation of college opportunity for students.

The depth of the challenge is evident in the extent of the growth of support for Pell grants during the Obama administration. The maximum award has increased by over one-quarter, and the number of recipients has doubled. Perhaps most remarkable from a neoliberal perspective, banks were cut out of the process, by an administration that had bailed out Wall Street after the 2008 collapse. But the administration was not able or willing to expand support for Pell grants to the extent it initially desired, when it created the so-called Summer Pell, and then subsequently withdrew that option. Budget austerity trumped investment in students' college education. And opposition to the growth, as to the 60 percent goal, revealed that a once largely bipartisan academic capitalism policy regime of privatization was being renegotiated.

At the same time, consistent with past neoliberal policy trends, the administration has expanded education tax credits, and it has done so for students whose annual family household income is up to $180,000, thereby benefiting the already advantaged. And while the administration has established a "pay as you earn" plan to make repayment of student debt easier, and it worked to prevent an increase in the percentage rate on student loans, it has not supported proposals to enable students to renegotiate their debt (as basically all other lenders can do) and to make student debt less onerous in terms of the consequences of default.

A second divergence, though, from the neoliberal pattern of previous decades is that college affordability and student debt in particular have become defined as problems to be solved, not conditions to be created, subsidized, and monetized for the extraction of private wealth. The condition of essentially having an educational mortgage has been challenged as unacceptable and unsustainable. Again in a nod to the idea of college being a public good, the administration has advanced a college cost and affordability initiative. Indeed, during his second term President Obama has translated a focus on college affordability into a push for free community college, at least for the first two years. Again, the Republican response points to a break in the bipartisan pattern of previous decades.

Yet again, however, there is considerable neoliberal continuity amid the challenge. In fact, in some regards the academic capitalist push arguably trumps the initiative's challenges to the regime. At the core of the race to the top for college affordability and completion is a neoliberal accountability leveraging of states and institutions to a level not seen in higher education previously, and one experienced thus far only at the K–12 education level. Moreover, the accountability push is not matched by a push for new investment—indeed, the measures of the administration consistently increase accountability pressures with an ongoing austerity agenda, measures that are prototypically neoliberal state strategies. Further, although there is a call for free community college, there is no leverage or funding for it, and the model privileges the most advantaged students, those who can go full-time. And finally, perhaps most emblematically of the academic capitalist policy regime, the administration is promoting free college in a sector that it has been systematically defined in terms of short-cycle workforce development, not just underplaying but undermining its role as a collective and individual path of social mobility and increased social equity.

A third policy divergence from the bipartisan, neoliberal pattern of the past has been in the federal administration's stance toward for-profit higher education. As noted above, for-profit higher education is really for-subsidy higher education. It has succeeded in cornering a very large, indeed disproportionate share of the financial aid market, to the point that these entities are almost entirely dependent on federal subsidy.

Although the Obama administration has not challenged the legitimacy of such subsidy, even in a time of austerity, it has aggressively pursued two agendas that have had a significantly adverse effect on major players in proprietary higher education. One is a formal policy agenda to ensure accountability and consumer protection in the realm of proprietary higher education. A second is the pursuit of lawsuits against major for-profit higher education corporations. The former agenda in some sense fell well short of its initial aims to require institutions to demonstrate that graduates obtain "gainful employment" at wages/salaries sufficient to repay their student loans. But the consistent promotion of this agenda, and the use of the bully pulpit to question the extent to which in many cases for-profit colleges and universities were delivering on their promise of good employment have had significant effects on student demand for proprietary higher education. And the prosecution of major proprietary players in the market for various sorts of fraud has similarly impacted the entire sector's public image. Neither of these initiatives fall within what could be considered a neoliberal agenda, for both represent a sustained assault on private providers, if not on the entire concept of for-profit higher education.

### Patents

Before the 1980 Bayh-Dole Act, federal policy placed discoveries made with federal grant funds in the public domain. Universities were able to secure patents on federally funded research only when the federal government, through a long and cumbersome application process, granted special approval. Few universities engaged in patenting before 1980.[37] The Bayh-Dole Act directly signaled the inclusion of universities in profit taking. It allowed universities and small businesses to retain title to inventions made with federal R&D monies. In the words of the act, "it is the policy and objective of the Congress . . . to promote collaboration between commercial concerns and nonprofit organizations, including universities."[38] Bayh-Dole "explicitly recognized technology transfer to the private sector as a desirable outcome of federally financed research, and endorsed the principle that exclusive licensing of publicly funded technology was sometimes necessary to achieve that objective."[39]

Bayh-Dole shifted the relationship between university managers and faculty in several important ways. As potential patent holders, university trustees and administrators could see all research generated by faculty as relatively easily protected intellectual property. Faculty, too, could better conceptualize their discoveries as products or processes—private, valuable, and licensable—not necessarily as knowledge to share publicly with a community of scholars.[40] The Bayh-Dole Act gave new and concrete meaning to the phrase "commodification of knowledge." The act streamlined universities' participation in the marketplace.

Bayh-Dole was presented as a support for small businesses, which the Reagan administration had deemed as engines of economic growth. In 1983, however, Reagan extended Bayh-Dole's coverage to large corporations through executive order. After 1983, any entity performing federal research and development (R&D) could patent and own discoveries made in the course of research, a shift that contributed to the privatization and commercialization of research across all categories of performers, including large corporations.

The Federal Courts Improvements Act of 1982 created a new Court of Appeals for the Federal Circuit (CAFC), which handled patent appeals from district courts, thereby ending "forum shopping" in intellectual property cases, creating a more uniform approach to patents. The new court led the way for a greatly strengthened approach to intellectual property. "Before 1980, a district court finding that a patent was valid and infringed was upheld on appeal 62% of the time; between 1982 and 1990 this percentage rose to 90%."[41] The CAFC led the patent office to offer broader protections through patents. "There are now patents for genetically engineered bacteria, genetically altered mice, particular gene sequences, surgical methods, computer software, financial products, and methods for conducting auctions on the web. For each of these, there would have been before 1980 at least serious doubt as to whether or not they would be deemed by the PTO [US

Patent and Trademark Office] and the courts to fall within the realm of patentable subject matter."[42]

University administrators and faculty members were well aware that strengthened intellectual property protection made patentable knowledge more valuable. The Small Business Innovation Development Act of 1982 mandated that federal agencies with annual expenditures of more than $100 million devote 1.25 percent of their budgets to research performed by small businesses, on the grounds that they were crucial to economic recovery. Universities strongly opposed this legislation, making the case that it diverted the mission agencies from funding university research.[43] Ironically, as universities became more deeply involved in academic capitalism, they increasingly took equity positions in small enterprises started by their faculty, often with funding provided by the Small Business Innovation Development Act.[44]

Equity deals did not occur frequently among research universities until the 1980s. The number of equity deals spread among research universities, slowly at first, and then, starting in the 1990s, quite rapidly. Taking equity positions rather than licensing intellectual property and receiving royalties became a market strategy for research universities. According to Feldman, Feller, Bercovitz, and Burton, equity provides three advantages over licensing: first, equity gives universities options or financial claims on companies' future income; second, equity deals align the interests of the university and the firm with regard to the rapid commercialization of technology; and third, equity signals interested investors about the worth of the technology.[45] These scholars attribute the rapid growth of universities taking equity positions to organizational learning through technology transfer offices.

In 2002, Feldman, Feller, Bercovitz, and Burton surveyed sixty-seven Carnegie I and II research universities that had active technology transfer operations. Of these institutions, 76 percent had taken equity in a company; altogether, they had participated in 679 equity deals. Public universities took more equity in companies than private universities, even though thirteen of the public universities (19% of the total sample) were prohibited by state laws from holding equity in companies. Ten of these public universities were able to circumvent state statutes by forming independent entities, or 501(c)(3)s—usually research foundations or other intermediary institutions—that were able to take equity in corporations based on faculty intellectual property. Although the study does not deal with which set of universities, public or private, initiated the first equity deals, this market strategy spread rapidly between both sets of universities, and even more rapidly among the publics than the privates, despite the barriers to public institutions taking equity. Both sets of institutions adopted similar strategies, geared to increasing their external revenue streams.

During the 1980s, as universities' intellectual property activity and potential grew, state systems and universities and colleges initiated or began to develop and change their patent property policies. They moved from minimal policies to more expansive ones, some of which dramatically changed the way intellectual property is handled. The following data, which illustrates current practices, is drawn from a study of eighteen colleges and universities, both public and private, in six states, and it addresses royalty splits, categories of persons covered by policies, exceptions to the policies, and conflicts of interest.[46]

The above pattern of academic capitalism has continued through the first fifteen years of the twenty-first century. In some regards, it has even heightened in its intensity and concentration. As recent research has shown, particularly in private research universities, there has been both a greater concentration of corporate capital's representation on boards of trustees, and a corresponding channeling of research and technology activity into realm reflecting that pattern of board representation.[47] More than that, following a neoliberal pattern of privileging the private (in this case, not-for-profit) providers, there is a growing divergence between the levels of access to corporate capital that public and private universities have, to the detriment of the former in the competitive research and faculty marketplaces.

## ROYALTIES

The various patent policies offered a wide range of royalty splits among faculty, department or college, and university. All were sufficient to provide strong incentives to patent. The greatest incentives were for the faculty, who were able to put the income in their bank accounts, as compared with all others, who had to use the revenue stream generated by patents for institutional purposes. The policies that were most generous to faculty split royalties fifty-fifty with faculty. At the bottom of the range of royalty splits, faculty received one-third of the royalty income. Private universities tended to be less generous than public ones, with many offering faculty one-third of the income from their licenses. When policies were changed over time, they usually gave faculty a lower percentage of royalties.

## PERSONNEL COVERAGE

Categories of persons covered by patent policies were elaborated on by many state system or college and university policies over the years. In the 1970s and 1980s, a number of patent policies covered only "inventors." By the mid-1990s, they included faculty, staff, graduate students, postdoctoral fellows, nonemployees who participate in university research projects, visiting faculty and, in a very few policies, undergraduates.

## EXCEPTIONS

Universities had long claimed ownership of discoveries made by faculty; the decisive court cases were heard in the 1950s. Initially, however, there were exceptions to universities' ownership claims to intellectual property patented by faculty. If faculty made the discoveries on their own time, using their own resources, and not availing themselves of university facilities, they could claim a patent for themselves—for example, if they invented something in the summer, in their garage workroom. As the academic capitalist knowledge-learning regime developed, definitions of time, resources, and facilities used were specified to the point where it was very difficult for faculty to assert any claims. For example, several policies had guidelines that indicated that if researchers depended on anything other than routinely available office equipment and commercially available software, or library materials generally available in nonuniversity locations, they were making substantial use of university resources.

Initially, state system and institutional policies addressed only patents. Over the years, the forms of intellectual property that were covered multiplied. Among those included were licensing income, milestone payments, equity interest, mask work (which charted the topography of a semiconductor chip product), material transfer agreements, tangible property (cell lines, software, compositions of matter), and trade secrets.

## MANAGERIAL CAPACITY

System and institutional patent policies delineated academic capitalism practices that greatly expanded market managerial capacity in colleges and universities. The new functions were many: surveying institutional employees' intellectual property activity to ensure capture by the system or institution; reviewing and evaluating faculty disclosures; licensing technology; supervising royalty flows, including the distribution of funds within institutions; reinvesting funds in new market activities; litigating to defend intellectual property; evaluating intellectual property for institutional equity investments; monitoring and occasionally administering corporations in which the institution held equity; overseeing initial public offerings (IPOs); and developing and monitoring market activity for conflict-of-interest issues. As colleges and universities become more involved in academic capitalism, they hired more managerial professional staff. Expanded managerial capacity institutionalized business activity in colleges and universities by allowing segments of institutions to directly engage the market.

The multiple forms of market activity pursued by universities, together with the faculty's close involvement in them, created many opportunities for conflicts of interest. Factors that expanded the possibilities of conflicts of interest for faculty were increased magnitude of personal compensation; growing numbers of financial relationships between a creator and a company; greater commitment of a faculty member's time to a company; faculty or administrators holding equity in a company; the involvement of trainees or students in a company; and the involvement of patients or human subjects in company research trials. In other words, the risk of conflicts of interest increased the more closely faculty members or creators participated in market activity, yet intellectual property policies continue to aggressively promote this close involvement.

A dramatic example of university patenting and licensing is provided by Onco-Mouse, a genetically engineered animal that reliably reproduces characteristics of various human cancers. It was created in Harvard Medical School laboratories in the early 1980s through the manipulation of cancer-causing genes. Onco-Mouse was patented by Harvard and licensed by DuPont for sale as a research tool. The patent was contested by a number of groups opposed to the patenting of living organisms, but it was upheld by the Canadian Supreme Court.[48]

The mouse research tool quickly became the standard in global cancer research that focused on the ways in which cancers develop and that tested new treatments for breast, prostate, and other forms of cancer. The cost of the mouse created access problems for some researchers. In 2001, DuPont, Harvard, and the National Institutes of Health signed an agreement that made the mouse more readily available to university researchers. However, DuPont will not allow the mouse research tool to breed, nor to be used in industry-supported research. Many groups, for example breast-cancer activists, think these restraints retard the development of a broad understanding of cancers and treatments for them. They argue that the mouse tool was developed in large part with public research funds and should not be privately owned. Rather, it should be freely available to all researchers.[49]

Although patents are concentrated in biology and engineering fields, they are increasingly being granted in other areas. For example, Carnegie Mellon University developed a series of Cognitive Tutor products that were licensed to Carnegie Learning, a company which spun out of the university in 1998. This instructional math software is based on artificial intelligence, integrating technology and print curricula into realistic problem situations. The company has claimed that minority and nonminority students using the program perform at a much higher level in classes, as well as improve their SAT scores.[50] However, Math Curriculum Kits—which cover Bridge to Algebra, Algebra I, Geometry, Algebra II, and Integrated Math for home users—cost $99 each, prices sufficient to deter many users.[51]

Before 1981, fewer than 250 patents per year were issued to universities. Between fiscal year (FY) 1991 and FY 1999, annual college and university invention disclosures increased by 63 percent (to 12,324); new patents filed grew by 77 percent (to 5,545); and new licenses and options executed by universities increased by 129 percent (to 3,914).[52] Since 1980, at least 3,807 new companies have been formed that were based on a license from an academic institution, including the 494 established in FY 2001. Colleges and universities received an equity interest in 70 percent of their startups in FY 2001, compared with 56 percent in FY 2000. At the end of 2001, 159 institutions reported that 2,514 startups were still operating. When similar statistics are reviewed in the National Science Foundation's *Science and Engineering Indicators 2010*, invention disclosures grew from 13,700 in 2003 to 17,700 in 2007. Patent applications increased from 7,200 in 2003 to 10,900 in 2007. Startup companies based on university inventions rose from 348 in 2003 to 510 in 2007. By 2009, there were 3,148 cumulative operating startups associated with US university patenting and licensing activities.[53]

While technology transfer brings external revenue to colleges and universities, it also takes funds from them. In FY 2001, colleges' and universities' adjusted gross license income was $1.071 billion, and running royalties on product sales were $845 million.[54] However, the median net royalty per university has only climbed from $440,000 in 1996 to $950,000 in 2005. In 2007, 161 universities received $1.9 billion from net royalties. In other words, there are winners and losers. Most royalties accrue to a few patents and the universities that hold them. In 2007, many university technology transfer offices reported negative incomes. Colleges and universities or state systems had to pay for legal fees and for their technology transfer offices. In 2001, legal fees were $161 million. The magnitude of nonreimbursed legal fees has increased about 250 percent over the eleven years that the Association of University Technology Managers (AUTM) has surveyed technology transfer activities. AUTM makes the case that about 40 percent of these costs are reimbursed through the legal process. However, these costs could be substantially higher, since AUTM explicitly modified its definition of legal fees in 1999, omitting major litigation, to better focus on benchmarking patent prosecution costs.

In the 1980s, many smaller universities and colleges received patents; the one hundred largest universities held only 82 percent of all patents. However, that trend was reversed in the 1990s, and the one hundred largest universities received more than 90 percent of all patents awarded. Income from patents was also concentrated in the top one hundred.[55] In 2005, the top R&D-performing universities continued to dominate, accounting for 95 percent of patents.

Patents dramatically illustrate the growth of the academic capitalist knowledge-learning regime. Patents, licensing and running royalties, startup companies, and universities holding equity positions in corporations built on faculty patents are not *market-like* behaviors; they are *true* market behaviors that involve nonprofit institutions in profit taking. Yet colleges and universities are not market entities, because they are chartered differently from corporations and do not disburse profits to shareholders. Instead, funds from external market revenues are put back into the institutions. In some ways, colleges and universities that patent are able to cross the traditional borders between public and private, engaging in practices that best meet their needs for generating external revenues. If patenting, which is expensive, fails to lead to licenses and royalties, the state bears the cost in the case of public institutions. Similarly, the startup corporations initiated by universities are in many ways a form of state-subsidized capitalism, although there are few penalties for failure. The income from royalties and licenses is tax free, so long as the profits are returned to the university, even if the profits are earmarked for the further development of technology transfer. Public universities try to defend their patents by invoking the Eleventh Amendment. Although patenting and technology transfer are generally portrayed as win-win endeavors, a relatively small number of large research universities are the only ones to generate substantial external revenues. For many smaller colleges and universities, the cost of maintaining a technology transfer office exceeds any revenues.[56]

## Copyrights

In the 1980s, many universities became involved in patenting; in the late 1980s and 1990s, a substantial number of them developed copyright policies. In the 1990s, new copyright legislation was enacted as digital technologies and telecommunications grew rapidly. The new laws strongly emphasized the protection of digital forms of creative expression, including new forms of intellectual property such as courseware, multimedia, electronic databases, and tele-immersion. Changes in the copyright law opened up opportunities for academic capitalism in areas other than the physical and life sciences, which had been the primary fields participating in the patent phase of the academic capitalism knowledge regime. Faculty from all fields were involved with copyrights, because copyright applied to student instructional materials, thus making academic capitalism not just a knowledge regime, but also a knowledge-learning regime.

The Telecommunications Act of 1996 dramatically altered the industry's regulatory framework. Before 1996, the 1934 Communications Act, as implemented through the Federal Communications Commission, authorized separate monopolies: broadcast, cable, wire, wireless, and satellite. The 1996 Telecommunications Act deregulated these various industries, creating a competitive climate that favored growth of the Internet, the web, and e-business, all of which utilized previously separated communications media in new patterns. The deregulation of telecommunications created numerous possibilities for an academic capitalism knowledge-learning regime, ranging from software to distance education.

The Digital Millennium Copyright Act (DMCA) of 1998 protects digital property by prohibiting unauthorized access to a copyrighted work, as well as unauthorized copying of a copyrighted work. The DMCA is far reaching and covers an array of technologies, from webcasting to hyperlinks, online directories, search engines, and the content of the materials made available by these technologies. Not only are citizens (and students) penalized for unauthorized access, but devices and services that circumvent copyrights are also prohibited. The law very deliberately seeks to develop electronic commerce and its associated technologies by strengthening protections for all forms of digital property. There are some exceptions, the broadest being for law enforcement and intelligence. The other exceptions are quite narrow.

The DMCA has a special section on distance education. Generally, the DMCA seems to take the position that purchasing or licensing digital materials should be a cost born by distance educators, as is the case with hardware and software. Currently, exemptions for the educational use of digital products are only for traditional classrooms that offer "systematic instructional activity by a nonprofit educational institution or governmental body," or for students who are in situations that make them unable to access such classrooms.[57] In other words, there is no exemption for distance-education networks not tied into conventional instruction. Fair use offers an exemption that might apply to distance education, but there is not yet a body of case law that clarifies how this would work. Moreover, if a US educational institution transmits courses to students in other countries, the law is not clear as to which will apply, US law or the law of the country receiving the transmission.

As it currently stands, the DMCA offers traditional colleges and universities an advantage in developing distance education. For the time being, they are best able to make use of such educational exemptions as exist, because of the physical classroom requirement. They also benefit because for-profit distance-education organizations are currently unable to access federal financial aid for their students. (However, the Department of Education has provisionally agreed to a change in these regulations, which will provide federal aid for students taking for-profit distance-education courses.) Traditional colleges and universities have every incentive to try to capture a sizable market share of distance education before for-profit competition explodes.

The Technology, Education and Copyright Harmonization (TEACH) Act was passed in 2002. TEACH attempted to modify provisions of the DMCA that constrained the delivery of distance education. TEACH allows educators greater freedom than that provided by the DMCA with regard to copyrighted materials. For example, the new law allows the display and performance of most works, unlike the DMCA, which limited broad classes of work, particularly those that had entertainment as well as instructional value. The DMCA confined free use of copyrighted materials to classrooms; TEACH allows institutions to reach students through distance education at any location. Unlike the DMCA, TEACH also lets students retain material for a short time. Further, TEACH permits digitization of analog works, but only if the work is not available in digital form.[58]

However, TEACH also has many restrictions. Copyrighted material used in distance education must be part of "systematic mediated instructional activity"; be supervised by an instructor; be directly related to the teaching plan; be technologically limited (protected) to enrolled students; and provide information about copyright protections attached to the works. The works may not be retained by students, and dissemination cannot interfere with the technological protections embedded in the works. TEACH assigns the responsibility for monitoring and policing copyrights to universities, steering universities in the direction of developing copyright policies, disseminating them, and staffing copyright offices. The act applies only to accredited nonprofit institutions, which must institute copyright policies that provide informational materials about copyrights to faculty, students, and staff. Generally, the TEACH provisions are designed to permit the use of digitized products and processes in distance education, but they are also framed to protect the material and property of copyright holders, especially for commercial developers of educational materials.

As was the case with patent policies, copyright policies moved from minimal policies to more expansive policies, some of which dramatically changed the way intellectual property is handled. The following data, which illustrates current copyright practices, is drawn from the same study of eighteen colleges and universities, both public and private, in the same six states that we used for the patent policies. As with patents, we look at the way copyright policies address royalty splits, categories of persons covered by policies, and exceptions to the policies.[59]

Institutional claims to their faculty's copyrighted materials are different from institutional claims to patents. Historically, many faculty published and held copyrights to scholarly and artistic materials, including instructional materials, that they created in the course of their employment at colleges and universities. They contracted with a variety of commercial publishing houses to produce and distribute their works. However, the stakes in scholarly publishing, with the exception of textbooks, were relatively small, and institutions were not interested in them. As our analysis of copyright policies demonstrates, this seems to be changing as the increased use of information technology mediates instruction. Institutions are aggressively advancing claims to shares of faculty intellectual property in copyrights, beginning with technology-mediated products. This is a sharp break with the past and potentially affects all faculty, regardless of field or institutional type.

Generally, our argument is that universities and colleges have initiated an aggressive pursuit of external revenues based on instruction and curriculum, and a number of faculty have cooperated, participating in the commercialization of instructional materials. State system and institutional copyright policies were very often introduced after patent policies, and they are substantively different from patent policies, following their own legal and product trajectories. We make the argument that knowledge in the public domain is increasingly being treated as raw material, which can be transformed into products sold for (potential) private profit or generate external revenues for colleges and universities. Over time, there is no case in which the intellectual products covered in the policies became less restrictive. Instead, the most comprehensive coverage is found in the most recent policies, providing evidence of institutions' increasingly expansive claims to copyrightable works.

## ROYALTIES

There is substantial variation among institutions on copyright royalties, with the faculty's share of royalties ranging from a high of 75 percent to a low of 33 percent. Still, the shares accorded to faculty at all institutions are generous. In contrast, none of the institutions give the growing numbers of nonfaculty employees involved in creating educational materials—for example, managerial professionals who create web pages or course materials—any shares in royalties.

## PERSONNEL COVERAGE

As with patent policies, the categories of coverage in copyright policies also expanded over time. Copyright policies cover not only full-time and part-time faculty, but also a wide range of other categories of people: classified staff, student employees, appointed personnel, graduate assistants and teaching associates, persons with "no salary" appointments, and visiting faculty and managerial professionals. Even faculty who are employed at other institutions but who work on research projects at institutions with aggressive patent policies are included in the coverage. However, there are a few cases in which coverage has not expanded. For example, only faculty are covered by the copyright and computer-software policies at several institutions. There are also cases in which the expansiveness of policies is extraordinary with regard to students. For example, one institution's policy stated that not only were students who were using substantial university resources or who were employed by the university covered by the policy, but also any student not employed by the university who created copyrightable intellectual property. Faculty using such volunteer, nonemployed students in their scholarly work projects were requested to have students sign a form that gave ownership of the property to this university.[60]

## EXCEPTIONS

Historically, universities and colleges excepted faculty creative works from institutional ownership, and advanced claims to faculty members' copyrightable intellectual products only under certain conditions. One condition was when a work produced by faculty was specified as "work for hire." The other was when faculty work that was copyrighted was specified as "within the scope of employ-ment." This language reversed the universities' traditional position with regard to their faculty's copyrightable intellectual property and enables colleges and universities to claim the material created by faculty. In their separate studies of research universities, Laura Lape and Ashley Packard both noted the greatly in-creased number of college and university intellectual property policies that have work-for-hire and within-the-scope-of-employment language, giving institutions a broader claim to property.[61]

Examples of introducing and expanding work-for-hire and within-the-scope-of-employment language are provided by some universities in our sample. Per-haps the most extreme example comes from the University of Utah. In 1970, this university's policy held that their faculty owned almost all of their copyrighted material, with one important exception: "Notwithstanding any other university policy provision, unless other arrangements are made in writing, all rights to copyrightable material (except material which is placed on videotape using uni-versity facilities, supplies, and/or equipment) and all financial and other benefits accruing by reason of said copyrightable material shall be reserved to the author, even though employed by the university." The university only claimed rights to ownership when there was a specific contract between the university and a third party, or when the author was specifically hired to do the work. (In the case of videotapes, the university also claimed ownership when its "facilities, supplies, and/or equipment" had been used, a point we will subsequently explore in dis-cussing "substantial use" language.) In their 2001 revised policy, all intellectual work of University of Utah faculty is declared as work for hire: "Works created by University staff and student employees within the scope of their University em-ployment are considered to be works made for hire, and thus are Works as to which the University is the Owner and controls all legal rights in the work." In the revisions, the university agreed to transfer rights to their faculty in some in-stances, such as in the case of "traditional scholarly work," but it still claimed ownership if the materials were produced with the "substantial use" of univer-sity resources.

In many cases, faculty work for hire is defined fairly narrowly. For example, the University of Miami's policy refers only to "a project assigned to members of the faculty" that will be owned by the institution "only if so specified at the time of assignment by an instrument of specific detail and agreement." Similarly, in the State University of New York System's policy, "[faculty] Work for Hire shall mean work done . . . under campus consulting, extra service, or technical assistance arrangements either through contract, consultancy, or purchase order, but not within the Scope of Employment."[62]

Although work for hire is sometimes defined narrowly for faculty, this is generally not the case for managerial professionals. As greater numbers of managerial professionals are employed within colleges and universities, and as they become more involved in "production" activities—such as the development of copyrightable educational products—institutions not only expand the personnel covered by their policies, but they also define the intellectual products of these personnel as works for hire. For example, the policy of the University of North Texas reads: "Electronically published course materials created jointly by faculty authors and others, whose contributions would be works for hire, will be jointly owned by the faculty author and the University." In short, managerial professionals have no property rights, and by virtue of their involvement in the educational production processes, universities have expanded their ownership claims.

While many faculty may be excepted from college and university copyright polices with regard to their creative work, they frequently lose that exception if they make significant use of institutional resources in the creative process. Most policies in the eighteen institutions we studied had language about "use of institutional resources" or "substantial use of institutional resources." As with patents, universities and colleges made the case that faculty use of institutional resources entitled institutional claims to intellectual property. Ironically, the institutional resources used by copyrighting faculty were often information technologies which patenting faculty may have developed, and which the institution owned.

Given that the metaphor of academic capitalism invokes a sense not just of class domination but also of class struggle, it is worth noting another and very different sort of exception to the neoliberal pattern of increased institutional claims of ownership and control of faculty's intellectual property in the realm of copyrighted materials, particularly in the realm of distance education. That exception lies in collective bargaining settings, where faculty are unionized. It is evident that faculty's claims to property rights are greater here than in nonunionized settings.[63] It is also clear that faculty claims on the use and (re)use of copyrighted educational materials is greater, as is their claim on the proceeds of that intellectual property, in a few cases even when substantial university resources have been used.

However, less than half of the contracts in a national data base have such provisions. Moreover, when it comes to the most recent, advanced forms of copyrightable educational materials, in the form of hybrid classes and the like, which extend more broadly than distance education, less than 10 percent of contracts nationally have language or provisions. Thus, in this new circuitry of educational production in the new economy, there is almost nothing by way of provision for faculty members claims to their intellectual creations. Perhaps at least as important from the standpoint of considering the public domain, and of higher education as a public good, it is telling that there are virtually no examples of provisions that address this.[64]

Looking to the future, one potential opening here lies in the changes augured by the growth of contingent faculty to now be the "new faculty majority" (the name of arguably the most prominent and successful advocacy group nationally for contingent faculty). The union organizing of these faculty has taken on a "metro" character, organizing adjunct faculty in private universities into locals that reach across multiple campuses. At present, these campaigns and locals are negotiating contracts campus by campus. But in recognition of the reality that adjunct faculty often work at multiple campuses, it may be in the not too distant future that there will be metro-wide contracts. In that case, there is an opportunity for other forms of "disruptive innovation" for the common, public good in the realm of copyrightable educational materials.[65]

### Expanded Managerial Capacity

Most of the college and university policies we studied did not develop the equivalent managerial capacity for copyrighted materials as they had for patented discoveries—for example, taking an equity position in corporations based on faculty intellectual property. However, some universities were moving in that direction with regard to copyrights. The case of Brigham Young University (BYU) points to a growing internal capacity to commodify education on the part of universities. At BYU, "the Technology Transfer and Creative Works Offices have the responsibility to license or sell the technology or work; or they may sell university developed products to end users when sales and support do not interfere with the normal activities of campus personnel, and when the sale is consistent with the educational mission of the university." If they "deem" the action "consistent with the educational mission and academic purposes of the university," they can approve the creation of an "enterprise center" that will pursue such activity. BYU has a Center for Instructional Design for producing copyrightable works, a Creative Works Office to oversee "the business aspects of commercializing intellectual properties and [managing] copyright issues," and the potential of enterprise centers that will further develop and market copyrightable educational materials.

The policies of other institutions are not so elaborate, but they point to some development of managerial capacity for the pursuit of academic capitalism in the realm of educational materials. Overall, it is evident that universities are developing internal managerial capacity to create and commodify copyrightable educational materials. Such capacity and investment has not only been used to justify institutions' more aggressive ownership claims to such products, but it has also enabled the organizational production of materials independent of faculty. In contrast to patenting and technology transfer, colleges and universities can develop and produce copyrightable educational materials without the direct involvement of full-time faculty. Staff who are hired to participate in these production and commercialization activities, whether they are full-time managerial professionals or part-time faculty, generally have no claims to the proceeds of their labors, since their directed labor is regarded as work for hire, entirely within the scope of their employment.

Under many of the copyright policies we have considered, colleges and universities could hire managerial professionals to develop curricular materials and part-time faculty to deliver them, and the institution would own the courses. These policies often cover distance-education efforts on the part of colleges and universities, as copyrights became a significant source of possible institutional revenues as colleges and universities pursued distance education. An example of the success that colleges and universities look to achieve through the management of copyrights is provided by Web-CT. Murray Goldberg, a computer science professor at the University of British Columbia developed Web-CT, educational website software that serves as a platform for colleges and universities. The University of British Columbia spun it off as a private corporation, which "entered into production and distribution relationships with Silicon Graphics and Prentice-Hall and fast became a major player in the American as well as the Canadian higher educational market. By the beginning fall term of 1997, WEB-CT licensees included, in addition to the University of California, Los Angeles, and the California State University System, the public universities of Georgia, Minnesota, Illinois, North Carolina, and Indiana, and such private universities as Syracuse, Brandeis, and Duquesne."[66]

Although for-profits lobbied to change financial aid requirements that call for institutions to register their students for at least twelve hours of instruction, to offer less than 50 percent of their courses via distance education, and to prohibit bonuses or incentives to admissions officers for enrolling students, through 2009 the for-profits were unsuccessful in changing legislation. However, during the George W. Bush administration, rules about compensating recruiters for the numbers of students admitted were relaxed. Indeed, colleges and universities can now reward recruiters for the number of students that are admitted, although factors such as retention must also be considered. For-profits were also able to win exceptions and to modify or reinterpret various restrictions with regard to federal student financial aid. For example, the Distance Education Demonstration Program, started in 1999 in response to these restrictions, waived requirements for fifteen schools, and, in the ensuing years, the quantity of waivers rose, including for a number of for-profits. Moreover, the 50 percent rule does not apply to many vocational education, job-training, or professional programs.[67] As one financial aid site, displaying ads for the University of Phoenix and the American Public University (ironically, a for-profit distance learning institution), puts it, "as long as you are attending a nationally accredited program . . . you are eligible for the same federal and state financial aid as a student attending a brick and mortar school."[68]

The University of Maryland University College (UMUC) provides a distance-education story with an interesting twist with regard to the source of profits from academic capitalism. Although UMUC was designed as a for-profit venture based on private monies, it has succeeded by tapping into state monies from Maryland and federal contracts with the military. UMUC was created with private-sector investment, although it has received tens of millions of dollars in state appropriations—about $10 million in both 1999 and 2000, $15 million in 2001, and $20 million in 2002.[69] Its greatest success has been in securing military funding to provide education to servicemen and -women around the globe. More recently, UMUC was awarded a Tri-Services Education contract from the US Army, at a value of $350 million over ten years. Members of the military accounted for 47,000 UMUC enrollments in 2002, out of a total of 87,000 for all of UMUC.[70]

UMUC was initially conceived as a profit center for the University of Maryland. It was expected to bring in external revenues for the system as a whole by expanding enrollments, and by saving through both economies of scale and reduced instructional costs, the latter made possible by using digitized materials rather than live faculty. When UMUC's costs remained high, the state of Maryland increased its contributions, perhaps because clicks and mortar were cheaper than bricks and mortar. However, the largest external revenue stream has been from the federal government, in the form of funding for the education of those in the military services. As in several of the other examples we have considered, the state—at the level of the several states and the federal government—supplies the lion's share of external revenue for a system designed to tap private external revenue streams.

In recent years, however, for-profit distance-education providers have eclipsed UMUC's military contracts. For-profits account for 29 percent of active-duty students and 40 percent of the half-billion-dollar annual tab in federal tuition for all students in the military. The cost for attending for-profits (such as the University of Phoenix) is $250 per credit, as compared with $50 per credit at community colleges. Federal student financial aid was $478 million in 2008, more than triple the spending of a decade earlier. Military personnel are eager to enroll, because courses taken count toward promotion. Critics claim that for-profit courses are faster and easier than those offered by nonprofit or public colleges and universities, and they compare the University of Phoenix, which allows some students to earn an associate's degree in five weeks, with community colleges, where an associate's degree usually takes two years. Large for-profits seek out students in the military because they do not count with regard to the Department of Education's 10 percent rule, which requires 10 percent of for-profits' revenues to be other than federal aid. Indeed, the University of Phoenix derived 86 percent of its $3.77 billion in revenues in 2009 from the Department of Education, up from 48 percent in 2001. Even though for-profits have not yet been able to change the 10 percent rule, they are close to running on students' Pell grants and loans alone.

However, as noted in the section on financial aid, the actions of the Obama administration have reversed the direction of enrollments in the for-profit sector. In this regard, using the leverage of federal financial aid, on which proprietary higher education institutions are totally dependent, along with the leverage of consumer protection and fraudulent reporting practices, the policies of the Obama administration mark a significant break from an academic capitalist knowledge/learning regime that privileges private providers.

Notwithstanding the previous paragraph, though, under the Obama administration there has been a continued push for exploring new "business models" and modes of delivery in higher education. In addition, there has been a push to channel more students into the two-year sector, which is disproportionately distance education. Moreover, not a little of the energy that is driving expanded distance education numbers in the not-for-profit sector is the pursuit of a new revenue stream.

Thus, the networks and policies involved in academic capitalism are extraordinarily complex. In exploring business–higher education connections, most scholars have focused on research activities and on universities.[71] Yet the commodification of education involves a wider range of higher education institutions, and activities other than patenting. Copyrighting occurs not only in the sciences and engineering, but across all fields in higher education, and it holds out the possibility of generating new sources and forms of higher education revenue.

## Conclusion

Over the past thirty-five years, the academic capitalist knowledge-learning regime was instantiated in higher education. It is not the only knowledge-learning regime, however. It coexists uneasily with, for example, both the military-industrial-academic knowledge regime and the liberal education learning regime. While the academic capitalist knowledge-learning regime did not replace these other regimes, considerable space was created for it within colleges and universities. And it has become increasingly predominant, not only in terms of the network of public policies, but also in the employment structure (enhanced managerial capacity, expanded interstitial organizations and intermediating associations) of college and universities, and in the minds and practices of the members of the academy.

The academic capitalist knowledge-learning regime was not unilaterally imposed on universities by external forces. Actors within colleges and universities worked to intersect opportunities created by the new economy. For example, the states have created an array of new opportunities. Many states have adjusted their conflict-of-interest laws so that universities (as represented by administrators) and faculty (as inventors and advisers) can hold equity positions in private corporations, even when those corporations do business with universities. Again, these laws were not imposed on passive institutions. Universities often lobbied their state legislators to ensure that the conflict-of-interest laws were changed, as did, for example, Texas A&M University.[72] The changing political-legal climate provided new opportunities for faculty and administrators in an uncertain resource environment.

More than that, many other administrators, faculty, and staff now embody and express the logic and spirit of academic capitalism, in their everyday behaviors and language. This knowledge-learning regime is something not so much actively imposed on them as it is something that they enact having taken it as their own driving logic. Through various mechanisms, such a competitive, market orientation becomes a logic that tightly couples the technical practices of the professionals in higher education to the network of formal policy structures that characterizes the regime.[73]

For four decades, then, federal and state policies have increasingly framed students as consumers and indeed as customers of colleges and universities that market to, commercialize, and commodify them. Policies have stimulated civilian technology policy, and created and (re)regulated the telecommunications infrastructure and product development in ways that spill over to the higher education sector. Only the 1972 amendments to the Higher Education Act, which created what came to be known as Pell grants, were directed toward postsecondary education. The other legislative initiatives were developed primarily to transform the industrial economy to an information economy, and to connect the national economy with global markets. Nonetheless, actors in and segments of postsecondary institutions, ranging from research universities to community colleges, worked to articulate their departments, programs, and offices with the new economy.

Part of the process of aligning institutions to a logic of academic capitalism is more closely defining and directing the institutions in terms of the short-term revenue and prestige bottom lines of the institutions more than of the communities in which they are situated and the larger publics they serve. The private domain and interest of the institution begins to trump the public domain and broader welfare. Moreover, even within colleges and universities, there is an increasingly segmented focus that works to the benefit of selected students, areas of research, and educational products, processes, and programs more than contributing to the welfare of students, fields, and institutions as a whole. Those that reflect and are seen as intersecting with the new economy are privileged over others. As a result, some portions and types of students, fields, and colleges and universities are prospering, while others are declining or being cut.

Ironically, despite the term "academic capitalism," the knowledge-learning regime is turning colleges and universities away from the growth markets of students (i.e., lower income, first in their families to go to college, students of color, and immigrants). And too many colleges and universities are aspiring to be what their resource base ensures they can never be, turning their backs on types of knowledge and on applied research and educational functions better served to address public policy problems of the day. It seems a bad business model, and a bad model for fostering social, political, and economic development.

In some regards, the last decade has been characterized by considerable continuity in federal policy in patenting and copyright policy and practice, furthering the advance of the academic capitalist knowledge-learning regime. There are some signs of internal contradictions in the union activity of faculty, particularly in the organizing of adjunct faculty, which may offer some promise of challenge and change to the neoliberal pattern. By contrast, the realm of student financial aid policy points to something of a break in the continuous, bipartisan pattern of past decades. In some cases, that represents either a pause in or even a challenge to the trajectory of academic capitalism, though in other ways the Obama administration has implemented neoliberal policies with a vengeance. Yet in the case of proprietary higher education, the policies and initiatives of the past decade constitute a clear reversal of past practice, in ways that are working to protect the public domain if not the public purposes of higher education.

NOTES

1. See Donna M. Desrochers and Rita Kirshstein, *Labor Intensive or Labor Expensive? Changing Staffing and Compensation Patterns in Higher Education* (Washington, DC: Delta Cost Project, 2014); Adam Goldstein, "Revenge of the Managers: Labor Cost-Cutting and the Paradoxical Resurgence of Managerialism in the Shareholder Value Era, 1984 to 2001," *American Sociological Review* 77 no. 2 (2012): 268–94.

2. Sheila Slaughter, Scott L. Thomas, David Johnson, and Sondra N. Barringer, "Institutional Conflict of Interest: The Role of Interlocking Directorates in the Scientific Relationships between Universities and the Corporate Sector," *The Journal of Higher Education* 85, no. 1 (2014): 1–25; B. J. Taylor, Brendan Cantwell, and Sheila Slaughter, "Quasi-Markets in US Higher Education: Humanities Emphasis and Institutional Revenues," *The Journal of Higher Education*, 84, no. 5 (2013): 675–707.

3. Deborah D. Stine, *America COMPETES Act: Programs, Funding, and Selected Issues* (Apr. 17, 2009), Congressional Research Service Report RL34328, http://opencrs.com /document/RL34328/ [accessed Aug. 19, 2010].

4. Sheila A. Slaughter and Gary Rhoades, "Changes in Intellectual Property Statutes and Policies at a Public University: Revising the Terms of Professional Labor," *Higher Education* 26 (1993): 287–312; Sheila A. Slaughter and Gary Rhoades, "The Emergence of a Competitiveness Research and Development Policy Coalition and the Commercialization of Academic Science and Technology," *Science, Technology, and Human Values* 21, no. 3 (Summer 1996): 303–39.

5. Andrew M. Isserman, "State Economic Development Policy and Practice in the United States: A Survey Article," *International Regional Science Review* 16, no. 1–2 (1994): 49–110; Peter K. Essingner, *The Rise of the Entrepreneurial State: State and Local Economic Development Policy in the United States* (Madison: University of Wisconsin Press, 1988).

6. David E. Osborne, *Laboratories of Democracy* (Boston: Harvard Business School Press, 1988).

7. David Harvey, *A Brief History of Neoliberalism* (New York: Oxford University Press, 2005).

8. The same applies at the state level. States that have greatly increased their student aid programs usually have also increased merit scholarships, which tend to benefit the well-to-do. In other words, state policies have generally followed in much the same direction as federal ones. See Donald E. Heller, *The States and Public Higher Education Policy: Affordability, Access, and Accountability* (Baltimore: Johns Hopkins University Press, 2000).

9. Lawrence E. Gladieux and Thomas R. Wolanin, *Congress and the Colleges: The National Politics of Higher Education* (Lexington, MA: Lexington Books, 1976).

10. Committee for Economic Development, "A Strategy for Better-Targeted and Increased Financial Support," in *ASHE Reader on Finance in Higher Education*, ed. David W. Breneman, Larry L. Leslie, and Richard E. Anderson (Needham, MA: Simon and Schuster, 1996), 61–68.

11. Larry L. Leslie and Paul Brinkman, *The Economic Value of Higher Education* (New York: ACE/Macmillan, 1988). For more about higher economic development country (HED) markets and public versus private good, see Brian Pusser, "Higher Education, the Emerging Market, and the Public Good," in *The Knowledge Economy and Postsecondary Education*, ed. Patricia Albjerg Graham and Nevzer Stacey (Washington, DC: National Academy Press, 2002).

12. Ronald G. Ehrenberg, *Tuition Rising: Why College Costs So Much* (Cambridge, MA: Harvard University Press, 2000).

13. The Middle Income Assistance Act of 1978 provided grant aid to a greater number of middle-income students and took the $25,000 limit off the Guaranteed Student Loans. The Middle Income Assistance Act was an anomalous moment in student financial aid's movement toward a greater reliance on loans, and by the 1980s it proved too broad a welfare benefit for the neoliberal state. For details, see James C. Hearn, "The Growing Loan Orientation in Federal Financial Aid Policy," in *ASHE Reader on Finance in Higher Education*, ed. John L. Yeager, Glenn M. Nelson, Eugenia A. Potter, John C. Weidman, and Thomas G. Zullo (Boston: Pearson, 1998).

14. Thomas Kane, *How We Pay for College in the Price of Admission* (Washington, DC: Brookings Institution Press, 1999), 11.

15. Donald E. Heller, *The States and Public Higher Education Policy: Affordability, Access, and Accountability* (Baltimore: Johns Hopkins University Press, 2000).

16. *1998 Amendments to the Higher Education Act of 1965*, Public Law 105-244, Part F, Sec. 961—Liaison for Proprietary Institutions of Higher Education, 112 Stat. 1836–37.

17. Ehrenberg, *Tuition Rising*.

18. Larry L. Leslie and Gary Johnson, "The Market Model and Higher Education," *Journal of Higher Education* 45 (1974): 1–20.

19. DePaul University, *National and Regional Trends in College Tuition*, http://oipr.depaul.edu/TuitionReport/2002/surveyrep.asp/.

20. College Board, "$90 Billion Available in Student Financial Aid, with Scholarship Growth Outpacing Loan Growth," press release, Oct. 24, 2002, www.collegeboard.com/press/releases/18420.html.

21. College Board, *Trends in College Pricing 2009*, www.trends-collegeboard.com /college_pricing/.

22. Ibid.

23. Project on Student Debt, an Initiative of the Institute for College Access & Success, "Getting with the Program," *Issue Brief* (Oct. 2009), http://projectonstudentdebt .org/files/pub/getting_with_the_program.pdf.

24. National Center for Public Policy and Higher Education [NCPPHE], *Measuring Up 2008* (San Jose, CA: National Center for Public Policy and Higher Education, 2008), http://measuringup2008.highereducation.org, quotation on p. 15.

25. NCPPHE, *Losing Ground: A National Status Report on the Affordability of American Higher Education*, 2002, www.highereducation.org/reports/losing_ground/ar.shtml.

26. Project on Student Debt, *Quick Facts about Student Debt* (updated Jan. 2010), http://ticas.org/sites/default/files/legacy/fckfiles/pub/classof2013.pdf.

27. Michael S. McPherson and Mortimer O. Shapiro, *The Student Aid Game: Meeting Need and Rewarding Talent in American Higher Education* (Princeton: Princeton University Press, 1998).

28. Albert B. Crenshaw, "Price Wars on Campus: Colleges Use Discounts to Draw Best Mix of Top Students, Paying Customers," *Washington Post*, Oct. 5, 2002, A1.

29. Alvin E. Roth and Xiaolin Xing, "Jumping the Gun: Imperfections and Institutions Relating to the Timing of Market Transactions," *American Economic Review* 84 (1994): 992–1044.

30. Christopher Flores, "U. of North Carolina at Chapel Hill Drops Early-Decision Admissions," *Chronicle of Higher Education*, May 3, 2002, A38; "Harvard to Eliminate Early Admission," *Harvard University Gazette*, Sept. 12, 2006; "Princeton to End Early Admission," *News at Princeton*, Sept. 18, 2006.

31. Marcia Yablon, "Test Flight: The Scam Behind SAT Bashing," *New Republic*, Oct. 30, 2001, 24–25.

32. Eric Hoover, "Instant Gratification: On-Site Admissions Programs Let Applicants Know Immediately Whether They Have Been Accepted," *Chronicle of Higher Education*, Apr. 12, 2002, A39.

33. Kathleen F. Kelly, *Meeting Needs and Making Profits: The Rise of For-Profit Degree-Granting Institutions* (Denver: Education Commission of the States, 2001).

34. Project on Student Debt, *Quick Facts*.

35. Project on Student Debt, "New Default Rate Data for Federal Student Loans: 44% of Defaulters Attended For-Profit Institutions," press release, Dec. 15, 2009.

36. Carolyn P. Griswold and Ginger M. Marine, "Political Influences on State Policy: Higher-Tuition, Higher-Aid, and the Real World," *Review of Higher Education* 19, no. 4 (1996): 361–89.

37. David C. Mowery and Arvids Ziedonis, "Academic Patent Quality and Quantity Before and After the Bayh-Dole Act in the United States," *Research Policy* 31 (2002): 399–418.

38. *Bayh-Dole Act 1980*, Public Law 96-517, 94 Stat. 3019.

39. Adam B. Jaffe, "The U.S. Patent System in Transition: Policy Innovation and the Innovation Process," *Research Policy* 29, no. 4–5 (2000): 531–57.

40. Gary Rhoades and Sheila A. Slaughter, "Professors, Administrators, and Patents: The Negotiation of Technology Transfer," *Sociology of Education* 64, no. 2 (1991): 65–77; Gary Rhoades and Sheila A. Slaughter, "The Public Interest and Professional Labor: Research Universities," in *Culture and Ideology in Higher Education: Advancing a Critical Agenda*, ed. William G. Tierney (New York: Praeger, 1991), 187–211.

41. Jaffe, "U.S. Patent System."

42. Ibid.

43. Sheila A. Slaughter, *Higher Learning and High Technology: Dynamics of Higher Education Policy Formation* (Albany: State University of New York Press, 1990).

44. Henry Etzkowitz and Magnus Gulbrandsen, "Public Entrepreneur: The Trajectory of United States Science, Technology, and Industrial Policy," *Science and Public Policy* 26, no. 1 (1999): 53–62.

45. Maryann Feldman, Irwin Feller, Janet Bercovitz, and Richard Burton, "Equity and the Technology Transfer Strategies of American Research Universities," *Management Science* 48, no. 1 (2002): 105–21.

46. Slaughter and Rhoades, *Academic Capitalism*.

47. See Slaughter et al., "Institutional Conflict of Interest."

48. Harvard Medical School, "Statement Regarding Canadian Supreme Court 5–4 Decision Dec. 5, 2002 Denying the Patentability of OncoMouse in Canada," www .geometry.net/detail/basic_c/canadian_supreme_court.html.

49. Dorsey Griffith, "Researchers Roar over OncoMouse Restrictions," *Sacramento Bee*, Nov. 2, 2003.

50. Association of University Technology Managers [AUTM], *AUTM Licensing Survey: FY 2001* (Deerfield, IL: Association of University Technology Managers, 2003).

51. Carnegie Learning, math curriculum kits, https://store.carnegielearning.com/.

52. Council on Governmental Relations, *A Tutorial on Technology Transfer in U.S. Colleges and Universities* (Washington, DC: Council on Governmental Relations, 2003), www.cogr.edu/viewDoc.cfm?DocID=151742/.

53. National Science Foundation, *Science and Engineering Indicators 2010*, NSB 10-01 (Arlington, VA: National Science Foundation, 2010).

54. AUTM, *AUTM Licensing Survey*, 11–12.

55. National Science Board, *Science and Engineering Indicators 2002*, NSB 02-1 (Arlington, VA: National Science Foundation, 2002).

56. Slaughter and Rhoades, *Academic Capitalism*.

57. Senate Committee on the Judiciary, *Statement of Marybeth Peters, the Register of Copyrights, before the Senate Committee on the Judiciary*, on Technology, Education and Copyright Harmonization (TEACH) Act (S. 487), 107th Cong., 1st sess., Mar. 13, 2001, www.copyright.gov/docs/regstat031301.html.

58. Kenneth D. Crews, *New Copyright Law for Distance Education: The Meaning and Importance of the TEACH Act*, 2002, http://www.ala.org/Template.cfm?Section=Distance _Education_and_the_TEACH_Act&Template=/ContentManagement/ContentDisplay .cfm&ContentID=25939#/ [accessed Aug. 19, 2010].

59. Slaughter and Rhoades, *Academic Capitalism*.

60. Ibid.

61. Laura Lape, "Ownership of Copyrightable Works of University Professors: The Interplay between the Copyright Act and University Copyright Policies," *Villanova Law Review* 37 (1992): 223–71; Ashley Packard, "Copyright or Copy Wrong: An Analysis of University Claims to Faculty Work," *Communication Law and Policy* 7 (2002): 275–315.

62. Slaughter and Rhoades, *Academic Capitalism*, 143.

63. See Slaughter and Rhoades, *Academic Capitalism*; Gary Rhoades, Managed Professionals: Unionized Faculty and Restructuring Academic Labor (Albany: State University of New York Press, 1998).

64. Gary Rhoades, "Whose Property Is It? Negotiating with the University," *Academe* 87, no. 5 (2001): 38–43.

65. Gary Rhoades, "Disruptive Innovations for Adjunct Faculty: Common Sense for the Common Good," *Thought & Action* 29 (Fall 2013): 71–86.

66. David F. Noble, *Digital Diploma Mills: The Automation of Higher Education* (New York: Monthly Review Press, 2001), 31.

67. US Department of Education, Office of Postsecondary Education, "Distance Education Demonstration Program: Selected Waivers Granted" (Apr. 16, 2007), www2.ed .gov/programs/disted/waivers.html.

68. Jobmonkey, "Distance Learning, Part 3: Financial Aid," www.jobmonkey.com /blog/distance-learning-part-3-financial-aid.html [accessed Aug. 19, 2010].

69. G. A. Heeger, "President's Testimony to the Maryland General Assembly, February 8–9, 2001," online archives of presidential addresses, www.umuc.edu/president /testimony/2001/testimony.html [accessed Mar. 1, 2003].

70. University of Maryland University College [UMUC], "The UMUC News Page: UMUC Awarded Tri-Services Education Contract for Europe," 2003, www.umuc.edu /events/press/news143.html [accessed Feb. 28, 2003]; UMUC, "About Us," University of Maryland University College home page, 2003, www.umuc.edu/gen/about.html [accessed Feb. 28, 2003].

71. Norman E. Bowie, *University-Business Partnerships: An Assessment* (Lanham, MD: Rowman and Littlefield, 1994); Henry Etzkowitz, Andrew Webster, and Peter Healey, *Capitalizing Knowledge: New Interactions of Industry and Academe* (Albany: State University of New York Press, 1998).

72. Peter Schmidt, "States Push Public Universities to Commercialize Research," *Chronicle of Higher Education*, Mar. 29, 2002, A26–A27.

73. Michael Sauder and Wendy Nelson Espeland, "The Discipline of Rankings: Tight Coupling and Organizational Change," *American Sociological Review* 74, no. 1 (2009): 63–82.

# Contributors

## Editors

*Michael N. Bastedo* is a professor of education and director at the Center for the Study of Higher and Postsecondary Education, University of Michigan. His scholarly interests are in higher education decision making, particularly college admissions, stratification, rankings, and governance. In 2013, he received the Early Career Award from the American Educational Research Association. His most recent research, funded by the National Science Foundation and the National Center for Educational Statistics, has been reported by journalists at *The New York Times*, *The New Yorker*, *The Washington Post*, *Slate*, and *The Chronicle of Higher Education*, among others.

*Philip G. Altbach* is a research professor and the founding director of the Center for International Higher Education in the Lynch School of Education at Boston College. He was the 2004–2006 Distinguished Scholar Leader for the New Century Scholars initiative of the Fulbright program and has been a senior associate of the Carnegie Foundation for the Advancement of Teaching. He is the author of *Global Perspective on Higher Education*; *Turmoil and Transition*; and *Student Politics in America*, among other books. He is also a member of the Russian government's "5-100 University Excellence Commission" and other international committees.

*Patricia J. Gumport* serves concurrently as the vice-provost for graduate education, a professor of education, and the director of the Stanford Institute for Higher Education Research at Stanford University. Her most recent book is an edited volume, *Sociology of Higher Education: Contributions and Their Contexts*, also published by Johns Hopkins University Press (2007).

## Contributors

*Benjamin Baez* is an associate professor of higher education in the Department of Leadership and Professional Studies at Florida International University. He received his law degree in 1988 and his doctorate in higher education in 1997, both from Syracuse University. He has written two books, *The Politics of Inquiry: Education Research and the "Culture of Science,"* with Deron Boyles (State University of New York Press, 2009) and *Affirmative Action, Hate Speech, and Tenure: Narratives About Race, Law, and the Academy* (Routledge, 2002), and edited *Understanding Minority-Serving Institutions: Interdisciplinary Perspectives* with Marybeth Gasman and Caroline Turner (State University of New York Press, 2009).

*Peter Riley Bahr* serves as an associate professor at the Center for the Study of Higher and Postsecondary Education, University of Michigan. In his research, Dr. Bahr seeks to deconstruct student pathways into, through, and out of community colleges and into the workforce or on to four-year postsecondary institutions. His work has been published in a wide range of scholarly outlets, including the *Journal of Higher Education*, *Research in Higher Education*, the *Review of Higher Education*, and *Educational Policy*. In 2011, he was awarded the Barbara K. Townsend Emerging Scholar Award by the Council for the Study of Community Colleges.

*Joy Blanchard* is an assistant professor of higher education at Louisiana State University and a board member of the Education Law Association. Her research focuses on higher education law, primarily negligence liability, intercollegiate athletics, and faculty life. Joy received her doctorate from the Institute of Higher Education at the University of Georgia.

*Corbin M. Campbell* is an assistant professor of higher education at Teachers College, Columbia University. Her current research considers new ways to conceptualize and measure the educational quality of colleges and universities that more closely reflect the teaching and learning process, by contrast with distal measures focusing on resources, reputation, and student selectivity. Campbell was awarded the National Academy of Education/ Spencer Postdoctoral Fellowship (2015–16) and serves on a National Academies committee to assess interpersonal and intrapersonal competencies in college.

*Melanie E. Corrigan* is the director of national initiatives at the American Council on Education (ACE) where she is also the project director of ACE's national public service campaign on expanding access to higher education. Corrigan also serves as the primary research analyst for ACE's Division of Governmental Relations and Public Affairs. Previously, she served for six years at ACE in the Division of Government Relations and the Center for Policy Analysis.

*Peter D. Eckel* is senior fellow and director of leadership programs in the Alliance for Higher Education and Democracy at the University of Pennsylvania. Previously he was vice president for programs and research at the Association of Governing Boards. Eckel has written and edited numerous books, including *Changing Course: Making the Hard Decisions to Eliminate Academic Programs* and *Privatizing the Public University: Perspectives from Across the Academy*. At the American Council on Education he was the lead author of *The CAO Census*, the national study of chief academic officers. He serves as a trustee at the University of La Verne.

*Roger L. Geiger* is the Distinguished Professor of Higher Education at the Pennsylvania State University. He is the author of *The History of American Higher Education: Learning and Culture from the Founding to World War II* (Princeton University Press, 2015); *Tapping the Riches of Science: Universities and the Promise of Economic Growth* with Creso Sa (Harvard University Press, 2008); and *Knowledge and Money: Research Universities and the Paradox of the Marketplace* (Stanford University Press, 2004); and is the editor of *Perspectives on the History of Higher Education*.

*Lawrence E. Gladieux* is an independent higher education consultant. His clients have included the Century Foundation, the federal Advisory Committee on Student Financial Assistance, the National Center for Public Policy and Higher Education, the College Board, the Bill and Melinda Gates Foundation, and the US Department of Education. Previously, he served as executive director of the Washington Office of the College Board and the organization's executive director for policy analysis. Gladieux has presented testimony to Congress and written widely on issues of the high school-to-college transition, equity, access, and college affordability.

*Sara Goldrick-Rab* is a professor of educational policy studies and sociology at the University of Wisconsin-Madison, and founding director at the Wisconsin HOPE Lab. She is a senior scholar at the Wisconsin Center for the Advancement of Postsecondary Education and an affiliate of the Center for Financial Security, Institute for Research on Poverty, La Follette School of Public Affairs, and Consortium for Chicago School Research. As an assistant professor, Goldrick-Rab was named a National Academy of Education/Spencer Foundation postdoctoral fellow and William T. Grant scholar. In 2014, the American Educational Research Association honored her with its Early Career Award.

*Jillian Leigh Gross* is a doctoral candidate at the University of Michigan, Ann Arbor in the Center for the Study of Higher and Postsecondary Education. Her scholarly interests focus on organizational decision making in American community colleges and their global counterparts. In 2014–15 she was a Fulbright-Nehru student researcher exploring the translation of the community college concept in the Indian context.

*D. Bruce Johnstone* is the Distinguished Service Professor of Higher and Comparative Education Emeritus at the State University of New York at Buffalo and director of the International Comparative Higher Education Finance and Accessibility Project. His principal scholarship is in international comparative higher education, higher education finance, governance, and policy formation. Prior to teaching at the University at Buffalo, he held the posts of vice president for administration at the University of Pennsylvania, president of the State University College of Buffalo, and chancellor of the State University of New York System.

*Adrianna Kezar* is a professor of higher education at the University of Southern California and co-director of the Pullias Center for Higher Education. Dr. Kezar is a national expert on change, governance, and leadership in higher education, and her research agenda explores the change process in higher education institutions and the role of leadership in creating change. Kezar has authored 18 books/monographs, over 100 journal articles, and over 100 book chapters and reports. Her recent books include *How Colleges Change* (Routledge, 2013) and *Enhancing Campus Capacity for Leadership* (Stanford University Press, 2011).

*Jacqueline E. King* serves as the director of higher education collaboration for the Smarter Balanced Assessment Consortium. She is an expert in higher education access, student financial aid, and alignment with K-12. King spent fifteen years at the American Council on Education, serving most recently as assistant vice president and policy research advisor. At ACE, she founded the Center for Policy Analysis and led the K–16 alignment agenda, including efforts to ensure that higher education faculty had direct input on the Common Core State Standards. King received a doctorate in higher education from the University of Maryland, College Park.

*Aims C. McGuinness, Jr.,* is a senior associate with the National Center for Higher Education Management Systems, Boulder, Colorado. He was previously at the Education Commission of the States. He has advised many states on major higher education reforms and has been involved in international projects of the World Bank and the Organisation for Economic Co-operation and Development.

*Michael Mumper* is a professor of political science at Adams State University in Colorado. From 2007 to 2015, he served as that institution's provost and senior vice president for enrollment management. Previously, Mumper was professor and associate provost for graduate studies at Ohio University. His research has focused on federal and state higher education policy and the factors driving college tuition inflation. He is the author of *Removing College Price Barriers: What Government Has Done and Why It Hasn't Worked* (State University of New York Press, 1996). Mumper received a doctorate in government and politics from the University of Maryland, College Park.

*Anna Neumann* is a professor of higher education and chair of the Department of Organization and Leadership at Teachers College, Columbia University. Neumann's research examines teaching in urban institutions, with attention to improving first-generation undergraduates' subject-matter learning. Current projects analyze teaching strategies for advancing students' understandings of core ideas in the humanities, social sciences, and sciences, and professional development for teaching improvement. An elected member of the National Academy of Education and fellow of the American Education Research Association, Neumann is a recipient of AERA's Division J Exemplary Research Award and past president of the Association for the Study of Higher Education.

*Robert M. O'Neil* is a professor of law emeritus and former director of the Thomas Jefferson Center for the Protection of Free Expression at the University of Virginia. He served as president of the University of Wisconsin System from 1980 to 1985 and of the University of Virginia from 1985 to 1990. He has also served as a trustee of several corporations and nonprofit agencies, including the Carnegie Foundation for the Advancement of Teaching and the Educational Testing Service. He is currently a senior fellow of the Association of Governing Boards of Colleges and Universities, and director of the Ford Foundation Difficult Dialogues Initiative.

*Laura W. Perna* is the James S. Riepe Professor and founding executive director of the Alliance for Higher Education and Democracy at the University of Pennsylvania. She is also president of the Association for the Study of Higher Education and past vice president of the Postsecondary Division of the American Educational Research Association. Her research examines the ways that social structures, educational practices, and public policies promote and limit college access and success, particularly for individuals from lower-income families and racial/ethnic minority groups. With Joni Finney, she recently published *The Attainment Agenda: State Policy Leadership for Higher Education* (Johns Hopkins).

*Gary Rhoades* is head of the Department of Educational Policy Studies & Practice, and professor and director at the Center for the Study of Higher Education,

University of Arizona. He was previously on leave serving as general secretary of the American Association of University Professors. Rhoades' scholarship focuses on the restructuring of academic institutions and of professions in the academy, as well as on science and technology policy, and comparative higher education. His books include *Managed Professionals* (SUNY, 1998), and, with Sheila Slaughter, *Academic Capitalism and the New Economy* (Johns Hopkins University Press, 2004).

*Roman Ruiz* is a predoctoral researcher at the Alliance for Higher Education and Democracy at the University of Pennsylvania and has served as a summer research fellow at The Pell Institute for the Study of Opportunity in Higher Education. His research interests include college access policies and precollege interventions designed to increase postsecondary enrollment and degree attainment for historically underrepresented student populations. His current work examines the role of place and geography as determinants of college access and student college choice.

*Lauren T. Schudde* is an assistant professor in the Department of Educational Administration at the University of Texas at Austin. She studies processes that contribute to socioeconomic inequalities in postsecondary degree attainment and subsequent labor market outcomes. Schudde is a research affiliate of the Center for Analysis of Postsecondary Education and Employment at Teachers College's Community College Research Center and of the Population Research Center at the University of Texas at Austin.

*Sheila Slaughter* is the Louise McBee Professor of Higher Education in the Institute of Higher Education at the University of Georgia. Professor Slaughter's scholarship concentrates on the relationship between knowledge and power as it plays out in higher education policy at the state, federal, and global levels. Together with Gary Rhoades, she is the author of *Academic Capitalism and the New Economy: Markets, State and Higher Education* (Johns Hopkins University Press, 2004).

*Daryl G. Smith* is a senior research fellow and professor emerita of education and psychology at the Claremont Graduate University. Prior to her faculty position, she was a college administrator for twenty-two years. Her research and writing have focused extensively on diversity issues in higher education—institutional transformation, faculty diversity, diversity in STEM fields—and she is the author of *Diversity's Promise for Higher Education: Making It Work* (Johns Hopkins University Press, 2015), and editor of *Diversity in Higher Education: Emerging Cross-national Perspectives on Institutional Transformation* (Taylor & Francis, 2014).

# Index